A PICTORIAL HISTORY OF
THE UNITED STATES ARMY

1776
1812
1846
1861
1898
1918
1941
Today

Norman Rockwell

INTRODUCTION

Telling the complete story of the United States Army in photographs, maps, charts, and other illustrations is a task that probably should not have been tackled by one man, but I am a firm believer in accepting challenges. When I was asked if I could and would do a pictorial history of the Army, I jumped at the chance. It wasn't only the challenge. Fundamentally it was the recognition of the great need for a comprehensive yet concise pictorial presentation of the history of our Army. During my twenty-five years as a commissioned officer serving in Army and Air Force assignments, in positions from remote sites to ones in the Pentagon's Department of Defense and during the last ten years as a military author and lecturer, I have had hundreds of requests for such a book. I could refer such inquiries to existing histories, some with a scattering of illustrations, some with none. But it was the pictures these people wanted. They wanted to see what the uniforms, the generals, the battles, and all the rest looked like. They wanted to see the Army as they read about it.

I decided to try to locate a picture of every important event and person in the long and colorful history of the United States Army, beginning with the colonists who took up arms to defend their homes in the years before the Revolutionary War and concluding with the conflict in Vietnam. Photographs were not available for the entire period, of course. For the years beginning with the Civil War for which a photographic record does exist, the very best of the available photographs have been chosen. In some cases the quality seems poor when compared with the work of today's combat cameramen, but it represents the best done on the subject at that time. To cover the events for which there is no photographic record, I have chosen, after studying many thousands of pictures, the best available illustrations— some of them the product of skilled artists who worked in their studios, and others the work of men, often soldiers, who made sketches on the scene.

All the machinery was set in motion, and the work began. In the course of my research I met Charles B. MacDonald, the Army's top civilian historian, who suggested that I make use of a definitive text entitled *American Military History, 1607–1958* (U.S. Army ROTC Manual 145–20). This was a series of monographs prepared by Army historians to give Reserve Officer Training Corps students an understanding of the part played by the Army in American history. The text covered the subject so well that I made generous use of it. I am deeply indebted to Mr. MacDonald for his suggestion and for permission to use the material.

I have also taken advantage of the vast amount of research done by Army historians, and used portions of their three-volume photo history of the U.S. Army during World War II and the two-volume photo history of the Korean War.

Altogether, over 1,000 individuals and organizations have contributed to this book. Space does not permit my naming the many people who helped. I am deeply grateful to all of them; sometimes it was for just one or two photographs of an elusive subject and sometimes it was for hundreds of photographs covering a whole war.

As for organizational and other sources—I feel compelled to name at least some of them: the Military History Department of the U.S. Army; the Magazine and Book Branch of the Department of Defense; the *Army Information Digest;* the Institute of Heraldry; the Army Photographic Files; the National Archives Audio-Visual Branch; the Library of Congress Prints and Photographs Division; the Smithsonian Institution's Military History Division; the *American Soldier Series;* the National Park Service; the Maryland Historical Society; *Frank Leslie's Illustrated Newspaper;* the Metropolitan Museum of Art; *Harper's Weekly;* the Wisconsin State Historical Society; New-York Historical Society; *McClure's Magazine; Gleason's Pictorial;* the New York Public Library; the U.S. Military Academy Archives; *Century Magazine;* Lossing's *Field Book of the Revolution;* the Library of Congress' *American Battle Art, 1755-1918;* Henry Loomis Nelson and H. A. Ogden's *Uniforms of the Army of the United States;* Steele's *American Campaigns;* the American Battle Monuments Commission's *American Armies and Battlefields in Europe;* Tome's *Battles of America;* and the Fort Ticonderoga Museum.

Several of the United States Army's museums supplied material—the Benton Small Arms Museum, Springfield Armory, Mass.; the Corps of Engineers Museum, Fort Belvoir, Va.; the Ordnance Museum, Aberdeen Proving Ground, Md., the Patton Museum, Fort Knox, Ky.; Signal Corps Museum, Fort Monmouth, N.J.; the Special Warfare Center Museum, Fort Bragg, N.C.; Missile Park Museum, White Sands, N.M.; and the West Point Museum, West Point, N.Y.

And I am indebted to Norman Rockwell and the Brown and Bigelow Company for permission to use Mr. Rockwell's painting of American soldiers on the jacket.

Gene Gurney

FOREWORD

Almost two centuries have passed since the United States Army was formed and the long parade of heroic young Americans in Army uniform began. Whether the uniform was the Continental Buff and Blue or one of the myriad shades that preceded our present Army Green, the wearers have established an unchallenged record of courage and devotion to their country.

A PICTORIAL HISTORY OF THE UNITED STATES ARMY presents a comprehensive account, in words and in pictures, of this enviable record of performance. It contains valuable reference material for the military historian, and should be a rewarding reading experience for anyone interested in the history of the United States.

HAROLD K. JOHNSON
General, U.S. Army
Chief of Staff

CONTENTS

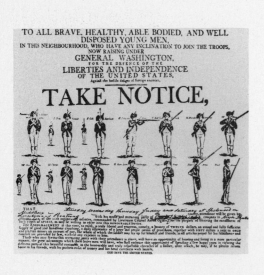

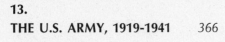

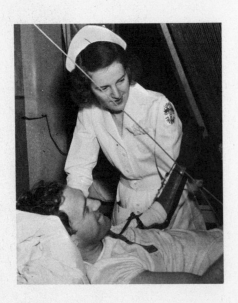

COLOR SECTIONS

MEDAL AWARDED TO LEE.

When Captain John Smith and his colonists arrived in Jamestown from England in 1607, they brought with them a supply of muskets, pikes, swords, armor, and other military equipment.

CHAPTER 1

THE SOLDIER IN COLONIAL AMERICA

The first American national army did not come into being until 1775 when thirteen English colonies in North America banded together to throw off British rule. The influences that went into the shaping of this army were many and varied, deriving from American experience since the first settlement at Jamestown in 1607 and from European experience that went back many centuries.

In colonial America neither formal battles in the open nor formal sieges were the normal modes of making war. America was a new continent, heavily forested and sparsely populated. The main enemy that the English colonists had to contend with during the first century after settlement was the primitive and savage Indian, who neither knew the rules of formal warfare nor cared to learn them. This, plus the fact that colonial society from its very beginning developed along more democratic and individualistic lines than society in England or continental Europe, combined to produce different forms of military organization from those of Europe and different methods of employing them on the battlefield.

When the white man came, the Indian relied on bow and spear, tomahawk and knife, but he soon learned the value of the white man's musket and was not long in obtaining quantities of them in trade for his valuable furs. With bow or musket, his method of fighting was the same. Indian tribes had no organized system of war; warriors simply formed voluntary bands under war chiefs and took off on the warpath. In battle each Indian fought a separate opponent without regard for his fellows, seeking to acquire as many scalps as he could. Indians avoided pitched battle whenever possible, seeking instead victory by surprise and careful utilization of cover and concealment. Only when they had the advantage did they close in for hand-to-hand combat. In such combat the Indian brave lacked neither skill nor courage. But knowing little and caring less about the rules of civilized warfare, he slaughtered men, women, and children indiscriminately. The favorite Indian tactic was a surprise raid on an isolated settlement. When the settlers organized a pursuit, the Indians lay in wait and ambushed them.

The white man soon adapted his tactics to the Indian's, quickly learning the value of surprise and stealth himself. To avoid ambush he sent out scouts as the Indian did; instead of fighting in the closed formations of Europe, he too adopted the open formation and fought from behind trees, rocks, and fences. In such fighting more depended on individual initiative and courage than on strict discipline and control.

The white settler learned to benefit from some of the enemy's weaknesses. For all their cunning, the Indians never learned the lesson of proper security and did not post guards at night. Nor did they like to fight in winter. Thus expeditions into the Indian country used as their favorite technique an attack on an Indian village at dawn and in the winter season. This attack almost invariably came as a surprise, and the white men, imitating the savagery of their opponents, burned the Indian's villages, sometimes slaughtering braves, squaws, and papooses.

1

An artist's conception of the retreat of Lieutenant Colonel George Washington (foreground) and his men from Great Meadows, near Fort Duquesne, in 1754.

The famous Peale portrait of George Washington in the uniform of a colonel in the Virginia Militia. It was painted at Mount Vernon in 1772.

Carlyle House in Alexandria, Virginia,
Braddock's headquarters in 1755.

A wood engraving of the battle that cost Braddock his
life. The mortally wounded general has fallen from his
horse.

Map—Braddock's expedition.

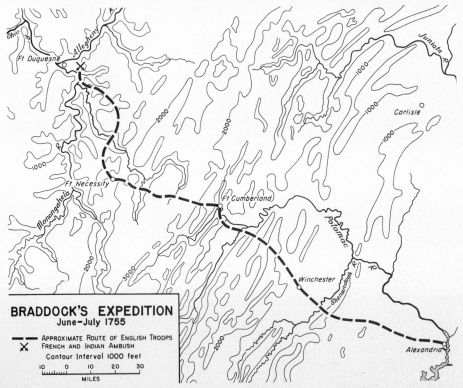

BRADDOCK'S EXPEDITION
June–July 1755

- – – APPROXIMATE ROUTE OF ENGLISH TROOPS
- ✕✕ FRENCH AND INDIAN AMBUSH
  Contour Interval 1000 feet

10 0 10 20 30
MILES

Ohio R.
Ft Duquesne
Allegheny
Juniata R.
Carlisle
Ft Necessity
Monongahela
Ft Cumberland
Potomac R.
Winchester
Shenandoah R.
Alexandria

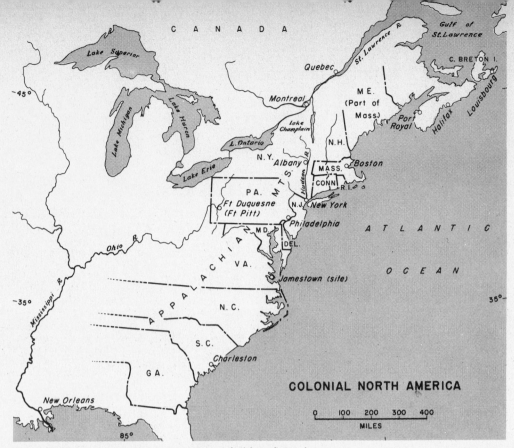

Map—Colonial North America.

In 1745 an all-colonial force, largely from New England, succeeded in taking Louisburg on Cape Breton Island from the French. This print shows General William Pepperell, the leader of the provincials, directing the siege of the fortress. Louisburg was returned to the French in 1748.

Louisburg as it appeared to a British engineer officer
when the fortress was under siege by British forces in 1758.

General Jeffrey Amherst, who led a British
army of 12,000 men at the 1758 siege of
Louisburg.

COLONIAL FORTS

The settlers tried to provide some permanent protection for their frontiers by erecting forts along the westernmost line of settlement in each colony, moving them forward as the line of settlement moved. These forts were not the elaborate earth and masonry structures of Europe, but simple rectangular enclosures, their walls constructed of upright pointed legs. Normally there were wooden blockhouses on each corner. These rude frontier forts served as points to which settlers and their families could retreat for protection in time of Indian troubles. Having no artillery, the Indians found them hard to take and could rely only on burning arrows to set them afire, on surprise attack, or on direct frontal assault. This last alternative was almost never used, as their war chiefs possessed no power to order any group of braves to undertake an assault in which they would suffer heavy casualties for the sake of gaining an objective.

COLONIAL MILITIA

For this sort of fighting, colonial governments relied not on professional soldiers but on the body of citizens. Each colony had its militia organization, normally based on the principle that every able-bodied male from sixteen to sixty should render military service. The militia was an ancient British institution, but since Britain's wars after 1660 were fought on the sea or in foreign lands, the militia there came to exist largely on paper, while professional soldiers and seamen fought Britain's battles. In the colonies, the old institution survived and took on new strength. Each member of the militia was obligated to appear for training a certain number of days each year and to hold himself in readiness for call in case of an Indian attack or other emergency.

A general call for the whole militia of a colony almost never occurred. Instead, the militia served as a training and mobilization base from which individuals or units could be selected for active operations. When a particular area of a colony was threatened, the colonial government would direct the militia commander in that area to call out his men. For expeditions into the Indian country, individuals from many local units were usually selected and formed into an organized force for the occasion. Selection was generally by volunteering, but local commanders could draft both men and property if necessary. As a rule, the selected men were obligated to serve for a stipulated length of time, normally the estimated length of the campaign. In Indian expeditions this was seldom more than six months.

For a military organization, the militia was a most democratic institution. Though general officers and regimental colonels were appointed by royal governors or the colonial assembly, company officers were elected by the men. This did not necessarily mean that any man might become an officer, though it clearly put a premium on popularity as well as ability. The expenses of providing distinctive uniforms and arms and the tradition of leadership in certain families normally kept the officers' commissions in the hands of the well-to-do.

Each militiaman was expected to provide his own weapons and clothing and food for a short expedition. The weapon in almost universal use in the colonies until about

An unknown Frenchman, who was probably at Louisburg during the siege, drew a figurative map showing the various stages of the action. It is reproduced here in three parts. The first (above) shows the British fleet at anchor (left) and an attempt to land troops (right).

1750 was the musket, generally the same type as that used by the European soldier. There were few if any bayonets; the colonial militiaman might well use a hatchet or hunting knife as a substitute in hand-to-hand combat.

Supply was not altogether an individual responsibility. Local authorities maintained reserve supplies of muskets to arm those too poor to buy them; they also collected stores of ammunition and sometimes small cannon that could be dragged along through the wilderness. For really long campaigns the colonial government had to take charge, the assembly appropriating the money to buy supplies and designating supply officers or contractors to handle purchasing and distribution. In this case there might be more cannon, but the use of anything but the smaller pieces of artillery was impractical because of the lack of roads and clear fields of fire in the forest. Cannon were more frequently used for defense of forts or towns.

Within each colony, the popular assembly exercised close control over all matters relating to the organization and use of militia, largely through its control of the purse. It must be kept in mind that there were thirteen militias,

not one, and that each of the thirteen was organized and administered under a separate set of laws. Each colonial government concentrated on the defense of its own frontiers, and cooperation among the militias of the various colonies was normally confined to specific Indian expeditions in which two or more colonies had a definite interest. Thus there appeared very early in our history a tradition of separatism among the various colonies that was to have lasting effects. The individual militiaman and his immediate commanders were apt to be bound by even narrower local ties and to show little enthusiasm in fighting for anything that did not affect their own community.

As a part-time citizen army the militia was naturally not a well-disciplined cohesive force like the professional army of the age. Its efficiency also varied from colony to colony and even from locality to locality within the same colony, depending on the ability and determination of commanders and the presence or absence of an enemy threat. When engaged in eliminating an Indian threat to their own community, militiamen might be counted on to make up in enthusiasm what they lacked in discipline and

This section of the map shows the Louisburg landing scene and the British advancing toward the fortress.

formal training, but when the Indian threat was pushed westward there was a general tendency for people along the seaboard to relax. Training days, one a week in the early days of settlement, fell to one a month or even one a year. Festivities rather than military training increasingly became the main purpose of these gatherings, and the efficiency of the militia in these regions declined accordingly. In some towns and counties, the military tradition of the earlier period was kept alive only by volunteers who formed units of their own within the militia such as the Ancient and Honorable Company of Artillery in Boston. On the frontier the situation was different, for Indian raids were still a constant threat, and the militia had to be constantly ready for instant action. There training days were more frequent, and the militia's efficiency in frontier warfare was the main guarantee of the settlers' survival.

Warfare with the Indians was not the only military problem of the colonial period. Between 1689 and 1763, in four great wars fought in Europe between various coalitions of states, France and England were invariably on opposite sides, and their respective colonies in North America inevitably followed suit. In fact one of the major issues, if not the major one, involved in all the fighting was control of the North American continent, for, as Britain was colonizing the eastern seaboard from Maine to Georgia, France was extending its power over Canada and Louisiana and asserting its claim to the Great Lakes region and the Mississippi Valley.

The character of much of the fighting in the colonial wars between the English and the French was the same as that in the Indian wars. The French did maintain garrisons of regulars in Canada, but never enough to bear the brunt of the fighting. Instead they relied heavily on Indian allies whom they equipped with firearms. The French constructed forts at strategic points and garrisoned them with small numbers of regulars, a few of whom were normally sent along with Indian raiding parties to supervise operations. The French were far more successful than were the English in promoting good relations with the Indians, and learned the lessons of forest warfare very quickly. Using these methods, the French gained many local successes, and indeed kept the frontiers of the English colonies in a continual state of alarm; but they were never able to achieve decisive results.

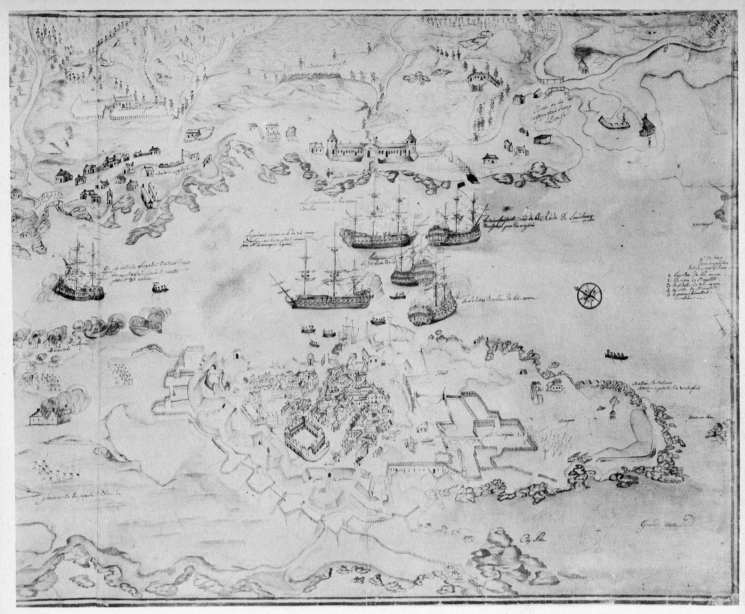

This section shows the fortress with the French fleet in the bay behind it. Louisburg surrendered on 26 July 1758.

VOLUNTEER FORCES

While the militia played an important part in the colonial wars, it had to be supplemented by volunteer forces of varying degrees of professionalism. For the expeditions against Canada, for instance, the primary reliance was necessarily on volunteer forces. Unlike the militia, volunteer forces were built from the top down. The commanding officers were first chosen by one of the colonial governors or assemblies, and the men were enlisted by them. The choice of a commander was made with due regard for his popularity in the colony and hence his ability to persuade officers and men to serve under him. The militia was the base from which the volunteers were recruited. The officers were invariably men whose ranks derived from the militia and whose total experience was in it. Volunteer forces were enlisted in the service and pay of one of the colonies and therefore were dependent upon appropriations of money made by that colony's assembly. Assemblies were usually parsimonious, and neither officers nor men were anxious to commit themselves for longer than a year or so. Volunteers were therefor enlisted usually only for a single campaign, not for long periods as in European armies. At the end of the campaign, they reverted to the militia, thus providing it with a leavening of experienced personnel.

The difficulties in securing a sustained and cooperative colonial effort forced the British to assumé an ever-increasing part of the burden of the wars in North America. Individual colonies were reimbursed for part of the expenses incurred in prosecuting the war, increasing numbers of British regulars were sent to North America, and finally certain colonial units were made part of the British regular establishment, and officers were appointed by the British to recruit Colonials for their regiments. These colonial units in the British establishment were the nearest thing to a regular force the Americans had before the Revolution.

THE FRENCH AND INDIAN WAR

All these methods of raising forces reached their culmination in the French and Indian War, the first truly large-scale conflict on the North American continent. The war began in America two years before it did in Europe when in 1754 a force of Virginia militia under Lieutenant Colonel George Washington was driven back from Fort Duquesne by the French and forced to surrender. The next year the British sent to America two regiments of regular troops under Major General Edward Braddock, a soldier of some forty-five years' experience on continental battlefields. Braddock's mission was to accomplish what the Virginia militia had failed to do—drive the French from Fort Duquesne. Accustomed to the parade-ground tactics and the open terrain of Europe, all Braddock's faith was in disciplined regulars and close-order formations. He had even more than the usual contempt of a regular British officer for militia and Indians. Early in June 1755, Braddock set out on the long march through the wilderness to Fort Duquesne with a total force of 2,200, including a body of Virginia militia. He was accompanied by Washington as an aide-de-camp. His force proceeded through the wilderness in traditional column formation with 300 axmen in front to clear the road, and a heavy baggage train of wagons in the rear. The heavy wagon train so slowed his progress that about halfway to Fort Duquesne he decided to let it follow as best it could and pushed ahead with about 1,300 selected men, 10 cannon, and a convoy of 30 wagons and several packhorses. In a ravine just past the Monongahela River on 9 July, 1755, Braddock's advance guard under Lieutenant Colonel Thomas Gage came under the fire of about 70 French regulars, 150 Canadians, and 650 Indians concealed in the forest. Instead of deploying his men in open formation and taking cover, Braddock advanced his force in mass formation to Gage's assistance, attempting to answer the concealed fire with volleys in traditional European fashion. The Virginians alone took to the woods and tried to answer Indian fire in Indian style. The volleys of the regulars were wasted on the air while the French and Indians poured in their fire with telling effect, decimating Braddock's troops and killing or wounding two-thirds of his officers. Mortally wounded himself, Braddock finally attempted to withdraw his force, but the belated order to retreat simply produced the panic that so frequently fell on regulars when their

officers were killed and their formations broken. The retreat became a wild flight that did not stop even when the terrified troops reached the baggage trains many miles to the rear. Despite the completeness of their victory, the French and Indian force was incapable of an effective pursuit, for the few French regulars present had little control over the Indians, who preferred to loot the battlefield and scalp the wounded.

The lessons of Braddock's defeat were not that regular forces or European methods were useless in America or that undisciplined American militia were superior to British regular troops. They were rather that tactics and formations would have to be adapted to terrain and the nature of the enemy, and that regulars, when employed in the forest, would have to learn to travel faster and lighter and take advantage of all the devices of cover, concealment, and surprise. Or, better still, they would have to employ colonial troops and Indian allies versed in this sort of warfare as the French had long since learned to do.

The British employed both methods in the ensuing years of the French and Indian War. Light infantry, trained as scouts and skirmishers, became a permanent part of the British Army organization. These troops were, when engaged in operations in the forest, clad in green or brown clothes instead of the traditional red coat of the British soldier, their heads shaved, their skins sometimes painted like the Indians'. The most proficient of the light infantry troops were special ranger companies recruited in the colonies and placed in the regular British establishment.

The French and Indian War was not entirely a war of forest engagements. Where British regulars had the opportunity to fight in the open, they showed the same superiority the woodsmen did in their native element. The final and decisive battle of the war was fought in the open field on the Plains of Abraham before the French citadel at Quebec in 1759. In this battle the training and discipline of the regulars and the initiative, determination, and courage of their commander, Major General James Wolfe, carried the day. In a daring move, Wolfe's men scaled the cliffs leading to the plains one night and appeared in

William Pitt (right), who passed over several senior generals and picked thirty-two-year-old James Wolfe to lead a British army of 9,000 men against the French at Quebec, with Wolfe before the latter's departure for Canada.

An anonymous eighteenth-century artist is responsible for this engraving showing the successive stages of action as General Wolfe's forces took Quebec. From bottom: British troops approach in barges; they scale the cliffs that night; the two armies face each other the next day; and the French begin to retreat.

General Wolfe was mortally wounded while leading a counterattack at Quebec on 13 September 1759. This engraving is based on a painting by the American artist Benjamin West.

traditional line of battle before the city the next morning. Major General the Marquis de Montcalm, the able French commander, accepted the challenge, but his troops proved unable to withstand the withering fire of Wolfe's exceptionally well-disciplined regiments.

The ultimate lesson of the colonial wars, then, was that European and American tactics each had their place, and either could be successful where conditions were suited to their use. But they also proved that only troops possessing the organization and discipline of regulars, whatever their tactics, could actually move in, seize and hold objectives, and thus achieve decisive results.

By the end of the French and Indian War, a new weapon had appeared on the frontier in Pennsylvania and to the southward, far better suited to use in guerrilla warfare than the musket. This weapon was later to gain fame as the Kentucky rifle. The effects of rifling a gun barrel, that is, of making spiral grooves that imparted a spinning effect to the bullet, giving it greater range and accuracy, had been known for some centuries in Germany and Switzerland. But the early rifles made there were too heavy and slow to load to be of military use. The Germans who settled in Pennsylvania developed, around 1750, a much lighter model far easier and faster to load. They used a bullet smaller than the bore, and a greased patch to keep the fit tight. This early American rifle could, in proper hands, hit a target the size of a man's head at 200 yards. Despite its superior range and accuracy, it was to take almost a hundred years of development before the rifle would supplant the musket as the standard infantry weapon, but, like the tactics of the American forest, it would have its place in any future war fought in America.

In the Indian wars and the colonial wars with France, Americans had gained considerable military experience, albeit much of it in guerrilla warfare along the frontiers that did not require the same degree of organized effort and professional competence as European-style warfare. Many colonial officers later to become famous in the Revolution— among them George Washington, Israel Putnam, Horatio Gates, Philip Schuyler, and John Stark—served their military apprenticeship in the French and Indian War, although none held high positions of command. In addition, certain traditions were established that continued to influence United States military policy and practices right down to the twentieth century. One of these was the tradition of the militia as the main reliance for defense and as a volunteer force for special emergencies. The fear of a standing army of professionals had already appeared. The colonial experience also established a strong tradition of separatism among the colonies themselves, for each had for a long period of years run its own military establishment. Within each colony, too, the civilian authority represented in the popular assembly had always kept a strict rein of control over the military, another tradition that was to have marked effect on American military development.

Certain characteristics of the American soldier that were to be fairly constant throughout all future wars had also made their appearance. He was inclined to be highly individualistic and to resent discipline and the inevitable restrictions of military life; he sought to know why he should do things before he would put his heart into doing them; and if in the end he accepted discipline and order as a stern necessity, he did so with the idea of winning victory as quickly as possible so that he could get back to his normal peacetime pursuits.

These traditions and these characteristics were the products of a society developing along democratic lines. The military strengths and weaknesses they engendered were to be amply demonstrated when the American soldier took up arms against the British in the American Revolution.

"Mort de Montcalm," by Jean-Baptiste Morret, shows the leader of the French forces at Quebec, Louis Joseph de Saint-Véran, Marquis de Montcalm-Gozon, after he was fatally wounded while trying to rally his fleeing army beneath the city walls.

Chief Pontiac agrees to let Major Robert Rogers and his troops pass through Indian country. The meeting took place in 1760 when the British were attempting to occupy forts surrendered by the French.

This engraving of Indians turning white captives over to British Colonel Henry Bouquet in 1764 is based on a drawing by Benjamin West.

The Kentucky rifle.

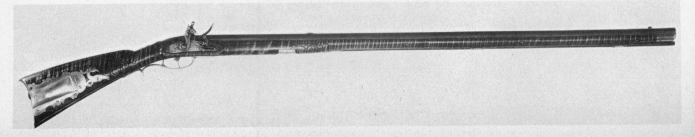

ARMY UNIFORMS OF THE EIGHTEENTH CENTURY

In colonial America the dress of the hunter was the cheapest and most easily procured. For that reason many of the men who fought in the French and Indian War were garbed in shirt and leggings. Their equipment included powder horns slung over the shoulder, bullet boxes and, of course, rifles. Washington, fond as he was of military formality and display, recommended hunting dress to his troops on the Virginia frontier in 1755, and in 1776 he repeated the recommendation to the soldiers of the Continental Army.

Some colonial military companies did adopt uniforms, and many of them were quite elaborate. In Connecticut the Governor's Foot Guard wore scarlet coats, bearskin hats, and brown gaiters. Members of the City-troop of Philadelphia dressed in brown coats with white facings, white breeches, high boots, and round leather caps decorated with a buck's tail and a silver cord. Brown was often used for military coats in colonial days and during the Revolution because brown dye was readily obtainable and brown cloth was manufactured throughout the country.

Independent military companies in the city of New York wore a variety of uniforms. In 1772 the Grenadier Company and the Light Infantry wore blue with red facings; the Fusiliers wore the same colors with bearskin caps; the blue coat of the German Fusiliers was trimmed with silver lace. The Sportsman Company wore green with crimson facings and small round hats. The Corsicans were dressed in short green coats and small round hats cocked

on one side and decorated with a red heart of tin engraved with the words "God and our Right." Around the crown were the words "Liberty or Death." The Bold Forresters wore green on their round hats which had one side turned up with a small brass plate carrying the word "Freedom."

Most of the Massachusetts and Connecticut militia wore scarlet, but the prevailing uniform of colonial times seems to have been blue coats faced with red; breeches were generally of buckskin. The uniform George Washington wore as a provincial officer has been described as blue with buff facings and buff waistcoat and breeches, although the 1772 portrait of him by Peale shows a blue coat with red facings and red waistcoat and breeches. Washington undoubtedly appeared at Cambridge to take command of the Army in the familiar blue and buff uniform.

In 1775 there were not enough uniforms in the Continental Army to distinguish the officers from their men. As a result, Washington was obliged to devise badges in order that rank might be indicated at sight. The following order was issued shortly after he took command: "As the Continental Army has unfortunately no uniforms, and consequently many inconveniences must arise from not being able to distinguish the commissioned officers from the privates, it is desired that some badges of distinction may be immediately provided; for instance, that the field officer may have red or pink colored cockades in their hats, the captains yellow or buff, and the subalterns green. They are

Left to right: A Virginia rifleman; a minuteman; a member of the Connecticut Governor's Foot Guard; and a member of the City-troop of Philadelphia.

to furnish themselves accordingly. The sergeants may be distinguished by an epaulette or stripe of red cloth sewed upon the right shoulder, the corporals by one of green." Washington also directed: "The general officers and their aides-de-camp will be distinguished in the following manner: The commander-in-chief by a light blue ribband worn across his heart betwen his coat and waistcoat; the major and brigadier general by a pink ribband worn in like manner; the aides-de-camp by a green ribband." After the order to field and line officers was issued, Washington directed that major generals' sleeves be distinguished from those of brigadier generals by a "broad purple ribband."

The first troops raised under the authority of the Continental Congress were riflemen from Virginia, Maryland, and western Pennsylvania. They wore shirts, ankle-length trousers that buttoned around the leg below the knee, and moccasins. Around the waist was a leather belt in which was stuck a hunting knife. A cartridge box and a powder horn usually hung from another belt worn over the shoulder.

The Continental Congress, aware of the curious variety of uniforms, or lack of them, in its army, decided in 1775 that the troops should be uniformed in brown, the men paying for their clothes by stoppages of pay, after the custom prevailing in the British service. But it was easier to decide the color than to procure the cloth. Some of the states undertook to make the soldiers for whom they were responsible presentable, and New York was more successful than any of the others. Even her troops, however, were clothed in different colors because the quartermaster had to buy whatever cloth was in the market. Troops appeared in blue, brown, and gray coats with facings of buff, white, crimson, blue, and green. A number of Pennsylvania regiments appeared in brown with buff or white facings, while others had blue coats with scarlet or white facings. Some of the men wore half gaiters, and all who could obtain them wore buckskin breeches. Occasionally the Continentals captured British uniforms which were dyed brown or blue if there was time; otherwise they were worn without change, causing serious mistakes on the battlefield.

Washington seems to have had little confidence in the ability of Congress or the individual states to provide clothing for the Army. While he was in New York in 1766 he issued a general order in which he said: "The General, being sensible of the difficulty and expense of providing clothes of almost any kind for the troops, feels an unwillingness to recommend, much more to order, any kind of uniforms, but as it is absolutely necessary that men should have clothes and appear decent and tight, he earnestly encourages the use of hunting shirts, with long breeches made of the same cloth, gaiter-fashion about the legs, to all those yet unprovided. No dress can be cheaper or more convenient in warm weather, and warm in cool weather, by putting on underclothes, which will not change the outward dress, winter or summer, besides, it is a dress justly supposed to carry no small terror to the enemy, who think every such person a complete marksman."

During the hard years of 1777 and 1778 all attempts to provide uniforms for the men were abandoned. Officers wore the remnants of their old militia dress; each coat or hat was what its wearer was able to procure, with no thought given to similarity of color. The enlisted men wore the clothes in which they had done their work at home. The men who underwent the hardships of Valley Forge were dressed in the apparel of private citizens. Many of them were coatless; many had no shoes and their heads were protected from the weather by handkerchiefs.

After 1778 the alliance with France raised the prospect that, in addition to help from the French army and fleet, arms and clothing would be made available to the Continental Army. It was probably in the hope that France would help provide the proper material for carrying it out that Washington issued this order in 1779: "The following are the uniforms that have been determined upon for the troops of these states respectively, so soon as the state of the public supplies will permit of their being furnished accordingly. And in the meantime it is recommended to the officers to endeavor to accommodate their uniforms to the standard, that when the men come to be supplied

Left to right: Two members of Pennsylvania regiments; a member of the 2nd South Carolina Regiment; and two riflemen in uniforms worn during the Revolutionary War.

14

Soldiers in the four types of uniforms ordered by George Washington in 1779. Left to right: The uniform for soldiers from New England; New York and New Jersey; Pennsylvania, Delaware, Maryland, and Virginia; and North Carolina, South Carolina, and Georgia.

This is the uniform that Lafayette chose for the light infantry corps he commanded during the Revolutionary War. It consisted of a blue coat with white facings and linings, white waistcoat and breeches, full black gaiters, a white crossbelt, and a round leather hat with a horsehair crest.

A brigadier general of the Continental Army and his aide-de-camp in 1780.

The artillery uniform.

Uniforms worn by officers during the Revolutionary War.

15

there may be a proportionate uniform." The order designated the uniforms by groups of states. The soldiers of New
Hampshire, Massachusetts, Rhode Island, and Connecticut
were to wear blue coats faced with white, and buttons and
linings white. The uniform of New York and New Jersey
troops was to be faced with buff, the buttons and linings
white. The men of Pennsylvania, Delaware, Maryland, and
Virginia were to wear blue faced with red, and those of
North Carolina, South Carolina, and Georgia blue faced
with blue, the buttonholes being edged with narrow white
lace or tape.

The artillery uniform remained the one chosen in 1777.
The coat was blue with red facings, lining, cuffs, lapels, and
collars; the skirts of the coat were fastened back in order
to show the red lining. There were three yellow buttons on
each cuff and at the large blue pocket flaps at the hips. The
waistcoat was white with twelve yellow buttons, and the
breeches were white. The rest of the uniform consisted of
black half gaiters, a white stock and ruffled shirt, a black
cocked hat bound with yellow braid, a black cockade and
a red plume. The men wore crossbelts and hangers; the
officers wore gilt epaulettes. In 1779 Washington ordered
a white center added to the black cockade to signify the
alliance with France, since the French wore white cockade
and coat.

Washington wanted his army to present as fine an appearance as the circumstances of the country and the condition of the treasury would permit when they joined forces
with the French under Rochambeau. In June 1780, from his
headquarters in Short Hills, New Jersey, he issued an order
which must have been obeyed by many of his officers only
with great difficulty. The order read: "As it is at all times
of great importance both for the sake of appearance and
for the regularity of service that the different military ranks

Uniforms of the commander in chief
and his staff at the end of the 18th century.

Left to right: Cavalry, infantry,
and artillery uniforms at the end of the eighteenth century.

The uniform of the commanding officer of
Washington's Life Guard in 1780. The Life Guard
was a special corps of mounted men attached
to the commander in chief.

The infantry uniform of 1796.

should be distinguished from each other, and more especially at present, the Commander in Chief has thought proper to establish the following distinctions, and strongly recommends it to all officers to endeavor to conform to them as speedily as possible. The major generals to wear blue coats with buff facings and linings, yellow buttons, white or buff underclothes, two epaulettes with two stars upon each, and a black and white feather in the hat; the stars will be furnished at headquarters. The brigadier generals, the same uniform as the major generals, with the difference of one star in place of two stars, and a white feather. The colonels, lieutenant colonels and majors, the uniform of their regiments and two epaulettes. The captains, the uniforms of their regiments and an epaulette on the right shoulder. The subalterns, the uniform of their regiment and an epaulette on the left shoulder. The aides-de-camp, the uniform of their rank and corps, or if they belong to no corps, of their general officers; those of the major generals and the brigadier generals to have a green feather in the hat, those of the Commander in Chief, a white and green. . . . All officers as will warrant as commissioned to wear a cockade and side arms, either a sword or a genteel bayonet."

This order, the first issued by Washington fixing the uniforms of general officers, indicates a brighter and more hopeful outlook for the Continental Army, but the promise of better times was not fully realized. The blue cloth which had been chosen for the uniforms could not be obtained, and in February and April 1783, Washington issued orders directing soldiers to reverse and repair their old coats.

The few troops that remained with Washington when he entered New York after its evacuation by the British were described by one young woman as "ill-clad." "But," she added, "they were our troops, and as I looked at them and thought upon all they had done and suffered for us, my heart and my eyes were full, and I admired and gloried in them the more because they were weatherbeaten and forlorn."

The small force that made up the U.S. Army after the Revolutionary War was divided into eight companies of infantry and two of artillery. Uniforms were based on the French military costumes of the period, with white the distinguishing color for the infantry and red and yellow for the artillery. Metal buttons, sword hilt, and epaulettes were gilt. The enlisted men of the infantry wore white belts, and those of the artillery, buff belts. Officers wore full gaiters, and enlisted men, half gaiters. In 1796 the infantry uniform changed somewhat—red replaced white for facings, cuffs, and collars, and officers were permitted to wear black top boots instead of gaiters.

How soldiers wore their hair was a continuing problem for the Army. The fashion of wearing it in long queues and covering it with grease and flour was not conducive to cleanliness, and during the Revolution numerous orders contained directions for the proper dressing of the hair. Flour for the hair was issued regularly to the troops, but during the war and later officers had much cause for complaint. An order issued in 1799 contained this paragraph: "The hair of the regimental officers, noncommissioned officers will be dressed uniformly, over a thin piece of wood with a rosette of black, one and a half inches in diameter; of ribbon for the officers and leather for the men." Another order, issued two years later, solved the hair problem by requiring that it be cut short.

Americaner Soldat.

These drawings are among the first to be made of Continental Army soldiers. The work of the German engraver Johann Martin Will, they bear the legend: "Accurate representation of an American soldier drawn and sent by an officer from Bayreuth, presently serving with the English in America. His clothing is made of coarse linen, he has a long musket and bayonet and is of robust health and endurance."

"The Boston Massacre" is the best known of all Paul Revere's engravings. The widely circulated drawing of a line of British soldiers firing point-blank into a group of unarmed citizens on the night of 5 March 1770, helped unite public opinion against the British.

CHAPTER 2

THE REVOLUTIONARY WAR

THE MILITIA AND THE MINUTEMEN

The Boston Tea Party

The immediate chain of events leading to the American Revolution began in December, 1773, when a group of Boston patriots dumped the tea aboard a British vessel into the harbor in violent protest against a British import duty on that commodity. In reprisal, the British closed the port of Boston, placed the whole colony of Massachusetts under the military rule of Major General Thomas Gage, and passed other repressive measures, collectively known as the "Intolerable Acts." These acts were interpreted by patriots throughout the colonies as evidence of British intent to reduce them all to complete subservience. Steps were taken to form revolutionary governments in each colony, and the First Continental Congress gathered at Philadelphia on 5 September 1774 to discuss concerted measures to protect American rights.

Simultaneously preparations for military resistance began. They consisted, for the most part, of establishing the control of the revolutionary governments over the militia in each colony and of shaping from it an effective military force. What happened in Massachusetts is of greatest significance. The revolutionary government there, fairly typical

of that in the other colonies, consisted of a Provincial Congress that took over from the old popular assembly, a central Committee of Safety, and various local conventions and committees in each township. The local committees forced the resignation of militia officers with Loyalist sympathies and reorganized the militia under patriot commanders. The Provincial Congress then, following the old colonial tradition of selection, directed officers in each township to enlist a third of their men into minutemen organizations to be ready to act at a moment's warning. Into the minutemen companies went the younger and more active members of the militia. The rest were organized into alarm companies as a reserve.

Lexington and Concord

The Provincial Congress and the local organizations also began to accumulate ammunition and other military stores. The major depot for these stores was established at Concord.

Information of these preparations leaked to General Gage in Boston, and on the night of 18–19 April 1775, he sent out an expedition of about 700 picked men under Lieutenant Colonel Francis Smith to seize and destroy the military stores at Concord. Despite Gage's efforts to pre-

Citizens of New York City are protesting the Stamp Act in this engraving. Their placard says: "England's Folly & America's Ruin."

The "Pennsylvania Journal and Advertiser" denounced the Stamp Act on 31 October 1765, the day before it became effective.

This is the Place to affix the STAMP.

This lithograph of the Boston Tea Party is the work of American artist Nathaniel Currier.

Part of the masthead of the "Massachusetts Sun" in 1774.

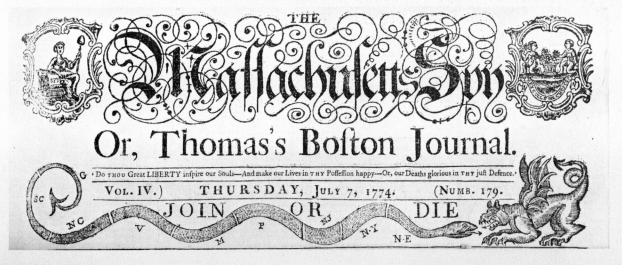

serve secrecy, preparations for the movement caught the eye of patriots in Boston, and two messengers—Paul Revere and William Dawes—rode out a few hours ahead of the British to give the alarm. When the British reached Lexington at dawn on 19 April, they found themselves confronted by a small force of local minutemen, drawn up in a line on the village green. Just who fired the first shot, the one "heard round the world," remains an intriguing mystery. Whoever did, it led the impatient and nervous British regulars, without orders from their commanders, to fire into the

minutemen, killing eight and wounding ten. The rest quickly dispersed and the British column proceeded to Concord, where the redcoats destroyed such of the military stores as they could find.

It was when the British began their return march to Boston that they first ran into serious difficulties. The alarm had been going out to farm and village, and both minutemen and alarm companies had been gathering. From behind trees and fences and from vacant houses along the road they poured their fire into the British column. Gage in

This cartoon was entitled "The Bostonian's Paying the Excise-Man, or Tarring & Feathering" when it appeared in London in 1774.

A Currier and Ives lithograph of Patrick Henry delivering his famous "Give me liberty or give me death" speech before the Virginia Assembly in 1775.

Boston received word of what was happening and sent a relief force with several pieces of artillery to join Smith at Lexington. The relief saved Smith's force from annihilation, but from Lexington to Charlestown the fire continued and the British had no surcease until they were safely under the protective guns of their fleet. The British lost about 273 men out of a total force of 1,500 to 1,800. The fact that the force was not wiped out was testimony to the poor marksmanship of farmers armed with muskets.

Lexington and Concord had tremendous psychological effect in arousing the colonies to determined resistance. Regardless of who fired the first shot, the British got the blame, and news of the events of 19 April was carried by messengers through the colonies to the southward. Military preparations in all the colonies were quickened and royal governors were forced to flee to British warships. In the immediate area around Boston, militia and volunteer forces from the other New England colonies rallied to join the Massachusetts men in a siege of Boston.

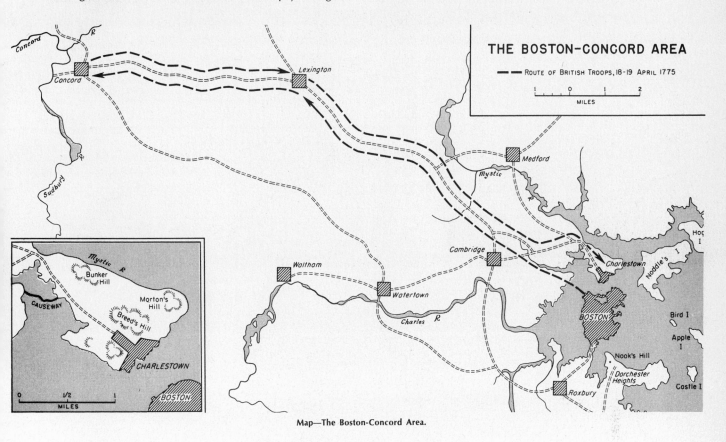

THE BOSTON-CONCORD AREA

– – – Route of British Troops, 18-19 April 1775

MILES

Map—The Boston-Concord Area.

Currier and Ives's "The Minute-Men of the Revolution."

A contemporary print of the Battle of Lexington on 19 April, 1775. The Lexington minutemen are shown dispersing at lower left and right.

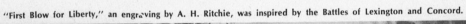

"First Blow for Liberty," an engraving by A. H. Ritchie, was inspired by the Battles of Lexington and Concord.

Capture of Fort Ticonderoga

In early May 1775, other New England forces led by Colonel Ethan Allen of Vermont and Colonel Benedict Arnold of Connecticut, seized the British fort at Ticonderoga, the strong point between Lakes George and Champlain on the water route betwen New York and Canada. Captain de LaPlace, the British commander, with a garrison of only about 40 men, surrendered without a fight. From there Arnold and Allen proceeded farther north to Crown Point, a fort the British demolished and evacuated before their arrival. These successes gave the Americans both strategic bases and valuable artillery pieces and other military supplies sorely needed for the siege of Boston, but it would take much time and effort to get the cannon there.

Fort Ticonderoga
after its restoration.

Ethan Allen's letter to Jonathan Trumbull, Governor of Connecticut, telling of the capture of Fort Ticonderoga and Allen's plans for taking "Lake Champlain and the fortifications thereon." Allen was turned back by a force of Canadian militia when he reached St. Johns, a British post on the Richelieu River.

Colonel Ethan Allen demanding the surrender of Fort Ticonderoga "in the name of the Continental Congress and the Great Jehovah!"

Colonel William Prescott and his men
fortifying Breed's Hill on the night of 16 June, 1775.

The Battle of Bunker Hill

In late May, Gage's force in Boston was reinforced from England, bringing it to a total of about 6,500 men. With the British reinforcements came three major generals of considerable military experience and reputation who were to play leading roles in the Revolution—William Howe, Henry Clinton, and John Burgoyne. All were anxious to take the offensive and get what Burgoyne referred to as "elbow room." However, it was the Colonials who first took the initiative and, on the night of 16 June 1775, threw up entrenchments on Breed's Hill on the Charlestown isthmus overlooking Boston from the north. The original intent had been to fortify Bunker Hill, nearer the narrow neck of the isthmus, but for reasons not clear even today, they decided to move in closer. Nevertheless, Bunker Hill was to give its name to the battle that ensued.

In moving onto Breed's Hill the Americans placed themselves in a position where they could easily have been cut off had the British landed in their rear at the neck of the isthmus. But other councils prevailed in Boston. Gage, with the approval of Howe, to whom tactical control was entrusted, decided on the morning of 17 June that the rebels must be dislodged before they could complete their works. Scorning elaborate maneuver, he evidently calculated

The American officer John Trumbull, who later painted this picture of the "Battle of Bunker's Hill," viewed the engagement from Roxbury Hill on the other side of Boston. Johann von Mueller, a German craftsman, made the engraving.

The artist Alonzo Chappell's version
of the Battle of Bunker Hill as engraved by John Godfrey.

This cartoon entitled "Bunkers Hill, or America's Head-Dress" appeared in 1776.

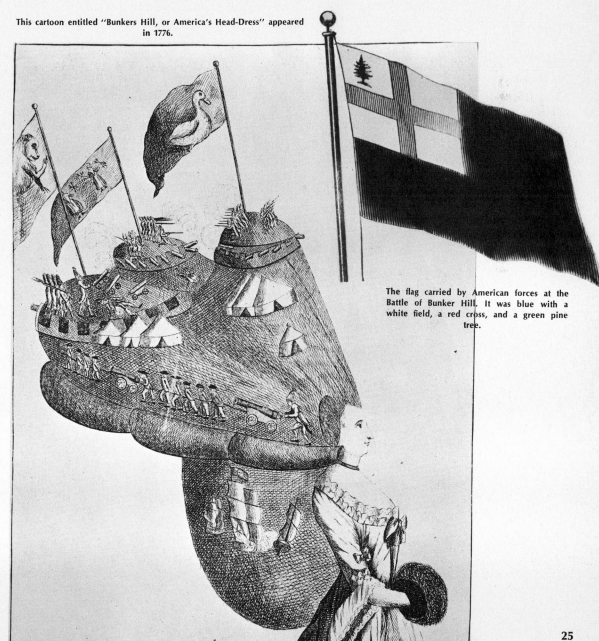

The flag carried by American forces at the Battle of Bunker Hill. It was blue with a white field, a red cross, and a green pine tree.

that the ill-trained American militia would disintegrate when faced with disciplined regulars, and that such a defeat administered in a direct attack on the hill would show the rebels the futility of resisting British power. Howe's force of around 2,200 men was ferried from Boston to Charlestown and in the midafternoon on 17 June began the attack on the American front and flanks. The Americans behind their entrenchments held their fire while the British regulars sweated up the hill under their heavy packs. When the redcoats came within 50 yards, the American opened a devastating fire. Twice the well-formed British lines broke and retreated, leaving large numbers killed and wounded on the field. By this time the Americans were nearly out of powder, and a third British attack with the bayonet carried the hill. The militia, without bayonets or other means of close-in defense, withdrew across the neck of the isthmus to the mainland. But Howe's victory had cost him more than 1,000 casualties to the American's 400, and his forces were too disorganized to undertake a pursuit. His experience at Bunker Hill made Howe thereafter wary of attacking

Americans in fortified positions, even under the most favorable circumstances. The British again retired to Boston and the siege was resumed.

The New England army that fought the Battle of Bunker Hill was hardly an army at all in the true sense of the word, but rather a conglomeration of militia and volunteers under the loose control of several military commanders. The general scheme adopted by the New England colonies after Lexington and Concord was gradually to replace the militia and minutemen by volunteer forces organized in the traditional colonial manner, the officers appointed and the men enlisted under them. None were enlisted, however, beyond the end of the year 1775, and the Connecticut men only until 10 December 1775. Each of the separate colonies appointed its own commanders and there was no overall commander for the whole force. Militia and minutemen units were the recruiting ground for the volunteer forces. While the enlistment of the volunteer force went on, militia units of various sorts continued to come and go.

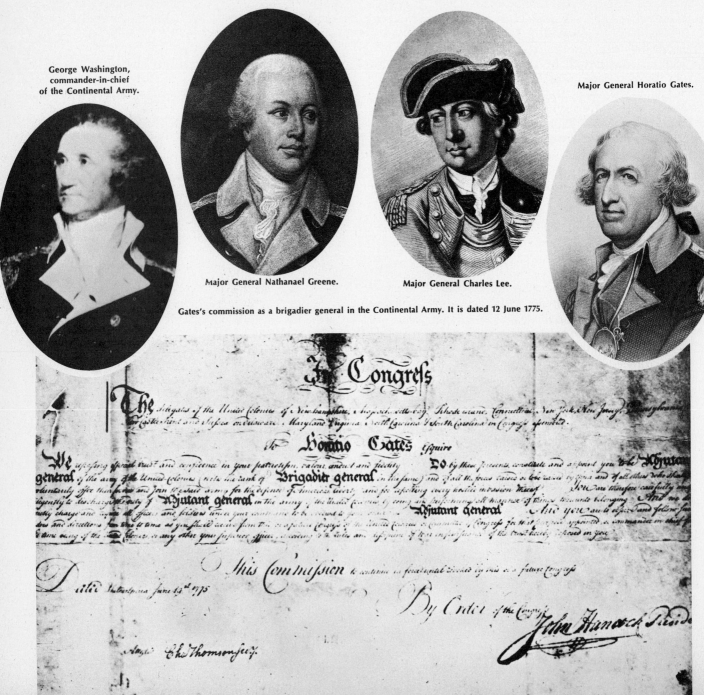

George Washington, commander-in-chief of the Continental Army.

Major General Nathanael Greene.

Major General Charles Lee.

Major General Horatio Gates.

Gates's commission as a brigadier general in the Continental Army. It is dated 12 June 1775.

THE CONTINENTAL ARMY: 1775–1776

The Massachusetts Provincial Congress, conscious of the necessity for enlisting the support of all the colonies in resistance to Britain, appealed to the Second Continental Congress then sitting at Philadelphia to adopt the new army. Congress did so on 14 June 1775—an anniversary date still remembered in the army of today. In view of the difficulty of transport and supply, no effort was made to raise proportionate forces from the other colonies to make the army at Boston a genuinely national one. However, ten companies of riflemen were authorized to be raised in Pennsylvania, Virginia, and Maryland, and enlisted until the end of the year. The choice of riflemen attested to the belief that specialists in the use of this new weapon would be a valuable adjunct to the musketry of New England. In recognition of the need for specialists of a different kind, Congress voted on 27 July 1775 to incorporate Colonel Thomas Gridley's regiment of Massachusetts artillery into the army.

The day after it voted to adopt the New England army, Congress chose George Washington to be its Commander in Chief. The choice was dictated as much by political and geographic considerations as by military ones. The New Englanders felt there was no better means of obtaining southern support than by choosing a southerner as continental commander. Washington's military experience was perhaps greater than that of any other southerner. His impressive appearance and his work in the military committees of Congress inspired the confidence of his fellow members. Of others who had greater military experience, none gave evidence of the same well-rounded personality, steadfast character, and political sagacity.

Washington himself recognized, when he accepted the command, that he lacked the military training, experience, and knowledge that it required. His whole military experience had been in frontier warfare during the French and Indian War. In that experience he had exhibited ample evidence of those qualities that make a natural leader of men —courage, initiative, perseverance, and resourcefulness— but he had never participated in operations on the scale of those he was now called upon to direct. Since 1758 he had been largely absorbed in the affairs of his large Mount Vernon plantation and in the political life of his native colony of Virginia. Nevertheless, he brought to his task traits of character and abilities as a leader that in the end more than compensated for his military deficiencies. Among these were a determination and steadfastness of purpose rooted in an unshakable conviction of the righteousness of the American cause, a scrupulous sense of honor and duty, and a dignity that inspired the respect and confidence of those around him.

Congress also provided Washington with a group of assistants, four major generals and eight brigadiers. The same mixture of geographical, political, and military considerations was evident in their choice. Two thirds of the generals came from New England since most of the troops under arms also came from there. Of the major generals the most notable was Charles Lee, an ex-British officer of considerable experience and reputation, and of the brigadiers, Horatio Gates, Richard Montgomery, and Nathanael Greene, the first two also former members of the British Army.

Washington described the army of which he formally took command on 3 July 1775 as "a mixed multitude of people . . . under very little discipline, order or government." The various colonial contingents were under different forms of organization and had different supply and pay systems. The size of regiments varied from 500 to 1,000 men. There were more than a dozen different kinds of muskets, almost all the property of the individual soldiers. Discipline was lax, with men coming and going between their homes and camp without much regard for the normal rules of military life. The respect ordinarily paid by soldiers to their officers was unknown. In the militia, privates selected their officers, and in the volunteer forces soldiers chose under whom they would serve. The officers had only the most elementary preparation for their positions and were, therefore, inefficient. The men, like all untrained soldiers, neglected field sanitation and did not take proper care of their persons or their camps. Shelters in which the men lived varied from tents to rude huts constructed of boards, brush, sailcloth, and turf. The arrival of the ten rifle companies from the South, after a remarkable march, added to the strength of the army but at the same time introduced a new element of discord. These men were primarily individualists and rejected all discipline. Finding few targets to engage their attention, they tended to waste ammunition and to become restless and troublesome. In sum, although the human material was good, it was untrained and there was no skilled cadre or doctrine to assist General Washington in their training. Both officers and men had to learn their jobs in the hard school of active operations and combat.

Major General Thomas Gage, the commander of all British forces in America at the outbreak of the Revolutionary War.

Washington was well aware that, although the enthusiasm of a day might sustain the soldiery for a Bunker Hill, the task of driving the British from Boston would require discipline, organization, and technical military competence. He therefore set out to create out of the volunteers a force that could fight in the manner of European regulars. Various punishments were instituted as a means of enforcing discipline—lash, pillory, wooden horse, and drumming out of camp. Elementary rules of sanitation were instituted. A strenuous effort was made to halt the random comings and goings of officers and men and to institute regular roll calls and returns of strength. Courts-martial sat almost constantly and many officers were dismissed.

The inculcation of discipline had to go on under extremely difficult circumstances. At the same time the siege of Boston had to be maintained and the army reenlisted in the Continental service rather than in that of the various individual colonies. Washington asked Congress for advice concerning the new establishment, and a committee of Congress visited camp in September, 1775. Out of conferences emerged a plan for an army of 26 regiments of infantry of 728 men each, plus 1 regiment of riflemen and 1 of artillery, 20,372 men in all, to be uniformly paid, supplied, and administered by the Continental Congress and to be enlisted to the end of the year 1776. In each of the 26 Regular infantry regiments there were to be 8 companies, each of 86 men and 4 officers, plus an 8-man regimental staff.

The plan meant reducing 38 regiments of irregular size to 28 of uniform size and a corresponding reduction of officers of all grades. Few officers were willing to accept a reduction in rank. The men also saw their first obligation to their familiar officers and were reluctant to remain in the ranks. Few would take service under any but officers of their own choosing, or in regiments from any locality but their own. The reenlistment proceeded slowly, and 10 December was fast approaching. This was the day when the Connecticut men were to go home, and no satisfactory force was available to replace them. Pressure was brought to bear to persuade the men to enlist or even to remain until the end of the month, but most went home anyway. Militia from Massachusetts and New Hampshire had to be hastily called in to fill their places.

On 1 January 1776, the changeover from the old to the new army formally took place. Enlistments were still far from sufficient to fill the 28 regiments, and men continued to come in slowly. Early in March 1776, when Washington set out to force the British out of Boston, his returns showed only 9,170 Continentals on the rolls. This failure to secure even for one year an army adequate to the task forced Washington to rely continually on short-term militia to supplement his regular force.

Just as serious as the manpower problem was the shortage of supplies. The colonies had long relied on England for their manufactured goods, and had no ready substitute for this source in 1775. Shortages in the army before Boston ran the whole catalogue of contemporary military supply—powder, muskets, cannon, cloth for uniforms, bayonets, camp kettles and other utensils, cartridge boxes, and salt. There was no shortage of provisions for the time being, though transportation problems and lack of salt to preserve meat threatened such shortages for the future. The Americans lost at Bunker Hill principally because they ran out of powder and had no bayonets. During the siege of Boston, Washington was reluctant to attack Gage not only because of the disorganized state of his army but also because of critical shortages of powder, cannon, and even muskets. Most of the departing militia and volunteers took their muskets with them since they were, for the most part, their private property. To halt this practice, Washington tried to purchase these muskets for incoming recruits, but on inspection he found many of them to be in such bad shape as to be useless. Spears were constructed as a substitute for bayonets, and indeed some men, for lack of muskets, were armed only with these spears.

The supply situation gradually improved during the long period of inaction before Boston that lasted from June 1775 to March 1776. Congress and the individual colonies sponsored voyages to the West Indies, where the French and Dutch had conveniently exported quantities of war materials. Washington put some of his troops on board ship, and this improvised navy succeeded in capturing numerous British supply ships. He also sent Colonel Henry Knox, later to become his Chief of Artillery, to Ticonderoga from where in the winter of 1775–1776 Knox brought some fifty pieces of captured cannon to Cambridge over poor or nonexistent roads in ice-bound New York and New England.

The Attack on Boston: 1776

With the arrival of the artillery and with his supply position generally much improved, Washington was finally ready in early March 1776 to attempt to drive the British from Boston. With the militia his army now numbered about 14,000. On 4 March, American infantry and artillery occupied Dorchester Heights, from which position their guns could dominate Boston from the south. Gage had meantime been succeeded by Major General William Howe, who had long had serious doubts of the feasibility of using Boston as the main base for the prosecution of the war. While he at first thought of launching an assault against Dorchester Heights, for several days the weather was too bad to permit sending boats across the harbor, and the American dispositions were such as to prevent any approach to the heights by land. The Americans took advantage of this enforced delay to fortify Nook's Hill, standing still closer and in a more threatening position to the city. Howe recognized the difficulty of his position and finally decided to evacuate the city, sailing to Halifax in Nova Scotia on 17 March. The British left behind in Boston large stores of military supplies, including 250 cannon.

The Attack on Canada

While Washington was organizing his army and gaining his bloodless victory at Boston, other American forces took the offensive in an effort to secure Canada as a fourteenth American colony, hoping to prevent its use as a British base in an invasion of the other thirteen. The American plan

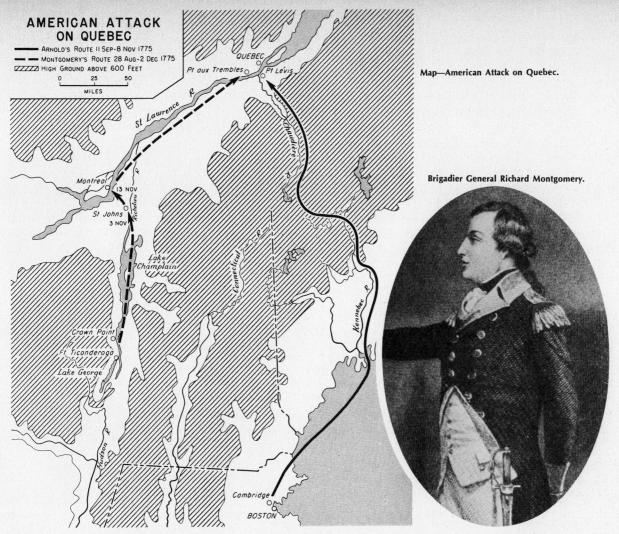

AMERICAN ATTACK
ON QUEBEC

▬▬▬▬ Arnold's Route 11 Sep-8 Nov 1775
▬ ▬ ▬ Montgomery's Route 28 Aug-2 Dec 1775
▨▨▨▨ High Ground above 600 Feet

0   25   50
MILES

Map—American Attack on Quebec.

Brigadier General Richard Montgomery.

called for a two-pronged attack on Quebec—one column under General Montgomery to proceed from Ticonderoga up Lake Champlain and the Richelieu River to the St. Lawrence, the other under Colonel Benedict Arnold to follow a more difficult and less known route up the Kennebec River in Maine, across the Height of Land, and down the Chaudière. The concept was a bold one in the light of existing shortages of manpower and supplies and the wild and difficult country through which the expeditions must pass. Time was of the essence since the men on these expeditions were, like those before Boston, initially enlisted only until the end of the year. Yet there was a bare chance of success, for the British Governor-General of Canada, Major General Sir Guy Carleton, had hardly 1,000 regulars at his disposal, and there were high hopes that the inhabitants of Canada, mainly French, would rally to the American cause.

Montgomery started early in September 1775 from Ticonderoga but was delayed in capturing the British fort at St. Johns until 3 November. From there he moved swiftly and on 13 November captured Montreal; by 22 November he had secured his position along the lower reaches of the St. Lawrence and was ready to move against Quebec. Yet this was too late for him to join Arnold in a surprise attack on the Canadian citadel. The latter had emerged at the

mouth of the Chaudière opposite the city on 8 November after a march through the wilderness that is one of the epics of American military history. Boats furnished by a contractor proved leaky, supplies of food ran short, and the portage between the Kennebec and the Chaudière was far more difficult than had been anticipated. One group of 400 men turned back at the halfway point. The rest went on, half-starved, sick, and exhausted. About 650 of them reached Point Lévis, slipped across the St. Lawrence in canoes at night, and clambered the steep banks to the Plains of Abraham on 12 November. This force proved inadequate for the capture of Quebec, and Arnold moved back to Point aux Trembles to await Montgomery.

Montgomery's force meanwhile had been seriously reduced by disease and desertion. The much-hoped-for aid from the Canadians did not materialize. Men whose enlistments expired at the end of the year had little stomach for further campaigning and many left for home. After leaving garrisons at St. Johns and Montreal, Montgomery had only 300 men with which to join Arnold. By the time he arrived, Carleton in Quebec had rallied a sizable force from among the English settlers in Canada.

Despite all the discouraging circumstances, Arnold and Montgomery refused to give up, and on the first snowy night, 30–31 December 1775, launched a desperate attack

29

on Quebec, timed in large measure because of the expiration of the men's enlistments on the next day. The attack was a failure, Montgomery was killed, and Arnold badly wounded in the leg. Arnold still refused to give up and continued to direct a siege from his hospital bed. He was later forced to relinquish command on 1 April 1776 after his leg was reinjured in a fall from a horse. During the siege, when the British in Quebec actually outnumbered their besiegers, smallpox broke out in the American Army, further depleting its ranks. Reinforcements arrived early in April, but they were overmatched by new arrivals of British regulars from England. Finally Carleton sallied forth in early June and drove the Americans back across the St. Lawrence at all points where they had penetrated into Canada. With an army ill-supplied and decimated by disease, Major General John Sullivan, the new commander, gave up the effort and fell back to the head of Lake Champlain.

The American failure before Quebec can hardly be attributed to any lack of leadership on the part of Montgomery and Arnold, both of whom exhibited daring, courage, and tenacity in the face of almost insurmountable obstacles. Few campaigns in our history have required equal physical endurance from both officers and men. It was mainly deficiencies in organization, training, discipline, and particularly in the system of short enlistments, combined with almost insuperable logistical obstacles, that defeated the Americans. And the defeat left the road open for a British invasion of New York from the Canadian base.

The War in the South: 1776

While the major theatre of war during the first year was in the North, events were also transpiring in the South that were to have major influence on the future course of the conflict. Shortly after Lexington and Concord, patriot militia drove British royal governors to seek refuge aboard warships off the coast and seized British military installations ashore with their stores. There was considerable Tory strength in the southern colonies, and the fleeing royal governors of Virginia and North Carolina urged the British Government to send an expedition to cooperate with these Tories in reestablishing British rule in the southern provinces. In response, the British Government organized a combined naval and military force under the joint command of General Clinton and Admiral Peter Parker to go south in early 1776.

Unfortunately for the British, the expedition was delayed, and by the time it arrived off the coast of North Carolina and Virginia, militia had dispersed the Tory forces organized in those colonies. Clinton therefore decided the British force must try to regain a base of operations at Charleston in South Carolina, the largest port in the southern colonies. But before Clinton and Parker could get to Charleston, the patriots had vastly strengthened the defenses of that city. Congress authorized the raising of 14 Continental battalions in the South and detached Major General Charles Lee from Washington's army to direct the defense of Charleston. In addition, South Carolina militia rallied in large numbers under Colonel William Moultrie. By the time Parker's fleet arrived off Charleston on 1 June 1776, fortifications in the harbor had been strengthened and were manned by nearly 6,000 men. Moultrie, contrary to the advice of Lee, who thought the post might well become a trap, concentrated his men in a fort on Sullivan's Island, later named Fort Moultrie. Parker's ships would have to pass this fort in order to enter the harbor. Parker landed Clinton's force on an adjacent island from which it was anticipated the British soldiers could wade the passage and join in the naval attack on Fort Moultrie. But on 28 June, when Parker signaled the attack, the water was too deep, and Clinton's army had to stand idly by while artillery in the fort wreaked havoc on Parker's fleet. Parker even had his breeches blown off. He had to reembark Clinton's troops and return north with his battered fleet to join Howe, who by then was concentrating both army and fleet for an attack on New York. The British were not to turn their attention southward again for almost three years.

The results of the first year were in no sense decisive on any front. The British had withdrawn from Boston to re-form and await reinforcements that would give them an army equal to the task of subduing the rebellious colonies. The American offensive against Canada had failed, as had the British effort to reestablish control of the southern colonies. The greatest American achievement of the year had not been a tactical one at all, but the creation of an army. Seriously imperfect as it might yet be, this army was nevertheless in being, a barrier to the concentrated effort the British would make the following year to subdue the colonies.

John Blake White's painting of the Battle of Fort Moultrie (opposite, top).

General William Moultrie. As a colonel he led the South Carolina Militia at Sullivan's Island, later renamed Fort Moultrie (opposite, center).

Heroism at Fort Moultrie: Sergeant Jasper replacing the flag while the bombardment that destroyed the original staff continues. Based on a painting by Johannes Adam Oertle (opposite, bottom).

The signing of the Declaration of Independence
at Philadelphia on 4 July 1776.

THE DECLARATION OF INDEPENDENCE: 4 JULY 1776

During the first year, the Americans fought ostensibly only to preserve their rights within the British Empire. The second year saw the adoption of the Declaration of Independence on 4 July 1776, proclaiming that the thirteen colonies "are and of Right ought to be Free and Independent States." This ringing declaration announced to the world the birth of a new nation and sharply defined the issues in the developing conflict, leaving little question that it would be a long and difficult one.

The articles of Confederation, stipulating the terms of union and granting Congress specific powers, were drawn up shortly after the Declaration of Independence, but jealousies among the states prevented their ratification until 1781. In the interim Congress did exercise most of the powers granted it under the Articles, but these were insufficient to enable it efficiently to direct the war effort. Congress had no power under the Articles either to levy taxes or to raise military forces directly under its own auspices. It could only determine the Confederation's need for troops and

New Yorkers respond to the announcement of the signing of the Declaration of Independence by pulling down the statue of George III on Bowling Green. They are assisted by soldiers from Washington's army.

money and set quotas for the states to meet in proportion to their population and wealth. The states seldom filled their quotas of men, never those of money.

Lacking an executive, Congress had to rely on various boards and committees to perform its executive functions. For handling affairs relating to the Army, Congress set up in June 1776 the Board of War and Ordnance chosen from its membership. This gave way in 1777 to a board composed of members from outside Congress. Neither of these arrangements worked well, and Congress was continually regulating purely administrative matters by action of the entire membership or appointing special committees to go to camp. Inspired by fear of seizure of political control by military leaders, Congress kept a suspiciously watchful eye on the military force and its commanders. Washington countered these suspicions very effectively by constantly deferring to congressional wishes. And he was rewarded by the assiduity with which Congress usually adopted his recommendations. The faults in military policy during the Revolution were due less to congressional failure to enact wise laws than to the lack of adequate governmental machinery to carry out the laws that were enacted.

Channels of administration and supply were confused and divided between Congress and the states. By the military provisions of the Articles, the states were responsible for raising troops for the Continental Army, for initially organizing and equipping them, and for appointing officers through the rank of colonel. Congress issued commissions for the officers selected by the states, and itself appointed all general officers. Once the Continental Army was in the field, Congress was also mainly responsible for administering and supplying it. Over the militia, which had to be so frequently called out to supplement the Continentals, Congress had no express control at all, though it frequently had to arrange for the supply and administration of militia forces operating with the Army.

The Continental Army was organized generally on the British model. It was mainly composed of infantry and artillery, with very little cavalry. The basic unit of organization was the regiment or battalion composed of 8 companies, instead of 10 as in the British Army. Organization above this level was highly flexible. A brigade was usually formed of several regiments and was commanded by a brigadier general; a division, by a similar grouping of several brigades commanded by a major general. Artillery was organized into a brigade of four regiments under a Chief of Artillery, Brigadier General Henry Knox, but the various companies were usually distributed among the infantry battalions. There were a small corps of engineers and an even smaller contingent of artificers, who handled the servicing and repair of ordnance. Supply and transport were under the supervision of the Quartermaster General, but civilians rather than service troops were usually employed to do the actual work.

On the advice of Washington, Congress provided him with a staff generally corresponding to that in the British Army. The most important staff officer was the Quartermaster General, responsible not only for transportation and delivery of supplies but also for arranging the camp, regulating marches, and establishing the order of battle of the

Army. In addition, the staff included an Adjutant General charged with issuing orders in the name of the commander and handling other administrative details; a Judge Advocate General responsible for legal affairs; a Paymaster General and Commissary General of Musters responsible for personnel administration; a Commissary General of Provisions responsible for procurement of food; a Clothier General responsible for procurement of clothing; a Chief Surgeon as head of the hospital service; and a Chief Engineer in charge of bridges and fortifications.

With the exception of the Quartermaster General, all these staff officers had primarily administrative and supply functions. For advice on matters of strategy and operations, Washington relied on a Council of War made up of his principal subordinate commanders. Aides-de-camp took care of routine headquarters work, such as the writing and delivery of orders, messages, and reports.

Both organization and staff work suffered from the confusion in the governmental levels at the top and from the other manifold troubles that plagued the Continental Army in general. Regiments organized by the various states inevitably had different forms of organization, different methods of drill, and different standards of discipline and training. Militia organizations usually provided additional variety to the pattern. Owing to the failure of the states to meet their quotas, regiments were constantly understrength. There were few Americans with knowledge or experience in staff work, and the direction of administrative and supply functions under conditions of divided authority and inadequate means was a task requiring a perseverance that even fewer possessed. Staff officers, like the men of the Continental Army, often found their private affairs more pressing than military service. Others resigned because they were simply overwhelmed by the immense difficulty of supplying and administering an army for which Congress was unable to provide the necessary means. As a result, both supply and administration were poorly handled and the proper functions of the administrative staff often devolved on an overworked commander and his aids.

With the evacuation of Boston the attention of both Washington and Howe shifted to New York. Both recognized that it was a position offering the British the greatest strategic advantage. It held a central position between New England and the colonies to the southward, and its sea approaches were well suited to amphibious landing. If there was any strategic approach by which the British could gain victory, it would be by driving from New York up the Hudson River and joining forces with British troops advancing down the lake and river chain from Canada, thus dividing New England from the rest of the country. New York also could provide a good jumping-off point for an advance on the seat of the Continental Congress at Philadelphia.

The Battle for New York

With these considerations in mind, in April and May 1776 Washington brought most of his army down from Boston to New York. His force on arrival numbered about 10,000 Continentals and militia. By dint of the efforts of Congress and the neighboring states, this force was raised by 26

August, the day the battle for New York began, to something over 20,000, the largest number Washington had under his personal command at any time during the Revolution. Most of the men were either militia or recently enlisted Continentals who had not been exposed to the discipline and training given the previous year before Boston. Only a few southern regiments that Congress had authorized in the interim were enlisted beyond the end of the year 1776.

Against Washington's heterogeneous force, General Howe brought from Halifax and England a body of 32,000 well-trained British and Hessian regulars, supported by a powerful British fleet under his brother, Admiral Lord Richard Howe. In early July 1776 the first part of the force arrived from Halifax and debarked on undefended Staten Island. There General Howe waited for a month and a half while the rest of the British land and naval forces sent from England gathered.

The geography of the area gave the Howe brothers an advantage that General Washington was all too slow in recognizing. The city of New York stood on Manhattan Island, separated from the mainland by the Hudson River on the New Jersey side and the Harlem River on the New York side. There was only one connecting link, Kingsbridge, over the Harlem River at the northern tip of Manhattan. Across the East River on Long Island, Brooklyn Heights stood in a position dominating the southern tip of Manhattan. With the naval forces at their disposal, the Howes could land troops on either Long Island or Manhattan proper and send their warships up the Hudson and East rivers a considerable distance.

Washington decided he must defend Brooklyn Heights on Long Island if he was to defend Manhattan; he therefore divided his army between the two places—the first step toward disaster. For all practical purposes, command on Long Island itself was also divided. Major General Nathanael Greene was first given the assignment, but when he came down with malaria, General Sullivan was sent over. Not completely satisfied with this arrangement, Washington at the last moment placed Major General Israel Putnam over Sullivan, but Putnam hardly had time to become acquainted with the situation and the terrain before the British struck. The American forces on Long Island, totaling about 10,000, were disposed in fortifications on Brooklyn Heights and in forward positions back of the line of thickly wooded hills that ran across the southern end of the island. Sullivan was in immediate command on the American left, Brigadier General William Alexander, Lord Stirling, on the right. Four roads ran through the hills toward the American positions. Unfortunately Sullivan, in violation of the principle of security, left the Jamaica-Bedford road unguarded, and it turned out that it was via this road that General Howe planned his main effort.

On 22 August 1776 General Howe landed on Long Island in force. Washington had hoped to draw him into a repeat performance of Bunker Hill, but this time Howe gave the Americans lessons in maneuver and surprise. Howe's plan called for an attack by a force of 5,000 on the American right under Stirling, a demonstration by a similar force on Sullivan's front, and the main attack on Sullivan's flank by a force of 10,000 moving up the Jamaica-Bedford

Road. It was an excellently conceived turning movement, and aided by the American failure to guard the Jamaica-Bedford Road, it worked perfectly. The demonstration on Sullivan's front lured his forces out from behind their fortifications into the open, where they were crushed between the demonstrating force and the flanking columns that took them by surprise. Though Stirling's Maryland and Delaware Continentals on the American right put up a valiant fight, it was a hopeless one, for the rest of the American front crumpled and inexperienced troops fled in terror before the British and Hessian bayonets. The remnants fell back to the entrenchments on Brooklyn Heights.

One of the great mysteries of the Revolution is why General Howe failed to follow up his success and launch a direct attack on the disorganized and panicky Americans on the heights. Perhaps it was because he had bitter memories of Bunker Hill, or perhaps because he looked on the destruction of Washington's army as of lesser import than the reconciliation of the country to British rule. In any case, he decided to take the fortifications on the heights by regular approaches in the traditional style of Vauban, a process that would require several days.

This delay enabled the Americans to escape, for Washington now realized that the position on Long Island was untenable and that at any moment the British Fleet might sail up the East River and cut off his entire force. Luckily wind and weather held up British warships. Boats were collected from all available sources around New York City, and skilled fishermen from Colonel John Glover's Marblehead Regiment were put to operating them. Despite several incidents that threatened disaster, the evacuation was successfully completed under the cover of darkness on the night of 29–30 August, and the British awoke the next morning to find their quarry gone.

Having reconcentrated his forces in Manhattan, General Washington deployed them at the danger points stretching from the city to Harlem Heights on the north end. Garrisons in Fort Washington and Fort Lee guarded the Hudson on the New York and New Jersey sides respectively. But morale was now at a low ebb; militia began to take off by companies, and there was a high rate of desertion among the Continentals. Beyond this, the position of the whole army was still precarious, for the British clearly had the capability of landing on the New York mainland in Washington's rear and isolating his force on Manhattan Island.

General Howe's next move, on 15 September, was not onto the mainland but in the center of Manhattan Island at Kip's Bay—the site of present 34th Street and East River but then well above the city. Connecticut militia posted at this point broke and ran without making any effective resistance to the British landing. Washington, seized by one of his rare fits of temper, raged at the troops and beat them with the flat of his sword but to no avail. All Howe had to do now was to move rapidly across the island in order to cut off American troops in lower Manhattan. But again he delayed, awaiting the landing and assembly of his whole force, and Putnam was able to bring the troops from the city up the west side of the island to join the rest of the American forces in new fortifications on Harlem Heights.

The day after Kip's Bay, a small battle occurred that

... the Honor and Success of the army, and the safety of our bleeding Country, depends upon harmony and good agreement with each other; ... he will be the best Soldier, and the best Patriot who contributes most to this glorious work, whatever his Station, or from whatever part of the Continent, he may come: Let all distinctions of Nations, Countries, and Provinces, therefore be lost in the generous contest, who shall behave with the most Courage against the enemy, and the most kindness and good humour to each other. ...

GENERAL GEORGE WASHINGTON
General Orders, Headquarters,
New York, 1 August 1776.

An excerpt from the general order Washington issued from his New York headquarters on 1 August 1776, in an attempt to reduce the friction among the various units of his army.

Major General John Sullivan.

Major General Israel Putnam.

gave evidence for the first time in the New York campaign that Americans, if well led, were capable of defeating regulars in the open field. Lieutenant Colonel Thomas Knowlton led a picked body of 120 men out to reconnoiter the enemy lines, and engaged in a spirited exchange of fire with British pickets. When Knowlton retried in an orderly manner, the British sent a detachment of 400 light infantry to follow him. Learning that the British detachment was unsupported, Washington laid a trap by having a small force demonstrate on the British front while a much larger one hid in the woods. At the same time Knowlton, reinforced by Virginia riflemen, slipped around to take the British in the rear. The British discovered the hidden force early enough and retired, but in their withdrawal they ran into Knowlton's

command. A sharp action followed into which both sides brought in reinforcements. The British were thrown back, but Washington decided to break off the battle when he saw that Howe was going to move up in force. The little victory on Harlem Heights did much to restore the morale of a defeated army. Knowlton, killed in action, left a fine example of courage and heroism for the American Army.

After a month of delay in front of Harlem Heights, in mid-October General Howe finally took the obvious course and landed at Pell's Point on the New York mainland in Washington's rear. Washington now quickly got out of the Manhattan trap, crossing the Harlem River at Kingsbridge and moving his army into position at White Plains. He left about 6,000 men behind in Fort Washington and Fort Lee

The Battle of Long Island: Forces under Lord William Alexander Stirling, an English nobleman who became a Continental Army officer, retreat before heavy British opposition on 27 August 1776.

under the command of General Greene. After a costly assault to gain one hill, Howe delayed an attack on Washington's main position, and Washington again moved away to the north toward the highlands. Howe now quickly seized the opportunity to interpose his army between Washington and the Hudson River forts, moving to Dobbs Ferry on the Hudson.

General Washington should have evacuated the forts and reconcentrated his army on the New Jersey side of the Hudson. But on the advice of Greene, he decided to hold on, and again divided his army into three main portions. One part, about 8,000 men, he left with Major Generals Charles Lee and William Heath at Peekskill and North Castle respectively to guard the passes through the high-

Washington's army leaves Long Island for Manhattan on the night of August 29–30.

lands, and moved with a second part, about 5,000 men, across the Hudson into New Jersey. General Howe then moved quickly against the third part, the troops defending Forts Washington and Lee. The attack against Fort Washington was supported by British warships on the Hudson, and the fort's garrison surrendered on 16 November after only spotty resistance. In this disaster the Americans lost nearly 3,000 men, mostly as prisoners of war, and large quantities of munitions. Three days later Major General Lord Charles Cornwallis landed with 4,500 men on the Jersey shore eight miles above Fort Lee, and Greene decided on a hasty evacuation. He got out with most of his men but was forced to leave almost all his supplies behind.

General Washington gathered the remnants of his army behind the Hackensack River, and began a rapid retreat across New Jersey with Howe's advance forces under General Cornwallis in rapid pursuit. With each step in the withdrawal the Army dwindled in strength, and few companies of New Jersey militia rallied to the cause. In early December the remaining force, only about 3,000 men, got across the Delaware into Pennsylvania just as Cornwallis was arriving in Trenton. But winter was approaching, and General Howe decided that the time for active campaigning was at an end. Instead of collecting boats and continuing the pursuit of Washington, as Cornwallis urged, Howe ordered his men into winter quarters, confident that he could shatter the small remaining rebel force with one blow the following spring. Howe placed garrisons at Perth Amboy, New Brunswick, Princeton, Trenton, and Bordentown, and sent a detachment to Rhode Island that captured Newport and remained as a garrison there. The rest of the British Army retired to winter among the delights of New York City.

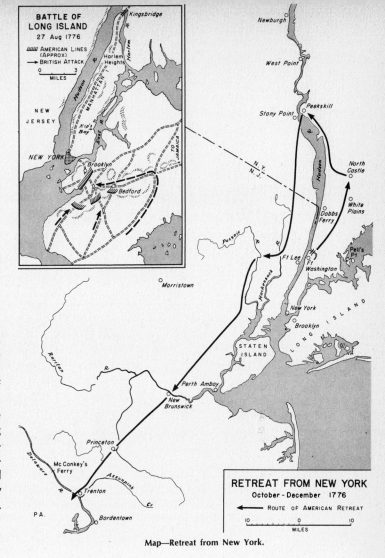

Map—Retreat from New York.

"I only regret that I have but one life to lose for my country." Connecticut Captain Nathan Hale was captured by the British on Long Island on 21 September 1776, and executed in New York City the next morning.

A British artillery officer made this drawing of the landing of General Cornwallis' forces in New Jersey on 19 November 1776.

A Currier and Ives lithograph of Washington supervising the loading of his men for the Delaware crossing.

The Lake Champlain Battleground

Meanwhile, on the old familiar battleground around Lake Champlain, the campaign of 1776 was ending more favorably for the Americans. With reinforcements that brought his total force to about 10,000 British, Hessians, Canadians, and Indian auxiliaries, Brigadier General Sir Guy Carleton sought to follow up his victories won in Canada in June, and pursued the retreating American forces down to the head of Lake Champlain with the obvious intention of driving through to form a junction with Howe in New York. To oppose him, Major General Philip Schuyler managed to raise a force of about 9,000 regulars and militia. It was not Schuyler, however, but Brigadier General Benedict Arnold, his subordinate, who seized the initiative. Arnold built a "fleet" of small boats on Lake Champlain and manned them with soldiers. This improvised navy was able so to delay Carleton's advance that mid-October found him only as far as Crown Point with the strong defenses of Ticonderoga still before him. To take Ticonderoga would require an orthodox siege operation, and with winter approaching Carleton prudently decided it was too late in the season. So he retired to Canada, leaving the British with no forward base from which to launch the next year's campaign, a fact that was to have immense strategic significance.

This successful defensive was at the time far overshadowed by the disastrous defeats Washington had suffered. The approach of the end of 1776 found the American cause at a low ebb. Three different forces remained in the field—Washington's army in Pennsylvania, Heath's and Lee's forces guarding the highlands along the Hudson, and Schuyler's army in New York. All were being rapidly depleted by desertion, disease, and the departure of militia units. Most appalling of all was the fact that the terms of enlistment of the major portion of the troops remaining expired at the end of the year 1776. In December 1776 Washington was faced with the same task that had proven so difficult under far better conditions a year earlier, the reconstitution of the Continental Army.

The New Army

Even before the defeats in New York, Washington had been urging on Congress the necessity of long-term enlistments and of offering sufficent inducement to keep experienced men in the service. After his bitter disappointments with militia and untrained Continentals, who ran away on Long Island and at Kip's Bay, his importunities became more urgent. On 2 October 1776 Congress finally responded by voting a new military establishment that on paper at least had the apearance of adequacy. Eighty-eight battalions of trops, about 60,000 men, were to be raised by the states and placed in the Continental establishment enlisted to "serve during the present war." Unfortunately this latter provision was weakened by another law permitting an alternative term of enlistment for three years.

Troops in the new establishment were not to be recruited directly into the Continental service but in various state lines. States would control the appointment of officers through the rank of colonel, but it was to be a truly Continental army raised from all the states in proportion to population. Quotas varied from 15 battalions respectively for Virginia and Massachusetts to 1 for Delaware and 1 for Georgia. A continental bounty of $20, 100 acres of land, and a new suit of clothes was authorized for each private or noncommissioned officer who enlisted.

In short, the new army was to be raised in accordance with the provisions of the unratified Articles of Confederation, and it promised to have all the weaknesses inherent in the military provisions of that document. The congressional legislation left many questions unanswered as to the extent of Washington's control or influence on appointments, promotions, and dismissals of the officers of the various state lines. There was soon ample evidence that political favoritism would play a more important part in state apointments than military ability, and that the old experienced officers already with the Army would be slighted in favor of new and inexperienced men. To regulate these questions, most of the state governors promised to send commissions to Washington's camp.

Neither new regiments nor state commissions put in their appearance during the dark days of December 1776. And Washington soon learned that few of the men of his existing army could be tempted even by the bounty to remain in the service. Schuyler, Heath, and Lee had much the same experience. It was evident that Congress had acted too late to provide an army to tide over the winter, and that few new troops would come in before spring 1777. Washington asked Congress for an increase from 88 to 110 battalions, less with any genuine conviction that the men could be raised to fill the entire quota than on the hope that "the officers of a hundred and ten battalions will recruit many more men than those of eighty-eight." The members of Congress, who had fled from Philadelphia to Baltimore, this time quickly acceded to Washington's wishes, voting on 26 December 1776 not only to grant him the right to raise the additional forces but also dictatorial powers for a period of six months to appoint and remove officers, to apply to the states for militia levies, and to seize private property and enforce martial law.

The vote of dictatorial powers was not the end that Washington was seeking, and indeed he used them very sparingly. He perceived that only by reawakening the spirit of the Army and of the people by some spectacular stroke could he hope to check the tide of despair and confusion that was sweeping the American states. Appraising the possibilities, he decided to concentrate all the troops available from the old Army of 1776 and strike a blow at the British before the end of December. Washington had been pressing General Lee to join him with the troops from Peekskill since he had begun the retreat across New Jersey, but Lee was dilatory, evidently placing his own military judgment above that of Washington. Finally Lee did move and—one might even say fortunately—he himself was captured by the British en route. His troops, their numbers dwindled from 5,000 to 2,000, came on to join Washington. Eight decimated regiments were also drawn from Schuyler's troops in New York. The arrival of about 2,000 Pennsylvania militia brought Washington's total force to something like 7,000 men by Christmas 1776.

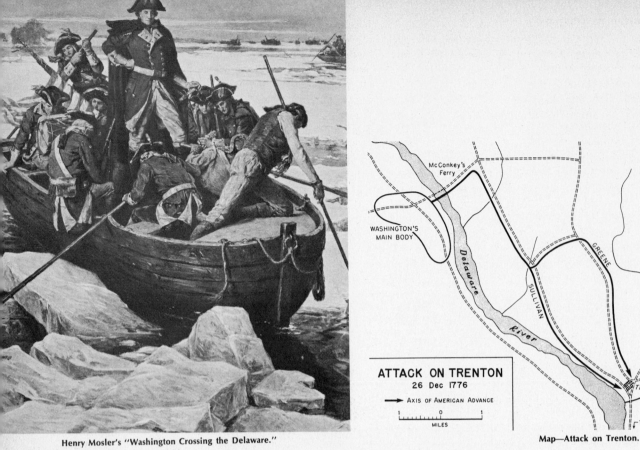

Henry Mosler's "Washington Crossing the Delaware."

ATTACK ON TRENTON
26 Dec 1776

→ AXIS OF AMERICAN ADVANCE

1   0   1
MILES

Map—Attack on Trenton.

"Capture of the Hessians at Trenton," by Colonel John Trumbull.

Washington Crosses the Delaware

The scattered British dispositions in New Jersey invited surprise attack. From a patriot butcher who passed as a Tory, Washington learned that the Hessian garrison at Trenton numbered 1,400 men and that its commander, Colonel Johannes Rall, was given to heavy drinking and neglect of security. Trenton therefore was chosen as the objective of a surprise attack to be delivered one hour before dawn on 26 December. Washington's plan called for the main force of 2,400 men to cross the Delaware at McConkey's Ferry, and then proceed in two divisions by separate roads running into the main street of Trenton from opposite ends. A supporting force, mainly militia, under Colonel John Cadwalader was to cross below near Bordentown and engage the Hessians at that point. A smaller force of militia under Brigadier General James Ewing was to cross directly opposite Trenton to block the route of escape across Assunpink Creek.

The main force was safely ferried across the Delaware by Colonel Glover's Marblehead men, despite the large cakes of ice in the river. It was 0300, 26 December, before they were all assembled and the silent march to Trenton began. Shoeless men left a trail of blood in the new-fallen snow. Meanwhile, Cadwalader was able to get only part of his force across and Ewing none. Disappointing though this was, it did not prevent the success of the main attack. The two columns, under Greene and Sullivan, converged on the town at 0800, later than scheduled but still in time to achieve complete surprise. Hessian sentries gave the alarm too late, for before the rest of the soldiery could be roused and formed in line of battle the two columns closed in on them from both ends of the town. Rall's efforts to rally his men failed and he himself was killed. Within an hour and a half after the attack began, the Hessians surrendered. Only 400 were able to escape to Bordentown. About 30 were killed and the prisoner count was 918. The Americans lost only 4 killed—2 from freezing—and 4 wounded.

Washington had hoped to continue to Bordentown, but learning that Cadwalader and Ewing had failed to cross in force, seeing that his men were exhausted, and desiring to get the captured Hessians and supplies to safety, he decided to return across the Delaware. But once across and the men rested, he determined to strike another blow. By an impassioned appeal to their patriotism coupled with a bounty of $10, he was able to persuade most of the men enlisted to the end of the year to volunteer to remain for six weeks longer. General Heath was ordered to join him with the remaining force left guarding the highland passes on the Hudson. Encouraged by the victory at Trenton, Pennsylvania, and New Jersey militia began to come in in greater numbers. By these expedients Washington was able to gather a sufficient force to put 5,200 men, about half militia, across the Delaware again on the night of 30–31 December 1776.

Meanwhile the British had not been idle. Cornwallis, their commander in New Jersey, also gathered most of his scattered forces, and on 2 January 1777, moved into Trenton with 6,000 men, taking a position confronting Washington along Assunpink Creek. Washington's back was to the Delaware, and Cornwallis was confident that he had no safe line of retreat. His men being exhausted from a long march, the British commander thought he could safely delay his attack until the following morning, 3 January. But Washington, learning of a road by which he could escape around the British rear, slipped away in the night, leaving campfires brightly burning to deceive the British. His objective was to seize British supplies at Princeton and New Brunswick.

By sunrise, when Cornwallis awoke to find no enemy in front of him, the American Army was within two miles of Princeton. There they ran into two British regiments just leaving Princeton to join Cornwallis. In the ensuing engagement the Americans inflicted heavy losses on these British regulars and drove them in disorderly retreat toward Trenton and New Brunswick. Washington had difficulty in restraining himself from following to New Brunswick but desisted, knowing that his men were exhausted and that Cornwallis would soon be behind him. Prudently he moved north to Morristown, where woods and hills afforded natural protection against British attack, and went into winter quarters there. From Morristown he could move quickly to counter any British effort to advance up the Hudson or overland against Philadelphia. But Howe had had enough of winter war. He withdrew all his troops from New Jersey save those along the Raritan River between New Brunswick and Perth Amboy. For six months the whole front was quiet.

In large measure, the victories at Trenton and Princeton accomplished what Washington had set out to do. They infused new life into the American cause, new confidence in the Army and its commander. Recruiting of the new Army was thus facilitated, and the militia encouraged to come in to hold the line while the new Army was being formed. Valuable military supplies had been taken from the British. In terms of territory, the greater part of New Jersey had been freed from British occupation, giving the patriot elements there an opportunity to deal with the numerous Tories who abounded in certain sections. All in all, Trenton and Princeton proved that the results of the New York campaign had not been so disastrous as it at first appeared. True the British had New York and some of the surrounding country, but only there and at Newport, Rhode Island, did they have footholds at the end of 1776. The Americans could well afford to trade a little space for a great deal of time.

Not the least important thing about Trenton and Princeton was the fact that they showed Washington to be a far abler general than his professional critics had thought after the defeats in New York. He had concentrated the remnants of an army dispirited by defeat and continued withdrawals, and with it he had executed a brilliant offensive, striking the enemy by surprise with superior numbers at critical points.

THE CAMPAIGNS OF 1777

Washington's hopes in 1777 for an army even approximately the size Congress had voted were doomed to disappointment. Of the 76,000 men authorized in 1776, only 8,000 had enlisted in the Continental service when Washington

Washington, bearing a standard, is waving his troops to the charge in this lithograph of the Battle of Princeton by Nathaniel Currier.

took the field in May 1777. The total enlistment for the year was 34,820, but nothing like this number was ever under arms at any given time. Battle casualties, sickness, and desertion kept the Continentals under Washington below 10,000 at all times, and the number in the northern army under Schuyler and Gates never exceeded 3,000. Those who did enlist for three years or for the duration gave the Continental Army a hard core of veterans, but since they were so few the old practice of supplementing the Continentals with militia had to continue.

The problem of securing and keeping good officers was also acute. Many were disappointed by appointments and promotions made by Congress and the states; practically all found their pay and the provision for retirement inadequate in view of the mounting cost of living. Some able men, like Colonel John Stark of New Hampshire, resigned. Others, like Benedict Arnold, whose promotion to major general was delayed while men with less brilliant records were advanced ahead of him, nursed grudges.

A brighter spot in the picture was the arrival of military supplies from France. The French court had been carefully watching the American revolt, seeking an opportunity to redress the balance of power in Europe so heavily tipped in England's favor by her victory in the Seven Years' War. In 1776 Congress sent a mission to France to seek supplies and financial aid and to sound out the French Government on the possibilities of entering the war on the American side. The French ministers preferred to move with caution, awaiting some proof of the American states' ability and determination to resist, but did agree to the secret dispatch of military supplies under the guise of a commercial transaction. The supplies arriving in early 1777 were the begin-

ning of what was to be a continuous flow. The French Charleville musket, an improved flintlock superior in some respects to "Brown Bess," eventually became almost the standard arm of the Continental infantry.

The supplies were accompanied by an influx of foreign officer volunteers, men of professional experience in European armies. While the Continental Army was sadly in need of professional guidance, most of these men were ill adapted to give it. Many were fortune seekers, who neither spoke English nor understood how to handle American citizen-soldiers. The American mission in Paris, anxious to secure good will abroad, at first issued commissions wholesale, much to the embarrassment of Congress and of Washington. On Washington's advice, Congress finally repudiated most of these commissions. Some of the foreign volunteers, however, were given positions of importance in the Continental Army and rendered invaluable service. To name only a few, Louis du Portail, a Frenchman, and Tadeusz Kosciuszko, a Pole, did much to advance the art of engineering in the Continental Army; Casimir Pulaski organized its first genuine cavalry contingent; and Baron Friedrich W. A. von Steuben provided effective instruction in organization and drill. The Marquis de Lafayette, an influential French nobleman who financed his own way, stood in a separate category and, at the age of twenty-one, was given a command as a major general under Washington.

Washington vs. Howe in Pennsylvania

The campaign of 1777 falls into two parts: the first, a conflict between Washington's and Howe's armies in Pennsylvania; the second, a struggle along the northern reaches of the Hudson. Washington perceived the connection be-

General Tadeusz Kosciuszko of Poland.

General Louis du Portail of France.

General Casimir Pulaski of Poland.

General Friedrich von Steuben of Prussia.

The Marquis de Lafayette, who became a general in the Continental Army at the age of twenty-one.

tween the two much more clearly than did Howe. The major portion of his army he kept with him in front of Howe, while he detached a small part to the northward to aid in defeating Burgoyne, including therein a contingent of riflemen well suited to operations in the wooded terrain of the north. A third force, reduced to an absolute minimum, he kept under General Putnam in the New York highlands to oppose any advance north by Clinton.

Both Washington and Howe spent the entire spring and most of the summer in fruitless maneuver in New Jersey. Uncertain as to Howe's intentions, the American commander constantly sought to keep in position to block a move either up the Hudson or against Philadelphia. Strong forts were built along the Delaware River to block any approach by sea to the Continental capital. Finally, in mid-August, Howe retired to New York, placed most of his army aboard ship, sailed down the coast and up Chesapeake Bay to Head of Elk in Maryland. Howe's intention to take Philadelphia was now abundantly clear, and Washington rapidly moved southward to meet him. On 11 September 1777 he took up a defensive position near Chad's Ford on Brandywine Creek, athwart the main road to Philadelphia, with a force of about 11,000 men.

A Currier and Ives lithograph of the first meeting of Washington and Lafayette in Philadelphia in August 1777.

The oath signed by Lafayette when he entered the Continental Army. Washington's signature is on the left.

Washington disposed his army in two main parts, one directly opposite Chad's Ford under General Sullivan guarding the right flank upstream where the creek was easily fordable at many points. Howe again, as on Long Island, conceived a turning movement that almost succeeded in trapping the American Army. While Lieutenant General Wilhelm von Knyphausen's Hessian troops demonstrated opposite Chad's Ford, a larger force under Lord Cornwallis marched upstream, crossed the Brandywine, and moved around to take Sullivan in the rear. American intelligence was faulty, and Washington was led to believe the main attack would develop on his front. Only at the eleventh hour did he get positive information of Cornwallis' movement. Sullivan was in process of changing front when the British struck him at 1600 and his men retreated in confusion. Meanwhile, Washington had hastily dispatched General Greene with two brigades to support Sullivan, and, in a valiant rear-guard action, Greene's troops saved the rest of the army from envelopment. The detachment of Greene weakened the front opposite the ford, and Washington had also to retreat before Knyphausen. Nevertheless, the trap was averted and the army retired in good order to Chester.

Washington's army still lay between Howe and Philadelphia, and was in good condition to fight. At Warren's Tavern on 16 September Washington almost took the British by surprise, but rain intervened, wetting the powder and ball of the American troops, who had few cartridge boxes. Washington then withdrew across the Schuylkill, leaving Brigadier General Anthony Wayne with a rear guard

on the other side of the river. A British contingent took Wayne's force by surprise and in a silent bayonet attack (the British regulars had even removed the flints from their guns) almost annihilated it. Howe followed with a feint at Washington's right, forcing the latter to move farther up the Schuylkill; whereupon he quickly recrossed the river and interposed his army between Washington and Philadelphia. On 26 September he moved into the city unopposed.

Once in Philadelphia, Howe dispersed his forces, stationing 9,000 men at Germantown north of the city, 3,000 in New Jersey, and the remainder in Philadelphia itself. Washington now sought to repeat his victory at Trenton by a surprise attack on the British contingent at Germantown. The plan was much like that used at Trenton but involved far more complicated movements of much larger bodies of troops. Four columns marching over separate roads were to converge on Germantown simultaneously. Sullivan and Greene with Continental divisions were to attack the British front and right respectively, while militia in two separate columns undertook the envelopment of both British flanks. All four columns were to arrive within two miles of the enemy's pickets at 0200, halt there until 0400, and make simultaneous attacks at 0500.

The columns started on the night of 3 October from a camp on Skippack Creek, about 16 miles north of Germantown, but failed to arrive in time to coordinate their attacks; the two militia columns never really got into the battle at all. A heavy fog hanging over the area at dawn made it difficult to distinguish friend from foe. Sullivan's

An artist's conception of the making of the first Stars and Stripes. The story that George Washington and two members of the Continental Congress asked Betsy Ross to make a flag with 13 stars and 13 stripes cannot be authenticated, but Congress did adopt such a flag on 14 June 1777. The Army flew the Stars and Stripes in battle for the first time at Bennington, Vermont, on 16 August 1777. Before then the various Army units had used a number of different flags.

column arrived first, a half hour before Greene's, and drove the British back in hard fighting until finally held up by British fire from the Chew House, a stone mansion, at the entrance to Germantown. At this moment Greene's men arrived and launched an attack on the British right, also with considerable success at first. But one of Greene's units departed without orders in the direction of the firing at the Chew House and in the dense fog exchanged fire with some of Sullivan's men. The British, with better discipline and cohesion, were able to re-form in the fog and send fresh troops into the fray. Some of the Americans ran out of ammunition; they had come into battle with but 40 rounds apiece. Whatever the cause, the seeming victory was suddenly turned into defeat. About 0900, the Americans began to retreat in disorder and left the British in command of the field. Howe followed cautiously for a few miles but was unable to exploit his victory.

Brandywine, Germantown, and all the intermediate maneuvers of 1777 revealed that, while both officers and men of the Continental Army were rapidly improving, they still had much to learn. Advances had been made by the artillery and engineers, but there was still a glaring lack of

cavalry. Even a small cavalry force should have been able to discover Cornwallis' movement at Brandywine, but Washington had none. Whether he appreciated the value of cavalry or understood its use is a debatable point. Other factors may explain his failure to organize the cavalry contingent authorized by Congress. Good cavalry horses were scarce north of Virginia; forage was difficult to obtain, and when obtained placed a heavy burden on an already overloaded transport system. Shortly after Brandywine, Major General Casimir Pulaski organized a small corps of cavalry, but even the efforts of this Polish cavalry expert were never crowned with outstanding success.

There were other deficiencies of even greater moment. The green Continental Army still lacked the discipline and organization necessary to enable it to move rapidly and efficiently and strike coordinated blows against the enemy, and the men still understood but poorly the use of the bayonet, the weapon with which the British soldier fought most effectively. These deficiencies were to receive primary attention in the training given during the bitter winter at Valley Forge.

A casualty of the Battle of Brandywine. Lafayette, who had leaped from
his horse to rally his troops, was hit
in the leg by a musket ball.

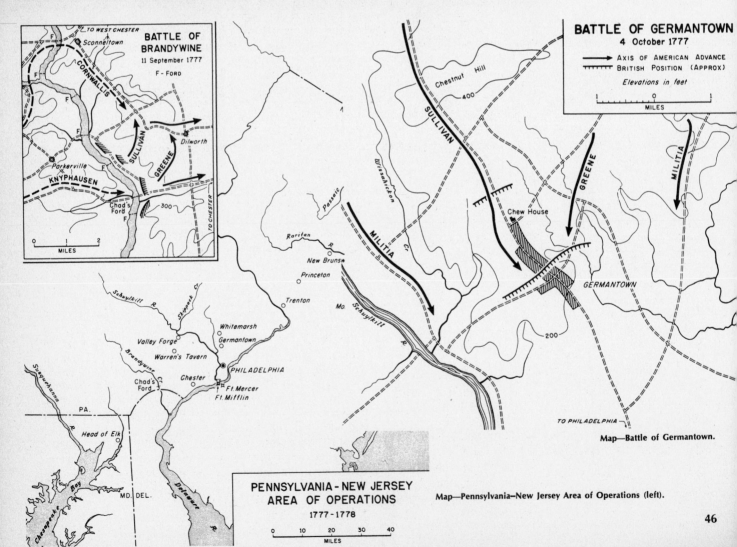

BATTLE OF BRANDYWINE
11 September 1777
F - FORD

TO WEST CHESTER
Sconneltown
CORNWALLIS
SULLIVAN
GREENE
Dilworth
Parkerville
KNYPHAUSEN
Chad's
Ford
300
TO CHESTER

0   1   2
MILES

BATTLE OF GERMANTOWN
4 October 1777

→ AXIS OF AMERICAN ADVANCE
⊥⊥⊥ BRITISH POSITION (APPROX)
Elevations in feet

1   0   1
MILES

Chestnut Hill
400
SULLIVAN
Wissahickon
Cr.
Chew House
MILITIA
GREENE
MILITIA
GERMANTOWN
200
TO PHILADELPHIA

Map—Battle of Germantown.

Passaic
Raritan R.
New Bruns.
Princeton
Trenton
Mo. Schuylkill R.

Schuylkill R.
Skippack Cr.
Whitemarsh
Valley Forge
Germantown
Warren's Tavern
Brandywine Cr.
Chester
PHILADELPHIA
Chad's
Ford
Ft. Mercer
Ft. Mifflin

Susquehanna R.
PA.
Head of Elk
MD. DEL.
Chesapeake Bay
Delaware R.

PENNSYLVANIA - NEW JERSEY
AREA OF OPERATIONS
1777-1778

0 10 20 30 40
MILES

Map—Pennsylvania—New Jersey Area of Operations (left).

This engraving of the Battle of Germantown
shows the British firing at American troops from the Chew House.

The War in the North

While Howe was moving on Philadelphia, Burgoyne was advancing south from Canada, confidently expecting to reach Albany by fall and thus forge a chain separating New England from the rest of the American states. Another force of 700 regulars and Tories and about 1,000 Indians was detached under Colonel Barry St. Leger to overrun American defenses in the Mohawk Valley and join Burgoyne before Albany. The American force gathered to oppose Burgoyne's army was initially a very weak one. There were 2,500 Continentals and militia under Major General Arthur St. Clair at Ticonderoga, the main defense work on Lake Champlain, and 450 Continentals at old Fort Stanwix, the center of American defenses in the Mohawk Valley. Dissension over command further weakened the American opposition. Major General Philip Schuyler, the New Yorker in command of the northern army, was unpopular with the New Englanders, who wanted to replace him with Major General Horatio Gates.

Transporting his army in boats on Lake Champlain, Burgoyne appeared before Fort Ticonderoga on 27 June 1777. Ticonderoga's defenses had been tremendously strengthened by Kosciuszko, the Polish engineer, but St. Clair did not have enough men to fortify and man two prominent hills overlooking the fort. The British placed artillery on these heights and forced St. Clair to evacuate; whereupon the whole American defense around Lake Champlain collapsed.

Schuyler fell back before Burgoyne to the mouth of the Mohawk, delaying the British advance by felling trees, destroying bridges, and scattering boulders along the route. The British army, with 59 pieces of artillery in its train, was slowed to a pace of about a mile a day. Supplies of food, forage, horses, oxen, and carts began to run short. Yet Schuyler's position was weak. His army gathered strength but slowly as he fell back. Washington detached troops from the main army and from Putnam's command in the highlands to join him, but the New England militia, reluctant to serve under Schuyler, rallied only in small numbers. By early August he had 4,500 men, but morale was low and desertion rife. Despite his troubles, Schuyler made the courageous decision to detach a force under General Arnold to go to the Mohawk Valley to relieve Fort Stanwix, besieged by St. Leger.

Moving down Lake Ontario to Oswego and on east to Fort Stanwix, St. Leger had arrived there on 2 August and paraded his force of regulars, Tories, and Indians before the garrison in an effort to persuade them to surrender. Seeing the Indians, the men in the garrison had little doubt of their fate if they laid down their arms, and determined to hold out at all costs. On 4 August a force of 800 militia commanded by Brigadier General Nicholas Herkimer set out to relieve the fort. St. Leger sent a group of Indians and Tories to ambush Herkimer in a ravine near Oriskany village, six miles from Stanwix. The militia, violating the principle of security, carelessly moved through the ravine in double file with no scouts on the flanks. The Indians suddenly opened fire from all sides. The surprise was far greater than that achieved against Braddock in 1755. But Herkimer was no Braddock. Mortally wounded in the leg, he had himself propped up against a great tree, whence he directed the militia in a bloody afternoon battle interrupted by a violent summer thunderstorm. Forming a great irregular circle behind the trees and fighting with tomahawk, pistol, musket, and knife, the militia finally beat off the Indian attack. They suffered so heavily themselves that they abandoned the effort to relieve Stanwix, but Oriskany had a telling psychological effect on the Indians, who had little love for such pitched battles.

Two weeks later, Arnold arrived in the Mohawk Valley with 950 Continentals just as St. Leger was completing approach trenches to Stanwix. Hoping to avoid a costly battle, Arnold devised a clever ruse to disperse St. Leger's Indians. Employing a half-wit Tory and a friendly Oneida Indian as his messengers, he spread the rumor that the Continentals were approaching "as numerous as the leaves on the trees." The Indians, who had special respect for any madman and wanted no repetition of Oriskany, fled from St. Leger's camp in panic, and the British leader was forced to abandon the siege. He would be of no aid to Burgoyne. Arnold, leaving a small garrison at Stanwix, returned to rejoin the American forces below Saratoga the first week in September.

By the first of September Burgoyne knew positively that Howe was on his way to Philadelphia and that he could expect little help from that quarter. The British commander was faced with a difficult decision—he could either attack, gain a decisive victory, and reach Albany before winter or retire to Ticonderoga. A gambler by nature, Burgoyne rashly decided to winter in Albany or lose his army. After some time spent awaiting the arrival of supplies, on 13–14 September 1777 he crossed the Hudson to the west side at Saratoga and prepared to advance against the American positions. About these positions or the terrain in front of him he knew little, for most of his Indians had deserted and his intelligence was as bad as his supply line.

Gates vs. Burgoyne and Victory at Saratoga

The American force opposing him had undergone marked changes. On 19 August it had got a new commander, General Gates, Congress having finally decided to defer to New England sentiment. Gates inherited a vastly improved situation. Militia from New England and New York rallied to the army. Arnold returned, and Washington sent a veteran regiment of riflemen under Colonel Daniel Morgan, an invaluable asset in subsequent forest fighting. By the time Burgoyne moved up to attack, the Americans outnumbered him 7,000 to 6,000, and their army was still growing.

Gates moved his army on 12 September into a strong position on Bemis Heights below Saratoga, directly athwart Burgoyne's route of advance. The Hudson was on the right; bluffs and woods were on the left. Its only weakness lay in the fact that there was a greater height to the west, dominating the position, which Gates failed to fortify.

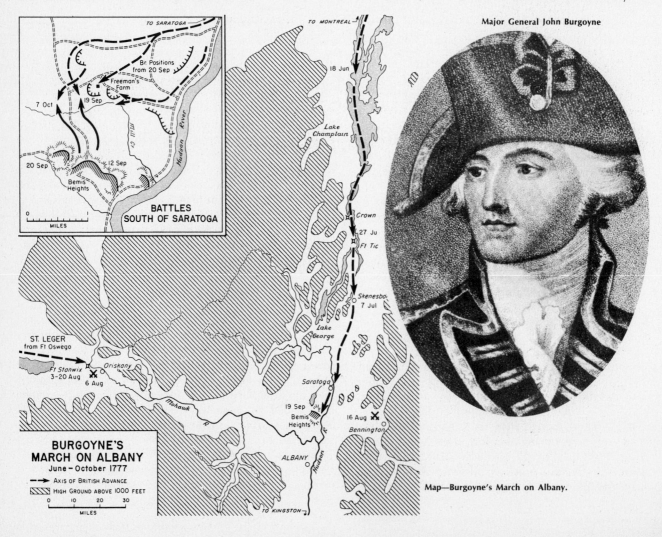

BATTLES SOUTH OF SARATOGA

BURGOYNE'S MARCH ON ALBANY
June – October 1777

Major General John Burgoyne

Map—Burgoyne's March on Albany.

An engraving of General Burgoyne speaking to his Indian allies during his drive toward Albany. In the battles that followed, the Indians failed to honor Burgoyne's request that they fight more like British soldiers and stop killing for scalps.

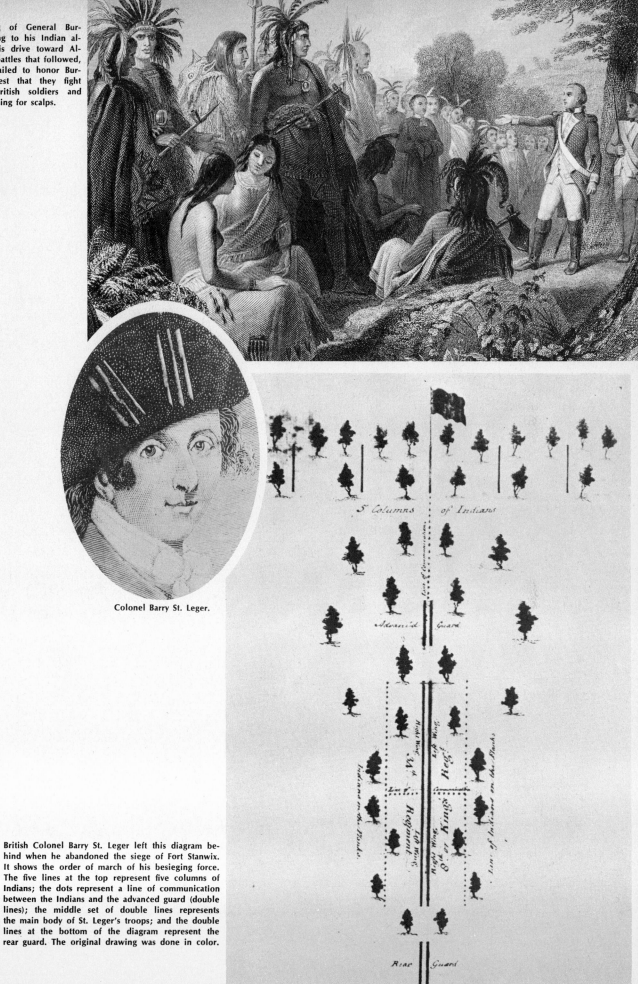

Colonel Barry St. Leger.

5 Columns of Indians

Line of Communication

Advanc'd Guard

Right Wing

Left Wing

34th Regiment

Indians on the Flanks

Line of Communication

Right Wing

Left Wing

8th or Kings Regt.

Line of Indians on the Flanks

Rear Guard

British Colonel Barry St. Leger left this diagram behind when he abandoned the siege of Fort Stanwix. It shows the order of march of his besieging force. The five lines at the top represent five columns of Indians; the dots represent a line of communication between the Indians and the advanced guard (double lines); the middle set of double lines represents the main body of St. Leger's troops; and the double lines at the bottom of the diagram represent the rear guard. The original drawing was done in color.

49

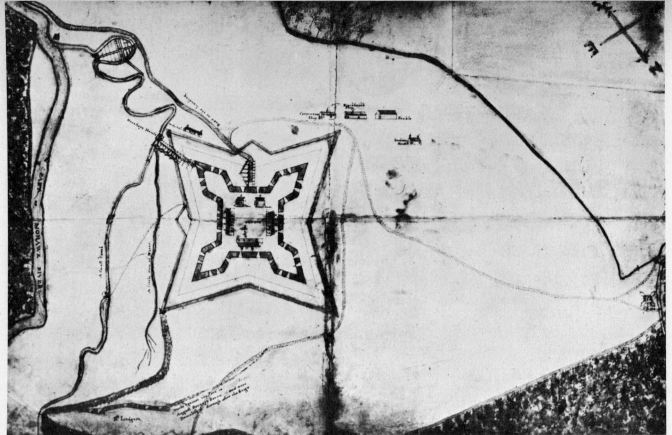

Fort Stanwix. The Mohawk River is at the left.

Major General Friedrich A. von Riedesel

Major General Philip Schuyler.

Burgoyne approached within four miles of the American position before he learned of its existence. But he subsequently obtained general information of American dispositions and learned of the unfortified height, which he made the principal objective of his attack on 19 September. Burgoyne sent Brigadier General Simon Fraser with 2,000 infantry and a brigade of artillery to seize the height on the American left, Brigadier General Hamilton with 1,100 against the American center, and Major General Friedrich A. von Riedesel with 1,100 Germans along the Hudson River. The attack had to be made through forests where neither British superiority in aritllery nor the bayonet could have telling effect. Each British column had to advance up a separate ravine out of contact with the others. Nevertheless, if Fraser could gain control of the height overlooking the American position, the plan had some chance of success.

Gates wanted to await the British attack within his lines on Bemis Heights, but Arnold persuaded him to send regiments forward on the left to block any British effort to flank the American position. One of these, Morgan's

An artist's conception of the battle at Bennington, Vermont, on 16 August 1777. At Bennington militia under Brigadier General John Stark defeated a force of Burgoyne's men who were trying to capture supplies belonging to the Continental Army (top).

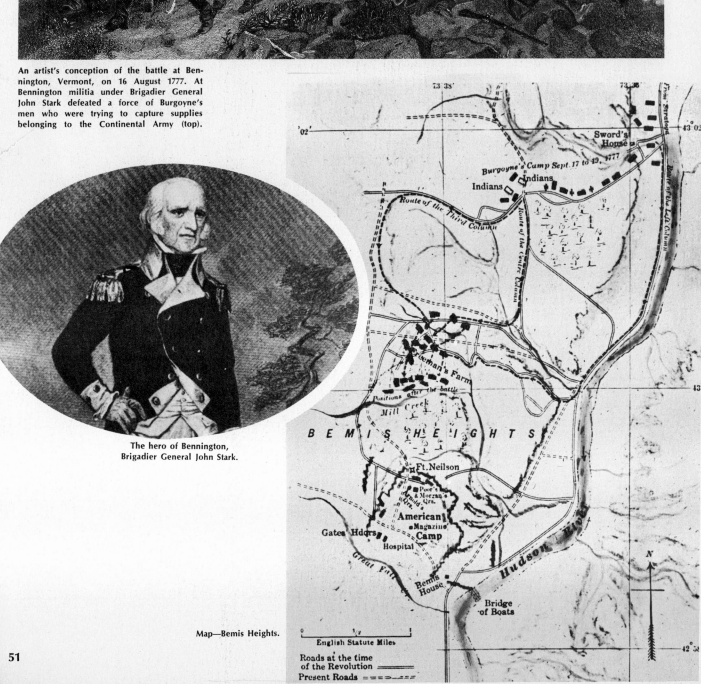

The hero of Bennington, Brigadier General John Stark.

Map—Bemis Heights.

The battle near Saratoga in which Major General Benedict Arnold was wounded while leading his men against a position held by Hessian troops.

riflemen, met Fraser's advance guard at a point south of Freeman's Farm, brushed it aside, and pushed forward, only to be repulsed by Fraser's main body. The battle then developed around this point. Gates sent several regiments to support Arnold, who expanded his attack against Hamilton in the center. Thinking he had found a weak spot between Fraser and Hamilton, Arnold called for still more reinforcements but Gates refused to send them. Then Riedesel moved into the battle, forcing Arnold's men back. The British held the field when night fell, but their losses were double those of the Americans, accurate rifle fire having taken a devastating toll. The American position on Bemis Heights was still secure.

Gates strengthened his entrenchments, fortified the height on his left, and awaited the attack he was sure Burgoyne would have to make. Militia reinforcements increased his force to more than 10,000 men by 7 October. Meanwhile, Burgoyne's position grew daily more desperate. Food was running out; the meadows were grazed bare by the animals; and every day more men slipped off into the forest, deserting the lost cause. American riflemen kept the British outposts under continual harassing fire. Burgoyne could gain little intelligence of American movements and dispositions. On 7 October he decided to make a reconnaissance in force to feel out the weak points in the American position. Learning of the British approach, Gates sent out a force, including Morgan's riflemen, to meet them. The British were repulsed and the Americans took the offensive. Arnold, who had been ordered to stay in his tent following

an argument with Gates, rushed into the fray and, according to some accounts, assumed direction of the offensive. In any event, the British were driven back to their fortified positions and suffered casualties five times those of the Americans. Two days later Burgoyne withdrew to a position in the vicinity of Saratoga.

Militia soon worked around to the rear of this position and cut Burgoyne's routes of escape. Having no news from General Clinton in New York, and despairing of relief from that quarter, Burgoyne surrendered his army, now reduced to 5,000, on 17 October. British troops at Kingston then hastily retreated to New York. Unfortunately the large militia force that had gathered under Gates also dissolved. Only the Continental contingents sent north by Washington returned to strengthen the main army.

Saratoga eliminated an important part of the British Army and delivered into the hands of the Americans large quantities of valuable military stores. It removed the danger of a British advance southward from Canada to split the American states in twain. Most important of all, it convinced the French Court that the time had come to enter the war on the side of the Americans. In February 1778 France negotiated a treaty of alliance with the American states tantamount to a declaration of war against England. French participation was to be the factor that finally and decisively tipped the scales in favor of the Americans. It is for this reason that Saratoga ranks as one of the decisive battles of history.

This lithograph of the surrender of General Burgoyne at Saratoga is based on a painting by Colonel John Trumbull.

SURRENDER OF GENERAL BURGOYNE
At Saratoga N Y October 17th 1777

1. Major Lithgow, Massachusetts
2. Colonel Cilly, New Hampshire
3. General Stark, New Hampshire
4. Captain Seymour, of Shelton's Horse
5. Major Hull, Massachusetts
6. Colonel Greaton, Massachusetts
7. Major Dearborne, New Hampshire
8. Colonel Scammell, New Hampshire
9. Colonel Lewis, quartermaster general, New Hampshire
10. Major General Phillips, British

11. Lieutenant General Burgoyne, British
12. General Baron Riedesel, German
13. Colonel Wilkinson, deputy adjutant general, American
14. General Gates
15. Colonel Prescott, Massachusetts Volunteers
16. Colonel Morgan, Virginia Riflemen
17. Brig. Gen. Rufus Putnam, Massachusetts
18. Lieut. Col. John Brooks, late Governor of Massachusetts
19. Rev. Mr. Hitchcock, chaplain, Rhode Island

20. Maj. Rob. Troup, aid-de-camp, New York
21. Major Haskell
22. Major Armstrong
23. Maj. Gen. Philip Schuyler, Albany
24. Brigadier General Glover, Massachusetts
25. Brigadier General Whipple, New Hampshire Militia
26. Maj. M. Clarkson, aid-de-camp, New York
27. Maj. Ebenezer Stevens, Massachusetts, Commanding the artillery

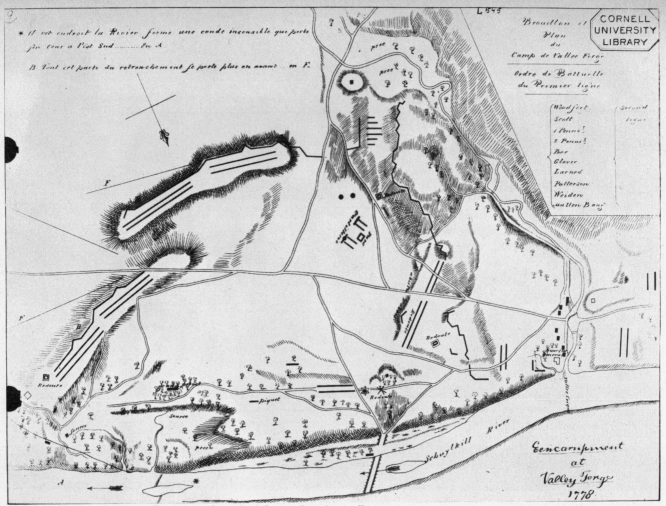

This map of the encampment at Valley Forge is the work of the French engineer officer Louis DuPortail, who supervised the construction of fortifications.

THE WAR IN 1778

Winter at Valley Forge

The news of Saratoga heartened Washington greatly as he moved into winter quarters at Valley Forge, but his own problems became too great to permit unrestrained rejoicing. The army at Valley Forge was soon in desperate condition, its men suffering almost unbelievable hardships. About one-half had no shoes or stockings, others no pants or blankets.

Weeks passed during which there was no meat, and a thin soup constituted the main course three times a day. The construction of fortifications to guard the valley had to come first, and it was not until well into January that the shivering army could get out of its tattered tents and into log huts. Fortunately, it was a relatively mild winter.

"The Prayer at Valley Forge." The engraving by John C. McRae is based on a story told by Isaac Potts at whose house Washington was quartered. While walking one day Potts came upon Washington at prayer. Feeling that he was upon holy ground, Potts quickly withdrew.

A replica of the cannon
that guarded Valley Forge.

Washington's headquarters
at Valley Forge.

An artist's conception of life at Valley Forge.

This is one of the huts reconstructed in the 2,000-acre Valley Forge State Park to tell the story of the Continental Army during the winter of 1777–1778. With the exception of the roof, it is a faithful reproduction of the huts that sheltered Washington's soldiers.

Valley Forge is mainly remembered today for the patriotism, perseverance, and devotion to duty of the small body of officers and men, less than 6,000 in all, that stayed with the Army during the winter of suffering in 1777–1778. Less well known are the reasons why the Army suffered. There was no real shortage of food or clothing in the country. The governmental and military agencies charged with procuring and delivering supplies simply failed to function efficiently.

The reconstructed hospital at Valley Forge.

The visit of a committee from the Continental Congress to Valley Forge in January 1778 provided the subject matter for this painting.

By 1780 the Continental Congress had issued almost $242,000,000 in paper money. It depreciated rapidly and farmers were reluctant to accept it in exchange for food and other supplies for the Army.

A supply train is bringing
food to Valley Forge
in this woodcut.

Reorganization of the Army in Early 1778

It is perhaps a measure of the extent to which mankind profits from adversity that the Continental Army emerged from Valley Forge a stronger, more effective force than before. Having successfully quashed a scheme to replace him with Gates, Washington was able to get Congress to accept his recommendations for reorganization of the Army in early 1778. Major General Nathanael Greene, Washington's ablest lieutenant, was made Quartermaster and Jeremiah Wadsworth, Commissary. These men introduced new efficiency in their departments that endured at least for a time. Despairing now of filling his battalions with men enlisted for the duration or three years, Washington got Congress to recommend to the states that the ranks be filled with men drafted from the militia for one year's service. Men enlisted for the duration or three years would count against state quotas as the equivalent of three one-year draftees.

Most important of all, the Continental Army, during its last months at Valley Forge, profited from professional instruction. Washington had long perceived the need for standardizing organization and training but had found no one qualified to carry out the task until Baron von Steuben appeared at Valley Forge in February 1778.

Steuben had seen service as a captain on Frederick the Great's staff during the Seven Years' War, and had mastered the elements of the Prussian military system, considered the best in Europe at the time. By 1778 he was seeking employment, and the French War Minister, aware of the American need for professional guidance, persuaded him to offer his services to the Americans.

Accepting Steuben at first only as a volunteer without rank, Washington sent him to inspect the camp at Valley Forge. The baron was appalled at what he saw. Different drill manuals and methods, British, French, and Prussian, and different forms of organization were in use in the various state lines. All units were understrength and some regiments were stronger than brigades, some companies stronger than regiments. There was general neglect of weapons and insufficient knowledge of their use in battle. Yet the discerning eye of the Prussian recognized in the men who had endured the rigors of Valley Forge the best of soldier material. Indeed, he thought, no European army could have held together under such hardships.

Impressed with the baron's judgment, Washington made him temporary Inspector General, a new staff office, and instructed him to work out a standard training program for the Continental Army. Steuben began to write out his drill lessons in French, having them translated into English by his own and Washington's aides. He then organized a model company and personally undertook to drill these men in the movements he was introducing. When he had progressed far enough with the model company, he extended the drill to the entire army, keeping the model company about six lessons ahead. Subordinate inspectors general were appointed for each brigade. To meet the problem of understrength, Steuben formed provisional battalions at full strength and rotated surplus officers and noncommissioned officers in the work of drilling, thus forming a cadre able to train the new recruits with whom it was hoped the ranks would be filled in the spring.

In this manner, Steuben taught the army to march in

Baron von Steuben (in long cloak)
drilling the Continental Army at Valley Forge.

regular columns of twos and fours in uniform step, to fire volleys at regular command, to change from column into line into column with precision, and to use the bayonet effectively. Though he used the Prussian model, he adapted it to the characteristics of the American soldier, eliminating all but the most essential maneuvers and motions. Form and ceremony he subordinated to the interest of practicality. Recognizing the importance of skirmishers in America, he took the lead in organizing elite companies of light infantry as part of every American regiment. He was also a pioneer in impressing on officers their obligations to the

A reproduction of the letter Washington sent Baron von Steuben at the end of the war to thank the Prussian officer for his "faithful & meritorious Services."

men they commanded. American officers, following British traditions, tended to regard their responsibility as only that of leading their men in battle. Steuben, by drilling the men himself and by attention to their sufferings and wants at Valley Forge, taught by example that the officer's responsibility extended to every phase of army activity. Steuben was quick to recognize that the American soldier had to be told why he should do things before he would do them well, and he applied this philosophy in his training program. His trenchant good humor and his outbursts of profanity, the only English he knew, delighted the soldiers of the Revolution and made the rigorous drill and discipline he instituted more palatable. Thus, ironically, a Prussian, whose traditions would seem to have been most alien to the American scene, first adapted the discipline and method of Europe to the ingrained individualism of the American soldier.

Pleased with Steuben's work, Washington secured his formal appointment as Inspector General, and in this post Steuben extended his work to other parts of the Army. The standard drill regulations developed at Valley Forge were formally codified in Regulations for the Order and Discipline of the Troops of the United States, the so-called Blue Book. For many years to come this was to be the official training manual of the American Army, and its influence is still alive in the United States Army of the present day.

While Washington's army underwent the trials of Valley Forge, Howe remained inactive in Philadelphia. Howe refrained from attacking not only because he disliked war, but also because Valley Forge was a well-nigh impregnable position. Moreover, he was sick of his role in the war and had already submitted his resignation. In the winter of 1777–1778 he was merely holding his army together until his successor, General Sir Henry Clinton, could take over.

58

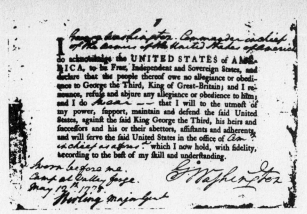

As required by a new law passed by the Continental Congress, Washington and his officers subscribed to an oath of allegiance to the United States of America in the spring of 1778. This is a facsimile of that oath that Washington signed on May 12.

Washington vs. Clinton at Monmouth

The British position was much altered by French entry into the war. Britain would now have to defend its far-flung possessions in the West Indies, the Mediterranean, and India and not fight solely in North America. The French fleet, much improved since the Seven Years' War, posed a definite threat at sea. The British Government decided that under these circumstances Philadelphia would be untenable and ordered Clinton, as soon as he assumed command, to evacuate the city and take his forces back to New York by sea. When he arrived in New York, parts of his army were to be detached to Florida, the West Indies, and Canada to protect these areas against French attack.

Clinton decided to evacuate the major portion of his army from Philadelphia by land rather than by sea, fearing the approach of a French fleet under Admiral D'Estaing. He began his march with about 10,000 men on 18 June 1778. Washington reoccupied Philadelphia immediately and then followed Clinton, undecided at first whether he should attack the British column while it was strung out on the road or merely try to harass its progress. The army he brought from Valley Forge was not only better trained but also larger than that of the previous year, new enlistments and militia draftees having brought its total strength to around 13,500 men. Additional troops of the New Jersey militia were in the field in a position to harass Clinton's movement.

The Battle of Monmouth as painted by Alonzo Chappell.

A Currier and Ives lithograph of "Molly Pitcher" (Martha or Molly Hays) manning a gun at Monmouth after her cannoneer husband suffered a mortal wound.

An engraving of Washington at his battlefield encampment on the night after Monmouth.

On 26 June Clinton arrived at Monmouth Court House with Washington's army close behind and the militia hovering about his flanks. All Washington's generals save Wayne and Lafayette advised against a direct attack. Despite this adverse advice, Washington finally decided to attack the first grand British division as it moved out from Monmouth. One part of the Army under Major General Charles Lee was to launch the attack, and Washington with the rest would move in to support it.

Lee at first declined command of the attacking force but, on learning it would include almost half the army, changed his mind. Yet he had little confidence in the success of the endeavor, and this probably explains his subsequent conduct. Lee moved forward on the morning of 27 June—a hot, sultry day—and made contact with the British near Monmouth. But he gave no clear orders to his subordinates, and apparently had no definite objectives, so that the ensuing battle degenerated into a series of

General "Mad Anthony" Wayne leading his men
against the British at Stony Point, New York.

Brigadier General Anthony Wayne.

separated skirmishes. Finally Lee gave the order to retreat and his force started back, no one apparently knowing what had gone wrong. Washington, moving up with the main force, met Lee, exchanged harsh words with him, and assumed direction of what now had to be a defense against a British counterattack. The general engagement that followed lasted until dark, the tide flowing one way and then the other. Casualties from sunstroke and heat prostration were almost as heavy on both sides as those from enemy fire. For the first time the Americans fought well with the bayonet, as well as with musket and rifle, and their battlefield behavior generally reflected the effects of the training at Valley Forge.

Both sides still held the field when night fell. In the night Clinton slipped away, as Washington had at Princeton, and in a few days successfully completed his retreat to New York.

THE STALEMATE OF 1779

Monmouth was the last general engagement in the North between Washington's and Clinton's armies. In 1779 the situation there became a stalemate and remained one until the end of the war. Washington set up a defense system around New York, its center at West Point on the Hudson. In late spring 1779 Clinton made his last serious effort to draw Washington out of his fortifications and into battle in the open field, descending in force on unfinished American installations forward of West Point at Verplanck's and Stony Points. But Washington refused to take the bait, and Clinton withdrew to New York, leaving small garrisons at the captured positions. Washington then launched a small counter-

offensive, more notable because it gave testimony to the improved skill of his soldiers than for its strategic consequences. General Wayne with an elite corps of light infantry moved swiftly down the Hudson in boats on the night of 15 July 1779 and took the British by surprise in a daring bayonet attack on Stony Point. The British garrison surrendered after only a brief struggle. Stony Point demonstrated the value of the new light infantry organization formed at Valley Forge and, even more than Monmouth, showed that trained American soldiers could now wield the bayonet as effectively as the British. But Wayne proved unable to take Verplanck's Point, and Washington finally ordered him to withdraw with his prisoners and captured supplies. Neither side made any further moves.

The only other serious threat to Washington's defenses came in 1780, not as the result of a British military movement but rather the treason of Benedict Arnold. Arnold had proved himself one of the most capable of American field commanders in the early stages of the war, but he lacked character and stability. Disgruntled by what he considered to be the failure of Congress to give proper recognition to his abilities, and tempted by the lucrative financial rewards offered by the British, Arnold finagled an appointment as commander at West Point and then entered into a plot to deliver this key post to the British. Washington discovered the plot just in time to foil it, but Arnold escaped to become a British brigadier.

Unable to accomplish anything decisive in the North, the British in late 1778 began to transfer their main effort to the South. Tory strength was greater in the South, and

I Benedict Arnold Major General do acknowledge the UNITED STATES of AMERICA to be Free, Independent and Sovereign States, and declare that the people thereof owe no allegiance or obedience to George the Third, King of Great-Britain; and I renounce, refuse and abjure any allegiance or obedience to him; and I do *Swear* that I will, to the utmost of my power, support, maintain and defend the said United States against the said King George the Third, his heirs and successors, and his or their abettors, assistants and adherents, and will serve the said United States in the office of *Major General* which I now hold, with fidelity, according to the best of my skill and understanding.

Sworn before me this 30th May 1778 at the Artillery Park Valley Forge

Benedict Arnold, hero of Quebec, Lake Champlain, and Saratoga—and traitor.

As part of his treason, Benedict Arnold arranged to have a link removed from the enormous chain that had been stretched across the Hudson at West Point to obstruct river traffic.

Head Quarters Robinsons House Sepr. 22d 1780

Permit Mr. John Anderson to pass the Guards to the White Plains, or below If He Chuses. He being on Public Business by my Direction

B. Arnold MGenl.

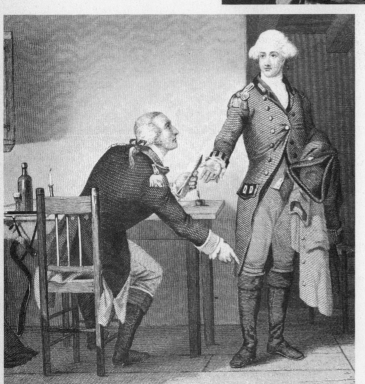

In this engraving Arnold is persuading his accomplice, British Major John André, to conceal secret papers in his boot.

A reproduction of the pass that Arnold gave to André who was traveling under the name "John Anderson."

André, wearing civilian clothes, is stopped and searched by three militiamen who find the incriminating papers. A Currier and Ives lithograph.

Currier and Ives's "The Escape of Sergeant Champe." Sergeant Champe took part in an attempt to abduct Benedict Arnold, who had defected to the British Army, and return him to Washington's headquarters. The attempt failed and Arnold became a brigadier general in the British Army.

A contemporary engraving of André's execution.

While awaiting execution as a spy, Major André sketched this self-portrait.

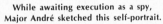

the area was closer to the West Indies, where the major portion of the British Fleet had to stand guard against the French. The King's ministers hoped to bring the southern states back into the British fold one by one, and from bases there and in New York, to strangle the recalcitrant North.

Georgia, a weak and thinly populated state, was chosen as the first objective; it was quickly overrun in the winter of 1778–1779 by two British forces, one sent from New York and the other moving north from Florida. Alarmed at the course of events, Congress sent Major General Benjamin Lincoln of Massachusetts south to Charleston in December 1778 to organize the southern effort. Lincoln gathered 3,500 Continentals and militia but failed in an effort to recover Georgia. In May 1779, while Lincoln was maneuvering along the Georgia border, the British commander, Major General Augustine Prevost, slipped away to besiege Charleston, and the city only barely managed to hold out until Lincoln returned to its relief.

Meanwhile Clinton, urged on by the British Government, had determined to push the campaign in the South in earnest. In late spring 1779 he sent a naval raiding force under Admiral George Collier into the port area inside Hampton Roads in Virginia, and Collier was successful in destroying such large quantities of supplies, ships, and installations that Virginia's ability to serve as a base for supply and reinforcement of the lower South was seriously affected. In October 1779 Clinton withdrew the British garrison at Newport and pulled in his troops from outposts around New York. By the end of the year he was ready to move south against Charleston with a large part of his force. Washington, at this time, had neither the men nor the supplies to enable him to divert more than small piecemeal reinforcements southward.

THE REVERSES OF 1780

On 12 May 1780, with Clinton's troops approaching within 250 yards of the American positions, Lincoln surrendered his entire force of 5,466 men, the greatest disaster to the American cause during the entire Revolution.

At the time Charleston surrendered, Colonel Abraham Buford with 350 Virginians, the last remaining organized American force in the South, was moving south to reinforce the garrison. Buford's force was overtaken at the Waxhaws, a district near the North Carolina border, on 29 May, and virtually annihilated by British cavalry under Lieutenant Colonel Banastre Tarleton, an able, daring, and

Major General Benjamin Lincoln who was in charge of the Continental Army's southern effort from December 1778 until the surrender of Charleston, South Carolina, in May 1780.

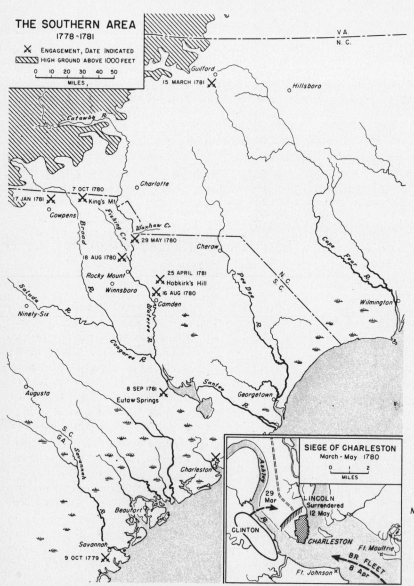

Map—The Southern Area.

Soldiers and civilians cooperating
in the unsuccessful defense of Charleston.

ruthless officer, whose name was to become anathema to patriots throughout the South. Tarleton surprised Buford with a sudden cavalry charge and slaughtered most of his men, refusing to honor the white flag Buford displayed.

After the capture of Charleston, American guerrillas, principally led by Brigadier Generals Thomas Sumter and Andrew Pickens and Lieutenant Colonel Francis Marion, harried British posts and lines of communication and battled the bands of Tories. A bloody, ruthless, and confused civil war ensued in the South, its character determined in no small degree by Tarleton's action at the Waxhaws.

The Defeat of General Gates in the South

On 22 June 1780 two understrength Continental brigades from Washington's army arrived at Hillsboro, North Carolina, and these became the nerve center of guerrilla resistance. In July, without consulting Washington, Congress named General Gates, the hero of Saratoga, commander of the Southern Department. Gates soon lost his northern laurels by adopting an aggressive plan hardly suited to his capabilities. Determining to attack the British post at Camden, he marched his army in great haste toward that point through Tory country where the men had to subsist on green corn. By the time he approached Camden, militia reinforcements had brought his force to 4,100 men, but stomach upsets left only 3,000 fit for duty, and of these but 900 were trained and disciplined Continentals. Gates made the additional mistake of detaching 400 men, including 100 Continentals, to go with General Sumter to raid a British wagon train.

Cornwallis learned of Gates's approach and hurried north from Charleston with reinforcements. With an army of 2,200, nearly all regulars, he contacted Gates's force outside Camden on the night of 15–16 August, but both commanders cautiously decided to await morning before

giving battle. In the morning, Gates deployed his force with the militia on the left and the Continentals under Major General Johann de Kalb on the right. The militia were still forming in the hazy dawn when Cornwallis struck, and they fled in panic before the British bayonets. DeKalb's Continentals put up a valiant fight but were so outnumbered once the militia fled that it was a hopeless one. Tarleton's cavalry pursued the fleeing Americans for 30 miles, killing or making prisoners of those who lagged in their flight. Gates himself fled too fast for Tarleton, reaching Hillsboro, 160 miles away, in three days. There he was able to gather only about 800 survivors of the southern Army. To add to the extent of the disaster, Tarleton caught up with Sumter and virtually destroyed his force in a surprise attack at Fishing Creek on 18 August.

Difficulties in the North

Defeat in the South was not the only discouraging aspect of the situation in 1780. In the North, the high patriotic enthusiasm of the early years waned as the war dragged on, and a creeping paralysis in the war effort set in. By 1780 the Continental currency had practically depreciated out of existence, rendering Congress impotent to pay the soldiers or purchase supplies, with the result that at Morristown, New Jersey, in the winter of 1779–1780 the Army suffered severe hardships. Congress could do little more than shift its responsibilities to the states, giving each the task of providing clothing for its own troops and furnishing certain quotas of specific supplies for the entire Army. Such a system proved entirely inadequate. Not only were the states laggard in furnishing the specific supplies, but when they did it was seldom at the time and place at which they could be most profitably used. This breakdown in the supply system was more than even General Greene as Quartermaster General could cope with, and in early 1780, under heavy criticism in Congress, he resigned his position.

Under such supply and financial difficulties, Washington was hard put to it to hold even a small army together. Recruiting of Continentals, difficult to begin with, became practically impossible when the troops could be neither adequately paid nor supplied and had to suffer such winters as that at Morristown. Both Congress and the states increased the bounties for enlistment again and again with little result except to create a large group of bounty jumpers who enlisted in one state only to desert and enlist in another and to cause resentment among the veterans who had enlisted earlier for much smaller inducements. The other expedient for securing men, the conscription of militia for one year's service, also failed to produce the numbers expected. The states adopted conscription reluctantly and applied it only sporadically.

While recruiting lagged, morale among the troops that did remain, ill-supplied and ill-paid, naturally fell. Mutinies in 1780 and 1781 were suppressed only by measures of great severity. That Washington did manage to maintain a force in being is a tribute both to his great leadership and to the devotion to duty of the great majority of his veteran officers and men.

THE FINAL BURST OF ENERGY, 1781

Congress made some efforts to remedy the situation toward the end of 1780. Colonel Timothy Pickering, an able administrator, was made Quartermaster General, and Robert Morris, a wealthy Philadelphia merchant, was induced to accept the position of Superintendent of Finance. Morris, working closely with Pickering, introduced a new policy of supplying the Army by private contracts, using his own personal credit as guarantee for eventual payment in gold or silver. Moreover, in 1781, the old cumbersome Board of War was abolished and a single full-time Secretary of War assigned its functions. General Lincoln, exchanged after

Charleston, was appointed to this position. To conform to reality, the authorized size of the Army was reduced from the 110 battalions voted in 1776 to 59 in 1781—50 of infantry, 4 each of cavalry and artillery, and 1 of artificers. If filled, these units would still have provided an army of around 40,000 but the regiments remained far below strength. Nevertheless, the net effect of the reforms was sufficient to make possible one great and decisive burst of energy in 1781.

Congress also provided new leadership in the South, this time accepting Washington's recommendations. General Greene replaced Gates in command; Brigadier General Daniel Morgan was assigned to command the light infantry under Greene; and Lieutenant Colonel Henry Lee was sent south with his legion, a mixed organization of cavalry and infantry, to provide a mobile force capable of cooperation with guerrilla units. Greene, Morgan, and Lee were to give the southern army the leadership it had long lacked, leadership that was to compensate, in some measure, for what that army lacked in numbers and material means.

General Nathanael Greene Takes Over in the South

At Charlotte, North Carolina, where he took over from Gates early in December, 1780, General Nathanael Greene found an army that, although numbering on paper 3,400, had only 1,500 present and fit for duty, and of these only 949 were Continentals. The army lacked clothing and provisions, and it had little systematic means of procuring them. Greene faced his problem realistically. He decided he must not, like Gates, rush into battle against a superior British force but would instead conduct essentially guerrilla operations, harrying Cornwallis' lines of supply and wearing down the strength of his army. He hoped for a gradual accretion of his own strength to the point where it would enable him eventually to defeat a weakened British army

The American attack on the British post at Camden, South Carolina, on 16 August 1780, is repulsed by Cornwallis' army.

in the field. As a first step he had his engineers explore and map the surrounding country so that no move would have to be made without some knowledge of the terrain. Next he determined to get out of the devastated area around Charlotte and into richer country, where he could live off the land. The best position, he found, would be at Cheraw Hill in South Carolina, but, since it was farther away from Cornwallis' camp than Charlotte, to move there with his entire army would give the inhabitants the impression he was retreating. He therefore decided to move only part of his army to Cheraw, and sent the rest under Morgan west across the Catawba into an area closer to Cornwallis' camp.

Puzzled by Greene's dispositions, Cornwallis divided his army not into two but three parts. He sent a holding force to Camden to contain Greene, and directed Tarleton with a fast-moving contingent of 1,100 infantry and cavalry to find and crush Morgan. With his main army he moved cautiously up toward North Carolina, confidently expecting to cut off the remainder of Morgan's force after its defeat by Tarleton. On 17 January 1781 Tarleton finally caught up with Morgan west of King's Mountain at a place called the Cowpens. There Morgan had determined to make his stand, with his back parallel to the Broad River a few miles in his rear and an open sparsely forested area on his front and right. Morgan's force was numerically almost equal to that of Tarleton, but it was three-quarters militia and his cavalry was much inferior.

Morgan fully understood the limitations of his militia, and adopted a plan whereby its capabilities could be used to full advantage. He selected a hill as the center of his position, and formed his main line of Continental infantry on it, deliberately leaving his flanks open, ordinarily a dangerous thing to do. Well out to the front of the main line he posted Pickens' militia riflemen in two lines, instructing the first line to fire two volleys and then fall back to the second, the combined line to fire until the British pressed them, then to fall back to the rear of the Continentals and re-form as a reserve. Behind the hill he placed Lieutenant Colonel William Washington's cavalry detachment, ready to charge the attacking enemy at the critical moment. Every man in the ranks was informed of the plan of battle and the part he was expected to play in it.

On finding Morgan, Tarleton ordered an immediate attack. His men moved forward in regular formation, were checked by the militia rifles but took the retreat of the first two lines to be the beginning of a rout and rushed headlong into the steady fire of the Continentals on the hill. When the British were well advanced, the cavalry struck them on the right flank, and Pickens' militia, having re-formed, drove out from behind the hill to hit the British left. Caught in a clever double envelopment, the British surrendered after suffering heavy losses. Tarleton managed to escape with only a small force of cavalry that he held in reserve.

Cornwallis was still near at hand with the main British Army, and Morgan had far too few men to risk a fight. He therefore swiftly marched to rejoin Greene, covering 100 miles and crossing two rivers in five days. Cornwallis, hoping to match the rapid movement of the Americans, destroyed all his superfluous supplies, baggage, and wagons. This action inspired Greene's next moves. Ignoring Morgan's advice to retreat west to the mountains where Cornwallis could not follow, Greene determined instead to move north toward Virginia, tempting Cornwallis to follow but keeping just far enough in front of him to avoid battle with his superior force. In this way he expected gradually to wear down Cornwallis' strength and exhaust his remaining supplies while he himself would gather strength. So Greene retreated, through North Carolina, up into southern Virginia, then back into North Carolina again, with Cornwallis always in hot pursuit.

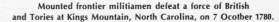

Mounted frontier militiamen defeat a force of British and Tories at Kings Mountain, North Carolina, on 7 Ocotber 1780.

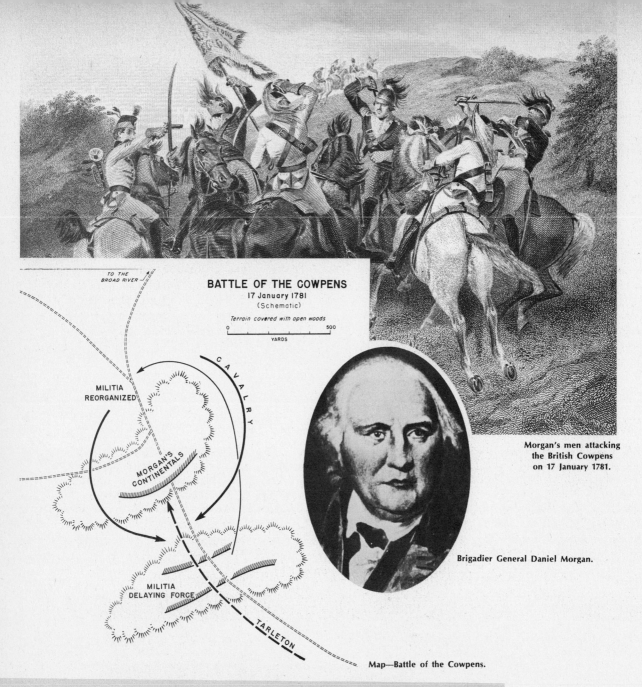

BATTLE OF THE COWPENS
17 January 1781
(Schematic)

Terrain covered with open woods

0   500
YARDS

TO THE
BROAD RIVER

CAVALRY

MILITIA
REORGANIZED

MORGAN'S
CONTINENTALS

MILITIA
DELAYING FORCE

TARLETON

Morgan's men attacking
the British Cowpens
on 17 January 1781.

Brigadier General Daniel Morgan.

Map—Battle of the Cowpens.

Throwing His Master. A British cartoon of 1781.

Colonel Francis Marion invites a British officer, who had come to negotiate an exchange of prisoners, to dine with him and his men in their swamp encampment. The engraving is by John Cartain, based on a painting by John Black White.

Marion and his guerrilla volunteers crossing the Pedee River in South Carolina. A Currier and Ives lithograph.

Cartoon—The Curious Zebra.

Rochambeau as the subject of a cartoon.

Lieutenant General Jean Baptiste Donatien de Vimeur,
Comte de Rochambeau.

Finally on 15 March 1781, at Guilford Court House in North Carolina, ground he had himself chosen, Greene halted and prepared to meet Cornwallis' attack. By this time he had 1,500 Continentals and 3,000 militia to the 1,900 British regulars Cornwallis could muster. Greene disposed his militia much as Morgan had at Cowpens. But this time, once the men had fired their volleys, they fled the field completely. The British finally won the battle, mainly because of the superiority of their artillery, but suffered casualties of about one-fourth of the force engaged. Greene withdrew his army to a point 10 miles away in much better shape than it had been at Charlotte six months earlier. Cornwallis, on the other hand, now had a decimated force and almost no supplies. It was impossible for him to maintain his position in the interior any longer. He withdrew to Wilmington along the coast where he could be supplied by sea, and from there decided to move northward to join the British forces General Clinton had sent to Virginia.

In late May 1781 Cornwallis arrived from Wilmington with the remnants of his army, and took command of all the British forces in Virginia, now numbering 7,000 men, nearly a third of the total British strength in America. Cornwallis had abandoned the lower South without even informing Clinton of his intention. He now proposed to carry out major operations in the interior of Virginia, but Clinton saw as little practical value in such a move as Cornwallis did in Clinton's plan to establish a base in Virginia and carry out a pincers movement against Pennsylvania. The two commanders were soon working at cross purposes. Cornwallis at first turned to the interior as if to pursue his own

French soldiers in Philadelphia.
Victory at Yorktown.

designs, and engaged in a fruitless pursuit of Lafayette north of Richmond. Then, on receiving Clinton's positive orders to return to the coast, establish a base, and return part of his force to New York, Cornwallis moved back down the Virginia peninsula and took up his station at Yorktown. At this small tobacco port on the York River, just off Chesapeake Bay, he proposed to establish the base that Clinton desired.

The Siege of Yorktown

Cornwallis' move to Yorktown gave Washington the opportunity to strike the decisive blow in cooperation with the French fleet that he had long awaited. He had learned that Admiral François de Grasse with a powerful French fleet intended to come to the American coast in late summer, and he persuaded the French commander at Newport, Lieutenant General the Comte de Rochambeau, to bring his 4,000 French troops to join him in New York. Rochambeau placed his army under Washington's command. The total combined Franco-American force numbered less than 10,000, and both Washington and Rochambeau soon decided they could make little progress against Clinton's 17,000 men in well-fortified positions. Then on 14 August, Rochambeau received word from de Grasse in the West Indies that he intended

to come to the Chesapeake later that month and that he could remain only until 15 October. De Grasse's proposed movement shaped Washington's plans. He saw immediately that if he could achieve a superior concentration of force on the land side while de Grasse held the bay he could destroy the British Army at Yorktown before Clinton had a chance to relieve it. Washington sent orders to Lafayette to contain Cornwallis at Yorktown, and then, after making a feint in the direction of New York to deceive Clinton, on 21 August started the major portion of his own and Rochambeau's troops on a rapid secret movement south to Virginia, leaving only 2,000 Americans behind to watch Clinton. The route lay overland through New Jersey, Pennsylvania, and Maryland to Head of Elk, Annapolis, and Baltimore, where an improvised flotilla of boats was readied to take the men down the Chesapeake and up the James River to a landing near Williamsburg.

On 30 August, while Washington was on the move southward, de Grasse arrived in the Chesapeake with his entire fleet of 24 ships of the line, and a few days later debarked 3,000 French troops to join Lafayette. De Grasse had wisely refused to heed the instructions of the French

Map—Washington's Official Map of Yorktown.

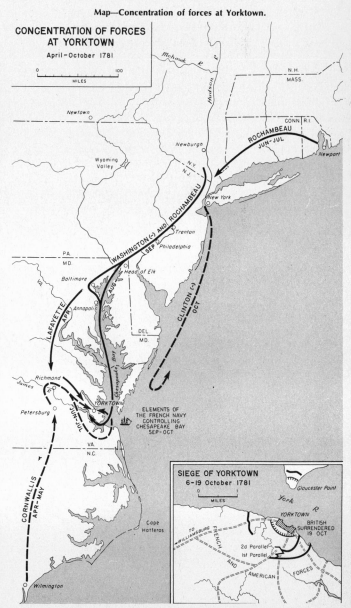

Map—Concentration of forces at Yorktown.

Government to divert 10 of his ships for convoy duty. In contrast, the British naval commander in the West Indies, Admiral Sir George Rodney, had divided his fleet, taking 3 ships of the line to England, leaving 3 in the West Indies, and sending only 14 north to join Admiral Thomas Graves's squadron at New York. Graves put out to sea in late August with 19 ships of the line, hoping either to intercept Barras' squadron or to block de Grasse's entry into the Chesapeake. He failed to find Barras, and when he arrived off Hampton Roads on 5 September he found de Grasse already in the bay. The French admiral sallied forth to meet Graves, and the two fleets fought an indecisive action off the Virginia capes. Yet the victory for all practical purposes lay with the French, for, while the fleet maneuvered at sea for days following the battle, Barras' squadron slipped into the Chesapeake, and the French and the American troops got past into the James River. Also at the end of the maneuvering, de Grasse got back into the bay and joined Barras, confronting Graves with such a decidedly superior naval force that he decided to return to New York to refit.

When Washington's army arrived on 26 September, the French fleet was in firm control of the bay, blocking Cornwallis' sea route of escape. Virginia militia poured in, and when the siege operation was begun on 6 October the army numbered over 16,000—8,845 Americans and 7,800 French regulars—to Cornwallis' 6,000 men. The decisive concentration of force had been achieved; it remained only to reap its benefits. Washington's main concern was to keep de Grasse in the bay long enough to complete the siege, and with Rochambeau and Lafayette's cooperation he got the French admiral to agree to extend his stay beyond 15 October if necessary.

The siege, carried on in traditional eighteenth-century fashion, was the type of operation in which the French were masters. Cornwallis obligingly abandoned his forward position on 30 September, and on 6 October the first parallel was begun 600 yards from his main position. Artillery was placed in position along the trench, and began its destructive work on 9 October. By 11 October the zigzag connect-

ing trench had been dug 200 yards forward, and work on the second parallel had begun. Two British redoubts had to be reduced by French and American light infantry in order to extend the line to the York River. This accomplished, Cornwallis' only hope was escape. On the night of 16 October he attempted to get his troops across the York to Gloucester Point, where the American line was thinly held, but a storm upset his plans. After this failure there was no other hope but relief from New York.

Clinton had been considering such a relief for some time, but there was doubt whether Admiral Thomas Graves's fleet at New York was equal to the task. Graves finally set sail on 17 October with 7,000 troops aboard. On that very day Cornwallis had begun negotiations on terms of surrender.

The Surrender of Cornwallis

After a destructive artillery barrage on the preceding day a British drummer on 17 October mounted the parapet before Cornwallis' defenses and beat a parley. Firing ceased and the next day commissioners from both sides met to agree on terms of surrender. On 19 October 1781 Cornwallis' entire army of 6,000 marched out to lay down their arms while the British band played an old tune called "The World Turned Upside Down."

So far as active campaigning was concerned, Yorktown ended the war. Both Greene and Washington maintained their armies in position near New York and Charleston for nearly two years more, but the only fighting was some minor skirmishing in the South.

Legend has it that Washington himself held the match that fired the first American siege gun at Yorktown.

Major General Charles Cornwallis.

SURRENDER OF LORD CORNWALLIS

At Yorktown Va. October 19th 1781.

The portraits of the French Officers were obtained in Paris 1787 and painted by Trumbull from the living men, in the house of Mr. Jefferson then Minister to France from the United States.

1. *Count Deuxponts*
   Colonel of French Infantry
2. *Duke de Laval Montmorency*
   Colonel of French Infantry
3. *Count Custine*
   Colonel of French Infantry
4. *Duke de Lauzun*
   Colonel of French Cavalry
5. *General Choizy*
6. *Viscount Viomenil*
7. *Marquis de St. Simon*
8. *Count Fersen*
   Aid-de-camp of Count Rochambeau
9. *Count Charles Damas*
   Aid-de-camp of Count Rochambeau
10. *Marquis Chastellux*
11. *Baron Viomenil*

12. *Count de Barras*
    Admiral
13. *Count de Grasse*
    Admiral
14. *Count Rochambeau*
    General en Chef des Francais
15. *General Lincoln*
16. *E. Stevens*
    Colonel of American Artillery
17. *General Washington*
    Commander in Chief
18. *Thomas Nelson*
    Governor of Virginia
19. *Marquis Lafayette*
20. *Baron Steuben*
21. *Colonel Cobb*
    Aid-de-camp to General Washington
22. *Colonel Trumbull*
    Secretary to General Washington

23. *Maj. Gen. James Clinton, New York*
24. *General Gist, Maryland*
25. *Gen. Anthony Wayne, Pennsylvania*
26. *General Hand, Pennsylvania*
    Adjutant General
27. *Gen. Peter Muhlenberg, Pennsylvania*
28. *Maj. Gen. Henry Knox*
    Commander of Artillery
29. *Lieut. Col. E. Huntington*
    Acting aid-de-camp of General Lincoln
30. *Col. Timothy Pickering*
    Quartermaster General
31. *Col. Alexander Hamilton*
    Commanding Light Infantry
32. *Col. John Laurens, South Carolina*
33. *Col. Walter Stuart, Philadelphia*
34. *Col. Nicholas Fish, New York*

**The surrender of Lord Cornwallis at Yorktown
as painted by John Trumbull.**

The Lessons of Victory

The lessons that might have been learned from the Revolution were many, for, although the Americans finally won, it was in spite of, rather than because of, their system of military mobilization and administration. The experience of the Revolution demonstrated first and foremost the need for strong, central direction in war and the subordination of state to national interests. If anything was made clear, it was that no efficient and uniform national army could ever be formed on the scale necessary for a major war as long as the individual states had primary responsibility for recruiting and organizing the regiments. The Revolution also

showed that the task of creating an army was a long and arduous one, that men must be enlisted for the duration of the war, that they must be subjected to a long period of training and discipline, and that there must be a sound and well-regulated system for the procurement and distribution of supplies. It also indicated that conscription, honestly, fairly, and uniformly administered, would be the most efficient and equitable system of raising such an army and that volunteers, even when encouraged by generous bounties, could not be persuaded to enlist in sufficient number. It did not prove that the militia system as such was a failure, only that militia or any other force on short-term enlist-

Announcing the surrender of Cornwallis in Philadelphia. A Currier and Ives lithograph.

ments and subject only to state control could never provide an effective and continuous force for a major war.

The men who drew up the Federal Constitution in 1787 profited from the experience of the Revolution and provided a central government with power to tax and raise military forces and a strong executive to carry out the decisions of Congress. The strictly military lessons of the Revolution were not so clearly appreciated or applied. The legend grew in America that an army could spring to arms overnight when the country was threatened. The legend took for its historical examples Lexington and Concord, Bunker Hill, Bennington, and King's Mountain and conveniently neglected the lessons of Long Island, Kip's Bay, Trenton, Germantown, Valley Forge, Stony Point, and Camden. The militia was credited with having won the Revolution, and the long, arduous process by which the Continental Army was forged into an effective fighting instrument was forgotten. Much of the valuable contribution of von Steuben was consequently lost, and military policy was too frequently shaped in terms of the legend.

As the defeated British leave New York,
the Stars and Stripes replaces the Union Jack.

WASHINGTON'S FAREWELL TO THE ARMY—

"With an heart full of love and gratitude I now take leave of you. I most devoutly wish that your latter days may be as prosperous and happy as your former ones have been glorious and honorable." With this simple and heartfelt statement General George Washington took leave of an Army that he had led through the trying days of the American Revolution.

Washington's triumphal return to New York City on 25 November 1783.

The commander-in-chief bids farewell to his officers on 4 December 1783.

WEST POINT

The United States Military Academy at West Point, New York, has occupied a colorful and important place in American history. Among its more than 26,000 graduates, it lists such names as Dwight D. Eisenhower, Douglas MacArthur, John J. Pershing, Ulysses S. Grant, and Robert E. Lee. Each year the Academy graduates about 600 new officers dedicated to a career in the service of their country.

The Academy was established officially on 16 March 1802, when Congress authorized a Corps of Engineers, set its strength at 7 officers and 10 cadets, and directed that they be stationed at West Point to constitute a military academy.

West Point had been a key Hudson River fortress during the Revolution and the new United States Military Academy began operations there on 4 July 1802, using buildings already in existence. The experience of the Continental Army during the Revolutionary War had demonstrated the need for trained military technicians in all branches of the service, and unsettled conditions since then had reinforced the need for better trained armed forces. In addition, Congress hoped that the Academy would encourage the practical study of the sciences at a time when many educational institutions ignored science completely.

West Point and its fortifications in 1780, as seen from across the Hudson River. The original drawing was the work of Major Pierre Charles L'Enfant, a French engineer serving with the Continental Army. L'Enfant later designed the basic plan for Washington, D.C.

This blockhouse, one of those that guarded West Point during the Revolutionary War, still stood when the Military Academy opened in 1802.

Another relic of the Revolution—Fort Putnam, shown here before its partial restoration in 1907–1910. The fort was designed by Colonel Tadeusz Kosciuszko and built in 1778. The restored fort is one of West Point's popular tourist attractions.

In 1812, when war with England appeared imminent, Congress increased the strength of the Corps of Cadets to 250 and stipulated that they be taught "all the duties of a private, a noncommissioned officer and an officer." The War of 1812 was the first of the many occasions on which Academy graduates served their country well. In addition to providing the wartime leadership so essential to success on the battlefield, Academy graduates participated in the building of roads, canals, and railroads, the mapping and deepening of rivers, and the exploration and settling of the West.

Under Colonel Sylvanus Thayer, the "Father of the Military Academy" and its superintendent from 1817 until 1833, the Academy began the emphasis on excellence in character and knowledge that has characterized its programs ever since. Both the academic and the military programs of the Academy have undergone changes in response to the changing needs of the country. After the Civil War, West Point dropped its strong emphasis on engineering subjects in favor of general training for all cadets. Several postgraduate schools were established to give special training in the various special branches of the service while the

West Point Cadets

In 1848.

1852.

In 1852.

In 1885.

77

Academy concentrated on turning out trained and capable Regular Army officers.

Before World War I, the Academy had substituted practical training in tactics and fieldwork for the mechanical drills that had constituted its military instruction. After that war one of the Academy's most famous superintendents, General Douglas MacArthur, modernized the entire curriculum to reflect the Army's experience during the war and changing world conditions after the war. He also instituted a strenuous program of compulsory physical education.

Recent changes in the Academy's curriculum have been the result of the increased technological character of weapons and military science in general. Greater emphasis has been placed on chemistry, nuclear physics, electronics, and astronautics. The worldwide nature of United States commitments has led to more instruction in the geography, history, government, economics, and ideologies of other countries.

In order to be accepted as a cadet at the United States Military Academy, a young man must be at least seventeen, but not older than twenty-one, a United States citizen, physically fit, of good character, and he must never have been married. After being nominated, usually by his United States Senator or Representative, although there are a few additional nominations, he must pass College Entrance Examination Board, medical, and physical aptitude tests. Those who qualify are highly capable young men. It is the Military Academy's mission to instruct and train them so that each graduate will have the qualifications and attributes essential to his progressive and continued development throughout a career as an officer of the Regular Army.

The Military Academy as it appeared in 1859.

The faculty in 1870.

This building housed the Military Academy Library from 1841 until 1962. It was replaced by a new library building in 1964.

Captain Robert E. Lee when he was Superintendent of the Military Academy in the early 1850's. At the beginning of the Civil War, Lee, a Virginian, resigned from the U.S. Army to fight for the Confederacy. Lee graduated from the Military Academy in 1829.

Cadet Training, 1904: Artillery practice.

Cadets at West Point in 1885.

The Military Academy Band in 1878.

The Military Academy Band in 1962. Band members must enlist in the Army for a minimum of three years; they are assured of permanent assignment to the Military Academy and an initial rank of specialist 5th class.

Winners of the major "A," class of 1915. Included in the group are Dwight D. Eisenhower, who commanded the victorious Allied armies in Europe during World War II and later became President of the United States (3rd from left, 2d row); James A. Van Fleet. commander of the Eighth Army during the Korean War (1st on left, top row); and Omar Bradley, commander of the U.S. armies in Europe during World War II (3d from right, top row).

80

The Battle Monument at Trophy Point. It is dedicated to soldiers and officers of the Regular Army killed in action during the Civil War.

The Cadet Chapel at night.

West Point today. The Academy's buildings and grounds occupy about 16,000 acres.

The Military Academy's coat of arms. It displays the Greek symbols of wisdom and military virtue, the helmet and sword of Pallas Athene, upon the American shield. "Duty, Honor, Country" (left) is the Academy's motto.

81

Graduation at West Point. After four years of hard work, the cadets receive bachelor of science degrees and appointments as second lieutenants in the Regular Army of the United States.

Bartlett Hall. In addition to classrooms and laboratories it contains the offices of the Departments of Electricity, Mechanics, and Physics and Chemistry.

Cadets on parade. The parade uniform is the one worn by American infantrymen in the War of 1812.

The cadet color guard.

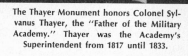

The Thayer Monument honors Colonel Sylvanus Thayer, the "Father of the Military Academy." Thayer was the Academy's Superintendent from 1817 until 1833.

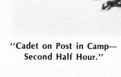

"Cadet on Post in Camp—
Second Half Hour."

"Cadet on Post in Camp—
Third Half Hour."

"Cadet on Post in Camp—
Last Half Hour."

Three sketches by Cadet James McNeill Whistler, who became one of America's most famous artists, and left the Academy before graduation.

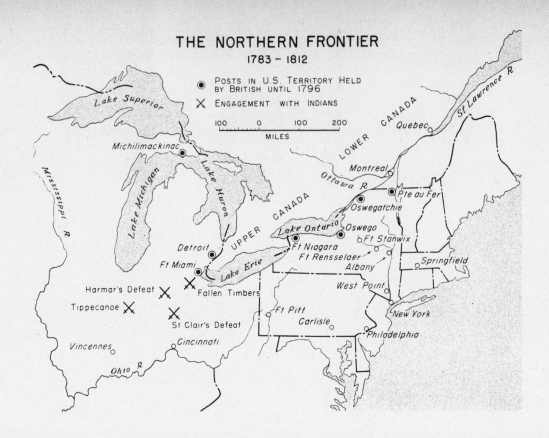

THE NORTHERN FRONTIER
1783 – 1812

● POSTS IN U.S. TERRITORY HELD
BY BRITISH UNTIL 1796

✕ ENGAGEMENT WITH INDIANS

100   0   100   200

MILES

Lake Superior

Michilimackinac

Lake Michigan

Lake Huron

LOWER CANADA

St Lawrence R

Quebec

Montreal

Ottawa R

Pte au Fer

Oswegatchie

UPPER CANADA

Lake Ontario

Oswego

Ft Stanwix

Detroit

Ft Niagara

Ft Rensselaer

Albany

Springfield

Ft Miami

Lake Erie

West Point

Harmar's Defeat ✕

Fallen Timbers ✕

Tippecanoe ✕

✕ St Clair's Defeat

Ft Pitt

New York

Carlisle

Philadelphia

Vincennes

Cincinnati

Ohio R

Mississippi R

CHAPTER 3

THE U.S. ARMY, 1783-1812

The definitive treaty of peace ending the Revolutionary War was signed on 3 September 1783. By then the Continental Army had all but disappeared. While the peace negotiations were in progress, Congress had wrestled with the question of demobilization, only to find itself becoming inextricably involved in a tangled web of postwar problems. Among the foremost of these were the matter of the Army's pay and the size of the peacetime establishment. Settlement of the pay accounts, which were months in arrears, and a decision whether officers were to receive half-pay for life, as they had been promised, hinged not only upon the outcome of the political struggle in Congress between those who wanted a strong national government and those who preferred the existing loose federation of sovereign states. During the winter of 1782–1783 the Army grew impatient. Having failed to obtain full redress from the state governments in the matter of pay and pensions, the officers were persuaded to look to Congress and to make common cause with the nationalists. Rumors that the Army would take matters into its own hands gained strength when several anonymous communications were circulated among the officers at Newburgh urging them not to fight if the war continued and not to lay down their arms if peace were declared unless their pay accounts were settled. Congress finally gave in to the arguments of the nationalists, agreed to pay the men their back pay, and decided to give the officers full pay for five years in lieu of half-pay for life.

Still the Government hesitated to disband the Army as long as the definitive treaty of peace was not ratified. With discontent mounting among the rank and file, Congress in May 1783 instructed Robert Morris to give the men three months' pay and directed Washington to furlough the "war men"—the soldiers who had enlisted for the duration of the war. By mid-June most of the common soldiers and many of the officers had started for their homes. On 3 November 1783 Washington, in his last general order, directed the Army to turn in its arms and disband. Congress had not, however, provided for a permanent establishment. Until it did so, a few Continentals would have to remain under arms to guard the military supplies at West Point and take over the ports and posts to be evacuated by the British. For these purposes Washington thought it necessary to retain in service one infantry regiment and a battalion of artillery totaling about 600 men.

THE COMPLICATIONS OF A PEACETIME ARMY

In the spring of 1784 the question of a permanent peacetime army became mixed up with the politics of state claims to western lands. The majority of men in the infantry regiment and artillery battalion that constituted the "Regular" Army were from Massachusetts and New Hampshire, and, because the rest of the Continental Army had been discharged, those states wanted to be rid of the financial burden of paying the extra pay that the legislatures had promised the men on enlistment. Congress refused to take over the responsibility unless the New England states would vote for a permanent military establishment. The New England representatives, led by Elbridge Gerry of Massachusetts, insisted that Congress had no authority to maintain a standing army, but at the same time they wanted the existing troops to occupy the western forts, which were situated on land claimed by the New England states. New York vigorously contested the New England claims to western lands, particularly in the region around Oswego and Niagara, and the delegates from New York refused to vote for any regular military establishment unless Congress gave the state permission to garrison the forts with its own state forces. The result was that attempts to establish a permanent national army failed.

The posts that had been the object of concern and discussion dominated the Great Lakes and the St. Lawrence River. Located on American territory south of the United States–Canadian boundary established by the peace treaty of 1783, they were in the hands of British troops when the war ended; but by the terms of the treaty they were to be turned over to the United States as speedily as possible. Congress was agreed on the necessity of maintaining a force in readiness to occupy the posts as soon as the British troops left. The problem was how and by whom the troops were to be raised. A decision was even more urgent because the Government was in the midst of negotiating a treaty with the Indians in the Northwest, and it was thought that a sizable force "to awe the Indians" would facilitate the negotiations. But the deadlock between the New England states and New York continued until early June 1784.

Finally, on the last two days of its session, Congress rushed through a compromise. To placate the New Yorkers and satisfy the economy-minded New Englanders, the existing infantry regiment and battalion of artillery were disbanded except for an artillery company of 58 officers and men at West Point and a detachment of 29 officers and men at Fort Pitt. The support of delegates who favored retaining a Federal army was obtained by tying the discharge of the existing force to a measure that provided for the immediate recruitment of a new force of 700 men, a regiment of 8 infantry and 2 artillery companies. By not making requisitions on the states for troops, but merely recommending that the states provide them from their militia, Congress favored most of the New England opposi-

tion on this score; by not assigning a quota for Massachusetts and New Hampshire, Congress satisfied the objections of most of the other states.

Four states were called upon to furnish troops according to the following quotas: 260 men from Pennsylvania, 165 from Connecticut, 165 from New York, and 110 from New Jersey. Lieutenant Colonel Josiah Harmar of Pennsylvania was appointed commanding officer. Only New Jersey and Pennsylvania showed any enthusiasm for raising the troops. By the end of September 1784 these two states had filled their quotas and had sent the men forward to the frontiers.

Meanwhile, Congress had learned that there was little immediate prospect of the British evacuating the frontier posts. Canadian fur traders and the settlers in Upper Canada had objected so violently to this provision of the peace treaty that the British Government secretly directed the Governor-General of Canada not to evacuate the posts without further orders. General Henry Knox, who had succeeded Washington as Commander in Chief of the Army, was informed by the British commander in Canada that he had received no instructions about the posts and that without instructions the British troops would remain. Then, the failure of the United States to comply with a stipulation in the treaty regarding the recovery of debts owed to Loyalists provided the British with an excuse to postpone the evacuation of the posts for twelve more years. Therefore, the New Jersey contingent of Colonel Harmar's force was sent to Fort Stanwix, in upstate New York, to assist in persuading the Iroquois to part with their lands. The remainder of the force moved to Fort McIntosh, 30 miles down the Ohio River from Fort Pitt, where similar negotiations were carried out with the Indians of the upper Ohio.

The postwar years had revealed a number of serious defects in the Federal Government. Rioting and disturbances in Massachusetts throughout the fall and winter of 1786–1787 supported the pessimism of those who feared the collapse of the new nation. A severe commercial depression following on the heels of the brief postwar boom caused particular distress among the back-country farmers. Angry mobs gathered in the Massachusetts hills, broke up the meetings of the courts, harried lawyers and magistrates out of the villages, and began moving toward the Government arsenal in Springfield. On 20 October 1786 Congress called on several of the states to raise a force of 1,340 officers and men to serve for three years. This time the

Fort McIntosh in the upper Ohio Valley.

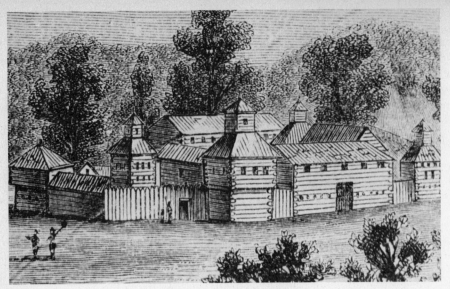

Fort Washington at Cincinnati, Ohio.

General Henry Knox, who succeeded George Washington as Commander-in-Chief of the Army. He was the first Secretary of War after the organization of the Federal Government in 1789.

Buildings at Fort Pitt. When the French controlled the Ohio Valley, the post was called Fort Duquesne.

Brigadier General Josiah Harmer.

86

New England States did not object to Congress taking action, but none of the troops voted by Congress reached the scene before the embattled farmers were dispersd by Massachusetts militia. In late January 1787 an attack on the Springfield Arsenal led by Daniel Shays was thrown back by a force of local militiamen with a "whiff of grapeshot." A few days later a large reinforcement of militia from the eastern part of the state arrived at Springfield and put an end to the disorders. Recruiting for the force authorized by Congress continued until the following April. By then about 550 men had been enlisted and the question of expense was becoming bothersome. Congress therefore directed the states to stop recruiting and to discharge the troops already raised, except two artillery companies which were retained as a guard for the West Point and Springfield Arsenals. Shays's "rebellion" was thus responsible for the first augmentation of the Federal Army. More important was its effect in helping to persuade Americans that a stronger government was needed.

THE CONSTITUTIONAL CONVENTION OF 1887

Rising concern over the ineffectiveness of the Federal Government, particularly in matters of finance and commercial regulation, finally led to the convening of a Constitutional Convention in the spring of 1787. Strengthening the military powers of the Government was one of the principal tasks of the Convention, a task no less important than establishing its financial and commercial authority. The general problem facing the Convention, that of power and the control of power, came into sharp focus in the debates on military matters, since the widespread suspicion of a strong central government and the equally widespread fear of a standing army were merged in the issue of the Government's military powers. Those who mistrusted a powerful government argued against a broad grant of authority not only in the field of taxation and commercial regulation, but in the matter of military affairs as well. Men like Alexander Hamilton, who sought to give the Federal Government wide latitude in handling both purse and sword, were also somewhat wary of standing armies. They, too, were concerned over the possible usurpation of political power by the military or its use by officeholders as an instrument for perpetuating their personal power.

In its final form the new Constitution gave the central Government adequate authority to raise and maintain an army without calling upon the states. By giving Congress the power to levy taxes, the Constitution provided the central Government with the necessary financial means and, by creating a separate executive branch, made it possible for the daily business of the Government to be conducted without constant reference to the states. In the division of powers within the Federal Government, those of declaring war and of raising armies and providing for a navy were assigned exclusively to Congress, although in time of emergency Congress has often vested the President with more or less discretion in the matter of raising and maintaining armed forces. An important innovation was the assignment of all executive power to the President. Thus the Secretary of War became directly responsible to the President, and

not to Congress. The Constitution specifically provided that the President should be Commander in Chief of the Army and Navy. As such his powers are exclusive, limited in their extent only "by their nature and by the principles of our institutions." The President therefore has the right to assume personal command of forces in the field, but for reasons of expediency he customarily delegates it. As Commander in Chief he is responsible for the employment and disposition of the armed forces in time of peace and for the general direction, when Congress has declared war and provided the means for carrying it on, of military and naval operations in war.

Washington, who had presided over the Constitutional Convention, became the first President under the new Constitution in March 1789, and on 7 August Congress created the Department of War. There was no change, however, in either the policy or the personnel of the Department. General Knox, who had been handling military affairs, remained in charge. Harmar, who had been given the rank of brigadier general in 1787, was confirmed in his appointment, as were his officers, and the existing establishment was taken over intact into the service of the United States.

In August 1789 the authorized strength of the Army amounted to 960 officers and men; actual strength, however, was about 750 or 800. All the troops, except the two artillery companies retained after Shays's Rebellion, were stationed along the Ohio River in a series of forts built after 1785 where they had been chiefly occupied in driving squatters out of the territory. This type of duty neither endeared Harmar to the settlers nor trained his men for Indian fighting.

Washington, as early as 1783, had expressed himself in favor of enlarging the Army. Furthermore, during Washington's two terms as President, the strategic position of the United States changed as a result of the outbreak of war in Europe. There was consequently a progressive increase in the authorized strength of the regular peacetime establishment from 1,283 officers and men in 1790 to 3,324 in 1796. In addition, Congress in March 1792 authorized the raising of three regiments to meet the temporary emergency caused by the Indians in the Northwest Territory, so that from 1792 to 1796 the total authorized strength of the Army, including the emergency forces, ranged from about 5,300 to 6,100 officers and men.

ACTION AGAINST THE INDIANS

To General Harmar fell the honor of leading the first regular troops that saw action after the Revolution, and with this honor he had to be content, for he derived no other from his campaign. Having decided to chastise the Indians in Ohio, Secretary Knox in June 1790 ordered Harmar to consult with Arthur St. Clair, Governor of the Northwest Territory, as to the best means of doing so. Under an authorization given to him the preceding fall, St. Clair called on Pennsylvania and Kentucky to send 1,500 militiamen to Harmar at Cincinnati. By the end of September, Harmar had assembled a motley collection of 1,453 men, including 320 regulars, with which he set out for the Indian country. After struggling through the wilderness for more than two weeks his force reached the neighborhood of the principal Indian villages near what is now Fort Wayne, Indiana. Instead of pushing on with his entire strength, Harmar on three successive occasions violated the principle of mass by sending forward small unsupported detachments of about 200 to 500 militia plus 50 or 60 regulars. The undisciplined militia could not be restrained from scattering in search of Indians and plunder, and, after two of the detachments suffered heavily in brushes with the Indians, Harmar took the rest of his army back to Cincinnati. His conduct was severely criticized, but a court of inqury, noting the untrained troops with which Harmar had been provided and the lateness of the season, exonerated him of blame.

The Defeat of General St. Clair

In the spring of 1791, Congress resolved to take stern measures against the Indians. A second infantry regiment was added to the Regular Army, and the President was authorized to raise a corps of 2,000 men for a term of six months, either by calling for militia or by enlisting volunteers into the service of the United States. Governor St. Clair was commissioned a major general and placed in command of the expedition. So slowly did recruiting and the procuring of supplies proceed that St. Clair was unable to set out before 17 September, more than two months after the date originally planned, and only by calling on the neighboring states for militia was he able to bring his force up to strength. When it finally marched out of Fort Washington (the army post at Cincinnati), St. Clair's force consisted of about 600 regulars, which was almost all the actual infantry strength of the U.S. Army, plus about 800 enlisted "levies" and 600 militiamen.

The general was determined not to repeat Harmar's tactical mistakes, and he carried his determination to the point of not sending out scouts on local reconnaissance. By 3 November, St. Clair had advanced about 100 miles northward from Cincinnati and was encamped for the night near the headwaters of the Wabash River. The next morning, just before dawn, a horde of about 1,000 Indians, which had surrounded the camp during the night, fell upon the unsuspecting troops. Untrained, low in morale as a result of inadequate supplies, and led by a general who was suffer-

ing from rheumatism, asthma, and "colic," the Army was thrown into confusion by the sudden assault. St. Clair and less than half his force survived unscathed. Out of approximately 1,400 men engaged in the action, about 637 were killed and 263 wounded. The rest fled back to Cincinnati in disorder.

Alarmed and outraged over the defeat of St. Clair, Congress doubled the authorized strength of the Army by providing for three additional regiments, two of which were to be infantry and the other a composite regiment of infantry and light dragoons. Although these new regiments were to be added to the Regular Army, they were intended as a temporary augmentation to be "discharged as soon as the United States shall be at peace with the Indian tribes."

The Victory of Anthony Wayne

Anthony Wayne, the dashing commander of the Pennsylvania Line during the Revolution, was appointed major general to succeed St. Clair. Recruiting began in midsummer, and in November 1792 Wayne moved his growing force from Fort Pitt to a camp about 30 miles down the Ohio River, where he spent the winter training and drilling his men. Correcting previous mistakes, General Wayne insisted on rigid discipline and strict training. Conscious of the welfare of his men, he saw to it that supplies were adequate and equipment satisfactory. At the same time the Army was reorganized into a "Legion," a term widely used during the eighteenth century and which had come to mean a composite organization of all combat arms under one command. In the reorganization of 1792 the Army, instead of being composed of regiments, was made up of four "sub-legions," each commanded by a brigadier general and each consisting of two infantry battalions, one battalion of riflemen, one troop of dragoons, and one company of artillery. To develop an esprit de corps, he had each sub-legion wear distinctive insignia. In honor of the reorganization, Wayne gave the name of "Legionville" to his camp on the Ohio.

In the spring of 1792 General Wayne took the Legion down the river to Cincinnati. While attempting to persuade the Indians to submit peacefully, he continued to drill his men. By early October the negotiations with the Indians had broken down, and the Legion set out over the route

Major General Arthur St. Clair.

Major General Anthony Wayne.

that Harmar and St. Clair had taken with more unfortunate results. Wayne was in even poorer health than St. Clair but of stronger will. Like St. Clair, he moved slowly and methodically, building a series of forts and blockhouses along his line of march. In spite of his efforts to improve morale, he found desertion as serious a problem as it had been for Harmar and St. Clair.

After spending the winter at one of the forts, the Legion continued its march northward, and on the site of St. Clair's defeat Wayne built Fort Recovery. Here, at the end of June 1794, the Indians attempted to repeat their earlier success by making a full-scale assault against the fort. In a daylong battle the Legion beat off the attack with such effect that when the Army resumed its march at the end of July the war chief of the Indians was at first disposed to accept Wayne's offer of peace. Reinforced by some 1,400 mounted militia, which brought his force up to about 3,000 men, Wayne advanced to within a few miles of Fort Miami, a post recently established by the British on the site of what is now Toledo, Ohio. There, on 20 August 1794, almost within sight of the British guns, the Indians again attacked. Wayne's men held their ground; then, with a furious bayonet charge they drove the enemy out of the cover of fallen trees that gave the Battle of Fallen Timbers its name. In the open prairie the Indians were at the mercy of Wayne's mounted volunteers, and in less than an hour the rout was complete.

Ignoring the protests of the British commander at Fort Miami, Wayne stayed where he was for several days, burning the Indian villages and destroying crops. Then, having accomplished his mission, he led the Legion back to Cincinnati. The western tribes, their resistance broken, finally agreed to make peace and cede their lands in Ohio to the United States by the Treaty of Greenville, 3 August 1795. Their submission had been hastened by news that England was about to evacuate the frontier posts, and British troops soon withdrew from United States territory.

WAR IN EUROPE INFLUENCES EXPANDED U.S. FORCES

While the United States was launching a new government, France had undergone a revolution, as a result of which Europe became embroiled in war. When Great Britain, in 1793, joined the coalition against France, the strategic position of the United States became precarious. At first France had hoped the United States would be a friendly neutral, if not an ally, and would permit French privateers to fit out and recruit crews in American ports. Britain, however, clamped down a blockade, and in the first year of the war seized at least 300 American merchant vessels. By signing Jay's Treaty, acquiescing in the British doctrine of contraband, the United States obtained a settlement of some longstanding problems, including the evacuation of the frontier posts, but only at the expense of domestic unity and peaceful relations with the French. Regarding Jay's Treaty as evidence of a pro-British policy on the part of the United States, France retaliated by seizing American vessels that were trading with the British, by sending secret agents to stir up the Creek Indians along the southern frontier, and by meddling in American politics in an attempt to bring about the defeat of the "pro-British" administration. In short, both France and England had adopted courses of action that threatened the peace of America. This was the legacy that President Washington handed over to his successor, John Adams, in 1797.

In 1797 the Army had an authorized strength of about 3,300 officers and men but an actual strength of about 3,000. The Legion type of organization and the troops that had been added for the temporary emergency in 1792 had been dropped in 1796, and the Army had returned to a regimental type of organization with four regiments of infantry of eight companies each, a corps of artillerists and engineers consisting of four battalions, and two companies of light dragoons. Each company was smaller in size than those of the Legion had been, and the four battalions of riflemen authorized for the Legion were discontinued.

"The Road to Fallen Timbers," a painting in the "U.S. Army in Action" series, shows the Legion driving the Indians from the protection of fallen trees.

During 1796 and early 1797 there was a limited redeployment into the Southwest, so that in the latter year 9 companies of infantry, about 2 companies of artillery, and the entire force of dragoons were stationed along the southwestern frontier. Up in the old Northwest there were 5 infantry companies at Detroit and small detachments at a dozen scattered forts elsewhere in the territory. Fort Washington, at Cincinnati, was the major installation and had perhaps a full regiment as a garrison. There were small harbor defense garrisons at New York, Philadelphia, Baltimore, Norfolk, Wilmington, North Carolina, and Charleston. The rest of the Army was stationed along the Canadian border from the lakes eastward and at the older posts like West Point, Carlisle, and Fort Pitt.

In the spring of 1798, with the country facing the prospect of a war with France, President Adams recommended an expanded defense program and Congress agreed to some of his proposals. Of the three regiments—one of infantry, one of artillery, and one of cavalry—which the administration recommended adding to the Regular Army, Congress authorized the additional artillery but failed to approve the cavalry. With respect to the infantry regiment, Secretary of War James McHenry proposed to Congress that the regiment act in the double capacity of marines and infantrymen. But instead of creating a regiment that would be a Jack-of-all-trades, Congress voted the U.S. Marine Corps into existence, making it part of the Army or the Navy according to whether the marines served on land or on shipboard. The number of companies in each of the four regular infantry regiments was increased from 8 to 10; a sizable sum for harbor defenses and ordnance was voted; and a "Provisional Army"—an emergency force that Adams had suggested the year before—was authorized.

The defects of short-term enlistments were avoided by setting the duration of the "existing differences between the United States and the French Republic" as the term of enlistment for the Provisional Army. However, when the President again asked for an increase in the Regular Army, Congress instead gave him authority to accept privately armed and equipped volunteer units for short-term service. Adams never made use of this authority, but went ahead with the plans to raise the 12 infantry regiments and 1 cavalry regiment that made up the Provisional Army. Washington was persuaded to come out of retirement to accept command as lieutenant general; Alexander Hamilton was appointed senior major general. By the beginning of 1799 officers had been appointed, and in May 1799 recruiting began. By the time the Provisional Army was disbanded in June 1800, about 4,100 men had been mobilized, assembled in camps, and given from 6 to 12 months' training. Preparation of new drill regulations, to replace von Steuben's, was begun under Hamilton's direction, but before the task was finished the French crisis had ended and the Provisional Army was discharged.

In a treaty signed on 30 September 1800, France agreed to recognize American neutrality and to refrain from seizing American vessels that were not carrying contraband. On the very next day France and Spain signed a secret treaty turning Louisiana over to France, and a few months later England and her allies made peace with France.

In the United States President Jefferson took office in 1801, committed to a policy of peace and economy.

John Adams, the second President
of the United States.

No. 176 EXCHANGE for 256. DOLLAR

SIR,   D'Etroit October 12, 179

AT ten days sight of this second of Exchange the first of the same tenor and date being unpaid, please to pay to Capt. Andrew McClary Pur. or order, the sum of Two Hundred and Fifty Six. Dolla which sum I have received of him in Cash, and charge the same as advice herewith to my Account.

C. Swan

To The Honorable
James McHenry Sect of war.

Caleb Swan, the Army's Paymaster General, signed this "ten days' sight draft" for $256.00 in 1797. It was drawn on James McHenry, Secretary of War in President John Adams' Cabinet, to pay Army Captain Andrean McClary.

JEFFERSON AND THE MILITARY

The Army did not feel the effect of his economy drive until he had been in office for a year. Until then the military establishment was much as Adams had left it after the Provisional Army troops had been discharged, with an authorized strength of 5,438 officers and men. Its actual strength, however, was about 4,000 officers and men. In the reduction of March 1802 the total strength of the Army was cut back to 3,220 officers and men, approximately what it had been in 1797 when Adams took office, but it was now more than 50 percent stronger in artillery. The cavalry arm was eliminated. This remained the regular peacetime establishment until the war with England in 1812. Additional forces were authorized in 1808 and 1812, but they were special, emergency forces not considered a part of the regular peacetime establishment.

West Point Military Academy Established

Ever since the Revolution, the Army had faced a lack of trained technicians, particularly in engineering science, and had depended largely upon foreign experts. To remedy this unsatisfactory situation, Washington, Knox, Hamilton, and others had recommended the establishment of a military school. During Washington's administration, the rank of cadet was created in the Corps of Artillerists and Engineers with two cadets assigned to each company for instruction. In the reorganization of the Army under Jefferson in March 1802, the engineers were separated from the artillery and a Corps of Engineers consisting of 10 cadets and 7 officers was created and assigned to West Point to establish a Military Academy. Within a few years the Academy became a center of study for the military sciences in general and a source of trained engineer officers. By 1812 the Academy

could list 89 graduates, 65 of whom were still in the Army and played an important part in building fortifications during the War of 1812.

The U.S. Acquires Louisiana

Not long after Jefferson became President, rumors—confirmed in 1802 by the French Government—reached America that France had acquired Louisiana from Spain. The news was upsetting to many Americans, including Jefferson. Up to this time the Mississippi Valley had not been regarded particularly as an invasion route. The problem of frontier defense had been chiefly one of pacifying the Indians, keeping the western territories from breaking away, and preventing American settlers from molesting the Spanish Now, with France, a strong, aggressive nation, as a neighbor the frontier problem became tied up with the question of security against possible foreign threats. Furthermore, the transfer of Louisiana to France was accompanied by restraints on American trade down the Mississippi. American settlers had been permitted by Spain to send their goods down the river and to store them at New Orleans. At the urging of France, Spain, just before transferring the colony, revoked the privilege of storing goods at New Orleans, an action which made it almost impossible for Americans to send goods out by this route. These considerations persuaded Jefferson to inquire about the possibility of purchasing New Orleans from France, and when Napoleon, anticipating the renewal of the war in Europe, offered to sell the whole of Louisiana, Jefferson quickly accepted. Thus, in 1803 the size of the United States was suddenly doubled. The Army was called upon to provide small garrisons for New Orleans and the other former Spanish posts on the Lower Mississippi, and preparations for exploring the newly acquired territory were hastened. Brigadier General James

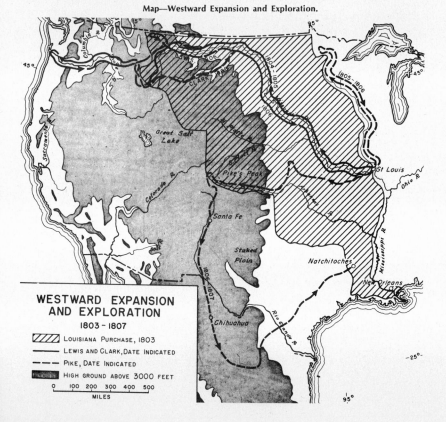

Map—Westward Expansion and Exploration.

WESTWARD EXPANSION AND EXPLORATION
1803 - 1807

- ///// LOUISIANA PURCHASE, 1803
- —— LEWIS AND CLARK, DATE INDICATED
- - - - PIKE, DATE INDICATED
- ▓▓ HIGH GROUND ABOVE 3000 FEET

0 100 200 300 400 500
MILES

Brigadier General James Wilkinson, who became governor of the northern portion of the Louisiana Territory in 1805. Wilkinson was the Army's senior officer.

Wilkinson, who had survived his own rascalities and the various reorganizations of the Army to become the senior officer, was appointed Governor of the Louisiana Territory.

A year before the purchase of Louisiana, Jefferson, with the reluctant consent of the Spanish Government, had decided to send an exploring party into the unknown territory west of the Mississippi. The acquisition of this territory now made such an exploration even more desirable. To lead the expedition, Jefferson chose Captain Meriwether Lewis and Lieutenant William Clark, both of whom had served under General Wayne in the Northwest. Leaving St. Louis in the spring of 1804, the party, including 27 enlisted men, traveled up the Missouri River, crossed the Rocky Mountains, and followed the Columbia River down to the Pacific, which was reached after much hardship in November 1805. On the return journey the party explored what is now central Montana, and returned to St. Louis in September 1806.

While Lewis and Clark were exploring beyond the Missouri, General Wilkinson sent out Captain Zebulon M. Pike on a similar expedition to the headwaters of the Mississippi. In 1807 Wilkinson organized another expedition. This time he sent Captain Pike, accompanied by the general's son, Lieutenant James B. Wilkinson, and 19 soldiers, westward into what is now Colorado. After exploring the region around the peak that now bears his name, Pike encountered some Spaniards, and his party was taken to Santa Fe. From there they were escorted down into Mexico, then back across Texas to Natchitoches, where, once more in American territory, they were released. The Lewis and Clark expedition and those of Captain Pike are great epics of the West, and contributed much to the geographic and scientific knowledge of the country.

THE ARMY VS. TECUMSEH'S SHAWNEE

After the Battle of Fallen Timbers, settlers had pushed rapidly into Ohio and beyond into lands still claimed by the Indians. In an effort to resist the encroachments, a tribal confederacy was organized by Tecumseh, chief of the Shawnee, and his brother, the Prophet. The Governor of the Indiana Territory, William H. Harrison, rejected Tecumseh's demands that the white settlers keep out. Urged on by the settlers, Harrison decided in the summer of 1811 to strike at the Indians before they could descend on the settlements. His scheme was approved by Secretary of War William Eustis, and 300 regular infantry were placed under his command, in addition to about 650 militia, including mounted riflemen. Moving north from Vincennes at the end of September 1811, Harrison built a fort on the edge of the Indian country and then continued on to the neighborhood of Tecumseh's principal village. Halting his force about a mile west of the village, Harrison on 6 November invited the Indians to a conference. The troops were encamped in the form of a trapezoid around their wagons and baggage on a piece of high wooded ground that rose above the marshy prairies. On the side facing the Indian village were a battalion of the regulars and 3 companies of militia. Along the opposite side, facing away from the village, were another battalion of Regulars and 4 militia companies. The mounted riflemen were posted on the flanks, except for 3 troops

Captain Meriwether Lewis and Lieutenant William Clark explore the unknown territory west of the Mississippi River.

located in the middle of the camp. Acting as spokesman in the absence of Tecumseh, who was in the South attempting to persuade the Creek to join the confederacy, the Prophet apparently promised that the Indians would not attack while Harrison's proposal for a conference was under consideration. Treacherously the Indians struck just before dawn on the 7th. Harrison's situation was very similar to that of St. Clair, and for a time there was grave danger of his force suffering the same fate. Furious hand-to-hand combat followed the Indians' wild charge, which at first threatened to overrun the camp. Although taken by surprise, the soldiers rallied, then mounted a counterattack. The end came when the cavalry charged in on the Indians and drove them from the field. The troops pushed forward to the Indian village and, finding it deserted, burned it. The entire force then started back to Vincennes, where it was disbanded. Harrison had lost 39 men killed and missing and had 151 wounded, of whom 29 died. The engagement by no means solved the frontier problem in the Northwest, and the outbreak of war with England eight months later overshadowed any permanent effects of the battle.

Close combat during the
Battle of Tippecanoe.

Brigadier General William Henry Harrison at the
Battle of Tippecanoe. In 1840 Harrison was elected
the ninth President of the United States. He died
a month after taking office.

SECOND CONFLICT IN EUROPE EMBROILS THE U.S.

In 1803 the brief period of peace in Europe had ended with the beginning of the second round of the great conflict between England and France. It was a much more serious affair than the earlier war, which had almost drawn the United States into the line-up against France. Both Britain and France adopted policies under which American merchant shipping, whether carrying contraband or not, was subject to search and seizure. In an attempt to insulate America from the war in Europe, President Jefferson and his successor, James Madison, tried to keep American merchant vessels at home, but their efforts failed to keep the United States from becoming embroiled in the war.

In February, 1808, President Jefferson submitted to Congress a proposal for augmenting the Army. He made two requests: (1) a volunteer force of 24,000 men who would be required to serve 12 months out of any 24 in a 5-year period and take 2 or 3 months' training every year during that period; (2) the addition to the Regular Army of 5 infantry regiments, 1 rifle regiment, 1 light artillery regiment, and 1 regiment of light dragoons, or approximately 6,000 men. Congress authorized the 8 additional regiments but rejected the volunteer force. Two years later, in January, 1810, the actual strength of the Army totaled 6,954 officers and men, of whom 2,765 belonged to the 3 regiments of the regular peacetime establishment and 4,189 to the 8 new regiments. Probably as an economy measure, the light dragoons of the additional force were equipped as light infantry and were not mounted until the outbreak of the War of 1812. No further additions to the Army were authorized until January 1812, when Congress voted 13 additional regiments totaling about 25,700 officers and men, and authorized the President to call 50,000 militiamen into service.

Six months later, on 18 June 1812, Congress declared war against England. A Senate proposal to declare war against France as well failed to pass by only two votes.

RECRUITING
POSTERS
OVER THE YEARS

Recruiting notice used in 1798–1799
during threatened war with France.

Recruiting for the Mexican War.

94

INSTRUCTIONS TO THE OFFICERS

APPOINTED TO RECRUIT

IN NEW-YORK,

FOR THE SERVICE OF THE

UNITED STATES OF AMERICA.

THE Honourable Continental Congress having re-confidered the refolution, of the 16th of September laft, for raifing eighty eight battalions to ferve during the prefent War with Great-Britain; and being of opinion that the readinefs of the inhabitants of the States, to enter into the fervice for limited times, in defence of their invaluable privileges, on all former occafions, gives good ground to hope that the fame zeal for the public good, will appear in future, when neceffity calls for their affiftance, and the uncertain length of time, which forces raifed during the continuance of the War may be compelled to ferve, may prevent many from enlifting, who would otherwife readily manifeft their attachment to the common Caufe by engaging for a limited time; have therefore, on the 7th inftant refolved to admit into their fervice, non-commiffioned officers and foldiers for the fpace of Three Years.

The encouragement you are to offer is fo great, as will, it is hoped, give you a choice of men and enfure you fuccefs, (to wit) a bounty of Ten Dollars in money to every non-commiffioned officer and foldier already enlifted for three years, and who has received the Continental Bounty of Ten Dollars, and to every other Recruit a bounty of Twenty Dollars, and alfo to each, a Suit of Cloths yearly, to confift for the prefent year of

Two linnen Hunting-Shirts,
Two pair of Hofe,
Two pair of Overhalls,
A leathern or woollen Waiftcoat with fleeves,
One pair of Breeches,
One Hat or leathern Cap, and
Two pair of Shoes.

Amounting in the whole to the value of Twenty Dollars more.

But each non-commiffioned officer or foldier, who fhall procure thofe articles for himfelf, and produce to the Paymafter of the regiment, a certificate thereof from the Captain of the company to which he fhall belong, fhall be entitled to receive the Twenty Dollars in money; befides which every non-commiffioned officer and foldier, who fhall enlift during the War, is to receive at the end of the War One Hundred Acres of Land, as a further encouragement.

2dly, You are to be careful to enlift none but healable-bodied Men, who fhall engage to ferve in the army of the United States of America, during the prefent War, or for the term of Three Years, unlefs fooner difcharged by Congrefs.

3dly, You are required to provide two diftinct enlifting rolls, one to be fubfcribed by fuch who fhall engage during the continuance of the War, and the other by fuch as fhall enlift for three Years if their fervices fhall fo long be required.

4thly, You fhall take the age, fize, complexion, colour of hair and eyes, and natural or accidental marks of every Recruit, with an account of the place of his birth and occupation.

5thly, You fhall embrace all opportunities to have Recruits drilled and difciplined, and for that purpofe you fhall difpatch them without delay, to fuch ftations or place of rendezvous, as fhall be appointed for that purpofe.

6thly, To every Recruit at the time of enliftment, fhall adminifter the Oath prefcribed by the Articles of War, publifhed by the Continental Congrefs.

7thly, You fhall appoint four active and capable recruiting Serjeants to affift you, in this Service.

8thly, If you fhall re-enlift for the War or for three Years, any non-commiffioned officer or foldier, who is at prefent in actual fervice for a fhorter time you are to give in his name and defcription to the Captain, to whofe company he fhall then belong, who is to take particular charge of him, that he be delivered over to his proper officer at the end of thefervice, for which he may to be pre-engaged or fooner if required.

9thly, You are to have your men muftered by the Commiffary of Mufters, the firft opportunity after enliftment, in order that they may receive their full bounty, Five Dollars of which only, you fhall pay to each Recruit, as an encouragement, at the time of enliftment.

10thly, For this purpofe you fhall receive from the Treafury of the State of New-York, the neceffary fums, of the expenditure of which you fhall keep a regular account and tranfmit it to the Treafurer at Fifh Kill.

After the Articles of War are read to the non-commiffioned officer or foldier, enlifted by the enlifting officer, or the commanding officer of the troop or company, the following Oath (or Affirmation, if the Recruit is concientioufly fcrupulous) fhall be adminiftered to him, before the next Juftice of the Peace, or Chief Magiftrate of any city, or town corporate, not being an officer of the army; or where recourfe cannot be had to a magiftrate, before the Judge Advocate.

" I fwear or affirm (as the cafe may be) to be true to the UNITED STATES OF AMERICA, and to ferve them honeftly and faithfully againft all their enemies or oppofers whatfoever; and to obferve and obey the Orders of the Continental Congrefs and the Orders of the General, and officers fet over me by them."

FISH-KILL: PRINTED BY SAMUEL LOUDON.

By order.
Robert Yates chairman of the Committee
of arrangour? in the ftate of
New York.

Fifh kill Nov 21 1776

Revolutionary War Recruiting Broadside

On 16 September 1776 the Continental Congress authorized payment of bounties to persons volunteering for military service for the duration of the war. New York State's committee for raising its quota of troops issued instructions to recruiting officers in the form of a broadside. Years later a copy of the broadside was submitted to the United States Government in connection with the claim for pension of a Revolutionary War widow. That copy, from which the above facsimile was made, is among the records of the Veterans Administration in the National Archives, Washington, D.C.

FREEMEN! OF TENNESSEE!

The Yankee War is now being waged for "beauty and booty." They have driven us from them, and now say OUR TRADE they muft and will have. To excite their hired and ruffian foldiers, they promife them our lands, and tell them our women are bountiful—that beauty is the reward of the brave.

Tenneffeans! your country calls! Shall we wait until our homes are laid defolate; until our women are vile, fo craven, as not to ftrike for his native land?

TO ARMS!

The underfigned propofe to immediately raife an infantry company to be offered to the Governor as part of the defenfe of the State and of the Confederate States. All thofe who defire to join with us in ferving our common country, will report themfelves immediately.

J. B. Murray.
H. C. Witt.

Neal & Roberts, Printers, Morriftown, Tenn.

May 17th, 1861.

30,000 VOLUNTEERS WANTED

COUNTY BOUNTY CASH DOWN $300
STATE BOUNTY 75
U.S. BOUNTY FOR NEW RECRUITS 502

TOTAL TO NEW RECRUITS $677
U.S. BOUNTY TO VETERAN SOLDIERS 100
TOTAL TO VETERAN SOLDIERS 777

$15.00 HAND MONEY
Paid any Party who brings a RECRUIT

Civil War Recruiting Posters

LINCOLN CAVALRY

Col. ANDREW T. McREYNOLDS, Commanding.

WANTED A FEW GOOD MEN!

In the field by 4th of July, if possible, who can furnish their own horses and equipments.

"EXTRACT FROM OFFICIAL ORDERS."
Allowances for Clothing for Cavalry, shall be $3 50 per month. Each Non-commissioned Officer, Private, and Musician, shall furnish Horse and Horse Equipments. [Equipments and Clothing valued for $50] In case the Horse is lost in action, the Government will pay 50 Cents a day is allowed for use of Horse.

FARRIERS and BLACKSMITHS, wanted for the above Regiment, PAY EXTRA.

This is the only Cavalry Regiment accepted by the United States Government for immediate service, and to serve during the War.

☞ Apply immediately to Head Quarters,
403 Walnut Street, Phila., or to William H. Boyd,
Box 661 Post Office.

☞ The person receiving this bill will please post it in a Conspicuous Place.

World War I and After
Recruiting Posters

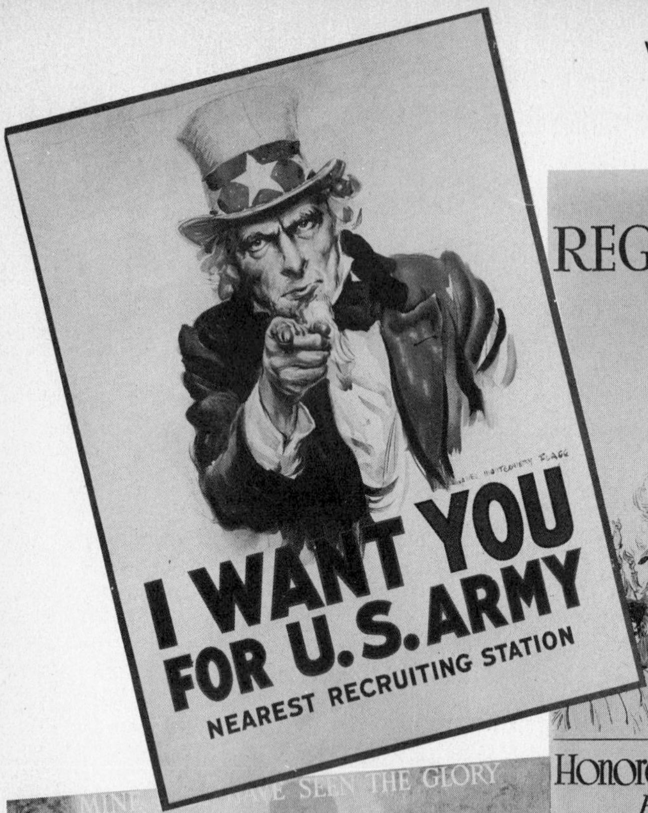
I WANT YOU
FOR U.S. ARMY
NEAREST RECRUITING STATION

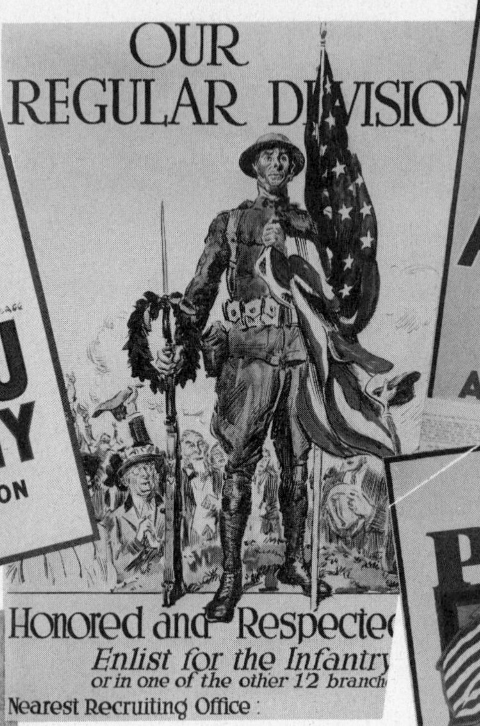
OUR
REGULAR DIVISION
Honored and Respected
Enlist for the Infantry
or in one of the other 12 branch
Nearest Recruiting Office :

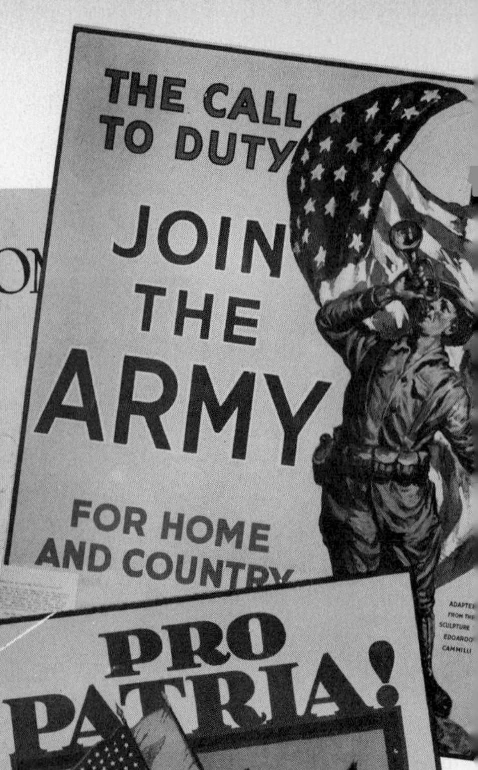
THE CALL
TO DUTY
JOIN
THE
ARMY
FOR HOME
AND COUNTRY

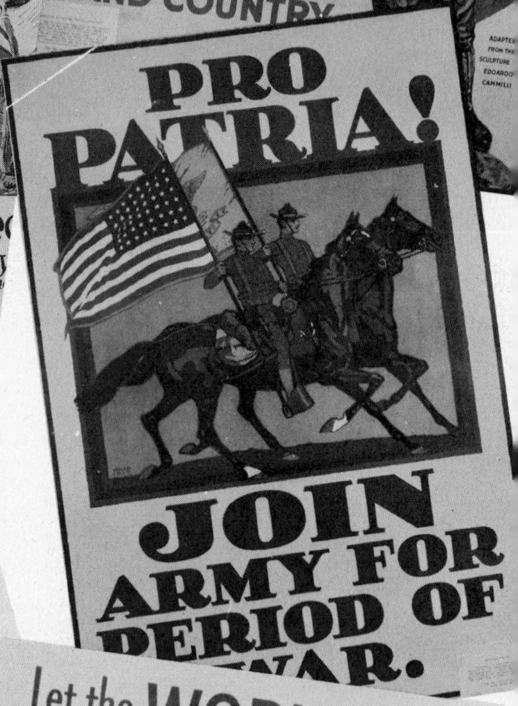
PRO
PATRIA!
JOIN
ARMY FOR
PERIOD OF

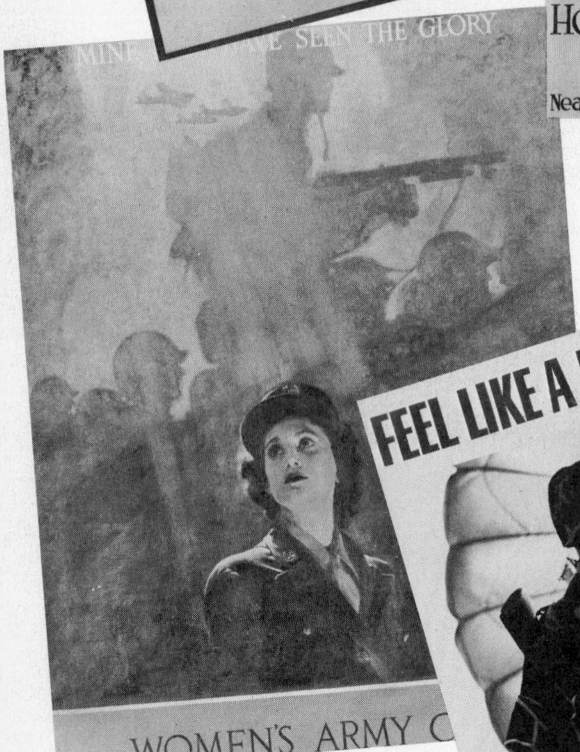
WOMEN'S ARMY C

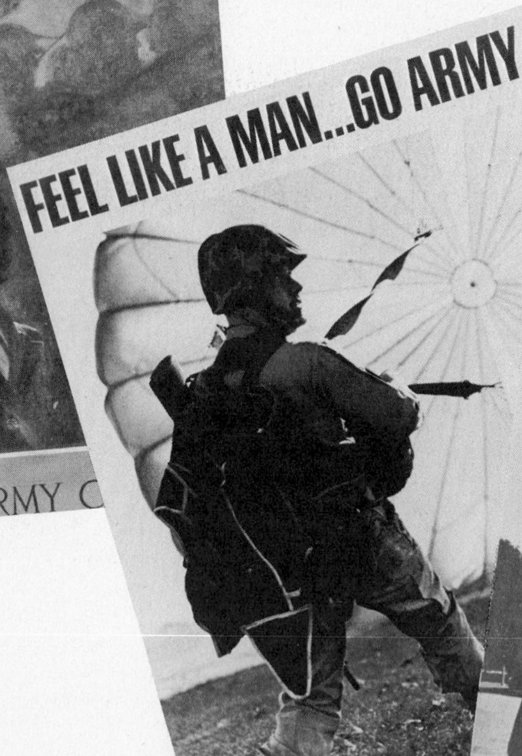
FEEL LIKE A MAN...GO ARMY

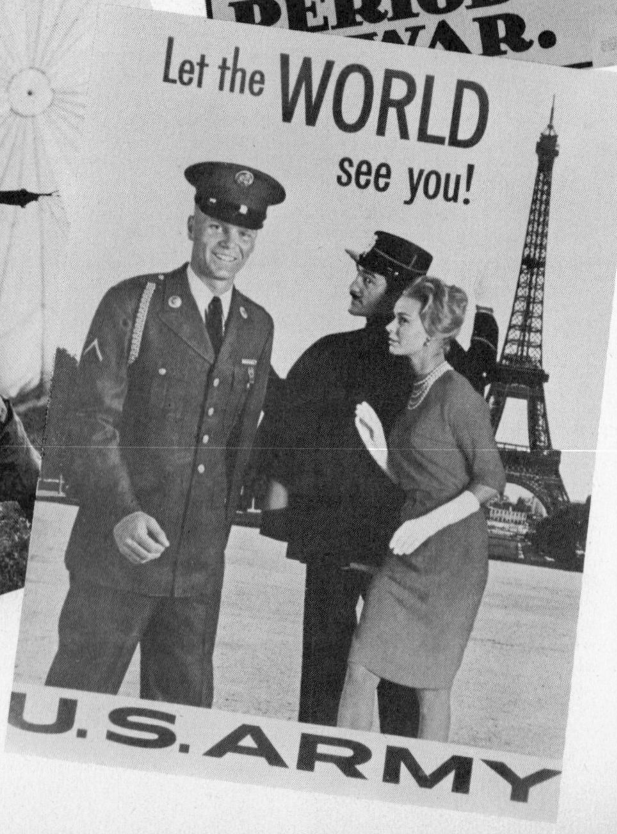
Let the WORLD
see you!
U.S. ARMY

THE PEOPLE of the State of New-York, by the Grace of GOD, free and Independent, TO _____ GREETING:

We, reposing especial trust and confidence, as well in your Patriotism, Conduct and Loyalty, as in your valor, and readiness to do us good and faithful service, have appointed and constituted, and by these presents Do appoint and constitute you the said _____ Captain _____ of a Company in the 11th Regiment of Cavalry _____ of our said State, whereof Volkert Peter Van Rensselaer _____ Esquire, is Lieutenant Colonel Commandant _____ You are therefore to take the said Company into your charge and care, as Captain _____ thereof, and duly to exercise the Officers and Soldiers of that Company in arms, who are hereby commanded to obey you as their Captain _____ and you are also to observe and follow such Orders and Directions as you shall, from time to time receive from our General and Commander in Chief of the Militia of our said State, or any other your superior Officer, according to the Rules and Discipline of War, in pursuance of the Trust reposed in you; and for so doing this shall be your commission, for and during our good pleasure, to be signified by our Council of Appointment.

In testimony whereof, WE have caused our Seal for Military Commissions to be hereunto affixed. WITNESS our trusty and well-beloved DANIEL D. TOMPKINS, Esquire, Governor of our said State, General and Commander in Chief of all the Militia, and Admiral of the Navy of the same, by and with the advice and consent of our said Council of Appointment, at our City of Albany, the second day of March in the Year of our Lord one thousand eight hundred and fourteen and in the thirty-eighth Year of our Independence.

Passed the Secretary's Office, the 26 day of April 1814

The commission issued to Captain Jerom Clark of New York's 11th Cavalry Regiment. It is typical of the commissions issued during the War of 1812.

CHAPTER 4

THE WAR OF 1812

At the outbreak of the War of 1812, the United States had a total population of about 7,700,000 people. The country was protected by a series of border forts along the Canadian boundary garrisoned by very small detachments of the Regular Army. The most important of these were Fort Michilimackinac, on the straits between Lake Michigan and Lake Huron, Fort Dearborn, near the present Chicago, Fort Detroit, and forts along the Niagara River and Lake Ontario, at Buffalo, Fort Niagara, Oswego, and Sackets Harbor. The actual strength of the Army in June 1812 totaled approximately 11,744 officers and men, which included an estimated 5,000 recruits authorized the preceding January. The United States Navy consisted of 20 vessels: 3 large 44-gun frigates, 3 smaller frigates of the **Constellation** class rated at 38 guns, and 14 others. They mounted an aggregate of slightly more than 500 guns. In addition, there were 62 small gunboats in commission, but they proved to be of little value.

In the six months before declaring war, Congress had readily authorized preparations for it, but not for the funds to carry out the preparations adequately. However, in the spring of 1812, two of the separate service departments necessary for a greatly enlarged military establishment had been provided. In March a civilian Commissary-General of Purchases and a Quartermaster Department had been created and given the function of procuring and purchasing all military stores and articles of supply, camp equipage, and transport. In May, Congress had made provision for an Ordnance Department, responsible for the inspection and testing of all ordnance, cannon balls, shells, and shot, the construction of gun carriages and ammunition wagons, and the preparation and inspection of the "public powder." The Corps of Engineers was enlarged by the addition of a company of bombardiers, sappers, and miners, and the Military Academy at West Point was expanded and reorganized. In addition to increasing the Regular Army, Congress had authorized the President to accept volunteer forces and to call upon the states for militia. In the week following the declaration of war, Congress merged the force authorized in 1808 with the Regular Establishment and voted an additional 8 regiments of infantry. This brought the total authorized strength of the Army up to approximately 44,500 officers and men.

Against the United States was ranged the strongest naval power in the world. The British fleet totaled about 600 fighting ships, of which more than 100 were large ships of the line, mounting 60 guns or more each. The British Army had from 90,000 to 100,000 men in service in 1812 and could draw replacements and reinforcement from a population of 18,000,000. Most of Britain's resources were tied up, however, in the war against Napoleon. For the time being, very little military and naval assistance could be spared for the defense of Canada.

On the basis of available resources, the two belligerents were more evenly matched. At the outbreak of the war, there were approximately 7,000 British and Canadian regulars in Upper and Lower Canada (now the province of Ontario and Quebec). There was one regiment of Canadian troops in New Brunswick, on the Atlantic coast, part of which was transferred to the theatre of operations later in the war. With a total population of only about half a million white inhabitants, Canada itself had only a very small reservoir of militia to draw upon. When the war began, Major General Isaac Brock, the military commander and civil governor of Upper Canada, had available 800 militiamen in addition to his regulars. Throughout the war, the two provinces put a total of about 10,000 militia in the field, whereas in the United States probably four hundred and fifty thousand of the militia saw active service, although not more than half of them ever got near the front. The support of the Indian tribes gave Canada one source of manpower that the United States lacked. After the battle of Tippecanoe, Tecumseh had led his warriors across the border into Canada, where, along with the Canadian Indians, they joined the forces opposing the Americans. Perhaps 3,500 Indians were serving in the Canadian forces during the Thames River campaign in southeast Ontario in the fall of 1813, probably the largest number that took the field at any one time.

An important element of weakness in the American position was the disunity of the country. In the New England States public opinion ranged from mere apathy to actively expressed opposition to the war. A good many Massachusetts and Connecticut shipowners fitted out privateers—privately owned and armed vessels that were commissioned to take enemy ships—but New England contributed little else to the war effort. Some of its citizens even defied the Government and sold grain and provisions to the British.

Canada also faced a disunity problem. Many inhabitants of Upper Canada were recent immigrants from the United States who had no great desire to take up arms against their former homeland. Other Canadians thought that the superiority of the United States in numbers and materiel strength made any defense hopeless. That General Brock, the British commander, was able to overcome this spirit of defeatism is a tribute to his leadership.

The basic United States strategy was simple enough. Americans could scarcely wait for a declaration of war before undertaking the conquest of Canada. The old invasion route to Canada by way of Lake Champlain and the Richelieu River led directly to the most populous and most important part of the enemy's territory. The capture of Montreal would cut the line of communication upon which the British defense of Upper Canada depended, and the fall of that province would become inevitable. But this invasion route was near the center of disaffection in the United States, and little local support in the shape of men and supplies could be expected. The West, where enthusiasm for the war ran high and where the Canadian forces were weak, offered a safer, if less strategically sound, theatre of operations. The initial assaults were therefore delivered across the Detroit River and across the Niagara River between Lake Erie and Lake Ontario.

THE INITIAL ATTACKS

The first blows of the war were struck in the Detroit area and at Fort Michilimachinac. Brigadier General William Hull, Governor of Michigan Territory, in command of operations in that area, arrived at Fort Detroit on 5 July 1814 with a force of about 1,500 Ohio militiamen and 300 regulars, which he led across the river into Canada a week later. At that time the whole enemy force on the Detroit frontier consisted of about 150 British regulars, 300 Canadian militiamen, and some 250 Indians led by Tecumseh. Most of them were at Fort Malden, about 20 miles south of Detroit, on the Canadian side of the river. General Hull had been a dashing young officer in the Revolution, but age and its infirmities had made him cautious and timid. Instead of moving directly against Fort Malden, Hull issued a bombastic proclamation to the people of Canada and remained at the river landing almost opposite Detroit. He sent out several small raiding detachments along the Thames and Detroit rivers, one of which returned after skirmishing with the British outposts near Fort Malden. In the meantime, General Brock, who was both energetic and able, had sent a small party of British regulars, Canadians, and Indians across the river from Malden to cut General Hull's communications with Ohio. Hull, fearing that Detroit would be

This caricature of the men recruited for the War of 1812 was published in 1832.

completely cut off from its base of supplies, on 7 August began to withdraw his force back across the river into Fort Detroit. The last American had scarcely returned before the first men of Brock's force appeared and began setting up artillery opposite Detroit. By 15 August five guns were in position and opened fire on the fort with considerable effect. The next morning Brock led his troops—about 700 British and Canadians and some 600 Indians—across the river, but, before he could launch an assault, Hull surrendered. Militiamen were released under parole; Hull and the regulars were sent as prisoners to Montreal. Later paroled, General Hull returned to face a court-martial for his conduct of the campaign, was sentenced to be shot, and was immediately pardoned.

On 15 August, the day before the surrender of Detroit, Fort Dearborn had also been lost. On that day, acting on orders from General Hull, the small garrison at Dearborn had evacuated the post and started out across the Michigan peninsula to Detroit, but it was almost immediately attacked and wiped out by a band of Indians, who then destroyed the fort.

Immediately after taking Detroit, Brock transferred most of his forces to the Niagara frontier where, at Lewiston, a force of New York militiamen was assembled under the command of Major General Stephen Van Rensselaer. General Van Rensselaer owed his appointment not to any military experience, of which he had none, but to his family position. Untrained and inept as he was in military art, Van Rensselaer at least fought the enemy—more than could be said of the Regular Army commander in that theatre, Brigadier General Alexander Smyth. By the beginning of October, Van Rensselaer had about 2,300 militiamen at Lewiston. General Smyth had 1,650 regulars and nearly 400 militiamen at Buffalo. Another force of regulars, about 1,300 strong, was at Fort Niagara. Opposite Van Rensselaer's camp lay the Canadian town of Queenston, protected by a fortified battery on the steep heights between the town and the Niagara River and defended by about 300 men, mostly British regulars. After one attempt had been called off, Van Rensselaer began crossing the river during the early morning hours of 13 October 1812. The first echelon of about 300 men, mostly regulars, were pinned down for a time on the riverbank below the heights, but, finding a path that had been left unguarded, the troops clambered to the summit, surprised the enemy, and drove them down into Queenston. A counterattack by the British, in which General Brock was killed, was repulsed. During the morning 600 or more reinforcements were ferried across the river, but less than half of them joined the troops holding the heights. Most of Van Rensselaer's militiamen flatly refused to cross, and General Smyth ignored his request for aid. Meanwhile, British and Canadian reinforcements had arrived in Queenston. Van Rensselaer's men, tired and outnumbered, put up a stiff resistance on the heights, but in the end were overwhelmed—90 Americans were killed and nearly 1,000 captured.

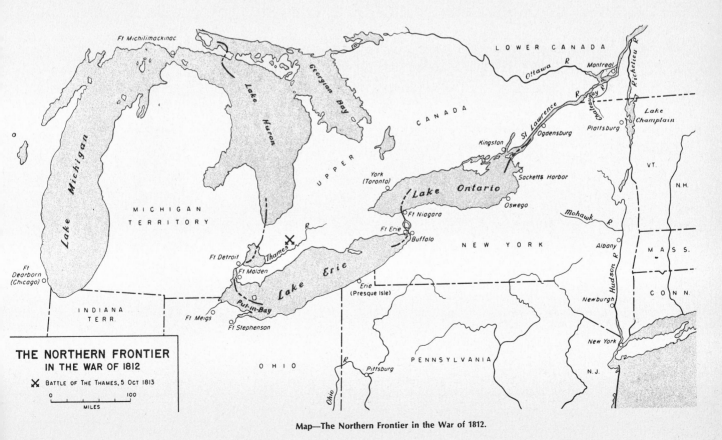

THE NORTHERN FRONTIER
IN THE WAR OF 1812

✕ Battle of The Thames, 5 Oct 1813

0   100
MILES

Map—The Northern Frontier in the War of 1812.

After the defeat at Queenston, Van Rensselaer resigned and was succeeded by the unreliable General Smyth who spent his time composing windy proclamations. Disgusted at being marched down to the river on several occasions only to be marched back to camp again, the new army, which had assembled after the battle of Queenston, gradually melted away. The men who remained lost all sense of discipline, and finally at the end of November the volunteers were ordered home and the regulars went into winter quarters. General Smyth's request for leave was hastily granted and three months later his name was quietly dropped from the Army rolls.

During the Niagara campaign the largest force then under arms, commanded by Major General Henry Dearborn, had been held in the neighborhood of Albany, more than 250 miles from the scene of operations. Dearborn had had a good record in the Revolutionary War and had served as Secretary of War during the Jefferson administration. Persuaded to accept the command of the northern theatre, except for Hull's forces, he was, at first, in doubt as to the extent of his authority, but when it was clarified he was reluctant to exercise it. Proposing to move his army, which included seven regiments of regulars with artillery and dragoons, against Montreal in conjunction with a simultaneous operation across the Niagara River, Dearborn was content to wait for his subordinates to make the first move. When Van Rensselaer made his attempt against Queenston, Dearborn, who was still in the vicinity of Albany, showed no sign of marching toward Canada. At the beginning of November he sent a large force north to Plattsburg and announced that he would personally lead the army into Montreal, but he got no farther than the boundary. At that point he turned around and marched his troops back to Plattsburg, where they went into winter quarters.

THE WAR AT SEA

If the land campaigns of 1812 reflected little credit on the U.S. Army, the war at sea brought lasting glory to the infant U.S. Navy. Captain Isaac Hull became the first hero of the war, when as commander of the **Constitution** he outfought and sank the British frigate **Guerrière.** Captain Hull's victory was the first of a series of single-ship actions in which the big 44-gun frigates **Constitution** and **United States** humbled the pride of the Royal Navy. At the same time, American privateers were picking off English merchant vessels by the hundreds. Altogether nearly 1,000 British vessels were captured by American privateers during the war. Having need of American foodstuffs, Britain was at first willing to take advantage of New England's opposition to the war by not extending the blockade to the New England coast; but by the beginning of 1814, the whole American coast was effectively blockaded. Of the 22 American warships that had managed to get to sea, only the **Constitution** and 4 smaller vessels were still operating when the war ended.

THE CAMPAIGN OF 1813

On land, the objects of the American plan of campaign for 1813 were the recapture of Detroit and an attack on Canada across Lake Ontario. For the Detroit campaign, the American troops were placed under the command of Brigadier General William H. Harrison, Governor of the Indiana Territory and the hero of Tippecanoe. The difficulties of a winter campaign were tremendous, but the country demanded action. Harrison therefore started north toward Lake Erie at the end of October 1812 with some 6,500 men. A sizable detachment, amounting to about 1,000 men, pushed on to a point nearly opposite Fort Malden, where they were defeated and brutally massacred by a slightly larger force of Canadians and Indians. Harrison then decided to suspend operations for the winter. Building two forts—Meigs and Stephenson—he posted his army near the Michigan border at the western end of Lake Erie.

The Ontario campaign was entrusted to General Dearborn, who was ordered to move his army from Plattsburg to Sackets Harbor, where Commodore Isaac Chauncey had been assembling a fleet. Dearborn was to move across the lake to Kingston, capture it and destroy the British flotilla there, then proceed to York (now Toronto), the capital of Upper Canada, to capture the stores at that place, and finally he was to cooperate with a force from Buffalo in seizing the forts on the Canadian side of the Niagara River. When the time came to move, Dearborn and Chauncey, hearing a rumor that the British forces in Kingston had been reinforced, decided to bypass that objective and attack York directly. About 1,700 men were embarked and sailed up Lake Ontario without incident, arriving off York before daybreak on 27 April. Dearborn, who was in poor health, turned over the command of the assault to Brigadier General Zebulon Pike, the explorer of the Southwest. The landing, about four miles west of the town, was unopposed. The British garrison of about 600 men, which occupied a fortification about halfway between the town and the landing, was overwhelmed after sharp resistance; but just as the Americans were pushing through the fort toward the town, a powder magazine or mine exploded, killing or disabling many Americans and a number of British soldiers. Among those killed was General Pike.

With General Dearborn incapacitated and General Pike dead, the troops apparently got out of hand. Public buildings in York were looted or burned and the provincial records destroyed. After holding the town for about a week, Dearborn's force recrossed the lake to Niagara to join an attack against the forts on the Canadian side of the Niagara River.

Meanwhile, Sackets Harbor had been almost stripped of troops for the raid on York and for reinforcing the army at Fort Niagara. At Kingston, across the lake, Sir George Prevost, the Governor General of Canada, had assembled a force of 800 British regulars in addition to militia. Taking advantage of the absence of Chauncey's fleet, which was at the other end of the lake, Prevost on the night of 26–27 May launched an attack on Sackets Harbor with his entire force of regulars. The town was defended by about 400 men from several outfits of the Regular Army and approximately 750 militiamen, under the command of Brigadier General Jacob Brown of the New York militia. Brown posted

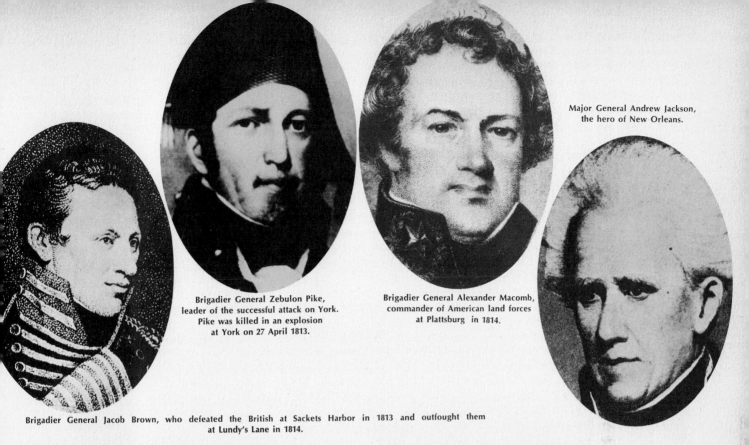

Major General Andrew Jackson, the hero of New Orleans.

Brigadier General Zebulon Pike, leader of the successful attack on York. Pike was killed in an explosion at York on 27 April 1813.

Brigadier General Alexander Macomb, commander of American land forces at Plattsburg in 1814.

Brigadier General Jacob Brown, who defeated the British at Sackets Harbor in 1813 and outfought them at Lundy's Lane in 1814.

his men in two lines in front of a fortified battery to cover a possible landing. The British landed under heavy fire, pressed rapidly forward, routed the first line, and pushed the second back into the prepared defenses. There the Americans held. The British then tried two frontal assaults but were repulsed with heavy losses. While they were reforming for a third attack, General Brown rallied the militia and sent them toward the rear of the enemy's right flank. This was the turning point. In danger of being cut off, the British hurriedly withdrew to their ships and sailed back to Kingston, having suffered serious losses.

On the same day that Prevost sailed against Sackets Harbor, General Dearborn at the western end of Lake Ontario was invading Canada with an army of 4,000 men. The operation began with a well-executed and stubbornly resisted amphibious assault led by Colonel Winfield Scott and Commandant Oliver Hazard Perry, USN, with Chauncey's fleet providing fire support. Outnumbered more than two to one, the British retreated, abandoning Fort George and Queenston to the Americans. An immediate pursuit might have sealed the victory; but Dearborn, lacking energy

and drive, waited several days and then sent a part of his command, some 2,000 men, after the enemy. The detachment advanced to within 10 miles of the British and camped for the night with slight regard for security. During the night a force of about 700 British attacked the camp and thoroughly routed the Americans. Some two weeks later, on 24 June, a smaller detachment, which had ventured 15 miles outside the fort, surrendered to a force of British and Indians that was half as large. After these reverses there was no further action of consequence on the Niagara front until the end of the year.

Hull's disaster at Detroit in 1812 and Harrison's unsuccessful winter campaign had clearly shown that any offensive action in that quarter depended upon first gaining control of Lake Erie. To build a fleet and seize control of the lake was the task that had been assigned to Commandant Perry. Throughout the spring and summer of 1813, except for the time he had joined Dearborn's force, Perry had been busy at Presque Isle assembling his fleet, guns, and crews. By the beginning of August his force was superior to that of the British in every respect except long-

The American fleet under Commodore Perry engages the British fleet on Lake Erie on 19 September 1813. The engraving by Benjamin Tanner is based on a drawing by John James Barralet.

range armament. Sailing up the lake, he anchored in Put-in-Bay, near the line still held by General Harrison in the vicinity of Forts Meigs and Stephenson, and there on 10 September Perry met the British fleet, defeated it, and gained control of Lake Erie.

As soon as the damage to Perry's ships and the captured British vessels had been repaired, Harrison embarked his army and sailed against Fort Malden. A regiment of Kentucky mounted riflemen, commanded by Colonel R. M. Johnson, moved along the shore of the lake toward Detroit. Outnumbered on land and open to attack from the water, the British abandoned both Forts Malden and Detroit and retreated eastward. After leaving a detachment to garrison the forts, Harrison set out after the enemy with Colonel Johnson's cavalry regiment, five brigades of Kentucky volunteers, and a part of the 27th Infantry, a force of about 3,500 men. On 5 October he made contact with the British on the banks of the Thames River about 85 miles from Malden. The enemy numbered about 2,900, of whom 900 were British regulars, and the remainder Indians under Tecumseh. Instead of attacking with infantry in the traditional line-against-line fashion, Harrison ordered Colonel Johnson to make a mounted attack. The maneuver succeeded completely. Unable to withstand the hard-riding Kentuckians, the British surrendered in droves. The Indians were routed, and Tecumseh, who had brought so much trouble to the western frontier, was killed. As a result of the victory, Lake Erie became an American lake, the Indian confederacy was shattered, the American position on the Detroit frontier was reestablished, and a large portion of Canadian territory was brought under American control.

On the other hand, the expedition against Montreal in the fall of 1813 was one of the biggest fiascoes of the war. It involved a simultaneous drive by two forces: one, an army of about 4,000 men assembled at Plattsburg on Lake Champlain under the command of Brigadier General Wade Hampton; and another, of about 6,000 men, which was to attack down the St. Lawrence River from Sackets Harbor under the command of Major General James Wilkinson. Relations between Hampton and Wilkinson were strained, with the two generals scarcely on speaking terms and no one on the spot to command the two of them. Neither had sufficient strength to capture Montreal without the other's aid; each lacked confidence in the other; and both suspected that they were being left in the lurch by the War Department. At first contact with the British, about halfway down the Chateaugay River, Hampton retreated and, after falling back all the way to Plattsburg, resigned from the Army. Wilkinson, after having a detachment of about 2,000 men severely mauled in an engagement just north of Ogdensburg, also abandoned his part of the operation and followed Hampton into Plattsburg.

The British scored again in December when they took advantage of the weakened state of American forces on the Niagara frontier to recapture Fort George and to cross the river and take Fort Niagara, which remained in their hands until the end of the war.

Perry's famous message to General William Henry Harrison after the Battle of Lake Erie.

We have met the enemy and they are ours. Two Ships, two Brigs one Schooner & one Sloop.

Yours, with great respect and esteem

O H Perry.

Commodore
Oliver Hazard Perry.

An engraving of Commodore Perry in action
during the Battle of Lake Erie.

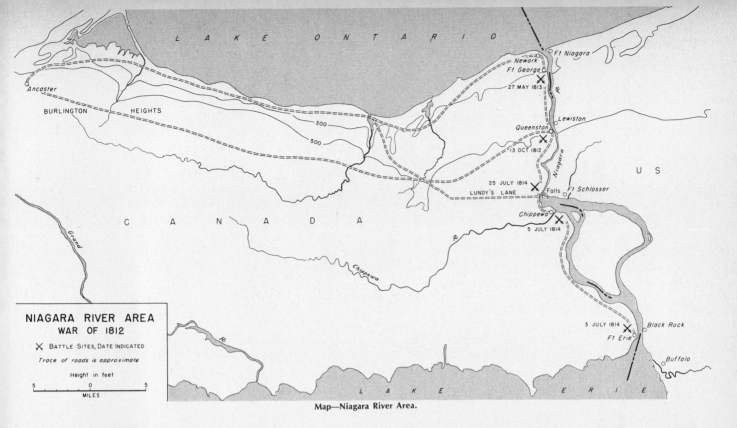

Map—Niagara River Area.

The map shows labels: LAKE ONTARIO, Ancaster, BURLINGTON HEIGHTS, 300, 500, Newark, Ft Niagara, Ft George, 27 MAY 1813, Queenston, Lewiston, 13 OCT 1812, US, CANADA, 25 JULY 1814, LUNDY'S LANE, Falls, Ft Schlosser, Chippewa R, Chippewa, 5 JULY 1814, Grand R, 3 JULY 1814, Black Rock, Ft Erie, Buffalo, LAKE ERIE.

NIAGARA RIVER AREA
WAR OF 1812
X BATTLE SITES, DATE INDICATED
Trace of roads is approximate
Height in feet
5 0 5
MILES

THE CAMPAIGNS OF 1814

After the setbacks at the end of 1813 a lull descended on the northern frontier. In March 1814 Wilkinson made a foray from Plattsburg with about 4,000 men and managed to penetrate about 8 miles into Canada before being stopped by some 200 British and Canadian troops supported by gunboats on the Richelieu River. It was an even more miserable failure than his attempt of the preceding fall. As a result of these and earlier setbacks, most of the senior generals were replaced by younger, more active officers, a change that came too late to affect the outcome of the war. Jacob Brown, who had been commissioned a brigadier general in the Regular Army after his heroic defense of Sackets Harbor, was promoted to major general and placed in command of the Niagara-Lake Ontario theatre, while thirty-eight-year-old George Izard received command of the Lake Champlain frontier and promotion

to major general. Six new brigadier generals were appointed from the ablest, but not necessarily most senior, colonels in the Regular Army, among them Winfield Scott, who had distinguished himself at the Battle of Queenston Heights and who now assumed command at Buffalo, where he threw himself energetically into the task of drilling and training his new recruits.

British control of Lake Ontario, which had been achieved by feverish construction activity during the previous winter, obliged Secretary of War John Armstrong to recommend operations from Buffalo. Disagreement within the President's cabinet delayed adoption of a plan until June. By this time Commodore Chauncey's naval force at Sackets Harbor was expected to be strong enough to challenge the British fleet, and a coordinated attack on the Niagara peninsula was decided upon. General Brown was instructed to cross the Niagara River in the vicinity of Fort

"Battle of the Thames." This portrayal of the shooting of Tecumseh by the victorious Americans on 5 October 1813 is the work of lithographer John Dorival. It was dedicated to President Andrew Jackson when it was published in 1833.

Erie and, after assaulting the fort, to move against Fort George and Newark or to seize and hold a bridge over the Chippewa River as he saw fit.

Brown accordingly crossed the Niagara River on 3 July with his whole force, about 3,500 men, took Fort Erie, and then advanced toward the Chippewa River, 16 miles away. There a smaller British force, including 1,500 regulars, had gathered to oppose the American Army. General Brown posted his army in a strong position behind a broad ditch or creek with his right flank resting on the Niagara River and his left protected by a swamp. In front of the American position was an open plain, beyond which flowed the

Chippewa River, and on the other side of the river were the British.

The next day, 5 July, when 1,300 men commanded by General Scott formed on the plain to parade in a belated celebration of Independence Day, they discovered that they would have a battle instead of a parade, for the British regulars had crossed the river without being detected and had taken up positions on the opposite edge of the plain. Scott ordered his men to charge and the British advanced to meet them. Alternately stopping to fire and then moving forward, closing the gaps torn by the volleys and artillery fire, the two lines approached each other.

Colonel James Miller and his regiment in action during the Battle of Chippewa.

They came together first at the flanks, while still 60 or 80 yards apart at the center, and at this point the British line crumbled and broke. By the time a second brigade sent forward by General Brown reached the battlefield, the British had withdrawn across the Chippewa River and were retreating toward Ancaster, on Lake Ontario. Scott's casualties amounted to 48 killed and 222 wounded; British losses were 137 killed and 304 wounded.

Brown followed the retreating British as far as Queenston, where he halted to await the arrival of Commodore Chauncey's fleet. After waiting two weeks for Chauncey, who failed to cooperate in the campaign, Brown withdrew to Chippewa, proposing to strike out across country to Ancaster by way of a crossroad known as Lundy's Lane from which he could reach the Burlington Heights at the head of Lake Ontario and the rear of the British.

When General Brown decided to pull back from Queenston, the British force at Ancaster amounted to about 2,200 men under General Riall; another 1,500 British troops were gathered at Fort George and Fort Niagara at the mouth of the Niagara River. As soon as Brown began his withdrawal, Riall sent forward about 1,000 men along Lundy's Lane, the very route by which General Brown intended to advance against Burlington Heights. A second force of more than 600 British moved out from Fort George and followed Brown along the Queenston road; while a third enemy force of about 400 men moved along the American side of the Niagara River from Fort Niagara. Riall's advance force reached the junction of Lundy's Lane and the Queenston road on the night of 24–25 July, the same night that Brown reached Chippewa, about three miles distant. Very much concerned that the British force on the opposite side of the Niagara would cut off his line of communication, and entirely unaware of Riall's force at Lundy's Lane, Brown on 25 July ordered Scott to take his brigade back along the road toward Queenston in the hope of drawing off the British force on the other side of the river. That force, however, had already crossed the river and joined Riall's men at Lundy's Lane. Scott had not gone far when, much to his surprise, he discovered himself face to face with the enemy.

The ensuing battle, most of which took place after nightfall, was the hardest fought, most stubbornly contested engagement of the war. For two hours Scott attacked and threw back the counterattacks of a numerically superior force of British, who, moreover, had the advantage in position. Then both sides were reinforced. With Brown's whole force engaged, the Americans now had about 2,900 men on the field against approximately the same number of British. At this point the British were forced back from their position and their artillery was captured. The battle then continued without material advantage to either side until just before midnight, when General Brown ordered the exhausted Americans to fall back to the camp across the Chippewa River. The enemy, equally if not more exhausted, remained where they were, unable to follow. Casualties on both sides had been heavy and about equal. The loss among officers was especially heavy. On the American side, both General Brown and General Scott were severely wounded, Scott so badly that he saw no further service during the war. On the British side, General Riall and his superior, General Drummond, who had arrived with the reinforcements, were wounded and Riall was taken prisoner. Both sides claimed Lundy's Lane as a victory, as well they might, but it put a halt to Brown's invasion of Canada.

This engraving, entitled "Capture of the City of Washington," appeared in "The History of England," by Paul de Rapin-Thoyras, published in 1816.

A few days after the Battle of Lundy's Lane the Americans withdrew to Fort Erie where they were besieged by the British at the beginning of August. The British abandoned the effort on 21 September after suffering extremely heavy casualties. A few weeks later General Izard arrived with reinforcements from Plattsburg and advanced as far as Chippewa, where the British were strongly entrenched. After a few minor skirmishes, Izard decided to cease operations for the winter. The works at Fort Erie **were** destroyed and the Army withdrew to American soil on 5 November.

During the summer of 1814 the British had been able not only to reinforce Canada but also to stage several raids on the American coast. In one of them, a force of some 4,000 British troops under Major General Robert Ross landed on the right bank of the Patuxent River and marched on Washington. At the Battle of Bladensburg, Ross easily dispersed a mixed force of about 5,000 that had been hastily gathered together to defend the Capitol. The British then entered Washington, burned the Capitol, the White House, and other public buildings, and returned to their ships.

This version of the burning of Washington was published in London in 1814.

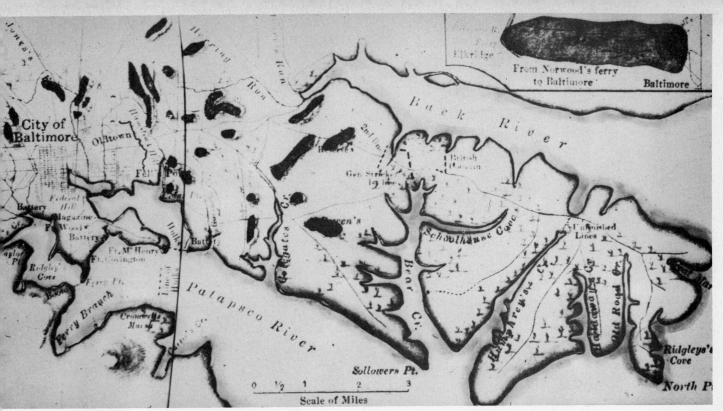

The Baltimore area at the time of the British attack.

A contemporary drawing of the land battle near Baltimore.

Baltimore was next on the schedule, but that city proved to be well defended. The approach by land was protected by a rather formidable line of redoubts and the harbor was guarded by Fort McHenry and blocked by a line of sunken gunboats. The Maryland militia succeeded in delaying the invaders and caused them considerable loss, including General Ross, who was killed. When the fleet failed to reduce Fort McHenry, the assault on the city was called off. Inspired by the sight of the American flag still flying over the fort after the bombardment, a young Washington attorney, Francis Scott Key, who was being detained on one of the British vessels, was moved to write a poem, "The Star-Spangled Banner." It was soon set to a popular tune of the day, and in 1931 became the American national anthem.

Two days before the attack on Baltimore, the British had suffered a much more serious repulse on Lake Champlain. After the departure of General Izard for the Niagara front, there had remained at Plattsburg a force of about 3,300 men under the command of Brigadier General Alexander Macomb. Supporting them was a small fleet under Commodore Thomas Macdonough. Across the border in Canada was an army of British veterans of the Napoleonic Wars, more than 16,000 strong. At the beginning of September 1814, Sir George Prevost, the Governor General of Canada, was ready to invade the United States. Moving slowly up the Richelieu River toward Lake Champlain, he crossed the border, and on 6 September arrived before Plattsburg with about 11,000 men. There he waited for almost a week until his naval support was ready to join the attack. With militia reinforcements, Macomb now had about 4,500 men manning a strong line of redoubts and blockhouses that faced a small river. Macdonough had anchored his vessels in Plattsburg Bay, out of gunshot from the British, but in a position to resist an assault on the

American line. On 11 September the British flotilla appeared and Prevost ordered a joint attack. There was no numerical disparity between the naval forces, but an important one in the quality of the seamen. Macdonough's ships were manned by well-trained seamen and gunners, the British ships by hastily recruited French-Canadian militia and soldiers, with only a sprinkling of regular seamen. As the enemy vessels came into the bay, the wind died and the British were exposed to a heavy raking fire from Macdonough's long guns. The British worked their way in, came to anchor, and the two anchored fleets began slugging at each other, broadside by broadside. At the end the British commander was dead and his ships battered into submission. Prevost immediately called off the land attack and withdrew to Canada the next day.

Macdonough's victory ended the gravest threat that had arisen so far. More important was the impetus it gave to peace negotiations then under way. News of the two setbacks—Baltimore and Plattsburg—reached England simultaneously, aggravating the war-weariness of the British and bolstering the efforts of the American peace commissioner to obtain satisfactory terms.

This version of the death of British General Robert Ross features a rocket (upper left). The British made frequent use of rockets in their campaigns against Washington and Baltimore.

A sketch of the attack on Fort McHenry.

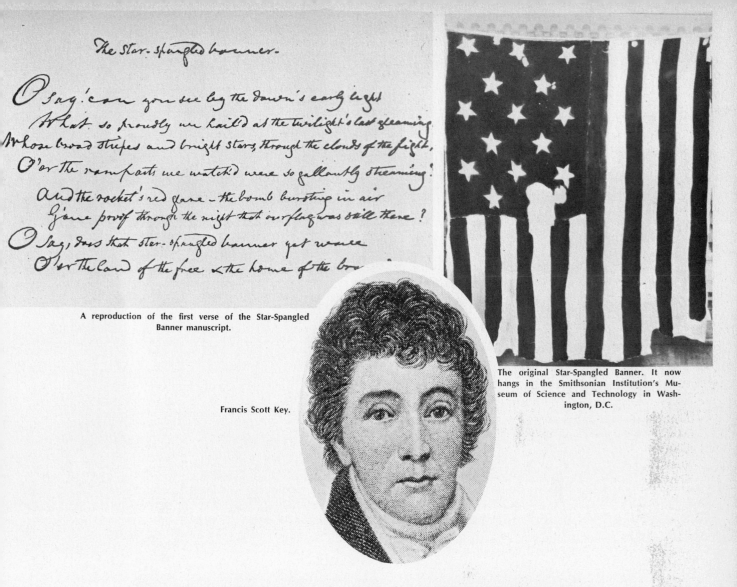

The Star-Spangled Banner.

O Say! can you see by the dawn's early light
What so proudly we hail'd at the twilight's last gleaming
Whose broad stripes and bright stars, through the clouds of the fight,
O'er the ramparts we watch'd were so gallantly streaming?
And the rocket's red glare - the bomb bursting in air
Gave proof through the night that our flag was still there?
O say, does that star-spangled banner yet wave
O'er the land of the free & the home of the brave.

A reproduction of the first verse of the Star-Spangled Banner manuscript.

The original Star-Spangled Banner. It now hangs in the Smithsonian Institution's Museum of Science and Technology in Washington, D.C.

Francis Scott Key.

This print, based on a painting by Hugh Reinagle, shows Commodore Thomas Macdonough defeating the British on Lake Champlain near Plattsburg on 11 September 1814.

However, the progress of the peace negotiations also caused the British to continue an operation that General Ross, before his repulse and death at Baltimore, had been instructed to carry out, namely, a descent upon the Gulf Coast, the object of which was the capture of New Orleans and a possible severing of Louisiana from the United States. Major General Sir Edward Pakenham, in command of the expedition, arrived at the mouth of the Mississippi on Christmas Day, 1814, to find his troops disposed on a narrow isthmus below New Orleans between the Mississippi River and a cypress swamp. They had landed two weeks earlier at a shallow lagoon some 10 miles east of New Orleans and had already fought one engagement. In this encounter, on 23 December, General Andrew Jackson, who had taken command of the defenses on 1 December, almost succeeded in cutting off an advance detachment of 2,000 British, but, after a three-hour fight in which casualties on both sides were heavy, he was compelled to retire behind fortifications covering New Orleans.

The main American position was on the east bank of the Mississippi, extending along a ditch stretching from the river to a swamp. Behind the ditch Jackson had raised earthworks and strengthened them with bales of cotton. The defenses were manned by about 3,500 men with another 1,000 in reserve. More than 20 pieces of artillery, including a battery of 9 heavy guns on the opposite bank of the Mississippi and the guns of a schooner, were prepared to support the American defenses.

After trying an artillery duel on 1 January, which the American gunners won, Pakenham decided on a frontal assault in combination with an attack against the American troops on the west bank. The main assault was to be delivered by about 5,300 men, while about 600 men under Lieutenant Colonel William Thornton were to cross the river and clear the west bank. For the main attack, Jackson was ready.

As the British columns appeared out of the early morning mist on 8 January, they were met with murderous fire, first from the artillery, then from the muskets and rifles of Jackson's infantry. The British were mowed down by the hundreds. Pakenham and one other general were killed and a third general badly wounded. More than 2,000 of the British were casualties, while American losses were trifling. As the main attack ended, Thornton's force on the west bank began its advance on the American position. Jackson had made inadequate preparations to meet in this quarter. The heavy guns of a battery posted on the west bank were not placed to command an attack along that side of the river, and only about 800 militia, divided in two groups a mile apart, were in position to oppose Thornton. Although the Americans resisted stubbornly, inflicting greater losses than they suffered, the British pressed on, routed them, and overran the battery. Had the British continued their advance, Jackson's position would have been indeed critical, but Pakenham's successor in command, appalled by the defeat of the main assault, ordered Thornton to withdraw from the west bank and rejoin the main force. Jackson failed to take the offensive. For ten days the shattered remnant of Pakenham's army remained in camp unmolested by the Americans, and then reembarked and sailed away.

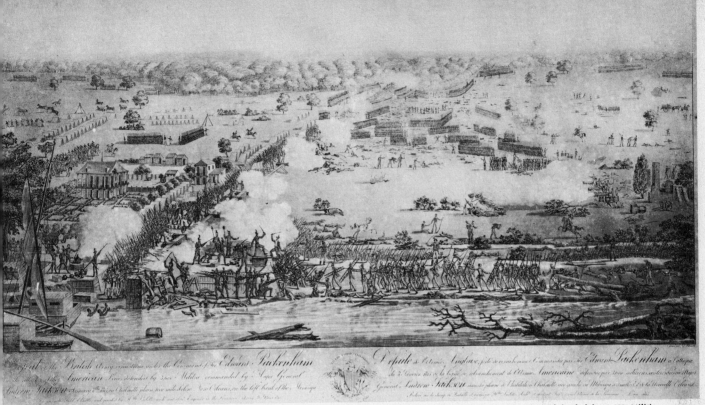

"Defeat of the British Army, 12,000 strong, under the Command of Sir Edward Pakenham in the attack of the American Lines defended by 3,600 Militia commanded by Major General Andrew Jackson." The perspective drawing is the work of Hyacinth Laclotte, "architect and assistant engineer in the Louisiana Army."

Engraver Francisco Scacki called his version of the Battle of New Orleans "A Correct View of the Battle Near the City of New Orleans."

General Andrew Jackson (on horse) is directing his forces in this pictorial representation of the Battle of New Orleans.

This print of the American position on the east bank of the Mississippi shows the bales of cotton that reinforced the earth-works.

A soldier removes an arrow from the leg of Lieutenant Sam Houston during fierce fighting with the Creek Indians at Horse-shoe Bend, Alabama, on 27 March 1814.

The death of the British commander, Major General Sir Edward Pakenham, as depicted in an early woodcut.

The victorious American forces are seen in action
in this engraving by H. B. Hall.

Jackson's fears that the attack would be renewed in some other quarter were realized when the British appeared off Mobile on 8 February. After the small fort that guarded the entrance to the harbor had capitulated, the way into the city lay open; but on 14 February news arrived that a peace treaty had been signed on 14 December 1814, three weeks prior to the Battle of New Orleans.

In the War of 1812 the artillery contributed conspicuously to American successes at Chippewa, at Sackets Harbor, at the siege of Fort Erie, and at New Orleans. The small Corps of Engineers, a branch which owed its efficiency partly to the services of foreign experts but chiefly to the United States Military Academy, also made important contributions. Graduates of the Academy completed the fortifications at Fort Erie, built Fort Meigs, planned the harbor defenses of Norfolk and New York, and directed the fortifications at Plattsburg.

Gunnery and engineering skill would have been of no avail without competent and experienced leaders. They were not available at the beginning, but by 1814 such leaders had been found. Officers like Winfield Scott, Jacob Brown, and Andrew Jackson proved worthy successors to the heroes of the Revolution.

Admiral Lord Gambier (left) and John Adams
shake hands after signing the Treaty of Ghent which ended the War of 1812.

Captioned "Dress the most distinguishing mark of a military Genius," this drawing appeared in Advice to Officers of the Army, published in Philadelphia in 1813. Among its recommendations "to Young Officers": "Your cross belt should be broad, with a huge blade pendent to it—to which you may add a dirk and a bayonet, in order to give you a more tremendous appearance."

JOHNNY BULL and the ALEXANDRIANS.

The British siege of Alexandria, Virginia, provided the subject matter for this cartoon.

This cartoon protested the use of Indian warriors by the British.

In "A Boxing Match, or Another Bloody Nose for John Bull," the figure representing the United States (right) assures his bleeding adversary that "we are an Enterprising Nation."

THE BADGE OF MILITARY MERIT—
ITS LEGACY IS THE PURPLE HEART

The Gen'l ever desirous to cherish a virtuous Ambition in his Soldiers as well as to foster & incourage every species of Merit, directs that when ever any singularly meritorious Action is performed the Author of it shall be permitted to wear on his Facings over the Left Breast the Figure of a Heart in Purple Cloth or Silk edged with narrow Lace or Binding. Not only Instances of unusual gallantry but also of extraordinary fidelity & essential service in any way shall meet with a due Reward. Before this Favour can be confered on any Man the particular Fact or Facts on which it is to be founded must be set forth, to the Commander in Chief accompanied with a Certificate from the Commanding Officer of the Regmt. & Brigade to which the Candidate for Reward belonged, or other incontestable Proof; & upon granting it the Name & Regmt. of the Person with the Action so certified are to be enroled in the Book of Merit which will be kept at the Orderly Office. Men who have merited this last Distinction to be suffered to pass all Guards & Sentinels which Officers are permitted to do.—From the original General Orders issued by General George Washington, Newburgh, New York, 7 August 1782.

The Badge of Military Merit of the American Revolution is the oldest decoration for valor, with the exception of the Cross of St. George of Russia. Only three of them were issued and only one of these exists today.

EARLY CONGRESSIONAL MEDALS

Before the establishment of the Purple Heart the American Government had given six medals to individuals—struck upon special occasions, but not a part of any organized, systematic plan of awards. These medals, both in their design and method of award, as well as in the circumstances which caused them to be awarded, were more a part of the tradition of the past than of that which was to develop in America in the future.

The first was given to George Washington, by a resolution passed by the Continental Congress and approved on 25 March 1776. The second was voted by Congress on 25 November 1777, to be given to General Horatio Gates for the defeat of the British under General John Burgoyne at Saratoga. This was a large medal, weighing more than 4 ounces, far too heavy to be worn as a decoration. The third was voted to Henry Lee—nicknamed "Light Horse Harry"—the father of Robert E. Lee, on 24 September 1779, in recognition of his attack upon the British at Paulus Hook, N. J., in July of that year, during which he captured 160 of the enemy without sustaining any loss to his own forces.

The next three awarded were unique, in that they went to enlisted men rather than officers, and that they were created by Congress with the specific understanding that they were to be worn as decorations by the recipients. These were the so-called "André" medals, given to the three American militiamen who captured the British intelligence officer Major John André, while he was an route to New York from West Point, wearing civilian clothes, after having plotted with Benedict Arnold for the betrayal of the American cause. The medals were awarded in 1780 to John Paulding, Isaac Van Wart, and David Williams.

THE "ANDRÉ" MEDAL

MEDAL AWARDED TO LEE

MEDAL AWARDED TO GATES

Subsequent to the Revolution the Purple Heart fell into disuse. Appropriately, it was reinstituted on the 200th Anniversary of the birth of George Washington. The inscription on the reverse of the revised medal reads "For Military Merit." Previously awarded for meritorious service as well as for wounds in action, it is now utilized solely as an award for wounds received in action.

Awarded to Commodore Oliver Hazard Perry after the Battle of Lake Erie.

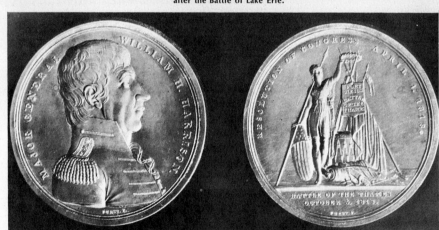

Awarded to Major General William Henry Harrison after the Battle of the Thames.

MEDAL AWARDED TO WASHINGTON

Awarded to Major General Winfield Scott after the Battles of Chippewa and Niagara.

117

A collection of military rifles. From top to bottom: the 1798 Whitney musket; the musket produced at the Government's Springfield and Harpers Ferry armories from 1844 until 1955; the 1903 Springfield rifle, used by the Army from 1903 through World War II; the Garand M1, the standard infantry rifle in World War II and Korea; and the fully automatic 7.62mm rifle adopted in 1957.

THE RIFLEMAN—KEY MAN IN ARMY HISTORY

by Stephen Ailes

Secretary of the Army (28 January 1964–1 July 1965)

The Army rifleman, bearer of a proud American tradition, is the latest in a long line of independent and self-sufficient men who earned this country's independence and who have protected it for 190 years. This tradition has its roots even before the American Revolution. When militia organizations formed the local defense of the American colonies, it was this militia, made up of men who brought their own arms, their own ammunition and their own powder who fought the battles of Lexington, Concord, and Bunker Hill. It was this militia, armed with their own weapons and considerable skill in marksmanship, and serving under the command of Colonel George Washington, who saved the remnants of Braddock's Army after the rout of the British regulars near Pittsburgh.

The United States Army traces its history to 14 June 1775 when the Second Continental Congress decided to raise "10 companies of expert riflemen." These constituted the nucleus around which the Continental Army was built. It is worthy of note that most of our men at Valley Forge were riflemen and that the teaching for which Baron von Steuben has become famous was that of the Manual of Arms and Infantry Tactics.

At one point shortly after the Revolutionary War, our Army consisted of only 80 men. During President Washington's administration, the Army was gradually increased to 3,300 men, mainly riflemen. During the same administration, Springfield Arsenal was established as a site for the manufacture of arms for the Army. Thus was established what has become a household word in military rifles. In its first year of production—1795—Springfield produced 445 muskets at a cost, with accessories, of about $25 each. They were copies of the French Charleville musket, 10,000 of which had been brought here by Lafayette.

It was with these muskets that Winfield Scott's Infantry was armed when they made such an impression on the British Commander at Chippewa in the War of 1812. When seeing those qualities which make riflemen great—courage, discipline, knowledge of their weapon—he exclaimed, "by God, those are regulars."

A series of basic changes to our weapons was made over the years. We rifled them and we adopted percussion caps. After some false starts, we got around to breech loaders. We improved the ammunition so that the cap, cartridge, and ball were combined. We picked up the bolt action. We went to semi-automatic weapons. Now we are attempting to make even greater progress by using extremely high-velocity projectiles. But during all of this period, we have been trying to provide the most effective weapon for the man who finally closes with the enemy, seizes, holds, and secures the land.

George Washington leads his army to victory at Princeton, New Jersey, on 3 January 1777. The Continental Army took pride in its firm ranks and in its bayonet charges.

By the time of the Mexican War, some 75 percent of our Army consisted of men with rifles. The men who carried the Confederacy to its height at Chancellorsville and who defended the Union so well at Gettysburg were riflemen. By this time, greater quantities of artillery had been made available, greater use was being made of cavalry and we were beginning to find better ways and means of moving supplies about the theatre of operations. Nonetheless, all our efforts to exploit technology were aimed at putting the rifleman on a critical piece of ground and helping him to stay there. It has been estimated that at the time of its highest strength, 83 percent of the Union Army of over a million men, were infantrymen.

Following that war, the Army was reduced to 25,000 and was dispersed to its stations on the frontier. Riflemen fought in 13 campaigns and over 1,000 engagements to maintain peace on the westward expanding frontier.

It was riflemen from the Regular Army and the militia who secured Cuba for the Cubans. Riflemen captured Puerto Rico and suppressed the Philippine Insurrection. It was a trumpeter in a rifle company who said, "I'll try, Sir," and scaled the wall and ran up the flag in Peking in 1900. Corporal Calvin P. Titus received the Medal of Honor for that exploit.

In World War I, which Laurence Stallings so aptly called the "Doughboys' War," we sent to Europe more than a million riflemen, and it was these American riflemen who broke the back of the veteran German Army. It was of these riflemen, their predecessors and successors, that General MacArthur so eloquently said:

"His name and fame are the birthright of every American citizen. In his youth and strength, his love and loyalty, he gave all that mortality can give. He

American infantrymen at Chippewa during the War of 1812. Their steady advance under heavy enemy fire caused the British commander to exclaim: "By God, those are regulars!"

119

needs no eulogy from me, or from any other man. He has written it in red on his enemy's breast.

"But when I think of his patience in adversity, of his courage under fire and of his modesty in victory, I am filled with an emotion of admiration I cannot put into words. He belongs to history as furnishing one of the greatest examples of successful patriotism. He belongs to posterity as the instructor of future generations in the principles of liberty and freedom. He belongs to the present, to us, by his virtues and by his achievements."

In World War II, despite the unprecedented requirement to provide an air force and to sustain worldwide lines of communications, we estimate that over two million of the men in Army uniform carried the war to the enemy with a rifle in hand.

As for the role of the rifleman in future wars, I can only say that we still count the strength of the Army in terms of divisions. We talk of a 14-division Army, a 16-division Army, or an 18-division Army—all else is ancillary. The cutting edge of a division consists of its riflemen and its tanks. And even the strongest supporters of Armor readily acknowledge that tanks cannot accomplish their tasks unless there are riflemen with them or near at hand. These riflemen continue to play the same role that the Continental Congress envisioned for those 10 companies of expert riflemen in 1775.

In recent years we have found ourselves faced with a new form of threat—the so-called war of national liberation. We prefer to call it guerrilla warfare or insurgency. As we looked about for ways and means of countering this threat, we once again found that many of the skills which we needed to pass on to our threatened Allies were the skills of the rifleman.

Men with rifles are now scattered throughout the world, helping our most immediately threatened friends in their fight against communist subversion. It is men trained to lead riflemen who are advising Vietnamese battalions. Our Special Forces teams are basically riflemen. One of the first skills they teach to the people of Viet Nam is that of self-defense with a rifle.

Today's concept of the land battle still places major emphasis on the rifleman. Most of the equipment we buy is designed in one way or another to help the rifleman do his job and to protect him while he does it. Artillery softens up enemy positions or knocks out enemy artillery. Armor exploits a weakness in the line, creates a breakthrough and overruns (or sometimes bypasses) positions which the infantry will then take and hold. The armored personnel carrier, as its name implies, is simply a device which enables the infantryman to ride to work protected from air burst artillery. Indeed, the Air Assault Division and the new mobility concept which has been under test is permitting the infantryman to ride to his task by air. Our sole purpose in that experiment has been to develop a better way to put

The 1st Battalion, 13th Infantry, at Vicksburg during the Civil War. Stiff resistance from Confederate riflemen (bottom) cost the 1st Battalion 43 percent of its men, but it carried the flag to the top of the hill.

120

One of the million U.S. riflemen
who fought in France during World War I.

The soldier of World War II with full field equipment.
He carried a rifle with bayonet, grenade bag, lensatic
compass, cartridge belt, first-aid pouch and package,
entrenching tool, haversack, bedroll, mess gear, and
canteen.

In Vietnam soldiers are often flown to battle,
but the rifle remains their most important weapon.

In Korea the bazooka was used against enemy tanks.

the rifleman at the decisive point on the battlefield, at the decisive time, in the best possible condition.

In the Army, we hold to the conviction that a man cannot be a soldier unless he knows how to use a rifle. As a result, every recruit spends over 25 percent of his training time during his eight weeks of basic training learning how to shoot the rifle accurately.

The effectiveness of the rifle, its range and its lethality depend entirely on the skill of the man who shoots it. This is why the Army spends so much time training the individual rifleman in marksmanship.

In 1798 Eli Whitney proposed an interchangeability of parts so that muskets he manufactured could be mass produced. Whitney finally received the approval of the new government to go ahead with his experiment. Starting from absolute zero since no machinery existed for such a project, Whitney accomplished his objective within eight years.

A major step in providing the American armed forces with the best in military arms occurred in 1841, when the Flintlock passed out of existence and was replaced by the United States Percussion Lock Musket, model 1842. The latter was a muzzle-loading rifle designed for use with the percussion cap. Originally known as the Jaeger, it was later called the Mississippi rifle. A limited number of these guns were turned out at the National Armories.

The breech-loading rifle was originally a muzzleloader which was converted into a single-shot cartridge breech-loader through a device conceived by E. S. Allin, master armorer of the Springfield Armory. The Allin conversion left intact the barrel lock, stock, and metal fittings of the model 1861 and 1863 rifle

---

muskets. However, a rectangular hole was set into each barrel. A breech block hinged to its forward end was lowered into the resulting aperture. A firing pin fitted in a hole drilled through the length of the breech block fired the cartridge when it was struck by the side hammer of the original lock.

The first magazine rifle to make the grade as a U.S. service arm was the Krag-Jorgensen, model 1892, a version of a Danish gun used by European armies. The Krag-Jorgensen was a .30 caliber centerfire, rifled with four grooves. The rifle was 49 inches long and weighed slightly more than 9 pounds. Its unusual magazine was constructed horizontally. Loose rounds were loaded from the right side of the rifle, while the right face of the magazine acted as a loading gate by swinging outward and down. With the loading gate closed, a follower spring pushed the cartridges to the left and up. The rifle could also be used as a single loader by use of a magazine cutoff located on the left side of the receiver.

The search for a gun which delivered a high rate of fire began as far back as 1903. In 1936 the goal was attained with development of the Garand—a gas-operated semi-automatic weapon which utilized the blow-back from gasses expended by its fired cartridges to cock the gun for the following round.

Early American military small arms development took place, to a large extent, at the Springfield Armory, Springfield, Massachusetts, and Harpers Ferry, Virginia. Both the Springfield and the Harpers Ferry Armories had their beginning in 1794 when the Third Congress authorized production of 7,000 new muskets and also provided for the establishment of two armories for their manufacture and storage.

THE INFANTRYMAN BADGE

COMBAT INFANTRYMAN BADGE

The Combat Infantryman Badge is authorized for service in World War II, Korea, Vietnam and Laos.

FIRST AWARD

SECOND AWARD

THIRD AWARD

EXPERT INFANTRYMAN BADGE

Awarded to an infantry officer, enlisted man or warrant officer with an infantry MOS who has satisfactorily completed the proficiency tests prescribed by Army regulations while assigned to an infantry unit of regimental or smaller size, while assigned to or attending a course of instruction at the United States Army Infantry School, or while on temporary duty at a testing headquarters for the sole purpose of taking the Expert Infantryman Badge Test.

Secretary of War John C. Calhoun, who reorganized the Army after the War of 1812.

Brigadier General Edmund P. Gaines, commander of the Army's Western Department.

Major General Jacob Brown, the first "Commanding General" of the Army.

CHAPTER 5

THE U.S. ARMY, 1815-1845

In February 1815, at the end of the War of 1812, the Regular Army totaled about 33,000 men, but a reduction of 20,000 was recommended by President Madison as soon as hostilities ended. Congress finally fixed the Army's strength at 10,000 men in addition to the Corps of Engineers, which was not changed. Eight regiments of infantry, 1 light artillery regiment, and 8 battalions of artillery were authorized; among the units that were abolished was the regiment of light dragoons. Provision was made for a "general staff," under the direction of the Secretary of War, with a membership of 2 major generals, each with 2 aides; 4 brigadier generals, each with 1 aide; an adjutant and inspector general, 2 adjutant generals, and 4 brigade inspectors; a quartermaster general, 2 deputy quartermaster generals, and 4 brigade quartermasters; a judge advocate; chaplains; and the superintendent and staff of the Military Academy. Also provided were the following departments: Ordnance, Medical, Pay, and Purchasing. The Army was reorganized on a territorial basis with 2 divisions: the division of the north, under Major General Jacob Brown, included 4 military territorial departments; the division of the south, under Major General Andrew Jackson, comprised 5 military territorial departments.

When Secretary of War John C. Calhoun took office in the fall of 1817, he was faced with two major problems—reorganizing the peacetime establishment, and meeting an outbreak of border warfare in the South. Neither problem was new, but Calhoun brought more energy and ability to bear on them than any Secretary had displayed since Secre-

tary of War Knox in Washington's Cabinet. In repetition of the experience of the Washington and Adams administrations, the Army after 1815 could not be maintained at its authorized strength, and Congress showed a disposition to cut the authorized strength back to the actual strength. At the end of 1817 the actual strength had fallen to about 8,200 men. A year later, in November 1818, it amounted to 7,676 officers and men.

Almost from the very moment he took office, Calhoun was faced with Congressional proposals to cut the strength of the Army, abolish the general staff, and discontinue the Military Academy at West Point. However, he was able to stave off Congressional action until 1821. The Secretary pointed out that, in proportion to the wealth and population of the country and to the number of military posts that required garrisons, the military establishment in 1815 was relatively smaller than that of 1802. A reduction in the staff, Calhoun argued, would have serious consequences. "It is in every service," he stated, "invariably the last in attaining perfection; and if neglected in peace, when there is leisure, it will be impossible in the midst of the hurry and bustle of war to bring it to perfection." By the fall of 1820 Calhoun's political opponents were able to muster enough support in Congress to pass an act reducing the Army to 6,000 men. Secretary Calhoun suggested that the reduction, if it had to come, could be effected by reducing the enlisted personnel of each company to half strength. In time of war this army could be quickly expanded to a force of approximately 19,000 officers and men. Congress rejected

Calhoun's plan, however, and reduced not only the company strength but also the number of regiments. The Act of 2 March 1821, which provided for the reduction, fixed the size of the Army at 4 artillery regiments and 7 infantry regiments. Each company of infantry was to consist of 42 privates, a drop of 26 from the previous figure. The Ordnance Department, by the same act, was merged with the artillery, and only one major general was provided for. The latter provision meant the retirement of General Jackson, who preferred appointment as Governor of Florida to demotion. The northern and southern territorial divisions were abolished and replaced by an Eastern and a Western Department, under the respective commands of General Scott and Brigadier General Edmund P. Gaines. One of the serious deficiencies in the War Department during the War of 1812 had been the lack of a senior line officer in the chain of command to act as adviser to the Secretary of War and the President. Calhoun rectified this mistake by bringing Major General Jacob Brown to Washington in a position which later became known as Commanding General of the Army.

During Calhoun's tenure as Secretary of War the line of military posts and trading houses was extended into the Indian territories west of the Mississippi, the supply and purchasing services of the Army were overhauled, and an improved diet was provided for the soldiers. Under his direction, General Scott prepared a new manual of infantry tactics, which Congress eventually adopted as the standard manual for both Regular Army and militia forces. Calhoun also proposed a "school of practice" for men in service, out of which in 1824 grew the Artillery School at Fort Monroe, Virginia. Unlike modern service schools, which instruct individuals, the Artillery School began by instructing an entire unit at a time, the unit being assigned to the station for a year's tour of duty. From a long-range point of view, one of Calhoun's most important measures was an order requiring Army surgeons to keep detailed day-to-day weather records at all posts. When these records were compiled twenty years later, they constituted the basic data for the first scientific study of weather in the United States, and the most complete data of that sort in the world.

WAR WITH THE SEMINOLE INDIANS

Before Calhoun had been at the head of the War Department a full week he found it necessary to order the Army into action on the southern frontier. The Seminole Indians in lower Georgia had for some time been engaging in sporadic raids and murders, retreating after each foray into Florida where they came under the protection of the Spanish flag. A crisis was reached when 50 Americans were murdered near an Army post in Georgia. Orders were sent to General Gaines permitting him to cross into Florida after the Indians but not to attack them if they took shelter at a Spanish post. In the following month, December 1817, General Jackson himself took command of operations. Interpreting the War Department's instructions as permission to launch a full-scale invasion, he proceeded to recruit a force of about 1,500 volunteers from Kentucky, Tennessee, and Georgia and an additional 1,500 friendly Creek Indians. For three months Jackson swept across northern Florida,

burning Indian villages, cleaning up the nests of marauders, and at the same time sweeping the Spaniards out of Spanish Florida. The news put Washington in a furor. Not only had Jackson, in violation of the Constitution, raised a military force and appointed officers (including a Creek Indian brigadier general) without Congressional authorization, but his operations had jeopardized some ticklish diplomatic negotiations with Spain and American relations with England. Among Jackson's prisoners were two British subjects, one of them a former lieutenant of Marines, whom he executed for inciting the Seminole and selling them arms. The British Minister to the United States entered a prompt protest, but after investigation the British Government disavowed the actions of the two men and let the matter drop. The Spanish Government protested vigorously, especially over Jackson's high-handed capture of Pensacola and his expulsion of the Spanish authorities. President Monroe was placed in a difficult situation, for negotiations with Spain on acquiring the whole of Florida and on an agreement on the Texas boundary had been in progress for some time. A compromise was finally worked out by which the American forces were withdrawn from Florida and the captured forts restored to Spain without repudiating General Jackson. On 22 February 1819, two weeks after the evacuation, Spain ceded all of Florida to the United States, and in return the United States accepted the Sabine River as its southwestern boundary.

THE ARMY PUSHES WESTWARD

Following a pattern established before 1812, the Army pushed westward ahead of the settlers, surveying, fortifying, and building roads. The stockades and forts built and garrisoned by the Army in Iowa, Nebraska, and Kansas became the footholds of settlement on the wild frontier. Just outside their walls could be found gristmills, sawmills, and blacksmith shops, all of them erected by the troops. On the site of many of these frontier forts flourishing cities were to grow up, their foundations laid by the brave men in blue who first blazed the trail westward.

In 1832, Captain Benjamin L. E. Bonneville and a detachment of 110 men from the 7th Infantry set out to study the western Indians in their native habitat. Disguised as fur traders, Bonneville and his men made their way into the heart of the Rockies where they spent five years among the Nez Percé and Flathead Indians. It was a venture that required courage and hard work. The information they accumulated about their customs and behavior was of great benefit to the Army in its later dealings with the Indians.

In 1842, Second Lieutenant John C. Frémont of the Topographical Engineers was sent out in command of another expedition. His mission was to explore and map the Platte River country for the benefit of emigrants moving over the Oregon Trail. Results were so valuable that the next year Frémont was again sent out, this time to try to find an easier route to the West Coast. After exploring the region of the Great Salt Lake and descending the Snake and Columbia rivers, he reached Sacramento. Returning, he crossed the Rockies at Denver and arrived back at his starting point in Kansas City, Missouri, in August 1844.

A battalion of mounted rangers had been organized in

An artist's conception of a Seminole attack on an Army fort.

1832 and expanded the following year into a regiment of dragoons—the first cavalry to appear in the Regular Army since 1815. Their purpose was to protect the overland routes pushing into California and Oregon. One detachment of five companies under Colonel Stephen W. Kearny left Fort Leavenworth, Kansas, on 18 May 1845, and returned 99 days later, having covered 2,200 miles.

Territorial expansion inevitably brought conflicts with the Indians. The Sac and Fox Indians, who had been pushed out of their tribal lands in western Illinois into the prairies west of the Mississippi River, began to show signs of restlessness in 1831 and started to move back to their old home. Their chief, Black Hawk, following the example of Tecumseh, tried to organize a confederacy of the various tribes. He also sought an alliance with the British in Canada, but the British were no longer interested in stirring up the Indians. Although blocked in his diplomacy, Black Hawk led his people, including about 500 warriors, across the Mississippi into Illinois. Brigadier General Henry Atkinson, in command at Fort Leavenworth, Kansas, was ordered to take the field with regulars of the 6th Infantry; the Governor of Illinois called out a large force of militia, most of them

mounted; and General Scott was ordered from the east coast with about 1,000 infantry and artillery. After an inconclusive brush between a detachment of the militia and Black Hawk's warriors, most of the Illinois volunteers returned home, leaving General Atkinson and his regulars to deal with the Indians. On 2 August 1832, Atkinson with about 500 regulars and as many volunteers as he had been able to collect, caught up with the Indians at the confluence of the Bad Axe River and the Mississippi. In a three-hour battle, in which more than 150 of the Indians were killed and wounded, Atkinson dispersed the foe and took Black Hawk prisoner. Five days after the battle General Scott arrived on the scene, having covered the 1,800 miles from Fort Monroe in Virginia in the unbelievably short space of 18 days. Only a small remnant of his force arrived with him, however. Scott had moved by water to New York, then up the Hudson and through the Erie Canal to Buffalo. At Buffalo the force embarked on four steamers for Chicago, but Asiatic cholera broke out and by the time Chicago was reached, one-third of the men had died or were incapacitated by the disease. Many others deserted in panic and helped to spread the epidemic.

Fort Brooke on Tampa Bay, established in 1824 when the Army began to move the Seminole from north to south Florida. The fort was also used during the Second Seminole War.

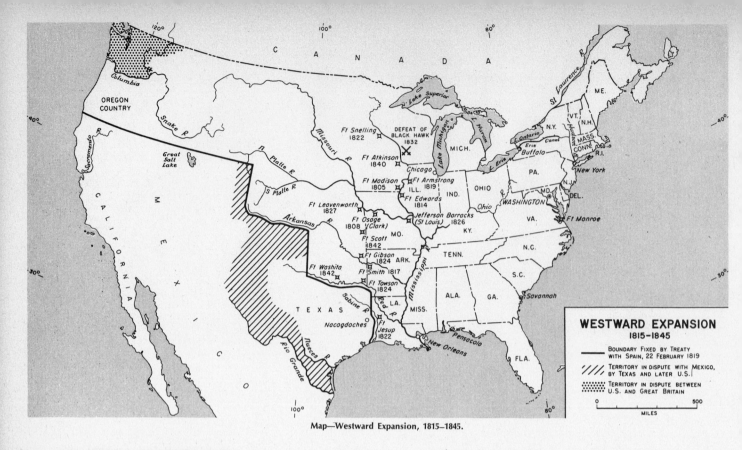

Map—Westward Expansion, 1815–1845.

WESTWARD EXPANSION
1815-1845

——— BOUNDARY FIXED BY TREATY
WITH SPAIN, 22 FEBRUARY 1819

/// TERRITORY IN DISPUTE WITH MEXICO,
BY TEXAS AND LATER U.S.

··· TERRITORY IN DISPUTE BETWEEN
U.S. AND GREAT BRITAIN

0   500
MILES

THE SECOND SEMINOLE WAR

On the southern frontier, the First Seminole War had been different from the western Indian wars in that it was an episode of the disintegration of the Spanish empire and part of the unfinished business of the War of 1812. The Second Seminole War, like the other Indian wars, began when the Seminole, after giving up their lands by treaty, refused to move out. The few U.S. troops stationed in Florida were badly reduced in December, 1835, when a detachment of 110 regulars was ambushed and slain; a second detachment of Florida volunteers and a few regulars were severely mauled. Although the part of Florida where conflict had broken out was in the Western Department, commanded by General Gaines, the War Department immediately sent General Scott to direct the operations against

the Seminole, principally because Gaines was expected to have his hands full with troubles that were brewing along the Texas frontier. While Scott was at Savannah assembling an army and planning an impressive three-pronged offensive, Gaines raised a force of about 1,000 men, mostly Louisiana volunteers, and embarked for Florida without waiting for instructions from the War Department. When he did receive word of Scott's appointment, Gaines ignored it, commandeered supplies that had been reserved for Scott, continued his advance, launched an attack and was saved only by the timely arrival of one of Scott's subordinates with reinforcements and more supplies. Gaines then returned to New Orleans, reporting that he had brought peace to Florida. Gaines was wrong, and when General Scott took to the field several months later with a

Major Stephen H. Long meets with a group of Pawnee Indians during his two-year (1819—1820) scientific expedition to the Far West. He returned with the report that the Great Plains area was "almost wholly unfit for cultivation."

smaller force than he had originally planned, he was unable to subdue a sizable force of Indians.

Over the next six years, three other commanders—Major General Thomas S. Jesup, Brigadier General Zachary Taylor, and Brigadier General Walker A. Armistead—tried and failed to drive the Seminole out of their dismal bogs and palmetto swamps. Finally, a campaign of extermination, like those waged by the early colonists, succeeded in routing the Indians out of the swamps and permitted the war to be officially ended. A total of something less than 5,000 regulars and perhaps 20,000 short-term volunteers had been engaged in the effort against approximately 1,000 Seminole warriors. Nearly 1,500 men had lost their lives in battle or from disease in order that 3,200 half-starved Indians might be shipped west.

Midway in the Seminole War trouble developed with the Creek Indians of southern Georgia and the Cherokee farther north. After a brief, bloodless campaign the Creek were forced to surrender and move west of the Mississippi, but the Cherokee presented a more formidable problem. More numerous than the Creek, civilized, led by educated chiefs, the Cherokee had adopted the white man's customs and had friends in Washington. But gold had been discovered on the Cherokee lands, and the whites were determined to turn the Indians out. In the summer of 1838 General Scott was instructed to remove the 15,000 Cherokee to lands in the present State of Oklahoma. With 2 regiments of regulars and a force of Georgia volunteers, Scott moved into the Cherokee country. Although the situation was tense, he succeeded, through tact and careful attention to the Indians' comfort, in persuading most of them to emigrate peacefully.

THE ARMY INCREASES ITS STRENGTH

To meet the needs of the Seminole War, Congress in 1838 authorized an increase in the strength of the Army, the first substantial increase since the War of 1812. It brought the

The Army's famous explorer, Colonel John C. Frémont, is planting the American flag on a high peak in the Rocky Mountains in this somewhat imaginative lithograph.

A pictorial representation of the opening of the last big battle of the Black Hawk shows soldiers on the deck of the steamer "Warrior" firing a cannon at an Indian raft. Shortly after the battle, which took place at the mouth of the Bad Axe River in August 1832, Black Hawk surrendered.

authorized strength up to nearly 13,000 by expanding the existing regiments and adding a new regiment of infantry. The Army then consisted of 8 regiments of infantry, 4 of artillery, 2 of dragoons (the second of which had been authorized in 1836), and the Corps of Engineers. Immediately after the Seminole War officially ended, the authorized strength was cut back to about 8,600 men by reducing the rank-and-file strength of the regiments. One of the regiments of dragoons was dismounted and converted into a rifle regiment, only to be remounted two years later, in April, 1844. Actual strength continued to be about 50 to 60 percent of the authorized strength, and in 1845, on the eve of the Mexican War, the Army numbered only 5,300 men. However, the principle of an expandible army appeared to have become firmly established in place of the elimination of units and the creation of new ones.

To provide men and replacements, a badly needed reform of the recruiting system had been undertaken in 1822. Until then, all recruiting had been done by the individual regiments, with widely unequal and not generally successful results. In an effort to bring the Army up to strength, General Brown in July 1822 instructed General Scott, commander of the Eastern Department, to open recruiting depots at New York, Philadelphia, and Baltimore for the purpose of enlisting men for the Army at large, not for specific units. The men accepted at these depots were given some training and then assigned to regiments on orders from the War Department. The General Recruiting Service, as it was known, immediately proved more successful than regimental recruiting. In the two years following its establishment, six additional depots were opened, three of them in the Western Department. Regimental recruiting continued along with the new system, and in times of emergency the General Recruiting Service also faced competition from volunteer units, but the system had been established on a solid footing, and proved its worth when the Mexican War made rapid expansion of the Army necessary.

Progress was also made in maintaining a corps of professionally trained officers. The Military Academy at West Point survived the disorganization and neglect brought by the War of 1812 and the removal of the wartime superintendant, Captain Alden Partridge. The difficulties incident to the superintendent's removal seem to have stemmed primarily from his interference with the faculty. Although popular with the cadets, he was a poor administrator. Under his successor, Captain Sylvanus Thayer, the Academy flourished. Thayer's great achievement was in organizing the academic course, a program of progressive instruction in French, mathematics, chemistry, the other physical sciences, and engineering, which presented these subjects as professional tools as well as for their cultural value. Thayer brought order to the disorder into which the Academy had fallen, allayed much of the opposition to the Academy within the Army, and established its traditions. By 1845 approximately 500 graduates of the West Point institution were in active service. Another 500 had resigned to enter civilian life, where they helped in building the first railroad and telegraph systems, laid out the new towns on the frontier, and constructed highways, canals, and bridges.

Although Indian affairs and a developing crisis along the Texas border occupied the immediate attention of the Army during most of the thirty years after 1815, the major problem of national defense involved the possibility of war with either England or France. The execution of a systematic and extensive program of harbor fortifications and the manning of the completed forts was the Army's responsibility. It was a weighty responsibility, since the coastline was long and the harbors and seaports were many. The fact that local workmen found employment on the construction projects usually meant that it was not difficult to obtain funds from Congress, and annual appropriations for the purpose ranged from $400,000 to $600,000. By 1826, 18 harbors and ports from the Penobscot River in Maine to the mouth of the Mississippi had been fortified with a total of 31 works of varying size. Although some were fairly elaborate, most fortifications consisted of sloping earthworks covered with grass and backed by stone or brick walls. By 1843 the harbor defense program had been extended to 40 coastal areas, and 69 fortifications either existed or were under construction. Two noticeable developments in the 1830's and 1840's were the greater emphasis on heavy guns (24- and 32-pounders and 8-inch heavy howitzers) and the declining importance attached to protecting the landward approaches to the forts.

TROUBLE WITH MEXICO

The military problems of the United States were complicated by the crumbling of the Spanish empire in America. Where this process created a vacuum, as in Florida and Louisiana, the United States had moved in. Elsewhere the process was hastened by the outbreak of revolution in the Spanish colonies, and in 1822, after the ratification of the Adams-Onis Treaty, the United States became the first nation of the world to recognize the independence of Spain's former colonies, including Mexico. Claiming as its northern boundary the line fixed by the Adams-Onis Treaty, Mexico adopted an immigration policy designed to attract American settlers to the uninhabited plains of Texas. Between the years 1825 and 1830, approximately 15,000 immigrants with several thousand Negro slaves poured into northern Mexico from the United States. In the end the policy was unsuccessful in cementing Texas to Mexico. The refusal of the United States to confirm the Adams-Onis boundary with Mexico, the persistent efforts of the United States to purchase part of Texas, the inability of American immigrants to cut their old ties completely, and the instability of Mexican politics resulted in 1830 in a reversal of Mexican policy, expressed in severe restrictions on immigration and landownership. The resulting discontent among the Texans flared into open revolt in 1835, and in the following year Texas proclaimed its independence. The Mexicans, under General Antonio López de Santa Anna, moved against the rebels and destroyed the garrison in the Alamo after a heroic siege that lasted 13 days. American volunteers rushed across the Sabine River to help the Texans, and for about five months during the summer and fall of 1836 a regiment of the Regular Army occupied the town of Nacogdoches, some 50 miles south of the boundary. On 21 April 1836, in the Battle of San Jacinto, the Texan general Sam Houston, with 743 raw troops, decisively defeated a force of about 1,600 veteran

An "Illustrated London News" engraving depicts a demonstration in Jersey City in 1845 in favor of the annexation of Texas. Similar demonstrations were held in other cities.

General Antonio López de Santa Anna.

Mexicans under Santa Anna, who was captured the next day. The United States recognized Texas as an independent republic in March, 1837.

In declaring their independence, most Texans meant only independence from Mexican rule. They hoped and expected that they would speedily be annexed to the United States, but the annexation question became tied up with the slavery controversy in the United States, and Texas became an issue of sectional and partisan politics. During the almost ten years that Texas existed as an independent nation Mexico made sporadic attempts to recover its lost province. Border raids marked by extreme ruthlessness and ferocity by both Texans and Mexicans kept the country in constant turmoil, particularly along the Rio Grande River.

Sam Houston.

An artist's conception of the action at the Alamo on 6 March 1836, the day it was captured by the Mexicans.

THE RED CROSS AND THE ARMY

THE AMERICAN NATIONAL RED CROSS

The American National Red Cross is chartered under the act of Congress approved 5 January 1905, pursuant to the treaties of Geneva or the treaties of the Red Cross to which the United States is a party.

The United States congressional charter charges the American National Red Cross with (1) furnishing volunteer aid to the sick and wounded of the armed forces and other victims of war in accordance with the spirit and conditions of the above treaties; (2) acting as a medium of voluntary relief and communication between the people of the United States and their armed forces; and (3) providing a system of national and international relief to mitigate the sufferings caused by pestilence, famine, fire, floods, and other great calamities, and devising and carrying out measures for their prevention.

The Red Cross is a membership organization supported entirely by voluntary contributions. There are 153 volunteers to every career worker.

In the discharge of responsibilities imposed by Federal statute and under military regulations, the American Red Cross acts in matters of voluntary relief and as a medium of communication between the people of the United States and members of its armed forces wherever they are stationed.

One of the first American Red Cross ambulance stations (1870).

Henry P. Davison, who in 1918 proposed the organization of the League of Red Cross Societies "for the promotion of good will wherever human life exists." Davison had been a partner in the banking firm of J. P. Morgan and Company before becoming chairman of the American Red Cross War Council in 1917. It was Davison's hope that the National Red Cross Societies would cooperate to serve humanity in time of peace as they had done during World War I.

American Red Cross services to the armed forces are free of charge and relate to the welfare of men and women in uniform and their families. These activities include social services for able-bodied and hospitalized service men and women and their dependents through field directors at military installations and in hospitals and through chapters in civilian communities.

Field directors stationed or providing service itinerantly at United States Army, Navy, Marine Corps, Air Force, and Coast Guard stations and hospitals at home and overseas, and working in cooperation with Service to Military Families in chapters throughout the United States and its possessions, provide a constant two-way flow of service. The American Red Cross contributes to the morale of service men and women and their families by helping with personal and family problems, furnishing financial assistance in emergencies, supplementing the military recreation program for able-bodied personnel on active duty in certain isolated areas overseas, and providing a program of social welfare services and medically approved recreation for the sick and injured in hospitals of the armed forces. Volunteers are recruited and trained by the Red Cross to take part in all of these services.

In time of war these Red Cross services are necessarily adjusted and expanded to meet the extraordinary needs that develop.

Service to Military Families is the program through which the Red Cross carries out in communities its responsibility for specific services to members of the armed forces and their families. In addition, it provides specific services to veterans and their dependents and to the dependents of deceased servicemen and veterans. These services are given without charge through the combined efforts of chapters and the national organization to assure a nationwide service that is uniform and effective.

The Service to Military Families program includes counseling in personal and family problems, reporting and communications service, emergency financial assistance, assistance in applying for Goverment benefits, and referral to other resources.

The Service to Military Families program of financial assistance recognizes priority of responsibility for assistance to wives and children of men in the armed forces, to veterans with disabilities resulting from military service, and to dependents of servicemen whose death resulted from military service.

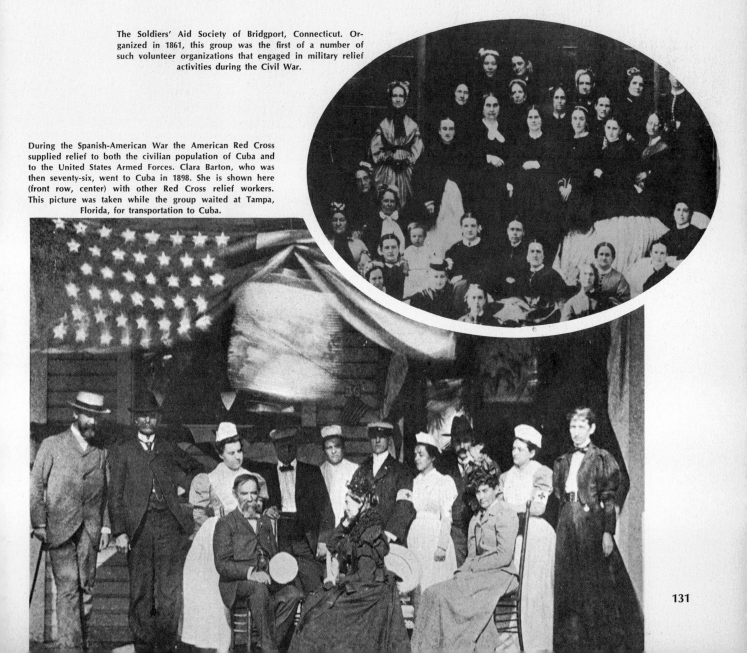

The Soldiers' Aid Society of Bridgport, Connecticut. Organized in 1861, this group was the first of a number of such volunteer organizations that engaged in military relief activities during the Civil War.

During the Spanish-American War the American Red Cross supplied relief to both the civilian population of Cuba and to the United States Armed Forces. Clara Barton, who was then seventy-six, went to Cuba in 1898. She is shown here (front row, center) with other Red Cross relief workers. This picture was taken while the group waited at Tampa, Florida, for transportation to Cuba.

Miss Jane Delano, founder of the American Red Cross Nursing Service (front row, center), and a group of her nurses aboard the S.S. "Red Cross" in September 1914. The nurses were part of 16 hospital units sent to Europe by the American Red Cross during the first year of the war. Each unit consisted of 3 surgeons and 12 nurses. One or more units was assigned to each of the belligerents. The S.S. "Red Cross" was especially chartered to carry medical personnel and supplies to the warring countries. It sailed under the Red Cross and American flags.

The first canteens operated by the American Red Cross in France were set up at the request of the French Government to serve French soldiers. Nearly a million men in transit or on leave in Paris were fed each month at the canteens. Here two canteen workers serve coffee and doughnuts to U.S. Army soldiers. During World War I the American Red Cross operated 130 canteens in France. The largest provided hotel facilities; the smallest were the "kitchens on wheels" that dispensed bouillon, coffee, tea, and cocoa in areas close to the front lines. These Red Cross canteens were popular with Allied as well as American servicemen.

This American Red Cross ambulance was used in the closing months of World War I and later for relief work in France.

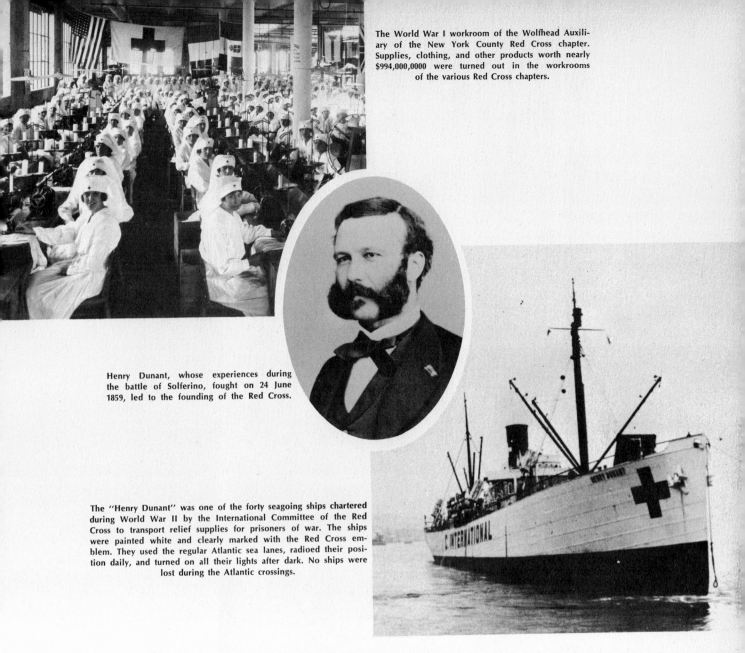

The World War I workroom of the Wolfhead Auxiliary of the New York County Red Cross chapter. Supplies, clothing, and other products worth nearly $994,000,0000 were turned out in the workrooms of the various Red Cross chapters.

Henry Dunant, whose experiences during the battle of Solferino, fought on 24 June 1859, led to the founding of the Red Cross.

The "Henry Dunant" was one of the forty seagoing ships chartered during World War II by the International Committee of the Red Cross to transport relief supplies for prisoners of war. The ships were painted white and clearly marked with the Red Cross emblem. They used the regular Atlantic sea lanes, radioed their position daily, and turned on all their lights after dark. No ships were lost during the Atlantic crossings.

Field directors stationed at Veterans Administration offices advise and assist Red Cross chapter workers in the preparation and development of evidence and other factual material required in individual cases to establish eligibility for veterans' benefits. They also appear before VA rating and appeal boards in behalf of veterans who have designated the American Red Cross as their representative. The national organization also provides for counsel and representation at the request of chapters in cases subject to the jurisdiction of the discharge review and retirement review boards of the armed services.

In VA hospitals, the Red Cross maintains a nationwide program of volunteer service to patients, with trained volunteers from local chapters assisting VA staff in hospital recreation, welfare, nursing, and rehabilitation programs.

At the request of the Department of Defense, the American Red Cross established the Supplemental Recreational Activities Overseas program. As the name implies, it is a recreational program planned for the personnel of the armed forces in selected overseas areas and supplemental to existing military and community facilities.

In Korea, clubmobile teams take recreational activities to the men of the Eighth Army in isolated areas.

In France, Morocco, and Turkey, Red Cross Centers located in selected communities adjacent to United States military installations aim to develop better understanding by providing opportunities for servicemen to participate in recreational activities with residents of the host community.

The Red Cross Blood Program makes blood and blood derivatives available, without charge for the products themselves, to people needing them. The program provides whole blood to hospitals in participating communities and blood derivatives to physicians and hospitals through Red Cross facilities and State health departments. The program's network of blood-collecting facilities is prepared to expand rapidly in any national emergency. A standby contract has been signed with the Department of Defense that designates the Red Cross as the coordinating agency to meet the blood requests of the Department in the event of a national crisis.

During World War II, as in past wars, the Red Cross emblem did not always guarantee protection. This American ambulance was hit by German shells during fighting in the Ardennes region.

Red Cross girl writing letter for wounded soldier of World War II. In addition to performing duties such as this, the American Red Cross operated clubs and motion picture theatres for the soldiers. The clubs served coffee, doughnuts, and ice cream, and sponsored musical programs, vaudeville shows, and dances. All was free of charge.

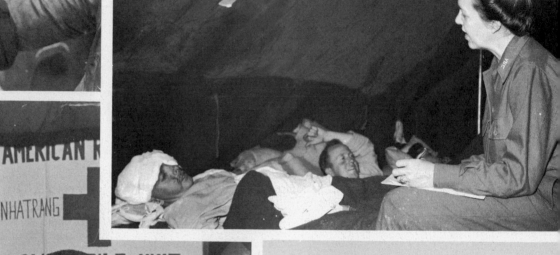

A lively jazz session in an American Red Cross center helps GI's forget about fighting.

Dr. Junod talking with a U.S. Army prisoner of war in Stalag VII A Moosburg, Germany, in 1943.

Dr. Roland Marti talks with a group of prisoners during a visit to Stalag XVII B during World War II.

The red cross on this helicopter evacuating wounded men during the Korean War places it under the protection of the Geneva Conventions.

One of the Red Cross medicosocial teams talks with prisoners of war in a camp in North Korea.

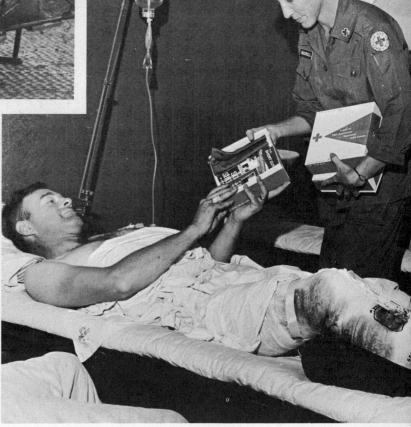

American Red Cross hospital field director Barbara J. Maxwell gives a Red Cross comfort kit to Staff Sergeant William C. Mullen. The kit contains soap, toothbrush and paste, razor, and other items for hospitalized servicemen who have lost their personal effects. The 1st Cavalry Division squad leader was in the 85th Evacuation Hospital in Qui Nhon after his leg was badly injured in a mine explosion.

The delegates of the International Committee of the Red Cross made more than 11,000 visits to prison camps during World War II. Their periodic visits, which involved the inspection of camp facilities and talks with prisoners, did much to ensure the observance of the Geneva Convention of 1929 regulating the treatment of prisoners of war.

THE INTERNATIONAL RED CROSS

The Red Cross had its beginning in the determination of one man to do something to relieve the suffering of the wounded in time of war. He was Jean Henri Dunant, a young Swiss businessman. In the summer of 1859 Henri Dunant left his home in Geneva to travel to northern Italy to negotiate with representatives of the French Emperor Napolean III in connection with a project involving the construction of windmills in Algeria.

Napoleon III had moved with his army into Italy to help the Sardinians in their attempt to regain their independence from Austria. When Henri Dunant arrived at Solferino on 24 June 1859, one of the fiercest battles of the century was raging. The injured were far too numerous for the meager medical facilities that had been set up for their care.

The fighting ceased at nightfall after more than fifteen hours of death and destruction. Some field hospitals had

One of the joint Red Cross teams
set up by the Korean armistice
visits Prisoner of War
Camp No. 1 in North Korea.

These happy American prisoners of war
are answering a last roll call before
being returned to the United Nations Command.

been set up during the day in houses, churches, and out in the open, but they were soon swamped by the wounded who needed help. Thousands more remained on the battle-field unable to reach the field hospitals. After the fighting was over and the French Army had won a costly victory, an attempt was made by both sides to collect the wounded. The search went on all night long, but in the morning there were still wounded lying with the dead on the battlefield.

Every building in the surrounding area was turned into a receiving station for the casualties. The largest number were taken to Castiglione, where the wounded overflowed into the streets and courtyards of the town. The few doctors worked without ceasing, but there were far too many wounded for them to handle. Food and water were available, but there was no way to bring them to the injured.

Henri Dunant was in Castiglione on that dreadful day. He went from one wounded man to another doing what he could to ease the terrible suffering. His one thought was to do what he could for the injured. The town of Castiglione was completely unprepared for the task of handling the hundreds of wounded men that filled its buildings and streets. Many of the townspeople were anxious to help but their efforts lacked any organization. This Henri Dunant set out to supply. He divided the workers into groups and gave each group a specific job to do. He impressed upon them that all the wounded were to be helped, friend and foe alike.

As the days became weeks the wounded who survived began to leave Castiglione for hospitals where they could receive proper medical treatment.

When he could do no more in Castiglione, Henri Dunant returned to Switzerland. His experiences in Castiglione haunted him; he could think of nothing else. He thought not only of the wounded he had seen after the Battle of Solferino, but also of the men who would certainly be wounded in any future war. At Castiglione they had succeeded in saving perhaps as many as 5,000 men. But 40,000 had been killed or wounded. If the help that had finally been available at Castiglione had been organized and ready at the beginning of the battle, how many more lives might have been saved?

Henri Dunant set about writing a description of his experiences during the Battle of Solferino and its aftermath. Three years later, in 1862, when he was thirty-four years old, he published **A Memory of Solferino.**

Henri Dunant's great contribution to the welfare of his fellowmen was his suggestion in **A Memory of Solferino** that in time of peace societies be formed to prepare for the care of the wounded in time of war, and that some sort of international body be set up to formulate the rules that would make such care possible anywhere in the world.

With much support behind his proposal, Dunant did not have to wait long for some action to be taken. In February 1863, the president of the Public Welfare Society of Geneva, a local philanthropic and charitable organization, appointed a temporary "Committee of Five" to take whatever steps it deemed necessary to begin the task of organizing societies of the kind Dunant had in mind. Before their first meeting ended, they had decided that an international conference should be held to formulate a plan for organizing national relief societies.

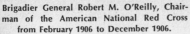

Brigadier General Robert M. O'Reilly, Chairman of the American National Red Cross from February 1906 to December 1906.

Plasma was one of the essential supplies put ashore during the Normandy invasion. Here, a casualty receives a transfusion on one of the invasion beaches. 13,000,000 pints of blood were collected by the American Red Cross during World War II.

Major General George W. Davis, Chairman of the American National Red Cross from December 1906 to November 1915.

Ex-presidents William Howard Taft and Woodrow Wilson are among the audience addressed by Mabel T. Boardman, Secretary of the Central Committee, American Red Cross. Taft was the head of the American Red Cross from November 1915 to January 1919.

General James F. Collins became the president of the American Red Cross on 1 April 1964. He was the Commander in Chief of the U.S. Army, Pacific, at the time of his appointment to the position as head of the American Red Cross. He is shown here (right), shortly before his retirement from the Army, meeting with the president of the Japanese Red Cross, Mr. Tadatsugu Shimadzu.

137

The first of two historic Red Cross conferences opened at Geneva on October 26, 1863. Dunant had toured the capitals of Europe, seeking support for the conference and extending invitations to attend. The other members of the committee meanwhile worked on preparations. Thirty-six delegates from fourteen European states were on hand when the conference began. In just four days they succeeded in drafting a series of resolutions and recommendations that would provide the basis for organizing national relief societies for the care of the wounded in wartime.

The delegates discussed the danger to the volunteers on the battlefield unless they could be readily identified as noncombatants. It was recalled that at Solferino a black flag had been flown over the first-aid posts, field ambulances, and hospitals. Both sides had agreed that they would not fire in the general direction of the black flags. However, in many countries the black flag denoted death, so the delegates rejected the idea of using it. What they wanted was a new symbol, one of life and hope.

The Committee decided that the volunteers should wear a white armband emblazoned with a red cross. The same emblem was to appear on all ambulances and hospitals.

It was inevitable that the symbol chosen would become quickly associated in the public mind with the organizations employing it and that the title "Society for the Relief of Wounded Combatants" would be replaced by the more easily remembered name, "Red Cross Society."

The arguments the delegates used must have been very persuasive, for Article 7 of the First Geneva Convention provides that "a distinctive and uniform flag shall be adopted for hospitals, ambulances, and evacuation parties [and that] an armlet may be worn by personnel enjoying neutrality but its issue shall be left to the military authorities [and that] both flag and armlet shall bear a red cross on a white ground." Except in the countries that use the red crescent or the red lion and sun as symbols, the medical services of the armed forces of the governments bound by the Geneva Conventions use the red cross in a white field as an identifying and protective symbol for official medical personnel and chaplains, vehicles used for the transportation of the wounded, hospital ships, trains, and planes, dressing stations and field and base hospitals, and neutralized buildings or zones.

Diplomats of fifteen European states were present on 8 August 1864, when the second historic conference opened at Geneva. After two weeks of work the delegates succeeded in drafting a treaty, or convention, that, when ratified by their governments, would bind them to accord humane treatment to the sick and wounded of the armies in time of war and to protect all those who were caring for the wounded. This agreement became known as the First Geneva Convention to differentiate it from the agreements that were made in later years. Twelve countries ratified the treaty on 22 August 1864. Others followed until by 1870 every major power and most of the smaller states of Europe had signed.

The United States was represented at the 1864 conference, but its representatives did not take an official part in the discussions.

After the 1864 conference, the Committee of Five took over the task of ensuring the observance of the Geneva Convention. In 1876 its name was changed to the International Committee of the Red Cross. Its membership has been enlarged, but it remains an independent body composed exclusively of Swiss citizens with a permanent headquarters in Geneva. The term "international" applies to its activities rather than to its membership. One of the Committee's most important functions is to see to it that the Red Cross societies of the various countries adhere to the four basic principles upon which the whole Red Cross movement is based and without which it could not hope to achieve its goal of relieving human suffering throughout the world.

Impartiality is the first of these Red Cross principles. Help is extended to the nationals of all countries without regard to race, color, or creed. Closely related to this is the tenet that the work of the Red Cross is universal in nature, reaching into every country no matter how remote. The third principle stresses the fact that although the National Red Cross societies consult and work with government agencies, they must remain independent of government control if they are to carry out the essential work of the Red Cross. Finally, the National Societies are to be strictly independent of one another, but they must stand ready to help should another National Society need it.

The International Committee of the Red Cross is one of the three bodies that make up the International Red Cross. The other two are the National Red Cross Societies of all the nations that accept the Geneva Conventions, and the League of Red Cross Societies. Each of these groups has its own special duties, which can be carried out quite separately. Sometimes they work jointly as the International Red Cross. For example, when fighting broke out in Korea, a Swiss delegate was sent by the International Committee of the Red Cross to see what help could be given to prisoners of war, and the League of Red Cross Societies appealed for teams from National Red Cross Societies for relief work among the civilian population.

Gradually a set of standards was drawn up which the national organizations had to meet if they wished to be recognized as National Red Cross Societies. Today a Society must use the title and emblem of the Red Cross, only in accordance with the terms of the Geneva Conventions.

In order to do their work the National Societies have to have the confidence and cooperation of their governments and at the same time they must retain their independence of action. One of the ways of achieving this is for the Societies to place themselves under the patronage of the president or the sovereign of their country. In monarchies the president of the National Society is usually a close relative of the sovereign. This is true in Thailand, Belgium, Iran, and Monaco. In Thailand the Queen is the President of the National Society. Princess Grace, the wife of the ruler of Monaco, is the President of the Monaco Red Cross Society, and Prince Albert, the brother of the King of Belgium, is President of the Belgian Red Cross. In republics the presidents of the National Societies are often leading citizens well known for their executive ability. In the United States General Alfred Gruenther, who was formerly Commander-in-Chief of the forces of the North Atlantic Treaty Organization, was head of the American Red Cross. And in 1965, retired Army General James F. Collins became the president, taking General Gruenther's place.

The third part of the International Red Cross, the League of Red Cross Societies, was organized immediately after World War I. During the war the efficient and humanitarian work of the Red Cross had won it worldwide approval and support. Mr. Henry P. Davison, who was chairman of the War Council of the American Red Cross, pointed out how splendidly the National Societies of the different countries had cooperated to relieve the suffering caused by the war, and proposed that they should unite themselves in a federa-

tion to maintain the same spirit of cooperation in peacetime. His proposal met with approval of the National Red Cross Societies who realized that such cooperation would increase the efficiency of their operations. On 1 February 1919 they formed a Committee of Red Cross Societies with representatives of the American, British, French, Italian, and Japanese Societies as members. The Committee was charged with working out and presenting to the Red Cross Societies a "programme of action on behalf of the general welfare of humanity."

The League represents the National Societies at the international level and encourages the establishment and development of new societies to further spread the work of the Red Cross throughout the world.

General George C. Marshall, president of the American Red Cross from October 1949 to December 1950, is shown here with General of the Army Omar N. Bradley during an Armed Forces blood donor program.

General Alfred M. Gruenther, president of the American Red Cross from January 1957 to March 1964, is seen here (right) with President John F. Kennedy during a White House historical conference.

The staff at the League's Geneva headquarters is drawn from its member societies, and they are rotated periodically. While in Geneva they work on an international level; whatever animosities that might exist between the citizens of various countries have to be put aside. It is not unusual for a conference to take place between nations of East and West Germany or the two Vietnams. In the case of East and West Germany, the two National Societies have been able to reach an agreement through the League and the International Committee of the Red Cross on such matters as the repatriation of prisoners and the reuniting of refugees with their families even though the two governments concerned do not officially recognize each other.

139

The staff at the League's Geneva headquarters is drawn from its member societies, and they are rotated periodically. While in Geneva they work on an international level; whatever animosities that might exist between the citizens of various countries have to be put aside. It is not unusual for a conference to take place between nations of East and West Germany or the two Vietnams. In the case of East and West Germany, the two National Societies have been able to reach an agreement through the League and the International Committee of the Red Cross on such matters as the repatriation of prisoners and the reuniting of refugees with their families even though the two governments concerned do not officially recognize each other.

Today over 90 National Societies are part of the League; their total membership has reached more than 130,000,000, and the number continues to grow.

More than a century has elapsed since the signing of the First Geneva Convention in 1864. That Convention has been supplemented by additional Conventions which have been agreed to by almost all the governments of the world. The Red Cross and the Geneva Conventions are closely interrelated. The Red Cross initiated the Conventions and worked for their ratifications as part of its efforts on behalf of the victims of war and disaster.

The First Geneva Convention in 1864, which was concerned primarily with land warfare, called for humane treatment of the wounded and protection for those who care for them. In 1899 the International Committee was instrumental in extending the provisions of the 1864 Convention to naval warfare. This agreement was known as the Hague Convention.

In 1906, when the original Geneva Convention was revised to bring it up to date, the humanitarian principle that had given rise to the Red Cross was clearly stated in the first article:

"Officers and soldiers and other persons officially attached to the armed forces who are wounded and sick shall be respected and cared for, without distinction of nationality, by the belligerent in whose power they may be."

The Hague Convention of 1907 also dealt with the treatment of prisoners of war, a matter in which the International Committee of the Red Cross had long been interested. The Regulations annexed to the IVth Hague Convention of 1907 freed prisoners of war from the arbitrary treatment to which they had hitherto been subjected. "Prisoners of War," read one article, "are in the power of the hostile Government, but not of the individuals or corps who capture them. They must be humanely treated." Disarmed, the prisoner of war was no longer at the mercy of his captor; he had a legal status.

Two articles have a special bearing on Red Cross work. One called for an official prisoner-of-war information bureau in each country, and the other permitted societies for aid to prisoners of war to pursue their work of mercy within the bounds set by military necessity.

After World War I, the International Committee of the Red Cross went to work on still another revision of the Geneva Convention. The result was the two Geneva Conventions of 1929. The first, for the "Relief of the Wounded and Sick in Armies in the Field," was a more complete and definite form of the 1906 Convention which it replaced.

The other, a big step forward in the field of international law, was the "Prisoners of War Code."

The war had indicated the need for more explicit regulations governing the care and treatment of prisoners. The 1929 Convention took the section of the Hague Regulations of 1907 relating to prisoners of war, and expanded it into 97 articles. It began by reaffirming the principle: "Prisoners of war are in the power of the hostile Government, but not of the individuals or corps who capture them." Some of its other provisions were:

"They shall at all times be humanely treated and protected, particularly against acts of violence, from insults and from public curiosity.

"Measures of reprisal against them are forbidden.

"Prisoners of war are entitled to respect for their persons and honor. Women shall be treated with all consideration due to their sex.

"Prisoners retain their full civil capacity."

The Prisoners Convention tried to fill up the gaps left in the text of 1907, seeking to define not so much the duties of prisoners of war as their rights and the obligations of the detaining power with regard to them.

One part of the 1929 Convention directly concerned Red Cross organizations and especially the International Committee. This was Part VI, entitled, "Bureaus of Relief and Information concerning Prisoners of War." Article 77 called for the establishment of official information bureaus and described in detail the way in which they should function. Article 78 repeated the authorization given to the recognized relief societies by the 1907 Convention. Article 79, which was new, sanctioned an earlier undertaking of the International Committee: the establishment of a Central Information Agency. The International Committee was mentioned twice more: in Article 87, which says that in the event of dispute between the belligerents regarding the application of the Convention, the Protecting Power may submit for the approval of the Powers in dispute the name of a person belonging to a neutral Power or a person "nominated by the International Red Cross Committee," who shall be invited to take part in the conference of the representatives of the belligerents in dispute, and in Article 88 on the organization of control: "The foregoing provisions do not constitute any obstacle to the humanitarian work which the International Committee of the Red Cross may perform for the protection of prisoners of war with the consent of the belligerants concerned."

The years immediately after World War II saw another revision of the Geneva Conventions. The International Committee of the Red Cross drew up a series of changes and additions based on its experiences during the war. These were presented at a diplomatic convention in Geneva in 1949 which was attended by representatives of over sixty nations. There were actually four separate revised Conventions. The First dealt with the "amelioration of the wounded and sick in armed forces in the field"; the Second Convention with the "amelioration of the condition of wounded, sick and shipwrecked members of the armed forces at sea"; the Third with the "treatment of prisoners of war"; and the Fourth with the "protection of civilian persons in time of war." These four Geneva Conventions of 1949, ratified by most of the nations of the world are in force today.

An engraving from "The Journal of William H. Richardson, a Private Soldier in the Campaign of New and Old Mexico" depicts a scene familiar to the inhabitants of Army camps during the Mexican War—soldiers washing clothes.

CHAPTER 6

THE MEXICAN WAR

War with Mexico was the inevitable result of the annexation of Texas to the United States because the United States then inherited the Texans' conflict with Mexico. The Mexican Government, which had served notice that the annexation of Texas would be considered an act of war, broke off diplomatic relations with Washington on 28 March 1845. President James Polk replied by dispatching troops into Texas and deploying the Navy along the Mexican coast. By midsummer of 1845, nearly 4,000 troops of the Regular Army plus a few mounted volunteers had been assembled between the Sabine and Nueces rivers under the command of Brigadier General Zachary Taylor, with advance headquarters at Corpus Christi.

Meanwhile, Polk tried to restore diplomatic dealings with Mexico. When Texas was part of Mexico, the southern boundary of the province had been the Neuces River, but on declaring independence the Texans had claimed the Rio Grande as their boundary. Polk sent a representative to Mexico with an offer to release Mexico from the payment of old claims in return for recognition of the Rio Grande as the southern boundary of the United States, but Mexico refused to receive him. As soon as the news of the rebuff reached Washington, the President ordered General Taylor to move into the disputed territory and establish himself on the Rio Grande.

Taylor led his command south to Point Isabel, while a fleet of supply vessels followed along the coast. After establishing his main base at Point Isabel, Taylor advanced to the Rio Grande with almost his entire force, and proceeded to build a fort opposite the Mexican town of Matamoros. He rejected the Mexican commander's demand that the Americans retire forthwith to Corpus Christi, and for almost two months the two forces watched each other across the river·while continuing their preparations for whatever might happen. Taylor's troops were regulars: the 3d, 5th, 6th, 7th, and 8th Infantry Regiments, Major Samuel Ringgold's "Flying Artillery," parts of two other artillery regiments, and a regiment of dragoons. All were understrength. Many of the enlisted men were of foreign birth. Some of them were unable to resist the temptation of the free land and immunity that Mexico offered to American deserters, a problem with which General Scott also had to contend later in the war.

Except for a few companies armed with a new percussion-cap musket, Taylor's men carried flintlocks that were little different from those used in the Revolution and the War of 1812. The troops were well officered, although few of the officers had ever commanded as large a body of men as they had under them on the Rio Grande. The elite of the army—at least it considered itself such—was the light, mobile horse artillery, trained in rapid battlefield maneuver. Commanded by Major Ringgold, the horse artillery was led by young officers, graduates of West Point, as most of the subalterns of the Regular Army were. The eyes and ears of the army were a volunteer force of Texas Rangers.

Map—The Mexican War.

THE MEXICAN WAR
1846–1847

→ AXIS OF U.S. ADVANCE
▨ HIGH GROUND ABOVE 6000 FEET

0   100   200   300
MILES

THE MEXICANS CROSS THE RIO GRANDE

As the Mexican forces in Matamoros grew in strength, they began to infiltrate across the river, north and south of the American fort, where some patrol actions occurred. The first clash in which Taylor's regulars were involved took place on 25 April 1846, when an American cavalry patrol was attacked north of the fort, and all the men killed or captured.

Concerned by the threat to his lightly held base and line of communication, General Taylor on 1 May withdrew the bulk of the army to Point Isabel. To hold the fort opposite Matamoros he left behind a small detachment of artillery and the 7th Infantry, under the command of Major Jacob Brown, with instructions to fire the heavy siege guns at regular intervals if the fort were attacked and in need of help. Early in the morning of 3 May the Mexican artillery

Brigadier General Zachary Taylor,
commander of the U.S. forces on the Rio Grande.

General Taylor's camp at Corpus Christi. The lithograph is based on a sketch by one of the general's junior officers, Captain Daniel Powers Whiting, who was trained in topographical drawing at West Point.

opened on the fort with heavy cannon and mortar fire. The bombardment continued for two days. On the morning of 5 May the garrison found itself surrounded by thousands of Mexicans, apparently moving into position for assault. The continued bombardment was causing damage, and there were some casualties. The next morning Brown decided, to begin sounding his signal guns. All that day and night the small garrison waited in uncertainty, expecting to be attacked at any moment and wondering whether General Taylor had heard the signal guns. Major Brown fell, mortally wounded, and ammunition began to run low. During the night of 7 May there was much activity in the Mexican camp; bugles sounded, but there was no assault. The next morning large numbers of the enemy were seen moving off in the direction of Point Isabel.

General Taylor had heard the signal guns and on the afternoon of 7 May had started back from Point Isabel with about 2,300 men to relieve the fort. The next morning, when a little more than halfway to the fort, his army came face to face with the enemy. The Mexicans, outnumbering Taylor by at least two to one and perhaps numbering as many as 6,000 men, were forming a line of battle to bar the road, their right flank on an elevation known as the Palo Alto and their left ending in a marshy area closely covered with scrub growth. Moving unhesitatingly to join battle, Taylor ordered his artillery to open fire to cover the deployment of his infantry into battle. The gun drill of the artillery was smooth and rapid and the fire was deadly. A Mexican column, still moving into position, was cut to pieces. The Mexican artillery in the center replied and for over an hour the battle raged as a cannon duel. When the Mexicans tried two wide flank attacks, American artillery raced around the line to meet and throw back one of the attacks. On the other flank, the 5th and 3d Infantry Regiments, forming in squares, scattered the Mexican cavalry. The dry grass had been set on fire by the gunfire, and a cloud of black smoke obscured the battlefield. Under the cover of this smoke screen, the American artillery moved into a new position and opened a destructive fire on the right flank of the Mexican line, throwing it into confusion.

Now, in the growing dusk, the Mexicans tried one last attack, their infantry advancing in line with flags flying and the band playing, but the American artillery tore the line to pieces and the battle ended as it had begun, with an artillery duel. As the guns ceased to fire in the darkness, the Mexicans fell back beyond the Palo Alto.

Americans Win at Palo Alto

General Taylor had lost only 9 men killed, one of whom was Major Ringgold, the artillery commander, for whom Fort Ringgold was later named, and 47 wounded. The Mexicans had over 700 casualties, of whom about 320 were killed, but replacements and reinforcements kept coming in from Matamoros.

The next morning Taylor resumed his march after sending out a strong advance party to locate the enemy. Word came back that the Mexicans were in a defensive position a few miles down the road, in a dry river bed (the Reseca de la Palma) that lay athwart the road along which Taylor was moving. It was a strong position. The Resaca provided natural breastworks for the Mexican infantry, whose flanks were protected by lagoons of standing water and thickets of cactus. The enemy artillery was in a position from which it could rake the main approach along the road.

Taylor ordered the "flying artillery" to advance and engage the Mexican batteries, and sent two infantry regiments forward on each side of the road in support of the artillery. In spite of heavy enemy fire the infantry formed in line and worked its way painfully through the brush. Losing sight of one another, the various units moved independently but their adherence to standard procedure gave the over-all effect of close coordination. When Lieutenant Randolph Ridgely, who had taken over Ringgold's command, was having difficulty with one Mexican battery placed squarely on the road, Taylor sent in his dragoons. Charging down the road, the cavalry drove the Mexicans from their guns, crossed the Resaca, turned, and discovered that the enemy artillerymen were back at their posts. Before the cavalry could charge the Mexican battery from the rear, however, Taylor's infantry had taken it and the road was

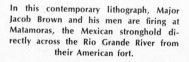

In this contemporary lithograph, Major Jacob Brown and his men are firing at Matamoras, the Mexican stronghold directly across the Rio Grande River from their American fort.

open. In the meantime the American infantry had turned the enemy's left flank, and the whole Mexican line broke and fled. The rout became a race to the Rio Grande, which the Mexicans won.

In the second day's battle, Taylor's losses had amounted to 33 men killed and 89 wounded. The enemy had suffered severely—well over a thousand men were killed and wounded and many more were drowned attempting to cross the Rio Grande. Second Lieutenant Ulysses S. Grant, who had been given temporary command of an infantry company on the second day, noted that the Mexican soldier was brave and would put up a good fight if well led. But they had not been well led and their marksmanship had been poor because of excessive powder charges in their musket cartridges. On the American side, Taylor, whose leadership in battle had already earned him two brevet promotions, was advanced to major general, and many of his subordinates were also promoted.

For want of boats to cross the Rio Grande, Taylor was compelled to stay until 18 May at the fort, which was later named Fort Brown in honor of its gallant commander. A year before, Taylor had requested the War Department to provide him with a pontoon train for river crossings, but he had never received the equipment. After 10 days spent collecting boats he began to move into Matamoros only to find that the Mexican Army had disappeared into the interior. A mounted detachment penetrated 60 miles to the south and returned to report that a move in force would be impossible because of the lack of water and forage in that direction.

Grass, ignited by gunfire, burns in the background of this representation of the Battle of Palo Alto.

Major Samual Ringgold (pointing) directs his wing of flying artillery during the Battle of Palo Alto. The skillful use of artillery was largely responsible for the American victory.

American dragoons, or mounted infantrymen, in action at Palo Alto.

One of the most melodramatic illustrations to come out of the Mexican War, "Death of Major Ringgold, of the Flying Artillery, at the Battle of Palo Alto," shows the mortally wounded artillery commander falling from his horse.

General Zachary Taylor at the Battle of Palo Alto, as sketched by one of his lieutenants. Taylor, who became a national hero during the Mexican War, was elected President of the United States in 1848.

President Polk Declares War on Mexico

On 9 May 1846, the day of the battle of Resaca de la Palma, President Polk called a cabinet meeting to discuss the Mexican situation. No news had come from Texas for some weeks. For all that Polk and the cabinet knew the Mexicans were going to permit General Taylor to remain on the banks of the Rio Grande unmolested. Polk suggested that he might draw up a war message for Congress on the basis of Mexico's refusal to pay the old American claims, and only Secretary of Navy George Bancroft insisted on waiting until the Mexicans committed an act of hostility against Taylor's forces. That evening a message came from the War Depart-

ment telling of the skirmish of 25 April, in which the American cavalry patrol had been wiped out. Polk immediately drafted a message declaring that a state of war existed. Congress passed the declaration, and President Polk signed it on 13 May. Congress then appropriated $10,000,000 to prosecute the war, doubled the strength of the Regular Army by setting the enlisted strength of a company at 100 men, authorized the President to call for volunteer units to a maximum of 50,000 men for a term of one year or the duration of the war, added a regiment of mounted riflemen to the Regular Army, and authorized the President to charter or purchase such vessels as might be suitable for the public service.

The Battle of Resaca de la Palma.

Fierce hand-to-hand combat at Resaca de la Palma on the day after the American victory at Palo Alto.

In this lithograph by Nathaniel Currier, General Taylor is ordering Captain Charles May, commander of a squadron of dragoons, to charge the enemy.

Captain May leads his squadron against the Mexicans. May is reported to have told his men: "Remember your regiment and follow your officers."

Captain May crowned his successful assault on the enemy line by capturing Mexican General La Vega (right) just as he was about to fire a cannon at American troops. A contemporary lithograph depicts the capture.

Dragoons in action.

Second Lieutenant Ulysses S. Grant who commanded one of the American infantry companies at Resaca de la Palma.

147

The President had gone into the war with at least one objective—to seize all of Mexico north of the Rio Grande and the Gila River and westward to the Pacific. His discussions with General Winfield Scott, the Commanding General of the Army, produced plans for a huge three-pronged thrust. Taylor, it was decided, should advance against Chihuahua. Another movement was to start from Fort Leavenworth, where a force mostly of militia and volunteers was being concentrated under the command of Colonel Stephen W. Kearny, and was to be aimed at Santa Fe. Its ultimate objective was California. The Navy was to blockade the east coast of Mexico from Tampico to Yucatan and capture the California coast in conjunction with Kearny. The campaign that eventually ended the war—the landing at Vera Cruz and the move on Mexico City—was a later addition to the plan.

General Scott, an experienced campaigner, realized the magnitude of the task. Mexico had a population of approximately 7,000,000 inhabitants. Its Regular Army, which included 15 infantry regiments and 4 artillery brigades, had about 30,000 names on the muster rolls, and the Central Government had more or less control over a large territorial militia. Particularly impressive to foreign observers was the Mexican light cavalry, armed with lance, carbine, and sword, of which there were 15 regiments. Twenty years of intermittent revolution and civil turmoil had given the Mexican soldiers plenty of experience in the field. Climate, geography, and disease were all on the side of the Mexicans. While President Polk had talked about a "quick war," Scott plunged into the intricate and stupendous problems of supply, transportation, communications, and mobilization, which had to be solved before operations on a grand scale could be conducted with any chance of success.

All through June and July volunteers and supplies poured into Matamoros. The new troops, units such as the Mississippi rifles commanded by Taylor's son-in-law, Colonel Jefferson Davis, made up in exuberance and spirit what they lacked in training and experience. Fortunately discipline was not one of the enemy's strong points. Some training, although not enough to satisfy all the regular officers, was given the new arrivals while Taylor waited for boats to take the army upriver and for the summer rains to stop.

GENERAL TAYLOR'S CAMPAIGN IN NORTHERN MEXICO

Instead of striking across the barren country directly for Monterey, Taylor had decided to move by boat and wagon train up the Rio Grande to the town of Camargo, 130 miles above Matamoros. From Camargo, a road led 150 miles southwest to Monterey and the other key cities of northern Mexico. By the end of July, Quartermaster General Thomas S. Jesup was able to send Taylor enough shallow draft river steamboats to begin the move, and by mid-August, 20 steamers were in operation between Matamoros and Camargo. But the ravages of disease, the necessity of keeping holding forces at critical points along the river, and a shortage of wagons limited the size of the force that started for Monterey at the end of August to a little more than 6,000 men, of whom about two-thirds were regulars.

On 17 September 1846 Taylor arrived before Monterrey. A force of from 7,300 to 9,000 Mexicans defended the city, but Taylor promptly moved to attack. He had organized his command into 3 divisions, 1 of volunteers, and 2 of regulars. After sending one of the divisions of regulars around to the west of the city to cut off the road to Saltillo and to attack from that side, Taylor moved in on the eastern outskirts with the remainder of his force. After two days of hard fighting both attacks succeeded in driving into the city proper. Then followed two more days of fighting such as Americans had never before experienced, except for the few Continentals that had pushed into Quebec with Montgomery and Arnold back in 1775. As in most Mexican cities, the houses of Monterey were strongly built of stone and adobe, forming solid walls along narrow streets that led to a central plaza. Each street was easily converted into a fortress. Painfully but relentlessly Taylor's men blasted down walls, chased the enemy troops from house to house and off the flat rooftops, and finally pushed them into the plaza. On 24 September the Mexican commander offered to surrender the city on condition that his troops be allowed to withdraw unimpeded and that an eight-week armistice go into effect. General Taylor agreed, and Monterrey was in his hands.

Monterrey as it appeared from a rooftop overlooking the main plaza.

The infantry storms Independence Hill to silence the Mexican fire slowing the advance into Monterrey.

General Taylor's army approaches Monterrey.

American troops attack at the Bishop's Palace in Monterrey.

The battle for Monterrey nears its end as General Taylor's men force their way into the main plaza.

President Polk and the administration received the news of the surrender terms with chagrin and disappointment, and promptly repudiated the armistice. In justice to Taylor it should be noted that it had been a tremendous feat to win the stronghold on any terms, that he had had a long line of communications to secure, and that, as far as he knew, his mission was not to win the war but merely to hold northern Mexico. By the time Taylor learned that he was expected to defeat the enemy in the field, not win cities, the armistice had almost expired.

While Taylor waited in Monterrey, the other prongs of the grand operation had been put in motion. Kearny had taken Santa Fe, and with a small force was on his way across the deserts and rugged mountains to California. Brigadier General John E. Wool with about 2,000 men was on the march from San Antonio, but instead of Chihuahua his objective now was the town of Parras, situated in a fertile region from which supplies for Taylor's army could be drawn. As General Wool approached Parras in mid-November, Taylor sent one of his divisions forward from Monterrey to occupy the city of Saltillo, a provincial capital and important road junction on the routes to Parras and Mexico City. Another detachment occupied the city of Victoria, capital of the province of Tamaulipas and about halfway between Monterrey and the port of Tampico, which had been taken and occupied by an American naval force. Thus at the beginning of December a large part of northern Mexico had come under American control. In the Far West, Kearny and his dragoons had reached San Diego after one of the most extraordinary marches in American history to find that a naval squardon had already seized the California ports with the questionable help of a force of California volunteers.

A strike at the heart of Mexico and the capture of its capital, Mexico City, and the defeat of the Mexican Army had been under discussion ever since Taylor's victories along the Rio Grande. The points at issue were who should command the expedition and what route should be taken. In June, while Taylor prepared to move against Monterrey, Scott had expected to take personal command of the army of the Rio Grande, and he had written to ask Taylor to press on into the heart of the enemy's country and take "the High Road to the capital of Mexico." However, if such an invasion route appeared to be too difficult, the War Department was prepared to consider making the attempt by way of Tampico or Vera Cruz, or some other place along the coast. General Scott, after deciding not to leave Washington for the time being and after further study of logistical and communications problems, began to urge approval of the Vera Cruz project. Taylor, too, after taking Monterrey, recommended an assault by way of Vera Cruz. Political decisions had delayed the appointment of a commander, and by this time Taylor was even less acceptable than Scott to the Administration. Finally, in mid-November, it was reluctantly decided to give General Scott command of the Vera Cruz expedition.

Scott in methodical fashion proceeded to draw up the requirements for the campaign. He needed 15,000 to 25,000 men, most of them regulars. During the next two months the able and hardworking Quartermaster General labored mightily to assemble supplies, munitions, and transports while Scott proceeded to Camargo to see what troops he could detach from Taylor's force. With the center of action shifting, there seemed to be no need for a large army in northern Mexico, so Scott detached practically all of Taylor's regulars—about 4,000 men—and an equal number of volunteers, who were ordered to rendezvous at Tampico and at the mouth of the Brazos River in Texas. Taylor was left with less than 5,000 men, all of them volunteers except two squadrons of dragoons and a small force of artillery.

The President of Mexico, General Santa Anna, had taken the field in person and had assembled in the neighborhood of San Luis Potosí an army of approximately 20,000 men. Word of Scott's expedition had leaked out to the newspapers and was known in Mexico City almost as soon as the preparations got under way. A captured dispatch revealed to Santa Anna the plans for depleting Taylor's army. The opportunity thus presented could not be ignored, and Santa Anna decided to strike northward against Taylor's weakened forces. Taylor was understandably concerned with his situation but ignorant of Santa Anna's intention. He assumed, as did General Scott and the War Department, that the Mexicans would make their main effort at Vera Cruz. Early in February 1847 Taylor moved all his troops except a small garrison out of Saltillo into a camp 18 miles south of the city. General Wool, who had been brought from Parras when Taylor's force was reduced and who had been occupying a position at Buena Vista, near Saltillo, was moved forward to the new camp a few days later. No tactical significance was attached to the shift. Taylor merely thought it would improve the morale of his troops to move them a few miles in the direction of the enemy, and he also hoped that it would persuade the inhabitants of Saltillo, who had

been driven away by frequent alarms, to return to the city. As late as 14 February, Taylor considered a Mexican advance on his position improbable.

The Rout of Santa Anna's Army of Buena Vista

A week later, on 21 February, an American scouting party came into camp with news that a force of several thousand Mexicans was approaching. It turned out to be the leading elements of Santa Anna's army. Taylor immediately drew back to Buena Vista, where the terrain offered better possibilities for defense, and prepared to engage the Mexicans.

At Buena Vista the high valley along which Santa Anna was approaching narrowed to a defile flanked by the shoulders of a rugged mountain ridge. The road from the south followed a stream up the valley and through the defile, and then continued over the ridge in the direction of Saltillo. As Santa Anna came up the valley he saw the bulk of the American forces posted on the ridges to the right of the road. At the head of the defile Taylor had placed a battery of artillery and a regiment of Indiana Volunteers. To the left of the defile, the right flank of the Americans was held by a Kentucky regiment. In all about 4,800 men were in position. Taylor had gone on to Saltillo with the Mississippi Rifle Regiment and a squadron of dragoons, leaving General Wool in command at Buena Vista. Santa Anna had perhaps 15,000 men on the scene.

General Taylor watching his troops in action during the Battle of Buena Vista.

Major Joseph H. Eaton, General Taylor's aide-de-camp throughout the Mexican War, made this sketch of the battleground at Buena Vista as it appeared on 23 February 1847.

Captain Bragg's artillery. It was to Captain Bragg that General Taylor is supposed to have said: "Give them a little more grape, Mr. Bragg."

"Volunteers for Texas," a cartoon of the time.

The Mexicans (right) have charged to within a few yards of the American guns at Buena Vista in this historically accurate lithograph by Nathaniel Currier. The next volley forced the Mexicans to retreat.

The Mexican general decided to make his main effort against the American left flank. The first day, 22 February 1847, was largely devoted to an attempt on the part of the Mexicans to outflank the American position. A brigade of Mexican light infantry moved toward a ridge the Americans had not occupied on the extreme left, seized it, and pushed back a force of dismounted American cavalry and riflemen who tried to counter the move, while a force of about 1,500 Mexican cavalry made a wide sweep along mountain roads toward Saltillo and the American rear. The next day, at dawn, the battle opened in earnest, with an attempt by the Americans to restore the left, which the Mexicans re-pulsed and countered by sending a division up the road against the American position at the head of the defile, only to be repulsed in turn.

Santa Anna next launched his grand assault on the American left, an attack by a column of two divisions. For half an hour the Americans—360 men of the 2d Indiana Regiment and a battery of 3 cannons—withstood the assault, pouring a heavy fire into the massed columns. When their commander ordered a withdrawal, the men turned, broke, and ran. Two adjoining regiments of mounted volunteers joined the flight and ran almost all the way back to Saltillo. A third regiment retired in good order to another position

"A New Rule in Algebra," a cartoon of the time.

along the ridge. At this critical point the artillery came at a gallop from the right flank and went into action on the exposed left, and almost simultaneously General Taylor arrived on the scene from Saltillo with Jefferson Davis' Mississippi Rifles and about half the men of the Indiana regiment whom he had rallied on the way. At the same time the Kentucky regiment came over from the right flank and joined the fight. The combined grape, canister, and musket fire of the Americans was more than the dense Mexican columns could stand, and they began to fall back. After a lull in the battle, the Americans took the initiative against what they believed to be a thoroughly shaken foe, only to be met by an entirely fresh division of Mexicans, Santa Anna's last reserves. Artillery was again hastily thrown into the breach, the first volley of canister stopping the enemy only a few yards from the muzzles of the guns. The next volley threw the Mexicans back in disorder, and the arrival of troops from the Mississippi and Indiana regiments at this point ended the battle. Santa Anna ordered a withdrawal to Taylor's old camp a few miles to the south. Apprehensive of what the next day would bring, the weary Americans rested that night on the battlefield with their arms beside them. But Santa Anna had had enough. He had lost 1,500 to 2,000 men killed and wounded. The cavalry column that

he had sent against Saltillo had been defeated and thrown back. With his army completely demoralized, there was nothing to do but retreat to San Luis Potosí. Taylor's losses were 265 killed, 450 wounded, and 26 missing, but his men had won the hardest battle of the entire war; their leaders had exhibited courage, initiative, and resourcefulness, and many of them were rewarded with brevet promotion.

Buena Vista ended any further Mexican threat to the Rio Grande and secured the American hold on Mexico's northern provinces. There was only one other action in that theatre during the rest of the war, a fight that took place in Chihuahua less than a week after Taylor's victory at Buena Vista. A force of 900 Missouri volunteers under Colonel Alexander W. Doniphan, detached from Kearny's command, had set out from Santa Fe early in February to pacify the region of the upper Rio Grande. After crossing the river at El Paso, Doniphan encountered a well-entrenched force of approximately 3,000 Mexicans, mostly local militia, and defeated them with great slaughter, killing 300 and wounding 500 while losing only 2 men killed and 7 wounded. Doniphan's force then continued to Parras and Saltillo and back to the United States by way of Camargo, an epic march of about 1,000 miles.

GENERAL SCOTT'S INVASION OF CENTRAL MEXICO

General Scott's army for the invasion of central Mexico had been assembling at the mouth of the Brazos River and at Tampico. Including the detachments drawn from General Taylor, most of which were at Tampico, Scott had 13,660 men of whom 5,741 were regulars. On 15 February 1847 advance elements left the Brazos for the rendezvous on Lobos Island, about 50 miles south of Tampico, from which the entire force sailed for Vera Cruz on 2 March. A beach two miles south of the city had been chosen for the landing after a reconnaissance by Scott and his staff in which the small vessel carrying the party narrowly escaped being struck by shells from the citadel. Had it been sunk, American military history might have taken an entirely different course, for in addition to the commanding general, the party on board included a number of young officers—Joseph E. Johnston, Pierre G. T. Beauregard, George G. Meade, and

Robert E. Lee. At 1800 on the evening of 9 March the landing commenced, and in the space of four hours more than 10,000 men went ashore in the heavy surf boats that had been brought along for the purpose. Not a shot was fired. The Mexican commander, having only about 4,300 men with which to defend the place, had decided to keep his entire force behind the city's walls.

To avoid casualties, Scott chose to take the city by siege and bombardment rather than by assault, but the seven mortars with which he was provided proved ineffective against the heavy stone walls and bastions of the citadel. The commander of the American naval forces, Commodore Matthew C. Perry, loaned Scott six heavy naval guns and crews. With these weapons the walls were easily breached and the defenders were soon demoralized. On 27 March 1847 Vera Cruz capitulated.

While General Scott was assembling his army at Lobos Island, naval Lieutenant Charles C. Barton made this sketch "on the spot." It shows part of the fleet waiting to transport Scott and 10,000 men to Vera Cruz.

Major General Winfield Scott at Vera Cruz.

Lieutenant Barton was on hand with his sketchbook when General Scott and his army landed on a beach near Vera Cruz on 9 March 1847. Sixty-five surf boats, rowed by naval crews, carried the soldiers from the transports to the beach.

When Vera Cruz refused to surrender to General Scott, the American fleet opened fire. This representation of the bombardment is by the lithographers Sarony and Major.

The most famous version of General Scott's landing is this lithograph by Currier and Ives.

One of General Scott's staff officers, Robert E. Lee, supervised the construction of the land battery, mounting heavy naval guns, that is firing on Vera Cruz in this lithograph. These are the guns that finally breached the city walls.

An artist's conception of Vera Cruz during the bombardment. Casualties were reported as "80 soldiers killed or wounded and not over a hundred civilians killed."

The victorious Americans are approaching the walls of Vera Cruz in this lithograph.

The Battle of Cerro Gordo

Because the yellow fever season was approaching, Scott was anxious to move forward into the interior uplands where the climate was more healthful, but he was not able to collect enough pack mules and transport until 8 April. The advancing force had its first encounter with the enemy at Cerro Gordo, about 30 miles from Vera Cruz, where Santa Anna with a newly raised army of approximately 12,000 men was occupying a strongly entrenched position in the mountain passes through which ran the road to Jalapa and Mexico City. A reconnaissance led by Captain Lee disclosed that the Mexican left flank was vulnerable. Scott decided to split his force and send two of his three divisions around Santa Anna's left to cut the only road by which the Mexicans could withdraw, while the third division, a volunteer outfit, made a frontal assault. The flanking movement won the day. Finding themselves surrounded, the Mexicans surrendered

in droves, although they had beaten off the frontal attack. It was a smashing victory for Scott; at a cost of only 431 men killed and wounded he had taken 3,000 prisoners, 4,000 muskets, and 43 cannon and had inflicted 1,000 to 1,200 casualties on the Mexicans. Santa Anna and the remnants of his army fled into the mountains. Scott moved on to Jalapa without delay.

The Americans were now about 60 miles from Vera Cruz. The capital of Mexico was 170 miles farther on, but the road lay open. Nevertheless, an immediate advance faced a number of difficulties. Scott had expected to replenish his provisions and forage at Jalapa, but in this he was disappointed. The army's supply of ready cash was running low, and most of the cavalry had to be detailed to escort wagon trains to and from Vera Cruz. Scott had heard nothing from General Taylor, only rumors that Taylor's army was at San Luis Potosí preparing to advance on the capital, so his own planning was made more difficult. The extremes of climate and unbalanced rations had sent large numbers of troops to the hospital; at the end of May, Scott reported more than 3,200 sick and wounded soldiers. The most serious of all his problems was the expiration of the term of enlistment of 7 volunteer regiments. Wounds, sickness, and the departure of the volunteers reduced the army to 5,820 effective noncommissioned officers and privates.

During the month after the battle at Cerro Gordo, Scott pushed cautiously forward to Puebla, where he stayed until the beginning of August awaiting reinforcements and the outcome of an attempt to negotiate a peace. Influenced no doubt by Taylor's armistice after Monterrey, perhaps by a desire to salvage some glory for his administration, and by the conviction that the military arm of the Government was not the proper instrument for negotiating with the Mexican Government, President Polk had dispatched a State Depart-

ment official, Nicholas P. Trist, with instructions to accompany Scott and to handle all peace negotiations. Scott had protested vigorously at the appointment, and, for a time, refused to have anything to do with Trist, but during the stay at Puebla the two men patched up their differences and decided that Santa Anna might be more quickly persuaded to acknowledge the defeat if something material were offered as an inducement. The Mexican President agreed that for $10,000 down and $1,000,000 to be paid when a treaty was ratified he would discuss peace terms. However, after the down payment was safely in hand, Santa Anna discovered that he could not prevail upon the Mexican Congress to repeal a law it had passed making it high treason for any official to treat with the Americans. It was clear that Scott would have to move closer to the capital of Mexico before Santa Anna would seriously consider terms of a peace.

A view of Cerro Gordo showing the rugged nature of the terrain.

American troops are attacking a strongly held Mexican position
in this lithograph of the Battle of Cerro Gordo.

The Advance on Mexico City

By the beginning of August, Scott, after leaving a small garrison in Puebla, had nearly 10,000 men available for the advance on Mexico City. His force was not suffciently large to provide protection for the road to Vera Cruz at the same time, so Scott decided upon a step of great daring, nothing less than to strike out from his base and abandon his line of communications with the coast. On 7 August the leading division moved out of Puebla toward Mexico City. Within a week the army had climbed up to the high and broad plateau on which the city lay and had come in sight of the outer defenses.

In front of Mexico City, in the direction from which Scott was approaching, lay three large lakes surrounded by low marshes. The roads leading to the city gates passed through these marshes over raised causeways guarded at their intersections by strongly fortified positions. Out of the marshy lowland rose an occasional steep hill which the Mexicans had likewise fortified. The most formidable of them was the citadel of Chapultepec, a massive stone fortress on top of a 200-foot hill situated about a mile from the city proper. In these positions in and around the city Santa Anna had disposed his army.

Two brisk and bloody actions were fought on 19–20 August, as a result of which the Mexicans were pushed back to the defenses just outside the city walls. An apparent disposition on the part of the Mexican Government to consider peace terms encouraged Scott to propose an armistice. Santa Anna quickly agreed. For two weeks Trist and representatives of the Mexican Government discussed terms until it became clear that the Mexicans would not accept what Trist was prepared to offer and were merely making use of the armistice as a breathing spell. On 6 September Scott called a halt to the discussions and prepared to assault the city. Two days later the most important outwork of Chapultepec was taken and the citadel itself fell on 13 September. Scott's troops pushed on from Chapultepec, and on the same night a small vanguard entered the gates of the city. At dawn on 14 September the Mexican authorities sent out a white flag. The garrison, led by Santa Anna, had slipped away during the night, but it had ceased to be an effective fighting force. Santa Anna promptly abdicated the Presidency, and shortly afterward the last remnant of his army, about 1,500 volunteers, was completely defeated while attempting to capture an American supply train on the road from Vera Cruz.

This drawing of Chapultepec and the strong fortifications around the summer palace of the President of Mexico was made by Sergeant Fabian Brydolf of the 15th Infantry.

The storming of Chapultepec by American troops on 13 September 1847. At left, soldiers are carrying the ladders that will be used to scale the walls.

General Scott and his army entering Mexico City's Plaza, in a sketch by the architect Carl Nebel. Nebel did a series of sketches based on his first-hand observations of the Mexican War.

The American Army Ruled Mexico

For two months the only responsible government in Mexico was the American military government under Scott. The collection of the revenues, the suppression of disorder, the administration of justice, all the details of governing the country were in the hands of the Army. When the Mexicans finally organized a government with which Commissioner Trist could negotiate a peace treaty, dispatches arrived from Washington instructing Trist to return to the United States and ordering Scott to resume the war. Knowing that now the Mexicans were sincerely desirous of ending the war and realizing that the Government in Washington was unaware of the true situation, both Trist and Scott decided to continue the negotiations.

The Treaty of Guadelupe Hidalgo, 2 February 1848

On 2 February 1848 the Treaty of Guadelupe Hidalgo was signed. Mexico recognized the Rio Grande as the boundary of Texas and ceded New Mexico (including the present states of Arizona, New Mexico, Utah, and Nevada, a small corner of present-day Wyoming, and the western and southern portions of Colorado), and Upper California (the present state of California) to the United States. The United States on its part agreed to pay Mexico $15,000,000 and to assume the unpaid claims against Mexico. Resisting public demands that the whole of Mexico be annexed and refusing to repudiate Trist and the treaty, President Polk sent the treaty to the Senate, where it was ratified after bitter debate. On 1 August 1848 the last American soldiers stepped aboard their transports at Vera Cruz and quitted Mexican soil.

In the conduct of military operations the United States had come a long way since the War of 1812. The American Army was better trained and disciplined and there was less reliance on short-term militia calls and more reliance on volunteers. Although the volunteers that were raised were for the most part given some intensive training before being sent into battle, their 12-month terms of enlistment still proved to be too short to permit the long-range planning of campaigns.

The supporting arms and services were generally of high quality. The artillery, consisting almost entirely of regulars, turned the tide at critical points in several battles. The success of the horse artillery demonstrated the value of mobility and justified the training that had been given the artillery in this respect in the years before the war. The engineers had little opportunity to display their technical knowledge in the building of defensive works except at Fort Brown, for the Americans had taken the offensive in every engagement except Buena Vista. Instead the engineers made their principal contribution as the eyes of Scott's army. A careful reconnaissance of the enemy position, conducted by the engineers, was generally insisted on by Scott before engaging in battle. The Quartermaster Department had faced a tremendous task. The theatre of operations was greater and the lines of communications more extended than in either of the earlier major wars. Considering the unprecedented demands, the logistical arrangements worked out with a minimum of confusion.

The Mexican War was unique in a number of ways. For the first time an American army engaged in house-to-house fighting in city streets. For the first time American forces were transported overseas to fight in a climate and over terrain entirely different from that to which they were accustomed. Although operations on the Great Lakes during the War of 1812 had involved amphibious landings and the use of water routes for transport and supply, the landing at Vera Cruz and the use of transport vessels by both Taylor and Scott in the Mexican War far surpassed those earlier operations, and for the first time steam-propelled vessels were used extensively. Finally, in the Mexican War an American army was required to establish and administer a system of military government over a defeated people.

Mexican Border Expedition. Ohio National Guard field artillery observation balloon near El Paso, Texas.

THE NATIONAL GUARD AND THE RESERVE

THE NATIONAL GUARD

The origins of the modern-day National Guard are found in the detachments of able-bodied young men who manned the defense perimeters of the early colonies. Forerunners even of the militia, these were the men who stood watch over Jamestown, the Massachusetts Bay Colony, and Plymouth.

Older, as a matter of fact, than the nation itself, the National Guard can point to the longest continuous history of any military organization in the United States.

Many modern National Guard organizations in the eastern States trace their ancestry back to militia organizations that fought alongside the British in the French and Indian campaigns. Later many of these same militiamen were arrayed against British regiments as our fledgling nation went about the business of breaking away from the English yoke.

The National Guard descendants of the Revolutionary militia today carry battle streamers embroidered with the names of the campaigns of 1776–1780; Virginia—Long Island—Trenton—New York—Princeton—Brandywine—Germantown—Monmouth—South Carolina—Saratoga—Connecticut—Boston.

The name "National Guard" first appeared on the scene in New York. This came about 25 August 1824, as a result of a visit to New York by the Marquis de Lafayette. The honor guard for the gallant French officer who contributed so heavily to the winning of United States independence was drawn from the 2d Battalion, 11th Regiment of Artillery of New York. This battalion was renamed the "Battalion of National Guards" in tribute to Lafayette's command of the Garde Nationale of the French Army in Paris in 1789. New York's "Battalion of National Guards" later became the famous 7th Regiment of Infantry, and on 1 October 1917 it became the 107th Infantry Regiment of the 27th Division.

As the nation grew, the outward appearance of the Guard changed.

It was, throughout the nineteenth century, an unwieldy and sprawling force which nevertheless contributed heavily to the winning of four major wars and hundreds of minor encounters. The major wars included service of State troops in the War of 1812, the Mexican War, the Civil War, and the War with Spain.

The modern face of the National Guard began to emerge in 1903 when Congressional legislation thrust the Federal Government into the picture by establishing procedures for a more direct and active part in organizing, training, and equipping the militia troops in line with the standards of the United States Regular Army.

Then, in the passage of the National Defense Act of 1916, official cognizance was taken of the name National Guard for the organized militia, and it was made to conform to the organizational structure of the Regular Army. As such, it became a component of the nation's organized peacetime establishment and, when called into active Federal service, it was an integral part of the Army of the United States.

In 1916, over 150,000 Guardsmen were mobilized under the call of the President and 110,000 served under General John J. Pershing along the Mexican Border.

"... The Whites of Their Eyes."

On the night of 16-17 June 1775, the Americans entered the Charleston Peninsula and erected fortifications on Breed's Hill, overlooking Boston. Next day, early in the afternoon, the British landed 7 regiments on the peninsula to drive them off, and so began the first battle of the American Revolution. The American line, of 5 militia regiments and 2 field pieces from the New England colonies, extended from Breed's Hill to the Mystic River, on the north.

"Remember the River Raisin" was the American battle cry after the massacre of the Kentucky Militia in January 1813. On the following October 5, at the Battle of the Thames in Upper Canada, the stage was set for vengeance.

"The Mississippi Rifles."
This scene depicts the First Mississippi Regiment, composed of "hard fighting Mississippi gentlemen," under the command of Colonel Jefferson Davis, attacking the formidable Mexican cavalry at Buena Vista, Mexico, on 23 February 1847. Made up of volunteer militiamen, familiar with hunting and firearms, this Regiment was armed with percussion rifles, then the most advanced weapons in use.

California Militia (Guard), 1846.

"Lafayette and the National Guard."
The visit of the Marquis de Lafayette to the United States in 1824-1825, as the guest of the President and the Congress, was in every way a triumphal procession. The 2nd Battalion of the 11th New York Artillery was one of the many militia commands that turned out in his honor. This unit adopted the name "national guard" in honor of Lafayette's celebrated "Garde Nationale de Paris."

World War I. Antiaircraft machine gun of the 101st Massachusetts Field Artillery, New England Coast Artillery, firing on a German observation plane at Plateau Chemin des Dames, France.

1st Cavalry, New York National Guard from Rochester, entraining at Yonkers for training maneuvers in Texas during the 1920's.

In 1941 Carolina maneuvers, the 29th Guard Division Blue Army successfully defends the main street of Albemarle, North Carolina, as the citizens of the town watch as interested spectators.

209th Guard Coast Artillery in Carolina Army maneuvers—Fall 1941.

Second Army maneuvers in Arkansas, September 1941. The 107th Ohio Cavalry Regiment of the Guard go into speedy action against the Red Army. Horses of the Regiment were loaded in Porté truck units. The Porté carries 8 horses and 8 men, plus one day's forage in each unit.

World War II. Guard soldiers of the 32nd Division resting after the capture of a Japanese position in New Guinea.

Post World War II. Minnesota National Guard training of regulars in heavy Army equipment.

New Jersey National Guardsmen ready to board transport for airborne exercise.

World War II. Guard infantrymen of the 35th Division advance cross-country near Rhineland, Germany.

The 115th Aerial Observation Squadron at a National Guard encampment near San Luis Obispo, California, in 1935.

Major General Winston P. Wilson, Chief of the National Guard Bureau (the Bureau is the composite Department of Defense headquarters for the Army and Air Guard units), flies an Army helicopter in many of his various Guard activities, 1966.

National Guardsmen training at Camp Drum, New York. Citizen soldiers in 1952 training period perform night firing exercises with 3.5 bazooka, resulting in a dramatic photograph.

In World War I the National Guard supplied 17 divisions, 11 of which became engaged in actual combat operations. Of the 8 American divisions rated "excellent" or "superior" by the German High Command, 6 were National Guard divisions. The best known of these divisions were the 42d (Rainbow) Division, a composite division composed of troops from all parts of the country. One of the brigade commanders of this distinguished division was a brigadier general named Douglas MacArthur.

Following a rapid and haphazard demobilization at the end of World War I, it was necessary for the States to rebuild the National Guard. Under postwar amendments to the National Defense Act of 1916, the National Guard was reorganized to consist of the same numbered divisions that had served during the war.

The amended National Defense Act established an Army of the United States to consist of the Regular Army, the Organized Reserve Corps, and the National Guard when called into Federal service. The National Guard remained a State force under the command of State authorities. The new act also provided for increased Federal assistance for the Guard.

The act of 5 June 1933 created a new component of the Army, the National Guard of the United States. This component, while identical in personnel and organization to the National Guard of the several States, was a part of the Army at all times and could be ordered into active Federal service by the President whenever Congress declared a national emergency.

In August of 1940 the President of the United States ordered the National Guard of the United States into active military service. Between 16 September 1940 and 1 October 1941 the National Guard brought into Federal service more than 300,000 men in 18 combat infantry divisions as well as in numerous nondivisional units, including 29 air observation squadrons. These troops immediately doubled the strength of the active Army.

Following World War II, National Guard units were demobilized and personnel returned directly to civilian life through Army separation centers. For a short period in the winter of 1945–1946 there actually was no National Guard.

On 13 October 1945 the Secretary of War approved a plan for reorganizing the Guard. The first four post-World War II units were extended Federal recognition on 30 June 1946. Air units of the National Guard were organized as a separate entity, and since that time the National Guard establishment has consisted of the Army National Guard and the Air National Guard.

During the Korean War more than 183,000 members of the post-World War II National Guard saw active service. Eight infantry divisions, 22 wings, and hundreds of other units of the Army and Air National Guard were ordered into Federal service.

The post-Korea National Guard rose in strength to over half a million men in March 1957. Subsequent strength cuts have reduced the current programmed strength to 419,000 in the Army National Guard and 77,000 in the Air National Guard (1965).

ROTC students from the Citadel, University of Connecticut, University of Georgia, University of Massachusetts, University of Mississippi, University of Pittsburgh, Princeton, and University of Rhode Island performing engineering construction work on a timber trestle bridge at the 1953 summer ROTC encampment.

A Reservist pulls a tree stump during construction of an airstrip while on Reserve duty with the 411th Engineer Aviation Brigade at Fort Belvoir, Virginia, in 1955.

A member of the 302nd Medical Battalion, U.S. Army Reserve, administers aid to a simulated patient during a training exercise at Fort Sam Houston, Texas, as a part of study under the Reserve Forces Act of 1955.

Reservists practice landing-craft operations in deploying their equipment.

167

All units and members of the Army National Guard of the United States and Air National Guard of the United States are in the Ready Reserve. In time of national emergency declared by the President, or when otherwise authorized by law, the Secretary of the Army or Secretary of the Air Force may order these units and personnel to active duty for not more than 24 consecutive months. In time of war or a national emergency declared by the Congress, or when otherwise authorized by law, they may be ordered to active duty for the duration of the war or emergency and for six months thereafter.

THE U.S. ARMY RESERVE— THE ORGANIZED RESERVE CORPS

The mission of the Organized Reserve Corps is to supplement the active Army establishment in the event of a national emergency by furnishing units (and additionally trained personnel, both officer and enlisted), which have been trained and organized for rapid mobilization, expansion, and deployment.

The Organized Reserve Corps is made up of two sections, the Officers' Reserve Corps and the Enlisted Reserve Corps.

The integral part of the Officers' Reserve Corps is the steady influx of new officers from the Reserve Officers' Training Corps (ROTC), which was established by the National Defense Act of 1916.

It is believed that the first recognition by law of the need for a ready reserve force was the Militia Act of 1792, against which a small number of organized militia forces was established. And on 28 July 1866 the President signed an Act which defined the Army as consisting of 45 regiments of infantry, 10 regiments of cavalry, and 4 regiments of artillery. Four of the infantry regiments were to be composed of men wounded in service, constituting the Veteran's Reserve Corps.

In 1908, Congress established a Medical Reserve Corps in which outstanding graduates of medical schools were appointed first lieutenants. The National Defense Acts of 1916 and 1920 further improved the reserve organization but the Army Reserve units of today, mainly, had not been established until after World War II. By 7 December 1941 more than 77,000 Reserve officers had been called to extended active duty as individuals, and thousands more were called during the war. This individual call-up precluded the possibility of calling Reserve units into service. Approximately 100,000 ROTC graduates served in World War II in grades from second lieutenant to brigadier general.

During the Korean War, more than 78,000 officers and 165,000 enlisted men of the Army Reserve served on active duty. This was in addition to some 43,000 Army Reserve officers already on active duty when the emergency began. The present structure of the Army Reserve has been brought about mainly through the provisions contained in the Universal Military Training and Service Act of 1951, the Armed Forces Reserve Act of 1952 and the Reserve Forces Act of 1955.

In 1959, the Reserve was reorganized under the Army pentomic concept which was designed to provide a modern, efficient Reserve structure with a capability of fulfilling the requirements of the initial phases of mobilization. (The Pentomic Army—"Penta" (5) plus "atomic"—is a reorganization which provides for replacement of the three regiments within a division with five battle groups.)

During the Berlin crisis in late 1961, both the Army Reserve and the National Guard were called to active duty in substantial numbers with most members being released by September 1962.

On 12 December 1964 Secretary of Defense Robert S. McNamara announced plans to transfer the unit structure of the U.S. Army Reserve to the National Guard and eliminate all Reserve units for which there was no requirement under current plans. The former proposal is subject to Congressional considerations, and the latter is taking place as conditions permit.

> "We must all—regulars and reserves, civilian and military, infantryman and engineer, active duty and retired—close ranks and strive in fact as well as in theory for a true unity of effort, purpose, and spirit which will weld all units, components and elements into 'One Army'."
>
> WILBUR M. BRUCKER,
> Secretary of the Army.

Member of the 112th Armored Division waves his column of M-48 tanks onward in a training exercise. This Division was one of the units called to active duty during the Berlin crisis of 1961-1962.

168

The Air National Guard received jets in 1954. This photograph taken in the 1950's shows the North American F-86A aircraft of the California 146th Fighter Wing.

During the 1950's the Air National Guard also received the Republic F-84F aircraft.

After World War II the Guard received North American P-51 aircraft.

Boeing C-97 Stratofreighters of the Guard's 146th Air Transport Wing (Heavy) are shown here on the flight line at the Van Nuys Air National Guard Base.

Reservists in basic combat training at Fort Lewis, Washington.

Reservists at Camp A. P. Hill, Virginia, while undergoing their two weeks' annual active-duty training, prepare a rocket launcher for action.

At Fort George G. Meade, reservists receive classroom instructions in use of Special Forces weapons.

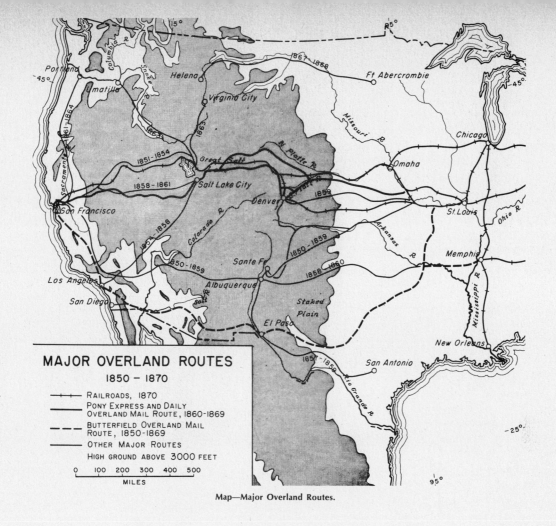

MAJOR OVERLAND ROUTES

1850 – 1870

├─┼─┤ RAILROADS, 1870
──────── PONY EXPRESS AND DAILY
OVERLAND MAIL ROUTE, 1860-1869
- - - - - BUTTERFIELD OVERLAND MAIL
ROUTE, 1850-1869
──────── OTHER MAJOR ROUTES
HIGH GROUND ABOVE 3000 FEET

0 100 200 300 400 500
MILES

Map—Major Overland Routes.

CHAPTER 7

THE U.S. ARMY, 1848-1860

The brief interval of peace between the end of the Mexican War in 1848 and the beginning of the Civil War in 1861 saw the Army reduced in strength at a time when it was assuming vastly greater responsibilities. The victory over Mexico and the settlement of the Oregon boundary question added a wide stretch of territory to the United States— much of it wild, rough, and inhospitable. The rich lands on the Pacific Coast and the discovery of gold in California were luring an increasing number of emigrants to the West across plains inhabited by such warlike Indian tribes as the Cheyenne, Blackfoot, Sioux, Pawnee, Ute, Comanche, and Apache. The Army protected the emigrants and settlers by guarding the several transcontinental wagon routes and by keeping the tribes in check throughout the vast spaces between the Mexican and Canadian borders. The Army was also responsible for exploring and surveying the new regions and for coastal fortifications.

CAMPAIGNS AGAINST THE INDIANS

The years between 1848 and 1860 saw a constant succession of marches, expeditions, and campaigns against the Indians. During the decade of the fifties there were no less than 22 distinct "wars," ranging from Florida to Arizona, and from the Missouri River to Oregon. In the year 1857 alone the Army sent out 37 separate expeditions that involved actual combat, plus many others that accomplished their missions without shedding blood. The extent of the campaigns is indicated by the fact that in 1858 the Army's regiments marched an average distance of 1,234 miles, each expedition carrying with it all its requirements from horseshoe nails to artillery.

All this was done in rough terrain in a part of the country where local procurement was nonexistent. Supplying the various frontier posts entailed great effort. In former years military posts had been located on or near navigable rivers, but now frontier posts were as far as 1,000 miles from inland waterways, making it necessary to transport supplies in wagons or by packtrains.

Merely getting troops to the frontier posts was a major effort. To reach the West Coast from the Mississippi River region required three months of arduous overland travel; every day's march required a tactical formation; every night's bivouac required all-round security. There were two other methods of reaching the West from the Atlantic Coast—the

Soldiers guarding
a stagecoach
in the 1850's.

The stage station
at Fort Kearney.

long, rough sea voyage around Cape Horn, or by ship to Panama, overland across the jungle isthmus, then by ship to the West Coast. However, these alternatives were also hazardous and unpleasant. In 1853 the chartered steamer **San Francisco,** loaded with 3d Field Artillery soldiers, their wives, and children, sank at the outset of a voyage from New York City around Cape Horn. It carried about 200 people to their deaths. The journey over the disease-ridden isthmus was also bad. One regiment lost 107 men to cholera and various fevers acquired in Panama.

Despite all these difficulties, the scattered garrisons and units of the Army substantially carried out their missions. Although the frontier would not and could not be com-

pletely pacified until the area was more densely settled, the emigrant wagon trains were, in the main, well protected. Indian forays against isolated settlements could not be stopped completely, but they were kept down in part by the Indian's knowledge that a foray was always followed by retaliatory action. Further, the constant warfare and alerts kept the individual units of the Army in a high state of tactical efficiency, although the necessity for garrisoning many dispersed posts (in 1857 there were 68 large, permanent forts, and 70 temporary forts) made brigade and division maneuvers impossible, and there were no brigade headquarters in the Army until the Civil War.

Sutter's Fort in northern California. Built as a private fort and taken over by the U.S. Army in 1846, Sutter's Fort is typical of pre-Civil War forts in the Far West.

Fort Harker in northern Kansas.

Two views of Fort Dodge, Kansas.
Top: inside the fort.
Bottom: the fort store.

Indian fighting in the 1850's.
A Currier and Ives lithograph.

Scene at Fort Bridger where Colonel Johnston's men spent the winter of 1857-1858 during the campaign against the Mormons.

General Albert Sidney Johnston. His successful handling of the Mormon mission won him a promotion to brigadier general. During the Civil War, Johnston, a native of Kentucky, served with the Confederate Army.

TROUBLE WITH THE MORMONS

Indians were not the only source of trouble. To the Utah Territory had immigrated the main body of the Church of Jesus Christ of Latter-day Saints, more popularly called the Mormons. Almost immediately after his inauguration in March 1857, President James Buchanan received reports that the Mormons were defying Federal authority. Although this was not strictly true, Buchanan believed it and acted accordingly. When he sent civil officials to the territory, he decided to send with them a strong body of troops. About 2,500 men—8 companies of the 2d Dragoons, the 5th and 10th Infantry Regiments, and 2 artillery batteries—went out under command of Colonel Albert Sidney Johnston. Before the column could enter the Great Salt Lake Valley, the alarmed Mormons skillfully separated the wagon train from the troops, burned the wagons, and captured many horses. Johnston's isolated force was compelled to spend the winter in the Rockies on short rations. In the spring of 1858 more troops started out from Fort Leavenworth—the 1st Cavalry, the remaining companies of the 2d Dragoons, 2 companies of light artillery, the 6th and 7th Infantry Regiments, detachments from the Mounted Rifles and the 3d Infantry, and a battalion of volunteers—to bring Johnston's strength to 5,500. An agreement was reached with the Mormons, and most of the troops were sent elsewhere before reaching Utah, but as late as 1860 the Army still had 8,282 men in the Department of Utah.

NEW DUTIES FOR THE ARMY ENGINEER

Fighting, though of primary importance, did not absorb all the Army's energies. During this period the Engineers were busy with seacoast fortifications and improving rivers and harbors. The method of building forts underwent some changes. Grass-covered slopes were abandoned in favor of vertical granite walls with the expectation that the guns of the fort would prevent invaders from landing and that long-range cannonading would decide the action. In 1853 responsibility for building the north and south wings of the Capitol in Washington, D.C., was transferred from the Interior Department to the Army Engineers. Captain Montgomery C. Meigs, who became Army Quartermaster General during the Civil War, directed the work and made extensive studies in acoustics, heating, and ventilation in the course of building the Senate and House Chambers. At the same time he supervised initial construction of an aqueduct designed to carry water from the Great Falls of the Potomac to the District of Columbia. The Topographical Engineers were constantly busy with surveys and exploration, generally in hostile Indian country, where every exploring party was a military expedition. The most significant and far-reaching explorations began in 1853; when Congress authorized comprehensive explorations to discover the best railway routes from the Mississippi River to the Far West. Several parties went out, one of which was wiped out by Indians in Utah. The reports of the expeditions resulted in recommendation of four routes which were substantially those eventually followed by the Northern Pacific, the Union Pacific, the Kansas Pacific, and the Southern Pacific when those railroads were built after the Civil War. Largely as a result of Secretary of War Jefferson Davis' recommendation, the United States, in 1853, bought from Mexico a tract of land south of the Gila River in New Mexico (the Gadsden Purchase) to provide a route to California that skirted the Rocky Mountains.

The difficulties of supplying the isolated frontier posts in the arid regions of the Southwest brought an interesting experiment in the use of camels. Davis thought that the camel, which for centuries had been used as a pack and riding animal in the deserts of Asia and Africa, might help solve the Army's supply problem. In 1856 he obtained a small appropriation from Congress and had 30 camels purchased and shipped to Texas where they were able to carry twice as much as a horse could pull in a wagon, and walk surefootedly over ground no wagon could traverse. The next Secretary of War, John B. Floyd, was so enthusiastic that he asked Congress for money to buy a thousand camels, but Congress refused to appropriate the funds. Nevertheless, the original camels and their descendants carried supplies in the Southwest until the Civil War, and some are reported to have carried the Confederate mails in Texas. The Civil War ended the U.S. Army's camel experiment, and the construction of the transcontinental railways after the war made further use of camels unnecessary.

One of the Army's biggest engineering projects during this period—building the north and south wings of the Capitol.

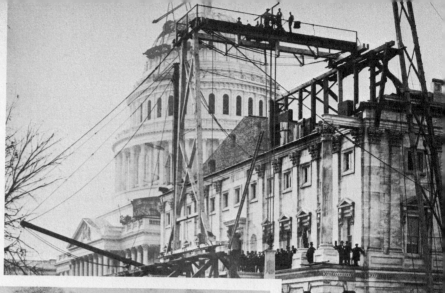

The "Explorer" carries Topographical Engineers on a Colorado River exploring expedition in 1857-1958. The engineers built the steam-driven craft before starting their journey.

En route to Texas.

Soldiers loading camels in Texas.

Jefferson Davis, the Secretary of War who suggested the camel experiment. During the four years he served as head of the War Department, Davis, an 1828 graduate of the Military Academy, raised the soldiers' pay, made improvements at army posts, at West Point and in coastal defenses, and encouraged exploration of the West. During the Civil War he was President of the Confederate States of America.

An early version of the covered wagon.

The "Army wagon." It was similar to the type used by commercial freight carriers.

The escort wagon. It replaced the "Army wagon" and carried a standard load of 3,000 pounds. Its maximum load was 5,000 pounds.

Officers of high rank used the Daugherty wagon.

NEW TYPES OF RIFLES INTRODUCED

Rifles, with their superior range and accuracy, had been used for military purposes in America during the eighteenth century, but their slow rate of fire compared with that of the musket had made it inadvisable to issue them to infantry of the line. However, an improved rifle was gradually replacing the smoothbore musket, as the Mississippi Rifles of the Mexican War, and the addition of two rifle regiments to the Army in 1855 bear witness. Nineteenth-century technological developments had made possible an accurate, dependable muzzle-loading rifle with at least as fast a rate of fire as the smoothbore musket. The earlier introduction of the percussion cap had made the musket much more reliable, and the application of this principle, together with the Minié ball, made the rifle, or rifled musket, a good military weapon. The Minié ball, perfected by Captain C. E. Minié, a French officer, was adopted by the U.S. Army in 1855. It was cylindro-conoidal in shape, and consisted of a lead shell tapering forward from its hollow base. To load and fire, the soldier bit open the paper cartridge, poured the powder down the barrel, rammed in the paper to seat the charge, and then rammed the bullet home. He then put the cap in place, full-cocked the piece, aimed, and fired. Sparks from the cap fired the powder. The force of the explosion expanded the hollow base of the bullet to fit the rifling, and the bullet left the barrel with considerably accuracy. Its maximum range was about 1,000–1,200 yards, and its effective range was about 400–600 yards as compared with 100–200 yards for smoothbore muskets. Rate of fire was a theoretical three rounds a minute, but it was seldom attained in practice. In 1855 manufacture of smoothbore muskets in national armories was stopped and the armories then began making only rifles. The Army also started converting its smoothbores into rifles. The work took time; by the end of 1858 the Springfield and Harpers Ferry Armories had manufactured only 4,000 of the new type of rifle, the Springfield .58. When the Civil War began, most state troops still had smoothbores, and both Federal and Confederate governments had to look to European sources for suitable weapons.

Like rifling, the principle of breech-loading to permit more rapid rates of fire was an old one, but it could not be put into practice until metallurgy and methods of accurate measurement had developed to a state that made possible a tight-fitting, but easy-moving, bolt that would withstand the force of a propellant charge and at the same time operate a firing pin. Many breechloaders were on the market in the 1850's. The Army began testing all available models, but it had not completed its tests by 1861. In 1860, however, Secretary Floyd prophesied that the breechloader would replace the muzzle-loader just as surely as the percussion cap had supplanted flint and steel. Effective breech-loading rifles required metallic rather than paper cartridges to prevent the escape of gases at the breech. Although metallic cartridges were invented in 1856, they were not produced in large numbers until after 1861.

Field artillery ammunition did not change substantially after the Mexican War. Grape and canister shell (high explosive and shrapnel), and solid shot were still standard. The outstanding new development came with the introduction of rifling into both field and coast artillery. As in the case of small arms, rifling greatly increased the accuracy and more than doubled the effective range of artillery, but rifled guns did not immediately supplant the smoothbores since this period also saw the introduction of artillery piece for light batteries—the 12-pound bronze cannon called the "Napoleon" after Napoleon III. It was a smoothbore, but a substantial improvement over older models.

The development of tactical doctrine did not entirely keep pace with the development of weapons, although some efforts were made in that direction. Secretary of War Davis prescribed light infantry tactics for all infantry units in an attempt to put the lessons of the Mexican War into practice and to fit tactical doctrine to the new weapons. In general, this meant reducing the line of the infantry from three to two ranks and placing increased emphasis on skirmishers, but tactics remained basically those of the eighteenth century. Formations were rigid; men stood shoulder to shoulder (it was very difficult to load a muzzle-loader lying down) in ranks, and intervals between units were small. These relatively dense formations would, in the early days of the Civil War, offer inviting targets to the field artillery and to riflemen. But some changes in tactics had been made, and the shock of battle in the Civil War would effect more.

1 CM.
1/2 IN.

Minié Ball.

THE ARMY FLAG

The Army Flag was dedicated and unfurled to the general public on 14 June 1956 at Independence Hall, Philadelphia, on the 181st anniversary of the establishment of the United States Army by the Continental Congress in 1775. Measuring 4 feet 4 inches by 5 feet 6 inches, the flag is of white silk with a blue embroidered central design of the original War Office seal. "United States Army" is inscribed in white letters on a scarlet scroll, with the year "1775" in blue numerals below. The Secretary of the Army designates the Army headquarters and agencies authorized an Army Flag.

In 1962 the Army Field Flag was authorized for issue to headquarters and other Army elements not authorized the Army Flag. Reversing the colors of the Army Flag, the Army Field Flag measures 3 feet by 4 feet; it is of blue silk with central design of the War Office seal in white and a white scroll with "United States Army" inscribed in scarlet. The year "1775" appears in white arabic numerals. On the top of the staff are the streamers representing battles and campaigns.

HERALDIC HISTORY OF THE DEPARTMENT OF THE ARMY SEAL

The Third Board of War, established by the Continental Congress on 29 October 1778, authorized under date of 8 March 1779 a seal for use in authenticating military commissions. This seal appeared on commissions as early as 7 January 1779, and the same design with minor changes was continued in use by the War Department until 18 September 1947 when it was redesignated for use by the Department of the Army.

No official description of the seal has ever been found, nor have any official colors been assigned to the various elements. It is customarily colored bronze and is described in heraldic parlance thus—

On a disk within a band inscribed "United States of America War Office" are the following symbols: On the right side (left from observer's viewpoint) a cannon in front of a drum with two drumsticks; below are three cannon balls. On the left side a mortar on a trunnion; below are two powder flasks. In the center is a Roman breastplate over a jupon. Above the breastplate is a plain sword, point upward, with pommel and guard, supporting a Phrygian cap between an esponton and an organizational color (on the right) and a musket with fixed bayonet and national color of the Revolutionary War period (on the left:) both flags have cord and tassels and flagstaffs with spearheads. Above is a rattlesnake holding in its mouth a scroll inscribed "This We'll Defend." Below the breastplate are the Roman numerals MDCCLXXVIII.

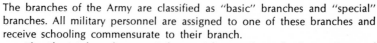
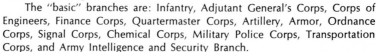
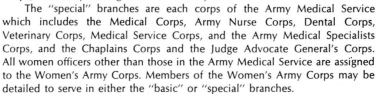

BRANCHES OF THE ARMY

The branches of the Army are classified as "basic" branches and "special" branches. All military personnel are assigned to one of these branches and receive schooling commensurate to their branch.

The "basic" branches are: Infantry, Adjutant General's Corps, Corps of Engineers, Finance Corps, Quartermaster Corps, Artillery, Armor, Ordnance Corps, Signal Corps, Chemical Corps, Military Police Corps, Transportation Corps, and Army Intelligence and Security Branch.

The "special" branches are each corps of the Army Medical Service which includes the Medical Corps, Army Nurse Corps, Dental Corps, Veterinary Corps, Medical Service Corps, and the Army Medical Specialists Corps, and the Chaplains Corps and the Judge Advocate General's Corps. All women officers other than those in the Army Medical Service are assigned to the Women's Army Corps. Members of the Women's Army Corps may be detailed to serve in either the "basic" or "special" branches.

ARMS AND SERVICES

The branches of the Army named above are further grouped into "Arms" and "Services." The Arms are those branches whose primary mission is to fight or directly support the fighting elements. These "Arms" are the Infantry, Armor, Artillery, Corps of Engineers, and Signal Corps.

The Services are those branches whose primary mission is combat service support and/or administration to the Army as a whole. Some branches have missions in both fields. The "Services" are Adjutant General's Corps, Corps of Engineers, Finance Corps, Quartermaster Corps, Army Medical Service, Chaplains, Judge Advocate General's Corps, Ordnance Corps, Signal Corps, Chemical Corps, Military Police Corps, Women's Army Corps, Transportation Corps, and Army Intelligence and Security Branch.

ARMY MAJOR COMMANDS

— Insignia, Headquarters, Missions —

U.S. ARMY ALASKA
FORT RICHARDSON, ALASKA

U.S. Army Alaska is a component of the unified Alaskan Command (ALCOM) whose area of responsibility for normal operations other than air defense and protection of sea communications is Alaska, including the Aleutian Islands and islands of the Bering Sea.

U.S. ARMY FORCES
SOUTHERN COMMAND
FORT AMADOR, CANAL ZONE

U.S. Army Forces Southern Command is an element of the unified U.S. Southern Command (USSOUTHCOM) whose area for normal operations, other than air defense and protection of sea communications, is Central (less Mexico) and South America. For MAAG activities and Service Training Missions only, the area includes all of Latin America.

U.S. ARMY PACIFIC
FORT SHAFTER, HAWAII

U.S. Army Pacific is an element of the unified Pacific Command (PACOM) whose area for normal operations is the Pacific Ocean and its islands (less Aleutians), the Bering Sea (excluding islands therein), the Eastern Indian Ocean area, Japan, Korea, and the countries of Southeast Asia.

U.S. ARMY EUROPE
HEIDELBERG, GERMANY

U.S. Army Europe is a component of the unified U.S. European Command (USEUCOM) whose area of responsibility for normal operations is Western Europe, including the United Kingdom, the Mediterranean and its islands, Turkey, and North Africa, west of Egypt.

U.S. ARMY SECURITY AGENCY
ARLINGTON HALL STATION, VA.

Performs specialized technical functions relating to the national security.

U.S. ARMY MATERIEL COMMAND
WASHINGTON, D.C.

Performs assigned materiel functions of the Department of the Army comprising research, development, engineering, testing and evaluation, procurement and production, integrated materiel inventory management, new equipment training, and technical intelligence; mutual security programs; and, as related to the CONUS wholesale supply and maintenance system, storage and distribution, transportation, maintenance, demilitarization, and disposal.

U.S. ARMY STRATEGIC
COMMUNICATIONS COMMAND
WASHINGTON, D.C.

Directs and controls those Army telecommunications elements which operate strategic radio, wire, and cable facilities, including those supporting the Defense Communications System.

U.S. CONTINENTAL ARMY
COMMAND
FORT MONROE, VIRGINIA

Responsible for recruiting, inducting, equipping, and training of enlisted personnel of the Army, and for organizing, training, equipping, and ensuring the combat readiness of assigned troop units.

**U.S. ARMY
AIR DEFENSE COMMAND
ENT AIR FORCE BASE, COLORADO**
Commands the Army component of the North American Air Defense Command (NORAD) and of the Continental Air Defense Command (CONAD).

**U.S. ARMY
INTELLIGENCE CORPS COMMAND
FORT HOLABIRD, MARYLAND**
Exercises central control of counterintelligence activities throughout the continental United States, and provides counterintelligence support to all U.S. Army elements within the continental United States.

**U.S. ARMY COMBAT
DEVELOPMENTS COMMAND
FORT BELVOIR, VIRGINIA**
Responsible for formulating and documenting current doctrine for the Army, and in anticipation of the nature of land warfare in the future, to determine the kinds of forces and materiel needed, and how these forces should be employed.

**U.S. ARMY FORCES
STRIKE COMMAND
FORT MONROE, VIRGINIA**
(No Insigne)
U.S. Army Forces Strike Command is an element of the unified U.S. Strike Command (USSTRICOM) which is responsible for providing a general reserve of combat-ready forces to reinforce other commands. USSTRICOM area for normal operations also includes the Middle East/Southern Asia and Africa south of the Sahara.

**MILITARY TRAFFIC MANAGEMENT
AND TERMINAL SERVICE
WASHINGTON, D.C.**
(No Insigne)
The Secretary of Defense has announced that effective 15 February 1965 a new single manager organization under the Secretary of Army, known as Military Traffic Management and Terminal Service (MTMTS), will assume responsibity for regulation of surface transportation of military cargo and personnel within continental United States. MTMTS also will be responsible for management of all military ocean terminals except those used by the Navy in support of the fleet.

THE ARMY TODAY

The United States Army continues to be a shield for the Nation. While events in recent years have profoundly reshaped its structure, the Army still has a global mission, mainly concentrated in Europe, Korea and the United States. It maintains 16 active Army divisions, 8 Army National Guard divisions and 12 Army Reserve training divisions. Concurrently, under a security assistance program, the Army helps America's allies attain adequate military capabilities to defend their freedom.

DEPLOYED FORCES

The deployment of Army forces overseas is vital to support national treaty commitments and to serve as a deterrent to aggression. Troops assigned to United States Army Europe and the Seventh U.S. Army are prepared to meet armed aggression against free world countries in Europe.

Eighth Army soldiers stationed in Korea continue to serve with distinction to help maintain the security of the Republic of Korea. This American presence has forged a stronger South Korea and provides evidence of our Nation's determination to honor its commitments.

SPECIALIZED COMMANDS

Diverse responsibilities of the Army within the United States are assigned to specialized commands.
● The U.S. Army Forces Command (FORSCOM), Fort McPherson, Georgia, is responsible for unit training and operational readiness of all deployable combat and support forces of the Active Army, Army National Guard, and U.S. Army Reserve.
● The U.S. Army Training and Doctrine Command (TRADCO), Fort Monroe, Virginia, provides professional training for the individual soldier in service schools and training centers, manages the Army ROTC program, and directs combat developments. It also supports individual and collective training in units.
● The U.S. Army Materiel Development and Readiness Command (DARCOM, formerly AMC), Washington, D.C., is responsible for the research and development of materiel, and the readiness of that materiel while in the hands of the troops.
● The U.S. Army Health Services Command, Fort Sam Houston, Texas, provides medical health services, medical training and education in health specialties.
● The Military District of Washington, Washington, D.C., is responsible for Arlington National Cemetery, the conduct of all joint military ceremonies as they relate to visits of foreign heads of state and other dignitaries (to the White House), for state funerals, and other support or contingency missions that may be directed.
● The U.S. Army Communications Command, Fort Huachuca, Arizona, provides for the Army's long distance, intercontinental communications complex operating throughout the world.
● The U.S. Army Criminal Investigation Command, Washington, D.C., performs and exercises centralized command authority, direction, and control of Army criminal investigative activities worldwide.
● The U.S. Army Recruiting Command (USAREC), Fort Sheridan, Illinois, recruits personnel from civilian life for the Active Army, examines and processes applicants for enlistment in the Armed Forces, and assists the U.S. Army Reserve in its recruiting efforts.

THE REGULAR ARMY DIVISIONS

The ground combat strength of 1966's Regular Army is embodied in 17 divisions—infantry, mechanized infantry, armored, airmobile, airborne. Organized under the ROAD concept, these divisions are deployed around the globe—in Germany, Santo Domingo, Hawaii, Korea, Vietnam, and the United States. Manned by alert, trained troops, commanded by outstanding professionals, they carry the punch that backs up our nation's global commitments. The 9th Infantry Division, recently reactivated, is not covered in detail. (Activated 1 February 1966.)

1st INFANTRY DIVISION
"The Big Red One"
Viet Nam

Distinctive Insignia of
non-color-bearing units.

FORMERLY stationed at Fort Riley, Kansas, the 1st Infantry Division's 2d Brigade deployed to Vietnam in July 1965, followed by the rest of the "Big Red One" during the build-up in October 1965. This marks the Division's first duty in the Far East. Its motto: "No Mission Too Difficult; No Sacrifice Too Great; Duty First."

Originally organized in 1917 as the First Expeditionary Division, it was redesignated as the 1st Division and in 1942 became the 1st Infantry Division. It was the first American division in World War I to meet the enemy, suffer casualties, capture prisoners, stage a major offensive and enter Germany. Returning to the United States in September 1919, its units were scattered along the eastern seaboard until August 1942 when the Division was sent to England for training. In World War II it made the first major landing against the European Axis powers, striking into North Africa where it hit Oran and engaged at Kasserine Pass and El Guettar. In July 1943 the Division invaded Sicily. In 1944 the Big Red One landed at Omaha Beach, then drove on through France and Germany. It was in Czechoslovakia when hostilities ended. After 10 years of occupation duty in Germany, the Division traded places with 10th Infantry Division at Fort Riley, then moved to Viet Nam in 1965.

2d INFANTRY DIVISION
"Indianhead"
Korea

IN 1965 in a transfer of units and colors minus personnel and equipment, the 2d Infantry Division replaced the 1st Cavalry Division in Korea.

Activated in Bourmont, France, on 26 October 1917, it was originally formed from Army and Marine Corps units with a Marine Corps brigadier general as its first commander. In World War I the unit won more decorations than any other American division, participating in six major campaigns. In World War II the Division landed in Normandy on 7 June 1944, fought through France and Germany, and had reached Pilsen, Czechoslovakia, when the European fighting ended. The Division arrived in Korea in early August 1950, where it was utilized in fire brigade action, moving swiftly to counter enemy threats, then meeting the Chinese Communist Forces as the war expanded.

3d INFANTRY DIVISION
"The Marne Division"
Germany

Distinctive Insignia of
non-color-bearing units.

COMBAT-READY and highly mobile, the 3d Infantry Division constantly engages in hard training in practical field exercises to fulfill its mission as part of the front-line shield of NATO. Known as the Marne Division, its unofficial slogan is "Nous Resterons Là" ("We're Staying There") from a remark by its commanding general when asked what the Division intended to do in the face of an all-out German attack in World War I.

Organized on 21 November 1917, the Division went

overseas in April 1918 and earned six battle streamers in World War I campaigns. In November 1942 the Division went overseas again to land in North Africa, then on to Sicily, Anzio and the Southern France invasion. The Division returned to the United States in 1946, and in September 1950 went to Korea where it engaged in eight campaigns. The Marne Division claims 49 Medal of Honor winners—tops for any United States Army division.

> MEMORABLE MOMENT. Not one, but three are recorded—one in each of the three wars it has fought. In World War I, the division's baptism under fire on the Marne River early in 1918 won its name and motto. In World War II, the division's action in clearing the Colmar Pocket resulted in its being awarded the Distinguished Unit Citation and French Croix de Guerre with Palm. In the Korean War, the Marnemen distinguished themselves in smashing the infamous Iron Triangle, winning the second of its two Korean citations.

4th INFANTRY DIVISION
"Ivy Division" or "Famous Fourth"
Fort Lewis, Washington

Distinctive Insignia of
non-color-bearing units.

AS PART OF ARSTRIKE, the 4th Infantry Division has participated in exercises from Alaska to Puerto Rico and from Europe to the Philippines. Organized at Camp Green, North Carolina, in December 1917, the Division arrived in France during May-June 1918, then took part in five campaigns and served seven months on occupation duty. It was inactivated 1 August 1919, then activated at Fort Benning in June 1940. After leading the Normandy invasion it participated in the First Army drive for the liberation of Paris. It breached the Siegfried Line in four places and took part in the Battle of the Bulge. It was deep in Germany when the fighting ended in Europe. Inactivated at Camp Butner, North Carolina, in March 1946, it was activated as a training division in July 1947 at Fort Ord, California, and went to Europe in 1951 as part of the NATO structure. It returned to the United States in September 1956, and became a component unit of STRAC in 1958. In 1961 it helped train activated units called to active duty during the defense forces buildup.

> MEMORABLE MOMENTS. The Division's World War II fight against four Nazi divisions in the Huertgen Forest and its contribution in repelling the German attack in the Battle of the Bulge.

5th INFANTRY DIVISION
(MECHANIZED)
"Red Diamond"
Fort Carson, Colorado

Distinctive Insignia of
non-color-bearing units.

THE 5th Infantry Division (Mechanized)—which became known to the Germans in World War II as the "Red Devils" —is now located at Fort Carson, Colorado. Its motto—"We will."

Probably inactivated and activated more often than any other Regular Army Division, the 5th was organized 11 December 1917 at Camp Logan, Texas. It fought through four campaigns in World War I, highlighting its actions with the crossing of the Meuse River at Dun, a feat hailed as "brilliant" by General Pershing. It was inactivated in 1921 at Camp Jackson, South Carolina, then activated in October 1939 at Fort McClellan, Alabama. It was one of the first U.S. units to go overseas in World War II, being based in Iceland in 1942. World War II found the Red Diamond retracing many of its earlier steps through France and Germany. Again it gained fame for river crossings under fire. It was inactivated in September 1946 at Camp Campbell, Kentucky, activated 15 July 1947 at Fort Jackson, South Carolina, inactivated 30 April 1950 at Fort Jackson, activated once more on 6 April 1951 and then inactivated 1 September 1953. On 25 May 1954 it was activated in Germany and inactivated in 1957 at Fort Ord, California. In February 1962 it was finally organized, this time as a mechanized ROAD division.

> MEMORABLE MOMENT: The assault crossing of the Rhine River on 22 March 1945.

7th INFANTRY DIVISION
"Bayonet Division"
Korea

Distinctive Insignia of non-color-bearing units.

Organized 1 January 1918 at Camp Wheeler, Georgia, the 7th Infantry Division went overseas in August 1918 and fought in the Lorraine campaign. It was inactivated in 1921, then activated 1 July 1940 at Fort Ord, California, and has been an active division ever since. In April 1943 it went to the Aleutian Islands, then fought on Kwajalein, Leyte, and in the Ryukyus. Immediately following the war, the Division occupied Korea, moving to Japan in late 1948. It returned to Korea in September 1950 as part of the United Nations force landing at Inchon. It penetrated to the Yalu River, border between Korea and Red China. Since the Japanese surrender in 1945, the Division has accumulated almost 7,000 days in Korea. On 1 July 1963, the Division was reorganized under the ROAD concept.

LIVING UP to their motto—"In War Invincible, In Peace Prepared"—the Bayonetmen today are stationed in Korea.

8th INFANTRY DIVISION
"Golden Arrow" "Pathfinders"
Germany

AS PART of the U.S. Seventh Army, the 8th's primary mission is to help bolster the NATO defense perimeter against any aggressor. Headquarters is located at Bad Kreuznach, Germany. Organized in January 1918 at Camp Fremont, California, the Division is sometimes called "Pathfinder" after the soldier and explorer John Frémont. Arriving in France after the Armistice was signed, one of its units, the 8th Infantry, became part of the Army of Occupation. Demobilized in September 1919, it was reconstituted as an inactive unit in 1923. In World War II, it landed in France on 4 July 1944 and took part in four campaigns. The Division was inactivated in November 1945. In August 1950 it was again activated at Fort Jackson, South Carolina, as an infantry division and in June 1952 was again reorganized at Camp Carson, Colorado, where it continued its training mission. In 1956 the Division "gyroscoped" to Germany, as a component of the Seventh Army. In August 1961 the 1st Battle Group, 18th Infantry, went to West Berlin where it reinforced the garrison during the Berlin Crisis.

MEMORABLE MOMENT. When in World War II Brigadier General Charles D. W. Canham, then the assistant division commander, confronted German Lieutenant General Hermann Barnard Ramcke in Ramcke's underground headquarters, the German addressed Canham through his interpreter: "I am to surrender to you. Let me see your credentials." Pointing to the infantrymen crowding the dugout entrance, Canham replied, "These are my credentials." Thus was born the division's slogan.

24th INFANTRY DIVISION
"Victory Division"
Germany

Distinctive Insignia of non-color-bearing units.

WITH headquarters in Southern Bavaria, the "Victory Division"—which has never served in the continental United States—together with units of West Germany's Bundeswehr, stands ready to combat any aggressor.

First organized in 1921 as the Hawaiian Division at Schofield Barracks, Hawaii, it was redesignated on 1 October 1941 as the 24th Infantry Division, and received its baptism of fire when Pearl Harbor was attacked. Three years later the Division stormed the beaches of New Guinea, seized Hollandia Airdrome, then participated in campaigns on Leyte and Luzon in the Philippines. In October 1945 it entered the Japanese homeland, remaining for nearly five years.

In July 1950, it was rushed to South Korea where it earned the Distinguished Unit Citation. It spearheaded the breakout from the Pusan Perimeter and the drive to the Yalu River. Returning to Japan in January 1952, it went back to Korea for the final months of hostilities in July 1953.

The "Victory" Division was transferred to Department of the Army control at zero strength in December 1957, then reorganized on 1 July 1958 in Germany, replacing the 11th Airborne Division being inactivated concurrently. Almost immediately, elements were used to form an airborne task force which was deployed for crisis duty in Lebanon. In July 1960, its men were alerted for the Congo crisis. After the Berlin Wall went up, the 1st Battalion, 19th Infantry moved to Berlin to augment the divided city's forces. The 24th has since been providing one battalion to serve with the Berlin Brigade, on a rotating basis.

25th INFANTRY DIVISION
"Tropic Lightning"
Viet Nam

Distinctive Insignia of
non-color-bearing units.

THE 25th Infantry ("Tropic Lightning") Division was activated at Schofield Barracks, Hawaii, just nine weeks before Pearl Harbor Day. On 23 December 1942 it landed on Guadalcanal, then secured the island of New Georgia in late 1943. On 11 January 1945 it landed on the island of Luzon, where it saw 165 days of continuous combat.

After five years of occupation duty in Japan it was rushed to Korea in July 1950. It engaged in defensive actions, then with other UN forces broke out of the Pusan Perimeter to drive the enemy deep into North Korea. When the Chinese attacked in November, the Division covered the withdrawal of UN forces, then counterattacked to free Seoul in March 1951, and assisted in driving the CCF into the "Iron Triangle" area north of the 38th Parallel. From January 1963 to December 1965 the Division sent troops to Viet Nam as aerial machine gunners nicknamed "Shotgunners."

MEMORABLE MOMENT: The Division's 165 continuous days of combat on the island of Luzon.

1st ARMORED DIVISION
"Old Ironsides"
Fort Hood, Texas

FIRST armored division to be organized in the U.S. Army, the 1st Armored was activated in March 1932 at Fort Knox, Kentucky, as the 7th Cavalry Brigade (Mechanized), and was designated as 1st Armored Division in July 1940. It was regarded as the parent of most of the succeeding armored units since it supplied so many cadres for newly organizing divisions. As the first armored command to go overseas in World War II, it landed in Algeria, fought through the Tunisia Campaign, then landed in 1943 between Salerno and Paestum in Italy. In January 1944 it entered the Anzio beachhead and finally broke out of the ring of German resistance and pushed on to Rome—the first American unit to enter an enemy capital in World War II. It was inactivated in April 1946, then activated at Fort Hood in March 1951 during the Korean War. "Old Ironsides" was reduced in strength in November 1957 to a single Combat Command "A." On 3 February 1962, the Division was again brought up to strength as a Regular Army division under the new ROAD concept. In October 1962, the 1st was declared a member of the Strategic Army Corps and almost simultaneously the Division carried out its first STRAC mobility test. Responding to the Cuban crisis the entire Division moved to Fort Stewart, Georgia. While in the Southeast, 12 of its battalions took part in amphibious training maneuvers in southeastern Florida. The Division returned to Fort Hood on 20 December. In spring 1964, men of Old Ironsides traveled 1,500 miles to the Mojave Desert to participate in Exercise Desert Strike.

MEMORABLE MOMENTS: One of the 1st Armored Division's finest moments came in North Africa on 9 May 1943, when the German Afrika Corps led by Field Marshal Erwin Rommel, hopelessly crushed, surrendered to the American II Corps. "Old Ironsides." after many months of hard fighting, processed thousands of the surrendering soldiers.

2d ARMORED DIVISION
"Hell on Wheels"
Fort Hood, Texas

FAMED as Patton's "Hell on Wheels" division, the 2d Armored is located at Fort Hood, Texas, as part of the Strategic Army Forces.

Organized 15 January 1940, it is the only Army armored division that has been on continuous active duty. Under command of General George S. Patton, Jr., the Division prepared for overseas service during stateside maneuvers in the early '40s. Thereafter, the "Hell on Wheels" division fought in North Africa, Sicily, and throughout Europe. It was part of the force that eliminated the German "bulge" in December 1944 and was the first American unit to enter Berlin the next year. After peacetime service at Camp Hood, Texas, the 2d Armored moved to Europe in 1951 as part of the "Mailed Fist of NATO." In 1957 the Division returned to Fort Hood where it trained recruits. In three and a half years, the 2d trained more than 90,000 soldiers in basic military skills.

The Berlin crisis brought a change in mission; it became a full combat-ready tactical unit in 1961, and in 1962 it became the first regular armored division to be assigned to the Strategic Army Corps. In 1963 it participated in the history-making Exercise Big Lift. Elements of the Iron Deuce also participated in the 1964 Exercise Long Thrust X. In early 1964 the Division became the first armored division in the United States to receive the Army's new Main Battle tank, the M-60, subsequently used in the 1964 U.S. Strike Command Exercise Desert Strike.

> **MEMORABLE MOMENTS:** Chosen to be the first American unit to roll into fallen Berlin on 4 July 1945, it was also picked to provide the honor guard for President Truman during the Potsdam Conference.

3d ARMORED DIVISION
"Spearhead Division"
Germany

Distinctive Insignia of
non-color-bearing units.

STATIONED in Germany, the 3d Armored Division plays a key role in the defense of Western Europe as part of the NATO shield of defense. Known as the "Spearhead Division," it was organized in April 1941 at Camp Beauregard, Louisiana, with a cadre drawn from the 2d Armored Division. In September 1943 the Division underwent further training in England, and on 23 June 1944 hit Omaha Beach and received its baptism by fire in the hedgerow country near Saint-Lô. It joined VII Corps forces to close the Argentan-Falaise gap, routing the German 7th Army and continuing on through the Siegfried Line to enter Cologne and then on across the Rhine. The Division was at Dessau on the Elbe River when hostilities ended in Europe. After a brief tour of occupation duty in Germany, the Division was inactivated in Germany in November 1945. In mid-1947, the Spearhead was reactivated as a training division at Fort Knox, Kentucky. The Division continued to train new soldiers until April 1955, when it became a combat division and participated in operation Gyroscope. After a period of intensified training the 3d Armored Division came back to Germany in the spring of 1956 to become part of U.S. Seventh Army.

> **MEMORABLE MOMENT:** The 90-mile, one-day march on the Paderborn to seal off the Ruhr in World War II.

4th ARMORED DIVISION
Germany

Distinctive Insignia of
non-color-bearing units.

NOW stationed in Germany supporting NATO's first line of defense, the 4th Armored's mission is to help maintain peace by being constantly combat ready. This means intense training and participation in the various exercises staged by Seventh Army.

The 4th Armored Division was organized at Pine Camp, New York, on 15 April 1941, and served initially as a training unit. In 1943 it moved to England, and on 11 July 1944 it landed at Utah Beach in the Normandy invasion. The Division fought through the Brittany Peninsula, drove across France, then across the Saar River to establish a bridgehead. When the Germans launched their Ardennes offensive, the 4th Armored raced 150 miles northwest into Belgium in 19 hours to help relieve the besieged 101st Airborne Division at Bastogne. Six weeks later the 4th Armored plunged across the Moselle River, then crossed the Rhine and fought on into Czechoslovakia by the end of hostilities. Following the war, many elements of the Division were on occupation duty in Europe as Constabulary before being inactivated. On 15 June 1954, the Division was activated at Fort Hood, Texas. Three years later it was back at the scene of its wartime conquests, this time as an ally.

> **MEMORABLE MOMENT:** The Division's drive into Belgium to relieve the defenders of Bastogne in the Battle of the Bulge.

1st CAVALRY DIVISION (AIRMOBILE)
"The First Team"
Viet Nam

Distinctive Insignia of
non-color-bearing units.

THE ARMY'S new 1st Cavalry Division (Airmobile) is currently involved in the Viet Nam War in the central highlands of Viet Nam. The division was formed in August 1965.

The Division claims three famous "firsts"—first in Manila, first in Tokyo, and first in Pyongyang, capital of North Korea. Formally activated on 13 September 1921 at Fort Bliss, Texas, the 1st was made up of units tracing back to days when cavalry guarded frontiers against Indian raids or patrolled the Mexican border—the 1st, 5th, 7th, and 8th cavalry Regiments. In 1943 the Division was dismounted, sailed for Australia, and in 1944 stormed ashore on Los Negros. The Division landed on Leyte, then went on to Luzon where a flying column made a 100-mile thrust through enemy-held territory to free prisoners of the infamous Santo Tomás prison camp; the rest of the Division followed to liberate Manila. On 8 September 1945 it entered Tokyo.

The Division remained on occupation duty in Japan until the outbreak of the Korean War. On 18 July it carried out the first amphibious landing at Pohangdong, then pushed north to capture Pyongyang, capital of North Korea. In December 1951 it moved to Japan where it stayed until 1957 when it was returned to Korea. It served in Korea until August 1965 when the colors of the 1st Cavalry Division were flown to Fort Benning where the new airmobile division was organized and then deployed in Viet Nam.

82d AIRBORNE DIVISION
"All American"
Fort Bragg, North Carolina

Distinctive Insignia of
non-color-bearing units.

THE BULK of the 82d Airborne Division is presently located at Fort Bragg, North Carolina. However, the 1st Brigade is still serving as part of the Inter-American Peace Force in the Dominican Republic. Living up to its motto of "All the way," it is prepared to go anywhere, anytime, and fight. It stages training and field exercises from Alaska to the jungles of Panama.

Activated in August 1917 at Camp Gordon, Georgia, as the 82d Division, it participated in three campaigns in World War I. It was demobilized in 1919, then in 1921 reconstituted in the Organized Reserves. Ordered into active military service in March 1942, it became the Army's first airborne division. It made the first division-size combat jump in Sicily, occupied Naples, and sent some units to the Anzio beachhead. After moving to England where it was reinforced, it spearheaded the Normandy invasion, liberated the French city of Sainte-Mère-Eglise. Later it jumped into the Netherlands and seized bridges across the Maas and Wall rivers at Nijmegen. Committed next in the Battle of the Bulge, the Division dented Von Rundstedt's northern salient, breached the Siegfried Line in two places, crossed the Rhine and Elbe rivers and occupied Berlin as "America's Guard of Honor."

In May 1964 the 82d was reorganized as a ROAD division and became a member of ARSTRIKE. As such it is prepared to deploy rapidly to trouble spots anywhere in the world as it demonstrated in April 1965 when it was deployed to the Dominican Republic during the crisis there.

> MEMORABLE MOMENT: On the nights of 9 and 10 July 1943, members of the 505th and 504th Parachute Infantry Regiments plunged into the darkness behind enemy lines near Gela, Sicily —marking the first division-size parachute operation in the history of the United States Army.

101st AIRBORNE DIVISION
"Screaming Eagles"
Fort Campbell, Kentucky

A MAJOR component of the United States Strike Command, the 101st Airborne Division, except for one brigade, is stationed at Fort Campbell, Kentucky, where it was reorganized 21 September 1956 to pioneer the Army's pentomic concept.

Known as the "Screaming Eagles," the Division history reflects the changes in warfare and in U.S. Army organization in recent years. Partially organized as the 101st Division in World War I, the unit was demobilized in December 1918 before its organization was completed. Reconstituted in 1921 the division was organized in June of that year with headquarters at Milwaukee, Wisconsin. On 15 August 1942 the division was ordered to active military service at Camp Claiborne, Louisiana, as the 101st Airborne Division.

In World War II one of its members was the first to land in occupied France to mark the drop zone prior to the Normandy invasion. The Division dropped before the 4th Infantry Division came ashore at Utah Beach, then in September 1944 staged the airborne operation into Holland. Units were thrown into the line at Bastogne to hold that key town during the Battle of the Bulge. It was the commanding general of the Division, General Anthony C. McAuliffe, who gave the famous rejoinder "Nuts" to the German demand for surrender there. The Division is one of the few divisions to be cited as a whole for the Distinguished Unit Citation. One of its brigades has been deployed to Viet Nam and is currently conducting operations against the Viet Cong.

9th INFANTRY DIVISION

Distinctive Insignia of
9th Infantry Division
non-color-bearing units.

Activated 1 February at Fort Riley, the 9th Infantry Division will be organized under the ROAD concept. It will include 9 maneuver battalions, a cavalry squadron, an engineer battalion, and division artillery. It will have 3 brigade headquarters, an aviation battalion, signal battalion, and the

typical support command setup with headquarters company and band, administration company, medical battalion, supply and transport battalion, and a maintenance battalion. In addition, there will be a division headquarters and headquarters company and a military police company.

Standard in a ROAD setup are brigades numbered one through three—1st, 2d, and 3d Brigade—consisting of a headquarters and headquarters company. Under the ROAD organization, any of the other elements of the division can be attached to any brigade upon decision of the commander during field problems or combat. This flexible arrangement makes it possible to tailor a fighting force for any type of warfare.

The Infantry units will be the 2d, 3d and 4th Battalions, 39th Infantry; 2d, 3d and 4th Battalions, 47th Infantry; 2d, 3d, and 5th Battalions, 60th Infantry. The 5th Battalion, 60th Infantry will be mechanized. The Cavalry is the 3d Squadron, 5th Cavalry, and the maintenance battalion will be the 709th. Artillery organizations will be the 1st Battalion, 11th Artillery; 2d Battalion, 4th Artillery; 3d Battalion, 34th Artillery; and 1st Battalion, 84th Artillery. There will also be an Honest John battalion, known as the 3d Battalion, 28th Artillery.

9th INFANTRY DIVISION BATTLE CREDITS
(Campaign Streamers)
World War II
Tunisia • Sicily • Normandy • Northern France •
Ardennes • Rhineland • Central Europe

Proud heritage of the 9th Infantry Division —"The Old Reliables" whose deeds of valor reverberated across North Africa, Sicily, Central Europe in World War II—joins the 16 other regular divisions of the active Army.

Divisions Inactivated and Reactivated Since 1967:

23d Inf Div	Activated	25 Sep 67	7th Inf Div	Inactivated	2 Apr 71
6th Inf Div	Activated	24 Nov 67	23d Inf Div	Inactivated	29 Nov 71
6th Inf Div	Inactivated	25 Jul 68	9th Inf Div	Activated	21 Apr 72
9th Inf Div	Inactivated	25 Sep 69	7th Inf Div	Activated	21 Apr 72
24th Inf Div	Inactivated	15 April 70	5th Inf Div	Activated	21 Sept 75
5th Inf Div	Inactivated	15 Dec 70	24th Inf Div	Activated	21 Sept 75
4th Arm Div	Inactivated	10 May 71			

FLAGS are signs and symbols of the Army organizations. Whenever the Army undergoes a major reorganization, some familiar symbols may disappear, to be replaced by others representing the new types of organizations.

Under current ROAD (Reorganization Objective Army Divisions) structure the active Army will have four types of divisions—Infantry, Mechanized, Airborne, and Armor. (The 1st Cavalry was organized as an Infantry division.) While basic organic structure is the same for all, composition of each type may be varied by the "mix" of the combat battalions, according to mission.

The accompanying charts show all the types of flags authorized for the ROAD divisions. Several of these are new; a few of the old types have disappeared, including the distinguishing flag for Division Train Headquarters and the organizational colors for the Transportation Battalion and the Ordnance Battalion. An explanation of the designs of the new types of flags follows.

Headquarters of each brigade of a division has a distinguishing flag with the background (field) divided into two equal vertical stripes of the same colors as the distinguishing flag for the division headquarters—i.e., red and blue for Infantry, Infantry (Mechanized) and Airborne divisions; red and yellow for Armored divisions and the 1st Cavalry Division. The shoulder sleeve insignia of the division (in a smaller size than used on the flag for the division) is in the upper part of the flag on the line where the colors meet, and below it is the brigade number. This combination of colors, insignia and numeral identifies the type of division, specific division, and specific brigade of the division. The guidon for the brigade headquarters company is, of course, of the same design as the distinguishing flag for the brigades.

Headquarters, Support Command has a distinguishing flag showing connection with the division. The background has three vertical stripes that repeat the colors of the division flag in equal amounts but the red has been divided to make a stripe at each end of the flag. The number of the Support Command (which is the number of the division) is in the center of the flag. For the 1st Cavalry Division Support Command the designation "CAV" follows the number to distinguish it from the flag for the 1st Armored Division Support Command. The guidon for the Headquarters Company repeats the design.

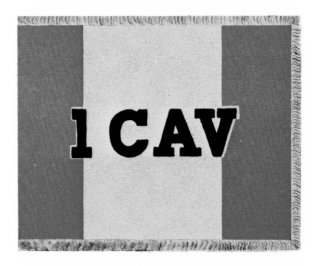

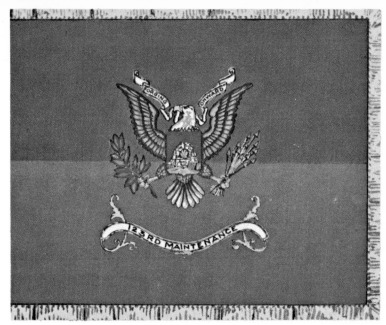

Maintenance Battalion is another new type comparable in organization to the Supply and Transport battalion. As in the case of the Supply and Transport battalion, the background of the organizational color and the guidons show a combination of colors—in this instance, crimson for Ordnance and brick red for Transportation. The Maintenance battalion inherits the history and coat of arms of the Ordnance battalion of the Division. In the Airborne Divisions, this battalion is already known as the Maintenance battalion. Under the reorganization, there is no change in name—only a change in the background color of the organizational color and in the design of the guidons.

Aviation Battalion is not assigned to a specific Army branch and, therefore, the background color of the organization color is teal blue. Guidons for the companies of the battalion are also teal blue. The insignia is that for units not assigned to a branch. To distinguish Aviation battalions from other units using the teal blue guidons, the companies of the Aviation battalions are identified by "AVN" after the battalion number above the insignia. The battalion color does not need such identification because the name is on the scroll below the eagle. The Aviation battalion of the division will have a new coat of arms.

Supply and Transport Battalion combines similar services that were formerly performed by units of different branches. Because this new type battalion is a combination of branches, no one branch color or insignia is appropriate. The background of the battalion color is a combination of the first named branch color of the two predominant branches in the new battalion—i.e., buff for Quartermaster and brick red for Transportation. The guidons for the companies of the Supply and Transport battalion are divided in the same way and no branch insignia is used. The Supply and Transport battalion inherits the history of the Quartermaster company of the division, which in most cases was previously a Quartermaster battalion. Historic coats of arms of Quartermaster battalions are being redesignated for the new battalions and are being used on the battalion colors.

191

Infantry Divisions
7th Inf Div Illustrated

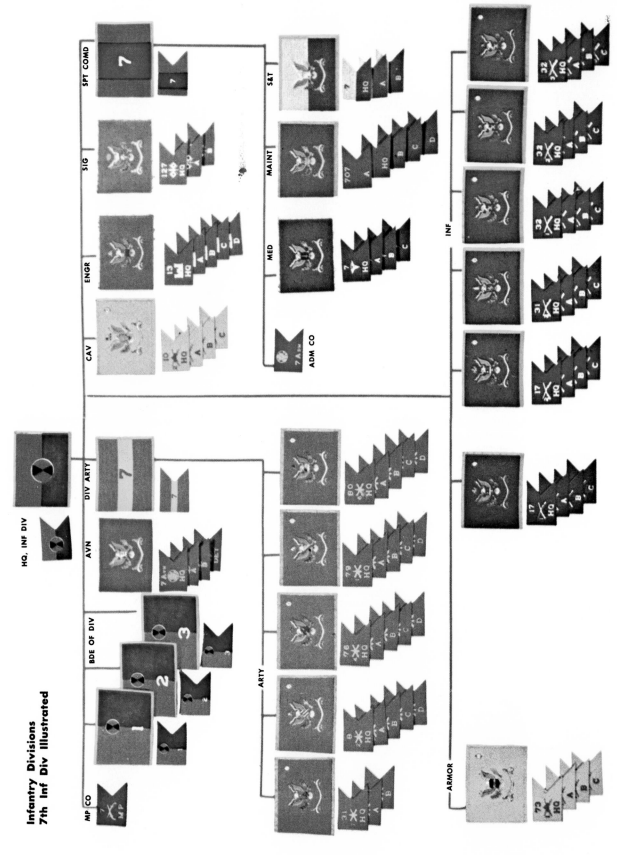

Armored Divisions
1st Armored Div Illustrated

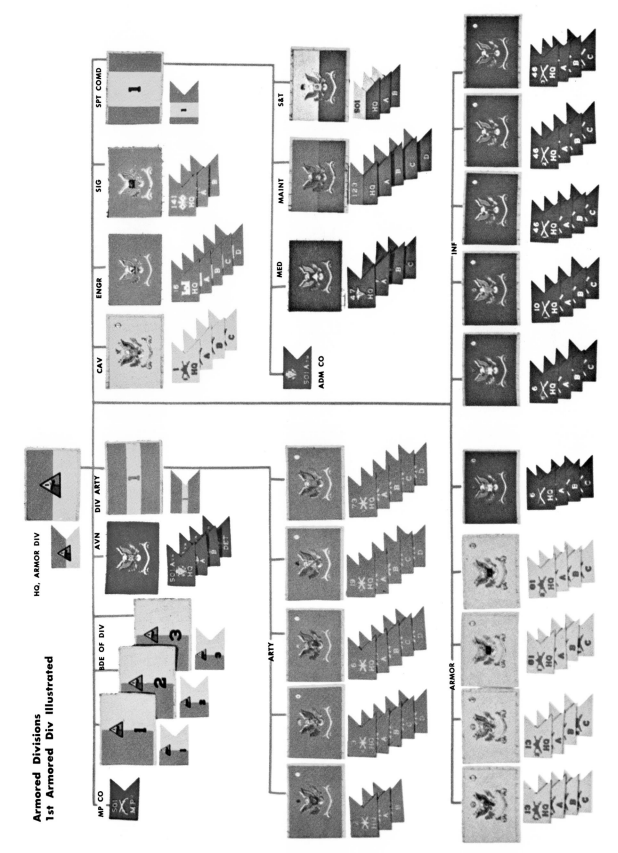

1st Cavalry Division

The 1st Cavalry Division, which is organized as an Infantry Division, has flags similar to those for an Armored Division except for some of the guidons. The Cavalry battalions organized as Infantry are authorized the old red and white Cavalry guidons which have no branch insignia.

194

Fort Sumter under bombardment. Although begun in 1829, the fort was still unfinished in 1861, and less than half of its intended capacity of 140 guns were available for defense.

CHAPTER 8

THE CIVIL WAR

The American Civil War was, after the Napoleonic struggles, the largest and longest major conflict in the Western world during the nineteenth centry. It was the last American war in which infantry attacked in the open in dense formations, but it also saw the employment of railroads, balloons, the telegraph, steamships, armor plate, revolving turrets, rifled artillery, long-range rifles, and even breechloaders. Not all these were new, but in the Civil War they were used on an unprecedented scale.

PRELUDE TO WAR

The election of Abraham Lincoln to the Presidency in 1860 triggered the states of the Deep South into enacting ordinances of secession and taking possession of Federal property, including forts, arsenals, and navy yards, within their borders. By February 1861 seven states—South Carolina, Georgia, Alabama, Florida, Mississippi, Louisiana, and Texas—had declared themselves out of the Union and had set up in Montgomery, Alabama, a provisional government calling itself the Confederate States of America. Its President, Jefferson Davis, was a U.S. Military Academy graduate who, like Mr. Lincoln, had seen service in the Black Hawk War. Subsequently Davis had resigned from the Army to become a planter, distinguished himself as a regimental commander in the Mexican War, and had served as United States Senator and Secretary of War. By the time Mr. Lincoln took the Presidential oath on 4 March 1861, the only places within the Confederacy that were effectively controlled by the U.S. Government were Fort Pickens at Pensacola and Fort Sumter in Charleston harbor. Eight slave states—Delaware, Maryland, Virginia, North Carolina, Ken-

tucky, Tennessee, Missouri, and Arkansas—remained within the Union but strongly secessionist opinion prevailed in several of them.

The actions of the dissident states had a disrupting effect on the Regular Army, which on 1 January 1861 consisted of 1,098 officers and 15,304 enlisted men mostly stationed in the West to ensure peace on the Indian frontier. Most, but not all, of the Southern-born officers resigned their commissions and offered their services to the Confederate government. Some Northern-born officers joined the Confederates, but most stayed in the U.S. Army. The enlisted men could not resign. Almost to a man, they remained faithful to their oaths.

Fort Sumter Falls

President Lincoln was determined to maintain the Union and to hold Fort Sumter and Fort Pickens (and the latter did stay in Union hands), but he had to move cautiously. He was anxious to avert civil war, eager to avoid any act that would drive the eight remaining slave-holding states out of the Union, and well aware that he was not backed by a unanimous public opinion in the North. Major Robert Anderson, Sumter's commander, had earlier withdrawn his tiny garrison from the indefensible Fort Moultrie in Charleston Harbor. Since then he had been virtually besieged by a growing Confederate force. In January 1861 an unarmed supply vessel attempted to bring in reinforcements and supplies for Anderson's men, but was fired on by Confederate batteries and withdrew. President Lincoln, after receiving conflicting counsel from his civilian and military advisers, decided to succor the fort by dispatching a sea-

195

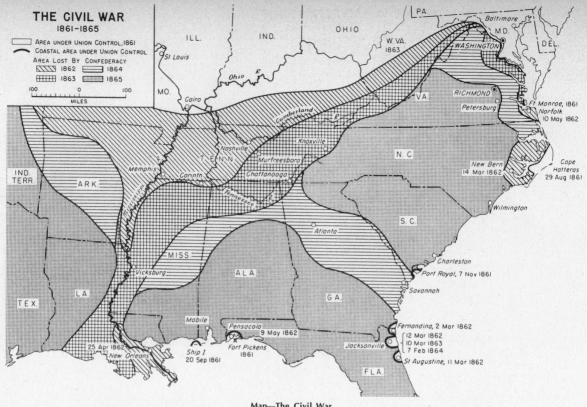

THE CIVIL WAR
1861-1865

Area under Union Control, 1861
Coastal area under Union Control
Area Lost By Confederacy
1862 1864
1863 1865

100   0   100
MILES

Map—The Civil War.

borne expedition, and he so notified the Governor of South Carolina. But the Confederates lost patience. On 12 April 1861, after Anderson had rejected a demand for his surrender, Confederate cannon ringing the harbor's shore began a 34-hour bombardment. Fort Sumter returned the fire, but the result was inevitable. Anderson surrendered with the honors of war and on 14 April, his 90-man garrison saluted the United States flag and marched aboard ship for New York. This incident was minute in itself, but the rashness of the Confederates in committing an overt act of war removed any difficulties from Lincoln's path. It crystallized a large body of Northern opinion in favor of preservation of the Union, and gave the President the resolution to act swiftly and decisively.

Acting under authority vested in him by the Militia Act of 1795, Lincoln immediately called upon the governors of the loyal states to furnish 75,000 militiamen to suppress the rebellion. These men were to serve for three months, the maximum time possible under the law. The response from most of the states was so enthusiastic that nearly 100,000 men were offered. On the other hand, the President's decision to use force led Virginia, North Carolina, Tennessee, and Arkansas to join the Confederacy. (Virginia's western counties refused to secede, however, and remained in the Union.) Virginia's secession lost to the United States the services of Colonel Robert E. Lee, a distinguished officer whom Lieutenant General Winfield Scott, General in Chief of the Army, had decided should have the field command of the forces in the event of war. Colonel Lee, though personally opposed to slavery and to secession, felt that he could not honorably fight against Virginia, his native state. He resigned from the U.S. Army, joined the forces of Virginia, and shortly thereafter rose to the rank of general in the Confederate Army.

This lithograph, by Currier and Ives, shows the Fort Sumter garrison returning the Confederate fire.

196

A typical recruiting broadside. This one was issued in Philadelphia in May 1862.

"The Hero of Fort Sumter." A photograph of Major Robert Anderson taken by George S. Crook when Anderson commanded the defenses of Charleston Harbor. Crook later became the chief combat photographer of the Confederacy. The Civil War is the first American war for which there is an extensive photographic record.

Lincoln Enlarges the Army

Now that war seemed inevitable, and with four more states in the Confederacy, Lincoln declared a blockade of the entire Confederate coastline, and called a special session of Congress to begin on 4 July 1861. Correctly anticipating that Congress would approve his actions, on his own authority he established 40 regiments of U.S. Volunteers (42,034 men) to serve for three years or for the duration of the war, and called for men to serve in the regiments. He also increased the Regular Army by 1 field artillery regiment, 1 cavalry regiment, and 8 infantry regiments (actually 9 were added), or 22,714 men, and the Navy by 18,000 men. The discrepancy in numbers is explained by the fact that the previously existing regular infantry regiments, like those of the militia and the new U.S. Volunteers, were 1-battalion regiments, while the new regular infantry regiments were to have 3 battalions of about 800 men each. As it turned out, however, the 3-battalion regiments were never recruited up to strength. Until the end of the war, despite increased inducements to join the regulars, men preferred the larger bonuses, laxer discipline, and more neighborly atmosphere of the Volunteers. The response to

the various Presidential calls was so enthusiastic that men poured into the state and Federal camps faster than they could be housed, equipped, and trained and Lincoln was forced to ask the governors to slow down the induction of recruits. The task of raising and organizing the troops was initially handled by the Treasury while the War Department provided arms and supplies. The War Department did not control the raising of the armies until 1862. Actually, the mobilization of forces in 1861, although accompanied by the confusion that resulted from inexperience, compared favorably with mobilization for the First and Second World Wars. Although President Lincoln did not, despite the warnings of General Scott, anticipate the length or scale of the war which faced him, his foresight was remarkable and called up far larger forces than the United States had ever before possessed.

The combat efficiency and state of training of the new units varied from good to very poor. Some of the state militia regiments were well trained and equipped; others were regiments in name only. The soldiers of the green Volunteer regiments often elected their own company officers; these in turn were supposed to select all the field-grade officers except the regimental commanders, who

197

In this drawing by Alfred R. Waud, one of the best of the Civil War combat artists, President Lincoln and General Winfield Scott are reviewing a regiment of three-year volunteers, probably in the early summer of 1861.

were appointed by the state governors. In other instances the governors commissioned all officers. Similar practices had always been followed among United States volunteer forces. These practices were based in part on the belief that soldiering, whether on the level of the squad or the regiment, was something that a man of good sense and good will could easily master. Although many of the newly made officers proved enthusiastic, devoted to duty, quick, and eager to learn, many incompetents were also commissioned. Before the end of 1861, however, officers were being required to prove their qualifications before examin-ing boards, a practice which Congress soon made mandatory. Those found unfit were allowed to resign. The President, frequently acting upon the advice of governors and members of Congress, commissioned all U.S. Volunteer officers above the rank of colonel. The majority of the first generals' commissions in the Volunteers went to regulars on active duty, to former regulars like George B. McClellan who had resigned from the Army to pursue civilian careers, and to those who had held Volunteer commissions in the Mexican War.

A sketch by Waud of a funeral procession in Washington in May, 1861. The dead man, Colonel Abram S. Vosburgh, had commanded the 71st New York Regiment assigned to the defense of Washington. The United States Capitol, still under construction, can be seen in the background.

Union Army Camps.

Fort Albany, erected in 1861 for the defense of Washington. Located on the Virginia side of the Potomac River, Fort Albany was constructed by the three-month volunteer troops of the 25th New York Regiment.

Camp Bates, a cavalry post on the upper Potomac near Poolesville, Maryland.

During the first year of the war the 5th New York Volunteer Infantry occupied this camp at Federal Hill, Baltimore, Maryland. The 5th, known as Duryee's Zouaves, was one of a number of Civil War regiments that adopted the colorful uniforms of the French colonial service.

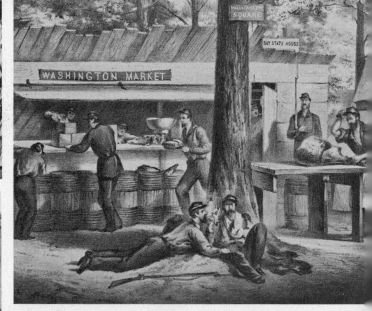

Entitled "Commissary Department," this lithograph shows supplies being distributed at the camp of the 6th Massachusetts Regiment of Volunteers near Baltimore in 1861.

Camp Dennison, 16 miles northeast of Cincinnati, one of the biggest mobilization and training centers in Ohio.

The Regular Army, in 1861 and for the duration of the war, was kept intact, although this policy was criticized on the ground that the regular units should have been broken into cadres and used to train the Volunteers (who, after First Bull Run, poured in by the hundreds of thousands). But in 1861 the President did not foresee a long war and the regular units were needed on the frontier until trained men could replace them. Until Volunteer commissions were opened to all regulars in 1862, they were promoted very slowly in comparison with inexperienced Volunteers who began their military careers as full colonels. But the slow promotion probably worked to a regular's advantage, for he obtained tactical experience in command of small units before being catapulted into command of large ones. Ulysses S. Grant and William T. Sherman, for example, both Military Academy graduates who had resigned from the Army, specifically asked for regimental commands, for which they felt qualified, rather than the higher rank that might easily have been theirs.

In most camps food was prepared in large iron kettles and served in tin plates and cups. Staple items of the Union soldier's diet were "salt horse and hard-tack" (salt beef and a thick, very hard cracker), dried beans, rice, cornmeal, and dried vegetables.

STRATEGY OF THE RIVAL CAPITALS

The two sides, the United States of America and the Confederate States of America, readied themselves for battle in the spring of 1861. The rival capital cities faced each other across a 100-mile stretch of rolling country that rivers and streams formed into cross-compartments. Richmond (after Virginia seceded, the Confederates had moved their capital there) was a railroad center and the site of the only ironworks in the South at the outbreak of war. It had some purely military value, as did Washington, which possessed the largest naval gun factory on the continent. But the psychological importance of Washington to Northern prestige and morale was too great to allow the Confederates to capture it, even if it had possessed no military value. The Confederates felt similarly about Richmond. Thus a lunge in the direction of one capital was sure to bring out a contending army.

Most Southerners, underestimating the North's devotion to the cause of Union and its military capacity, thought in terms of no war, or a short easy one, or of foreign intervention. Many in the North also thought in terms of a short

Richmond's Tredegar Works. One of the few manufacturing plants in the South, it produced machinery, cannon, submarines, torpedoes, and plates for iron-clad ships.

The capitol building at Richmond, Virginia. Richmond, the largest city in the Confederacy and 110 miles from Washington, D.C., became the Confederate capital in May, 1861.

war that would end with the capture of Richmond. This view was in sharp contrast to that held by General Scott, who as General in Chief was the ranking officer of the U.S. Army. He commanded all the military departments and field armies and was the chief military adviser to the Secretary of War and the President. The old veteran, who moved his headquarters to Washington to be in close touch with the President, recommended that time be taken to train an army of 85,000 men, and that a stringent naval blockade of the entire coastline be enforced to strangle the South economically. Then the Army should advance down the Mississippi to divide and conquer the Confederacy. This was the concept which the press ridiculed as the "Anaconda Plan." It was the general plan by which the North won the war, although its manpower estimates were too modest.

The Defense of Washington

With partly trained militiamen, almost untrained U.S. Volunteers, and one new battalion of regulars defending Washington in July 1861, the total Federal forces at hand numbered about 50,000 men. They were commanded by Brigadier General Irwin A. McDowell, recently promoted from the rank of major. Almost three months had elapsed since the President had called out the militiamen, and their terms of service were about to expire. To defend Richmond, General Pierre Beauregard had posted about 20,000 Confederates at Manassas, a road and rail junction some 30 miles southwest of the Federal Capital. (Until the U.S. Navy could be expanded, a seaborne advance against Richmond was out of the question.) In the Shenandoah Valley, Brigadier General Joseph E. Johnston commanded some 11,000

A gun emplacement at Fort Totten, part of the defense network around Washington. The picture was taken by Mathew B. Brady, the famous Civil War photographer.

Battery Rodgers on the Potomac in Alexandria, Virginia. It protected the river approach to Washington.

Confederate soldiers. At Martinsburg, West Virginia, 18,000 Union troops under Brigadier General Robert E. Patterson were charged with responsibility for keeping Johnston in place. Other Federal and Confederate forces, including a Federal unit under Major General Benjamin F. Butler at Fort Monroe, Virginia, were holding various posts, junctions, and mountain passes. Neither side was well trained although the Confederates had started earlier and probably had a slight edge over the Federals.

Lincoln Orders Advance Against Richmond

Northern public opinion, as evidenced by newspaper editorials and speeches in Congress, demanded immediate action in the form of an advance against Richmond. General Scott warned against starting a campaign before the troops were fully trained but President Lincoln, anxious to use the three-months militiamen before their terms expired, aware that the Confederates were far from seasoned, and cherishing the belief that one defeat would make the South quit, wanted action. Scott, perhaps influenced by erroneous intelligence reports that indicated Washington was in danger of attack, acceded and McDowell was directed to prepare a plan of operations. In brief, his plan as accepted in late June called for Butler and Patterson to prevent the Confederate forces facing them from reinforcing Beauregard while McDowell, with about 30,000 troops committed to the assault and 10,000 in reserve, advanced against Manassas to outflank Beauregard's position. The plan was a good one but it was badly executed.

It was 16 July before McDowell had enough men and moved out, trailed by Congressmen, newspapermen, and hucksters, along the Warrenton Turnpike (now U.S. Route 29). Everything depended on a rapid march, if the Union troops were to hit Beauregard before anyone could reinforce him. But the 35,000 troops—the largest army assembled on the North American continent up to then—marched slowly, even straggled, and McDowell did not force them to speed up. It was 18 July before the Army had covered the 20 miles to Centreville, about 4 miles east of the Stone Bridge over Bull Run. From there McDowell's advance guard pushed the Confederate outposts back. The Warrenton Pike crossed Bull Run over the Stone Bridge, and numerous dirt roads led to the fords. The country was fairly rough, cut by streams, and thickly wooded, so that it provided good defensive positions. While McDowell's main body waited at Centreville for the Army wagon trains, his leading division advanced against the fords, found them stoutly defended, and retired. Sure that his green troops could not force their way over Bull Run under fire, McDowell tarried for two more days, 19 and 20 July, concentrating his troops while engineers reconnoitered for an undefended ford. When they found one that seemed undefended at Sudley Springs, northwest of the Stone Bridge, McDowell decided to envelop the Confederate left flank on 21 July and destroy the Manassas Gap Railway to keep Johnston from reinforcing Beauregard. This was a good idea, but the Confederates had moved too fast.

On 17 July spies in Washington had informed Beauregard of McDowell's move, and he at once telegraphed the information to Richmond. President Davis, also using the telegraph, ordered up reinforcements and directed Johnston to proceed to Manassas at once. By adroit maneuvering, and by employing a cavalry screen led by a promising young colonel named J. E. B. Stuart, Johnston was able to move 9,000 effectives by rail to Manassas before McDowell attacked. Beauregard had already deployed six and one-half brigades to defend the fords, and the timely reinforcements gave him four more. Johnston ranked him, but as Beauregard had already prepared a battle plan, Johnston let him control the battle.

The Battle of Bull Run

Holding one division plus one brigade and artillery at Centreville in reserve, McDowell planned a diversionary attack by one division in the vicinity of the Stone Bridge. The main effort was to be executed by two divisions, under his direct command, which were to advance in column to the right, cross the Run at Sudley Springs, and envelop the enemy flank and rear. Once the main body had forced the Confederates away from the Stone Bridge, the diversionary division would cross and join the attack.

Map—Battle of Bull Run.

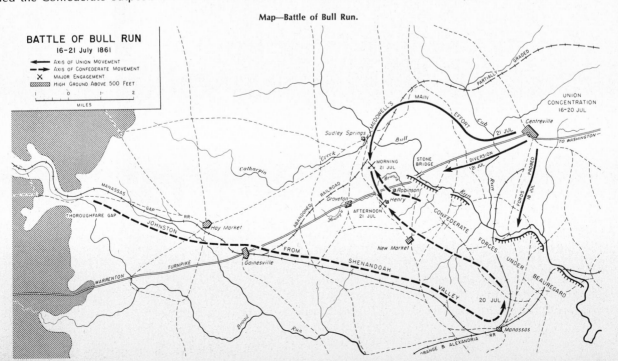

203

Currier and Ives's lithograph of the Battle of Bull Run shows a group of Zouaves and the rebel Black Horse Cavalry in fierce combat.

McDowell's leading division, the one scheduled to make the diversionary attack, moved out so slowly along the Warrenton Pike on the morning of 21 July that it delayed the movement of the two enveloping divisions. The diversionary attack against the Stone Bridge was feebly executed and failed to deceive the Confederates. McDowell's enveloping column reached Sudley Spring at 0900, rather than 0700 as originally scheduled, and drove southeast while Beauregard, warned by courier and by a wigwag flag signaler, made ready. At first the Federal attack went well, forcing the Confederates to cross the Pike to a flat-crested ridge where they rallied to the brigade led by Brigadier General Thomas J. Jackson, who on this day won the nickname "Stonewall." The troops fought bitterly for about two hours, as McDowell collected 10,000 men to attack 7,000 Confederates. But Beauregard was able to counterattack with fresh troops, some of whom wore blue uniforms and were thought to be comrades by the Federals until too late. The Federal units lost cohesion and soldiers left the field individually and in groups. Panic broke out among some who fled but several of the regiments marched away in an orderly manner. As in so many Civil War battles there was no pursuit, except for some harassing by cavalry and artillery.

Bull Run was not an important action in itself, but it highlights many of the problems and deficiencies that were typical of the first years of war. A clash between large, ill-trained bodies of recruits, it was disorderly and confused. Neither commander was able to employ his whole force effectively. Of McDowell's 35,000, only 18,500 crossed Bull Run, to suffer about 2,900 casualties, including missing. Beauregard, with about 32,000 men, got only 18,000 into action and lost about 2,000. Instead of placing himself in the army's rear where he could exercise effective control, McDowell led the enveloping column and acted more like a subordinate than an army commander as he valorously led individual regiments into the attack. Similarly, Beauregard rode up and down the front, encouraging individual

units and men. Some of his orders were vague and confusing, and others were never delivered. The confusion that arose from the welter of uniforms led to the adoption of gray for all Confederate troops, and blue for the Federals. Further, the Confederate flag, the "Stars and Bars," had looked dangerously like the Stars and Stripes when no wind was blowing, causing the Confederate command to adopt the famous battle flag with the Cross of St. Andrew.

After First Bull Run, Northern leaders began to grasp the nature and scope of the struggle while their deceptively easy victory convinced some Southerners that little more would be required. President Lincoln and Congress set to with a will to raise and train the vast armies that would be needed. On 22 July the President signed a bill which authorized enlistment of 500,000 volunteers to be raised by the several states to serve for three-year terms, except that at the end of six months the soldier had the option of discharge or continuing his enlistment. This law also rigidly fixed the ratio of field artillery and cavalry to infantry, and authorized brigades of four or more regiments with three or more brigades per division. Three days later the law was amended to provide for the enlistment of the 500,000 volunteers for the duration of the war. The response was enthusiastic. With recruits pouring in, it was obvious that the Army's prewar staff and administrative machinery was too small for its tasks. In August Congress provided for an Assistant Secretary of War and a chief of Ordnance, and authorized additional inspectors general, surgeons and assistant surgeons, adjutants general, commissaries, engineers, topographical engineers, quartermasters, and ordnance officers, as well as the employment of medical cadets and female nurses, and called for the appointment of one Christian chaplain for each regiment. Jewish chaplains were provided for in 1862.

The Army of the Potomac

McDowell had done his best but President Lincoln decided the task of commanding the forces around Washington—

shortly thereafter designated the Army of the Potomac—was beyond him. On Scott's advice, Major General George B. McClellan, who had a series of small but heartening victories in West Virginia, was appointed to command the Army of the Potomac. Before the year was out Scott took advantage of a new law and retired from active service, and Lincoln appointed McClellan as General in Chief. Acting on McClellan's assurance that he could handle two jobs, Lincoln retained him in command of the Army of the Potomac as well.

By the end of 1861 the Volunteers had been organized into 560 regiments of infantry, 82 of cavalry, and 15 of field artillery; actual strength of the Regular Army totaled 19,871 men. Following established usage and statutory requirements, McClellan organized his Army of the Potomac into 10,000-man divisions, each consisting of 3 infantry brigades, 1 cavalry regiment, and 4 6-gun field artillery batteries, and the other Union armies followed suit. The assignment of a cavalry regiment to each division was never fully carried out, for cavalrymen were used for a multiplicity of duties—as pickets, wagon train escorts, and messengers. This practice contrasted with that of the Army of Northern Virginia, as Johnston's command came to be called after Bull Run, where cavalry was treated as a separate arm, and grouped first as a division and finally as a corps.

Except for the capture by Union forces of Forts Hatteras and Clark, North Carolina, and Port Royal, South Carolina, and a drawn battle at Wilson's Creek, Montana, in August, there were no significant ground actions during the latter half of 1861. A badly executed reconnaissance at Ball's Bluff on the Potomac River by a Union detachment on 21 October, however, had results that were far-reaching. A Volunteer officer and former Senator, Colonel Edward D. Baker,

was killed, and a congressional committee decided to investigate. Out of this investigation came the Joint Congressional Committee on the Conduct of the War, which by searching out graft and inefficiency was to do valuable work but not without vexing the President and most of his generals.

As winter of 1861–1862 wore on, McClellan, a perfectionist who was prone to exaggerate his difficulties and the enemy's strength, drilled and trained his Army of the Potomac, while the armies of the western forces under his general command seemed to be accomplishing little. The President, impatient for offensive action, took command himself, and issued his General War Order No. 1 on 27 January 1862. The order, besides telling the armies to obey existing orders, directed that a general movement of the United States land and sea forces against the Confederacy be launched on 22 February 1862. Lincoln apparently acted only to get McClellan to move, but when he issued his order, important action was about to begin in the West.

ACTION IN THE MIDWEST: 1862

Union forces beyond the Appalachians were organized into two separate commands: one, under Brigadier General Don Carlos Buell with headquarters at Louisville, Kentucky, and the other, under General Henry W. Halleck with headquarters at St. Louis, Missouri. Facing Buell and Halleck were 43,000 scattered and ill-equipped Confederate troops under General Albert Sidney Johnston. Charged with the mission of keeping the Federals out of Kentucky, and holding Tennessee and the Mississippi River, they occupied a long line of forts and camps extending from Cumberland Gap in western Virginia through Bowling Green, Kentucky, to the Mississippi. With most of the roads in the region virtually

"Battle of Logan's Cross Roads." At Logan's Cross Roads, near Somerset, Kentucky, on 19 January 1862, Union forces prevented a Confederate advance into Kentucky. The sketch of the battle was made by Private Alfred E. Matthews.

"Union Forces Crossing Fishing Creek," another drawing by Private Matthews, shows several regiments of Ohio Volunteers crossing a tributary of the Cumberland River on their way to assist the Union army at Logan's Cross Roads. The reinforcements arrived after the battle was over.

impassable in winter, rivers and railroads provided Johnston with a line of communications. To protect a lateral railroad where it crossed rivers' in Tennessee, the Confederates had built Fort Henry on the Tennessee River and Fort Donelson on the Cumberland River.

Halleck and Buell were supposed to be cooperating with each other, but without any assurances from Buell, Halleck, in early February of 1862, decided to effect a strategic penetration of the center of Johnston's line. He sent 17,000 men under Brigadier General Ulysses S. Grant, supported and transported by armored gunboats and river craft under Flag Officer Andrew H. Foote, up the Tennessee River to seize Fort Henry. While Grant was landing and moving overland to the fort, the Confederate commander sent most of his men to Fort Donelson. On 6 February, after gunboats had shelled Fort Henry, it was surrendered before Grant's troops arrived.

The Fall of Fort Donelson

Grant turned against Fort Donelson at once. He sent some of his troops by boat down the Tennessee to its confluence with the Cumberland, thence up the latter to Fort Donelson. The rest moved through the sleet, snow, and mud of the Tennessee winter across the 10-mile neck of land sepa-

rating the forts. Reinforced up to a strength of about 25,000, Grant's army invested Fort Donelson on the evening of 12 February. Johnston, sure that the fall of Donelson would jeopardize his entrenched camp at Bowling Green, hurried 12,000 reinforcements to Fort Donelson, and retired toward Nashville with 14,000 men. Even without reinforcements, Fort Donelson was a strong position. Standing 100 feet above the river, it embraced an area of about 100 acres; the river and two creeks formed a moat that completely surrounded it Grant and Foote first attempted to reduce it by the gunboat bombardment that had succeeded at Fort Henry, but the gunboats suffered such severe damage that they withdrew. Grant then prepared for a long siege, as he did not think his troops well enough trained to assault successfully. However, the Confederates essayed a sortie which failed and Grant was able to attack successfully. Some Confederate troops escaped, but 11,500 men surrendered on 16 February. Meanwhile, Buell had advanced on learning of Fort Henry's surrender. He reached Bowling Green the day Fort Donelson fell. Grant's bold advance, coupled with Buell's move, cracked the Confederate Cumberland Gap–Bowling Green–Mississippi River line and forced the Confederates out of Kentucky and much of Tennessee. Johnston withdrew to Corinth, Mississippi, averaging 14 miles a day on the march.

A lithograph of the battle at Fort Donelson on the Cumberland River in Tennessee. When the Confederate garrison decided to surrender and asked for terms on 15 February 1862, Union General Ulysses S. Grant sent back a reply that became famous: "No terms except unconditional and immediate surrender can be accepted. I propose to move immediately upon your works."

The first Union dress parade in Nashville, Tennessee, on 4 March 1862. Nashville was abandoned by the Confederate Army after the surrender of Fort Donelson.

This lithograph showing Federal gunboats, under the command of Flag Officer Andrew H. Foote, bombarding Island No. 10 in the Mississippi River near New Madrid, Missouri, is the work of Currier and Ives. The fortified island was surrendered on 7 April 1862.

The Bloody Battle of Shiloh

As theatre commander, Halleck naturally received much credit for these victories. When President Lincoln decided to unify the command of the western armies in March, he placed Halleck in charge of more than 100,000 men, organized into 4 armies—Brigadier General Samuel Curtis' Army of the Southwest in Missouri and Arkansas, Grant's Army of the Tennessee, Buell's Army of the Ohio, and Major General John Pope's Army of the Mississippi.

Halleck decided to concentrate Grant's and Buell's armies and move against Johnston's Army of the Mississippi in Corinth. He ordered Buell to Savannah on the Tennessee River and dispatched Grant's troops up the Tennessee to

Pittsburg Landing, about nine miles from Savannah. Johnston, meanwhile, had received some reinforcements, though not all he needed. Well aware of the Federal's movements, Johnston decided to attack Grant at Pittsburg Landing, where Shiloh Church was located, before Buell could join him. His army, 40,000 strong, marched out of Corinth on the afternoon of 3 April. Two dirt roads led through thick forests to Shiloh, 22 miles away, but heavy rains had turned them into bogs. It was late afternoon on 5 April when the Confederates reached a point about two miles from Grant's front, and Johnston decided to postpone his attack until the next morning.

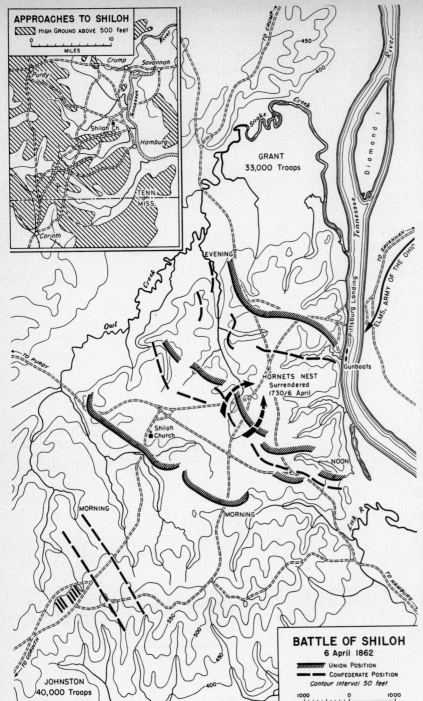

APPROACHES TO SHILOH
High Ground Above 500 feet
MILES

GRANT
33,000 Troops

EVENING

HORNETS NEST
Surrendered
1730/6 April

Shiloh
Church

NOON

Gunboats

TO SAVANNAH

ELMS, ARMY OF THE OHIO

Pittsburg Landing

MORNING

MORNING

Lick R.

TO HAMBURG

TO PURDY

Owl

TO CORINTH

JOHNSTON
40,000 Troops

BATTLE OF SHILOH
6 April 1862

Union Position
Confederate Position
Contour Interval 50 feet

1000   0   1000
YARDS

Map—Battle of Shiloh.

The fighting at Shiloh on April 7
as sketched by Private Alfred E. Matthews.

After "Bloody Shiloh" Federal troops followed the retreating Confederates to Corinth, Mississippi, 20 miles to the southwest. Private Matthews made this sketch of the march.

Johnston's men burst out of the woods early on 6 April, so early that the surprised Federals turned out into their company streets from their tents to fight. Some fled to the safety of the river, but most of the regiments fought stubbornly and yielded ground slowly. By afternoon the Confederates had attained successes all along the line, but they had become badly disorganized and Johnston himself had been mortally wounded in leading an assault. General Beauregard, Johnston's successor, suspended the attack for the day and attempted to straighten out and reorganize his command. That evening Grant's sixth division and advance elements of Buell's army reached Shiloh. Grant counterattacked the next morning, regained the lost ground, and the Confederates withdrew to Corinth. Shiloh was the

bloodiest battle fought in North America up to that time. Of 63,000 Federals, 13,000 were casualties. The Confederates lost 11,000. Buell's presence had prevented Johnston from defeating the Union armies in detail. Grant came in for much denunciation for being surprised, but President Lincoln loyally sustained him. "I can't spare this man; he fights."

FAILURE OF THE PENINSULAR CAMPAIGN

Meanwhile in the East, operations aimed at the capture of Richmond were under way. McClellan, who had been relieved as General in Chief but who still commanded the Army of the Potomac, recommended a seaborne move to Fort Monroe, Virginia, at the tip of the peninsula formed

The Confederate camp at Corinth. The lithograph is based on a painting by Conrad Wise Chapman, an ordnance sergeant with the 59th Virginia Regiment. The Southerners abandoned Corinth on 30 May 1862.

The gunboats "Tylor" and "Lexington" are firing in support of the hard-pressed Union forces at Shiloh in this lithograph. Both gunboats were converted side-wheel river steamers.

by the York and the James rivers, to be followed by an overland advance up the peninsula. If the troops moved fast, he maintained, they could cover the 70 miles to Richmond before Confederate General Joseph E. Johnston could concentrate his forces to stop them. Although Lincoln did not like the plan, he gave it his approval providing McClellan left behind enough men to ensure the safety of Washington and hold Manassas. McClellan gave the President his assurances, but failed to point out that he considered the Federal troops in the Shenandoah Valley to be covering Washington. In listing the forces he had left behind, McClellan counted some men twice and included several units in Pennsylvania that were not under his command, a piece of carelessness that was to cost him dearly.

Embarkation for the Peninsular Campaign began at Alexandria, Virginia, on 17 March 1862, and by 4 April advance elements of the Army of the Potomac had moved out of Fort Monroe against Yorktown. On 3 April, however, the commander of the Washington defenses had reported that he had insufficient force to protect the city. In addition, Stonewall Jackson had become active in the Shenandoah Valley. Lincoln directed his Secretary of War Edwin Stanton to hold one of the two corps which were awaiting embarkation at Alexandria, and Stanton detained 30,000 men.

Map—Peninsular Campaign.

PENINSULAR CAMPAIGN
MAY–JULY 1862

////// UNION POSITION
ттттт CONFEDERATE POSITION
- - - ➤ AXIS OF CONFEDERATE MOVEMENT
Roads and positions are approximate

Contour Interval 100 feet

5   0   5
MILES

Hanover

STUART

Yellow Tavern

13-15 June

Mechanicsville   26 JUNE
Gaines Mill   Cold Harbor
27 JUNE
RICHMOND

White House

Fair Oaks   Savage Sta.
31 MAY   29 JUNE

30 JUNE
Glendale
1 JULY
Malvern Hill

Bermuda Hundred

Harrison's Landing   2 JULY

PETERSBURG

McClellan Threatens Richmond

Recognizing McClellan's threat to Richmond, the Confederate garrison at Yorktown made ready to delay McClellan while Johnston hurried his army to the peninsula. Meanwhile, Confederate authorities in Richmond had ordered a spectacularly bold diversion. With a small force Stonewall Jackson attacked Federal troops at Kernstown, Virginia, on 23 March, and suffered defeat. But it was a strategic victory, for by calling attention to Jackson's threat to Harpers Ferry at the junction of the Potomac and Shenandoah rivers, and perhaps to Washington, it diverted forces from McClellan. The equivalent of three Federal divisions was sent out at once to destroy Jackson. Jefferson Davis and his military adviser, General Robert E. Lee, noting the reaction in Washington, sent Jackson reinforcements in April while Lincoln and Stanton, using the telegraph and what military knowledge they had, devised plans to bottle Jackson up and destroy him. Stonewall Jackson was a most outstanding field commander who used hard fighting, rapid marches, surprise and deception to neutralize and defeat Federal forces three times larger than his own. He prevented another strong Federal force from joining McClellan in May, when 20,000 men were diverted to the Shenandoah Valley, where they stayed, accomplishing little, until the end of June, and by then the Peninsular Campaign had ended in failure.

When McClellan reached the peninsula in early April, he decided not to wait for his whole army but to begin the advance to Yorktown at once in order to gain time and ground before Johnston could concentrate his forces. Confederate Major General John B. Magruder, a master of deception, was holding Yorktown with some 10 to 15 thousand men. By clever ruses and deceptive maneuvers he so dazzled McClellan that the latter, instead of brushing Magruder

Fortress Monroe, at Old Point Comfort on the tip of the peninsula formed by the York and James rivers. Called the "key to the South," Fort Monroe served as a base for the Army of the Potomac during the Peninsular Campaign.

aside, spent a month in a siege. As a result, Johnston was able to move his army, now equal to two-thirds of McClellan's, to Yorktown. McClellan, after emplacing heavy guns and constructing complicated siege works, planned to assault on 5 May. But Johnston, who wanted to fight the decisive action closer to Richmond, decamped on 3 May and withdrew slowly up the peninsula with his cavalry, under Brigadier General J. E. B. Stuart, covering the rear. Led by its cavalry, the Army of the Potomac set out in pursuit. On 16 May McClellan established his headquarters and main base at White House on the Pamunkey River, and by 25 May two corps of the Army of the Potomac had turned southwest toward Richmond and crossed the Chickahominy River; the remaining three corps were on the north side of the river.

Johnston and the Confederates Attack at Fair Oaks

The Chickahominy, which divided the Army of the Potomac, was usually a sluggish, shallow stream, but drenching rains on 30 May made it unfordable. McClellan had provided bridges, but the rains washed out most of them and weakened the others, and the two parts of his army were effectively separated. Johnston, grasping a chance to defeat the Federals, struck on 31 May near Fair Oaks. His plans called for his whole force to concentrate against the isolated corps south of the Chickahominy, but his staff and subordinate commanders were not up to the task of executing them. Assaulting columns became confused, and attacks were delivered piecemeal. The Federals, after some initial reverses, held their ground and bloodily repulsed the Confederates. Johnston suffered a severe wound at Fair Oaks, and

Federal forces are capturing a rebel lunette, or earthwork, near Yorktown, Virginia, in this lithograph. The action took place on 26 April 1862.

(Below) A temporary camp occupied by picket reserves during the fighting near Yorktown. When on duty pickets manned advance posts to watch for surprise enemy attacks.

211

Part of General McClellan's supply dump near Yorktown where he collected equipment for his advance toward Richmond.

President Davis replaced him with General Lee. While McClellan waited for the weather to clear, Lee pulled back closer to Richmond and started fortifications which would enable him to protect Richmond with a relatively small force while he used the main body of his army offensively in an attempt to cut off and destroy the Army of the Potomac. He also ordered Jackson out of the Shenandoah Valley toward Richmond with all possible speed. Jackson eluded his pursuers and traveled by rail, wagon, and on foot in such secrecy that the Federals did not know where he was until his troops were about to deliver their first attack.

Lee struck before McClellan resumed his advance. At Mechanicsville, on 26 June, he attempted to roll up McClellan's right flank north of the Chickahominy and cut the line of communications between it and the base at White House. The Confederates' timing and coordination were off and McClellan successfully withdrew southeast to a stronger position at Gaines' Mill where 57,000 Confederates attacked 34,000 Federals on 27 June. The fighting was severe, for on both sides the troops were equally well trained and valorous. Numbers told, however, and the Federal line broke. Darkness fell before Lee could exploit the opportunity, and the Federals took advantage of the night to cross to the south bank of the Chickahominy where the main body of the Army of the Potomac was encamped.

Lee Attacks at Malvern Hill

With his line of communications to White House cut, McClellan decided to abandon it and shift his base to Harrison's Landing on the south side of the peninsula. This move, which involved 90,000 men, the artillery train, 3,100 wagons, and 2,500 head of cattle, began on the night of 27–28 June. By the first day of July McClellan had concentrated the Army of the Potomac in a strong position on a commanding plateau at Malvern Hill, northwest of Harrison's Landing. There was a good field of fire to the front. The flanks were protected by streams. Massed artillery, ready to sweep all approaches, lay in supporting positions, and gunboats on the James River were ready to fire in support of the left flank. The Confederates' assembly area, somewhat more than 300 to 400 yards north of Malvern Hill, was broken and wooded, traversed by a swamp, and barely passable. When, on the morning of 1 July, Lee's attempt to knock out the Federal artillery by counterbattery fire failed, he decided that Malvern Hill was too strong to attack. But later when a shifting of Federal troops deceived him into thinking that they were withdrawing, he changed his mind and attacked, a decision that cost heavily. Lee sustained 5,000 casualties in this, the last action of the Peninsular Campaign. Next day, 2 July, the Army of the Potomac fell back to Harrison's Landing and dug in. After reconnoitering McClellan's position on 3 July, Lee ordered his exhausted

Currier and Ives's version of the Battle of Fair Oaks, Virginia, on 31 May 1862. Confederate General Joseph E. Johnston was wounded during the engagement.

This Brady photograph
of a Union artillery battery
was taken near Fair Oaks.

The commander of the Army of the
Potomac, Major General George S. Mc-
Clellan. The photograph was taken by
Mathew B. Brady.

Putting up an observation balloon near
Yorktown in 1862. Both sides made some
use of balloons for observation purposes.

A Federal cavalry charge at Gaines' Mill, Virginia. It took place
on 27 June 1862, as the Union army was retreating from Richmond.

213

men back to the Richmond lines for rest and reorganization.

Casualties on both sides in the Peninsular Campaign—during which Brigadier General Daniel C. Butterfield devised the bugle call "Taps"—were heavy. The Federals lost some 15,849 men killed, wounded, and missing. The Confederates, who had done most of the attacking, lost 20,614 men out of a total of 95,481 men engaged.

President Lincoln, abandoning the idea of exercising command over the Union armies in person, on 11 July 1862 selected as new General-in-Chief, Henry W. Halleck who had won acclaim for his victories in the West. It was Lincoln's intention that Halleck exercise field command himself, and direct the various Federal armies in close concert to take advantage of the North's superior strength. If all Federal armies coordinated their efforts, Lincoln reasoned, they could strike where the Confederacy was weak or force it to strengthen one army at the expense of another, and thus eventually wear the Confederacy down, destroy the various armies, and win the war. Lincoln was destined to be disappointed by Halleck, who seldom attempted to exercise field command or assume responsibility for strategic direction of the armies. He acted more as military adviser to the President than as a commander, but in this advisory capacity he performed a valuable function by serving as a channel of communication between the President and the field commanders. He translated the President's ideas into terms the generals could comprehend, and expressed the soldiers' views in language that the President understood.

LINCOLN FORMS THE ARMY OF VIRGINIA

Shortly before Lincoln appointed Halleck, he had also decided to consolidate the various Union forces in the Shenandoah Valley and other parts of western Virginia—some 45,000 men—into the Army of Virginia. He appointed Major General John Pope to command this force. When Halleck took over as General-in-Chief, Pope's scattered army was in western Virginia, and the Army of the Potomac, close to 100,000 strong, was at Harrison's Landing. Between them lay

Richmond and Lee's Army of Northern Virginia. Despite the fact that the two Union armies vastly outnumbered Lee's, the President and Halleck were concerned by the dispersion of forces, and on 3 August Halleck ordered McClellan to withdraw by water from the peninsula to Aquia Creek on the Potomac and to effect a speedy junction at Fredericksburg with Pope. Embarkation began on 14 August. Pope, meanwhile, acting on orders from Washington which aimed at concentrating the two Union armies between Washington and Richmond, began posting the Army of Virginia in the region of Sperryville and Warrenton, with the exception of one division which was defending the depot at Falmouth across the Rappahannock from Fredericksburg.

Lee, dauntless and resolute, realized that his Army of Northern Virginia was in a dangerous position between Pope and McClellan, and in an equally dangerous position if McClellan and Pope united. Pope's presence in western Virginia forced him to divert a strong force eventually totaling 24,000 men under Stonewall Jackson. Jackson's column left Richmond on 13 July, marched northwest, and reached Gordonsville on 19 July with the intention of blocking Pope. Lee, knowing that McClellan was leaving Harrison's Landing, marched out of Richmond with the rest of the Army of Northern Virginia, and arrived at Gordonsville on 15 August. He had about 55,000 men to Pope's 45,000, and resolved to outflank and cut off Pope before the whole of McClellan's vast army could be brought to bear.

Moves and Countermoves:
Major General Pope vs. General Lee

Pope was dangerously exposed, for the Federals seem to have expected Lee to stay near Richmond. But in a stroke of luck, Union cavalrymen captured copies of Lee's orders which were promptly forwarded to Pope. Seeing his danger, Pope withdrew the Army of Virginia to the north bank of the Rappahannock. Several days of feints and maneuvers followed as Lee probed for openings across the fords of the Rappahannock. Then J. E. B. Stuart's troopers overran

Soldiers of Major General Nathaniel Banks's II Corps attack Confederate forces under Stonewall Jackson at Cedar Mountain, Virginia, on 9 August 1862. After receiving reinforcements, Jackson drove Banks from the field.

Pope's headquarters in a dashing raid and seized documents which showed that two corps of the Army of the Potomac were marching west from Aquia and would join Pope within two days, as would a reserve division of the Army of Virginia. These forces totaled 20,000, and the rest of the Army of the Potomac, Lee learned, was at Aquia Creek and Alexandria, within five days' march. To add to Lee's problems, heavy rains caused the Rappahannock to rise so high that it could not be forded. Lee acted quickly and boldly to escape the threatening disaster. To divert Pope, he sent Jackson off on a wide turning movement through Thoroughfare Gap in the Bull Run Mountains around the right flank of the Army of Virginia, and next day followed the same route with the divisions commanded by Lieutenant General James Longstreet.

Pope took note of Jackson's move, but first assumed that it was pointed toward the Shenandoah Valley. Then Jackson, covering nearly 60 miles in two days, came in behind Pope at Manassas on 26 August, destroyed supplies there, and moved westward. Pope marched and countermarched his forces for two days trying to find the elusive Jackson who turned on 28 August and attacked Pope at Groveton, then made ready for defense. Next day, Pope, whose dispositions failed to take Lee's other force into account, walked into Lee's trap, which was designed to lure him into battle before the Army of the Potomac could arrive in strength. Pope attacked Jackson, whose divisions held a strong position behind the embankment of an abandoned railroad, and was repulsed with heavy casualties.

The Confederate hospital at Cedar Mountain. The private dwelling in the center of the photograph served as a field hospital for the 1,100 Confederate soldiers who were wounded during the fighting on 9 August.

The next day passed uneventfuly until about noon when Pope attacked north of the Warrenton Pike. Massed Confederate artillery broke the first assault, but the Federals pushed on valiantly until Lee sent some of Longstreet's troops to bolster Jackson, who then drove back the attackers. Longstreet pushed east toward Bald Hill and when Pope sent men to hold this vital eminence, Jackson pushed back the weakened force on his front. Pope, who had fought hard but with less skill than his opponents, admitted defeat and led his army back to Washington, fighting an enveloping Confederate force at Chantilly on the way. The troops reached the Capital defenses about 3 September. Lee had successfully defeated one formidable Union army in the presence of another even larger one.

The Army of Virginia is Dissolved

On 1 September, as the Army of Virginia was withdrawing to Washington, Halleck, acting on Lincoln's instructions, gave McClellan command of all forces in the area of the Capital, including the Army of the Potomac and Pope's army. The Army of Virginia was dissolved and its component units assigned to the Army of the Potomac. Pope was sent to a command in Minnesota. The Union authorities hoped that

McClellan would be able to devote several months to training and reorganization, but in this they were disappointed.

DAVIS AND LEE LAUNCH AN INVASION OF THE NORTH

For a complicated set of political and military reasons, Davis and Lee, decided to take the offensive and invade the North. Lee did not immediately stop for rest but moved out of Chantilly, northward across the Potomac near Leesburg and on to Frederick, Maryland, where he rested for two days. Because the Union garrison at Harpers Ferry threatened his line of supply and retreat, Lee sent Jackson's column back across the Potomac against the garrison, and some of Lieutenant General James Longstreet's men posted themselves on the heights on the north side of the Potomac overlooking Harpers Ferry. The remainder of Lee's army crossed the Blue Ridge Mountains and headed for Hagerstown, about 25 miles northwest of Frederick, with Stuart's cavalry screening the right flank. In the meantime McClellan's cavalry had reported Lee's general location, and McClellan marched the Army of the Potomac—90,000 men organized into 6 corps—northwest from Washington to Frederick, which was reached on 12 September.

Major General Phil Kearny (on horseback) directing a rear-guard action at Chantilly, Virginia, aimed at keeping Lee from cutting off the retreat of Federal troops to Washington. Kearny was successful, but he was killed during the fighting, which took place on 1 September 1862.

Union troops (below) winning a victory at South Mountain, Maryland, on 14 September 1862.

216

Then came a stroke of luck for McClellan. Lee, in assigning missions to his command, had detached Major General D. H. Hill's division from Jackson and attached it to Longstreet, and had sent copies of his orders, which prescribed routes, objectives, and times of arrival, to Jackson, Longstreet, and Hill. But, in the absence of the modern "distribution list" which shows exactly how many copies of a document are prepared and to whom they go, Jackson was not sure that Hill had received the order. He therefore made an additional copy of Lee's order and sent it to Hill. One of Hill's orders, wrapped around some cigars, was somehow left behind in an abandoned camp and were picked up on 13 September by Union soldiers and rushed to McClellan. This gave McClellan an unmatched opportunity to defeat Lee's scattered forces, but he did not start the troops moving until next morning and did not urge them on. Lee, informed of the lost order, sent all available forces to hold the mountain gaps, so that it was nightfall on the 14th before McClellan got through to the west side of the mountains.

A Draw at Antietam

Lee then retreated to Sharpsburg, Maryland, on Antietam Creek. He reached there on 15 September and decided to fight. The decision was bold to the point of recklessness, for Lee was pinned in between Antietam Creek and the Potomac River with no room for maneuver and he was greatly outnumbered. Jackson had taken Harpers Ferry the same day and was marching hard to join him, but his leading elements would not arrive until 16 September. Fortunately for Lee, McClellan delayed his attack until 17 September, when he launched an uncoordinated series of assaults which drove back the Confederates in places and came within an inch of breaking their line. But McClellan, having committed 5 corps to the attack, would not commit his reserve. Jackson's last division arrived in time to head off the final assault, and at the day's end Lee still held most of his ground. As in nearly all Civil War battles, casualties were heavy. Of 70,000 Federal troops engaged 13,000 were killed, wounded, or missing. The 40,000 Confederates lost 8,000. McClellan did not resume the attack the next day, and Lee withdrew unmolested to Virginia. Tactically, Antietam ended in a draw.

This photograph of the bridge at Antietam was taken shortly after the major fighting ended.

BURNSIDE REPLACES McCLELLAN

In early November of 1862 the Army of Northern Virginia was divided between Culpeper, south of the Bull Run Mountains and east of the Blue Ridge and Winchester in the valley. McClellan was at Warrenton making ready to attack Lee, but his military career was about to end. His slowness, his failure to accomplish more at Antietam, and perhaps his rather arrogant habit of offering gratuitous political advice to his superiors, coupled with the intense anti-McClellan views of the Joint Congressional Committee on the Conduct of the War, convinced Lincoln that he could retain him no longer. He replaced McClellan as commander of the Army of the Potomac with Major General Ambrose E. Burnside, who had won some distinction in operations that gained control of ports on the North Carolina coast and who had led a corps at Antietam. Burnside accepted the post with reluctance.

Abandoning McClellan's plan to strike at Culpeper, Burnside evolved a plan to demonstrate with part of his army while the main body advanced rapidly to Falmouth on the north bank of the Rappahannock, crossed the river on pontoon bridges, seized Fredericksburg, and moved along the railroad toward Richmond. If successful, this move would place the 120,000-man Army of the Potomac between Lee and his principal base. To achieve greater ease of tactical control, Burnside created three headquarters higher than corps—the Right, Center, and Left Grand Divisions under Major Generals Edwin V. Sumner, Joseph Hooker, and William B. Franklin, respectively—with 2 corps plus cavalry assigned to each Grand Division. The success of Burnside's plan depended on speed; he had to get across the river and take the high ground behind Fredericksburg before Lee could get there.

The Army of the Potomac vs. the Army of North Virginia

Things went well at first. The Right Grand Division reached Falmouth on 17 November, ahead of Lee, and was followed shortly by most of the rest of the army with one important exception—the pontoon trains. These were at Harpers Ferry, and did not reach Falmouth until 25 November. The Rappahannock could have been forded, but Burnside feared that rain or snow might flood the river and cut off the troops on the far bank. Meanwhile Lee, who had organized the Army of Northern Virginia into 2 corps under lieutenant generals, plus cavalry and reserve artillery, had detected Burnside's movement and deduced his intentions. He rushed the I Corps under Longstreet from Culpeper to the high ground behind Fredericksburg. Jackson then followed from Winchester, and by the time Burnside was ready there were 78,500 Confederate soldiers waiting to receive the attack. At this point Burnside might well have changed his plan, since it was based on the assumption that there would be little or no opposition to his river crossing and seizure of the high ground, but he decided to carry on.

On 11 December Burnside's engineers began laying the pontoon bridges. There was no trouble on the left, but on the right Confederate sharpshooters posted in houses and buildings (the civilian occupants had left) shot them off the boats. Artillery shelled the city, but Union infantry had to ferry over and clear the town of the covering Confederate brigade before the bridge-laying could proceed unmolested. By afternoon of 12 December all the assault units were over the river.

After an artillery duel, the dense Union columns moved out to the attack on the morning of 13 December. On the left, where the ridge was low, part of the Left Grand Division found a weak spot in Jackson's line, and drove in to seize the ridge, but as Burnside had weakened that part of the assault, the Federals could not hold against Jackson's counterattack. On the right, the troops had to cross about a mile of open ground to reach Marye's Heights, which

Longstreet was holding. In addition, a drainage canal lay to its front, and at the foot of Marye's Heights and parallel to the ridgeline was a sunken road with stone walls behind which Longstreet had posted four ranks of riflemen. In a series of assaults the Union soldiers pushed their way to the foot of Marye's Heights, but the attack failed, with heavy casualties. In the course of the day's action the Army of the Potomac lost 12,600 men, the Army of Northern Virginia, 5,300. Planning to resume the attack on 14 December, Burnside pulled his men back to the river, but his corps commanders talked him out of renewing the assault. He held his position for two days, then withdrew across the Rappahannock. Lee did not follow.

President Lincoln and General McClellan in the latter's tent at Antietam on 3 October 1862. Lincoln had come to Antietam to urge McClellan to take the offensive in the hope of ending the war.

Lincoln with McClellan and members of the general's staff during the Antietam visit.

This lithograph shows General Burnside's men constructing pontoon bridges across the Rappahannock River under fire from Confederate sharpshooters in Fredericksburg.

THE STATE OF THE ARMIES AT THE BEGINNING OF 1863

Civil War battles were bloody and costly, but even so, the death rates from disease in both armies were higher than those from battle casualties. Thus the year 1863 had found the ranks of both armies seriously depleted. Lincoln had asked for 300,000 more volunteers on 2 July 1862, but only 85,000 men responded immediately. Therefore, on 3 March 1863, Congress passed the Enrollment Act, the first national draft law in United States history, which law made able-bodied males between twenty and forty-five years of age liable for national military service. The Enrollment Act was not popular, and its exemptions made it possible for many to escape military service entirely. Comparatively few men were drafted into the Federal service, but by stimulating volunteering the Enrollment Act had its desired effect.

In 1863, the highest United States decoration, the Medal of Honor, authorized by Congress on 12 July 1862, was awarded for the first time. It went to six soldiers who had demonstrated extraordinary valor in a daring raid behind the Confederate lines near Chattanooga.

Along with awards for valor, the Civil War saw a general improvement in the lot of the individual soldier. The more severe forms of corporal punishment were abolished in the Army in 1861. An effort was made to extend medical services beyond the mere treatment of battle wounds, and as an auxiliary to the regular medical service, the volunteer U.S. Sanitary Commission fitted out hospital ships and hospital units, provided male and, for the first time in the U.S. Army, female nurses, and furnished clothing and fancier foods than the regular rations. Similarly, the U.S. Christian Commission augmented the efforts of the regimental chaplains and even provided, besides songbooks and Bibles, some coffee bars and reading rooms.

Currier and Ives evidently published their lithograph of the Battle of Fredericksburg before the battle was over. It is entitled "Bombardment and Capture of Fredericksburg, Virginia, 11 December 1862," although the Union forces withdrew on 13 December without ever taking the city.

Some Civil War Military Hospitals

At the outbreak of the Civil War, the Army Medical Bureau was totally unprepared to care for the thousands of sick and wounded soldiers that straggled into Washington and other cities from the battlefields. In the emergency, the United States Sanitary Commission, organized with the sanction of the War Dept. and supported by private contributions, provided hospital care and other forms of aid. Its services were similar to those of the Red Cross in later wars—help for the soldier in field, camp and hospital, relief for the disabled and assistance for dependent families. By 1863 the reorganized Army Medical Service was establishing general hospitals and staffing them with trained doctors and nurses, but until the end of the war, the need for hospital services far outstripped what could be provided.

Soldiers' Rest, Alexandria, Virginia. One of the lodges established by the Sanitary Commission to care for soldiers not well enough to rejoin their regiments and not ill enough to be treated in the crowded military hospitals, Soldiers' Rest was conveniently located near the Alexandria railway station.

Mount Pleasant Hospitals, Washington, D.C. Completed in April 1862, Mount Pleasant was the first of the "pavilion hospitals" constructed during the Civil War. Its capacity was enlarged by the erection of the 57 tent-pavilions in the foreground.

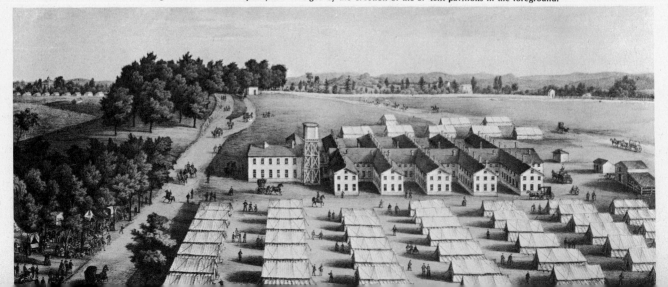

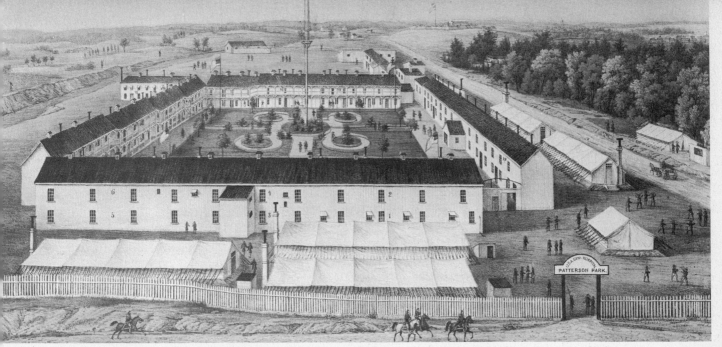

Patterson Park General Hospital, Baltimore, Maryland. Patterson Park is typical of many of the general hospitals constructed by the Army Medical Service—long barrack-like buildings around a central court.

Armory Square Hospital, Washington, D.C. Built in the summer of 1862, Armory Square cared for the sick and wounded of the Army of the Potomac. Its site was selected for easy access by water and rail.

Hospital Varian, Hamburg, Tennessee. Named for Dr. William Varian, the medical officer in charge, Hospital Varian was one of a number of tent hospitals established near Hamburg to care for the sick and wounded after the Shiloh campaign. The worst cases were sent back to their home states on hospital boats.

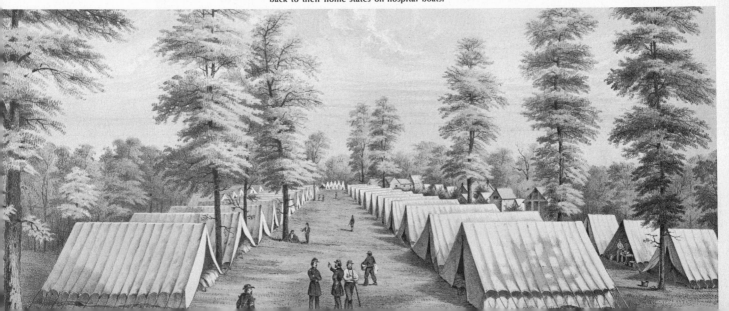

By 1863 the war had entered what General William T. Sherman called its professional phase. The troops were well trained and had had ample experience in combat. Commanders had pretty well mastered their jobs, and were deploying their forces fairly skillfully in accordance with the day's tactical principles. The infantry usually marched in column but attacked and defended in a line of two ranks. The brigade was the basic maneuvering unit, and it formed for the attack with regiments in a two-rank line. The division usually attacked in column of brigades, the second 150 to 300 yards behind the first, the third a similar distance behind the second. Terrain and skirmishers protected the flanks if no units were posted on either side. As most men were using single-shot muzzle-loaders, they still had to stand shoulder to shoulder in order to load conveniently and to get enough firepower. Attacks started in close order, but troops often scattered for cover and concealment when they came under fire, and thereafter advanced by short rushes supported by fire from neighboring units. No assaults were delivered frontally with fixed bayonets, and throughout the war most of them failed. The reasons for these failures lie in the longer range and greater effectiveness of Civil War rifles and field artillery and in the enthusiasm and skill with which the soldiers entrenched and used such features as ditches, trees, logs, and stone walls.

The main support for the infantry was provided by field artillery. Rifled guns of relatively long range were available, but the standard pieces were the 6-pound and 12-pound smoothbore, muzzle-loading, bronze "Napoleons" with ranges varying from 320 to 1,660 yards. The troops preferred the older to the rifled guns for several reasons. Rifled cannon were harder to clean; their projectiles were not as effective; their greater range could not always be effectively used; and finally, the rifled guns had flat trajectories, while the higher trajectories of the smoothbores enabled gunners to put fire on reverse slopes. Smoothbore projectiles were the same as those used in the Mexican War: solid shot, shell, canister, and shrapnel.

Cavalrymen, armed with saber, pistol, and breech-loading carbine, rode to the scene of battle but usually fought on foot. The broken and heavily wooded terrain of most battles was poor country for mounted men with drawn sabers, and the range and accuracy of the Springfield .58 rifle made it next to impossible for mounted men to attack infantry in position. With their superior speed and mobility, cavalrymen were particularly useful for screening, reconnaissance, and in advance guard actions in which they seized and held important hills, river lines, and road junctions pending the arrival of infantry. In these engagements they dismounted and fought with their breech-loading carbines, which had a faster rate of fire but shorter range than the infantry rifle.

The opening day of the Battle of Stone River, 31 December 1862. General William Rosecrans' Union troops (two lines at left) were forced to fall back before the engagement ended.

Union troops charge across the Stone River to resume the battle on 2 January. When Federal reinforcements arrived at the end of the day, the Southerners withdrew. The indecisive battle produced 13,000 Union and 12,000 Confederate casualties.

THE VICKSBURG CAMPAIGN: 1863

At the beginning of 1863 only the posts in the Vicksburg and Port Hudson areas prevented the Union from controlling the entire length of the Mississippi and splitting the Confederacy in two. Vicksburg was almost perfectly located for defense. At that point on the river, bluffs rose as high as 250 feet above the water, and extended for about 100 miles from north to south. North of Vicksburg lay the Yazoo River and its delta, a gloomy stretch of watery, swampy bottomland extending 175 miles from north to south, 60 miles from east to west. The ground immediately south of Vicksburg was almost as swampy and impassable. Furthermore the Confederates had fortified the bluffs from Haynes'

Bluff on the Yazoo, some 10 miles above Vicksburg, to Grand Gulf at the mouth of the Big River about 40 miles below. Vicksburg could not be assaulted from the river, and sailing past it was extremely risky since the river formed a great U there, and Vicksburg's guns threatened any craft that tried to slip by. For the Union troops to attack successfully, they would have to get to the high, dry ground east of town. This would put them right in Confederate territory between two enemy forces. Lieutenant General John C. Pemberton commanded some 30,000 men in Vicksburg, while the Confederate supreme commander in the area, General Johnston (now recovered from his wound) concentrated forces at Jackson, Mississippi, 40 miles east of Vicksburg.

Admiral Porter's fleet under heavy fire from the rebel batteries at Vicksburg on the night of 16–17 April 1863. All but one transport survived the bombardment to carry Grant's troops across the river a few days later.

Map—The Vicksburg Campaign.

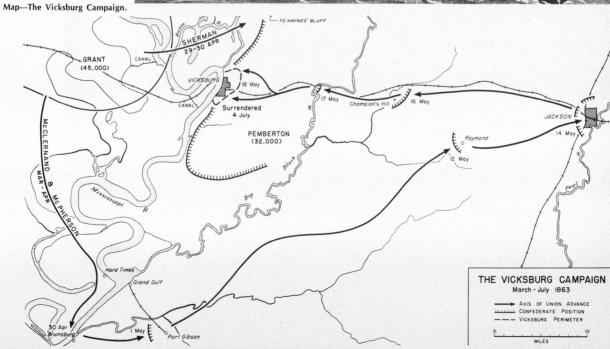

THE VICKSBURG CAMPAIGN
March - July 1863

→ AXIS OF UNION ADVANCE
⊥⊥⊥⊥ CONFEDERATE POSITION
- - - VICKSBURG PERIMETER

0   10
MILES

223

During late winter and early spring of 1863, with the rains falling, the streams high, the swamps at their wettest and muddiest, and overland movement impossible, the Army of the Tennessee, under Ulysses S. Grant, set to work digging canals. The purpose of the canals was to clear an approach by which troops could sail to a point near the high ground east of the river without being fired on by Vicksburg's guns, but the canals were failures.

In March, working in close cooperation with the local naval commander, Flag Officer David D. Porter, Grant evolved a plan of surprising boldness. He decided to use part of his force above Vicksburg to divert the Confederates while the main body marched southward overland on the west side of the Mississippi, crossed to the east bank, and struck out inland with five days' rations to live off a hostile country without a line of supply or retreat. Porter's gunboats and other craft on the river north of Vicksburg were to slip past the batteries during darkness and then ferry the troops over from the west to the east bank.

While the XV Corps under Major General William T. Sherman demonstrated near Vicksburg, Major General John A. McClernand's XIII Corps and Major General James B. McPherson's XVII Corps started southward. The rains let up in April, the waters receded slightly, and overland movement became somewhat easier. Even so, the movement south took one month. On the night of 16–17 April, Porter led his river fleet past Vicksburg, whose guns started a heavy bombardment once the move was discovered. Luckily, all but one transport made it safely. Starting on 30 April, Porter's craft ferried the troops eastward over the river at Bruinsburg below Grand Gulf, and the march against Vicksburg was ready to begin.

Grant's army, less Sherman's corps which followed a week later, captured Port Gibson on 1 May, then waited for Sherman. Grant had decided he must defeat Johnston who was gathering troops at Jackson before attacking Vicksburg. He moved out northeastward and by 12 May he was in position to interpose his force between Johnston and Pemberton and cut the Confederate line of communications. The next day Sherman and McPherson marched against the city of Jackson, with McClernand following in reserve, ready to hold off Pemberton. The leading corps took Jackson on 14 May, and drove its garrison eastward. While Sherman occupied Jackson, the other two corps started for Vicksburg. Pemberton tried to hold them off, fighting hard at Champion's Hill (16 May) and Black River Bridge (17 May)

but was defeated and shut up in Vicksburg. In 18 days, Grant's men had marched 200 miles and won four victories, living off the country except for the five days' rations they had carried. Grant assaulted Vicksburg on 18 May, and again on 22 May. When both attacks failed, he established a base on the Yazoo 12 miles away and began a siege.

The fall of Vicksburg was only a matter of time, with Sherman keeping Johnston away and the Federals advancing their approaches toward the Confederate works. Inside Vicksburg food was short, and troops and civilians were soon reduced to eating mules and other unconventional fare. Shells pounded the city. The front lines were so close that the Federals could throw hand grenades into the Confederate works. The Confederates had no grenades, but occasionally managed to fling back Federal grenades before they exploded. By 1 July the Union troops, having completed their approaches, were ready for another assault. But Vicksburg was starving, and Pemberton asked for terms. Grant offered to parole all prisoners, and Vicksburg surrendered on Independence Day. Since Grant was out of telegraphic contact with Washington, the news reached the President via naval channels on 7 July, the day before Major General Nathaniel P. Banks's 15,000-man army, having advanced up from New Orleans, captured Port Hudson, Louisiana. The whole river was now repossessed by the Union and the Confederacy sliced in two.

Hooker Replaces Burnside

In the East, General Burnside had been replaced as commander of the Army of the Potomac by Major General Joseph Hooker. The new commander had won a reputation as an intrepid and competent division and corps commander. Under his able administration, discipline and training improved. Morale, which had fallen after Fredericksburg, rose as Hooker regularized the furlough system and saw to it that rations of good quality, supplied by the War Department, were delivered to his front-line troops. Abolishing Burnside's Grand Divisions, Hooker returned to the orthodox corps, of which he had 7 of about 15,000 men each. He also took a long step toward improving his army by reorganizing the cavalry, which up to now had been assigned a multiplicity of diverse duties and was split up into small attachments. Hooker regarded cavalry as a combat arm of full stature, and he concentrated his cavalry units in a corps of three divisions under Brigadier General George Stoneman.

"The Civil War in America. Southern Refugees Encamping in the Woods Near Vicksburg." This engraving appeared in the "Illustrated London News" on 29 August 1863. It depicts citizens of Vicksburg who had fled the city to escape the daily bombardments during the siege that lasted from 22 May until 4 July. Other refugees lived in the caves outside the city.

224

Hooker Fails to Envelop Lee's Army

With Lee holding Fredericksburg, Hooker, whose strength totaled about 134,000 men, planned a double envelopment which would place strong Union forces on each of Lee's flanks. He ordered three of his infantry corps to move secretly up the Rappahannock and ford the stream, while two more corps, having conspicuously remained opposite Fredericksburg, crossed below the town. Two more corps were in reserve. The cavalry corps, less one division which was to screen the move, was to raid Lee's rear to divert him. Hooker's plan was good, but he executed it poorly. The three corps secretly moved up the river on 27 April, and two days later crossed the Rappahannock and advanced to a principal road junction at Chancellorsville. They were now in the Virginia Wilderness, a low, flat area of scrub timber and narrow dirt roads in which movement and visibility were extremely limited. That same day two corps under Major General John Sedgwick crossed the Rappa-hannock below Fredericksburg. The two remaining corps then moved up to join Hooker at Chancellorsville. At first everything went according to plan, save that Stoneman's raid failed to divert Lee. One of Stuart's brigades kept Stoneman under surveillance while the main body of the Confederate cavalry stayed with Lee and provided him with much more information about Hooker than Hooker ever obtained about Lee. But Hooker, by moving strong forces to each of Lee's flanks had won the first round.

General Lee, with 60,000 men, had been preparing plans to invade the North once again, but Hooker's action forestalled them. By morning of 30 April, Lee was aware of what was up and knew that he was threatened by double envelopment. A less bold and resolute man would have retreated southward at once, but Lee, leaving a part of his army to hold Marye's Heights at Fredericksburg, started for Chancellorsville with the main body.

A Confederate camp at Warrington Navy Yard, Pensacola, Florida, in 1861.

"Night Amusements in the Confederate Camp." This engraving, which appeared in the "Illustrated London News" in January 1863, shows Sweeny, "the most famous banjo-player in the Southern States" (in tent). He is playing for a Negro dancer. On both sides, the campfire was the center of camp social life.

When Lee began to move, Hooker in turn changed his plan and assumed the defensive. He established a line in the forest, felled trees for an abatis, and constructed earth-and-log breastworks. The line faced generally south with its left flank protected by the Rappahannock; however, the right flank was unsupported by any strong natural feature.

Lee brought his main body up and on 1 May made contact with Hooker's strong left. That same day Stuart's cavalry discovered the location of Hooker's vulnerable right flank, and late that afternoon brought the news, together with information about the roads, to Lee. Conferring that night with Stonewall Jackson, Lee made another bold decision. Facing an army much greater than his own, an army that was threatening to envelop and destroy him, he decided to divide his army and envelop the envelopers. Accordingly, Lee committed about 20,000 men against Hooker's left to hold it in place while Jackson with 25,000 men made a wide 15-mile swing to get beyond the right flank.

Jackson's force, in a 10-mile-long column, moved out at daybreak on 2 May, marching southwest first, then swinging northwest to get in position. The Federals noted the beginning of his march and realized something was afoot but were unable to intercept Jackson or determine his intentions. In late afternoon Jackson reached the Orange Turnpike near Wilderness Tavern. He was now west of Hooker's right flank. Here the woods thinned out a little and it was possible to form a line. Time was running short, so Jackson hastily deployed his force. Shortly after 1700 his leading division, shrieking the wild Rebel Yell, struck and drove Major General Oliver O. Howard's XI Corps out of position. Jackson pressed forward but was halted by a combination of darkness, fresh Union troops, and the disorganization of his own. As Jackson and his staff returned to the Confederate lines in darkness, soldiers of a North Carolina regiment failed to recognize the party and fired on it. Jackson was severely wounded and died eight days later.

During the night of 2–3 May, Stuart, who had assumed command of Jackson's II Corps, re-formed his lines. Hooker then launched local counterattacks against Stuart's right with some success, but on the morning of 3 May Hooker withdrew his whole line although he had a strong force between Lee's two divided and weaker forces. Stuart

A sketch by Southern artist Adalbert John Volck depicts General Jackson (standing at left with folded hands) at prayer in his camp. Jackson, a devout Presbyterian, reportedly arose to pray several times on the night before a battle.

"Lee and His Generals." Although they never assembled as a group during the course of the war, this lithograph shows the commander of the Confederate forces (on white horse) with his leading generals.

"Winter Campaigning." Sketched near Falmouth, Virginia, on 21 January 1863, by the combat artist Alfred R. Waud, this drawing shows the Army of the Potomac moving through rain and mud in a futile attempt to launch an attack on Lee's army on the opposite side of the Rappahannock River.

promptly renewed the attack and the two wings of Lee's army made contact and pressed forward. During the morning a Confederate shell struck a porch pillar of the house that served as Hooker's headquarters. Unfortunately the general was on the porch. A piece of the pillar hit him on the head, knocked him down, and from then on until the end of the battle he was dazed and incapable of exercising effective command. But he did not relinquish it, and neither the next senior general nor the surgeon dared declare him unfit. Meanwhile Sedgwick, who shortly after Jackson's attack

received orders to proceed through Fredericksburg to Chancellorsville, had assaulted Marye's Heights. He carried them about noon of 3 May, after a morning-long fight, but Lee then detached troops against Sedgwick, pressed him on his front and rear, and forced him off the road and northward over the river. While Lee made ready for a full-scale assault against the Army of the Potomac on 6 May, Hooker ordered a withdrawal to the north bank of the Rappahannock. Total Union casualties numbered about 17,000; the Confederates lost 13,000.

The railroad in this photograph was one of the Army of the Potomac's vital supply lines during its operations in Virginia.

The Army of the Potomac's Ninth Army Corps embarking at Aquia Creek, Virginia, for Fort Monroe in February 1863. The embarkation lasted four days.

At a camp somewhere in Virginia in 1863, a newspaper vendor sells copies of "Harper's Weekly" and Philadelphia, New York, and Baltimore papers.

An Army of the Potomac infantryman on guard near Fredericksburg. The sketch was done in January 1863 by Edwin Forbes who recorded a variety of Civil War scenes.

Edwin Forbes' "studio" at Rappahannock Station, Virginia. Like several other Civil War artists, Forbes, who worked for "Frank Leslie's Illustrated Newspaper," traveled with the army and lived in its camps.

The Army of the Potomac moves toward Chancellorsville on the night of 30 April 1863.

A Currier and Ives lithograph showing the intense fighting that characterized the Battle of Chancellorsville. The engagement, which extended from Chancellorsville, ten miles eastward to Fredericksburg, resulted in 12,800 Confederate casualties, including General Stonewell Jackson, and 17,000 Union casualties.

This may be the first photograph of the U.S. Army in combat. It was taken near Fredericksburg.

The Union hospital at Chancellorsville, sketched by Edwin Forbes on 2 May. At the left a surgeon is operating out of doors.

Lee Advances North From Fredericksburg

In early June General Lee began moving his units north from Fredericksburg. In his advance he used the Shenandoah and Cumberland Valleys, for by holding the east-west mountain passes he could readily cover his approach route and line of communications. Hooker soon got wind of the move and on 9 June his cavalry, now commanded by Major General Alfred Peasonton, surprised Stuart at Brandy Station, Virginia. Here on an open plain was fought one of the few mounted, saber-swinging, cut-and-thrust cavalry combats of the Civil War. Up to now the Confederate cavalry had been superior, but Union cavalry was improving and Stuart was lucky to hold his position. The Federals learned that Confederate infantrymen were west of the Blue Ridge heading north, and Hooker immediately moved to protect Washington and Baltimore and to destroy Lee. As Lee's Army of Northern Virginia moved through the valleys and deployed into Pennsylvania, the Army of the Potomac moved north on a broad front to the east. It crossed the Potomac near Leesburg on 25 and 26 June. By then Lee, forced to disperse because of scanty supplies, had extended his infantry corps from McConnelsburg and Chambersburg on the west to Carlisle on the north and York on the east. When, on 28 June, Lee learned from Longstreet that the Army of the Potomac was north of the river, he ordered his Army to concentrate at once between Gettysburg and Cashtown.

Meade Replaces Hooker

After Chancellorsville, Lincoln, though advised to drop Hooker, had kept him in command of the Army of the Potomac, pointing out that he would not throw away a gun because it has missed fire once. But Hooker, while advancing northward, became embroiled in an argument with General in Chief Halleck over the merits of holding Harpers Ferry. When Halleck insisted that Harpers Ferry be held, Hooker requested relief and was quickly removed. Major General George G. Meade, appointed in his place, started north on a broad front at once, but soon decided to fight a defensive action in Maryland, and issued orders to that effect. However, not all his commanders received the order, and events overruled him.

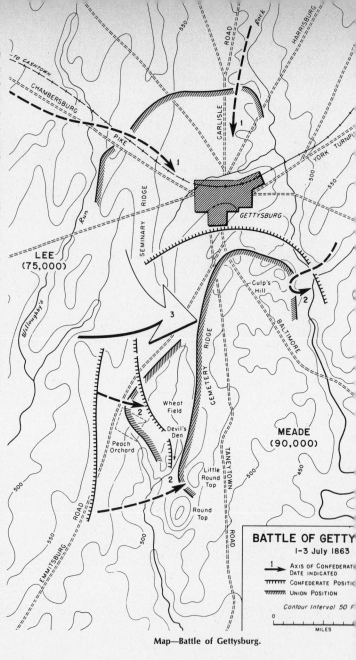

Map—Battle of Gettysburg.

The Gettysburg battlefield with Little Round Top, where a fierce battle raged on 2 July, in the left foreground, and Culp's Hill, where the fighting began on 3 July, at right center.

The Battle of Gettysburg

During the afternoon of 30 June the advance guard of the Union 1st Cavalry Division, covering the left of Meade's army, encountered Confederates from Lee's III Corps in Gettysburg. In the vicinity of the village were several strong tactical positions, and Gettysburg was the junction of twelve roads which led to Harrisburg, Philadelphia, Baltimore, and Washington, and to the mountain passes to the west controlled by Lee. The local commanders rushed reports and recommendations to their superiors, who forwarded them upward, and both armies, still widely dispersed, started moving toward Gettysburg.

The Union cavalrymen, dismounted, fought a delaying action against advance troops of the III Corps northwest of Gettysburg until Meade's I Corps arrived. Elements of Meade's XI Corps soon followed, but the Confederate II Corps came down from the north and drove the Federals back through Gettysburg. The Federals finally held firm on Cemetery and Culp's Hills. Lee, who reached the field about 1400, decided to wait for Longstreet's I Corps, which was still several miles west of Gettysburg, before renewing the attack. The Confederate positions extended in a great curve from northeast of Culp's Hill westward through Gettysburg, thence south on Seminary Ridge. The Federals, with interior lines, held the key points of Culp's Hill, Cemetery Hill, Cemetery Ridge, and Little Round Top.

More and more Union troops marched in. Four whole corps and two-thirds of two more were present by 0900, 2 July; 6 corps were on hand by noon, as well as the reserve artillery, and the VI Corps, having made a 34-mile forced march, began arriving at 1400. Meade had completed his dispositions by 0900. His line was very strong with two exceptions. In the confusion, Little Round Top was left occupied only by a signal station when the 1st Cavalry Division was dispatched to guard the army trains and not replaced. And the commander of the III Corps, Major General Daniel E. Sickels, on his own responsibility, had moved his line forward from the south end of Cemetery Ridge to higher, more defensible ground near the Peach Orchard, so that his corps lay in an exposed salient. On the Confederate side, Lee had not been able to attack early; reconnaissance took time, and Longstreet's leading division, which was to make the attack, did not arrive until after noon. It was 1500 when Longstreet's men, having deployed, advanced toward Little Round Top and the Devil's Den. At this point Meade's chief engineer, discovering that no infantry held Little Round Top, persuaded the commander of the V Corps, Major General George Sykes, to send two brigades and some artillery to the knoll. They arrived just in time to hold the summit against a furious Confederate attack. When this attack bogged down, Longstreet threw a second division against the Peach Orchard; this cracked Sickels' line and drove as far as Cemetery Ridge before Meade's reserves halted it. As the day ended the Federals held all their main positions. The Confederates had been fighting hard and with great bravery, but their attack had never engaged the Union front decisively at any point.

Meade, after requesting the opinions of his corps commanders, decided to defend, rather than attack, on 3 July. He surmised that Lee, having attacked his right and left, would try also for his center, and he was right. Lee had at first planned to launch a full-scale, coordinated attack all along the line but then changed his mind in favor of a massive frontal assault by 15,000 men against the Union center, held by Major General Winfield Scott Hancock's II Corps. About 1400, after an artillery duel in which the Confederates failed to knock out the Federal artillery, the 15,000 men, under command of Major General George E. Pickett, attacked eastward from Seminary Ridge along a mile of front. The assault force—47 regiments altogether—moved at a walk until it reached the Cemetery Ridge, then broke into a run. Union artillery, especially 40 Napoleons on the south end of Cemetery Ridge and some rifled guns on Little Round Top, opened fire and forced Pickett's right over to the north. Despite heavy casualties the Confederates kept their formation until they came within rifle and canister range of the II Corps. The four brigades composing the left of Pickett's first line were heavily hit but actually reached and crossed

"General Hancock at Gettysburg" as painted by Frank Brisco. Sent to Gettysburg on 1 July to study the situation, Hancock recommended to General Meade that a battle be fought there.

231

a stone wall defended by a II Corps division only to be quickly cut down or captured. Pickett's survivors withdrew to Seminary Ridge, and the fighting was over except for a suicidal mounted charge by Union Cavalry which Longstreet's right flank units easily halted.

Of 90,000 effective Union troops and 75,000 Confederates, there were more than 51,000 casualties. The Army of the Potomac lost 3,155 killed, 14,529 wounded, and 5,365 prisoners and missing. Of the Army of Northern Virginia, 3,903 were killed, 18,735 wounded, and 5,425 missing and prisoners.

Lee retired at once toward the Potomac, but the river was flooded and it was several days before he was able to cross. President Lincoln, naturally pleased over Meade's defensive victory and elated over Grant's capture of Vicksburg, thought the war would end in 1863 if Meade launched a resolute pursuit and destroyed the Army of Northern Virginia on the north bank of the Potomac. But Meade, who

might have been suffering from what today would be called combat fatigue, did not move at once, and Lee safely returned to Virginia on 13 July. Gettysburg was the last important battle in the East during 1863. The action now shifted to Tennessee.

The Army of the Cumberland

Lincoln had long wished to push an army into the strongly Unionist east part of Tennessee and he now prodded Major General William S. Rosecrans, the commander of the Army of the Cumberland, who began an advance from Murfreesboro to Chattanooga during July 1863. Chattanooga's location made it one of the most important cities in the South. From Chattanooga the Confederates could threaten the Ohio River and prevent a Union penetration of the southeastern part of the Confederacy. If the Union armies pushed through Chattanooga, they would be in position to attack Savannah, Georgia, or even Richmond from the rear.

Pickett's charge against the center of the Union line on the afternoon of 3 July. When Federal reinforcements arrived, Pickett and his men withdrew under heavy fire with a loss of nearly 6,000 men.

This is Currier and Ives's version of the fighting at Gettysburg on 3 July.

232

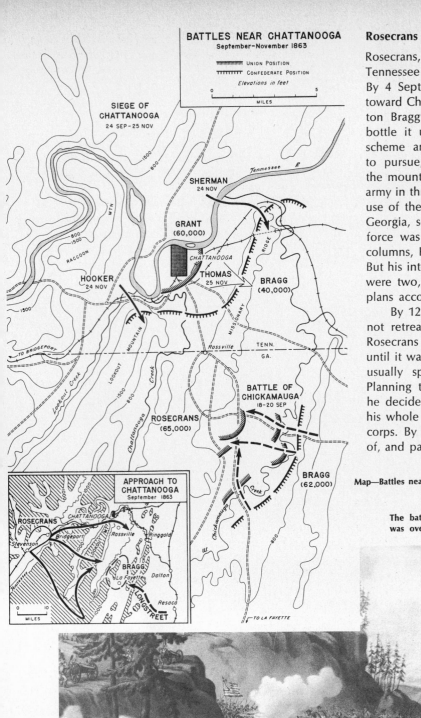

BATTLES NEAR CHATTANOOGA
September–November 1863

━━━━━ UNION POSITION
─┬┬┬┬─ CONFEDERATE POSITION
Elevations in feet

0 — — — — 5
MILES

SIEGE OF
CHATTANOOGA
24 SEP-25 NOV

Tennessee R.

SHERMAN
24 NOV

GRANT
(60,000)

CHATTANOOGA

HOOKER
24 NOV

THOMAS
25 NOV

BRAGG
(40,000)

TO BRIDGEPORT

Rossville

TENN.
GA.

BATTLE OF
CHICKAMAUGA
18-20 SEP

ROSECRANS
(65,000)

BRAGG
(62,000)

Chickamauga

Creek

TO LA FAYETTE

APPROACH TO CHATTANOOGA
September 1863

CHATTANOOGA

ROSECRANS

Bridgeport
Rossville
Ringgold

Stevenson

BRAGG
La Fayette
Dalton

LONGSTREET

Resaca

0 — 10
MILES

Rosecrans Advances on Chattanooga

Rosecrans, with his army, reached the north bank of the Tennessee River near Stevenson, Alabama, on 20 August. By 4 September he was across the river and on his way toward Chattanooga. He planned to approach General Braxton Bragg's Army of Tennessee from the southwest and bottle it up in Chattanooga, but Bragg saw through the scheme and slipped away southward. Rosecrans decided to pursue, even though there were few passes through the mountains and no good lateral roads. He dispersed his army in three columns over a 40-mile front in order to make use of the various passes, and followed Bragg to Lafayette, Georgia, some 22 miles south of Chattanooga. Because his force was three times as large as any one of the Union columns, Bragg anticipated that he could defeat Rosecrans. But his intelligence service had failed him; he thought there were two, rather than three Union columns, and prepared plans accordingly.

By 12 September, Rosecrans was aware that Bragg was not retreating in disorder but was getting ready to fight. Rosecrans ordered an immediate troop concentration, but until it was accomplished, his corps were vulnerable. Bragg, usually speedy in executing attacks, delayed this time. Planning to push Rosecrans southward from Chattanooga, he decided to wait for Longstreet in order to concentrate his whole force against what he thought were two Federal corps. By 17 September he was occupying a position east of, and parallel to, Chickamauga Creek.

Map—Battles near Chattanooga.

The battle at Chickamauga, Georgia, in September 1863. When it was over, the Army of the Cumberland had been driven back to Chattanooga, Tennessee.

Confusion at Chickamauga

When Longstreet's three leading brigades arrived on 18 September, Bragg decided to cross the creek and attack. The Federals, with two corps now almost concentrated, defended the fords so stoutly that only a few Confederate units got over. During the night, however, more slipped across, and by the morning of the 19th about three-fourths of Bragg's men were over.

With the arrival of the third Union corps on the 19th, Bragg faced a much stronger force than he had anticipated. The battlefield was heavily wooded, with few landmarks, and units had some difficulty maintaining direction. Fighting went on throughout the day with all units engaged, but in piecemeal fashion. The Federal lines were broken several times, but counterattacks restored all positions, and by nightfall the Federals still controlled the roads to Chattanooga. That night Lee's "war-horse," Longstreet, arrived with two more brigades. As he went looking for Bragg to report to him, he got lost in the woods. Encountering some soldiers, he asked them what unit they belonged to. When they replied with numbers—Confederate divisions were named for their commanders—he realized he was in the presence of Union troops, hastily rode off in the darkness, and eventually found Bragg.

When Bragg renewed the attack the next morning, Rosecrans received an erroneous report that one of the Federal units was not supported, so he ordered another unit to move in and help. But he had become confused and designated a unit which was already in line of battle. As this force obediently abandoned its position, Longstreet, just beginning his attack, saw the hole and drove into it at once. Some units retreated in disorder all the way to Chattanooga and swept Rosecrans along with them for about half the distance. Rosecrans, considering he had been defeated, went on to Chattanooga to organize it for defense. Major General George H. Thomas, with about two-thirds of the disorganized army, stood fast and checked Longstreet with a counterattack delivered on foot by a brigade of mounted infantry armed with repeating rifles. The attacks continued all day and Thomas' resolute stand and the valorous performance of the 19th Infantry won for him and the unit the title "Rock of Chickamauga." The next day Thomas retired into Chattanooga.

Bottled Up in Chattanooga

Rosecrans' army, having started out offensively, was now shut up in Chattanooga and Burnside, in eastern Tennessee, was too far away to render immediate aid. There were no strong Confederate units north of Chattanooga, but Rosecrans' line of communications was cut anyway. The Nashville and Chattanooga Railroad ran through Confederate territory into town, and river steamers could get only to within eight miles of Chattanooga. Supplies had to come over the mountains in wagons, but Confederate cavalry managed to destroy many precious wagons. Also the mountain roads were breaking down under the heavy traffic in wet weather. Rations ran short at Chattanooga. Men went hungry and horses and mules began to die of starvation.

Rosecrans' problems had been receiving earnest consideration in Washington. On 23 September the President met with Secretary Stanton, General Halleck, and others to determine what could be done. As General Meade in the east was not then active, they decided to detach two corps, or 20,000 men, from the Army of the Potomac and send them by rail to Tennessee under command of General Hooker, who had been without active command since his relief. The 1,200-mile journey, involving four changes of trains, got under way on 25 September, a day after Bragg's army established itself in front of Chattanooga. A month later the supply line was reopened.

Grant Takes Command of the Mississippi Military Division

Chickamauga had caused Stanton and his associates to lose confidence in Rosecrans. For some time Lincoln had been dubious about the general, who, he said, acted "like a duck hit on the head" after Chickamauga, but he did not immediately choose a successor. Finally, about mid-October, he decided to unify command of all the western armies and to vest it in General Grant, who still commanded the Army of the Tennessee. He now became commander of the Military Division of the Mississippi, which embraced the Departments and Armies of the Ohio, Cumberland, and Tennessee, and included the vast area from the Alleghenies to the Mississippi River north of General Banks's Gulf Department. Thomas replaced Rosecrans, and Sherman was appointed to command Grant's old army.

Positions and camps of part of the Army of the Cumberland at Chattanooga in the fall of 1863 with Lookout Mountain in the background.

234

The Battle of Missionary Ridge on 25 November 1863. The battle ended with the Confederate forces in full retreat.

Grant's Victory at Chattanooga

In early November Bragg weakened his besieging army at Chattanooga by sending Longstreet's force after Burnside in eastern Tennessee. This reduced his strength to about 40,000 just as Sherman arrived with Grant's old Army of the Tennessee. The troops immediately at hand under Grant—Thomas' Army of Cumberland, Sherman's Army of the Tennessee, and Hooker's two corps from the Army of the Potomac—now numbered about 60,000. Grant characteristically decided to resume the offensive with his entire force.

Hooker took Lookout Mountain on 24 November. On the same day Sherman crossed the Tennessee at the mouth of Chickamauga Creek and gained positions on the north end of Missionary Ridge. He attacked southward along the Ridge on 25 November but failed to gain. Grant's plan had initially provided for Thomas to attack the western face of Missionary Ridge only after Hooker had pushed southeastward from Lookout Mountain and enveloped Bragg's left. But Grant's mind was flexible, and when Sherman's attack stalled he switched plans. To help Sherman, he directed Thomas to take the rifle pits at the foot of the west slope of Missionary Ridge. These rifle pits were the first of three lines of Confederate trenches. Thomas' troops drove forward and seized the pits, and then themselves took control of this phase of the battle. Coming under fire from the pits upward and in front of them, they kept going. When Grant observed this movement he was at first concerned but, when he saw it succeeding, he gave it additional suport. Thomas' troops drove up all the way to the top, and in the afternoon Hooker swept the southern end of Missionary Ridge; the Union troops then had the unusual experience of seeing a Confederate army in precipitate retreat. Grant pursued Bragg the next day, but one Confederate division skillfully halted the pursuit while Bragg retreated and concentrated his Army. Grant's victory at Chattanooga cleared practically all of Tennessee for the Union.

Grant Assumes Command of All Union Armies: February, 1864

In February 1864 Congress revived the rank of lieutenant general, which until then had been held by only two U.S. Army officers, George Washington and Winfield Scott. President Lincoln promoted Grant to lieutenant general on 9 March, relieved Halleck as General in Chief, and put Grant in his place. Sherman succeeded to Grant's western command of three armies. Lincoln for years had been seeking a man who would accept responsibility and effectively control all the Union armies, operating them in concert with one another to bring the superior resources of the Union to bear against the South, win decisive victories, and end the war. McClellan and Halleck had disappointed him, but in Grant he found the man he wanted.

Plans for Winning the War

Plans for winning the war were developed by Lincoln and Grant during the spring of 1864. Grant elected to accompany Meade's Army of the Potomac in its southward advance rather than occupy a Washington office, but he was never very far from the Capital, and the President visited him frequently. Also the telegraph kept them in constant touch. The President gave Grant much wider latitude in exercising strategic control over the armies than he had given to McClellan and Halleck, doubtless because Grant was willing to accept responsibility and because Lincoln had confidence in Grant's ability and resolution.

The organizational machinery which Lincoln and Grant devised to control the armies was remarkable for its smooth efficiency. Grant, as General in Chief, reported to Stanton and to the President, keeping them informed on the broad aspects of his strategic plans and informing them in advance of the armies' requirements in men and munitions. For the conduct of operations he maintained a small staff at his headquarters in the field. Grant's job, administratively, was

Two Union soldiers, one of them wounded, in a deserted camp. Because of limited medical knowledge, the Civil War soldier's chances of surviving a wound were only one in seven.

The Volunteer Refreshment Saloon in Philadelphia, Pennsylvania, one of two such volunteer operations in Philadelphia, where soldiers from the North changed trains. The Volunteer Refreshment Saloon fed nearly 900,000 soldiers during the Civil War in a dining room (bottom, center) that could seat 1,200 people at a time. The Cooking Department is depicted at lower right. There was also a Washing Department (lower left). "Soldiers' Guides," Bibles, prayer books, and newspapers were given to those who asked for them.

Punishing a thief. Although punishments varied from regiment to regiment during the Civil War, thieves were often stripped of their military insignia and marched out of camp.

very large, for under him were 17 different field commands that embraced more than half a million men. He dealt directly with Meade and used Halleck, who had loyally stepped down and assumed a new post as Army Chief of Staff in Washington, as a channel of communication with the other army commanders. Halleck eased the heavy burden of studying the commanders' reports and plans for Grant by preparing brief digests, so that Grant's time was not taken up by too many routine details. Men and munitions continued to be sent forward to the armies by the General Staff in Washington under Stanton's keen and exacting supervision.

As a military commander, Grant was married to the principle of the offensive. His plans called for the Union armies to move toward a common center in a vast, concentrated effort that for size and distance was hitherto unsurpassed in modern war. As Grant saw it, in the past the Union armies had not pulled together but had acted like a balky team. The Confederates had been able to use their interior lines and railroads to shift troops from one theatre to another, but Grant intended to stop that. He planned to hold Lee with the Army of the Potomac and defeat the Army of Northern Virginia in a decisive engagement while the western armies executed a wide, swinging movement through the South which would, in effect, envelop the whole country east of the Mississippi.

Grant ordered the Army of the Potomac to drive southward against Lee. He directed Butler, who now commanded the Army of the James at Fort Monroe, to advance up the peninsula, menace Richmond, capture it if possible, and destroy the railroads south of the city in order to cut Lee's main supply route. If Butler captured Richmond, Lee could not retire into the city's entrenchments. Major General Franz Sigel, commanding a small force in the Shenandoah Valley, was to lead a raid up the valley in an attempt to divert the Confederates away from Richmond, and perhaps get at Lee from the rear. In the West the three armies under Sherman were to advance southward from Chattanooga to break up and destroy the Army of Tennessee, which was now commanded by Johnston, then push into the Confederacy's interior and damage its war-making resources.

This engraving of a sharpshooter on picket duty with the Army of the Potomac is based on a painting by the American artist Winslow Homer, who drew combat pictures for "Harper's Weekly" during the Civil War. The weapon most used by Federal forces was the United States Rifle Musket, Model 1861, called the "Springfield" because it was manufactured at the arsenal in Springfield, Massachusetts. The English Enfield Rifle Musket, Model 1853, the Spencer Repeating Carbine, and the Henry Repeating rifle were also used.

"Soldier's Burial." Over half a million Americans died from wounds or disease during the Civil War. The simple ceremony depicted here was often impossible under battle conditions.

ORD.   WEITZEL TERRY   CROOK   SEDGWICK   GRANT.   PARKE.   WRIGHT.   HANCOCK.   WARREN   HUMPHREY.
             SHERIDAN.   RAWLINS.   MEADE.

Ulysses S. Grant and his generals in the campaign against Richmond. General Grant is standing at center with Sheridan seated at his right and Meade seated at his left.

The Offensive Against Lee Begins

Meade's and Sherman's widely separated armies moved out to the attack on the morning of 4 May 1864. The Army of the Potomac crossed the Rapidan River and attempted to slip around Lee's right flank to envelop him and defeat him decisively while Butler cut his line of communications. Grant had decided to go by Lee's right, rather than his left, so as to use the Potomac River to ease the supply problem. Even so, the army trains numbered 4,000 wagons. When the army halted near Chancellorsville to allow the wagon trains to get through on 5 May, Lee struck at Meade's right flank. Grant and Meade swung the troops into line and fought back. The fighting, consisting of assault, defense, and counterattack, was close and desperate. Artillery could not be used effectively since there were few open spaces, and observation was limited. The dry woods caught fire, and some of the wounded died miserably in the flames. Lee attacked again on 6 May and drove the Federals back, but neither side renewed the fight on 7 May.

After an encounter with Lee, other Union commanders had usually retired and tried to postpone any further clashes with the great general. But Grant remained unruffled and renewed his attempt to push south around Lee's flank and interpose the Army of the Potomac between Lee and Richmond. On 7 May he drove south toward Spotsylvania, a key road junction. Lee detected the move and, using roads generally parallel to Grant's, also raced toward Spotsylvania. Confederate cavalry units were able to harass and slow Grant, so that Lee got there first. He quickly built strong earth-and-log trenches on commanding ground covering the roads leading to Richmond. General Philip H. Sheridan's

cavalry would have been useful to Grant in this race, but Meade had dissipated the cavalry corps' strength by using two divisions to guard his already well-protected trains. This provoked an argument between Meade and Sheridan which Grant resolved in favor of Sheridan. Grant regrouped the cavalry, and gave Sheridan a free hand when the latter promised to stop raids by Stuart's cavalry. Sheridan thereupon led his corps southward in a long raid toward Richmond which had as its objective a decisive action with Stuart. Sheridan fought a running series of engagements that culminated in the victory at Yellow Tavern in which the gallant Stuart was mortally wounded. The South was already short of horses and mules, and Sheridan's 16-day raid ended forever the offensive power of the cavalry of the Army of Northern Virginia.

From 9 to 20 May the Army of the Potomac struck at Lee's fortifications and was bloodily beaten back. On two separate occasions the Federals actually broke through the trenches and split Lee's army in two, but in each case the attackers became disorganized, supporting elements did not or could not come to their aid, and Confederate counterattacks were delivered with such ferocity that the gains could neither be exploited nor held. On 20 May, Grant decided the line was too strong to break and sideslipped south again, still trying to envelop Lee's right flank.

With inferior forces, Lee refused to come out from behind entrenchments to get beaten in decisive open battle. He retired to the North Anna River and built positions that Grant decided not to attack. Instead he moved south again. Butler, meanwhile, had advanced up the peninsula toward Richmond but did not capture it or cut Lee's railroads,

The camp of Grant's II Corps on the James River near City Point, Virginia. City Point, at the junction of the James and Appomattox rivers, was captured by Union forces on 4 May 1864.

City Point became the supply center for Grant's campaign. This photograph, made in 1864, shows supplies for City Point being loaded into wagons on the banks of the James.

Equipment and ammunition stockpiled at City Point in 1864.

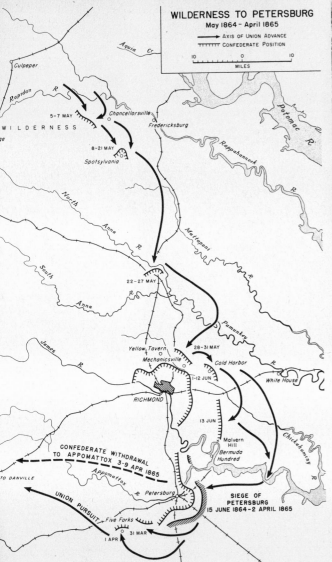

WILDERNESS TO PETERSBURG
May 1864 – April 1865

→ AXIS OF UNION ADVANCE
⊤⊤⊤ CONFEDERATE POSITION

10   0   10
MILES

Culpeper

Aquia Cr.

Rapidan R.

5–7 MAY   Chancellorsville
Fredericksburg

WILDERNESS

8–21 MAY
Spotsylvania

Rappahannock R.

Potomac R.

North Anna R.

Mattapони

22–27 MAY

South Anna R.

Pamunkey R.

James R.

Yellow Tavern   28–31 MAY
Mechanicsville   Cold Harbor
White House

1–12 JUN

RICHMOND

13 JUN

Chickahominy R.

Malvern Hill
Bermuda Hundred

CONFEDERATE WITHDRAWAL TO APPOMATTOX 3–9 APR 1865

Appomattox R.

TO DANVILLE

Petersburg

UNION PURSUIT   Five Forks

SIEGE OF PETERSBURG
15 JUNE 1864–2 APRIL 1865

31 MAR

1 APR

Map—Wilderness to Petersburg.

239

for Beauregard outmaneuvered him in May and bottled him up at Bermuda Hundred between the James and the Appomattox Rivers. Lee, therefore, easily made his way into Richmond defenses. With the armies facing each other along six to eight miles of front on 3 June, Grant ordered an assault against Lee's center at Gaines' Mill (Cold Harbor). The attack was badly planned, though bravely executed, and the Confederates repulsed it with gory efficiency.

Casualties Are Enormous

Thus far Grant, though fighting constantly, had failed to achieve a single major objective in the East. He had inflicted some 25,000 to 30,000 casualties on Lee, but Federal casualties in that bloody summer numbered 55,000 to 60,000, and the newspapers were calling Grant a butcher. Lincoln, in July, had to call for another half million volunteers with deficiencies to be made up by the draft.

"Battle of the Wilderness." The three-day Battle of the Wilderness was fought in a tangle of underbrush and trees after Grant's army crossed the Rapidan River during the drive toward Richmond. This lithograph depicts the action on 6 May 1864. Losses were very heavy on both sides.

This photograph was taken at Grant's temporary headquarters at Massaponax Church, Virginia, when the general met with his staff prior to the Battle of Cold Harbor (Gaines' Mill). Grant is leaning over a bench to examine a map held by General Meade.

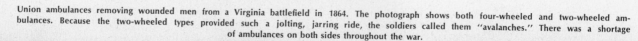

Union ambulances removing wounded men from a Virginia battlefield in 1864. The photograph shows both four-wheeled and two-wheeled ambulances. Because the two-wheeled types provided such a jolting, jarring ride, the soldiers called them "avalanches." There was a shortage of ambulances on both sides throughout the war.

Since Lee was strongly entrenched in Richmond, Grant now altered his plans. He decided to cross the James River east of Richmond and attack Petersburg, through which ran all the railways and main roads connecting Richmond with the south. If he could take Petersburg, he could either starve Lee into surrender or force him out of his trenches to fight. By 14 June, Grant had assembled his men on the north bank of the deep, wide James which they crossed on a 2,100-foot pontoon bridge. Lee, expecting Grant to attack between the Chickahominy and James rivers, did not interfere with the move.

Failure and Siege at Petersburg

Grant's leading elements, having crossed the river and deployed, came up in front of Petersburg on 15 June. Inasmuch as Lee had been deceived about Grant's intentions, the city was held by only a handful of Confederate soldiers under Beauregard and could have been taken handily on 15 June. But the Union commanders on the spot had not understood Grant's intentions either. While they dawdled, Lee found out about the movement, and quickly moved into Petersburg. A heavy Union assault on 18 June failed. On the last day of July a large mine tunneled under the Confederate

The Battle of Cold Harbor on 3 June 1864. The Union army of 60,000 men failed to break through the strongly fortified Confederate lines.

Civil War engineers constructed this pontoon bridge across the James River to enable Grant to move against Petersburg.

Civil War engineer officers.

A Union battery
before Petersburg.

The "Battle of the Crater" on 30 July 1864. Alfred R. Waud has sketched what was, in Grant's words, "a stupendous failure" for the Union side at Petersburg. After tunneling under enemy lines and exploding 8,000 pounds of gunpowder, Union troops attacked in the huge crater that resulted, only to be cut down by massed artillery and rifle fire.

A photographic wagon
"on location" near Petersburg.

works was exploded, opening a large breach in the Confederate line. However, the succeeding infantry assault was poorly managed and it failed, with over 4,000 casualties. Grant thereupon undertook siege operations, an effort which continued on into the next year. It was position warfare, a war of trenches and sieges, conducted ironically enough by two masters of mobile warfare. Mortars were used extensively, and heavy siege guns were mounted on railway cars and brought up. Grant extended his lines to the left, in a westerly direction, as he still sought to get around Lee's right, and operated against Lee's left to prevent him from shortening his line and achieving a higher degree of concentration. Lee moved his lines to counter Grant, so that the two commanders were, in effect, maneuvering their fortifications.

While Grant and Lee were hammering each other in the vicinity of Richmond, Federal troops had been moving up the Shenandoah Valley to threaten Lee from the rear. Now that he was firmly in place at Petersburg and could spare some troops, Lee decided to ease the pressure by sending Major General Jubal A. Early with one corps to raid northward through the Shenandoah Valley. Entering the valley from the south in early July, Early advanced. The Union commander, Major General David Hunter, received confusing orders from Washington and retired up the valley, but when he reached the Potomac he turned west into the safety of the mountains, thus uncovering Washington. Early saw his chance and drove through Maryland toward the Capital. Delayed by a Union force on 9 July, he reached the northern outskirts of the city on 11 July, and skirmished

Battle-weary Union soldiers in the trenches at Petersburg.

The first Federal wagon train enters Petersburg at the end of the siege in April 1865.

Union artillery at Fort Brady in 1864. During the siege of Petersburg, Union forces constructed the fort on a high bluff overlooking the James River. Fort Brady is typical of the Union forts built during the Civil War.

briskly in the vicinity of Fort Stevens. He did not know that an interested spectator in a black frock coat and tall silk hat stood behind the fort's parapet—the Commander in Chief of all the armed forces of the United States, Abraham Lincoln. That same day a force hastily dispatched by Grant reached Washington. Early, who was only raiding, realized he was engaging troops of the Army of the Potomac, and made off the next day. Although he was outnumbered by Union forces in the vicinity, he escaped safely.

Sheridan Put in Command of Washington Forces

Up to then Grant had not been paying close attention to the Union forces in the Shenandoah Valley, but on President Lincoln's instructions he now reorganized them. Deciding that Early had eluded superior forces because they had not been under a single commander, Grant abolished the four separate departments in the vicinity of Washington and formed them into one command embracing Washington, Western Maryland, and the Shenandoah Valley. After discussing the problem with Lincoln and General Hunter, he put Sheridan in command in August with orders to follow Early to the death.

Sheridan spent the rest of the year in the Shenandoah Valley. Employing and coordinating his infantry, cavalry, and artillery in a manner that has won the admiration of military students ever since, he met and defeated Early at Winchester and Fisher's Hill in September, and shattered him at Cedar Creek in October. To stop further raids and prevent the crops of the fertile valley from being used to feed Lee's army, Sheridan devastated it.

The Confederate prison at Salisbury, North Carolina. Opened in 1862, Salisbury consisted of an abandoned cotton factory and some former boarding houses surrounded by a wooden fence. Although this picture shows a group of well-dressed prisoners, some of them playing baseball, conditions at Salisbury became very bad in 1864 when 7,500 prisoners were moved there from Richmond. Both water and food were scarce, and disease was prevalent. Between October 1864 and February 1865 3,479 of 10,321 prisoners died at Salisbury.

Private William C. Schwartzburg of the 24th Wisconsin Volunteers drew this sketch of Libby Prison in Richmond. Schwartzburg himself was probably held elsewhere in Richmond because only officers were confined at Libby Prison, a former warehouse. After a series of Union cavalry raids on Richmond in 1864, the prisoners held at Libby Prison were moved to Macon, Georgia.

Camp Douglas, Chicago, Illinois. Camp Douglas, opened in 1861 as a training camp for Illinois volunteers, was later used to house Confederate prisoners.

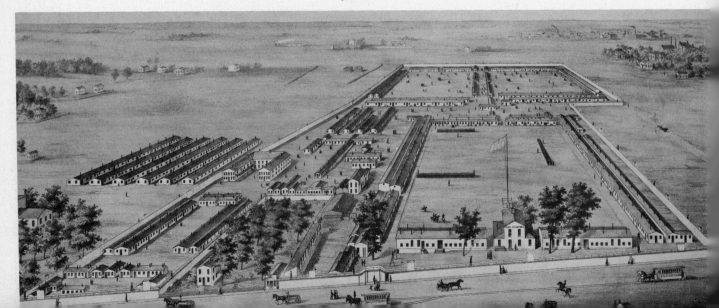

Andersonville Prison. One of the most notorious of all Civil War prisons, Andersonville was opened in 1864 to receive enlisted prisoners transferred there from the north. By May the stockade held 12,000 prisoners and over a thousand men had died. The death wagon at lower left carries the sign "Dead, 12,877."

While Grant and Meade were fighting Lee, and Sheridan was pursuing Early and burning the Shenandoah Valley, Sherman with his great force of 105,000 men in three armies had been advancing from Chattanooga to Atlanta. Facing him were two corps of the Army of Tennessee under Johnston. This force was shortly joined by Polk's Army of Mississippi to bring Johnston's whole force, including cavalry, to about 65,000 men. Sherman's mission was the destruction of Johnston's armies and the capture of Atlanta, which, after Richmond, was the most important industrial center in the South.

Sherman Moves South in Atlanta

Sherman had moved out on 4 May 1864, the same day the Army of the Potomac crossed the Rapidan. Johnston, realizing how seriously he was outnumbered, decided to go on the defensive, preserve his forces intact, hold Atlanta, and delay Sherman as long as possible. There was always the hope that the North would grow weary of the costly struggle, and that some advocate of peaceful settlement might defeat Abraham Lincoln in the election of 1864. From 4 May through mid-July, the two forces maneuvered against each other. There were daily fights but few large-scale ac-

Sheridan defeats Early in the Shenandoah Valley—at Winchester, Virginia, on 19 September 1864.

Sheridan defeats Early in the Shenandoah Valley—at Cedar Creek, Virginia, on 19 October 1864.

Burning cotton near Memphis. The official Confederate policy was to burn cotton rather than let it fall into Union hands. In this engraving from the "Illustrated London News" for 9 August 1862, Federal scouts have surprised a group of cotton burners.

The metal shortage in the South produced this etching in which church bells are being offered to the Confederate Army to be melted down and cast into cannon. Several requests were made for bells during the war.

"Going to the Commissary for Rations." After Union forces occupied an area, the local population often had to depend on the Federal Government for food, especially during the winter months. In this drawing, Southern women are on their way to a commissary to pick up food.

tions. As Sherman pushed south, Johnston would take up a strong position and force Sherman to halt, deploy, and reconnoiter. Sherman would then outflank Johnston, who in turn would retire to a new line and start the process all over again until he was forced back to positions in front of Atlanta.

Johnston had done his part well, slowing Sherman so that he had covered only 100 miles in 74 days. Now Johnston, his forces intact, was holding strong positions in front of Atlanta, his main base. But Jefferson Davis had grown impatient with Johnston and his tactics of cautious delay. In July he replaced him with Major General John B. Hood, a much more impetuous commander.

On 20 July, while Sherman was executing a wide turning movement around the northeast side of Atlanta, Hood left his fortifications and attacked at Peach Tree Creek. When Sherman beat him off, Hood pulled back into the city, Sherman unsuccessfully tried cavalry raids to cut the railroads and then began extending fortifications on 31 August. Hood, who had dissipated his striking power in his assaults, gave up and retired to northwest Alabama, and Sherman marched into Atlanta on 1 and 2 September.

Sherman's Plans for a March to the Sea

The fall of Atlanta and Hood's withdrawal raised the question of Sherman's next mission, and his new proposals proved him an able strategist as well as a consummately bold and aggressive commander. Abandoning the idea of catching up with Hood, he suggested that he send two corps of about 30,000 men back to Thomas at Nashville, where Thomas would raise and train more men and be in position to hold Tennessee and deal with Hood if he came north. He recommended that he himself take four corps of about 62,000 men, cut his communications, live off the country, and march to the seacoast through the very heart of the Confederacy, meanwhile devastating and laying waste all farms, railways, and storehouses in his path. When he reached the coast, he reasoned, he could get to a port and make contact with U.S. naval forces. Neither Grant nor Lincoln was hidebound in thought, but their reaction to the plan was less than enthusiastic. That they accepted it at all was proof of their confidence in Sherman.

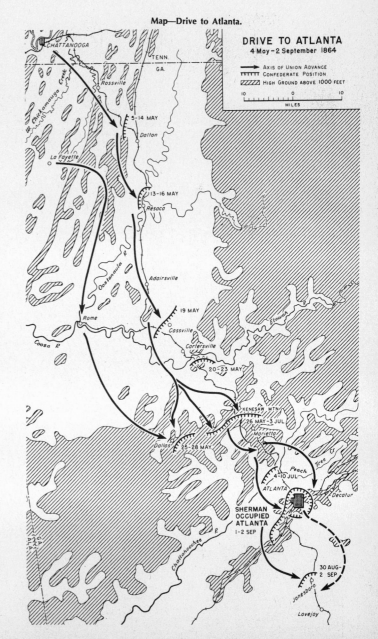

Map—Drive to Atlanta.

DRIVE TO ATLANTA
4 May – 2 September 1864

→ AXIS OF UNION ADVANCE
⊥⊥⊥⊥ CONFEDERATE POSITION
////// HIGH GROUND ABOVE 1000 FEET

10   0   10
MILES

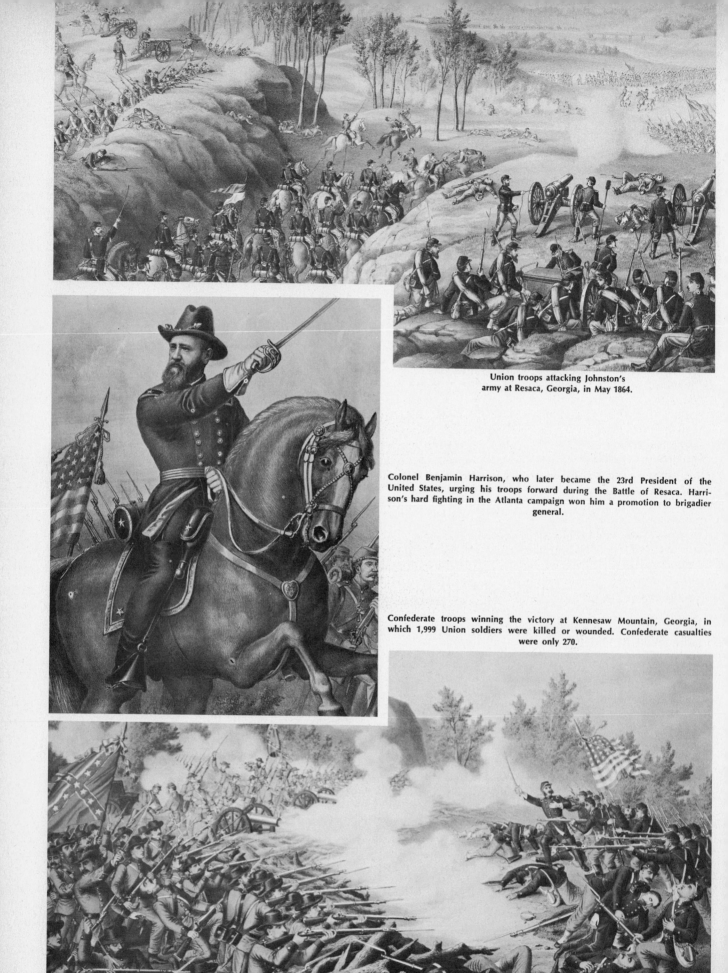

Union troops attacking Johnston's
army at Resaca, Georgia, in May 1864.

Colonel Benjamin Harrison, who later became the 23rd President of the
United States, urging his troops forward during the Battle of Resaca. Harrison's hard fighting in the Atlanta campaign won him a promotion to brigadier
general.

Confederate troops winning the victory at Kennesaw Mountain, Georgia, in
which 1,999 Union soldiers were killed or wounded. Confederate casualties
were only 270.

Fighting near Atlanta on 22 July 1864. After several skirmishes
on the outskirts, Sherman occupied Atlanta on 1 September.

After destroying Atlanta's military installations—much of the city itself was burned either by accident or design—Sherman's troops set forth on 12 November and headed for Savannah, Georgia. They planned to live off the country but carried a 20-day emergency supply of rations in the wagon train. Operating on a 60-mile-wide front, they systematically burned and destroyed crops, cotton gins, cattle, railways, and storehouses as they marched along. There was no fighting, and the march became something of a rowdy excursion. As might be expected from troops engaged in a mission of destruction with their spirits not tempered by the presence of a Confederate army, discipline, which was never overly strong in Civil War armies, seems to have broken down. As a consequence, in addition to the destruction carried out officially, there was a good deal of looting. Sherman's army reached Savannah on 10 December; Confederate forces evacuated the city on 21 December; and Sherman offered it as a Christmas present to the Nation.

Thomas Routs Hood in Tennessee

The two corps Sherman sent to Thomas were under the command of Major General John M. Schofield. While they were on their way to Nashville the aggressive Hood pushed north again and with 30,000 men attacked Schofield at Franklin, Tennessee. The battle, which opened after 1600 on 30 November and ended at dusk, was short, sharp, and furious. Schofield beat Hood off, inflicting 6,000 casualties and losing 2,300. Next day Schofield brought his men into Nashville.

General Thomas, the Rock of Chickamauga, belonged to the last bootlace school of soldiering. In comparison with Grant and Sherman, he was slow. But he was also sure. He had collected and trained troops and horses, and had made ready to attack Hood on 10 December, but a snow and sleet storm on 9 December made any movement impossible. Grant meanwhile became so impatient that he did not accept Thomas' assurances that he would strike soon and decided to relieve him of command. He actually started for Nashville in person, but before he arrived, the weather improved and Thomas hit Hood on 15 December, driving him back in an attack that military students have regarded as virtually faultless. He then renewed the fight and drove Hood from the field in almost complete disorder. A scattering of Hood's men got back across the Tennessee, but his army was never again an offensive threat.

General Sherman reviews his troops in Savannah, Georgia, in January 1865. After taking Savannah, Sherman sent this message to President Lincoln on 22 December: "I beg to present you as a Christmas gift, the city of Savannah, with one hundred and fifty heavy guns and plenty of ammunition, also about twenty-five thousand bales of cotton."

This group, photographed in an unidentified camp, illustrates the diverse nature of the population of Civil War camps.

At a camp near Brandy Station, Virginia, members of a Massachusetts regiment play games or sit around and talk in their off-duty time.

Life in Camp

Training was a regular part of camp life. This photograph shows a Union gun squad during a practice session.

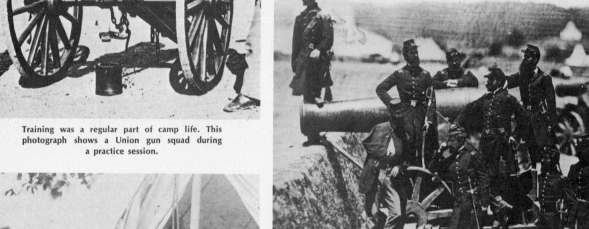

Every camp underwent several inspections in the course of a year. Here a gun emplacement is under scrutiny.

Mathew B. Brady took this photograph of a colonel and a general (holding bottle) in what was probably the general's tent. The camp bugler stands by at left.

250

The exterior of a sutler's tent at the headquarters of the 1st Brigade, Horse Artillery, Brandy Station, Virginia. The sign on the tent reads "A. Foulke, Sutler."

Organized bands, such as that of the 10th Veteran Reserve Corps in this photograph, were very popular with Civil War soldiers. The bands provided music for drill and gave occasional evening concerts for the troops.

Grant's Final Push: 1965

The operations of 1864 were continued in 1865. Grant and Meade hung on to Lee. The General-in-Chief and Sherman decided that the latter could accomplish more by marching overland from Savannah toward the Army of the Potomac, tearing up communications as he went, than by taking ships to Virginia, and Sherman started north in January. He moved through Wilmington, North Carolina, the Confederacy's last port, in February 1865, and pushed on.

At Petersburg, toward the end of March, Grant renewed his efforts to get at Lee's right flank. By now Sheridan's cavalry and the VI Corps had returned from the Shenandoah Valley, and the total force immediately under Grant numbered 101,000 infantry, 14,700 cavalry, and 9,000 artillery. Lee had 46,000 infantry, 6,000 cavalry, and 5,000 artillery. On 29 March, Grant began his move. While Sheridan and the cavalry pushed out ahead by way of Dinwiddie Court House in order to strike at Burke's Station where two rail-

A large naval force under Admiral David D. Porter bombards Fort Fisher at Wilmington, North Carolina. By January 1865 Wilmington was the only major port still under Confederate control.

roads intersected, Grant's main body moved to envelop Lee's right. But Lee caught on and moved west. Sheridan had advanced to Five Forks, a road junction southwest of Petersburg, where he encountered a strong Confederate force under General Pickett—cavalry plus two infantry divisions—which Lee had dispatched to forestall Sheridan. Pickett attacked and drove Sheridan back to Dinwiddie Court House, but there Sheridan dug in and halted him. Pickett then entrenched at Five Forks.

Grant renewed his attack against Lee's right on 2 April with an assault that broke the Confederate line and forced it back, and the Confederates withdrew toward Petersburg. With his line stretched very thin, Lee was forced to abandon Richmond and the Petersburg fortifications. He struck out and raced west toward the Danville Railroad, hoping to get to Lynchburg or Danville, break loose, and eventually join forces with Johnston. But Grant had him in the open at last. He pursued relentlessly and speedily, with troops behind (east of) Lee and south of him on his left flank while Sheridan dashed ahead with the cavalry to cut Lee off. A running fight ensued from 2 through 6 April during which Lee's rations ran out and his men began deserting and straggling by the thousands. Finally, Sheridan pushed his men to Appomattox Court House, squarely athwart Lee's line of retreat.

In this Currier and Ives lithograph, Union troops are landing to begin the attack on Fort Fisher. The fort surrendered on 15 January 1865.

The Battle of Five Forks, Virginia. At Five Forks on 1 April 1865, Union troops (on the left) finally broke through the Confederate line. It was the last major battle of the Civil War.

A Richmond street.

After Five Forks, Lee was forced to abandon the Petersburg fortifications and Richmond. A contemporary print depicts the fire that raged in Richmond on the night of April 2 after the retreating Confederate Army burned its supplies. Citizens of Richmond are fleeing the fire on the bridge at center.

A general view of Richmond after the fire.

Confederate equipment
left behind in Richmond.

Lee and Grant (seated at center)
at the McLean House at Appomattox.

Lee's Surrender at Appomattox: 9 April 1865

Lee decided that he could accomplish nothing by more fighting. Sadly, he went to Grant. The two great leaders met at the McLean house in Appomattox on 9 April 1865. The handsome, well-tailored Lee, the very epitome of Southern chivalry, asked Grant for terms. Reserving all political questions for his own decision, Lincoln had authorized Grant to treat only purely military matters. Grant, though physically less impressive than Lee, was equally chivalrous. He accepted Lee's surrender, allowed the Confederates to keep their horses and mules, furnished rations to the Army of Northern Virginia, and forbade the soldiers of the Army of the Poto-

mac to cheer or fire salutes in celebration of their victory over their old antagonists. Johnston surrendered to Sherman at Hillsboro, North Carolina, on 26 April; other Confederate forces gave up the struggle; and the grim fighting was over.

In this costly war, the U.S. Army lost 138,154 men killed incident to battle, 221,374 died of other causes, bringing the total Union dead to 359,528. The number of wounded in action totaled 280,040 men. Figures for the Confederacy are less exact, but at least 74,524 were killed incident to battle, 59,297 died of disease, and from 25,976 to 30,716 died in Northern prisons.

This representation of the surrender shows Confederate soldiers (left) turning in their muskets. Lee (left center) is offering to turn in his sword, and Grant is refusing it.

Lincoln and his victorious generals: From left: Admirals Porter and Farragut, the President, General William T. Sherman, General George H. Thomas, General Ulysses S. Grant, and General Philip H. Sheridan.

The Army of the Potomac parades in Washington. During the Grand Review on 23 and 24 May 1865, 150,000 veterans passed the reviewing stand occupied by President Andrew Johnson (who had succeeded to office upon Lincoln's assassination), General Grant, and members of the Cabinet.

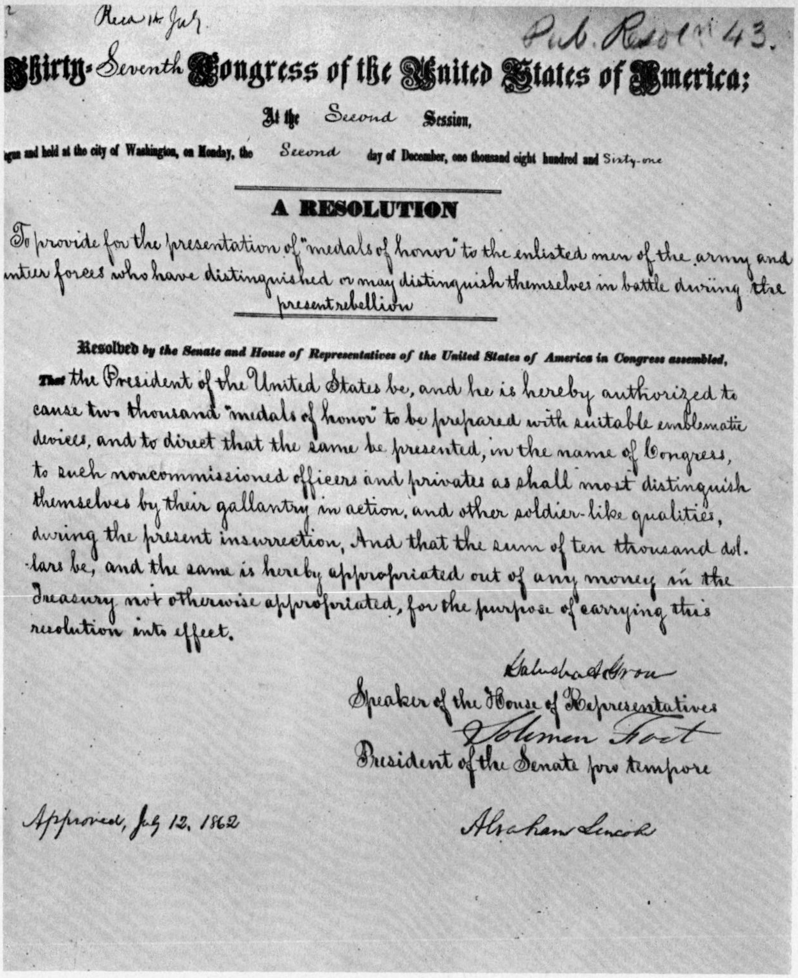

Recd 1st July

Pub. Resol. No. 43.

Thirty-Seventh Congress of the United States of America;

At the Second Session,

gun and held at the city of Washington, on Monday, the Second day of December, one thousand eight hundred and Sixty-one

A RESOLUTION

To provide for the presentation of "medals of honor" to the enlisted men of the army and unteer forces who have distinguished or may distinguish themselves in battle during the present rebellion

Resolved by the Senate and House of Representatives of the United States of America in Congress assembled, That the President of the United States be, and he is hereby authorized to cause two thousand "medals of honor" to be prepared with suitable emblematic devices, and to direct that the same be presented, in the name of Congress, to such noncommissioned officers and privates as shall most distinguish themselves by their gallantry in action, and other soldier-like qualities, during the present insurrection. And that the sum of ten thousand dollars be, and the same is hereby appropriated out of any money in the Treasury not otherwise appropriated, for the purpose of carrying this resolution into effect.

Galusha A. Grow
Speaker of the House of Representatives
Solomon Foot
President of the Senate pro tempore

Approved, July 12, 1862

Abraham Lincoln

The law that established the Medal of Honor

THE MEDAL OF HONOR

The Medal of Honor stands at the top of the "Pyramid of Honor," the term used by the Army to describe the degrees of heroism and their corresponding decorations. The Nation's second highest decoration, the Distinguished Service Cross, is awarded to members of the Armed Forces who distinguish themselves "by extraordinary heroism **in connection with military operations** against an armed enemy." Army regulations also provide that the heroism involve extraordinary risk of life. The criteria for the Medal of Honor are even more rigid. The risk of life involved must be **"above and beyond the call of duty,"** and, for the Army's Medal of Honor, it must involve **"actual conflict with an enemy."** Further, the heroic act must be conspicuous because of its "gallantry and intrepidity." The words "gallantry and intrepidity" mean almost the same thing as "bravery and courage," but in our language they are the most impressive words we can use to describe bravery and courage. Their use indicates the requirement that the deed have a certain nobility and selflessness that leaves no doubt that it was without equal. Such distinctions are hard to draw, and in making such a decision the Department of the Army is careful to rely on the judgment of mature and judicious officers with extensive combat experience.

The Medal of Honor awarded by the Army (and also the Air Force because of its historic association with the Army) is different both in appearance and origin from the comparable award made by the Navy. The Army Medal of Honor was created by an act of Congress signed by President Lincoln on 12 July 1862. The law provides that the Medal be awarded "in the name of Congress," and this is why it is often called the Congressional Medal of Honor.

The symbols used in the Army's Medal of Honor are rich in tradition. The 13 stars on the ribbon represent the original states, and the eagle stands for the Nation itself. The laurel wreath surrounding the five-pointed star is based on the actual laurel wreaths placed on the heads of Julius Caesar and the other great heroes of ancient Rome. In the center of the star is the head of Minerva, the ancient Roman goddess of wisdom and technical skill.

Several other things about the Medal of Honor make it unique. It is the only American decoration worn suspended from the neck; it entitles qualified sons of the recipient to appointments to the United States Military Academy without regard to quota requirements; it entitles recipients to free transportation on military aircraft when space is available; it entitles the recipient to a pension of $100 per month from the time the recipient reaches age 50; it is the only decoration awarded in the name of Congress; and it has been the subject of special legislation to protect it from imitation and abuse. However, it is the deeds themselves that have really made the Medal of Honor great, for no law or practice could substitute for the gallantry,

The Medal was redesigned and patented for protection against duplication.

The first U. S. Army Medal of Honor as established by law, July 12, 1862.

The ribbon design was changed because of imitations by non-military organizations.

the intrepidity, and the risk of life above and beyond the call of duty that make up the record of the Medal's winners.

The first actual award of the Army's Medal of Honor was made on 25 March 1863. It went to six soldiers for their exploits as members of the Mitchell Raiding Party. In one of the most thrilling episodes of the Civil War, they had slipped deep into Confederate territory and captured an entire train. Their objective was to destroy the bridges on the long railroad in order to cut off the whole State of Tennessee. This would prevent Confederate reinforcements reaching the site of planned Federal attacks. Of the 22 men in the raiding party, 19 eventually received the Medal of Honor.

The practice of awarding the Medal sometime after the deed of heroism was at first quite common. In fact, the first deed for which the Medal of Honor was awarded occurred on 13–14 February 1861—before the Medal was created—and the award itself was not made until 4 January 1894. It went to Bernard J. D. Irwin, a young Irish immigrant who in 1861 had been graduated from a New York medical school. His citation relates that he voluntarily took

command of a party that made its way through hostile Indian territory to rescue a detail surrounded by an Apache war party.

The many great campaigns of the Civil War afforded numerous opportunities for demonstrating the extraordinary heroism that merits the Medal of Honor. The citations are full of such phrases as: "saving a wounded comrade under murderous fire," "voluntarily extinguishing the burning fuse of a shell which had been thrown into the lines of the regiment by the enemy," and "among the first to mount the enemy's works in the assault, he received a serious bayonet wound in the face, was struck several times with clubbed muskets, but bravely stood his ground, and with his sword killed the man who bayoneted him." The citations cover such great battles as the Wilderness, Vicksburg, Gettysburg, and countless smaller but no less violent actions. They include the story of fifteen-year-old Private Nathaniel Gwynne of the 13th Ohio Cavalry, who lost his arm in a heroic action at Petersburg, Virginia. The gallant soldiers of the Civil War provided the first standards of heroism which the Medal of Honor still symbolizes.

The Indian Campaigns that marked the Nation's push westward were a different type of warfare from that of the Civil War. But just as they are today, the soldiers of the U.S. Army were called upon to demonstrate their capability for fighting any type of conflict. Their deeds emphasized that bravery is not limited to locale or type of enemy. Between 1861 and 1891, Army forces fought Comanches, Apaches, Sioux, Sheepeaters, and many other tribes. The history of that period on the Western Plains paints a vivid picture of the ambushes, massacres, and fierce hand-to-hand combat that has become a part of the Medal of Honor story. The citations include such strange names as Blanquet, Elastousoo, and Nantaie—gallant Indian Scouts—along with more familiar names like Taylor and O'Sullivan.

The Spanish-American War and later actions within the former Empire of Spain added another chapter in the history of the Army's Medal of Honor. All 30 of the Medal of Honor winners in the Spanish-American War were cited for action in Cuba. Almost without exception, these men were awarded the Medal for braving heavy enemy fire to rescue wounded comrades who had fallen in front of the American lines. Six were commissioned officers, the rest were sergeants, corporals, and privates. Their actions were part of a struggle that brought important international responsibilities to the United States.

One of these new international responsibilities was the development of the Philippine Islands, which were ceded to the United States as a result of the war with Spain. Before the United States could progress toward the goal of Philippine independence, it was first necessary to subdue the insurgent native bands of Emilio Aguinaldo and the fanatical Moros. Between 1899 and 1913, the Army pursued this important and difficult task.

MacARTHUR, ARTHUR, Jr.
Rank and Organization: First Lieutenant, and Adjutant, 24th Wisconsin Infantry. Place and Date: At Missionary Ridge, Tennessee, 25 Nov. 1863. Entered Service at: ———. Birth: Springfield, Massachusetts. Date of Issue: 30 June 1890. Citation: Seized the colors of his regiment at a critical moment and planted them on the captured works on the crest of Missionary Ridge.

Typical of the Army's Medal of Honor winners during the Philippine Insurrection was Thomas Sletteland. Born in Norway and entering the Army at Grafton, North Dakota, his official citation tells how he performed his extraordinary act of bravery near Paete, Luzon, and "single-handed and alone defended his dead and wounded comrades against a greatly superior force of enemy." Seth L. Weld of Altamont, North Carolina, won his Medal of Honor at La Paz, Leyte, in 1906. His citation reads, "With his right arm cut open with a bolo, went to the assistance of a wounded constabulary officer and a fellow soldier who were surrounded by 40 Pulajanes, and using his disabled rifle as a club, beat back the assailants and rescued his party."

Troubles along the Mexican border in the early 1900's led to numerous conflicts and the awarding of still another Medal of Honor in 1911. The recipient, Julien E. Gaujot, entered the Army at Williamson, West Virginia, and had risen to the rank of captain. On 13 April 1911, his unit, Troop K of the 1st United States Cavalry, was at Aqua Prieta, Mexico, where it was pitted against a large force of Mexican rebels. According to his official citation, he "crossed the field of fire to obtain the permission of the rebel commander to receive the surrender of the surrounded forces of Mexican Federals and escort such forces,

CLARKE, POWHATAN H.
Rank and Organization: Second Lieutenant, 10th United States Cavalry. Place and Date: At Pinito Mountains, Sonora, Mexico, 3 May 1886. Entered Service at: Baltimore, Maryland. Birth: Alexandria, Louisiana. Date of Issue: 12 March 1891. Citation: Rushed forward to the rescue of a soldier who was severely wounded and lay, disabled, exposed to the enemy's fire, and carried him to a place of safety.

together with five Americans held as prisoners, to the American line."

Calvin P. Titus, a former trumpeter in Company E, 14th United States Infantry was one of four Medal of Honor winners during the Boxer Rebellion.

The Boxer Rebellion is the name given to a bloody campaign waged by a group of Chinese who were fanatically opposed to all foreigners in China. Known as "the Boxers," they eventually trapped the foreign diplomats, missionaries, and Chinese Christians in the legation quarter of the great walled city of Peking. American soldiers, along with other foreign troops, were called upon in 1900 to break through and rescue the besieged group.

When units of the 14th United States Infantry finished their long march on the Chinese capital city in 1900, they were barred from the imprisoned group by the 30-foot wall of the city. It was then that Private Titus came forward to volunteer and spoke his now famous words, "I'll try, sir!"

Throwing aside his rifle and equipment, Titus began to climb at a point where the wall and a projecting bastion joined. Grasping at exposed stones, digging his toes into crevices created by long exposure to the elements, expecting at any moment to be knocked down by a rifle butt or a bullet, he slowly inched his way to the top. The Chinese, Titus discovered to his immense relief, had failed to occupy this section of the wall.

Other men following Titus' lead joined him, some bringing with them ropes for pulling up weapons and ammunition. By late afternoon of the same day, Company E, 14th Infantry, was firmly encamped within the Legation grounds, and victory in Peking was assured.

Trumpeter Titus' words in volunteering for his dangerous mission have come to stand for the heroic spirit of the Medal of Honor winners. "I'll try, sir!"

Around the World War I period several things were done to protect the Medal of Honor as the highest award of the Nation. An act of 1916 laid down the criteria that the action involved must be "actual conflict with the enemy, distinguished by conspicuous gallantry or intrepidity at the risk of life above and beyond the call of duty." The act of 9 July 1918 created the Distinguished Service Cross and the Silver Star. These actions reflect the feeling that one medal was not enough because there are degrees of bravery depending on the circumstances.

One man has been said to symbolize the new high standards for the Medal of Honor that have prevailed since the beginning of World War I. He was Lieutenant Samuel Woodfill, whom General Pershing called "America's greatest Doughboy." Woodfill was a Regular Army sergeant of long experience when the war began, and had been commissioned lieutenant shortly before his eventful "big day" of combat.

Like most official citations, the one that describes Woodfill's heroic deeds condenses a lot of action into the fewest possible words. Actually his action extended over a period of several hours. That is one reason why many ground fighting experts regard Woodfill's exploit as the ideal example of a trained, skillful, and efficient ground fighter. Here is what the official Medal of Honor book has to say:

Samuel Woodfill was another Medal of Honor winner of World War I. A first lieutenant in the 60th Infantry, 5th Division, he was leading his company against the enemy at Cunel, France, on 12 October 1918, when his line came under heavy machine-gun fire, which threatened to hold up the advance. Followed by two soldiers at 25 yards, this officer went out ahead of his first line toward a machine-gun nest and worked his way around its flank, leaving the two soldiers in front. When he got within 10 yards of the gun it ceased firing, and four of the enemy appeared, three of whom were shot by Lieutenant Woodfill. The fourth, an officer, rushed at Lieutenant Woodfill, who attempted to club the officer with his rifle. After a hand-to-hand struggle, Lieutenant Woodfill killed the officer with his pistol. His company thereupon continued to advance, until shortly afterwards another machine-gun nest was encountered. Calling on his men to follow, Lieutenant Woodfill rushed ahead of his line in the face of heavy fire from the nest, and when several of the enemy appeared above the nest he shot them, capturing three other members of the crew and silencing the gun. A few minutes later, this officer for the third time demonstrated conspicuous daring by charging another machine-gun position, killing five men in one machine-gun pit with his rifle. He then drew his revolver and started to jump into the pit, when two other gunners only a few yards away turned their gun on him. Failing to kill them with his revolver, he grabbed a pick lying nearby and killed both of them. Inspired by the exceptional courage displayed by this officer, his men pressed on to their objective under severe shell and machine-gun fire.

Another renowned Medal of Honor winner from World War I was the tall mountaineer from Tennessee, Sergeant Alvin C. York. Marshal Foch of the French Army said his action was "the greatest thing accomplished by any soldier of all the armies."

At the time of his famous exploit, York was a corporal and squad leader in Company G, 328th Infantry. During the Meuse-Argonne Offensive in the fall of 1918, the 328th was engaged in action in the Châtel-Chéhéry sector of France. Shortly after dawn on 8 October, York's unit was ordered to attack a railroad across the Aire River. His platoon, spearhead of the attacking battalion, was suddenly raked by murderous machine-gun fire. Reaching the cover of nearby trees, York discovered that he was the only remaining noncom. He immediately took command. York and his seven remaining men overran one machine-gun nest and captured its crew. York then went on alone to reconnoiter the high ground ahead. Almost at once the enemy defenders pinned him down by fire from as many as 35 machine guns. Like his famous ancestor Davy Crockett, York was a crack shot. He methodically began to pick off the enemy gunners as they lifted their heads to aim at him. After at least ten gunners had been silenced, six German soldiers left their positions and raced toward him. He picked them off one by one. Once again he directed his firing at the individual machine gunners. His incredible accuracy began to create panic in the well-entrenched defenders, who now had lost 22 men to this lone American. His repeated demands for their surrender had at first seemed preposterous. But now

YORK, ALVIN C.—Sergeant
Citation: On 18 October 1918, in the Argonne Forest, after his platoon had suffered heavy casualties and three other noncommissioned officers had become casualties, Corporal York assumed command. Fearlessly leading seven men, he charged with great daring a machine-gun nest which was pouring deadly and incessant fire upon his platoon. In this heroic feat the machine-gun nest was taken, together with 4 officers and 128 men and several guns.

RICKENBACKER, EDWARD V.
Rank and Organization: First Lieutenant, 94th Aero Squadron, Air Service. Place and Date: Near Billy, France, 25 September 1918. Entered Service at: Columbus, Ohio. Birth: Columbus, Ohio. G.O. No.: 2, W.D., 1931. Citation: For conspicuous gallantry and intrepidity above and beyond the call of duty in action against the enemy near Billy, France, 25 Sept. 1918. While on a voluntary patrol over the lines, Lieutenant Rickenbacker attacked seven enemy planes (five type Fokker, protecting two type Halberstadt). Disregarding the odds against him, he dived on them and shot down one of the Fokkers out of control. He then attacked one of the Halberstadts and sent it down also.

their commander came out under a white flag. Calling upon his own men for the first time, York accepted the surrender of 90 Germans. With his seven men, York prepared to lead his prisoners back to the American lines. This meant marching through a line of trenches filled with German infantry. As he approached the enemy-filled trench with his strange party, York demanded the surrender of the whole force. Now completely demoralized by the gallantry, intrepidity, and sharpshooting of one American soldier, the remaining Germans raised their hands in surrender. Altogether, York and his men took 132 German prisoners. This unique action will be remembered always as a perfect example of personal bravery combined with the skill to make that bravery most effective.

A total of 95 soldiers received the Medal of Honor in World War I. Among the other great doughboy heroes were Colonel "Wild Bill" Donovan of New York National Guard's noted "Fighting 69th" Regiment; Sergeant Mike Ellis of the 1st Division, who captured 6 machine guns and 44 prisoners; and Private George Dilboy from the 26th Division, who

took a machine-gun crew with his bayonet in spite of painful leg wounds. At the time of his action, Dilboy was AWOL from the hospital where he had been under treatment for earlier wounds.

It was once suggested to General of the Army Dwight D. Eisenhower that he deserved the Medal of Honor for his leadership of American forces in Europe. He disagreed emphatically, saying it was a Medal for soldiers who fought the enemy at close quarters. Later, when he was Chief Executive, he told one Medal winner, "Son, I would rather have the right to wear this than be President of the United States."

In World War II the jungles of the South Pacific, the deserts of North Africa, the mountains of Italy, and the plains of Western Europe all provided opportunities for the kind of combat that has always produced Medal of Honor winners.

A popular song about one World War II Medal of Honor winner made his name famous. Rodger Young's deeds were among the most selfless of the war. During his high school days, Rodger Young's eyesight and hearing were impaired as the result of a head injury he incurred playing basketball. But he managed to get into the Army. In the South Pacific, Young rose to squad leader in the 148th Regiment although he was the smallest man in the unit. Then, because of his increasing deafness, he asked to be demoted to Private; he felt his deafness might endanger his men in combat.

On 31 July 1943, Private Young's regiment was facing a Japanese force in the steamy jungles of New Georgia Island. The fighting became fierce, and Young's platoon found itself several hundred yards ahead of the main group. As darkness fell they began quietly to withdraw to prevent being cut off and surrounded. As they made their way through the undergrowth, a machine gun opened fire behind them.

Private Young asked the platoon leader to hold the men in place until he took care of the machine gun. He began to crawl back toward the enemy position. Soon Young was severely wounded, but continued crawling toward the machine-gun nest. He had reached hand grenade range when he was hit again. Meanwhile, his platoon had been able to return to the main force. When the unit advanced again the next day, his comrades found Rodger Young dead. But where the Japanese machine-gun nest had been there was only a small crater. Rodger Young had lived long enough to throw his grenade.

The popular song named for him included this fitting verse:

"On the island of New Georgia in the Solomons
Stands a simple wooden cross alone to tell
That beneath the silent coral of the Solomons
Sleeps a man, sleeps a man remembered well."

Another Medal of Honor winner of World War II was Captain Robert E. Roeder, 350th Infantry, who distinguished himself at Mt. Battaglia, Italy, on 27–28 September 1944. His official citation speaks for itself:

"For conspicuous gallantry and intrepidity at the risk of life above and beyond the call of duty. Captain Roeder commanded his company in defense of the strategic Mt. Battaglia. Shortly after the company had occupied the hill, the Germans launched the first of a series of determined counterattacks to regain this dominating height. Completely exposed to ceaseless enemy artillery and small-arms fire, Captain Roeder constantly circulated among his men, encouraging them and directing their defense against the persistent enemy. During the sixth counterattack, the enemy, by using flamethrowers and taking advantage of the fog, succeeded in overrunning the position. Captain Roeder led his men in a fierce battle at close quarters, to repulse the attack with heavy losses to the Germans. The following morning, while the company was engaged in repulsing an enemy counterattack in force, Captain Roeder was seriously wounded and rendered unconscious by shell fragments. He was carried to the company command post, where he regained consciousness. Refusing medical treatment, he insisted on rejoining his men. Although in a weakened condition, Captain Roeder dragged himself in a sitting position. He began firing his weapon, shouted words of encouragement, and issued orders to his men. He personally killed two Germans before he himself was killed instantly by an exploding shell. Through Captain Roeder's able and intrepid leadership, his men held Mt. Battaglia against the aggressive and fanatical enemy attempts to retake this important and strategic height. This valorous performance is exemplary of the fighting spirit of the Army of the United States."

MacARTHUR, DOUGLAS.
Rank and Organization: General, United States Army, Commanding United States Army Forces in the Far East. Place and Date: Bataan Peninsula, Philippine Islands. Entered Service at: Wisconsin. Birth: Little Rock, Arkansas G. O. No.: 16, 1 April 1942. Citation: For conspicuous leadership in preparing the Philippine Islands to resist conquest, for gallantry and intrepidity above and beyond the call of duty in action against invading Japanese forces, and for the heroic conduct of defensive and offensive operations on the Bataan Peninsula. He mobilized, trained, and led an army which has received world acclaim for its gallant defense against a tremendous superiority of enemy forces in men and arms. His utter disregard of personal danger under heavy fire and aerial bombardment, his calm judgment in each crisis, inspired his troops, galvanized the spirit of resistance of the Filipino people, and confirmed the faith of the American people in their armed forces.

The fighting conditions in Korea were as difficult as any in the Army's long history. Once again the U.S. Eighth Army proved that the individual fighting man is still the most important element of success in battle. It has been said that the U.S. Eighth Army was the finest fighting force in American history. The valor of the Army's Medal of Honor winners contributed immeasurably to this reputation.

One of these brave men was Lloyd L. Burke who, like

MURPHY, AUDIE L.—Infantryman.

Near Holtzwihr, France, on 26 January 1945, Second Lieutenant Audie L. Murphy, 15th Infantry Regiment, 3rd Infantry Division, jumped on a burning tank destroyer and manned its machine gun against two companies of attacking enemy infantry supported by six tanks. Alone and exposed to fire from three sides, Lieutenant Murphy was wounded in the leg, but continued firing and brought the attack to a halt, thereby saving his company from possible encirclement and destruction.

MIYAMURA, HIROSHI H.—Sergeant

Sergeant Hiroshi H. Miyamura of Gallup, New Mexico, an Army infantryman who was released from a Communist prisoner-of-war camp on 20 August 1953, is presented the Medal of Honor by President Dwight D. Eisenhower during a ceremony at the White House. Sgt. Miyamura was awarded the Medal for his actions while serving as a squad leader of a 3d Infantry Division machine gun platoon, in action against the enemy near Taejon-ni, Korea, on 24–25 1951. The fact that he earned the Medal of Honor was kept secret until his release.

Rodger Young, was of "stature small, but of courage so tall." "Scooter" Burke, who was born and raised in Arkansas, won his Medal in Korea while serving as a first lieutenant with Company C, 5th Cavalry Regiment. He distinguished himself by conspicuous gallantry and outstanding courage near Chong-dong on 28 October 1951.

When intense enemy fire had pinned down leading elements of his company during an attempt to secure commanding ground, Burke left the company's command post to rally and urge the men to follow him toward three bunkers impeding the advance. Dashing to an exposed vantage point, he threw several grenades at the bunkers. Then, returning for an M1 rifle and rifle grenade adapter, he made a lone assault, wiping out the first position and killing the crew.

Closing on the center bunker he lobbed grenades through the opening and, with his pistol, killed three of its occupants who attempted to surround him. Ordering his men forward, he charged the third emplacement, catching several grenades in mid-air and hurling them back at the enemy. Inspired by his display of valor his men stormed forward, overran the hostile position, but were again pinned down by increased fire.

Securing a light machine gun and three boxes of ammunition, Burke dashed through the impact area to an open knoll, set up his gun and poured a crippling fire into the ranks of the enemy, killing approximately 75.

Although wounded, he ordered more ammunition, reloaded, and destroyed two mortar emplacements and a machine-gun position with his accurate fire. Cradling the weapon in his arms, he then led his men forward, killing some 20 more of the retreating enemy and securing the objective.

His Medal of Honor citation states, "Lieutenant Burke's heroic action and daring exploits inspired his small force of 35 comrades to overcome an estimated defending enemy force of 300 troops. His unflinching courage and outstanding leadership reflect the highest credit upon himself, the Infantry, and the United States Army."

Sergeant Ola L. Mize served in Korea with Company K, 15th Infantry Regiment, and joined the annals of America's great fighting heroes near Surang-ni on 10–11 June 1953.

Company K was committed to the defense of "Outpost Harry," a strategically valuable position, when the enemy launched a heavy attack. Learning that a comrade on a friendly listening post had been wounded, Mize moved through the intense barrage, accompanied by a medical aid man, and rescued the wounded soldier.

MEDAL OF HONOR RECIPIENTS.	
(By Conflict).	
Civil War	1199 [1]
Indian Wars	415 [2]
War with Spain	30
Philippine Insurrection	70
Boxer Rebellion	4
Mexico, 13 April 1911	1
World War I	95
World War II	293
Korean War	78
	2,185 [3]

[1] 1,200 including one soldier who received the Medal twice.
[2] 419 including 4 soldiers who received the Medal twice.
[3] Ten awards were made by special acts of Congress to Charles A. Lindbergh, Major General Adolphus Greeley, and to the Unknown Soldiers of World War I, World War II, and Korea, and those of Belgium, Great Britain, France, Italy, and Romania after World War I.

On returning to the main position, he reestablished an effective defense system from which his troops inflicted heavy casualties on determined enemy assault forces which had penetrated into trenches within the outpost area. During his fearless actions he was blown down by artillery and grenade blasts three times, but each time he dauntlessly returned to his position, tenaciously fighting and successfully repelling hostile attacks.

When enemy onslaughts temporarily ceased, he took his few men and moved from bunker to bunker, firing through the apertures and throwing grenades at the foe. When an enemy soldier stepped out from behind a fellow soldier, prepared to fire, Mize killed him, saving the life of his comrade. After rejoining the platoon, moving from man to man, distributing ammunition, and shouting words of encouragement, he observed a friendly machine-gun posi-

tion being overrun. He immediately fought his way to the position, killing 10 of the enemy and dispersing the remainder. Fighting back to the command post and finding several friendly wounded, he took a position to protect them. Later, securing a radio, he directed friendly artillery fire upon the attacking enemy's routes of approach. At dawn he helped regroup for a counterattack which successfully drove the enemy from the outpost.

The United States Army is extremely proud of these and all the many other recipients of the Army Medal of Honor. They represent the ideal of fighting man and patriot. Each year, as the Army celebrates the anniversary of its Medal of Honor, its members can draw increased inspiration from their stories in preparation for the difficult tasks that may lie ahead. Their century of valor is one of the finest chapters in the history of military conflict.

OLIVE, MILTON L.—Pfc.

Private First Class Milton L. Olive III distinguished himself by conspicuous gallantry and intrepidity at the risk of his own life above and beyond the call of duty while participating in a search and destroy operation in the vicinity of Phu Cuong, Republic of Viet Nam, on 22 October 1965. Private Olive was a member of the 3d Platoon of Company B, 2d Battalion (Airborne), 503d Infantry, as it moved through the jungle to find the Viet Cong operating in the area. Although the Platoon was subjected to a heavy volume of enemy gunfire and pinned down temporarily, it retaliated by assaulting the Viet Cong positions, causing the enemy to flee. As the platoon pursued the insurgents, Private Olive and four other soldiers were moving through the jungle together when a grenade was thrown into their midst. Private Olive saw the grenade, and then saved the lives of his fellow soldiers at the sacrifice of his own by grabbing the grenade in his hand and falling on it to absorb the blast with his body. Through his bravery, unhesitating actions, and complete disregard for his own safety, he prevented additional loss of life or injury to the members of his platoon. Private Olive's conspicuous gallantry, extraordinary heroism, and intrepidity at the risk of his own life above and beyond the call of duty are in the highest traditions of the United States Army and reflect great credit upon himself and the Armed Forces of his country.

263

A lithographic representation of the execution of 38 Sioux Indians sentenced to death after the massacre of 500 Minnesota settlers in 1862. The mass hanging took place in Mankato, Minnesota.

CHAPTER 9

THE U.S. ARMY, 1865-1898

The ink on the surrender document at Appomattox was scarcely dry before war-weary citizens were demanding the immediate demobilization of the Union Army. Out of the 1,034,064 volunteers on 1 May 1865, more than 800,000 had been demobilized by November. Taking into consideration the vastly increased responsibilities of the Army, General Grant had proposed that a standing army of 80,000 men be maintained, but the Secretary of War whittled his request down to a force of 50,000 which, without the addition of new units, could be expanded to 82,600. By September 1866 the strength of the Regular Army had dwindled to 38,545, but in the following year it climbed to 53,962, a postwar peak from which it thereafter steadily declined.

In 1866 the Army had 5 regiments of artillery, 10 of cavalry, and 45 of infantry. Each artillery and cavalry regiment was composed of 12 companies, and each infantry regiment of 10. Also, provision had been made for 1,000 Indian scouts. For administration the Army was divided into 19 territorial departments and 5 geographical divisions, but this was to fluctuate considerably in the ensuing years. In 1878 the Regular Army consisted of 2,153 officers and 23,254 enlisted men organized into 5 regiments of artillery, 10 of cavalry, and 25 of infantry; this organization was to remain fairly constant until 1898.

After the Reconstruction period, most of the U.S. Army was widely dispersed in small units along the frontier. A garrison usually consisted of one company of infantry and one of cavalry, but frequently a single company was the only protection for many miles of territory. Under such conditions there could be little uniformity within regiments. For example, in 1882 all of the Army's cavalry regiments were distributed among 55 posts in the Indian country. Major General John M. Schofield called the country's scattered military establishment a "police force and not an army." But in spite of its smallness and dispersion, the post-

Civil War Army successfully performed three important missions: the elimination of the threat posed by French-supported Emperor Maximilian in Mexico; occupation of the southern states; and suppression of dissident Indians and restoration of order on the Western frontier.

MEXICO POSES A THREAT

In 1861 when the United States was preoccupied with the Civil War, French and British troops marched into Mexico with the ostensible purpose of restoring order and collecting debts owed their nationals. The British soon recognized the imperialist design of Napoleon III for what it was and withdrew. The United States protested the French action but could do nothing more than that until after Appomattox.

In May 1865, General Sheridan with an army of about 50,000 men was ordered to Texas. Although he took no aggressive action, Sheridan's force posed a threat that was not lost on the Maximilian government or its French sponsor. Finally, in 1866 the United States flatly demanded that Napoleon III recall his soldiers and he did so in January 1867. Maximilian was later defeated by the Mexicans, his government was overthrown, and the Mexican republic was restored.

THE ARMY OCCUPIES THE SOUTH

While Sheridan's forces were deployed along the Mexican border, other Army units were engaged in occupation duties in the South. The period of reconstruction in the South can be broken into two distinct phases. During the first, which lasted until 1870, the South was under military government. Ten of the former Confederate states were divided into five military districts, each commanded by a major general. During the second phase, with civil control restored, the Army was used to maintain law and order and to uphold the civil authority. In 1877 occupation responsibilities were terminated, and Army troops remaining in the South performed the usual garrison duties.

One of the least-wanted tasks given the Army during this period was the administration of the Freedmen's Bureau created by Congress on 3 March 1865 to help former slaves adjust to a life of freedom. The Bureau furnished food and clothing to needy Negroes, helped them find employment, secured homesteads for the Negroes on public lands, established schools and hospitals for them, and protected their civil rights in unfriendly Southern communities. The commissioner of the Freedmen's Bureau was Major General Oliver O. Howard, who divided the South into ten districts, each with an assistant commissioner in charge. A considerable number of Army officers were assigned to the Bureau until 1872 when it was discontinued.

THE INDIAN WARS

The third important mission confronting the Army in the decades after the Civil War was the protection of the white settlers that were thronging to the trans-Mississippi West as the railroad steadily pushed its way through the hostile Indian country. From 1865 to 1891 there were 13 different campaigns and at least 1,067 separate engagements with the Indians. The principal tribes involved were the Comanche, Modoc, Apache, Northern Cheyenne, Sioux, Nez Percé, Bannock, Piute, and Ute.

In 1849 the administration of Indian affairs had been taken away from the War Department and entrusted to the Department of the Interior, whose agents either were inexperienced in the administration of Indian affairs or deliberately cheated their charges. Even under conditions of hostility, these agents furnished Indians with the latest models of repeating rifles and plenty of ammunition, either because it was financially profitable to do so or because they naïvely believed that the Indians wanted the weapons to kill buffalo. Only after the work of the Indian agent had failed and the Indians were on the warpath was the Army called in.

A campaign against the Indians was an unpleasant assignment. The press was apt to be deeply critical of the Army whether it won or not; campaigning resulted in a very high percentage of deaths and permanent maiming not only as a direct result of the fighting but also from nonbattle causes such as freezing and sunstroke; and a campaign meant long absences from the small pleasures of post life and from families who had to remain behind in the dangerously undermanned forts.

War With the Sioux

Some of the first post-Civil War Indian campaigns were against the Sioux. After the suppression of the Sioux uprising in Minnesota in 1862, most of the Sioux nation had moved westward into the Dakotas. In 1866 the Army built and garrisoned posts on the Bozeman Trail, which led through the Sioux country toward the gold mines of Montana. The Indians protested by harassing the new garrisons. On 21 December 1866 Chief Crazy Horse, with about 2,000 Sioux, Cheyenne, and Arapahoe warriors, attacked an Army train sent out from Fort Phil Kearny to secure wood. Captain William J. Fetterman, who had previously bragged that he could ride through the entire Sioux nation with 80 men,

An Army camp in the Lava Beds during the Modoc campaign.

A Modoc sharpshooter. Most Modoc Indians wore white man's clothes.

Covering the Modoc Campaign. A newspaper correspondent with the
Army in the Lava Beds.

was ordered out to relieve the besieged train. Rashly, and
contrary to orders, he moved against the main body of
Indians. He probably was drawn into an ambush by a common Indian trick of retreating with a small body into a
killing ground surrounded by a larger force. Not a white
man survived. The incident had a sobering effect on the
rasher elements of the Army; they now realized that fighting the Indians was something considerably more than what
in the Civil War would have been termed a patrol action.

The "Wagon Box Fight" on 2 August 1867 had a happier
ending. Once again soldiers were cutting wood for Fort
Kearny. They were guarded by a small force under Captain
James Powell, who had improvised a barricade of wagon
beds from which the wheels and axles had been removed.
Suddenly his outposts warned him that large Indian force
was riding toward the barricade, and Captain Powell assembled his force behind the wagon boxes. When the
Indians had charged to within 50 yards, the soldiers opened
fire. So rapid and accurate was their fire that the Indians
had to pull back and re-form before charging again. Six
times they charged and six times they were driven back.
Finally the Indians withdrew, taking an estimated 180 dead
and wounded with them. Thirty-two U.S. Army men had
stood up against a hostile force of about 1,500 men and
won. Unlike Fetterman, Powell had not underestimated the
Indians, but was dismounted and ready.

Throughout the period of the Indian Wars there was an
almost constant succession of small skirmishes and raids by
Indian war parties that burned and pillaged, stole horses
and cattle, and killed or captured the settlers. They would
usually attack suddenly and then disappear. The Army would
learn of a raid only after it had happened; it would then
rush to the scene and take up the trail, sometimes days later.
Often the troops were unable to catch the miscreants, for
the Indians were considerably more mobile than the American cavalrymen.

To deal with the problem, General Sheridan launched
a series of winter campaigns in 1868–1869. Because of
scarcity of forage, the Indians were inactive during the
winter months, whereas the U.S. forces, which carried their
forage in their trains, could continue operations. General
Sheridan's troops moved against the Cheyenne, Arapahoe,
and Kiowa in the upper Arkansas region with the purpose
of driving them back to their reservations. This was successfully accomplished, partly by operations in the field and

The Peace Commission tent in which the Modoc, Captain Jack,
shot General Canby.

partly by a threat to kill two Kiowa chiefs who had been
held as hostages.

War With the Modoc

In 1872 the Army launched a campaign against the Modoc
on the Pacific Coast. The Modoc had been removed from
their lands and placed on the same reservations as the
Klamath, their enemies. Being stronger, the Klamath bullied
the Modoc and in general made life intolerable for them.
As a consequence, the Modoc quit the reservation and went
back to their tribal lands, where they came into conflict
with settlers.

The commanding officer of the Department of the
Columbia, Brigadier General Edward R. S. Canby, suggested
placing the Modoc on a separate reservation. However, the
Commissioner of Indian Affairs insisted that the Army dis-
arm the Modoc and return them to their old reservation.
Captain James Jackson and Company B, 1st Cavalry, received
the assignment. At dawn on 29 November 1872 they surrounded the Modoc and their chief, Captain Jack. The
Modoc surrendered a few old muzzle-loaders, but, when
an attempt was made to arrest the leaders, pistol-firing broke
out with each side suffering a few casualties. The Indians
then withdrew to the easily defensible lava beds east of
Mount Shasta, where they were reinforced to a strength of
about 120 men. Well armed and provisioned from caches
they had stored there the entrenched Modoc successfully
resisted an attack by a hastily organized force of about 400
men—half regulars and half civilians.

Contrary to the recommendation of General Canby, the
Indian Bureau appointed a peace commission with Canby
as its head. Because of mutual distrust and suspicion, the
commission did not meet with Captain Jack and his party
until April 1873, and then the Indians came armed; General
Canby and another commissioner were killed.

Brigadier General Jefferson C. Davis, who succeeded
General Canby as departmental commander, renewed the

Indian Scouts on picket duty with the U.S. Army in the Modoc Campaign.

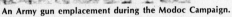

An Army gun emplacement during the Modoc Campaign.

campaign. After mortar fire delivered by crews from the 4th Artillery drove the Indians away from their water supply, they were defeated, and on the first day of June 1873 the last of the Modoc surrendered. This time the recommendations of General Canby were followed, and the Modoc were given a new reservation.

War With the Sioux and Cheyenne

The next important campaign was against the Sioux and Cheyenne. In November 1875 the Indian Inspector reported to the Commissioner of Indian Affairs that these Indians were getting out of hand, and recommended that they be sent back to their reservations. When they refused to return, it became necessary for the Army to take action. General Sheridan planned an attack employing three converging columns—south, west, and east under Major General George Crook and Colonels John Gibbon and George A. Custer respectively. Gibbon and Custer were under the command of Brigadier General Alfred H. Terry, the commander of the Department of the Dakotas. General Crook was in command of the Department of the Platte.

In late February 1876 General Crook concentrated 10 troops from the 2d and 3d Cavalry and 2 companies of the 4th Infantry at Fort Fetterman, and on 1 March moved out toward the Powder River. During the night the cavalry, under Colonel Joseph J. Reynolds, preceding Crook's column, located a Cheyenne village near the mouth of the Little Power River. At dawn Reynolds' force attacked from three directions, driving the Indians out, destroying over 100 lodges with ammunition stores, and capturing a large band of ponies, before the Cheyenne could recover from their initial surprise and fight back. Colonel Reynolds suddenly ordered a withdrawal, leaving behind his dead and, it is alleged, one wounded. By then the troopers, who had removed their heavier outer clothing, were suffering greatly in the extreme cold. The Indians pursued, harassing the troops, and during the night they recaptured their ponies. General Crook arrived shortly after, but because of the inclement weather, the defeat of Reynolds, and the encumbrance of 6 wounded and 66 frostbitten men, he was

forced to return to his fort. General Terry's forces had not yet moved out, having been held back by the severity of the weather and the necessity of assembling the 7th Cavalry.

It was late in May when General Crook left Fort Fetterman again, this time with 15 companies of cavalry and 5 companies of infantry. He reached the Tongue River, where he left his supply trains, and then moved to and across the Rosebud River. On 17 June he encountered a Sioux-Cheyenne force of about 1,500 under Chief Crazy Horse. The fight was indecisive; 11 dead Indians were found on the field, and Crook lost 9 killed and 21 wounded. General Crook then returned to his trains and awaited supplies and reinforcement. Meanwhile, the two columns under General Terry had finally started. Colonel Gibbon with 450 men—6 companies of infantry and 4 companies of cavalry —marched east from Fort Ellis in Montana along the north bank of the Yellowstone River to the mouth of the Big Horn where General Terry ordered him to a halt.

A larger force of about 12 companies of cavalry and 6 companies of infantry moved out of Fort Abraham Lincoln, and on 7 June established a supply camp at the confluence of the Powder and Yellowstone rivers. A reconnaissance party from the camp found a heavily traveled Indian trail that led south along the Rosebud and then west across the mountains, apparently toward the Little Big Horn River. Using this information, General Terry made his plans. Colonel Custer was to take all of the 7th Cavalry and follow the trail found by the reconnaissance party. If he found that the trail led to the Little Big Horn, Custer was not to follow it but was to sidestep south in order to prevent the Indians from escaping around his left and give the slower-moving infantry under Colonel Gibbon more time to move up. General Terry was to join Colonel Gibbon's force and move south along the Big Horn to a junction with Custer at some point on the Little Big Horn.

Custer's Last Stand

Custer followed the Indian trail up the Rosebud for about 20 miles and found that it did lead to the Little Big Horn River, but for some unknown reason he failed to sidestep south according to plan. Instead, he continued toward the Little Big Horn, where he found a large Indian encampment which he decided to attack. Custer separated his attacking force into three battalions, each beyond supporting distance of the other. Major Marcus A. Reno with three companies was sent into the valley at the point where the trail

The steamer "Far West." It carried supplies and served as General Terry's headquarters during the campaign of 1876.

Sitting Bull, one of the Indian leaders in the war against the whites that culminated in the Battle of the Little Big Horn.

Low Dog, a fighting chief at Little Big Horn.

met the river. Custer was to attempt to enter the valley about three miles lower down. Captain Frederick W. Benteen was to scout the country to the left.

Reno's three companies forded the river, dismounted, and fought on foot. Overwhelmed by numbers, they were forced to withdraw back over the river and take a position on the high bluffs overlooking it. Here Reno was joined by Captain Benteen, who with three companies had been about two miles to the left of Reno until the fight started and he had been ordered by Custer to return. When he came to the river, Benteen realized it would be impossible to force a crossing because of the large number of Indians blocking the way, so he joined Reno's hard-pressed force on the bluffs. They were soon surrounded by an overwhelming Indian force that took up a commanding position overlooking the troops. A bitter fight ensued in which the cavalry suffered severe casualties, but upon the approach of General Terry and Colonel Gibbon, the Indians withdrew.

The movements of Custer and his five companies of cavalry are shrouded in mystery. All that is definitely known is that the entire command moved into an ambush, dismounted, and was destroyed by the Indians. A single horse, Comanche, survived and, for the rest of his days, appeared saddled but riderless at all 7th Cavalry parades.

The Indians had won a resounding victory over the U.S. Army and it was imperative that the Army immediately take steps to rectify the situation. All posts in the military division of the Missouri were stripped for reinforcements, 24 companies of artillery were reequipped as infantry, Generals Terry and Crook were reinforced, and the Indians on the Sioux reservations were disarmed and dismounted. General Sheridan then launched a series of expeditions that lasted through that winter and the next. Most of the Sioux were driven back into their reservations, but a small group under Chief Sitting Bull fled to Canada. At this time Congress authorized more cavalry—2,500 cavalrymen could be added, but the total strength of the Army was not to exceed the authorized strength of 25,000.

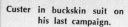
Custer in buckskin suit on his last campaign.

Curley, one of Custer's Indian scouts and reputedly the only survivor of Little Big Horn.

George Armstrong Custer in a photograph taken about 1865. As one of the most brilliant Union cavalry officers, Custer won several promotions during the Civil War and attained the rank of brevet major general. After the war, in his permanent rank of lieutenant colonel, he was assigned to the 7th Cavalry on the frontier. The wide hat, shirt, and tie he wears in this picture were of his own design.

General Custer (center) and a grizzly bear he killed with the help of Colonel Ludlow (far right) during an Army exploring expedition in the Black Hills in 1874-1875. Posing with Custer and Ludlow are the Indian Bloody Knife (far left) and Custer's orderly, Private Noonan.

The Battle of the Little Big Horn on 25 June 1876. The artist has placed General Custer (firing two hand guns) in the center of the picture.

In Custer Battlefield National Monument, a large granite memorial now marks the grave where most of the slain victims of the Battle of the Little Big Horn were buried. Custer Battlefield National Monument, which contains the portions of the battlefield where the most severe fighting occurred, is part of the National Park System.

This picture of the Little Big Horn battlefield was taken sometime in 1876.

Campaign Against the Nez Percé Indians

In the summer of 1877 a campaign was launched against the Nez Percé Indians, a hitherto peaceful tribe. Angered by being forced out of the Wallowa Valley and by the murder of their chief's brother, a group of Nez Percé raided a white settlement and killed 20 settlers. Although Chief Joseph had once counseled peace with the white men, he saw that war was inevitable and joined his tribesmen. The Nez Percé were well trained and disciplined, and Chief Joseph was an excellent tactician. An Army force of over 90 men, sent out to bring the recalcitrant tribesmen back to the reservation, ran into a well-planned ambush in White Bird Canyon to the east of the Wallowa Valley and was routed.

Major General Oliver O. Howard, the commander of the Department of the Columbia, then set out with a force of about 400 men from the infantry, cavalry, and artillery.

He caught up with the Indians at the Clearwater River on 11 July 1877. In the engagement that ensued Chief Joseph and his men, though they fought well, were forced back over the river. Moving east over the Lolo Trail, they encountered a trail-block of about 140 soldiers and civilians, but Chief Joseph, using trails unknown to the whites, managed to evade the blockade and proceeded south along the Bitter Root River, leaving Howard's force far behind. At the Big Hole Basin, Chief Joseph rested his tribe, thinking he had outdistanced the Army. However, Colonel Gibbon, alerted by telegraph, was closing in with six infantry companies and some volunteers—a total force of about 200 men. At dawn Gibbon attacked the unguarded Indian camp from three directions and took it within 20 minutes. Chief Joseph, displaying remarkable ability, rallied his warriors for a counterattack and soon had his adversaries on the defensive. For three days the Indians besieged Gibbon and his men, who were finally saved by the arrival of General Howard. Chief Joseph and his band escaped.

At dawn on 30 September 1877, Colonel Nelson A. Miles with 6 companies of infantry, 5 cavalry companies, and 2 field guns attacked Chief Joseph's camp in the Bear Paw Mountains. Though surprised, the Indians soon recovered and dug in. On 4 October, after a four-day battle, Chief Joseph and the remnants of his band surrendered. In 11 weeks, he had moved his tribe, 1,600 miles, engaged 10 separate U.S. commands in 13 battles and skirmishes, and in nearly every instance had either defeated them or fought them to a standstill. General Sherman rightly termed the campaign against the Nez Percé "one of the most extraordinary Indian Wars of which there is any record."

Major General George Crook.

Campaign Against the Apache Indians

Other equally arduous campaigns were under way against the Apache in the Southwest. This tribe was notorious for extreme cruelty as well as for cunning and endurance. Bitter warfare had long existed between the Apache and the white settlers, neither of whom gave or asked for quarter.

Between 1871 and 1874 General George Crook, then a colonel, had been in command of the Department of Arizona. His policies for dealing with Indians on the warpath and for administering the Indian reservations proved very successful. He used Apache as scouts, issued strict instructions that a column in pursuit must never give up an Indian trail, and strongly emphasized the use, care, and training of mule pack transport. The troops were trained by long conditioning marches and long reconnaissances.

When Crook was ordered north in 1874, Arizona was at peace. The Indian Bureau then took over the reservations and tried to confine the Indians, a process that stirred them up and caused trouble. Victorio, Geronimo, and other Apache chiefs began to shuttle back and forth across the international boundary between the United States and Mexico, committing many depredations as they traveled. The Army went out on numerous punitive expeditions, but nothing decisive was achieved as long as the American troops had to stay on their side of the border. In 1880, however, Victorio was captured and killed by the Mexicans. Two years later a treaty was signed by the American and Mexican Governments permitting troops of either country to cross over the boundary in unpopulated regions when in hot pursuit.

Geronimo.

General Crook's force of soldiers and Indian scouts at Wilcox, Arizona, just before the start of the expedition into Mexico in 1883.

General Crook with his favorite riding mule and the Apache scouts Dulchy (left) and Alchiso. Mules were used on Apache duty because the cavalry horse could not live on the pine burrs and sword grass of the arid southwest.

Troop A, 6th Cavalry, posed for this picture during the hunt for Geronimo in 1885.

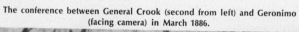

The conference between General Crook (second from left) and Geronimo (facing camera) in March 1886.

General Crook, in the Southwest again after his Sioux campaigns, decided to take advantage of the treaty to punish the Apache, Chato, who had been actively raiding up and down the border. In May 1882 a cavalry troop located Chato's camp 200 miles south of the border. Although the troop was unable to capture the camp, the Apaches decided that they had had enough. Geronimo, Chato, and the other chiefs surrendered and returned to their reservation in southeastern Arizona. The administrators of the reservation were Army officers, who kept the Indians quiet for two years.

In May 1885, when the reservation was again under control of the Indian Bureau, Geronimo and his tribesmen slipped off the reservation. Twenty troops of cavalry moved toward the border in a fruitless effort to intercept the Apache. The pursuit continued into Mexico where, in January 1886, Captain Emmet Crawford with 80 Apache scouts located and attacked the principal hostile camp about 200 miles south of the border. The Indians had agreed to parley, when an unexpected attack by Mexican irregulars killed Crawford, and the negotiations were delayed. Later, at a conference near the border with General Crook, Geronimo agreed to surrender if certain conditions were granted. Crook acquiesced, but shortly thereafter Geronimo broke his pledge and disappeared with some of his band into the Sierra Madres. General Sheridan, who did not like the terms to which General Crook had agreed, held that the flight of Geronimo negated the agreement with the Apache who remained. Crook, who felt that he had given his word, asked to be relieved and was succeeded by Major General Nelson A. Miles.

Captain Henry Lawton's 2,000-mile pursuit of Geronimo during the summer of 1886 provided the subject for this painting by the famous Western artist Frederic Remington.

Geronimo and some of his followers pose for a picture in San Antonio a few days after their capture on 4 September 1886 ended the last big Indian war.

Miles set up a system of observation posts on high peaks covering the critical area, and sent small, mobile columns into Mexico. One of these, under Captain Henry W. Lawton, pursued Geronimo for more than 2,000 miles. In two skirmishes Lawton captured much of Geronimo's ammunition and supplies, and many of his horses, though the Indians themselves escaped. Finally Lieutenant Charles B. Gatewood, who was highly respected by the Apache, secured the surrender of Geronimo by going to the chief's camp and persuading the Indians to agree to a surrender conference with General Miles.

In Nevada during the winter of 1889–1890 the preachings of an Indian mystic threatened to start a general Indian war. The Sioux were particularly influenced, for they had long been dissatisfied. When they streamed off their reservation into the Bad Lands by the hundreds, about half of the U.S. Army went after them. The large number of troops deployed left the Indians little alternative but to return to their reservations, and by January 1891 the danger had subsided. This was the last of the Indian Wars.

THE ARMY IS IMPROVED

A simpler and more efficient type of infantry drill was adopted which a recruit could learn in a much shorter period of time than it took him to master the one previously in use. In 1866 Congress, recognizing the Military Academy's broadening responsibilities, specified that the superintendent, who had previously been an engineer, could come from any branch of the Army, and West Point thereafter changed from a strictly scientific school to one of general education and training for all branches of the Army.

Also in 1866 Congress passed an act requiring all permanent camps or garrisons to maintain schools for enlisted men. After 1894 all recruits had to be able to read and write.

In the latter part of 1867 General Grant reestablished the Artillery School at Fort Monroe. Two years later a Light Battery School was opened at Fort Riley, Kansas. It was discontinued in 1871 because of the Indian Wars, but reopened in 1892 as the School for Cavalry and Light Artillery. Starting in 1868 an officer from each of the territorial departments was sent to Washington to secure signal instruction from the Chief Signal Officer; the curriculum was later broadened to include courses in meteorology. In 1881 the School of Application for Infantry and Cavalry was opened at Fort Leavenworth, Kansas, and in 1885 the Engineer School of Application was opened at Willets Point, New York.

During the years between the Civil and Spanish-American Wars the Army carried out numerous civil assignments. When the United States purchased Alaska from Russia in 1867, the Army was sent there to act as a temporary caretaker until Congress provided some form of civil government. As events turned out, the Army remained in charge of the territory for ten years, during which time it explored the territory, set up several posts, maintained law and order, and regulated the affairs of the native population. When in June 1877 the last of the troops were withdrawn, military control over Alaska ceased. For the next twenty years there were no troops in Alaska except for exploring parties.

Between 1865 and 1898 the Army Engineers were busy wtih coastal fortifications; river and harbor improvements and the surveys for them; the protection of the navigable waters of the United States; the geodetic and hydrographic survey of the Great Lakes; surveys for the defense of the coasts; military surveys into the interior; geographical and geological explorations; construction of public buildings and grounds in the District of Columbia (in this period the Army completed many public buildings, including the Capitol, the Washington Monument, and the State, War and Navy Building); the construction of lighthouses; and the demarcation of the boundary between the United States and Canada.

The Army also maintained a vast network of meteorological stations scattered throughout the country for the securing and distribution of the latest information on the weather. It played an important role in the tremendous expansion of the railroads after the Civil War, and many of the engineers who superintended the construction of the trans-Mississippi railroads were former Army officers.

There was, however, a dark side to the picture. Because of the small size of the Army and its wide dispersal, most of its officers received no training in the handling of large units. The few remaining veterans of the Civil War were now too advanced in years. Moreover, the power and insularity of the bureau chiefs stifled all initiative. Under the existing system, no effective plans could be made for war and mobilization. The archaic organization of the War Department was to demonstrate its complete inefficiency in the conflict that broke out in 1898.

Cavalrymen at target practice.

Troop F, 2nd Cavalry, at Fort Riley, Kansas, in 1897.

Second Lieutenant Joseph F. Herron
of Troop H, 1st Cavalry,
in formal dress, 1896.

Sergeant F. W. Klopfer of Troop
H, 4th Cavalry (second from left),
and Indian scouts at Fort Stanton,
New Mexico, in 1885.

Returning to camp after ten days in the field, 1897.

Winter patrol.

A 9th Cavalry camp at Camp Cook, Nebraska.

Training horses
to lie down at
Fort Washington, Wyoming.

The Troop C, 1st Cavalry,
football team in 1895.

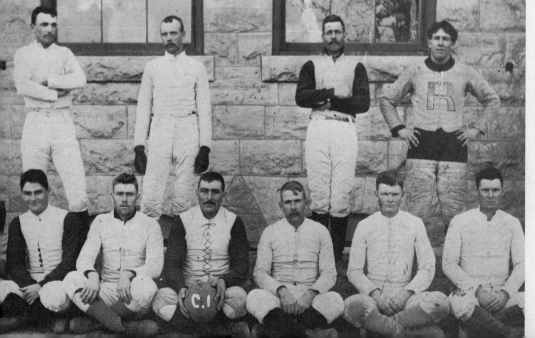

The tables are set for Thanksgiving dinner for Troop H, 1st Cavalry, at Fort Sill, Oklahoma.

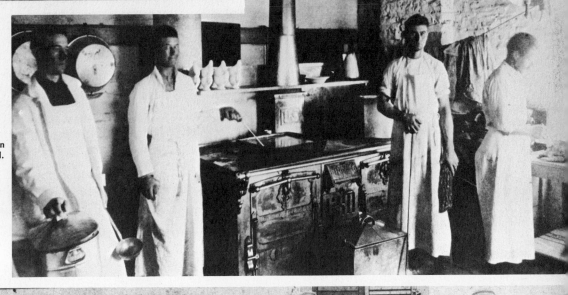

The kitchen at Fort Sill.

The Troop K, 8th Cavalry, baseball team in 1895.

"My Bunkie," Schreyvogel's most famous painting, was based on a story told to him by a trooper. It shows a mounted soldier, in full gallop, swinging a dismounted trooper up into the saddle beside him while other troopers hold the Indians at bay.

WINNING THE WEST

For thirty years after the Civil War the Indians of the Plains fought a losing battle to protect their lands from westward-moving settlers. The Sioux, Cheyenne, Ute, Apache, Comanche, and other Western tribes were fierce and cunning fighters, all the more so because the white man threatened them with extinction.

Ranged against the desperate Indian warriors were the U.S. Army troopers stationed at posts throughout the West. They, too, were fighters of skill and courage. The troopers led a hard life, and their mortality rate was high, but they eventually succeeded in subduing the Indians and bringing peace to the West.

The American public, often critical of the Army, displayed great interest in its campaigns against the Indians, and this interest was reflected in the literature and art of the period. One of the artists whose works became popular was Charles Schreyvogel (1861–1912), a native of New York and an artist for a firm of advertising lithographers. Schreyvogel, who had been interested in the West since childhood, spent the summer of 1893 on a Ute reservation in Colorado where he observed the life of the Indians and of the troopers stationed nearby. He visited the West again in 1900.

Using the knowledge he gained on his western trips, Schreyvogel began to paint scenes featuring troopers and Indians for calendars. After his painting "My Bunkie" won an award from the National Academy of Design in 1900, his works with their realistic portrayal of troopers and Indians, usually in violent combat, became very popular. A number of them are reproduced here.

In "Attack at Dawn" a cavalry unit is attacking an Indian camp.

"Defending the Stockade" depicts an Indian attack on a military post.

"Custer's Demand," depicting Lieutenant Colonel George Armstrong Custer and his aides meeting with four Indians, was the cause of a dispute between Schreyvogel and another famous artist of the West, Frederic Remington, who challenged the authenticity of the colors used in the painting. Mrs. Custer came to Schreyvogel's defense with a letter in which she wrote: "I think the likeness excellent, the composition of the picture and the harmony of color admirable." She went on to say that soldiers on the frontier were allowed great freedom of dress. Custer himself always wore a red necktie, buckskins, and a wide-brimmed felt hat.

"Remember the Maine"

The destruction of the battleship Maine as depicted in a contemporary lithograph. Two hundred and sixty men were killed in the explosion in Havana Harbor on 15 February 1898.

CHAPTER 10

THE WAR WITH SPAIN
THE PHILIPPINE INSURRECTION
THE CHINA RELIEF EXPEDITION

Few periods in American history have witnessed a greater and more significant change in national policy than the years at the turn of the century when the United States began to emerge as a world power. With the disappearance of the frontier (officially in the 1890 census) the energy that had gone into westward expansion sought new outlets. Most of it went into industrial and internal development, but enough was left over for ventures beyond the sea.

Of immediate concern to most Americans was the area in and around the Caribbean. This concern was demonstrated when an insurrection broke out in the island of Cuba in 1895. The American people, normally sympathetic to the aspirations of colonials for independence, favored the insurgent cause, and sympathy for the Cubans mounted when Spain adopted stern measures to deal with the revolt. In

January 1896, Spain sent a new governor, General Valeriano Weyler, to the island. Weyler tried to stop the depredations and terrorism of the insurgents by introducing a harsh reconcentration system. Under it, noncombatants (men, women, and children) were herded into concentration camps and garrisoned towns and prohibited from leaving them under pain of death and forfeiture of property. Without sufficient supplies to keep them alive, they perished miserably by the thousands. While Grover Cleveland was President of the United States, the demands for intervention and war with Spain made little headway. His successor, William McKinley, was also opposed to taking action, but ambiguous policy and lack of firmness enabled the advocates of war to determine the course of events.

EVENTS LEADING TO WAR WITH SPAIN

Their success was made easier by two events that took place early in 1898. The first was the publication of a private letter written by Dupuy de Lôme, the Spanish Minister to the United States. This letter, purloined from the Post Office in Havana, characterized President McKinley as "a weakling . . . a bidder for the admiration of the crowd" and "a would-be politician who tries to leave a door open behind him while keeping on good terms with the jingoes of his own party." Public indignation in the United States ran high over the affront to the President, which the speedy resignation of De Lôme did little to calm. It was viewed as a national insult.

The other incident was the sinking of the United States battleship **Maine** in Havana harbor after an explosion which ripped the vessel apart and killed 260 members of the crew. Although the cause of the disaster was never definitely established, there was little doubt in the minds of most Americans that Spanish treachery was responsible. Newspapers the country over demanded war, and the country rang with the cry, "Remember the **Maine** " and the tune, "There'll Be a Hot Time in the Old Town Tonight."

Caught in a storm of public emotion which it had done little to combat, the Administration made weak, last-minute efforts to avert conflict. But a peaceful solution was no longer possible. An ultimatum sent to Spain on 27 March 1898 demanded the end of the reconcentration policy, an amnesty, and the right of the United States to act as arbitrator between the Spanish Government and the insurgents. Spain seemed ready to agree to such terms, provided a way could be found to do so without bringing about the overthrow of the Spanish monarchy. This required time and patience on the part of the American public and their representatives in Congress, but both had run out.

On 19 April, Congress passed a joint resolution proclaiming Cuba free and independent and authorizing the President to use land and naval forces to expel Spain from the island. Attached to the resolution was the "Teller Amendment," which altruistically disclaimed "any disposition or intention to exercise sovereignty, jurisdiction or control" over Cuba following the elimination of Spanish authority.

The joint resolution, when signed by McKinley the next day, amounted to a declaration of war. It was followed immediately by a Presidential order to blockade Cuba, and by 22 April an American naval squadron was off Havana. On the same day Congress voted to double the size of the Regular Army, and empowered the President to issue a call for 125,000 volunteers from the several states.

The Army Unprepared

When war broke out the Regular Army's 28,000 men were scattered throughout the country at many different posts. Individually the troops were well trained, but the Army as a whole was unprepared for war in practically every other respect. It lacked a mobilization plan, a well-organized high command, and experience and doctrine in combined operations. Units larger than a regiment were nonexistent, and those of regimental size were rarely assembled in one place. Only a few older officers had ever seen a unit as large as a brigade, and still fewer had any experience in commanding one. As for the National Guard, it numbered around 100,000 men, composed mostly of infantry units, whose training, discipline, and equipment were, with rare exceptions, lamentable. Few had any acquaintance with military matters beyond close-order drill and company administration. Equipment of all sorts was either scarce or obsolete. To make matters worse, the organization of the National Guard varied from state to state, and so, to all intents and purposes, there were as many different armies as there were states. All were exceedingly jealous of their prerogatives and suspicious of any move that might be interpreted as bringing them under Regular Army control. There was also a question about the legality of sending the National Guard abroad to serve. In the light of these considerations, the absorption of the National Guard into the Army was considered unwise. The Volunteer Army Act passed on 22 April, therefore, was so framed that National Guard could serve as state volunteer units with the sanction of the respective governors.

Answering the Call for 125,000 Volunteers.

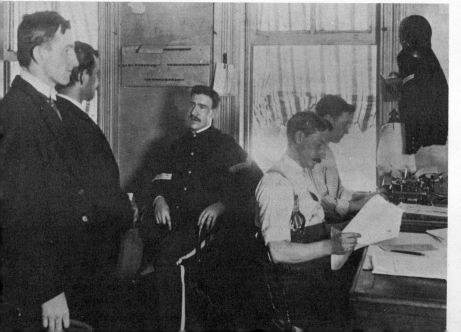

Filling out enlistment papers: An Army corporal talks to a group of potential volunteers.

Taking the oath.

Exchanging civilian
clothes for Army uniforms.

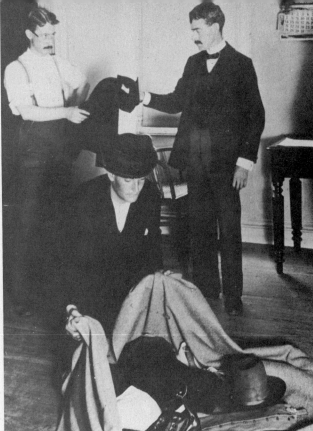

Moving South. The 21st Infantry leaves Plattsburg, New York.

Early in April, as war was approaching, Major General Nelson Miles, Commanding General of the Army, urged the concentration of the entire Regular Army at Chickamauga Park, Georgia, where it would be "equipped, drilled, disciplined and instructed in brigades and divisions and prepared for war service." But Russell A. Alger, the Secretary of War, who was hardly on speaking terms with Miles, had different ideas. Alger had been a general officer in the Civil War, and considered himself fully competent to run the Army. Disregarding the advice of the Commanding General, he ordered the cavalry and artillery to Chickamauga and the infantry to New Orleans, Tampa, and Mobile, his main purpose apparently being to concentrate the infantry at points where it could make a quick descent upon Cuba.

Company K, 9th Massachusetts, marches through Clinton, Massachusetts, prior to its departure for Tampa.

Like many others, Alger believed that Spain would withdraw from the island at a show of force, and that the war would end in a few weeks without any fighting. Most military experts were less optimistic, however, and pointed out that the Spanish Army was in a position to make a stand, and that months, rather than weeks, would be required to drive it from Cuba.

General Miles preferred a small force of about 80,000 men to a large one predominantly composed of volunteers. Such an army, he believed, would be more effective because it could be more quickly trained and equipped. As events proved, he was right, but the Administration, Congress, and the people thought otherwise. In response to public demand, the number of volunteers that could be called was soon raised from 125,000 to 267,000. The fact that about a million men offered their services indicated that the war was looked upon as a glorious national picnic that nearly everyone wanted to attend. Not until the volunteers were exposed to the hardships of camp life in the South did enthusiasm decline. There, instead of picnic conditions, they found utter confusion. Volunteer officers were untrained, equipment and supplies short, sanitary conditions disgraceful, food tainted, medical service woefully inadequate, and weapons and ammunition obsolete. Thousands lacked such essentials as underwear, socks, and shoes, and those who were clothed in uniforms wore woolens designed for use on the western Plains, not for wear in southern camps during the summer or campaigns in the tropics. The Regular Army fared better than the volunteers, but most of its members also failed to receive proper clothing before the fighting was over.

Logically, the long period of strained relations with

Spain should have produced some plan for military operations in Cuba. Actually, there was no plan. The preparation of war plans would have been the duty of a general staff, not of officers burdened with routine administrative duties, but there was no true general staff. Consequently the United States went to war without any coordinated plan, and quite ignorant of such basic matters as the strength, disposition, and capabilities of the Spanish in Cuba or of the Cuban insurgents, whose ally the United States automatically would become the moment war broke out. Nor was much thought given before the war to organizing for amphibious warfare. Joint Army-Navy planning for an attack on a hostile shore, the most complicated of all military operations, awaited the outbreak of hostilities. Even accurate maps of Cuba, essential to intelligent planning, were practically nonexistent. As a result of these failures, all planning had to be undertaken after hostilities broke out. Fortunately for the United States, the Spanish were even more inept. Meanwhile the Army languished in the filth and heat of the concentration areas, growing daily sicker, more restless, and more disillusioned.

ACTION IN CUBA

On 19 May Spanish Admiral Pascual Cervera's fleet slipped into Santiago Bay. Composed of four armored cruisers and two destroyers it had sailed across the Atlantic directly into the center of operations, skillfully eluding a superior hostile fleet. As a naval achievement, the voyage was an unqualified success. But this success was the Spanish Fleet's first and last. In entering Santiago Bay, Cervera had virtually sealed the fate of his fleet. His move brought the American Fleet together and gave the armed forces a definite objective.

The Navy at once blockaded the port and dispatched a force of marines to establish a naval base on Guantanamo Bay. After a minor action, the first on Cuban soil involving Americans, the site was taken. At the same time the forts and batteries commanding the entrance to Santiago Bay were subjected to naval bombardment, but without success. Fearful of Spanish coast defenses and mines, Rear Admiral T. Sampson hesitated to risk his ships in running the channel. Instead, he sought to prevent the escape of Cervera's fleet by ordering the collier **Merrimac** sunk across the channel. The attempt failed and Sampson was confronted with the choice of forcing an entrance into the bay or calling for land forces to take the batteries that his ships could not silence. He decided to call for assistance.

Eager to get the Army into action, the War Department at once directed Major General William R. Shafter to embark from Tampa for Cuba. His orders gave him the choice of moving directly on the forts dominating the entrance to Santiago Bay or driving into the interior to take Santiago from the rear. To issue orders to move an Army to Cuba was one thing, to get it there was quite another.

For weeks harassed and bewildered officers and War Department officials struggled with the problem of getting the expedition under way. A worse embarkation port could hardly have been chosen, for Tampa had only one pier and was served by a single-track railroad.

On 11 June, the embarkation of some 17,000 men finally got started. It lasted four days, an operation which, if properly organized, could have been accomplished easily in eight hours. But the embarkation was anything but organized. No detailed and coordinated plan existed and no staff was on hand to direct the movement. Little attention was given to proper loading for a combat mission. Men, supplies, and equipment were loaded into ships helter-skelter without regard to the order in which they might have to be discharged in case resistance was encountered during the landing. So confused did the embarkation become that some regiments actually took matters into their own hands, commandeering railroad cars and equipment meant for other units and even fighting on the pier in an effort to board transports. Yet somehow, someway, men and supplies were loaded and the expedition finally set off.

Mealtime at Tampa.

The port at Tampa.

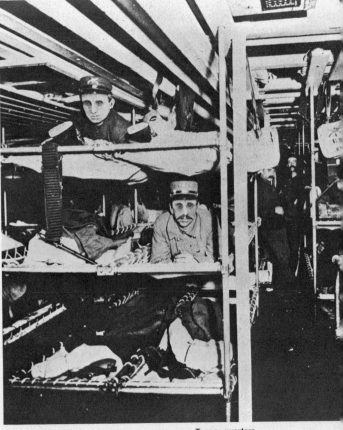

Troop quarters
on one of the transports.

284

Inspecting the troops before disembarkation.

Boarding a transport for Cuba.

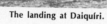
The landing at Daiquíri.

Landing at Daiquiri

By 20 June, the transports reached a point off Santiago. Shafter immediately conferred with Sampson, who urged him to land his troops near the fort on the east side of the entrance to the bay, storm it, and then drive the Spanish from the battery positions on the opposite side. The Navy would then sweep the mines from the channel and enter Santiago Bay to engage the Spanish fleet. Shafter, after looking at the fort perched on a hill rising sharply from the sea to a height of 230 feet, concluded that it was too difficult a position to take without heavy artillery. He decided, instead, to follow the advice of General Calixto Garcia, commander of the Cuban insurgents in the area, and land his army at Daiquíri, 18 miles east of Santiago Bay. After making a feint west of the bay to throw the Spanish off guard, the force began to move ashore, following a heavy naval shelling aimed at driving out any Spaniards who might be in the neighborhood. Fortunately the area was unde-

fended. By failing to oppose the landing, the Spanish lost a splendid opportunity, for the debarkation was if anything more disorganized and confused than the embarkation at Tampa.

That a landing could have been accomplished in the face of determined resistance is extremely doubtful. No plans had been made for an amphibious assault, and units got ashore as best they could, with or without equipment. Many captains of chartered merchant ships refused to take their vessels inshore, and some, in fright, actually fled the scene and had to be rounded up by the Navy. Horses were gotten ashore by the simple expedient of dropping them overboard and letting them swim. Unfortunately some swam out to sea and were lost before someone thought of stringing them together and leading them ashore with boats. The landing that should have taken hours actually took days, but thanks to Spanish military inefficiency catastrophe was avoided.

Cuban insurgents
at Daiquirí.

After the landing of some 6,000 troops on the first day, the march on the city of Santiago began despite the criticism of the Navy, which still hoped the force would move against the positions guarding the entrance to the bay. Shafter's plan was simple enough—a quick drive toward Santiago by the most direct route, which meant by the one road leading to the city through Siboney, a village on the coast. About 12,000 Spanish troops were thought to be in entrenched lines around Santiago, but their exact location was not known. On 23 June, Brigadier General Henry W.

Map—Siege of Santiago.

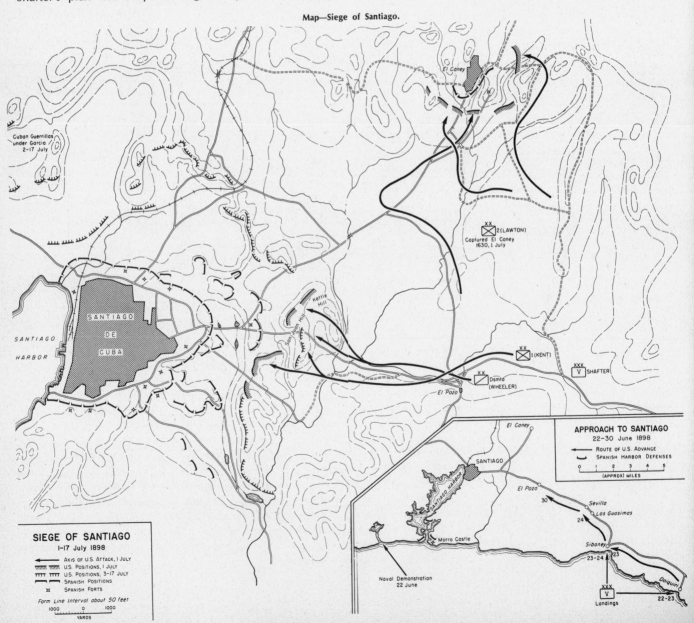

Lawton, commanding the vanguard, reached Siboney and captured it without difficulty. His orders directed him to establish a perimeter defense behind the beach so that further debarkation operations could be moved to that area. This was done, and Siboney from that time on became the base for the operation. While Lawton was reorganizing to continue the advance as directed, Brigadier General Joseph W. Wheeler, a veteran of the Confederate Army, stole a march on him and pushed on toward Santiago with his dismounted cavalry division. At Las Guasimas, he ran into the rear guard of a retiring Spanish force, which inflicted some casualties. No serious delay was suffered, however, since the Spanish had no intention of making a stand beyond Santiago's outer defenses.

The push toward Santiago as recorded in contemporary lithographs: Above: an attack on the Santiago fortifications. Below: the battle at Las Guásimas.

One of the Signal Corps' observation balloons in Cuba.

Moving ammunition to the front during the siege of Santiago.

A Gatling gun detachment in action near Santiago. The Army used machine guns for close support for the first time during the siege of Santiago.

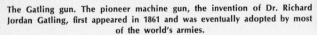

The Gatling gun. The pioneer machine gun, the invention of Dr. Richard Jordan Gatling, first appeared in 1861 and was eventually adopted by most of the world's armies.

Attack on San Juan Hill and El Caney

The most important of these defenses were along a series of ridges known collectively as San Juan, and in the village of El Caney to the north. To prevent Santiago from being reinforced and to cut its water supply, Shafter decided to attack El Caney first and then follow with a frontal assault on the San Juan positions. Only two hours were allowed for the capture of El Caney, an estimate that proved overly optimistic. General Lawton, who was to take the fortified village, moved out on time, but because of poor roads and difficult terrain conditions he was unable to begin the assault on schedule.

The force assigned to take the San Juan heights, commanded by Major General Jacob F. Kent, waited more than two hours for the El Caney attack to get under way before beginning its attack. It was a poorly coordinated effort, and within a short time units of the attacking force became badly disorganized. Part of the confusion resulted from the heavy artillery fire that a Signal Corps captive balloon brought upon the troops as it was being towed along in the advancing front line. Another factor was the extremely hot weather. The heat prostrated General Shafter, who weighed over 300 pounds, and prevented him from directing the battle. Poor communications and inadequate staff work also contributed to the lack of direction. Subordinate officers rose to the

288

Preparing to move forward on July 1. The road to Santiago ran over the heavily fortified San Juan heights.

The 16th Infantry under fire from Spanish artillery on the San Juan heights.

Lieutenant Colonel Theodore Roosevelt (center) and his Rough Riders at San Juan Hill.

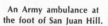

An Army ambulance at the foot of San Juan Hill.

289

Troops of the 10th Cavalry at rest on San Juan Hill.

Spanish prisoners taken at San Juan Hill.

Lieutenant Colonel Theodore Roosevelt, the commander of the Rough Riders.

After the battle. Rough Riders prepare to defend their newly won positions on San Juan Hill.

290

occasion, however, restored order, and stormed enemy positions with a medley of troops. Lieutenant John H. Parker, commander of a Gatling gun detachment, for example, sought and received permission to move his guns into line and join the infantry attack. This use of weapons heretofore considered suitable only for defense proved highly successful. The close support given the infantry helped establish fire superiority and contributed much to the restoration of the offensive spirit, without which the San Juan heights could not have been taken. Kettle Hill, a knob separate from the main ridge, was taken by dismounted cavalry units, among them the famous Rough Riders. It was in this action that Lieutenant Colonel Theodore Roosevelt distinguished himself.

Meanwhile, the attack on El Caney finally got started. At first it made little headway. Some 500 Spanish troops in a strong position protected by barbed wire resisted stubbornly until their ammunition gave out and they were forced to retire. The capture of the stronghold was further delayed because Lawton had to withdraw a volunteer regiment from the fight when the black powder cartridges it used betrayed its position, bringing heavy enemy fire on American lines. He also initially deployed his artillery in such a manner that it could not properly support the advance. Late in the battle the artillery was moved forward to positions from which it could effectively shell enemy defenses, and the attack proceeded at a more rapid pace. With the fall of the village all the outer defenses of Santiago were in American hands. Shafter now faced the problem of what to do next.

Before him lay the enemy's well-organized second line of defense, and behind that, the more formidable inner defenses, strongly protected by barbed wire. Despite his victory, Shafter's position was not an enviable one. His troops were exposed to enemy fire which they could not return effectively, and malaria, yellow fever, and the approaching hurricane season threatened their health and safety. To attempt to storm the city without sufficient artillery to blast a way through the barbed wire and batter entrenched positions would be suicidal. Shafter's first inclination was to withdraw to higher ground about 4 miles from the city, but this move was vetoed by the War Department. He next tried to persuade the Navy to run the channel and attack the city from the bay, but neither Sampson nor his superiors in the Navy Department in Washington would risk the fleet in running batteries that they had called upon the Army to take. No one person below the President himself had command authority over both Army and Navy forces in the area, and since McKinley was not inclined to exercise it, the differences between the Army and the Navy threatened to develop into a public debate between spokesmen of the two services. In fact, the debate had already begun when Spanish action brought it to an abrupt halt.

The Spaniards Surrender Santiago

While Shafter and Sampson were worrying about their problems, the Spaniards faced far more serious ones. In Santiago ammunition and food were low, and there was little hope of getting more of either. Near-famine conditions prevailed, seriously affecting the health and morale of both troops and inhabitants. Despite the strength of their de-

Brigadier General Joseph W. Wheeler, commander of a dismounted cavalry division at Santiago.

Brigadier General Henry W. Lawton, in command during the successful attacks on Siboney and El Caney.

fensive position, it seemed to the Spanish leaders after San Juan and El Caney that the fall of the city was inevitable. But there was one hope. Since Santiago was a military objective only because Cervera's fleet had found refuge in its harbor, the departure of the fleet for some other Cuban port probably would induce the U.S. Navy to follow and possibly the Army also. In any event there was nothing to be gained by leaving the fleet in the port and letting it fall into the hands of the enemy without a fight. Admiral Cervera's superiors in Madrid ordered him to attempt to escape with his fleet as soon as the fall of the city seemed imminent. Cervera, considering escape hopeless, objected, but finally obeyed orders. Suddenly on the morning of 3 July, while Sampson and Shafter were in conference ashore discussing their differences, the Spanish Fleet emerged from the narrows of the bay and made for the open sea, hoping to reach the port of Cienfuegos. A dramatic running battle ensued which ended in the complete destruction of the entire enemy fleet. The victory was decisive and ended whatever hopes the Spanish still had of holding out successfully in Santiago.

The destruction of the Spanish fleet in Santiago Bay on July 3.

A few days later General Shafter and General José Toral, the defender of Santiago, met between the lines to discuss the fate of the city. Shafter convinced Toral that honorable surrender was his only course. The U.S. general would have permitted the Spanish garrison to withdraw from the city without arms, but Washington insisted on unconditional surrender. Toral, who at first refused to capitulate on that basis, finally agreed after a long-range naval bombardment of Santiago which caused more fright than damage. On 16 July terms were signed which provided for the surrender of the 11,500 troops in the city and some 12,000 others situated at Guantanamo, San Luis, and other places from 25 to 60 miles away. The next day a formal surrender ceremony was held which ended in a round of handshaking between the erstwhile enemies.

After the fall of Santiago, General Miles, who had arrived in Cuba to take personal command of the Army, moved to Puerto Rico with 3,000 men. His original plan was to land at Cape Fajardo on the northeastern corner of the island, establish a base there to which reinforcements could be sent, and then move on San Juan, the capital on the north coast. While at sea, he decided to land at Guanica

U.S. General William Shafter and Spanish General José Toral meet between the lines to discuss the surrender of Santiago. The formal surrender of the city took place on July 17.

This picture was taken at the religious services on July 17 where General Wheeler announced: "I am pleased to say there will be no more fighting; the enemy has surrendered."

Raising the American flag over the
governor's palace in Santiago.

on the southeastern coast. Why he changed plans is not clear, but there is good reason to believe he was motivated as much by a desire to dispense with the services of the Navy in the operation against San Juan as to deceive the enemy. In any event, no harm was done, for the landing met no opposition. The city of Ponce, just east of Guanica, was taken without trouble and immediately turned into an Army base. Meanwhile, additional troops under Major General John R. Brooke were landed at Guayama, also on the south coast, and within a short time the island was overrun by four columns. There was some light resistance, but the population as a whole received the American troops with enthusiasm. Only one problem arose—how to get enough American flags to bedeck government buildings and properly celebrate the expected annexation to the United States. Campaigning in Puerto Rico was indeed a picnic.

There was little bloodshed, no serious hardship, and plenty of fun.

Back in Cuba the Army met its worst problems after the surrender of Santiago. They were caused not by Spanish troops but by more deadly enemies—malaria, typhoid, and yellow fever. So serious did the situation become that a group of senior officers drew up a joint letter addressed to General Shafter in which they called for the immediate evacuation of the Army from Cuba. When this "round robin" letter was dispatched to General Shafter, it was also leaked to the press with the result that officials in Washington read the letter in the newspapers before they were informed of its contents by the commanding general in Cuba. Its publication caused a sensation, coming as it did just when peace negotiations were beginning. The whole business was very unmilitary, very indiscreet, and very embar-

American troops in the field hear the best news of all:
the war is over.

Sick call during the siege of Santiago. While yellow fever was a constant threat, the chief causes of illness among American soldiers in Cuba were malaria and dysentery.

Hospital-tent patients at the U.S. base at Siboney. The picture was taken on 8 July, 1898.

rassing to General Shafter, but it did bring action. American troops were immediately brought back and placed in an isolated camp on Montauk Point at the tip of Long Island. Some 20,000 of the 35,000 who passed through the camp were ill, but most of them eventually regained their health. It was at Montauk Point that the troops finally were able to shed their woolen clothing and don cotton uniforms.

THE BATTLE OF MANILA

The last military action of the war with Spain was the battle for Manila. In response to a request for 5,000 men from Commodore George Dewey, who had been in command of Manila Bay since 1 May, the War Department had organized a force with Major General Wesley Merritt in com-

mand. The first contingent of 2,500 arrived in Manila on 1 July and was gradually built up until it reached 11,000 shortly after Merritt arrived on 25 July. As American strength increased, the need for help from Filipino insurgents decreased. Their leader, Emilio Aguinaldo, who had hoped for recognition of his Philippine Republic, was far from pleased with the American buildup. Relations grew strained as it became clear that the Americans were determined to take Manila with a minimum of Filipino aid. A partial reason for this determination was that the Spanish early in the siege had indicated a willingness to surrender the city, provided it was not exposed to undisciplined insurgents afterward. But the main reason was that Washington was trying to make up its mind about the future of the islands, and

294

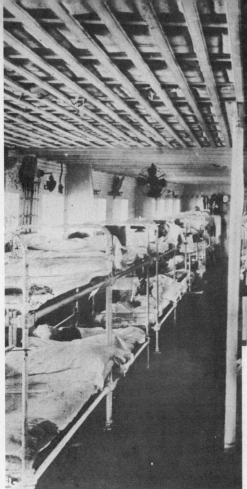

Ward 3 on the "Relief."

The operating room of the "Relief"

The hospital ship
"Relief" off Siboney, Cuba.

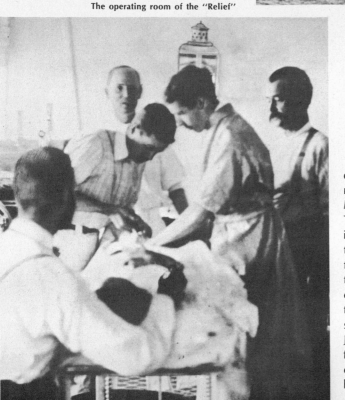

did not want to be handicapped by obligations or commitments to a native government. As a result, both Dewey and Merritt had to adjust their actions to a policy in the making. This was not an easy thing to do for it meant resistance to insurgent aspirations and demands without bringing matters to a breaking point. To make the situation even more difficult, the insurgents held a line around Manila between the U.S. lines and the city walls. Before an advance on the city could be arranged without the insurgents, their positions would have to be occupied by American troops. With skill and tact, this feat was accomplished by the end of July, the Filipinos leaving reluctantly but peacefully. Plans for the final assault moved rapidly thereafter, if a negotiated operation can be called an assault. Arrangements for a bloodless action had been completed and everything

The Army in the Philippines: American infantrymen on the firing line.

seemed to be in perfect order when the attack began, but it did not proceed as planned. The advance became confused in the rice paddies before the city. Insurgent bands moving on the flanks became intermingled with American troops approaching the Spanish forward positions, and firing broke out. The American firing stopped when the Spanish failed to reply, but the insurgent fire continued. It seemed for a time that the token assault would become a serious affair, but after some difficulty the firing was reduced sufficiently to permit the Spanish to capitulate. The fact that the war had officially ended two days before was not yet known in Manila, and on 14 August formal surrender terms were signed.

THE PHILIPPINE INSURRECTION

The collapse of Spanish power and the approaching transfer of the islands to the United States brought a rapid deterioration of Filipino-American relations. Aguinaldo and his followers were as determined as ever to be free, and on 4 February, as the treaty with Spain was about to be ratified by the U.S. Senate, hostilities broke out around Manila. The Army, having defeated the Spanish forces, was now faced with the far more serious task of suppressing a native revolt. For this Major General Elwell S. Otis, who succeeded General Merritt, had some 21,000 men on hand. Since many of these were volunteers about to be returned to the United States, he could count on only 12,000 effectives. His control of the islands scarcely extended beyond Manila since the insurgents held a semicircular line of blockhouses around the city with a force estimated by some to number 40,000 men. The reaction of the Army to the revolt was immediate and determined. In a battle which lasted two days the insurgents lost about 3,000 men and the Army of Occupation 250.

The outbreak convinced the United States that a larger force was needed to meet the challenge to its control. Ten volunteer regiments were raised, and within seven months nearly 35,000 reinforcements were on their way to the Philippines. The fighting that followed was influenced by terrain, climate, and differences in weapons. The natives fought with bolos as often as with rifles, and their attacks were met with small arms fire and bayonet charge. Gatling guns, used effectively against the Spanish, were too unwieldy for jungle warfare; for the same reason, little artillery was used.

Signaling for reserves to advance during the attack on Manila.

The Manila fortifications after the American flag had replaced the Spanish colors.

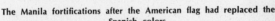

Until reinforcements arrived General Otis could not undertake an all-out offensive, but he did seize Malolos, the insurgent capital, and the islands of Panay, Cebu, and Negros. By April, Otis was ready to undertake a general offensive in Luzon, the center of insurgent resistance. It began with a two-pronged advance, one under General Lawton on Santa Cruz and the other under Major General Arthur MacArthur up the central plain from Malolos toward San Fernando. Both drives were successful, and by mid-May organized resistance in central Luzon was seriously weakened. A shortage in manpower and the approaching rainy season then temporarily halted the offensive until October,

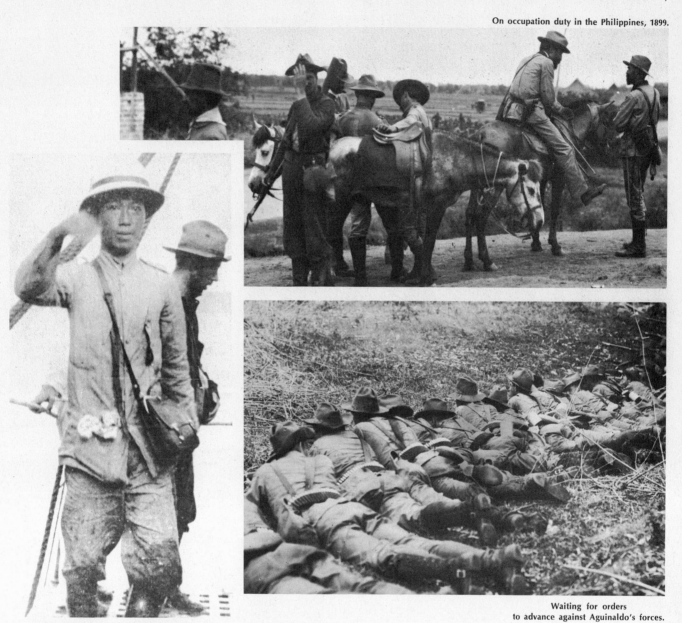

On occupation duty in the Philippines, 1899.

Aguinaldo boards an American gunboat
after his capture in March 1901.

Waiting for orders
to advance against Aguinaldo's forces.

An American battery in action
against the insurgents.

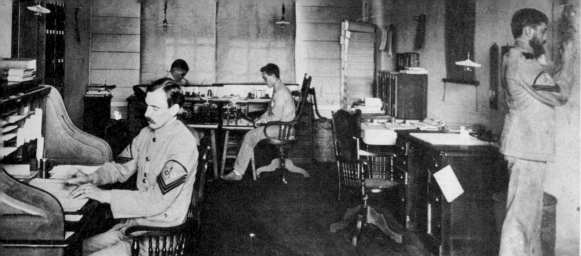

A U.S. infantry camp in China.

when it was resumed. To cut off Aguinaldo's retreat to the mountain fastness of northern Luzon, Otis planned to continue the advance up the central plain with his main force and send two smaller forces around each flank, the one on the right by way of the Lingayen Gulf. The operation failed to trap the insurgent leader, but it dispersed much of his band. Aguinaldo himself was not taken until March 1901. In southern Luzon Otis was equally successful, and by March 1900 it and the neighboring Visayas were both under control. Mindanao and the Sulu Archipelago, inhabited by the warlike Moros, were occupied next and organized resistance ended, but not the fighting. In some respects the 13 months between May 1900 and June 1901 were the most difficult of the insurrection. Fighting was bitter and brutal, with little quarter given or asked. The Army fought over 1,000 separate engagements, and casualties surpassed those of the earlier period. The fighting finally ended in April 1902, except for spasmodic outbreaks which continued for years.

THE CHINA RELIEF EXPEDITION

Meanwhile, the United States Army had also seen action in China. Aroused by the ruthless exploitation of their country, many Chinese had accepted the preachings of the "Boxers," fanatical members of a secret society dedicated to the extermination of "foreign devils" and the eradication of their influence. Under the leadership of Prince Tuan and encouraged by the reactionary Dowager Empress, the Box-

American artillery bombarding the Great Wall at Peking.

298

Major General Adna R. Chaffee, commander of the U.S. force, supervises his artillery.

Reilley's Battery. This was the unit that blasted the gates to Peking's Inner or "Forbidden" City.

ers and their supporters proceeded to carry out their program. Hundreds of hated foreigners and Chinese Christians were slain. A climax occurred on 20 June 1900 when the German Minister was murdered while on his way to protest against the indignities of the Boxers. Convinced by the incident that they were no longer safe in Peking, many foreigners and Chinese converts took refuge in the legation compound, where they were immediately besieged by thousands of Chinese, including some troops from the Chinese Army.

The powers reacted at once by organizing a relief expedition. Because the United States was involved in military operations in the nearby Philippines, it was in a position to make a substantial contribution to the international force. Manila became a main base and, by agreement with Japan, Nagasaki was used as a secondary base. The latter proved very valuable as a distribution point for men and supplies from the states. In less than three weeks after receiving their orders, the 9th Infantry and a battalion of marines were landed at Taku, the Chinese port closest to Peking. Major General Adna R. Chaffee, commander of the United States force, and others soon joined them, bringing the American contingent up to 2,500 men; it was surpassed in strength only by the Russians and Japanese. On 13 July the relief expedition, composed of American, British, French, Japanese, and Russian troops, attacked and took the walled city of Tientsin after a 15-hour battle during which the city was badly damaged. Its fall opened the way to Peking 75 miles away.

The Fall of Peking

Early in August the allied force, now numbering about 18,000 men, began its advance on the capital through a region infested with Boxers and their sympathizers. Several sharp skirmishes were fought with serious losses, but by 12 August the force was at the gates of Peking, and two days later succeeded in taking the Outer City, thereby ensuring the relief of the beleaguered legations. In this action two companies of the 14th Infantry scaled the Tartar wall and covered the British as they entered the city in force. A final assault on the Inner or "Forbidden" City was made the next day after an American artillery unit known as "Reilley's Battery" blasted the gates that blocked the entrance. With the fall of the "Forbidden" City the important military operations came to an end. Order was restored in Peking, but not without unnecessary violence and much looting by some of the European contingents, which did not add to the reputation of foreigners in China. Mopping-up operations also were undertaken in the provinces, particularly Chih-li, where Boxer influence was still strong. Meanwhile reinforcements, including a large contingent from Germany, continued to arrive. An international army of occupation, commanded by Field Marshal Count Alfred von Waldersee, was set up and in a few months succeeded in wiping out the last traces of resistance in the provinces. In return for the concessions made by the Chinese Government, the powers agreed to evacuate all troops but legation guards by the fall of 1901. All of them did so except Russia, which continued to maintain a strong force in southern Manchuria and the province of Chih-li.

With proportionately few troops, the American contribution to the success in quelling the trouble in China was great enough to establish itself thereafter as a strong voice in all future Far Eastern problems.

Two soldiers in the round leather hat with a bearskin crest that replaced the three-cornered cocked hat of the Revolutionary War. Their uniforms are blue with red facings, cuffs, and collars.

A group of officers in uniforms of the War of 1812. The major general (seated) and the brigadier general at his left are wearing blue, close-buttoned, single-breasted coats. An artillery officer in a blue uniform is reporting to the major general.

ARMY UNIFORMS OF THE NINETEENTH CENTURY

The U.S. Army began the nineteenth century in uniforms very little changed from those worn during the Revolutionary War. By 1813, however, the old three-cornered cocked hat had disappeared to be replaced, first by a compressible three-cornered hat, or chapeaux bras, for officers and round leather hats with bearskin crests for enlisted men, and then by the shako. Instead of the long cutaway coat, soldiers wore close-buttoned, single-breasted coats with very high collars. Facings disappeared as did red collars and cuffs. The blue coat of the infantry and artillery was shortened and called a coatee. It was worn with trousers and waistcoats of blue in winter and nankeen in summer.

On social occasions knee breeches and shoes were the prescribed wear. An order issued in 1813 read in part: "Where etiquette requires shoes, breeches agreeable to the uniform are to be worn with yellow knee-buckles instead of strings, yellow buckles in the shoes, a chapeau bras instead of the cap. No plumes."

Another order, issued in 1816 in response to requests for an "undress" uniform more comfortable than the regular military costume, prohibited "undress uniform, and all other dresses resembling the military without conforming to regulations." The same order directed that "black cockades with yellow eagles will always be worn by all officers of the army."

Although they were changed from time to time, the various arms of the service continued to wear distinctive colors. In 1825 the light artillery wore yellow and red pompons on the forage cap; the artillery, yellow; the grenadiers, red; the light infantry, white and red; the infantry, white; and rifles, green. Later scarlet became the color of the artillery, Saxony blue of the infantry, orange of the dragoons, and yellow of the cavalry.

The campaign, or battle, dress adopted during the Mexican War represented a big change in the direction of simplicity, although full dress, especially for officers, remained elaborate and colorful. Artillerymen, for example, wore bright scarlet trimmings; infantrymen, Saxony blue (replaced in 1852 by sky blue); riflemen, medium or emerald green; and dragoons, orange. The pompon, which also carried the distinguishing colors, had become a small round ball by the 1850's.

Dark blue flannel blouses, light blue trousers, dark blue forage caps and gray canteens and blankets were the standard infantry uniform of the Civil War, but troops were per-

Soldiers of the War of 1812: (from left) an infantryman; a rifleman; and an artilleryman. The infantry and artillery coats were blue, the trousers summer-wear nankeen. The rifleman's coat and trousers were gray.

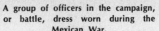

A group of officers in the campaign, or battle, dress worn during the Mexican War.

Army officers in the short frock coats and cloth shakos worn in the 1830's.

A subaltern of dragoons (right) in blue coat and light-blue trousers with yellow stripes and an ordnance sergeant in a blue coat and light-blue trousers with a dark blue stripe. The dragoon's rank of second lieutenant is indicated by two buttons on gold-lace slash flaps on his cuffs. The sergeant's grade is indicated by four buttons on yellow slash flaps on his cuffs, heavy yellow worsted braid on his epaulettes, and his red sash. Both uniforms were worn in the 1830's.

mitted a certain amount of latitude in what they wore for marching and fighting. Dark blue jackets trimmed in yellow were issued to the enlisted men of the Civil War cavalry; the dark blue jackets of artillerymen were trimmed in scarlet.

In the years after the Civil War, Army uniforms became more elaborate. Epaulettes and sashes reappeared. Officers wore gold sword knots and shakos decorated with plumes and gilt. Even the once plain black felt hat was decorated with braid and cords. Coats became shorter, and everyone, except general officers, wore sky-blue trousers.

In 1881 helmets similar to those worn by the Germans in the Franco-Prussian War were adopted by the U.S. Army for all its troops. Those of field officers were decorated with plumes, cords, and tassels, while the helmets of enlisted men were spiked. The summer uniform hat was a white helmet.

During this period the regulations covering swords, which were a required part of the officers' uniform, came under the criticism of the Army's Inspector General: "In the artillery the company officers of foot troops have one sword, the officers serving with light batteries have another, and finally the field officers and adjutants another.

"In the infantry the company officers have one kind of sword, while field and staff have another. The lieutenant of artillery who joins his foot battery secures for himself an infantry sword; he soon finds himself assigned to one of the light batteries for duty, and he procures a light artillery sword. If he is then so fortunate as to be appointed adjutant to his regiment, he provides himself with a cavalry saber. Aside from the hardships that such outlays cause to those concerned, it increases the luggage that the officer must carry about with him. I do not know of any sufficient reason why one pattern of sword should not meet all the requirements of any one branch of the service."

In the same report the Inspector General noted the absence of waterproof clothing for the use of the troops, even though such clothing was in general use by civilians.

Because of the tropical climate in which it was fought, the Spanish-American War produced several changes in the uniform of the U.S. Army. Khaki, first worn by the British in India, replaced blue cloth, although only regulars were able to obtain issues of it. Many volunteer troops fought the entire war in their heavy uniforms, but in some cases khaki trousers were worn with the blue shirt. Canvas leggings protected the soldier against tropical insects and plant spurs, replacing leather boots. Headgear consisted of either a wide gray felt hat or a high cork helmet covered with khaki broadcloth or cotton drilling. As the nineteenth century ended, the full-dress uniform continued to be blue, but khaki had taken over in the field.

An infantryman (left) and a rifleman play checkers while (from left) an engineer, a dragoon, a musician and a light artilleryman watch. All are wearing uniforms of the early 1850's.

Soldiers of the Mexican War: (from left) a foot-rifleman, or voltigeur; two infantrymen; and a dragoon.

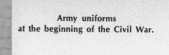

A first lieutenant of the Corps of Engineers and an infantry first sergeant in the
field during the Civil War.

Campaign uniforms of the Civil War. From left:
an artillery officer, an infantry officer, and
infantrymen.

303

General Grant (seated), General Meade (with paper) and other Civil War officers. The felt hats they wear in this drawing resemble civilian hats of the period except for gold cords.

By 1874 the coat of the foot trooper's dress uniform had become shorter and his shako lower. Mounted men (center) wore shorter coats than foot soldiers, and helmets adapted from those worn by the German army.

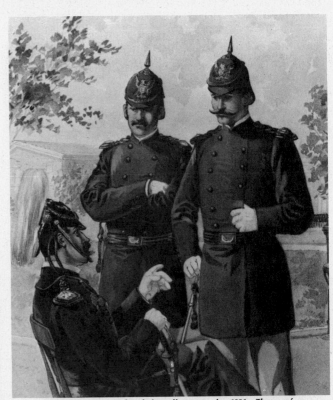

Helmets were ordered for all troops in 1881. Those of mounted officers (left) were decorated with plumes, cord, and tassel. Foot officers had spikes in their helmets, as did enlisted men.

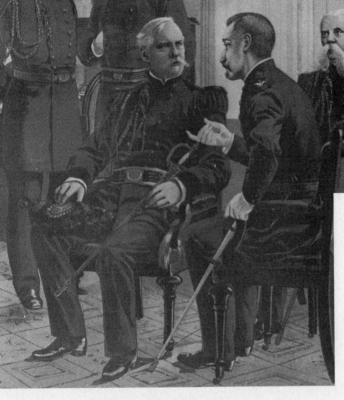

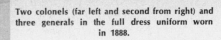

Two colonels (far left and second from right) and three generals in the full dress uniform worn in 1888.

The Army winter overcoat of 1888.

An infantryman (left) and two cavalrymen in the 1888 dress uniforms of their arms of the service.

A group of officers in the khaki field uniform of the Spanish-American War.

Khaki-clad
enlisted men in Cuba.

A major of the Army's Medical Department (left) in the old blue field uniform. With him is a field artillery private in the dark blue kersey trousers worn by some of the troops in Cuba.

306

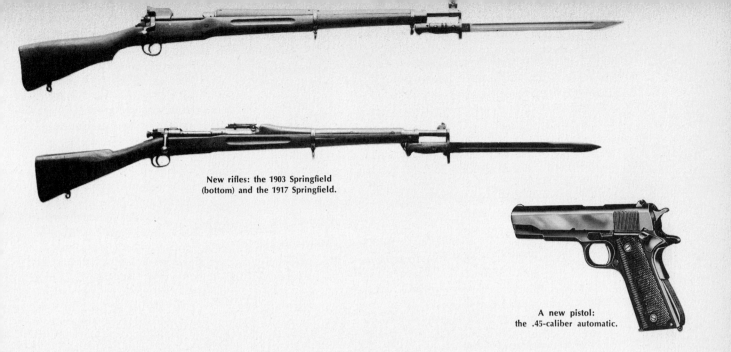

New rifles: the 1903 Springfield
(bottom) and the 1917 Springfield.

A new pistol:
the .45-caliber automatic.

CHAPTER 11

THE U.S. ARMY, 1898-1917

The end of the nineteenth and the beginning of the twentieth century witnessed not only the emergence of the United States as a world power but also the intensification of international rivalry throughout the world. Most of the great European powers sought to strengthen their alliances and alignments and improve their diplomatic positions. By 1907 two rival alliances, the Triple Alliance, composed of Germany, Austria-Hungary, and Italy, and the so-called Triple Entente, France, England, and Russia, faced each other in uncertain peace.

Although not directly aligned with either of the two great European groups, the United States, nevertheless, began to give increased attention to the development of its military establishment. As a nation with newly acquired overseas possessions, it emphasized strengthening the Navy as its first line of defense without, however, neglecting the Army.

IMPLEMENTS OF WAR CHANGE RADICALLY

In response to technical and industrial progess and to rising international tensions, implements of war underwent rapid change around the turn of the century, forcing reforms in military organization, administration, and tactics. The new era found governments more willing than before to spend a larger portion of their national income on armaments and to adopt new ideas and weapons. Armies began to pay serious attention to developments in small arms, particularly the machine gun; they improved their artillery

and ammunition; and they acquired such new equipment as the motor vehicle, telephone, wireless, telegraph, and the airplane.

In the United States, the Krag-Jorgensen rifle, with which a part of the infantry was armed in the Spanish-American War and the Philippine Insurrection, gave way in 1903 to the improved bolt-action, magazine-type Springfield rifle. In it the Army had a rifle that was probably the best in the world. About the same time, the .45-caliber automatic pistol was developed for close fighting. Its adoption was based on experience in the Philippines where the U.S. forces had needed a side arm capable of stopping an attacking bolo-throwing fanatic in his tracks. More significant was the further development of the rapid-firing machine gun. In the 1880's a true automatic weapon using the recoil from a fired cartridge to bring the next into firing position had been invented by Hiram Maxim. About the same time John M. Browning invented a machine gun that utilized escaping gas from a fired shot to actuate a mechanism that brought another shell into place. The Army used some automatic weapons in the Spanish-American War, but it was not until World War I that their deadly effectiveness was fully demonstrated.

No munitions underwent greater changes in the late nineteenth and early twentieth centuries than artillery and artillery ammunition. Muzzle-loading cannon typical of most Civil War artillery gradually gave way to breechloaders. Smokeless powder was introduced, permitting a more rapid rate of fire since it eliminated the need of waiting for smoke clouds to clear after each round. When the hydro-pneumatic recoil system was adopted for artillery, still greater speed and accuracy were attained, because it overcame the backward roll that displaced an artillery piece from its position and permitted it to be refired immediately following a quick check for proper orientation on the target.

Improvement in explosives and the machining of guns and shells added greater accuracy and longer range. This in turn permitted indirect fire by a variety of guns. Artillery was divided in general into three classes: mortars, howitzers, and guns, each class differing in the trajectory of the projectile it fired. For example, a mortar lobbed shells at short range in a high curve, usually over high obstructions; a gun discharged projectiles in a flat curve; and a howitzer delivered its shells in a curve between the two. These differences in artillery were of little significance in the days when ranges were short, but the new and more powerful explosives made possible longer ranges and greater penetrating power. As a result, mortars temporarily fell into disuse, only to be revived in World War I as an infantry weapon for close fighting in trench warfare. Howitzers and guns, on the other hand, became standardized, the former for fire against enemy positions in fortified areas, the latter, with their longer range and high penetrating power, for use against more distant targets. Neither required a cannoneer to see his target.

The startling rise in the effectiveness of infantry and artillery weapons tended to restrict the role of cavalry and decrease its importance in certain areas. Against an enemy armed with machine guns and rapid-firing artillery, the heavy cavalry charge, which occasionally in the past had proved decisive in battle, could no longer prevail. Although still effective for reconnaissance, for combat in open country against a poorly equipped foe, and for dismounted action, cavalry was gradually relegated to a secondary role.

ELIHU ROOT RE-FORMS THE ARMY

In the demobilization that followed the War with Spain the U.S. Army suffered less loss of strength than in previous postwar periods, partly because the country still had military commitments, particularly in the Philippines. There was also a growing realization on the part of the American people that as a world power, the United States could no longer afford to allow its defenses to wither away completely. No one appreciated this more than Elihu Root, who became Secretary of War in 1899 and immediately began to prepare the Army for its new role. After studying the Army's experiences in the War with Spain, he became convinced that most of its mistakes could be traced directly to faulty military organization, specifically, the division of authority, in existence since the early nineteenth century, under which the Commanding General of the Army exercised discipline and control over the troops in the field while the Secretary of War, working through his bureau chiefs, handled administration and fiscal matters. Root recommended the elimination of dual control over the Army and the restoration of command in strictly military matters to the Army. Under his plan a Chief of Staff would take the place of the Commanding General of the Army

and be the responsible advisor and executive agent of the President through the Secretary of War. The formulation of Army policy, however, would remain under civil authority. Despite the opposition of diehards, Congress accepted Root's proposal in February 1903. But to pass a law was one thing; to change a system, hallowed by tradition, was another. The subordination of the bureau chiefs, in particular, proved to be a difficult task and was not quickly accomplished.

The second reform recommended by Root was the creation of a General Staff Corps, a group of selected officers free to devote full time to matters of policy and the preparation of military plans. In all previous national emergencies, Root pointed out, plans were drawn up hastily by officers already staggering under the load of other duties. Again Congress listened and adopted Root's recommendation. As a result, the Army, for the first time in its history, was in a position to develop a group of officers capable of scientific planning for war in time of peace. One of the early products of the new General Staff was the Field Service Regulations, published in 1905.

To keep the Army abreast of new ideas and requirements, several reforms affecting the noncombat services and the Special Staff also were introduced. The Medical Department was reorganized to include a Medical Corps, a Hospital Corps, an Army Nurse Corps, a Dental Corps, and a Medical Reserve Corps, the last designed to attract civilian physicians to serve during national emergencies. In 1912 the Subsistence and Pay Department was combined with the Quartermaster to create the Quartermaster Corps. An attempt was also made in that year to establish an Enlisted Reserve Corps, but without success, largely because the framers of the legislation did not provide for the payment, promotion, or training of the reservists. How complete the failure was is indicated by the fact that only 16 enlisted men were enrolled in the Enlisted Reserve Corps by 1914.

Annual maneuvers for units of regimental and occasionally larger size helped raise the professional qualifications of the Army, as did a reorganization of Army schools. A number of new schools were established for advanced and specialized study. Among them was the Army War College, opened in November 1903 to acquaint experienced officers with the problems of the War Department and to prepare them for high command in the field. An Army signal school was established in 1905, indicating the growing military importance of rapid signal communications. The Field Artillery School opened in 1911 and the School of Musketry in 1913.

Because of the disturbance in the Philippines and the need of troops to protect and garrison Alaska, Hawaii, and other overseas areas, a large part of the Regular Army served abroad after 1898. Even after the Philippine Insurrection was officially declared suppressed in mid-1902, American troops could not be withdrawn, for much remained to be done in stamping out scattered resistance and organizing and directing a native force known as the Philippine Scouts. Although the authorized strength of the Regular Army was 100,000 officers and men, organized into 30 infantry and 15 cavalry regiments supported by a corps of artillery, it did not reach that number. As a result, it could not fully meet

Ready for takeoff.
The Wright plane
at Fort Myer, Virginia, in 1908.

As spectators on the ground watch, the
Wright plane circles Fort Myer during
the 1908 tests.

The Army's first aviator, Lieutenant T. E.
Selfridge, lost his life when the Wright
plane crashed at Fort Myer on 17 September 1908.

Elihu Root. As Secretary of War from August
1899 until February 1904, he reorganized the
Army and created its General Staff.

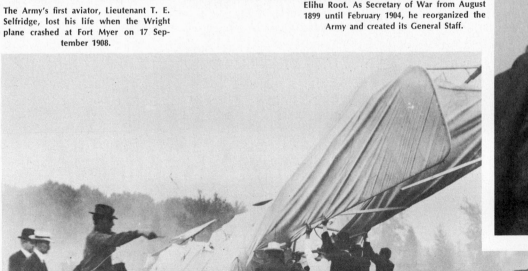

the requirements of both home defense and commitments abroad. Congress, therefore, decided to provide for the country's defense needs by strengthening the National Guard.

The Militia Act of 1903 provided the National Guard with Federal funds, prescribed drill at least twice a month, supplemented the drill periods with short annual training periods, and patterned the guard's organization and equipment after the Regular Army's. However, no National Guard unit could be called to Federal service without the consent of the governor of the state, and then not for more than nine months; no guardsman could be ordered to such service unless he volunteered; and no guard officer could be removed by any agency of the Federal government. These restrictions left the National Guard relatively free from Federal control. Changes introduced between 1908 and 1914 gave the President the right to prescribe the length of Federal service and, with the advice and consent of the Senate, to appoint all officers of the guard while in Federal service.

To improve training and to break down the barriers that had plagued relations between the Regular Army and the militia since the birth of the Nation, joint maneuvers were held from time to time after 1902. While these maneuvers failed to produce all the results sought, they encouraged coordination between the two components and helped to create a better integrated, more harmonious defense force, capable of immediate participation in a major conflict.

In response to changing conditions, the artillery in 1907 was divided into the Coast Artillery Corps and the Field Artillery. The purpose of the former was to plot and prepare underwater mine fields and to man the heavy guns in the new harbor defenses that had been constructed to protect American ports against hostile fleets. Its mission was not unlike that of the Navy. The Field Artillery, on the other hand, remained in the field army and its main mission, the support of the infantry in battle, was unchanged.

Experience in the Spanish-American War, observations of military developments abroad, and the Army's annual maneuvers all pointed to the need of permanent, self-sufficient units, composed of the combined arms. Regiments, the largest peacetime units then in existence, afforded no training in the command of large units or in meeting the special problems of supply and administration created by brigades and divisions. To remedy the situation the General Staff in 1910 drew up a plan for three permanent infantry divisions to be composed of Regular Army and National Guard regiments. However, difficulties arose along the Mexican border before the plan could be put into operation. Instead, a provisional "maneuver division" was hastily organized in 1911 and its component units were ordered to the border in the hope that an immediate show of force would discourage further disturbances.

What actually happened was disappointing. No division could be assembled quickly. Regular Army troops had to be collected from widely scattered points in the continental United States, and every post, depot, and arsenal had to be denuded to scrape up the necessary equipment. Even so, when the "maneuver division" was finally brought together, it was far from fully operational since none of its regiments were up to strength or adequately armed. Fortunately, the efficiency of the "maneuver division" was not put to a battle test, and within a short time the division was broken up and its component units returned to their home stations. An effort was made to organize the scattered military posts so that their garrisons could join one of three paper divisions, but this was hardly more than a short step in the direction of the mobile, well-trained, and well-equipped force required.

The Wrights brought an improved version of their plane to Fort Myer in 1909. This picture was taken during a test flight. The Army accepted the plane in August of that year and it became "Aeroplane No. 1, Heavier-than-Air Division, United States aerial fleet."

The Army's interest in aeronautics goes back to the captive balloons used during the Civil War. Interest in heavier-than-air flying equipment, powered by the internal combustion engine, also began early; in fact, it began before a successful flight was made. In 1898 the War Department subsidized Dr. Samuel P. Langley's experiments, but withdrew its support in 1903 when his ill-fated plane crashed into the Potomac River. Perhaps as a result of Langley's failure attempts on the part of Wilbur and Orville Wright to prove that their machine could pass Army tests were at first rebuffed, and it was not until late in 1908 that their plane was given a trial. The results of the test indicated that the Army had a promising new weapon within its grasp. But when Congress was asked for funds to further its development, the request was denied. Meanwhile, other nations were paying considerably more attention to the weapon that was to influence warfare so profoundly. By 1913, France, Russia, Germany, and England were spending millions annually on aviation. Even Mexico was spending $400,000 yearly at a time when the United States was devoting only $125,000 to aviation. In July 1914 Congress authorized the creation of an Aviation Section in the Signal Corps to be composed of 60 officers and 260 enlisted men. But this group accomplished little, partly because the young air enthusiasts in it received only grudging and tardy support from their superiors. Consequently, only a few planes were available on the Mexican border in 1916, and most of them broke down. When the United States entered World War I, the Army discovered that it had been left behind in aviation by startling developments abroad, not only in equipment but in organization and doctrine as well. Its pilots were required to learn as they fought in foreign aircraft, for not a single American-made fighter plane reached the Western Front before the armistice, despite the millions of dollars poured into the effort to catch up with the other powers.

The Army's second airplane, a Wright Type B lent to it by publisher Robert F. Collier, at Fort Sam Houston, Texas, in 1911.

Two of the Army's pioneer aviators.

311

THE ARMY BUILDS THE PANAMA CANAL

A logical result of the emergence of the United States as a world power with a primary interest in the Caribbean was the construction of an interocean canal. The strategic need of such a waterway had been deeply impressed upon the American people during the Spanish-American War by the long voyage of the battleship **Oregon** from Puget Sound on the west coast around South America to Cuban waters where it arrived just in time to participate in the destruction of Cervera's fleet off Santiago. President Theodore Roosevelt was widely supported when he rather arbitrarily set diplomatic and political machinery in motion to acquire the sole right to complete the canal begun earlier in Panama by the French company headed by Ferdinand de Lesseps, builder of the Suez Canal. Toward the end of 1903, all political obstacles had been overcome sufficiently to permit work on the project to begin as soon as Congress appropriated funds and decided who should do the work.

After considerable deliberation and negotiations with a civilian engineering firm, the conclusion was reached that building the canal was a job for the Army rather than private enterprise. A commission of Army officers under Colonel George W. Goethals, who served as Chairman and Chief Engineer and a little later as Civil Governor of the Canal Zone as well, was set up to supervise the task of construction. An able soldier and expert administrator, Goethals pushed construction to completion in eight years. In this task he was ably supported by the Army's Medical Department which rigidly applied the principles of field sanitation and the knowledge acquired in the Cuban occupation. Malaria was quickly brought under control, yellow fever, the curse of the Tropics, was wiped out, and the Canal

An early stage in the construction of the Panama Canal.

Major General George W. Goethals. As a colonel he was placed in complete charge of construction work on the Panama Canal.

Pedro Miguel locks in July 1910.

Zone was transformed from a pesthole into a healthy and attractive place for human habitation. The canal, a lasting monument to the technical ability and efficiency of the Army, reduced the heavy cost of maintaining an enormous fleet in both the Atlantic and Pacific since it permitted vessels to move quickly to any point of need in either ocean. On the other hand, it created a strategic point in the continental defense system which required for its protection the strongest and most up-to-date facilities manned by permanent highly trained garrisons.

PERSHING'S PURSUIT OF VILLA IN MEXICO

As has already been noted, in 1911 border disturbances had threatened to upset the peace between Mexico and the United States. Internal trouble in Mexico led to further disturbances culminating in a surprise attack on Columbus, New Mexico, by General Francisco Villa and some 1,500 men. A number of American troops and civilians were killed in the raid which took place on 9 March 1916. Considerable property was destroyed before units of the 13th Cavalry drove off the raiders. The following day, President Wilson ordered Brigadier General John J. Pershing into Mexico to assist the Mexican Government in taking Villa.

On 15 March the punitive expedition entered Mexico in "hot pursuit." It chased Villa through unfriendly territory for hundreds of miles, never quite catching up with him but managing to disperse most of his followers. Although Mexican President Carranza could not suppress Villa, he soon showed that he had no desire to have the United States do the job for him by protesting the continued presence of American troops in Mexico and insisting on their withdrawal. Carranza's attitude, plus orders from the War Department forbidding attacks on Mexicans that were not followers of Villa, made it extremely difficult for Pershing to deal effectively with Villa and his band. Some clashes with government troops actually took place, the most important one at Carrizal where scores were killed or wounded. The action once again created a critical situation, and led President Wilson to call 75,000 National Guardsmen into Federal service to help police the border. War probably would have broken out then and there but for the bitter struggle raging in Europe. Anxious not to become involved

in Mexico at a time when relations with Germany were deteriorating, Wilson agreed to submit the disputes arising out of the punitive expedition to a joint commission for settlement. Some time later the commission ruled, among other things, that the American unit commander involved in the Carrizal affair was at fault. In January 1917, as the relations between the United States and Germany approached the critical stage, the expedition was withdrawn.

Although Pershing failed to capture Villa, the activities of the American troops in Mexico and along the border were not wasted effort. The dispersal of Villa's band put an end to serious border incidents. More important from a military point of view was the intensive training in the field received by both the Regular Army and the National Guard on the border and in Mexico. Many defects in the Military Establishment, especially in the National Guard, were uncovered in time to correct them before the Army was thrown into the cauldron of war in Europe. One other result that can be attributed to the experiences of the Army on the border, in part at least, was the passage of much-needed new legislation affecting national defense.

THE NATIONAL DEFENSE ACT OF JUNE 1916

In June 1916 Congress passed a National Defense Act which made possible the retention of the National Guard on the border as long as necessary by empowering the President, when authorized by Congress, to call it into Federal service for the duration of a national emergency, not merely for the nine months permitted under the act of 1903. Congress also reasserted the principle embodied in law since 1792 that all able-bodied men between the ages of eighteen and forty-five were subject to military service. In reaffirming this principle, Congress made possible the translation of an indefinite military obligation into compulsory service in time of war, thereby paving the way for the passage of the Selective Service Act of May 1917. The National Defense Act provided for an Officers' Reserve Corps and an Enlisted Reserve Corps, the latter to be formed from men who wished to enroll after completing active duty. Maximum Regular Army strength was increased to about 288,000 men, organized into 65 infantry, 25 cavalry, and 21 artillery regiments, 91 coast artillery companies, and the necessary service units to support them. To fill the recognized need for large-sized tactical organizations in being rather than

General Francisco (Pancho) Villa.

U.S. cavalrymen pursuing Villa in April 1916.

The leader of the punitive expedition, Brigadier General John J. Pershing (right foreground), and some of his troops crossing a river in Mexico.

on paper, these units were assigned to brigades and divisions. The National Guard was authorized up to 425,000 men. The act also provided for increased support of military training in colleges and summer camps, an important and necessary step in meeting an expanding army's need for officers. The flaw in the bill was the provision which required increases to be spread over a period of five years. Failure to provide for immediate enlargement left the Army with only some 5,000 officers and 123,000 men in the Regular Army and 8,500 officers and 123,000 men in the National Guard on the eve of America's entry into World War I.

Lieutenant George S. Patton, who won fame as a World War II general, was Pershing's aide in Mexico.

A U.S. Army supply depot in Mexico.

THE MILITARY HISTORY OF THE FLAG

Flags are almost as old as civilization itself. Archeological records abound with these symbols and devices of mankind.

The dictionary defines a flag as "a light cloth bearing a device or devices . . ."; but even the most ardent realist must admit that a flag is more than mere cloth and color. Indeed, any effort to explain the flag fully is as hopeless as an attempt to describe the soul.

THE FIRST STARS AND STRIPES.

Birth of the present United States Flag is tied so closely with the birth of the U.S. Army that today we celebrate Flag Day on 14 June, the anniversary of the Army. But before adoption of the original Stars and Stripes, in 1777, varying forms of flags with red and white alternating stripes were used at different times and places. And other flags, too, were used by various units. On many occasions men fought under flags never used again, and now almost forgotten. Some of the flags of the Revolutionary era are shown here.

PERSONAL EMBLEM OF COMMODORE HOPKINS' FLAGSHIP, 1775.

BENNINGTON FLAG.

MOULTRIE.

WASHINGTON'S CRUISERS.

BUNKER HILL FLAG.

315

The Grand Union Flag

The Grand Union flag, sometimes called the "First Navy Ensign" and the "Cambridge Flag," among other designations, was the immediate predecessor of the Stars and Stripes. This type of flag was carried on the flagship "Alfred" on 3 December 1775 as the naval ensign of the Thirteen Colonies, after Commodore Esek Hopkins assumed command of the Navy built by Congress. It was hoisted by General Washington in January 1776, at Cambridge, Massachusetts, as the standard of the Continental Army, and it was also carried ashore by the Marines who made an expedition to the Bahamas in March of 1776. As the flag of the Revolution, it was used on many occasions before 14 June 1777, when the Continental Congress authorized the Stars and Stripes. The canton, with its crosses of St. George and St. Andrew, indicated our relation with the "mother country" until the severance of those ties brought about its replacement with the white stars in a blue field. Washington later wrote that it was flown at Cambridge "out of compliment to the United Colonies."

The First Stars and Stripes

The Stars and Stripes, whose birthday we observe on 14 June, was created on that date, in 1777, when the Continental Congress resolved: "That the flag of the thirteen United States be thirteen stripes, alternate red and white: that the union be thirteen stars, white in a blue field, representing a new constellation." The first Army flag had the stars arranged in a circle, presumably based on the idea that no colony should take precedence. The first Navy Stars and Stripes, flown by the man-of-war "Guerriere" when she sailed from Boston on 25 July 1818, for Cowes, England, had the stars arranged in staggered formation in alternate lines and rows of threes and twos on the field of blue. However, on 9 September 1818, the Board of Navy Commissioners received a directive from President Monroe that "the Flag of the United States shall conform to the pattern, herewith transmitted, viz: twenty stars in a blue union, and thirteen stripes, red and white, alternately, according to the Act of Congress passed on the fourth of April last; of which you will please to give due notice to the Naval Commanders, and the necessary directions for making the Flags."

Fifteen Stars and Stripes

Following an Act of Congress on 13 January 1794, this was the flag of our country from 1795 until 1818. The addition of the two stars and two stripes came with the admission of Vermont, 4 March 1791, and Kentucky, 1 June 1792, into the Union. This type of flag figured in many stirring episodes. It inspired Francis Scott Key to write the "Star-Spangled Banner"; it was the first flag to be hoisted over a fortress of the Old World, when Lieutenant Presley N. O'Bannon, of the Marine Corps, and Midshipman Mann, of the Navy, raised it above the Tripolitan stronghold in Derne, Tripoli, on 27 April 1805; it was our ensign in the Battle of Lake Erie; and was flown by General Jackson at New Orleans. Fearing that too many stripes would spoil the true design of the flag, Congress passed a law on 4 April 1818 returning the flag to its original design of thirteen stripes and providing for a new star to be added to the blue field as additional States came into the Union. Thus, for nearly a quarter of a century, this flag with its fifteen stars and stripes was the banner of our growing Nation.

Speaking of the Flag of the United States, President Woodrow Wilson once said:
"This Flag, which we honor and under which we serve, is the emblem of our unity, our power, our thought and purpose as a nation. It has no other character than that which we give it from generation to generation. The choices are ours. It floats in majestic silence above the hosts that execute those choices, whether in peace or war. And yet, though silent, it speaks to us—speaks to us of the past, of the men and women who went before us, and of the records they wrote upon it."

The Flag of Liberation

The Stars and Stripes, which in 1941 flew over the United States Capitol on 8 December when we declared war on Japan and on 11 December when we declared war on Germany and Italy, has indeed proved to be the "flag of liberation." This same flag went with President Roosevelt to Algiers, Casablanca, and other historic places, and flew over the conquered cities of Rome, Berlin, and Toyko.

The Stars and Stripes that flew over Pearl Harbor on 7 December 1941 rippled above the United Nations Charter meeting at San Francisco and over the Big Three conference at Potsdam. This same flag was flying over the White House on 14 August 1945, when the Japanese accepted surrender terms.

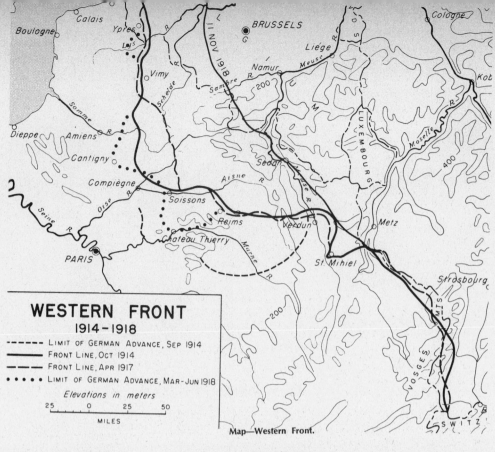

WESTERN FRONT
1914–1918

- - - - - - LIMIT OF GERMAN ADVANCE, SEP 1914
———— FRONT LINE, OCT 1914
- - - - FRONT LINE, APR 1917
• • • • • LIMIT OF GERMAN ADVANCE, MAR-JUN 1918

Elevations in meters

25   0   25   50

MILES

Map—Western Front.

CHAPTER 12

WORLD WAR I

Shortly after the beginning of trouble with Mexico, the long period of peace between the armed camps in Europe suddenly ended and the Continent burst into flame. The spark that set it off was the assassination of the heir to the Austro-Hungarian throne by a fanatical Serbian nationalist in the Balkan city of Sarajevo on 28 June 1914. Supported by the German Government, which believed a localized settlement possible, the Austro-Hungarian Government sent an ultimatum to Serbia, making demands that were rejected; whereupon Austria-Hungary declared war. Events moved swiftly, and by 4 August, Germany, France, Russia, England, and Belgium were drawn into the struggle, while Italy, a lukewarm member of the Triple Alliance, declared itself neutral. Before the conflict ended, many other nations were drawn into it. Turkey and Bulgaria joined Austria-Hungary and Germany, while Japan, Italy, China, the United States, and others joined the Allies. Europe was the center of military activity, but campaigns were also fought in Asia and Africa, and almost every ocean witnessed some naval activity. All told, about 65,000,000 men were mobilized of whom 10,000,000 were killed. In lives lost and wealth expended no previous war in history approached it in magnitude.

German strategy in case of war on two fronts called for the quick destruction of the French armies in the west before Russia could mobilize, then a rapid shifting of forces to the east and the defeat of the Russian armies at will. During the first few weeks of World War I it appeared that the German plan might succeed. But the Germans made two serious mistakes. The first was the modification of the "Schlieffen Plan," prepared years before the war by Germany's famous Chief of Staff, Count Alfred von Schlieffen. That war plan had aimed at encircling the French armies by a wide sweep through the Low Countries and northern France and then crushing them against fixed German fortifications in Lorraine. But the Germans, by withdrawing units from the right flank to bolster the Eastern Front and shifting troops to the center, found themselves in the summer and fall of 1914 incapable of enveloping the French.

The second major German error was the underestimation of the time it would take the Russian Army to mobilize and launch an attack on Germany. The Russians began to move much sooner than the Germans expected. To meet the danger, the Germans withdrew two corps from the west and sent them to the Eastern Front. Before they arrived, however, the German forces already in the east destroyed the Russian armies in the battles of Tannenberg and Masurian Lakes in August and September 1914. Had the two corps been retained in the west where they were badly needed, it might not have been necessary for the Germans to withdraw to positions behind the Aisne River after losing the critical Battle of the Marne in September.

After the Battle of the Marne the Allies vigorously attacked the Germans on the Aisne but failed to dent their skillfully chosen and well-organized positions. The stalemate along the Aisne was followed by a "race to the sea," in

Cavalry leaving Berlin after the declaration of war in August 1914.

German airmen before a mission in June 1917.

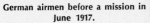

Shock troops of the German Army cutting their way through barbed wire entanglements.

which each side sought to envelop the northern flank of the other in successive battles. By October the race was over, neither side having won. Fortunately for the Allies they retained all the channel ports west of Ostend. Loss of these ports would have seriously handicapped England in supplying her forces on the Continent and would have given the Germans valuable bases for future naval operations.

With the flanks of both opposing armies securely protected by the sea on the north and by neutral Switzerland on the south, the only hope of victory for either side lay in a successful penetration of the line of the other. The story of the war on the Western Front from that time until the end of hostilities deals largely with the efforts of first one belligerent and then the other to break through its opponent's defense system. Against a well-dug-in defender, skillfully coordinating terrain with firepower, no attacker, however high his offensive spirit, could hope to prevail without first attaining overwhelming superiority in men and weapons. Because of superior long-range artillery and greater skill in the use of field fortifications, barbed wire, machine guns, mortars, and grenades, the Germans initially enjoyed an advantage. To overcome it, the Allies had to raise and train vast armies and produce munitions and supplies on an unprecedented scale. In industrial potential,

Field Marshal Paul von Hindenberg, chief of the German Army's General Staff (center) at his Western Front headquarters in June, 1917, when the military situation was very favorable to Germany, and German morale was high.

The German submarine "U-139." In 1915 the "U-139" sank the British liner "Lusitania" with a loss of 1,195 lives.

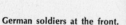

German soldiers at the front.

economic strength, and manpower the advantage was distinctly with the Allies. The unanswered question was: could it be transferred to the battlefield in time to prevent the Germans from breaking the deadlock and winning a decision?

It was natural for the American people, drawn as they were from many nations and chiefly from those at war, to display an intense interest in the struggle in Europe. Ignoring the admonition of President Wilson to remain "impartial in thought as well as in action," most Americans soon took sides. The side they chose was determined as much by emotion as by knowledge of the underlying

causes of the conflict. Despite the strong passions exhibited, there was at first little desire to become involved. The tradition of noninvolvement in European affairs was still firmly fixed in the American mind, but as time went on and the conflict grew more violent and bitter, the spirit of neutrality gradually weakened.

From the start both sides interfered with the trade of nonbelligerents. The British Navy dominated the seas and blockaded not only Germany but neutral European nations as well. The British arbitrarily added to the list of prohibited items many commodities not normally considered contraband of war under international law, blacklisted firms suspected of trading directly or indirectly with the Central Powers, and ordered neutral shipping into British ports for search. Germany, unable to use its surface fleet, resorted to submarines to stop the flow of supplies to the Allies, thereby inaugurating a new type of blockade, the legality of which was at once questioned. To meet this threat, Great Britain armed merchant vessels and directed them to fire at submarines on sight. Contending that the protection of international law did not extend to armed merchantmen, Germany retaliated by ordering enemy cargo ships sunk without warning. As was to be expected, the Germans could not avoid errors of identification. A climax was reached in 1915 when the British liner **Lusitania** was sunk off the coast of Ireland with the loss of 1,195 lives, including 124 Americans.

THE UNITED STATES IS DRAWN INTO THE WAR, APRIL 1917

The United States protested the violation of neutral rights by both belligerents but in stronger terms to Germany since its actions involved the destruction of life. In April 1916, after President Wilson threatened to break off diplomatic relations unless it discontinued unrestricted submarine warfare, Germany agreed not to sink passenger ships and to warn all other vessels before attacking them, provided they offered no resistance. For a while the promise was kept and tension eased. But early in 1917, following Allied rejection of a peace offer, Germany announced a return to unrestricted submarine warfare in a zone covering the approaches to Great Britain and France; whereupon the United States at once severed diplomatic relations.

The succession of events now hastened the United States along the road to war. Early in March American opinion was shocked by the publication of an intercepted German message to the Mexican Government, the Zimmerman note, which proposed an alliance between Germany and Mexico if the United States entered the war. Shortly afterward, President Wilson announced that American merchant ships would be armed, and on the same day an American ship was sunk under circumstances which for the first time permitted no excuse whatever on grounds of error. In the next few days four more American ships fell victim to German U-boats. Six Americans lost their lives. With public opinion aroused, Congress on 6 April 1917 declared war on Germany.

In returning to unrestricted submarine warfare, the German Government was fully aware that it risked war with the United States. It had taken the risk largely because German naval leaders were confident that unrestricted submarine warfare would bring the Allies to their knees before American arms could become a decisive factor. The decline in Allied morale also gave Germany hope of ultimate victory. France, Italy, and Russia were all showing signs of war-weariness, and the Germans had every reason to believe that Russia at least might soon be eliminated from the war, permitting them to concentrate most of their military strength in the west.

The German Army, therefore, went on the defensive in the west during 1917, shortened its lines to save manpower, and concentrated its strength in the east where a revolutionary Russian government headed by Alexander Kerensky had launched a last offensive. When it failed, the Germans counterattacked. The Russian armies disintegrated rapidly; the Kerensky government was overthrown; and by November the Bolsheviks under Lenin and Trotsky, who had come to power with the connivance of Germany, agreed to talk peace. After several months of haggling over terms, during which the Germans advanced to the outskirts of St. Petersburg, the Bolsheviks on 3 March 1918 signed a treaty at Brest-Litovsk taking their country out of the war. Russia's collapse released enough men and guns to enable Germany to gain a temporary numerical superiority on the Western Front for the first time since the early days of the war.

General Pershing Arrives in France, June 1917

Shortly after entering the war the United States sent elements of the American Expeditionary Force under Major General John J. Pershing to France, where they arrived in June 1917. The choice of Pershing proved to be an excellent one; he was professionally competent, a natural leader, a thorough organizer, and a strict disciplinarian. During his career in the Army he had carried out every mission given him with imagination and vigor.

After studying Allied needs in men and arms, Pershing advised the War Department to prepare to send 1,000,000 trained men to Europe within a year and to lay plans for raising a total force of 3,000,000—a figure that was later increased to 4,000,000 by the War Department. The strength

Major General John J. Pershing, Commander in Chief of the American Expeditionary Forces, arrives in France on 13 June 1917.

321

of the Army at the time was about 200,000 men, 65,000 of whom were National Guardsmen in Federal service. To increase the Army twentyfold and train it was a tremendous task, one that would require considerable time even under the most favorable conditions.

Many uninformed people had visions of hundreds of thousands of "Yankees" pouring into France within a short time to give the Allies the overwhelming numerical superiority needed to drive the invader across the Rhine and bring the war to a close. As the months passed with the arrival of nothing more than a token force, the high hopes of the spring and summer of 1917 gave way to disillusionment. What many failed to appreciate was that raising a military force of several million men involved more than merely calling them to the colors. For such a task existing facilities, equipment, and instructors were completely inadequate.

The Selective Service Act of May 1917

It was clear from the start that the time-honored volunteer system could not provide all the men needed by the Army. A form of conscription was required, but conscription was not popular, many Americans believing that compulsory service was unbefitting a free people, particularly if administered by military authority. Newton D. Baker, the Secretary of War, hoped to overcome this opposition by placing the draft machinery in the hands of civilian boards. Based on Baker's proposal, Congress passed the Selective Service Act on 19 May 1917. The act established a National Army and required all males between the ages of twenty-one and thirty to register for service, later, the age was raised to forty-five. The law also permitted volunteering for the Regular Army, National Guard, Marine Corps, and Navy. It specifically prohibited the twin evils of the Civil War period, the hiring of substitutes and the payment of bounties to induce enlistments.

On 5 June 1917 the first million men registered for service, and from this initial reservoir of manpower conscripts were chosen by lot. Within three months, the first draftees, numbering 180,000, were selected, screened, and sent to training camps. Other contingents followed periodically thereafter until the end of the war, when conscription was suspended. About 67 percent of the men serving in the Army during World War I were brought in under the Selective Service Act. Under the system, 2,810,296 men were selected and delivered to the armed forces in less than 18 months.

Officer Selection

The selection and training of officers for the National Army was a far more difficult task than providing men for the ranks. When war broke out there were less than 9,000 officers in Federal service. About 200,000 were needed. In previous wars appointments directly from civilian life had largely met officer requirements, often to the detriment of the men in the ranks. In World War I the Army attempted to select prospective officers on the basis of proved leadership and capacity to command. Only specialists, such as doctors and individuals qualified for duty in supply and technical services, received direct commissions. Officers for

other assignments were obtained from qualified enlisted men of the Regular Army, from the Reserve Officers' Training Corps and Student Army Training Corps in colleges and universities, and from officer training camps. The last produced most of the officers commissioned during the war. Candidates for commissions were carefully selected for the camps and then subjected to intensive training for a period of about three months. Those who made the grade, about 60 percent of the number originally enrolled, were commissioned in the new National Army. Their capacity for leadership far exceeded that of the average officer in any previous war. It was largely these new officers who led the troops that helped defeat Germany in 1918, winning by their deeds the respect of friend and foe alike.

Reorganization of the Army

Reports from observers in Europe early in the war convinced the War Department that the existing organization of the Army, particularly the infantry division, was not suited for the type of war that was being fought on the Western Front. A division capable of greater and longer-sustained driving power was needed. On the recommendation of General Pershing the strength of the infantry division was therefore increased to 27,000 men—later 28,000—and the division was reorganized into 2 infantry brigades of 2 regiments each, a field artillery brigade, a regiment of combat engineers, 3 machine gun battalions, and supporting service troops. These changes made the American infantry division roughly twice the size of the British, French, and German infantry divisions of the time. The enlarged division, though unwieldly and difficult to control, had tremendous striking and staying power, the characteristics that experience proved were most needed to crash through enemy defenses on the Western Front.

The War Department organized 62 divisions during World War I. At the close of the war 43 of these had been sent to France and 19 others were in various stages of organization and training. At first the National Guard and National Army divisions comprised men from particular areas, but, as fillers and replacements from all parts of the land were assigned to these divisions, they became almost as thoroughly mixed as the Regular Army divisions.

Establishing a New System of Logistics

Probably the most difficult organizational problem that the Army had to deal with in World War I was the establishment of a smooth-functioning logistical system for both the Zone of Interior and the theatre of operations. To support it, the resources of the nation were mobilized as never before. Most of 1917 was devoted to the retooling and expansion of industrial plants, to the construction of barracks and facilities to house troops, and to estimating requirements and letting contracts. New weapons were slow in rolling from factories, and many of the first men drafted were trained with dummy or obsolete weapons. To speed up the arming of troops the War Department adopted the British Lee-Enfield rifle modified to take U.S. ammunition. Manufacture of the Springfield .03 rifle was curtailed, and the 600,000 available were issued to Regular Army units only. The British and French supplied machine guns and automatic rifles for most of the Army. But those troops reaching France after 1 July 1918 were armed with Browning machine guns and automatic rifles that proved to be far more reliable and effective than those bought from the Allies. The artillery used by the Army was acquired in large part from the French. Planes and tanks were furnished by both France and Great Britain. The United States did produce an excellent 12-cylinder Liberty airplane engine, which was put into the British de Havilland 4, an observation and daytime bombing plane. The United States succeeded in manufacturing some aircraft for war purposes, but, on the whole, its plane production program was unsuccessful, particularly in the categories of fighters and bombers. For those, the United States remained dependent on the Allies through-

out the war despite untold millions spent on development.

Transportation is one of the most critical elements in any logistics system. The shipment of some 2,000,000 men across 3,000 miles of ocean was the major movement problem confronting the United States in World War I. The problem was the more difficult because there was no previous experience to guide those dealing with a task of such magnitude. Success demanded an unprecedented number of ships of all kinds, the organization of ports, the construction of piers, warehouses, roads, railroads, and planning and coordination all along the line of communications from the source of production to the point of delivery in the theatre of operations.

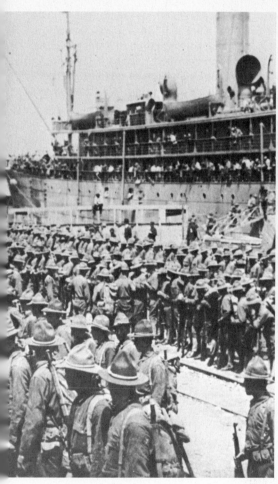

The "Leviathan," formerly the German liner "Vaterland," in service as an American troop transport.

The first American troops arrive at Saint-Nazaire, France, on 26 June 1917.

A convoy of transports en route to Europe. Almost 50 percent of the transports landed in England, and the troops traveled by train and Channel steamer to France.

Shortly after the first contingent of American troops arrived in France, the Allies began to exert pressure to have them fed into their armies ostensibly for training purposes. Actually they sought replacements to bolster the sagging strength of their battalions. General Pershing, with the full support of the War Department, opposed the demands on the ground that integration would destroy confidence and national pride, two main characteristics in a successful fighting force, and prevent the training of his higher officers in command and staff responsibilities. The commander of the AEF was not so obstinate in his view, however, that he clung to it at the cost of Allied defeat, for he offered the unrestricted use of his troops in the crisis created by the German breakthrough in March 1918. Instead of allowing his troops to be parceled out, Pershing sought and obtained an area near Lorraine where his forces could concentrate, train, and eventually fight. The buildup was slow at first, but it speeded up rapidly during the spring and summer of 1918.

Pershing Reorganizes the AEF

The size and complexity of the AEF convinced General Pershing that success in battle would be impossible without efficient staff work. This required a large number of trained officers using a common system under uniform methods. After studying British and French staffs, Pershing adopted an organization largely patterned after that of the French. The staff had three main divisions, a general staff, a technical staff, and an administrative staff. The general staff was divided into sections which varied in number depending upon size of the command. For Pershing's headquarters (GHO) and army headquarters there were five sections: G-1, Administration; G-2, Intelligence; G-3, Operations; G-4, Coordination (Supply Replacements); and G-5, Training. In corps and division headquarters the number of general staff sections was limited to three. A chief of staff was responsible for the coordination of the general staff and the technical and administrative staffs at all headquarters down to and including the division.

To train staff officers, Pershing set up a staff college near Chaumont and directed that only graduates of the school would be assigned to vacancies in staff positions. The result was that uniformity soon supplanted variety in staff organization and operations. It made possible the skillful management of the largest force of U.S. troops ever assembled in the field up to that time.

French Marshal Ferdinand Foch (left) and General Pershing at the latter's headquarters at Chaumont.

En route to a training area in France. American units received intensive training in an area to the rear of the front lines, then served in a quiet sector with French or British troops, and finally completed training in a sector of their own.

THE GERMANS LAUNCH THEIR OFFENSIVE: MARCH 1918

By the end of 1917 German hopes of winning the war through unrestricted submarine warfare were fading. But there still was time to strike a decisive blow in the west before the full strength of American arms could be brought to bear. With more troops available as a result of the collapse of Russia, Germany decided to resume the offensive. Field Marshal Erich von Ludendorff selected the Somme area for the attack, hoping that a breakthrough there would drive a wedge between the French and the British and that a British defeat would cause the French to lose heart and agree to peace.

On 21 March the first blow fell with shattering force on the British. Their lines were pierced, and for a time it looked as though the German advance might develop into a pursuit. By 26 March Amiens, a strategically located rail center, was in serious danger. If it fell, continued cooperation between the French and British armies would be difficult if not impossible. In the crisis Ludendorff hurled 20 fresh divisions into the battle, but they were repulsed. On 27 March when a gap was created between the French and British armies, German troops, exhausted and out of supplies, were unable to exploit the situation. Allied reserves moved rapidly into the threatened area by rail and succeeded in plugging the gap. By the end of the month the German

American soldiers on duty at an outpost in the Vosges region in March 1918. The position was destroyed by gunfire a few minutes after the picture was taken.

Americans on patrol near Badonviller in the Vosges region.

The 28th Infantry of the 1st Division going "over the top" at Cantigny on the morning of 28 May 1918. The 1st Division was the first American unit to enter the line on an active battlefront.

drive, bogged down in mud and debris, had lost its momentum, and by 5 April the offensive was definitely over. Tactically the Germans had won a brilliant victory. Leading units had succeeded in breaking through the Allied positions and had advanced 40 miles in 8 days, taking 70,000 prisoners and 1,100 guns and inflicting about 200,000 casualties. But strategically the offensive was not successful. The British Army, although seriously battered, was not destroyed; Amiens was not captured; and lateral communications between the Allies were not disrupted. For their gains the Germans had paid a high price in human life, particularly in the shock divisions whose trained men could least be spared.

The Allies Hold in Flanders

Despite the indecisive battle on the Somme, General Ludendorff clung to his basic plan to destroy the British Army before dealing with the French and the Americans. On 9 April he chose to strike in the Lys area in Flanders, north of the previous point of attack. As before, he succeeded initially in overrunning British positions and inflicting heavy damage. So desperate was the situation that Field Marshal Sir Douglas Haig, the British commander-in-chief, issued a "backs to the wall" order, urging his troops to fight to the end. He also appealed to Marshal Ferdinand Foch, the newly appointed Supreme Commander of the Allied Forces, for help, thus putting the principle of unity of command to its first great test. The Supreme Commander, convinced that the British could hold and determined to regain the initiative, refused to commit his reserves to battle. His decision proved to be sound. The British held, and, as on the Somme, the Germans failed to win a decision. On 29 April, having committed 46 divisions to action, General Ludendorff called off the offensive. For a few weeks quiet reigned on the Western Front, punctuated only by local attacks, air battles, and a long-range artillery bombardment of Paris.

The Germans Attack Chemin des Dames

Still hoping to defeat the British and roll them back to the channel ports, Ludendorff planned to renew the battle in Flanders as soon as he had regrouped his forces. To attain surprise, he decided on a diversionary attack on the Chemin des Dames, a dominant ridge east of the Aisne River. The position had become a quiet sector to which battle-weary Allied divisions were sent to recuperate. The assault on the Chemin des Dames began on 27 May following a short but intensive shelling of Allied lines. The bombardment was the more effective because much of the defending force had been deployed well forward by the local commander. By the end of the first day the Germans had reached all their objectives, advancing 13 miles and taking most of the bridges across the Aisne before the French could destroy them. This unexpected success led Ludendorff to change his plans. What he had conceived as a diversionary attack to prevent the French from supporting the British, he now decided to turn into a major offensive. He rushed reserves forward and ordered the advance to continue in the hope that the momentum of the attack would enable the Germans to establish bridgeheads across the Marne for future use should he decide on a drive toward Paris.

The Battle of Château-Thierry

By 29 May the Germans had reached Château-Thierry, less than 40 miles from Paris, and the situation looked very dark indeed for the Allies. In the crisis the French commander appealed to Pershing for help. He responded with two divisions. The 3d Division was rushed to the scene by rail and motor, arriving just as the Germans prepared to cross the Marne. In a three-day battle beginning 1 June every German effort to establish a bridgehead was repulsed. West of Château-Thierry, the 2d Division, including a brigade of marines, was comitted to action along the Château-Thierry–Paris road. There, too, the Germans were checked in a series of bitterly fought local actions which culminated in an American attack that recaptured Belleau Wood and the villages of Bouresches and Vaux. The price paid at Belleau Wood was high, but the action changed German opinion on the combat effectiveness of American troops from one of open skepticism to respect.

Though checked, the offensive on the Aisne was a tactical success for the Germans. But it left them in a dangerous salient, its western side supplied mainly by an exposed railroad that ran close to the Allied lines and through the town of Soissons. Ludendorff held on to this weak positions because of the adverse effect a withdrawal would have on German morale. His decision to stay led later to a counteroffensive in which American forces played a leading role.

The Allies Capture Cantigny

Meanwhile, in another sector, American troops undertook their first offensive. Following the German attack on the Somme, the 1st Division was assigned an active sector west of the farthest point of German advance. This was considered the hottest spot in the line. On high ground to the front lay the village of Cantigny, which afforded the Germans good observation of Allied lines and concealed their own activities. Its capture would reverse the situation and give a much-needed boost to Allied morale. On 28 May, as the Germans broke through on the Aisne, the 1st Division, supported by American and French artillery and French tanks and flamethrowers, launched its attack. Success was immediate and complete. Cantigny was not only taken but held against strong German counterattacks. This engagement, though only a local affair, proved the ability of the American soldiers to fight offensively and bolstered sagging Allied morale.

The cars in this picture are taking soldiers of the 2d Division to a rest camp. The Division had just completed a tour of duty in the front lines.

Responding to a request from the French for help, the U.S. 3d Division leaves for Château-Thierry in June 1918.

A 3d Division machine-gun crew in position at Château-Thierry.

American troops in the public square at Château-Thierry.

The bridge at Château-Thierry was blown up to prevent a German crossing of the Marne River.

The Germans Plan Two Attacks

As a result of their first three offensives of 1918, the Germans had driven three salients into the Allied defenses. Although the supply line of each salient was vulnerable, Ludendorff still retained the initiative and held to his basic plan—the defeat of the British in Flanders. To retain the initiative he had to act soon, for the balance in manpower was shifting rapidly to the Allies as American troops arrived by the hundreds of thousands monthly, permitting Foch to create the strategic reserve needed to assume the offensive. The Germans planned two attacks. The first was to pinch off Rheims which, if successful, would protect the supply of the Marne salient and draw in Allied reserves. The second, to take place 10 days later and much larger in concept, was a renewed attack on the British Army in Flanders, but as events turned out it was never undertaken. The attack on Rheims failed to achieve surprise. General preparations, usually well-kept secrets in the past, leaked out of Berlin or were spotted from the air, while detailed plans were learned from captured prisoners. This information enabled Foch to rearrange his reserves and take other defensive measures before the Germans struck.

In anticipation of the attack the Allies were deployed in depth with a main line of resistance about 2,500 yards behind an outpost line. Between the two lines fortified positions had been established to break up the attack. Artillery was also deployed in depth so that it could support both the outpost and the main line, while reserves were held in readiness to counterattack in case of a breakthrough. As a result of these defensive preparations the enemy was himself surprised when he launched his offensive on 15 July and was stopped far short of his objective. Two American divisions, the 3d and the 42nd, participated in the battle, winning high praise for their conduct. The failure of this offensive, which, although planned only as a diversion, German troops had come to regard as "a Peace Offensive," had a demoralizing effect on them. It convinced Foch that the time for a counterstroke had come at last.

THE ALLIES LAUNCH THEIR OFFENSIVE: JULY 1918

The area chosen for the Allied offensive was the Marne salient. Assault units were to attack along its entire front with the main blow directed at the northwest base of the salient near Soissons. Spearheading the attack was the French XX Corps composed of the U.S. 1st and 2d Divisions and the French 1st Moroccan Division. Since U.S. divisions were numerically stronger, the force actually was four-fifths American. Troop concentrations were carried out with the utmost secrecy some distance behind the lines. Only at the last moment were assault units rushed forward, one United States division moving at night over muddy roads and then into jump-off positions at double time.

The Battle of the Marne

The attack was launched early in the morning of 18 July behind a heavy barrage. Surprise was complete, and the initial assault was so powerful that it quickly overran the German front lines and forward artillery positions. By 0800 Allied troops had advanced three miles and captured the high ground south of Soissons, thus assuring the fall of that stronghold and the ultimate success of the battle. Elsewhere along the front Allied forces, heavily reinforced with American divisions, made uniform progress. Realizing his position had become untenable, Crown Prince Wilhelm, who commanded the German armies in the area, ordered a gradual withdrawal from the salient. In order to save supplies and equipment, the Germans prepared successive defense positions and stubbornly and skillfully defended them. By 3 August, with the salient evacuated, the Germans were in strong positions behind the Aisne and Vesle rivers. Attempts on the part of the U.S. 4th and 32d Divisions to drive them from these positions failed and the offensive was over.

A pontoon bridge across the Marne River—an example of the work of the Army's engineers.

An American division moving up to the front to take part in the Allied counterattack on the Marne in July 1918.

More American troops headed for the front.

A machine-gun unit of the 26th Division prepares for action on July 19. That night the Germans began to evacuate positions south of the Marne River.

Soldiers of the 26th Division examine an 8-inch Austrian howitzer left behind by the retreating Germans.

When this picture was taken on July 19, an artillery unit was moving a gun to a new position.

American artillery deployed in a field during the Allied counterattack.

A soldier with one of the flares used to call for an artillery barrage at night.

An artillery unit rests during a lull in the fighting.

A French tank with American forces south of Soissons. All the tanks used by the AEF were of French or British manufacture.

This was an American command post and first-aid station near Soissons in July 1918.

Moving artillery
during the counterattack.

Wreckage of a German ammunition train
destroyed by American artillery.

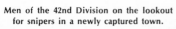

Mounted American soldiers supervise the
movement of German prisoners captured
at Belleau Wood.

Infantrymen in position near the Ourcq
River on 29 July 1918.

Men of the 42nd Division on the lookout
for snipers in a newly captured town.

A 42nd Division dugout.

These Americans moving up to attack at Beuvardes north of the Marne River are wearing gas masks. The road had been gassed by the enemy.

A 4th Division staff conference early in August when the division was located near the Vesle River.

Engineers exploding a mine left behind by the retreating Germans.

Moving out. An American unit loads its equipment on railroad cars at Château-Thierry at the conclusion of the Aisne–Marne offensive.

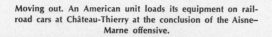

The battle had numerous and far-reaching results. It eliminated the German threat to Paris, upset Ludendorff's cherished plan to attack the British again in Flanders, gave the Allies important rail communications, demonstrated beyond further doubt the effectiveness of American troops on the offensive, firmly established Allied unity of command, and so dimmed German aspirations for victory that even Ludendorff thereafter no longer hoped for more than a stalemate. Most important of all, the initiative passed to the Allies.

The conduct of American troops in the Aisne–Marne offensive strengthened Pershing's case for an independent American army and a separate sector on the Western Front. This had been the original plan, but it had lapsed in the crisis produced by the German offensives. As the danger passed, Pershing pressed the issue again. Foch was sympathetic and, after a series of conferences, agreed to the organization of the U.S. First Army and assigned it a sector in the Saint-Mihiel area. Within a short time most of the American divisions then in France were assembled there. Three remained under French command along the Vesle, where they were badly needed.

While the battle to flatten the German salient on the Marne was at its height, Foch called a conference of his commanders to plan future Allied operations. He proposed first to reduce the three main German salients in order to improve lateral communications between Allied sectors, shorten the line, and set the stage for a general offensive. He assigned the reduction of the Saint-Mihiel salient to Pershing, who had requested it. Since joint effort was gradually reducing the Marne salient at the time, the only question remaining was who would deal with the Amiens salient. The final decision called for a joint British-French operation under Haig's direction.

The World War I soldier had his own weekly newspaper, "The Stars and Stripes." Written, edited, and published by and for the U.S. soldier in France, "The Stars and Stripes" had a peak circulation of 522,000.

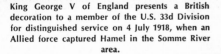

King George V of England presents a British decoration to a member of the U.S. 33d Division for distinguished service on 4 July 1918, when an Allied force captured Hamel in the Somme River area.

Two YMCA workers lead a song session at Château-Thierry. The YMCA was one of seven welfare organizations that operated officially in the AEF.

333

Mail call. In December 1918, a record month, 131,900 sacks of mail were received by the AEF and 25,532 bags were sent to the U.S.

These off-duty soldiers were lucky enough to find a pretty girl to talk to.

An Army photographer in the ruins of a French town. The Army's Signal Corps sent 38 divisional photographic units to France. They took motion, still, and aerial pictures.

334

Marshal Haig Advances on Amiens

Marshal Haig decided on a simple converging attack directed at the center of the salient with the British Fourth Army attacking from the northwest while the French First Army hit from the southwest. On 8 August the British struck with 10 divisions in the line; 45 minutes later, on schedule, the French moved in with 8 divisions. The mass of British infantry, advancing with the tanks behind a rolling barrage, shattered the German lines, capturing 1,600 prisoners and 200 guns in the first two hours. An hour later advance elements, including cavalry, had penetrated German defenses to the extent of 9 miles, forcing a general withdrawal to lines held by the Germans in 1915. The French advance, while not as spectacular, nevertheless contributed to the success of the engagement. As Ludendorff said, it was a "black day" for the German Army. Eager to exploit the advantage gained, Foch urged Haig to continue the attack, but the British commander, realizing that he was up against a well-integrated defense system which could be broken only after long and heavy artillery preparation, recommended an attack farther north between Amiens and Miraumont. To this Foch reluctantly agreed. The new drive opened on 21 August but encountered a stubborn defense in depth and counterattacks which soon brought it to a halt. Since Haig had committed only part of his force, he was still able to apply pressure elsewhere along his line. By the end of August he had forced the Germans back to the original positions from which they had started their offensive. The Amiens salient had disappeared.

The elimination of the Amiens salient left only one major salient, Saint-Mihiel, still in the hands of the enemy. Its reduction had been assigned to the American Army. Pershing lost no time in preparing for the attack. He faced numerous problems, including shortages in artillery, aircraft,

and tanks. Borrowing needed units and equipment from the French, he made up some deficiencies. The offensive was about to be launched when Foch, anxious to take advantage of the successes around Amiens before the Germans recovered, proposed to reduce the size of the Saint-Mihiel operation Pershing had planned and to disperse excess American units among the French and British armies. To exploit the recent successes was, of course, sound, and Pershing fully appreciated that, but he now obstinately refused to permit his army to fight except as an independent force. Two days later he agreed to a new plan that left his force intact but limited the objective of the Saint-Mihiel operation so that the American army could undertake a major offensive between the Meuse River and the Argonne Forest about ten days later.

The American Offensives on Saint-Mihiel

The plan committed Pershing and his staff to the task of preparing and launching two offensives within 23 days in areas 40 miles apart, a tough assignment never before attempted on the Western Front by a single army. However, it was a mission which, if successful, would establish the reputation of the American Army. The original plan for the Saint-Mihiel offensive was quickly modified. It now called for a simultaneous attack on the two sides of the triangular-shaped salient. One American corps was to attack the western face, delivering its main blow fairly close to the base of the triangle, while two corps attacked the southern face, with their main blow falling halfway between the base and apex. Both forces were to meet approximately in the center of the salient, pinching off all enemy forces caught in its nose. A French corps was to make a secondary attack against the nose and exploit whatever success the two main attacks achieved.

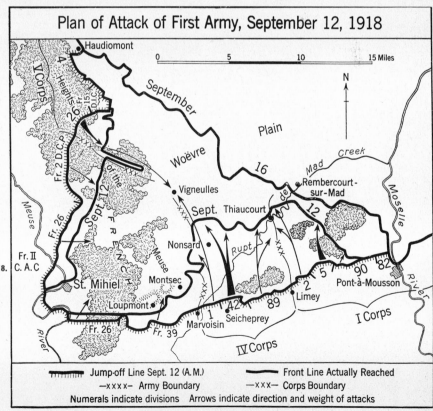

Map—Plan of Attack of First Army, 12 Sept. 1918.

Reserves, part of the force of 550,000 Americans and 110,000 French involved in the offensive, advancing toward Saint-Mihiel.

Moving up for the Saint-Mihiel offensive. The road shown here was typical of most roads in the area.

"No man's land" in the southern part of the Saint-Mihiel salient. The photo shows the nature of the terrain over which the First Army fought.

A French light tank, manned by Americans, crossing a trench during the Saint-Mihiel operation.

An American 75mm gun crew in action.

Dugouts behind the 89th Division's jump-off line.

The town of Saint-Mihiel soon after its capture. American engineers built the pontoon bridge in the left foreground.

Searching a prisoner
taken during the offensive.

Prisoners moving to the rear (foreground)
and supplies moving up during the Saint-
Mihiel offensive.

337

Supported by 3,000 guns, largely French, 1,500 planes, mostly British and French, and 267 French light tanks, the American attack opened on 12 September. Everywhere the Germans, who had been preparing to evacuate the salient, gave way, and by the end of the first day the Americans had reached all their objectives. The advance might have gone farther, but Pershing called a halt because of the coming Meuse–Argonne offensive. It was the first major World War I victory won by the American Army under its own command. The operation eliminated the danger to the rear of the Allied strongholds of Nancy and Verdun, improved Allied lateral communications, and deprived the Germans of excellent defensive positions covering the approaches to the fortress of Metz and the coal mines of Briey.

Foch Plans a General Offensive

Even before the reduction of the Saint-Mihiel salient, Foch had come to believe that a general offensive aimed at driving the enemy across the borders was possible before winter slowed down operations. The Allies now had unquestioned superiority in men and equipment, and their morale was high as the result of the victories in the Aisne–Marne and the Amiens areas, while that of the Germans was showing increasing signs of decline. Only a rapid and orderly evacuation, combined with systematic destruction of roads, railroads, and bridges, could prevent German defeat. To forestall an orderly enemy withdrawal, Foch planned an offensive that would yield two key railroad junctions that tied in enemy lateral rail communications with those from Germany. Two powerful converging attacks were to be made, one by the British, the other by the American army with Aulnoye and Mézièes as their respective objectives. To further the success of the two main blows, the French armies were to exert pressure all along their line and protect the flanks of both British and American armies while a newly created Belgian-French-British army group in the north, commanded by King Albert of Belgium, drove toward

Ghent. The date set for the commencement of the offensive was the last week in September. This barely allowed time for preparations, particularly for the Americans who still had the reductions of the Saint-Mihiel salient to accomplish.

For the next few weeks the U.S. First Army was busy planning operations and switching troops in and out of the concentration area between Verdun and the Argonne Forest. The task was complicated by the fact that so many U.S. divisions were engaged in the Saint-Mihiel battle at the time and by the necessity of making all movements at night in order to avoid observation by the enemy. All told about 820,000 troops with their equipment were involved—220,000 French moving out of the area as 600,000 Americans moved in. As a logistical operation it was a brilliant success for which a young staff officer, Colonel George C. Marshall, won well-deserved acclaim.

Since the Germans had no exposed flanks, Pershing had to plan a frontal attack powerful enough to effect a breakthrough. Terrain features and objectives led him to decide to make his main attack between the Meuse River and the western edge of the Argonne Forest, a zone roughly 20 miles in width. He massed three corps in the area disposed in line. Each corps was to attack with two divisions in the assault and one in reserve. Three other divisions were held as an army reserve available for use where needed as the battle developed.

The country through which the attack was to be made favored the defense. On the east were the heights of the Meuse, which afforded the enemy excellent observation; on the west was the Argonne Forest, high, rugged, and heavily wooded. In the center a ridge running north and south dominated the valley of the Meuse to the east and the valley of the Aire to the west. On the ridge were the heavy fortified positions of Montfaucon, Cunel, and Barricourt, which American troops would have to capture before they could make any appreciable progress. Behind the entire front the Germans had built an elaborate defense system organized in depth. It contained three completed

American soldiers in Flirey on 13 September.

A monument erected in Flirey by the residents of the area honors the American divisions that fought near there.

In Vigneulles the victorious Yanks changed the name of Hindenburg Strasse to Wilson, U.S.A.

American officers take over the German canteen in Monsard. The 1st Division had occupied Monsard by noon on 12 September.

main lines and a partially completed fourth farther to the rear on ground of great natural strength. In addition, the Germans had converted villages, woods, hills, and other natural obstacles between the lines into strong points to serve as centers of resistance to break up an attack.

Strong as this defense system was, Pershing hoped the weight of the attack would carry his army through the first three lines without loss of momentum and enable him to open up German flanks to attack and bring about that state of open warfare for which his men were trained. In case quick success did not attend his first effort, he planned to continue the attack until it penetrated the enemy defenses and then to join with the advancing French at Granpré, cross the Meuse, and advance northward to cut the strategic Sedan–Mézières railroad. The plan was simple enough, but, because of the large force involved, the inexperience of many of his newly arrived divisions, and the nature of the terrain, Pershing expected coordination to be difficult.

339

American engineers repairing the road through Fey-en-Haye. The destroyed village was later rebuilt on a new site.

A patrol prepares the way for a 42d Division advance on 14 September.

This house served as headquarters for an American battalion after its capture on 13 September.

A detachment comes out of the line on 15 September.

Balloons were used by both sides to deliver propaganda behind enemy lines. Here, Allied propaganda is being floated to the German lines.

This Austrian observation balloon floated over Tarnopol on the Eastern Front. It was a captive balloon, i.e., fastened to the ground by long cables.

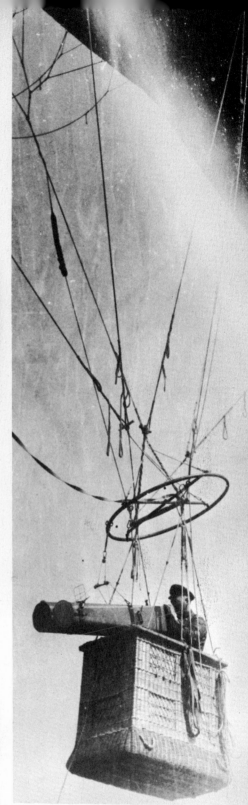

A German observer on the Western Front using a long-range photographic camera.

Maneuvering an American observation balloon during the Saint-Mihiel offensive. The Army's Air Service had 33 balloon companies in France.

341

Observation balloons were popular but dangerous targets for World War I airmen. The greatest of the American "balloon busters" was Lieutenant Frank Luke who shot down 14 balloons in a little over two months of combat.

Army Air Service pilots ready for patrol duty. When the war ended, the Air Service had 45 combat squadrons at the front.

HOW TO STOP THE WAR.

Do your part to put an end to the war! Put an end to your part of it. Stop fighting! That's the simplest way. You can do it, you soldiers, just stop fighting and the war will end of its own accord. You are not fighting for anything anyway. What does it matter to you who owns Metz or Strassburg, you never saw those towns nor knew the people in them, so what do you care about them? But there is a little town back home in little old United States you would like to see and if you keep on fighting here in the hope of getting a look at those old German fortresses you may never see home again.

The only way to stop the war is to stop fightin That's easy. Just quit it and slip across <No Man's l and join the bunch that's taking it easy there waitin exchanged and taken home. There is no disgr hat bunch of American prisoners will be w mly as you who stick it out in thes vise and over the top.
re in the g sing ta arg

An example of the propaganda the Germans dropped behind the American lines.

A mobile antiaircraft gun.

The highly flammable balloon burns as it falls to the ground.

Two American observers parachute from their balloon after an attack by a German aviator. American pilots wore no parachutes, but balloonists always did.

An observation balloon tender with two machine guns for driving off enemy aircraft.

The enemy had mobile guns too.

Machine gunners firing at a German plane during the Meuse-Argonne offensive.

Machine gunners brought down this German plane.

Because troops in transit were especially vulnerable to attack by enemy aircraft, this artillery unit moving to the front carried a mounted machine gun.

The Meuse–Argonne Offensive Succeeds

Early in the morning of 26 September the offensive began with an artillery preparation lasting about three hours. At 0530 the infantry jumped off. The assault divisions promptly took the forward positions, and by the end of the first day had made excellent progress everywhere except in two places, Montfaucon and the Argonne Forest. In the next few days the first two defense lines were captured, but the advance ground to a halt before the enemy's third line, upsetting Perishing's hope for a quick breakthrough. The battle now entered its second phase. The reasons for the collapse of the initial assault, other than stubborn enemy resistance, were numerous. Tank support proved ineffective, and supply broke down because of congestion and poor roads. More important was the inexperience of the divisions that were receiving their first taste of battle. Three had to be replaced by veteran outfits as soon as a lull in the battle permitted, not an easy task considering the condition of the roads serving the front lines. Nevertheless, it was accomplished by 1 October, and the stage was set for a renewal of the attack.

Between 4 October and the end of the month, the U.S. First Army slowly drove its way through the third German line. Casualties mounted as the enemy threw in reserves and stubbornly contested every defensible position. Gains were limited but significant because the grueling struggle forced the enemy to draw units from other parts of the front and commit them to battle. In the air the enemy introduced the "battle squadron" to strafe front-line troops, and Colonel William Mitchell made the first large-scale bombing raid, upsetting enemy preparations for a counterattack. During this period the Argonne Forest was cleared and the attack was extended east of the Meuse River. By mid-October enough divisions were in action to necessitate the organization of the U.S. Second Army under the command of Major General Robert L. Bullard; Major General Hunter Liggett was appointed to command the First Army, and General Pershing then assumed command of the army group.

Having finally penetrated the third main enemy line, the Americans were in a position to reap the harvest of success. Fresh outfits replaced exhausted divisions; most of the Allied units serving with the AEF were released and withdrawn; roads were built and repaired; and the supply system was improved. The Germans in the meantime had so strengthened their fourth line that it, too, had to be penetrated before open warfare was possible. On 1 November the attack reopened with the usual artillery preparation. The infantry assault that followed was highly successful; V Corps in the center advanced six miles in the first day, forcing the Germans to withdraw in a hurry to save their units west of the Meuse. Three days later units of III Corps crossed the river and headed toward Montmedy. By 7 November the heights before Sedan were seized, denying the Germans the use of the Sedan–Mézières railroad. Sedan could probably have been taken by the American First Army shortly thereafter had not Foch altered its left boundary to permit the French to capture the city which had witnessed the capitulation of the French Army to the Prussians in 1870. Almost a million and a quarter American troops were engaged in the Meuse–Argonne offensive before it ended. The price paid was heavy, some 120,000 casualties, but the military results were decisive. And in his futile effort to hold, Ludendorff was forced to pour rapidly diminishing reserves into the battle, thereby making it possible for Allied arms to register spectacular gains elsewhere on the Western Front.

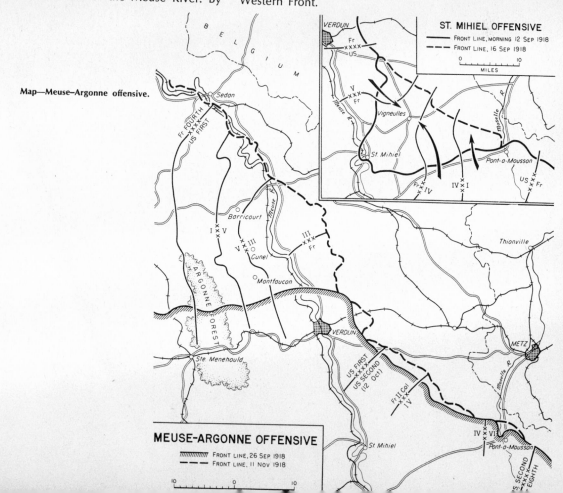

Map—Meuse–Argonne offensive.

Men of the 77th Division wait near their jump-off line for the beginning of the Allied attack on the morning of 26 September.

An American artillery unit in action near Varennes.

Troops of the 28th Division in Varennes after its capture on 26 September. The Division's headquarters was located at Varennes until 30 September.

American-manned tanks moving forward on the first day of the Meuse–Argonne offensive.

Some of the men wounded on the first day of the Meuse–Argonne
offensive were treated in a wrecked church.

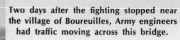
Two days after the fighting stopped near the village of Boureuilles, Army engineers had traffic moving across this bridge.

A camouflaged road in the Meuse–Argonne area.

An American front-line trench.

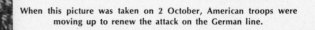
When this picture was taken on 2 October, American troops were moving up to renew the attack on the German line.

348

One of the U.S. Army's ration dumps
in the Meuse–Argonne area.

Religious services at Verdun during the Meuse–Argonne offensive.

After a visit to the ration dump,
a ration party returns to the trenches.

This is what happened when a tank and a supply wagon were caught in the explosion of a German mine.

The First Army's 155mm artillery in action.

Infantrymen wait in foxholes during a 1st Division probe on 11 October 1918.

The guns in this picture were captured from the enemy.

A 14-inch naval gun firing from a railway mount near Verdun. It was one of three such guns positioned near the village of Charny to shell enemy communication centers 20 miles away.

The World War I Army was only partly motorized. The AEF purchased 243,039 horses and mules during the conflict, of which France supplied 135,722 at an average cost of $379.81 each. The picture was taken during the Meuse-Argonne offensive.

A traffic jam at Esnes, an important road center during the Meuse–Argonne operation.

Artillerymen firing during a gas attack in the Argonne Forest area.

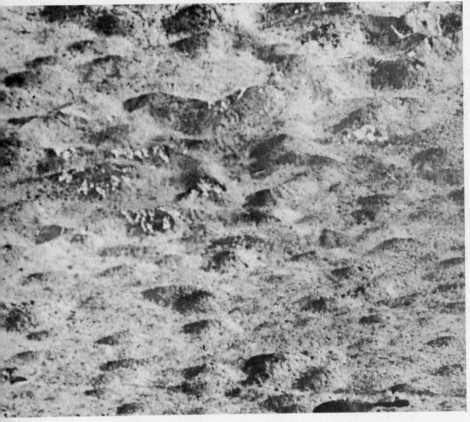

On the sending end of a gas attack.

After the battle—shell holes and mine craters on the Meuse–Argonne front.

Other Allied Victories

The successes gained by the AEF in the Meuse–Argonne offensive were matched by the Allies on other sectors of the front. By 5 October the British had penetrated the true Hindenburg Line, and a month later they took Aulnoye, a strategic rail junction upon which German supply depended. In their offensive they had the use of two American divisions, the 27th and the 30th, which participated in some of the bloodiest fighting of the war. In Flanders King Albert's Belgian-British-French army pushed ahead until it slid to a temporary halt in Belgian mud. As soon as ground condi- tions improved, King Albert's army renewed the attack, re- gaining the entire coast of Belgium before the armistice. During the last ten days of this operation two American divisions, the 37th and 91st, saw action. The French, whose mission was to apply pressure in the center between the American and British zones, also did well. They were assisted by two American divisions, the 2d and 36th. All along the Western Front success was so gratifying that a major opera- tion against Metz seemed possible before the end of the year. Plans for the attack to begin on 15 November were well under way when the armistice came.

A Formidable Foe

German officers
on an inspection trip.

German artillery
on the Champagne front.

Transporting a wounded
soldier to a first-aid station.

A first-aid station
directly behind the battle line.

353

A German hospital train.

A trench in the Hindenburg Line. This picture was taken on 3 November 1918.

Kaiser Wilhelm II (saluting) during a visit to the Western Front in December 1917. The Crown Prince is at his left.

One of the German Army's long-range cannon. It is being moved to a new location.

354

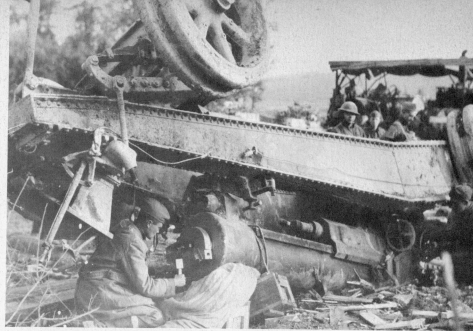

An example of German marksmanship—a direct hit on a 155mm tractor-drawn gun belonging to the U.S. First Army.

The American docks at Nantes on 3 November 1918. Nantes was the AEF's third largest port.

Supplying the AEF

An American-operated narrow-gauge train loaded with supplies for the troops.

Frenchwomen loading supplies at the U.S. Army's Quartermaster Depot No. 1 at Nevers.

The Army also used its trains to move civilian property from the front-line areas.

Muddy roads made it difficult to transport supplies by truck or wagon. Engineers (left) are working on this road.

Salvation Army workers made the doughnuts they gave to the troops.

When they could, the French supplied the troops with food and drink.

These Army engineers have found their own source of supply—a ruined house.

The burros are delivering water to troops stationed in the Saint–Mihiel sector.

The infantryman carried some of his own supplies. This column is moving through a captured town in the Meuse–Argonne area on 3 November 1918.

The Armistice of 11 November 1918

Disheartened by the inability of his armies to hold the Allied attacks, Ludendorff, as early as 29 September, had informed his government that Germany could not win and advised it to seek peace. The Imperial Government reacted by notifying President Wilson of its willingness to accept terms based on his earlier announced "Fourteen Points." Wilson could not respond at once, for he was not sure that all the Allies were willing to negotiate with the Imperial Government. Meanwhile, the fighting continued with disastrous results for the Germans. An offensive in Italy in late October forced them to reinforce that tottering front. At the same time the Allies were advancing all along the Western Front. A last desperate plan of the German Navy to break out and challenge the British Grand Fleet failed when the German sailors mutinied and seized the port of Kiel. Within a few days several other cities in northern Germany fell to the mutineers, who set up soldiers' and sailors' committees reminiscent of the events in Russia 18 months before.

Early in the crisis Ludendorff was relieved. On 9 November a German republic was proclaimed and the Kaiser fled to Holland. German emissaries crossed the lines to discuss terms with Allied representatives in a railroad car near Compiègne where agreement was reached on an armistice which took effect at 1100 on 11 November. It provided for: (1) the withdrawal of the German armies from occupied territory within two weeks; (2) the surrender of most of Germany's artillery, machine guns, planes, rolling stock, and trucks; (3) the immediate return of Allied prisoners of war; (4) the evacuation of the west bank of the Rhine; (5) the demilitarization of a six-mile strip on the east bank; (6) the relinquishment to the Allies of Mainz, Coblenz, and Cologne (7) the surrender of all submarines; and (8) the internment of the German fleet in neutral or Allied ports. These military and naval terms were supplemented by equally severe economic and political provisions.

Allied forces immediately moved in to occupy the west bank of the Rhine and the three designated cities. President Wilson at first was reluctant to occupy any territory, but under urging he agreed to permit the American army to take over the area around Coblenz.

For the first time since the establishment of the nation, the United States had departed from its traditional policy of noninvolvement in European affairs. Resources, industry, accumulated wealth, and manpower were harnessed in a war effort unprecedented in history. The U.S. Army, raised largely by conscription, was slow getting into action, but, once there, it gave an impressive account of itself. For the first time since the Civil War vast numbers of men were mobilized, put into uniform, equipped, trained, and committed to battle. Unprepared though the Army was when the war broke out, it grew and learned rapidly. By the summer of 1918 enough men and supplies had arrived at the Western Front to turn the tide of battle in favor of the Allies. In the Meuse-Argonne offensive American troops fought the greatest battle in which the Army had been engaged up to that time. They met and drove back the best troops in Europe in a dogged, grueling battle which helped convince the enemy that further resistance was useless. Many costly mistakes were made, particularly in the field of logistics, airplane production, and replacements, but many things were done well. Conscription was introduced and handled inexpensively and justly; officers were selected on the basis of merit and qualifications; the complexities of trench warfare were mastered without sacrifice of fundamental operational concepts; morale was kept at a high level both in the Army and on the home front; and finally, mobilization was handled with speed and without serious impairment of the Army's efficiency or disruption of the nation's economic life.

357

The Meuse–Argonne Cemetery, one of the six permanent American military cemeteries established in France after World War I. A cemetery was also established in England and another in Belgium. The Meuse–Argonne Cemetery is located near Romagne.

World War I Cemeteries and Memorials in France

The Meuse–Argonne American Memorial at Montfaucon commemorates the victory of the U.S. First Army in the Meuse–Argonne offensive and the French armies that fought in that sector. The memorial's 180-foot shaft makes it the largest American war memorial in Europe. It was erected by the U.S. Government.

The names of the towns captured by American troops during the Saint-Mihiel offensive were carved above the columns of the Saint-Mihiel American Memorial at Montsec.

The Aisne-Marne American Memorial near Château-Thierry was erected by the U.S. Government to commemorate the American fighting in the Aisne-Marne region and the friendship and co-operation of French and American forces during the war.

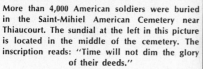

More than 4,000 American soldiers were buried in the Saint-Mihiel American Cemetery near Thiaucourt. The sundial at the left in this picture is located in the middle of the cemetery. The inscription reads: "Time will not dim the glory of their deeds."

The Aisne-Marne American cemetery is located below Belleau Wood. The majority of those who were buried there fought at Belleau Wood or along the Marne River.

359

This town near the Hindenburg Line was the target of American artillery before its capture on 2 November.

Weary American soldiers march through Saint-Juvin after being relieved from the front line early in November.

This picture was taken in Bar after the town was captured on 7 November. The bottom sign announced: "Bar open."

By November American troops had entered Belgium. Here, Army engineers repair damaged tracks near Waereghem.

American and French soldiers in the Meuse–Argonne sector on 3 November.

It was business as usual at a first-aid station in the Meuse–Argonne region on 8 November.

An artillery position abandoned by the retreating Germans.

French peasants in territory newly liberated from the Germans express their appreciation to American soldiers. When this picture was taken on 6 November, the Germans were retreating all along the battle line.

Peace Comes to the Western Front.

The 89th Infantry Division in Stenay two minutes before the Armistice took effect.

Marshal Foch's train at Compiègne. The Armistice was signed in the car in the foreground.

American soldiers celebrate the Armistice.

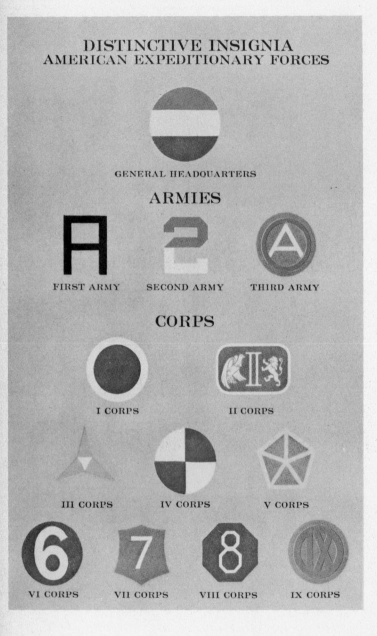

DISTINCTIVE INSIGNIA
AMERICAN EXPEDITIONARY FORCES

GENERAL HEADQUARTERS

ARMIES

FIRST ARMY   SECOND ARMY   THIRD ARMY

CORPS

I CORPS   II CORPS

III CORPS   IV CORPS   V CORPS

VI CORPS   VII CORPS   VIII CORPS   IX CORPS

DIVISIONS

1ST DIVISION   2D DIVISION   3D DIVISION

4TH DIVISION   5TH DIVISION   6TH DIVISION   7TH DIVISION

8TH DIVISION   26TH DIVISION   27TH DIVISION

28TH DIVISION   29TH DIVISION   30TH DIVISION   31ST DIVISION

32D DIVISION   33D DIVISION   34TH DIVISION

DIVISIONS

35TH DIVISION

36TH DIVISION

37TH DIVISION

38TH DIVISION

40TH DIVISION

41ST DIVISION

42D DIVISION

76TH DIVISION

77TH DIVISION

78TH DIVISION

79TH DIVISION

80TH DIVISION

81ST DIVISION

82D DIVISION

83D DIVISION

84TH DIVISION

85TH DIVISION

DIVISIONS

86TH DIVISION

87TH DIVISION

88TH DIVISION

89TH DIVISION

90TH DIVISION

91ST DIVISION

92D DIVISION

93D DIVISION

SPECIAL UNITS

SERVICES OF SUPPLY

ADVANCE SECTION S. O. S.

CHEMICAL WARFARE SERVICE

DISTRICT OF PARIS

AMBULANCE SERVICE

RESERVE MALLET

TANK CORPS

RAILHEAD

A.E.F. NORTH RUSSIA

REGULATING STATION

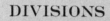

American soldiers, waiting for shipment home, examine captured German guns on display in Paris in November 1918.

CHAPTER 13

THE U.S. ARMY, 1919-1941

The Army of the United States, which totaled 3,710,563 on 11 November 1918, was reduced to about 19,500 officers and 245,000 enlisted men by the beginning of 1920. The War Department urged the establishment of a permanent regular force of about 600,000 and of a three-month universal military training system that would permit a rapid expansion to meet the requirements of a new major war, but Congress and public opinion rejected this proposal. Most Americans believed that the defeat of Germany and the exhaustion of the other European powers would prevent another major war on land for years to come. The possibility of war with Japan was recognized, but American leaders assumed that such a war, if it came, would be primarily naval in character. Indeed, the fundamental factor in the military policy of the United States during the next two decades was reliance on the United States Navy as the first line of national defense.

DEMOBILIZATION

When the fighting ended in France, almost all of the officers and men in the Army became eligible for discharge. The War Department had to decide how to muster them out as quickly and equitably as possible without unduly disrupting the national economy and at the same time maintain an effective force for occupation and other postwar duties. It decided in favor of the traditional method of demobilization by units as the one best calculated to achieve these ends. Units in the United States were moved to 30 demobilization centers located throughout the country, so that men after processing could be discharged near their homes. Units overseas were brought back just as rapidly as shipping space could be found for them, processed through debarkation centers operated by the Transportation Service, and then sent to the demobilization centers for discharge. In practice, the unit system was supplemented by a great many individual discharges and by the release of certain occupational groups, notably railroad workers and anthracite coal miners. In the first full month of demobilization the Army released about 650,000 officers and men, and within nine months nearly 3,250,000 were demobilized without seriously disturbing the American economy. A demobilization of war industry and disposal of surplus materiel paralleled the release of personnel, but the War Department kept a large reserve of weapons for peacetime or new emergency use. Despite the lack of much advance planning, demobilization was accomplished reasonably well. The Army was concerned at the outset because it had no authority to enlist men to replace those discharged, but a law passed in February 1919 permitted enlistments in the Regular Army for either one or three years. By the end of 1919 the active Army was almost entirely a regular volunteer force.

The military duties of the Army abroad and at home did not cease with the armistice. The United States had agreed to join Great Britain and France in a military occupation of western Germany, and for political rather than military reasons it had also joined in sending expeditionary forces into Russia. At home during 1919 and 1920 Army forces continued the guard on the border of Mexico required by revolutionary disturbances in that country, and, because of the lack of National Guard forces (not yet reorganized), the active Army had to supply troops on numerous occasions to help suppress domestic disorders arising chiefly out of labor disputes and race conflicts in a restless postwar America.

The newly activated U.S. Third Army, under Major General Joseph T. Dickman, crossed into Germany on 1 December 1918 to occupy a small segment of territory along the Rhine River centering on Coblenz. As many as nine divisions participated in the occupation during the spring of 1919. American troops had no unusual difficulties with the German populace, and soon after the peace conference ended in May 1919 the occupation forces were rapidly reduced. They numbered about 15,000 at the beginning of 1920. After rejecting the Treaty of Versailles, the United States remained technically at war with Germany until the summer of 1921, when a separate peace was signed. Thereafter, the occupying force was gradually withdrawn, and the last thousand troops left for home on 24 January 1923.

Homeward bound. The 28th Division entrains for Saint-Nazaire on 22 April 1919.

Embarkation at Saint-Nazaire.

The "Agamemnon" arrives at Hoboken, N. J., from France.

The 165th Infantry Division marches under the victory arch in New York City.

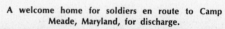
A welcome home for soldiers en route to Camp Meade, Maryland, for discharge.

The 339th Infantry Division in northern Russia in February 1919.

The revolutionary turmoil in Russia in 1918 induced President Wilson in August to direct Army participation in expeditions of United States and Allied forces that penetrated the Murmansk-Archangel region of European Russia and into Siberia via Vladivostock. The north Russian force, containing about 5,000 American troops under British command, suffered heavy casualties while guarding war supplies and communication lines south of the Arctic ports mentioned, before being withdrawn in June 1919. The Siberian force of about 10,000 under Major General William S. Graves had many trying experiences in attempting to rescue Czech troops and curb Japanese expansionist tendencies between August 1918 and April 1920. Together these two forces suffered about as many combat casualties as the Army expeditionary force of similar size had sustained in Cuba in 1898. After the withdrawals from Germany and Russia, the only Army forces stationed on foreign soil until 1941 were the garrison of about 1,000 maintained at Tientsin, China, from 1912 until 1938, and a force of similar strength dispatched from the Philippines to Shanghai for four months' duty in 1932. The Marine Corps, rather than the Army, provided the other small foreign garrisons and expeditionary forces required after World War I, particularly in the Caribbean area.

American troops disembarking
in China for duty at Tientsin.

A soldiers' club in China.

THE NATIONAL DEFENSE ACT OF 4 JUNE 1920

After many months of careful consideration, unfortunately not backed by any widespread popular interest, Congress passed a sweeping amendment of the National Defense Act of 1916. The new National Defense Act of 4 June 1920, which governed the organization and regulation of the Army until 1950, has been widely acknowledged to be the most constructive piece of military legislation ever adopted in the United States. It rejected the theory of an expansible Regular Army and established the Army of the United States as an organization of three components, the professional Regular Army, the civilian National Guard, and the civilian Organized Reserves (Officers' and Enlisted Reserve Corps). Each component was to be so regulated in peacetime that it could contribute its appropriate share of troops in a war emergency. The act was, in effect, an acknowledgment that throughout its history the United States had been unable to maintain a standing peacetime force capable of sufficient expansion to meet the demands of a great war, and that it had always been necessary to raise new armies of civilian-soldiers to achieve a large-scale mobilization. In contrast to earlier practice, the training of civilian components now became a major peacetime task of the Regular Army, and principally for this reason the Army was authorized an officer strength of 17,717—more than three times the actual officer strength of the Regular Army before World War I. At least half of the new officers were to be nonregulars who had served during the war. The act also provided that officer promotions, except for doctors and chaplains, were to be made from a list, a step that equalized opportunity for advancement throughout most of the Army. The Regular Army was authorized a maximum enlisted strength of 280,000, but the actual strength would depend on the amount of money voted in annual appropriations. The act authorized the Army to continue all of its arm and service branches established before 1917 and to add three new branches, the Air Service, the Chemical Warfare Service, and a Finance Department, the first two reflecting new combat techniques developed in World War I. The Tank Corps of World War I was absorbed by the Infantry. The act specifically charged the War Department with mobilization planning and preparations for the event of war. It assigned the military aspects of this responsibility to the Chief-of-Staff and the General Staff, and the planning and supervision of industrial procurement to the Assistant Secretary of War.

World War I experience both in Washington and in France had greatly strengthened the position and authority of the General Staff. In 1921 General Pershing became Chief-of-Staff, and under his direction the War Department General Staff was reorganized to include 5 divisions: G-1, dealing wtih personnel; G-2, with intelligence; G-3, with training and operations; G-4, with supply; and a new War Plans Division that dealt with strategic planning and related preparations for the event of war. These divisions assisted the Chief-of-Staff in his supervision of the military branches of the War Department and of the field forces. The field forces in the continental United States were put under the command and administration of 9 corps areas approximately equal in population, and those overseas in Panama, Hawaii, and the Philippines under departments with similar author-

ity. The division rather than the regiment became the basic Army unit, especially in mobilization planning, and each corps area was allocated 6 infantry divisions—1 Regular Army, 2 National Guard, and 3 Reserve. The defense act had contemplated a higher organization of divisions into corps and armies, but no such tactical organizations existed in fact for many years. The principal organizational change in the 1920's came in 1926 with the establishment of the Air Corps as an equal combat arm and with provision for its enlargement and modernization.

Between 1920 and 1941 education for and within the Army received far greater attention than ever before. This reflected the emphasis in the National Defense Act on preparedness in peacetime as well as the increasing complexity of modern war. The United States Military Academy and the Reserve Officers' Training Corps program furnished most of the basic schooling for new officers. Thirty-one special service schools provided branch training. The largest of these was the Infantry School, located at Fort Benning, Georgia. The branch schools trained officers and enlisted men of the civilian components as well as those of the Regular Army and, in addition, furnished training through extension courses. Three general service schools provided the capstone of the Army educational system. The oldest of them, located at Fort Leavenworth, Kansas, and known after 1928 as the Command and General Staff School, provided officers with the requisite training for divisional command and general staff positions. In Washington the Army War College and, after 1924, the Army Industrial College trained senior officers of demonstrated ability for the most responsible command and staff positions.

One of the major purposes of the National Defense Act was to promote the integration of the Regular Army and the civilian components by establishing uniformity in training and professional standards. In practice this fell considerably short of full realization; nevertheless, the new military system saw an unprecedented amount of military training of civilians in peacetime. It brought the regular out of his traditional isolation from the civilian community, and it acquainted large numbers of civilians with the problems and views of the professional soldier. Altogether, the civilian components and the groups in training that contributed to their ranks had an average strength of about 400,000 between the wars. The end result of the civilian training program was an orderly and effective mobilization of National Guard and Reserve elements into the active Army in 1940 and 1941.

The absorption of the National Guard into the Army during World War I had left the states without any Guard units after the armistice. The National Defense Act of 1920 contemplated a National Guard of 436,000, but its actual peacetime strength was stabilized at about 180,000. This force relieved the Regular Army of any duty in curbing domestic disturbances within the states from 1921 until 1941, and stood ready for immediate induction into the active Army whenever necessary. The War Department, in addition to supplying regular officers for instruction and large quantities of surplus World War I materiel for equipment, applied about one-tenth of its military budget to the support of the Guard in the years between the wars. Guardsmen engaged in 48 armory drills and 15 days of field training each year. Though not comparable to active Army units in readiness for war, the Guard was much better prepared by 1939 than it had been when mobilized for Mexican border duty in 1916. Numerically, the National Guard was the largest component of the Army of the United States between 1922 and 1939.

The civilian community had, of course, a very large number of trained officers and enlisted men after World War I, and this assured the Army of a natural reservoir of manpower for a decade or more after the war. Only a very few of these men joined the Enlisted Reserve Corps, but large numbers of officers maintained their commissions in the Officers' Reserve Corps through five-year periods, during which they received further training through school and extension courses and in brief tours of active duty. The composition of the Officers' Reserve Corps, which numbered about 100,000 between the wars, gradually changed as its ranks were refilled by men newly commissioned after training in Reserve Officers' Training Corps (ROTC) or in the Citizens' Military Training Camp (CMTC) program.

The National Defense Act of 1920 gave impetus to a greatly enlarged and better-regulated ROTC program. By 1928 there were ROTC units in 325 schools, about 225 of them being senior units enrolling 85,000 students in colleges and universities. Regular Army officers detailed as professors of military science and tactics instructed these units, and about 6,000 men graduating from them were commissioned each year in the Officers' Reserve Corps. The ROTC also contributed large numbers of officers and enlisted men to National Guard units. This inexpensive program paid rich dividends when the nation again mobilized to meet the threat of war in 1940 and 1941.

The Army's CMTC program, a very modest alternative to the universal military training system proposed in 1919, provided about 30,000 young volunteers with four weeks of military training in summer camps each year. Those who completed four years of CMTC training became eligible for Reserve commissions, the CMTC thus providing another, though much smaller, source for the rolls of the Officers' Reserve Corps and the National Guard.

When the National Defense Act was adopted in June 1920, the Regular Army numbered about 200,000—about two-thirds the maximum strength authorized in the act. In January 1921 Congress directed a reduction in enlisted strength to 175,000 and in June 1921 to 150,000. A year later Congress limited the active Army to 12,000 commissioned officers and 125,000 enlisted men, not including the 7,000 or so in the Philippine Scouts. Regular Army strength was stabilized at about this level until 1936. Appropriations for the military expenses of the War Department also became stabilized during this same period, amounting to about $300,000,000 a year. This was about half of what a full implementation of the National Defense Act had been estimated to cost. The United States spent rather less on its Army than on its Navy during these years, in line with the national policy of depending on the Navy as the first line of defense. War Department officials, especially in the early 1920's, repeatedly expressed alarm over the failure of Congress to appropriate enough money to carry out the terms of the National Defense Act. They believed that it was essential for minimum defense needs to have a Regular Army with an enlisted strength of 150,000 or, after the Air Corps Act of 1926, of 165,000. As the Chief-of-Staff pointed out in 1933, the United States ranked 17th among the nations in active Army strength, although foreign observers rated its newly equipped Army Air Corps 2d or 3d in actual power.

In equipment the Air Corps offered a marked contrast to the rest of the Army. For almost two decades ground units had to get along as best they could with weapons left over from World War I. The Army was well aware that these old weapons were becoming increasingly obsolete and that new ones were needed. For example, the Chief-of-Staff in 1933 described the Army's tanks—except for a dozen experimental models—as completely useless for employment against any modern unit on the battlefield. Although handicapped by very small appropriations for research and development, Army arsenals and laboratories worked continuously during the 1920's and 1930's to devise new items of equipment and to improve old ones. Service boards, links between branch schools and headquarters, tested pilot models and determined the doctrine for their employment so that it could be incorporated into training manuals. But not much new equipment was forthcoming for ground units in the field until after Army appropriations began to rise in 1936.

ACTUAL ARMY STRENGTH AND DUTIES

For a number of years only about one-fourth of the officers and one-half of the enlisted men of the Regular Army were available for assignment to tactical units in the continental United States. Many units existed only on paper; almost all had only skeletonized strength. Instead of 9 infantry divisions, there were actually 3. In May 1927 one of the infantry divisions, a cavalry brigade, and 200 planes participated in a combined arms maneuver in Texas, but for the most part regular units had to train as battalions or companies. The continued dispersion of skeletonized divisions, brigades, and regiments among a large number of posts, many of them relics of the Indian wars, was a serious hindrance to the training of regulars, although helpful in training the civilian components. Efforts to abandon small posts continued to meet with stubborn opposition from local interests and their elected representatives in Congress. In the infantry, for example, the 24 regiments available in the United States for field service in 1932 were spread among 45 posts, with a battalion or less at 34. Most of the organic transportation of these units was of World War I vintage, and the Army did not have the money to concentrate units for training by other means. Nor were there large posts in which they could be housed. The best training of larger units occurred overseas in the fairly sizable garrisons maintained by the Army in Hawaii, the Philippines, and Panama. In the early 1930's the depression had the immediate effect of cuts in appropriations and pay, which further reduced the readiness of Army units for military service.

The most conspicuous employment of the Army within the United States during these years of peace was a variety of nonmilitary tasks that only the Army had the resources and the organization to tackle quickly. In floods and blizzards and hurricanes it was the Army that was first on the spot with cots and blankets and food. In another direction, Army Engineers expanded their work on rivers and harbors for the improvement of navigation and flood control. For four months in 1934 the Air Corps, on orders from the President, took over the carrying of the air mail for the Post Office Department. The most important and immediately disruptive of these nonmilitary duties began in the spring of 1933, after Congress passed an act that put large numbers of jobless young men into reforestation and other reclamation work. President Roosevelt directed the Army to mobilize these men and thereafter to run their camps without in any way making the Civilian Conservation Corps (CCC) program a military project in disguise. Within seven weeks the Army mobilized 310,000 men in 1,315 camps. For more than a year the War Department had to keep about 3,000 regular officers and many noncommissioned officers assigned to this task, which meant that tactical units were stripped of their leadership. Unit training was brought to a standstill, and the readiness of units for immediate military employment was almost destroyed. In the second half of 1934 the War Department called a large number of Reserve officers to active duty to replace the regulars, and by August 1935, 9,300 Reserve officers (not counted in active Army strength) were serving with the CCC.

CLOUDS OF WAR IN 1931 LEAD TO ARMY REORGANIZATION

The clouds of war began to form again in 1931 when the Japanese seized Manchuria. In Europe, Hitler came to power in 1933, and by 1936 Germany had denounced the Treaty of Versailles, embarked on rearmament, and occupied the demilitarized Rhineland. Hitler's partner in dictatorship, Italy's Mussolini, began his career of aggression by attacking Ethiopia in 1934. In the face of these developments the United States made significant adjustments in its foreign policy; it recognized Soviet Russia in 1933; voted eventual independence for the Philippines in 1934, liquidated its protectorates in the Caribbean area, and in Latin America actively pursued the Good Neighbor policy. No radical change in American military policy followed, but beginning in 1935 the armed forces received substantially larger appropriations. Army improvements during the next three years reflected not only the increasingly critical international situation but also the careful planning of the War Department during General Douglas MacArthur's tour as Chief-of-Staff from 1930 to 1935. His recommendations led to a reorganization of the combat forces and a modest increase in their size, and were accompanied by more realistic planning for using the manpower and industrial might of the United States for war if that should become necessary.

The central objective of the Chief-of-Staff's recommendations was to establish a small, hard-hitting force ready for emergency use. In line with this objective the Army wanted to mechanize and motorize its regular combat units as soon as it could, and to fill their ranks so that they could be trained effectively. The Army also needed a new organization to control the training of larger units and teams

of combined arms in peacetime, and to command them if war came. For these purposes the War Department between 1932 and 1935 created four army headquarters and a General Headquarters Air Force organization in the continental United States under the command of the Chief-of-Staff. Under the supervision of these headquarters, beginning in the summer of 1935, regular and National Guard divisions and other units trained together each year in summer maneuvers and other exercises. Significant joint Army-Navy exercises had been held even earlier in the spring of 1932. In 1935 Congress authorized the Regular Army to increase its enlisted strength to the long-sought goal of 165,000. This increased was accompanied during the following years by substantially greater expenditures for equipment and housing, so that by 1938 the Regular Army was considerably stronger and more nearly ready for action than it had been in the early 1930's. But in the meantime the strength and power of foreign armies had been increasing even more rapidly.

Major General Edward A. Kreger, the Judge Advocate General of the A (left), administers the oath of office to the Army's new Chief of Staff, Gene Douglas MacArthur. General MacArthur was Chief of Staff from 1930 until 1

In the slow rebuilding of the 1930's the Army concentrated on equipping and training its combat units, for mobile warfare rather than for the static warfare that had characterized operations on the Western Front in World War I. Even so, its concept of mobility proved to be too limited. Through research the Army managed to acquire some new weapons that promised increased firepower and mobility as soon as equipment could be produced in quantity. In 1936 the Army adopted the Garand semiautomatic rifle to replace the 1903 Springfield, and during the 1930's it perfected the mobile 105-mm howitzer that became the principal divisional artillery piece of World War II. It also developed light and medium tanks that were much faster than the lumbering models of World War I. In units, horses gave way to motors as rapidly as new vehicles could be acquired, but here, too, there were inadequate plans for new mechanized units. To increase the maneuverability of its principal ground unit, the division, the Army decided after field tests to triangularize the infantry division by reducing the number of its infantry regiments from four to three, and to make it more mobile by using motor transportation only.

THE PROTECTIVE MOBILIZATION PLAN OF 1937

Modern war is so complex and modern armies are so demanding in equipment that industrial mobilization for war must precede the large-scale employment of manpower by at least two years if a war is to be fought effectively. The Army's Industrial Mobilization Plan of 1930 established the basic principles for harnessing the nation's economic strength to war needs, and revisions of this plan to 1939 improved the pattern. Manpower planning culminated in the Protective Mobilization Plan of 1937, prepared under the direction of General Malin Craig, then Chief-of-Staff. Under this plan the first step was to be the induction of the National Guard to provide, with the Regular Army, an Initial Protective Force of about 400,000. The Navy plus this defensive force would then protect the nation while the Army engaged in an orderly expansion to planned strengths of one, two, and four million, as necessary. With the development of mobilization planning there evolved for the first time before actual hostilities a definite training plan, which included the location, size, and scheduling of replacement training centers, unit training centers, and schools, detailed unit and individual training programs, and the production of a variety of training manuals. While these plans were useful in guiding the mobilization that began in the summer of 1940, it turned out that the planners had set their sights too low. They assumed a maximum mobilization of World War I dimensions, whereas World War II was to call forth more than twice as many men for the Army and proportionately an even greater industrial effort. The plans also assumed, until 1939, that mobilization for war would come more or less suddenly instead of relatively slowly during many months of nominal peace.

The German annexation of Austria in March 1938 followed by the Munich crisis in September of the same year awakened the United States and the other democratic nations to the imminence of another great world conflict. The new conflict had already begun in the Far East, where Japan invaded China in 1937. After Germany seized Czechoslovakia in March 1939, war in Europe became inevitable because Great Britain and France decided that they must fight rather than yield anything more to Hitler. Then Germany invaded Poland on 1 September 1939, and France and Great Britain responded by declaring war on Germany.

An overwhelming majority of the American people

General Malin Craig, the Army's Chief of Staff from 1935 until 1939.

The first Chief of the Army Air Corps, Major General Mason M. Patrick (left), and Brigadier General William Mitchell, the leader of the fight for airpower after World War I.

wanted to stay out of war if they could. This sentiment necessarily governed the actions of the United States Government and the prewar preparations of the armed forces between 1938 and 1941. President Franklin D. Roosevelt and his advisers, fully aware of the dangers of the situation, launched a limited preparedness program at the beginning of 1939. By then the technological improvement of the airplane had introduced a new factor into the military calculations of the United States. The moment was approaching when it would be feasible for a hostile power to establish air bases in the Western Hemisphere, from which the Panama Canal—the key to American naval defense—or the continental United States itself might be attacked. The primary emphasis in 1939 was therefore on increasing the striking power of the Army Air Corps. At the same time Army and Navy officers collaborated in drafting the RAIN-BOW plans that were to guide the preparations of the American armed forces. The focus of these plans in 1939 and 1940 was on hemisphere defense.

When the European war started, the President proclaimed a limited emergency and authorized increases in Regular Army and National Guard enlisted strengths to 227,000 and 235,000, respectively. When the quick destruction of Poland produced a lull in the war, the tempo of America's own defense preparations slackened. The Army concentrated on making its regular force ready for emergency action by providing it with modern equipment as quickly as possible, and by engaging 70,000 troops in the first genuine corps and army maneuvers in American military history. In April 1940, the successful German seizure of Denmark and Norway, followed by the quick defeat of the Low Countries and France and the grave threat to Great Britain, forced the United Statse to adopt a new and greatly enlarged program for defense.

Army officers at a CCC camp in the 1930's.

Two new Army weapons. Left: the Garand rifle with its inventor, John C. Garand; right: the 105mm howitzer.

THE ARMY EXPANSION IN 1940

Under the leadership of Chief-of-Staff General George C. Marshall and, after July, of Secretary of War Henry L. Stimson, the Army embarked in the summer of 1940 on a large expansion program designed to protect the United States and the rest of the Western Hemisphere. Army expansion was matched by a naval program designed to give the United States a "two-ocean" Navy strong enough to deal simultaneously with the Japanese Fleet in the Pacific and the naval strength that Germany and its new war partner Italy might acquire in the Atlantic if they defeated Great Britain. Both expansion programs had the overwhelming support of the American people, who, though still strongly opposed to entering the war, were now convinced that the danger to the United States was very real. Congressional appropriations between May and September 1940 reflected this conviction. The Army received six billion dollars for its needs during the succeeding year—a sum about equal to what had been granted for the support of its military activities during the preceding 16 years. The munitions program approved for the Army on 30 June 1940 called for procurement by October 1941 of all items needed to equip and maintain

a 1,200,000-man force, including a greatly enlarged and modernized Army Air Corps.

The Selective Service and Training Act of 1940

To fill the ranks of this new Army, Congress on 27 August approved induction of the National Guard into Federal service and the calling up of the Organized Reserves. Then it authorized the first peacetime draft of untrained civilian manpower in the nation's history in passing the Selective Service and Training Act of 16 September 1940. Selectees, Reserve officers to train them, and units of the National Guard, were brought into service as rapidly as the Army could construct camps to house them. During the last six months of 1940 the active Army more than doubled in strength, and by mid-1941 it numbered nearly one and a half million officers and men.

A new organization, General Headquarters, took charge of training the Army in July 1940. In the same month the Army established a separate Armored Force and subsequently Antiaircraft and Tank Destroyer Commands, which, with the Infantry, Field Artillery, Coast Artillery, and Cavalry, increased the number of ground combat arms to seven. The existing branch schools and a new Armored Force

President Franklin D. Roosevelt (left) inaugurates the first peacetime draft in U.S. history on 29 October 1940. After being blindfolded, Secretary of War Henry Stimson (behind table) drew number 158 from the lottery bowl.

School concentrated during 1940 and 1941 on improving the fitness of National Guard and Reserve officers for active duty, and in early 1941 the War Department established officer candidate schools to train men selected from the ranks for junior leadership positions. In October 1940 the four field armies assumed command of ground units in the continental United States and thereafter trained them under the supervision of General Headquarters. Major overseas garrisons were strengthened, and the Army established new commands to supervise the garrisoning of Puerto Rico and Alaska, where there had been almost no Army troops for many years. In June 1941 the War Department established the Army Air Forces to train and administer air units in the United States. In July it began the transformation of General Headquarters into an operational post for General Marshall as Commanding General of the Field Forces. By the autumn of 1941 the Army had 27 infantry, 5 armored, and 2 cavalry divisions, 35 air groups, and a host of supporting units in training in the continental United States. Many of these units were still unready for action, in part because the United States had shared much of its old and new military equipment with the nations that were actively fighting the Axis.

By early 1941 it had become apparent to Army and Navy leaders and to President Roosevelt that the United States might soon be drawn into full participation in the conflict. Regulars, National Guardsmen, Reserves, selectees, and volunteers had been fused during 1941 into a new Army, as large in numbers as the combined forces of North and South in the Civil War. Although raised for defense, this Army was trained and its equipment designed for offensive operations, providing a sure base for wartime expansion and ultimate victory in World War II.

Major General George S. Patton (left) and Lieutenant Colonel Mark W. Clark confer during Army maneuvers in the summer of 1941. Both men became famous World War II commanders.

President Franklin D. Roosevelt signs the declaration of war against Japan at 1610 on 8 December 1941.

CHAPTER 14

WORLD WAR II-EUROPE

Unknown to American political or military leaders, strong Japanese forces had concentrated in November 1941 for attacks on the two main centers of American power in the Pacific, Hawaii and the Philippines. Without warning, in the early morning hours of 7 December, powerful carrier-borne air forces smashed the Pacific Fleet at anchor in Pearl Harbor, Hawaii. The same day (8 December in that longitude), about noon, Formosa-based bombers caught the bulk of the U.S. Far East Air Force lined up on Clark and Iba Fields, not far from Manila in central Luzon, and virtually destroyed it.

The attack on Pearl Harbor was one of the most brilliant tactical feats of the war. From six carriers which had advanced undetected to a position 200 miles north of Oahu, some 350 aircraft came in through the morning mist, achieving complete tactical surprise. They bombed and strafed the neatly aligned planes on Hickam and Wheeler Fields, and carefully singled out major units of the Navy's Battle Force at anchor in the harbor. Fortunately, the Fleet's three carriers were away at the time, and the attackers failed to hit the oil tanks and naval repair shops on shore. But the blow was devastating enough. Almost 200 aircraft were destroyed, 8 battleships were sunk or badly damaged, besides numerous other vessels, and total casualties came to about 3,400, mostly killed. Japanese losses were only 29 aircraft and 5 midget submarines.

The attacks on Pearl Harbor and the Philippines effectively wiped out American striking power in the Pacific. The Philippines and other American possessions in the western Pacific were isolated and their loss became a foregone conclusion, while the Hawaiian Islands and Alaska lay open to invasion. As Japanese forces moved swiftly southward against the Philippines, Malaya, and the Netherlands Indies, Japan's Axis partners, Germany and Italy, declared war on the United States. For the first time in its history, the United States was embarked upon an all-out, two-front war.

In Europe the military fortunes of the anti-Axis powers had declined as the war expanded. Germany had crushed all her Continental opponents in the west and then attempted late in 1940 to destroy Britain's air forces as a prelude to an invasion across the English Channel. In the air battles over Britain in September 1940, the Royal Air Force won a brilliant victory, but during the following winter and spring, the waning threat of invasion had been replaced by the equally deadly and more persistent menace of economic strangulation. German aircraft pulverized Britain's ports and inland cities, while U-boats, surface raiders, and mines destroyed shipping.

In June 1941, however, the storm center of the war moved elsewhere. Only slightly delayed by the conquest of the Balkans, Hitler on 22 June 1941 hurled German might against the Soviet Union, the only remaining power on the European continent capable of challenging his ascendancy. By early December, when the onset of winter and stiffening Soviet resistance finally brought the advance to a halt, the German armies had driven to the suburbs of Moscow, inflicted huge losses on the Red Army, and occupied a vast expanse of European Russia embracing its most densely populated and industrialized regions. This, as it turned out, was the high tide of German success in World War II; Hitler, like Napoleon, was to meet disaster on the windswept plains of Russia. But in December 1941 few were willing to predict so much. British and United States leaders assembling in Washington at the end of that month (the ARCADIA Conference) to formulate plans for dealing with the crisis had to reckon with the probability that in the year to come, unless the Western Allies could somehow force Germany to divert substantial forces from the eastern front, the German steamroller would complete the destruction of the Soviet armies. Hitler would then be able, with the resources and enslaved peoples of all Europe at his command, to throw his full power against the West.

In this difficult situation the Allied leaders made a far-reaching decision which shaped the whole course of the war: they agreed that the first and main effort must go into defeating Germany, the more formidable enemy. Japan's turn would come later. Defeating Germany, it was recognized, would involve a prolonged process of "closing and tightening the ring" about Fortress Europe. Operations in 1942 would have to be defensive and preparatory, though limited offensives might be undertaken if the opportunity offered. Not until 1943 at the earliest could the Allies contemplate a return to the European Continent, "across the Mediterranean, from Turkey into the Balkans, or by landings in Western Europe."

Another important action taken at the ARCADIA Conference was the establishment of the Combined Chiefs-of-Staff (CCS). This was a committee consisting of the professional military chiefs of both countries, responsible to the President and Prime Minister for planning and directing the grand strategy of the coalition. Its American members were the Army Chief-of-Staff, General Marshall; the Chief of Naval Operations, Admiral Stark (replaced early in 1942 by Admiral Ernest J. King); and the Chief (later Commanding General) of the Army Air Forces, General Henry H. Arnold. In July 1942 a fourth member was added, the President's personal chief-of-staff, Admiral William D. Leahy. Since the CCS normally sat in Washington, the British Chiefs-of-Staff, making up its British component, attended in person only at important conferences with the heads of state. In the intervals they were represented in Washington by the four senior members of the permanent British Joint Staff Mission, headed until late in 1944 by Field Marshal Sir John Dill, the former Chief of the British Imperial General Staff. Under the CCS a system of primarily military subordinate committees grew up, assisting the CCS in such fields as strategic and logistical planning, transportation, and communications.

For control of American forces, Army planners suggested soon after Pearl Harbor the creation of a supreme U.S. military commander, who would be responsible to the President and be assisted by a joint Army-Navy general staff. This scheme was rejected owing to the Navy's objections. Instead, by February 1942 the Joint Chiefs-of-Staff (JCS), consisting of the U.S. members of the CCS, had emerged as the highest authority in the U.S. military hierarchy (though never formally chartered as such), and responsible directly to the President.

In other decisions during the spring of 1942, Britain and the United States agreed on a worldwide division of strategic responsibility. The U.S. Joint Chiefs-of-Staff were to be primarily responsible for the war in the Pacific, and the British Chiefs for the Middle East-Indian Ocean region, while the European-Mediterranean-Atlantic area would be a combined responsibility of both powers. China was designated a separate theatre commanded by its chief-of-state, Chiang Kai-shek, though within the United States sphere of responsibility. In the Pacific, the JCS established two main theatres, the Southwest Pacific Area (SWPA) and the Pacific Ocean Area (POA), the former under General MacArthur, the latter under Admiral Chester W. Nimitz. POA was further subdivided into North, Central, and South Pacific areas, the first two directly controlled by Nimitz, the third by his deputy, Admiral William F. Halsey, Jr. Later in 1942, the United States air and service troops operating in China, India, and northern Burma were organized as U.S. Army Forces, China-Burma-India, under Lieutenant General Joseph W. Stilwell. On various other far-flung lines of communications U.S. Army forces, mostly air and service troops during 1942, were organized under similar theatre commands.

AA	Antiaircraft	le.P.Kw.K.2s	*Leichter Personen Kraftwagen, K.2, Schwimmend* (light personnel vehicle, K.2, amphibian)
AC	Air Corps	LST	Landing ship, tank
AT	Antitank	LVT	Landing vehicle, tracked
BAR	Browning automatic rifle	LCVP	Landing craft, vehicle-personnel
cm.	Centimeter	LST	Landing ship, tank
DD	Duplex drive	M. G.	*Maschinengewehr* (machine gun)
DDT	Dichloro-Dithenyl-Trichloroethane	mm	Millimeter
DUKW	2½-ton 6x6 amphibian truck	OCS	Officer Candidate School
E-boat	Small torpedo boat (German)	Pak.	*Panzerabwehrkanone* (antitank gun)
Flak	*Fliegerabwehrkanone* (antiaircraft artillery gun)	Pz.	*Panzer*
Jaeg.	*Jaegdtiger* (tank-destroyer)	Pz. Kpfw.	*Panzerkampfwagen* (tank)
JU.	*Junkers* (designation of airplane built by company of that name)	SCR	Signal Corps Radio
K.	*Kanone* (gun)	s.F.H.	*Schwere Feld Haubitze* (medium field howitzer)
Kar.	*Karabiner* (carbine)	SHAEF	Supreme Headquarters, Allied Expeditionary Force
Kw.	*Kraftwagen* (motor vehicle)	Sig C	Signal Corps
Kw. K.	*Kampfwagenkanone* (tank gun)	SOC	Scout Observation Curtis
LBK	Landing barge, kitchen	SP	Self-propelled
LBV	Landing barge, vehicle	*Stu. G.*	*Sturmgeschuetz* (self-propelled assault gun)
LCI	Landing craft, infantry	*Stu. H.*	*Sturmhaubitze* (self-propelled assault howitzer)
LCI(L)	Landing craft, infantry (large)	*Stu. K.*	*Sturmkanone* (self-propelled assault gun)
LCM	Landing craft, mechanized	TD	Tank destroyer
LCP	Landing craft, personnel	TNT	Trinitrotoluene; trinitrotoluol (high explosive)
LCP(R)	Landing craft, personnel (ramp)	U-boat	Submarine
LCR(S)	Landing craft, rubber (small)	WAAC	Women's Army Auxiliary Corps
LCT	Landing craft, tank	WAC	Women's Army Corps
LCT(R)	Landing craft, tank (rocket)	USAFIME	U. S. Army Forces in the Middle East
LCV	Landing craft, vehicle	USSR	Union of Soviet Socialist Republics
LCVP	Landing craft, vehicle-personnel		

THE BUILDUP IN THE UNITED KINGDOM AND THE AIR OFFENSIVE, EUROPE

The buildup of the United States Army in the United Kingdom, from January 1942 until June 1944, with the huge amounts of supplies necessary to equip and maintain the forces and to prepare for the invasion of northern Europe was a tremendous undertaking. It involved the transportation of men and supplies across the Atlantic during a time when the German submarine menace was at its peak. The United States Navy played a vital role in transporting men and supplies and in protecting the convoys while en route. During this period the administrative task was enormous since facilities for quartering and training such large forces and for storing supplies and equipment had to be provided within the limited area of the United Kingdom. In October 1942 some of the units stationed in the United Kingdom were sent to the Mediterranean for the invasion of North Africa. The buildup continued after this, well-trained units arriving from the United States. As the time for the invasion of France approached, battle-tested units from the Mediterranean theatre were transferred to England to prepare for their part in the assault. In spite of the limited terrain available, large-scale maneuvers and realistic amphibious operations were conducted. In the early spring of 1944 joint exercises of the ground, sea, and air forces which were to make the attack in Normandy were held along the southern coast of England. The last of these exercises was held in early May, the units then moving to the staging areas and embarkation points for the invasion.

U.S. troops arriving in Belfast, Northern Ireland. The first U.S. troops to cross the Atlantic after the declaration of war by the United States went to Northern Ireland in January 1942. Shortly thereafter the center of concentration was transferred from Ireland to England and the rapid buildup of personnel commenced.

GREAT BRITAIN

0   50   100
    MILES

ATLANTIC

OCEAN

SCOTLAND

NORTH

SEA

NORTHERN
IRELAND
BELFAST

IRISH SEA

LIVERPOOL

EIRE

W A L E S

E N G L A N D

LONDON

○ BRISTOL

SOUTHAMPTON

PORTSMOUTH

PORTLAND

SLAPTON
SANDS

PLYMOUTH

WEYMOUTH

Lighters pull alongside the "Queen Elizabeth" to unload U.S. troops in Scotland. On one trip the "Queen Elizabeth" carried a record load of 15,028 troops. Between December 1941 and June 1944 the "Queen Mary" and the "Queen Elizabeth" transported a large portion of the total number of troops to the United Kingdom, running alone through seas in which their great speed was their chief protection against enemy submarines.

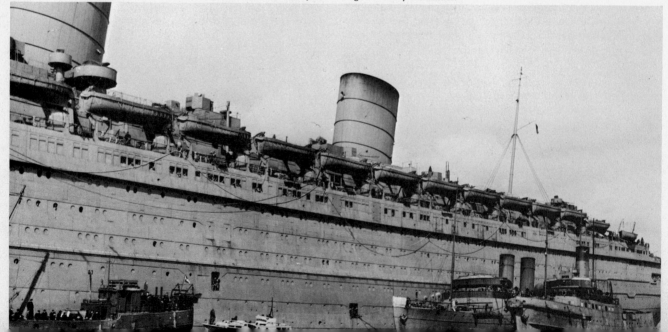

Training in Ireland, February 1942. Before leaving the United States, members of the U.S. armed forces normally had completed their training, but to keep the men at the peak of their fighting fitness programs in firing, field exercises, and special problems were begun under varying weather and terrain conditions. Men in their late teens or early twenties made the finest soldiers, as they had stamina and recuperative power far beyond that of older men. This physical superiority often determined the issue in heavy and prolonged fighting.

While the ground forces were being equipped and trained the Allied air forces bombed the fortress of Europe. The Royal Air Force Bomber Command carried out the air assault by night and the United States Eighth Air Force by day. The first U.S. participation in the bombing of Europe from British bases was on 4 July 1942, when American crews flew six British bombers. During the fall of 1942 the Eighth Air Force prepared the Twelfth Air Force for the invasion of Africa; and it was not until the beginning of 1943 that U.S. bombers began to attack Europe from England in large-scale raids. From that time on the attacks on Germany continued with increasing intensity and shattering power until, in February 1944, the German Luftwaffe attempted to sweep the U.S. bombers from the skies over Europe. After a battle of one week's duration over important industrial cities of Germany, the Luftwaffe was beaten and supremacy of the air was in Allied hands where it remained until the end of the war.

U.S. troops marching through the streets of a town in Northern Ireland escorted by a British sergeant. During the early months after the United States' entry into World War II a large part of the equipment was similar to that of World War I. In the succeeding months much was done to improve all types of equipment, and many of the changes may be seen in the pictures that follow.

Soldiers land from an assault boat during a training exercise in Scotland, July 1942. The base of fire of a U.S. rifle squad in World War II was the Browning automatic rifle (BAR). The man in right foreground is armed with this weapon. The two men behind the soldier with the BAR are armed with .30-caliber U.S. rifles.

A British police sergeant gives road direction to a U.S. first sergeant during a march. The helmet worn by the sergeant was standardized on 9 June 1941, and mass production began shortly thereafter. It replaced the earlier 1917 helmet shown in preceding pictures.

Infantryman with weapons. Soldier is holding a .45-caliber Thompson submachine gun; from left to right are: 60mm mortar, British antitank gun, .30-caliber U.S. rifle with bayonet attached, .30-caliber Browning machine gun, hand grenades, .45-caliber automatic pistol, .30-caliber U.S. rifle with grenade launcher attached, .30-caliber Browning automatic rifle, and 81mm mortar.

The sinking of a British liner without warning by a German submarine off the coast of Scotland on 3 September 1939 opened the Battle of the Atlantic, which continued until 14 May 1945 when the last U-boats surrendered at American Atlantic ports. Enemy submarines, traveling alone or in wolf packs, sank many Allied ships, but by the middle of 1943 the menace had been reduced to a problem. This was solved by the use of the interlocking convoy system that provided escort protection along the important convoy routes, small escort aircraft carriers and destroyer escorts, and planes, from which hunter-killer groups were formed to seek out and destroy the U-boats.

U.S. Navy plane attacks and sinks a German submarine in the North Atlantic, June 1943.

An engineer company at work on an airfield in England. By 1 June 1944 a total of 129 airfields was available in the United Kingdom for the Eighth and Ninth Air Forces. In addition there were 3 base air depots, 7 combat crew and replacement centers, 2 reconnaissance and 1 photographic reconnaissance fields, 19 troop carrier fields, 11 advance landing grounds, and 2 miscellaneous fields. Living quarters for more than 400,000 air force personnel had to be furnished, plus many thousands of square feet of space for storage.

Consolidated B–24 Liberators on a bombing mission over Europe.

Boeing B–17 Flying Fortresses dropping bombs on enemy installations in Bremen, Germany, while flak bursts around them. The first U.S. air unit to engage in combat over Europe was a light bombardment squadron. Flying British planes, six U.S. crews joined six RAF crews in a daylight attack against four airdromes in the Netherlands on 4 July 1942. On 17 August twelve B–17's, accompanied by four RAF Spitfire fighter squadrons, attacked the marshalling yards at Rouen, France, and successfully completed the first U.S. attack over Europe. From these small beginnings the number of planes taking part in the raids grew until the average per raid in 1943 was 570 heavy bombers, a figure that was to be almost doubled in 1944.

Three types of escort fighter planes over England. From top to bottom: Lockheed P–38 Lightning, North American P–51 Mustang, Republic P–47 Thunderbolt. P–47's were the first to join the British Spitfires in providing escort for heavy bombers; the P–38 was available in small numbers in October 1943, and the P–51 began to appear in January 1944. At first the 47's flew top cover, but before long they began to drop down and engage the enemy fighter planes. As the war progressed the escort opened out more and more until it became a huge net to envelop the enemy.

384

British fire fighters combating a fire started by bombs during a German night attack over London, February 1944.

A British Spitfire fighter chasing a German V-bomb over England. Only fast low-level ships, such as the British Spitfire or the U.S. P–47 or P–51, were good at this type of pursuit since the robot bombs averaged well over 300 miles per hour. These bombs, launched from sites along the invasion coast of France and the Low Countries, caused considerable damage in England, and in addition were a demoralizing factor in that one never knew when or where they would strike. The launching sites were placed on the list of targets for the Allied air forces, but because these sites could be easily moved and camouflaged they were not completely destroyed until the invasion forces took over the areas in which they were located. The first of the V-bombs appeared over England on 13 June 1944.

A V–1 Flying Bomb
that fell short of its target.

Anemometer and wind direction indicator being
checked by an enlisted man of a weather section.
Improvements in weather forcasting, instrument
bombing technique and equipment, and operating procedures had advanced so much that whereas in 1942 U.S. bombers could operate on an
average of only six days per month, in the last
year of the war they averaged twenty-two days.

Men of a service squadron salvaging a fuel
tank from the wing of a P–51. These tanks
helped to make the bomber escort planes
into long-range planes which gave fighter
protection to the heavy bombers. The tanks,
the fuel from which was consumed first, were
dropped when empty and the plane then
used gasoline from its permanent tanks.

P–51's in formation. Each plane in this formation has two wing tanks attached.

A fighter pilot, standing beside his plane in England, wearing an oxygen mask and helmet equipped with earphones. Over his leather flying jacket is a life preserver. The strength of the U.S. Air Force in 1940 was about 43,000 men and 2,500 planes. In early 1944 there were 2,300,000 men and 80,000 aircraft.

387

Bombs being unloaded at a U.S. Air Corps ordnance depot in England. After being stacked the bombs were covered with camouflage nets such as those behind tractors at left center of picture. Facilities for storing bombs in any other manner were limited. These stacks became common sights along the country lanes and roads in England during the war years. (1,000-pound bombs; crawler-type revolving crane on tractor mounting with Diesel engine.)

Bombs tumble from the bays of an overturned B-24 bomber. The plane was caught in a heavy flak belt while on a mission over Germany. During 1943 the enemy became much more aggressive as he shifted his fighters from the Russian front and the Mediterranean theater to western Europe. The German day fighters continually harassed U.S. heavy bombers, sometimes following them far out to sea on their withdrawal.

Aerial view of Schweinfurt, Germany, October 1943. This city was the center of the ball-bearing factories, one of the target priorities picked for destruction by the strategic air force. The order of these priorities was as follows: (1) submarine construction yards and bases, (2) aircraft industry, (3) ball-bearing industry, (4) oil industry, (5) synthetic rubber plants, and (6) military transport vehicle industry.

Bombs striking the ball-bearing factories at Schweinfurt, Germany, October 1943. Flak over the target was intense but good visibility enabled the bombers to make an accurate run, and more than 450 tons of high explosives and incendiaries were dropped in the target area. Heavy damage was inflicted on the major plants. The cost to the attackers was also severe. Sixty-two bombers were lost and 138 were damaged. Personnel casualties were 599 killed and 40 wounded. Such losses could not be sustained, and deep penetrations without escort were suspended. Schweinfurt was not attacked again for four months, and the Germans were given a chance to take countermeasures which they did with great energy and skill.

B-17's dropping bombs over Bremen, December 1943.

Heavy bombers on a mission over southwestern Germany, December 1943. Planes at upper level are Boeing B–17's; those at lower level are Consolidated B–24's. By April 1944 the Allies had achieved air superiority which permitted full-scale air attacks on Germany, an indispensable prerequisite for the invasion of Normandy.

Paratroopers having their parachutes inspected before taking off for a practice jump, England, October 1942. These troops were equipped with specially designed clothing and equipment including helmets with a new type fiber liner and chin strap, jump suits with large pockets that could be securely fastened, and boots that laced higher up the leg and had reinforced toes and stronger ankle supports.

Members of an airborne division loading a jeep ¼-ton 4x4 truck into a British Horsa glider.

By removing the tail section, the glider could be unloaded in approximately seven minutes. Airborne infantrymen in a U.S. glider. In this picture men are armed with .30-caliber U.S. rifles, a .45-caliber Thompson submachine gun, a 2.36-inch rocket launcher M1A1, and the .30-caliber Browning automatic rifle. Machine guns, mortars, and light artillery weapons were dropped by parachutes or brought in by gliders along with other supplies which made the airborne troops a compact fighting unit.

Paratroopers making a mass jump during their training in England. In practice jumps prior to the drop into Normandy there were numerous casualties. The injured were quickly cared for and the experience showed airborne medics what they could expect during the actual invasion.

A member of an engineer unit operating a multiplex machine in the process of preparing maps from aerial mosaics. Relief and other features were plotted from photographic diapositives, contained in the conical-shaped holders on the beam in background, to sheets on which control and check points have been plotted. Contours are being drawn on the maps by use of the multiplex machine. Contrary to general opinion, France was not a well-mapped country. During World War I detailed maps showed primarily trench fortifications and special small areas. The Engineers were responsible for making maps, which required the services of highly trained personnel.

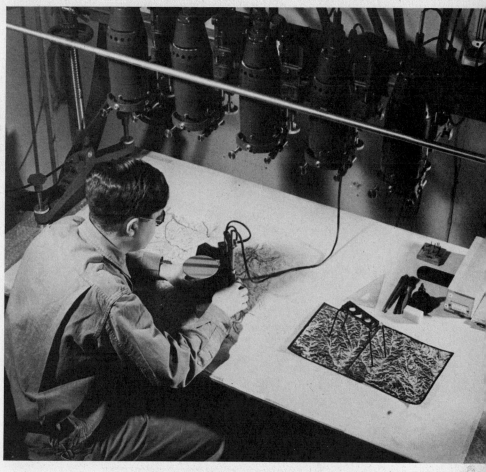

In this photo a technician is inking tracings on a contour map.

Members of an engineer topographical battalion preparing maps of Europe prior to the invasion of France. In 1944 more than 125,000,000 maps were printed for the invasion alone. An average of 867 tons of maps was shipped each month from the United States. In addition, 3,695,750 salvaged enemy maps were used for reverse side printing. Large-scale maps showing beach and underwater obstacles on the American and British assault beaches were produced by the U.S. Army Engineers in preparation for the invasion.

The Buildup in the United Kingdom-Ordnance

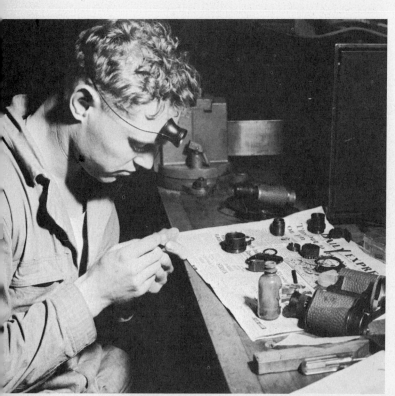

An ordnance specialist in the repair of optical equipment cleans a pair of field glasses, England, September 1942. Ordnance responsibility extended to "everything that rolls, shoots, is shot, or is dropped from the air." Its complete catalogue contained 35,000 separate items, ranging from watch springs and firing pins to 20-ton howitzers and 40-ton tanks.

Medium tanks in an ordnance depot, England. After a vehicle arrived in the United Kingdom there was much to be done before it could be issued to the using unit. Tanks were received from the United States with about 500 items of accessory equipment, including small arms, radio, tools, gunsights, and other incidentals, packed in waterproofed containers; many were coated with a rust-preventive compound. The job of preparing a tank took approximately fifty working hours. Accessories were unpacked, cleaned, tested, and installed; the motor and all mechanical components were checked and tuned. When a vehicle left the ordnance depot it was completely supplied, including ammunition and rations.

Artillery units training in England.

A repaired medium tank is given final check by ordnance personnel. Every tank, gun, or vehicle, damaged either by an accident or later in combat, which could be repaired meant one less new tank to be supplied. As the war progressed the medium tank underwent changes as did a great deal of other U.S. equipment. It became lower so as to present a more difficult target, the riveted hull was replaced by a welded or cast hull, and toward the end of the war the suspension system was changed. These, and other mechanical changes, with the addition of better armament and armor, made the vehicle a more formidable fighting machine, better able to combat enemy tanks.

A liaison plane flying over a battery of 105mm howitzers.

A 105mm howitzer motor carriage M7 on maneuvers in England, March 1943. This was an open-top, lightly armored vehicle and was the principal artillery weapon of an armored division.

155mm guns stored in England, 1944. After about 2,250 rounds had been fired, the barrel of the 155mm gun had to be replaced; in howitzers the number of rounds was higher.

20 Grosvenor Square, London, U.S. Headquarters
of the European Theatre of Operations.

U.S. enlisted men passing Number 10, Downing Street, residence and office of the
Prime Minister of Great Britain. During the period of the buildup in the British
Isles, activities and plans were formulated for the large and small units scattered
throughout the United Kingdom in a group of buildings located near the American
embassy in London. This group of buildings housed the offices of the personnel
whose task it was to coordinate the activity and training of units and, in addition,
to handle the problems relating to the buildup of supplies for the invasion.

Mail for units stationed in England being sorted. The handling of the mails through the Army Post Office
(APO) was a function of the Adjutant General's Department. Mail normally was delivered to the armed
forces with the least possible delay as it was an important morale factor for men stationed away from
home. During the last week of May 1944 an artificial delay of ten days was imposed on the forwarding
of all American mail to the United States and elsewhere, and the use of transatlantic telephone, radio,
and cable facilities was denied to American personnel. British mail was strictly censored by the military
authorities from April 1944 until the invasion on 6 June 1944. These precautionary measures were taken
to assure the secrecy of the coming invasion. In addition, a block was also placed on diplomatic cor-
respondence of all countries except the United States, Great Britain, and the USSR.

This soldier is firing a German rifle which was the standard shoulder weapon of the German Army and very similar to the U.S. rifle M1903.

Firing German weapons. In order to become familiar with German weapons and to learn the capabilities of enemy arms, U.S. infantrymen fired them during training in Northern Ireland in the spring of 1944. The men are firing a German standard dual-purpose machine gun.

A medical battalion quartered in tents, Cornwall, England.
A U.S. hospital installed in Quonset huts.

The hospital plan in the United Kingdom called for over 90,000 beds in existing installations, conversions, and new constructions. The program was later increased by 30,000 beds by using tents for the hospital units.

U.S. Army nurse, wearing a helmet and fatigue uniform, preparing an intravenous injection; a kerosene lamp provides illumination. Hospital personnel worked under conditions similar to those they might encounter upon their arrival on the Continent after the invasion. Army nurses gave widely varying types of skilled service, some of them in field hospitals and others in the general hospitals farther behind the lines. World War II was the first war in which nurses received full military benefits and real instead of relative officer rank. There were more than 17,000 Army nurses in the ETO in May 1945.

Caterpillar tractors and bulldozers stored at an Engineer depot to be used after the invasion of France.

An enlisted man on guard duty at a rail junction in Wales where American-made locomotives were stored. The United States shipped 1,000 locomotives and 20,000 railroad cars to the United Kingdom for use on the Continent after the invasion. In addition, 270 miles of railroad were constructed in England. The Transportation Corps was responsible for the movement of men and supplies by land and water, and for the operation and supply of a great deal of this equipment.

Men of a quartermaster unit storing field rations in a warehouse in England, March 1944. The U.S. Army was unquestionably better fed than any other in history. However, food in combat can never be the same as that in garrison or cantonment, since field rations must be nonperishable, compact, and easily carried by the individual soldier. Combat rations were improved as the war progressed, and C rations were supplied in a more varied assortment.

Engineer construction supplies stored in England in preparation for the invasion of Normandy. The large rolls of wire netting were to be used on the invasion beaches to make improvised roadways for vehicles.

Landing maneuvers for the invasion troops. Infantrymen landing from an LCI(L).

A combination gun motor carriage landing on the beach from an LCT. This was a highly mobile weapon, capable of a concentration of rapid fire, and designed for antiaircraft defense.

Engineers constructing a pontoon bridge in England during the training period.

Gun crew of an antiaircraft artillery group operating a 90mm gun near the coast of England, April 1944. In order to cope with the latest developments in the fields of high-altitude bombing, a 90mm antiaircraft gun with longer range, greater muzzle velocity, and a larger effective shell-burst area was introduced.

Members of an armored infantry regiment firing U.S. weapons during training in England. In 1941 the Ordnance Department began its experiments with the rocket launcher, which resulted in the invention of the 2.36-inch rocket launcher (bazooka). This was the first weapon of its type to be used in the war. Designed originally as an antitank weapon, it was used effectively against machine gun nests, pillboxes, and even fortified houses. It required only a two-man team—a gunner and a loader—and as it weighed only a little more than a rifle it could be carried everywhere.

The crew of a 60mm mortar firing at a simulated enemy position.

A half-track 81mm mortar carrier maneuvering on a road in England. The mortar could be used on the vehicle or separate from it.

The U.S. tank was designed as a weapon of exploitation to be used in long-range thrusts deep into the enemy's rear where it could attack his supply installations and communications. This required great endurance, low consumption of gasoline, and ability to move long distances without a breakdown.

Armored units participating in maneuvers in England.

Exhaust stacks and air-intake vents being installed on a medium tank.

After the installation was completed, the tank was tested off the coast of England. In addition to stacks, the tanks were further waterproofed by sealing all unvented openings with tape and sealing compound to render the hull watertight. Special attachments permitted rapid jettisoning of any waterproofing equipment which might interfere with satisfactory operation of the vehicles when on shore. These methods were first successfully used in the invasion of North Africa in November 1942. All vehicles which were to be driven ashore in Normandy under their own power, through water, and in the face of enemy fire, were waterproofed. Ordnance inspectors checked the vehicles in the marshalling yards a few hours before the tanks were loaded for the invasion.

Amphibian trucks carry supplies ashore from a coaster under the protection of a smoke screen during landing maneuvers.

Boat-landing drill during a training exercise, Slapton Sands near Weymouth, Devon, England, May 1944. The infantrymen shown here have their equipment as complete as it will be during the actual invasion landings. They are descending ladders into an LCVP.

A 2½-ton amphibian truck hitting the beach during maneuvers. These versatile trucks proved invaluable in bringing supplies to the beaches during the early stages of landing and during the buildup after the invasion of Normandy. During one of the amphibious exercises, which were made as realistic as possible, two LST's were sunk by German E-boats. In other respects the training was successful and valuable lessons were learned.

LCVP's circling near the mother ship while waiting for the signal to land on the beach during landing operation training at Slapton Sands.

Members of an armored unit being briefed at a marshalling area. At the conclusion of the training exercises in May all the assault, follow-up, and buildup troops moved from their camps to marshalling areas for final staging.

Men and equipment being loaded into LST's.

Men and equipment being loaded into LCVP's during the first days of June 1944 at one of the "hards" (paved strips running to the water's edge) in southern England for the invasion of Normandy. The training given the assault forces during the amphibious exercises were so thorough that the final loadings for the invasion were accomplished with a minimum of delay and confusion, and resembled another exercise more than the real thing. Two and one-half years after the first U.S. troops sailed for the United Kingdom, the training and preparation was completed, and the large invasion force of U.S. and Allied troops was to receive its real test in battle against the enemy.

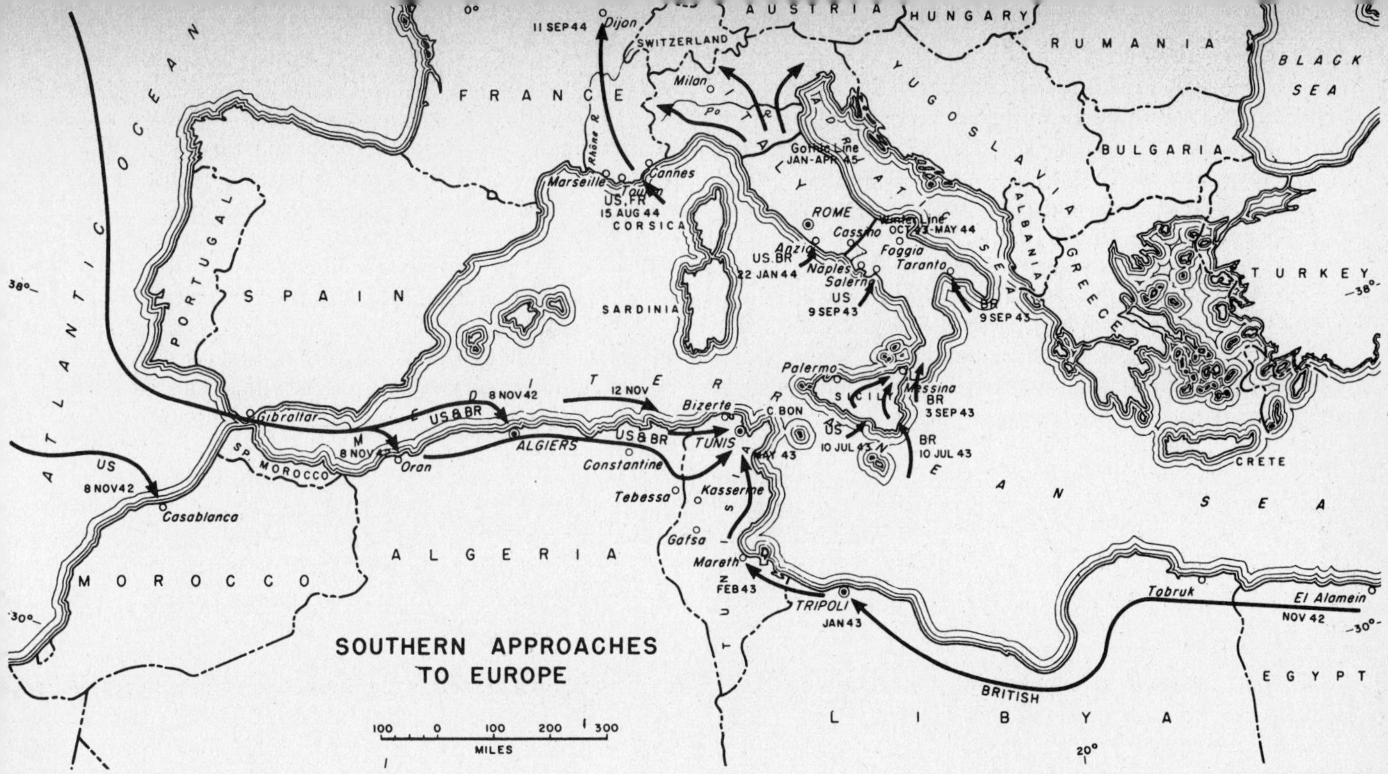
SOUTHERN APPROACHES TO EUROPE
ATLANTIC OCEAN
FRANCE
SWITZERLAND
AUSTRIA
HUNGARY
RUMANIA
BLACK SEA
YUGOSLAVIA
BULGARIA
ALBANIA
GREECE
TURKEY
PORTUGAL
SPAIN
ITALY
ADRIATIC SEA
SARDINIA
CORSICA
SICILY
CRETE
MEDITERRANEAN SEA
SP. MOROCCO
MOROCCO
ALGERIA
TUNISIA
LIBYA
EGYPT
Dijon
11 SEP 44
Milan
Po R.
Rhône R.
Marseille
Toulon
Cannes
US.FR
15 AUG 44
Gothic Line
JAN-APR 45
ROME
Anzio
US.BR
22 JAN 44
Cassino
Winter Line
OCT 43-MAY 44
Foggia
Naples
Salerno
US
9 SEP 43
Taranto
BR
9 SEP 43
Palermo
Messina
BR
3 SEP 43
US
10 JUL 43
BR
10 JUL 43
Gibraltar
US
8 NOV 42
Casablanca
Oran
8 NOV 42
US&BR
8 NOV 42
ALGIERS
12 NOV
US&BR
Bizerte
C. BON
TUNIS
MAY 43
Constantine
Tebessa
Kasserine
Gafsa
Mareth
FEB 43
TRIPOLI
JAN 43
BRITISH
Tobruk
El Alamein
NOV 42
38°
30°
0°
20°
100 0 100 200 300
MILES

NORTH AFRICA AND THE MIDDLE EAST

North Africa

The occupation of French North Africa by Allied troops was determined in July 1942 when the American and British Governments agreed to launch a Mediterranean operation in the fall of 1942. The invasion, designated as TORCH, was to coincide with a British advance westward from Egypt. Before American soldiers did any actual fighting in North Africa, however, and before the United States was at war, civilian and military observers had been informally attached in May 1941 to the U.S. military attaché in Cairo. This group was the beginning of a force whose primary function was to service and maintain lend-lease equipment from the United States, instruct the British in its use, and report on how it stood up under battle conditions. The U.S. Air Force also was performing missions in Egypt several months before the Allied landings in North Africa. All these activities contributed to the British victory at El Alamein in October 1942.

Allied troops sailed for North Africa from ports in both the United States and the United Kingdom. The U.S. Navy and the Royal Navy shared in supplying transports and naval escort and were able to prevent any serious losses through enemy submarine action. Vital air support was at first provided from aircraft carriers of both Navies and later by land-based planes of the Allied air forces utilizing recently captured airfields.

The Allies hoped to avoid French resistance to the landings by arranging for the assistance of patriotic Frenchmen ashore and by the participation in the operation of General Henri Giraud, a French military leader and former Army commander of great prestige who had escaped from France. These plans were only partly successful. The landings on the early morning of 8 November at beaches near Algiers, Oran, Casablanca, Port-Lyautey, Fedala, and Safi met resistance at all objectives. The opposition in Algiers and Safi collapsed quickly. Oran could be occupied only after considerable fighting. French forces, especially naval elements, in the neighborhood of Casablanca resisted strongly, but yielded on 11 November, a few minutes before the final assault on the city itself was to start. After a brief period of neutrality, most of the French forces in northwest Africa joined in the war against the Axis.

The Axis reacted to the Allied invasion by rushing troops to Tunisia by air and sea, and captured the local airfields and ports without opposition. British, American, and French troops drove eastward, and at the end of November and in early December launched their attack against the Axis bridgehead. The Allied advance, however, was stopped short of Tunis. Air superiority for the moment lay with the Axis. Lack of means to overcome the increased resistance, in addition to weather conditions which interfered with transport and flying, forced the postponement until 1943 of a renewed advance over the difficult terrain of northern Tunisia.

Meanwhile, the British Eighth Army was pressing German and Italian forces back from Egypt through Libya and reached the southern border of Tunisia in January 1943. Plans could then be perfected for a coordinated attack against the remaining Axis forces in North Africa by the British Eighth Army in the south and the Allied troops in the north consisting of the British First Army, the American II Corps, the French XIX Corps, and the Allied air forces. Attack by Axis forces at points of their own selection repeatedly interfered with Allied preparations. In February the enemy broke through Faïd Pass, and in a series of attacks advanced beyond Kasserine almost to the Algerian border. These attacks were stopped on 21-22 February when the enemy started his withdrawal, destroying bridges and mining the passes behind him.

But the Allied forces were closing in. After attacking and turning the Mareth position, the British Eighth Army defeated the enemy there and pursued him along the coast as far as Enfidaville, less than fifty miles from Tunis. Accelerated Allied air and naval attacks choked off the enemy's supply and weakened his resistance. At the same time the American II Corps was shifted northwest to a new sector on the left of the British First Army. Then, after severe infantry fighting, the American II Corps made an armored thrust to Mateur, and after a pause it pushed tank forces east to the sea, separating Bizerte from Tunis. Farther south the British First Army drove directly toward Tunis. On 7 May both Bizerte and Tunis were occupied, and by 13 May Axis capitulation was complete. The Allies had achieved their initial objective of opening the Mediterranean route to the Middle East and seizing bases in North Africa. At the same time they had inflicted a major defeat on the Axis Powers.

Allied strength in French North Africa had been brought to a total of about a million men. Much of this strength was not intended for the Tunisia Campaign but for later operations against Sicily and southern Italy. Elaborate training establishments were developed by the American Fifth and Seventh Armies and vast supply depots established with a view to future operations from the African base.

Persian Gulf Command

In June 1942 an American theatre of operations called U.S. Army Forces in the Middle East was established with headquarters at Cairo. Under this command were merged various groups and military missions that had been active in this area since the spring of 1941. American responsibilities for moving supplies to the Soviet Union led ultimately to a separation of the Persian Gulf activities of USAFIME and their establishment under an organization that was known from December 1943 to October 1945 as the Persian Gulf Command, with headquarters at Tehran, Iran.

From 1941 to 1945 the main business of the U.S. Army in the Middle East was to facilitate the supply of lend-lease goods to British and Soviet forces. This task involved the construction of docks, warehouses, shops, and highways as well as the operation of ports, a railroad, and a motor transport service in Iran. At the same time the Army constructed numerous airfields and bases, stretching across Egypt, the Anglo-Egyptian Sudan, Eritrea, Palestine, Saudi Arabia, Syria, Iraq, and Iran.

The Pyramids near Cairo, Egypt. For more than six months before the attack on Pearl Harbor, the United States had recognized the military importance of the Middle East. Lend-lease equipment was poured into Egypt to aid the British in the western desert. The type of transport plane shown above performed constant service in the Middle East area. It was known familiarly as "the work horse of the war." (Douglas C-47 transport, Dakota.)

Tanks at the Heliopolis U.S. ordnance repair depot. On Black Saturday, 13 June 1942, in a battle near Tobruk in Libya, British armor suffered severe tank losses inflicted by German 88mm antitank guns. This defeat caused a withdrawal to the El Alamein Line in Egypt.

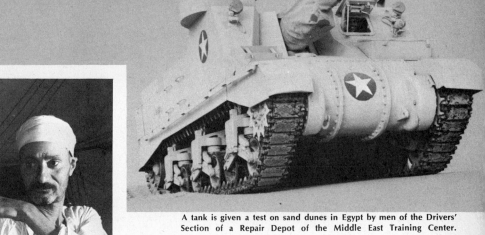

A tank is given a test on sand dunes in Egypt by men of the Drivers' Section of a Repair Depot of the Middle East Training Center.

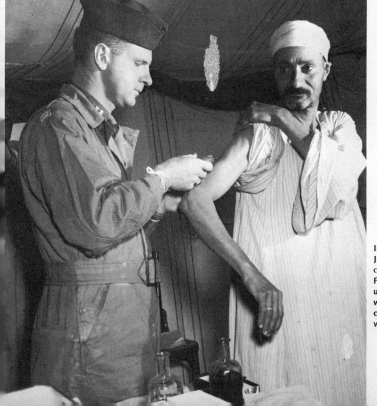

Inoculating Egyptian worker with typhus vaccine. In June of 1942 a separate command was formed in Cairo, called the U.S. Army Forces in the Middle East (USA-FIME). Natives working with U.S. personnel were usually under Army medical supervision. Those handling food were subject to physical inspection and received medical treatment and whatever immunization inoculations were indicated for the locality. The use of preventive medicine stopped the outbreak of epidemics.

409

Liberators bombing Ploesti oil field installations in Romania. The first U.S. air mission flown against any strategic target in Europe was on the Ploesti oil fields, a 12-bomber raid by B–24's from Egypt on 12 June 1942. The next raid on this target, 1 August 1943, was a low-level attack by 177 Liberators from Bengasi in Libya with the loss of 54 bombers. Refinery production was interrupted by these raids from Africa, but was not stopped until the spring of 1944 when continuous large-scale attacks were carried out from bases in Italy.

B–25's over the Western Desert in Egypt. The U.S. Air Forces were active in the Middle East several months before the Allied landings in North Africa. The first mission of these bombers was against the enemy-occupied port of Matruh on the coast of Egypt in July 1942.

The Landings

Troops on transport headed for French Morocco. Note rubber life belts on most of the men. These could be inflated instantly by means of gas cartridges in belts. In practice it was found that a fully inflated belt was not capable of supporting a soldier loaded down with his equipment. Men who found themselves in the water could not readily get rid of their packs and ammunition belts, and several drownings occurred during the landings.

Convoy bound for North Africa. Troops in the first landings approached their destinations in several large convoys, escorted by aircraft carriers and other warships. The convoy to Morocco originated in several ports of the United States on 23 October 1942, and when near the African coast separated into three major parts. The convoy steaming to the vicinity of Oran and Algiers left the United Kingdom on 26 October. Before passing through the Straits of Gibraltar it separated into two parts. Inside the Mediterranean the two sections overtook slower cargo convoys and continued on a course toward Malta until sundown of 7 November. That night each section wheeled southward and separated farther to reach several landing points near Oran and Algiers. Other convoys had already left both the United States and the United Kingdom before the attacks began.

Casablanca, the main objective on the Atlantic coast of Morocco. The landings were made at Fedala, farther north, in order to attack Casablanca overland, partly because of its very strong defenses and partly because of the necessity of capturing the port in usable condition. Casablanca was a naval base. The U.S. Navy had the mission of preventing French warships from interfering with the landings. American ships came under the fire of large coastal guns on El Hank Point, and engaged in running battles off Casablanca. Moored in the harbor was the battleship "Jean Bart" which also fired heavy shells to drive the American ships from their protective stations. After three days, when Casablanca was about to be attacked by ground, air, and sea bombardment and occupied by tanks and infantry, the city surrendered. The harbor was put to almost immediate use.

411

Directing landing-craft traffic off Fedala by means of semaphore flags. The port was captured and put into operation on D-Day, but because of its limited capacity, freighters had to stand offshore awaiting their turns to discharge cargo. In the meantime, unloading of ships went on with remaining assault craft. On the evening of 11 November a transport was torpedoed and sunk by submarine; a destroyer and tanker were damaged. The next day three additional transports were torpedoed and sunk. (Landing craft in picture: LCV; landing craft, mechanized, LCM(3); landing craft, personnel (Ramp), LCP(R).)

Infantry landing on the beach near Fedala. The landing itself was unopposed, but fighting developed just off the beach.

Unloading equipment in Fedala Harbor. Waterproofed jeep coming off LCV.

Warship passing the Rock of Gibraltar. This fortress was temporarily the Allied command post for TORCH. It was the only area on the European mainland under Allied control. Land-based aircraft did not take part in the beach assault phase, but aircraft were staged at the Gibraltar airport for takeoff for Africa as soon as airfields there were captured. A U.S. fighter group equipped with British Spitfires landed near Oran about noon on D-Day and aided in the fighting there; other planes flew to Algiers.

Light tank in Casablanca shortly after the surrender on 11 November. Only light tanks were brought ashore in assault craft; the medium tanks were unloaded in the port of Safi until D plus 2 and headed north toward Casablanca.

Radar sets near Casablanca. This type of set was part of the equipment of the invading forces. By the end of December 1942, 15 of these units were in operation as part of the air warning system of Casablanca. The searchlight automatically followed planes tracked by the radar. The city was almost at the maximum range of enemy bombers and was the target for few raids.

413

The beach of Les Andalouses, west of Oran. The landings here were unopposed.

Eastern part of Oran harbor. Early on 8 November two British ships (ex-U.S. Coast Guard cutters), carrying about 400 U.S. soldiers, entered the port between the moles shown in the distance. The ships came under point-blank fire from French naval vessels in the harbor and from shore batteries. They returned the fire but were sunk with great loss of life. When resistance in Oran ceased at noon on 10 November the port was cluttered with ships either sunk by British naval gunfire or sabotaged. Port installations had received only minor damage and were quickly put to use.

The plan for the capture of Oran and nearby airfields consisted of the frontal attack on the port itself and landings on both sides of the city at Mersat bou Zedjar and Les Andalouses west of Oran, and in the Golfe d'Arzeu east of Oran. Of the beach landings, those at Arzeu were much the largest and were made with little resistance. By afternoon of D-Day all opposition in the neighborhood had ceased.

Unloading supplies and laying prefabricated track on the beach in the Golfe d'Arzeu east of Oran.

Captured train at Saint-Leu on the Golfe d'Arzeu. The railroad from Casablanca to Tunis figured prominently in the planning of the African invasion. If the forces on the Mediterranean coast were to be cut off by sea, supplies could be carried by railroad from Casablanca. During the fighting in Tunisia and the buildup in Africa for the invasion of Europe, this railroad played an important part. After its capture it was repaired and improved. Locomotives and rolling stock were obtained from the U.S. to speed delivery of supplies.

Algiers, the most important objective of the North African invasion. The ultimate goals for the operation were Bizerte and Tunis, but because of the land-based enemy aircraft in Sardinia, Sicily, and southern Italy, it was decided to land no troops farther east than Algiers until airports had been captured. British-American elements at Algiers reembarked for a movement eastward to Bougie where they landed on 11 November. Bône was captured the following day by British paratroopers dropped from C-47's and by seaborne forces from Bougie. From there the advance toward Tunis started. Allied columns reached Djedeida, 12 miles from Tunis, on 29 November 1942, but rapid enemy buildup forced the Allies to abandon it on 13 December.

Troops loading into assault craft from transport prior to landing near Algiers. With minor exceptions, the landing craft were manned by Royal Navy personnel. Landings took place on beaches on both sides of the city as well as in the port itself. Although beach landings were not heavily opposed, one of the two British destroyer-transports making a frontal attack on the port had three boilers damaged by fire from shore but discharged her load of U.S. troops on a dock of 0520, D-Day. Some troops were surrounded and taken to a French military prison, others regained the ship before she was eventually driven off. The hostilities here ceased the same day, and the soldiers were set free by the French.

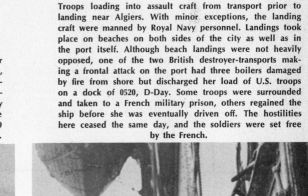

Antiaircraft defense over Algiers at night. The city suffered practically no damage during the invasion. On the first evening of its surrender it was bombed by enemy planes. This attack was followed by many others, mostly aimed at the concentration of shipping in the harbor. Damage was surprisingly small. Algiers became Allied Force Headquarters (AFHQ).

French prisoners of war captured during the invasion. The prisoners were released shortly after the end of hostilities, 11 November, and from then on fought on the side of the Allies. On 15 November orders were issued for the movement of French troops, then at Algiers and Constantine, to protect the southern flank of the American and British units advancing into Tunisia along the northern coast. The French were reinforced by U.S. troops, including tank destroyer units, and one of their assigned missions was the protection of advanced airfields in the Tébessa–Gafsa area.

Aviation engineers at Youks-les-Bains lining up for mess. This Algerian airfield near Tébessa and the Tunisian border was occupied by U.S. paratroopers on 15 November 1942. It became operational for P–38 fighter planes (Lockheed Lightnings) shortly afterward. During the first few weeks there were no provisions for landing after dark, and on 21 November six P–38's crashed while trying to land in the evening. It was not an improved field and there was no effective air-raid system. The first warning of enemy aircraft was frequently the strafing or bombing itself. When the rains started, operations were drastically reduced by mud.

Camouflaging medium bomber at Youks-les-Bains airfield. Camouflaging for hiding purposes in olive groves or on rough terrain was relatively successful; however, camouflaging an aircraft on a flat, featureless landing field was not practical except to deceive the enemy about the type or serviceability of planes. Note that the bomber above is minus both of its engines. (Martin B-26 Marauder.)

German Tiger tank. This heavy tank was encountered early in the campaign. The German High Command was particularly concerned with the performance of the Tiger in the defense of Tunis. Its high-velocity 88mm gun, equipped with a muzzle brake, could knock out Allied tanks before the latter could get within effective range; and within range, Allied tank guns could not penetrate its frontal armor. The Tiger sacrificed mobility for armor and firepower. To avoid weak bridges, it was equipped with telescopic air intake, exhaust extensions, and overall sealing that enabled it to cross rivers 15 feet deep, completely submerged on the bottom. The gun has a traverse of 360 degrees.

Faïd Pass. This opening in the eastern mountain chain was taken from a weak French garrison and held against U.S. and French counterattacks, 30 January–2 February 1943. Just before daylight, 14 February, very strong German forces came through Faïd Pass, and others came from south of the pass to drive the Americans from positions to the west. The enemy cut off and isolated three groups, on Djebel Ksaira and Garet Hadid southwest of the pass, and Djebel Lessouda northwest of it. On 15 February, an American armored counterattack to relieve the troops was made in strength far inferior to that required. Most of the troops were captured trying to escape. On 17 February, the American base at Sbeitla and the airfields at Thelepte were evacuated, as all troops were pulled back into the western mountain chain. The enemy then decided to continue his attack toward the northwest.

417

Captured German armor. The Mark IV medium tank was equipped with a 75mm cannon of higher velocity and range than any of the Allied tank guns then in use. It was generally superior to Allied tanks and was probably the best tank the enemy had until the Panther made its appearance in Italy, 1944. The Mark IV was used until the end of the war.

The eight-wheeled armored car with a 75mm howitzer was equipped with quite thin armor which was so well angled that machine-gun bullets and small fragments were not effective against it. It could be steered from both ends and had a speed of slightly more than 30 miles an hour.

Enemy Armored Equipment

General Sherman tank towing disabled half-track at Sidi bou Zid. This tank gradually re placed the M3 (General Grant) in Tunisia. Its principal weapon was the 75mm cannon Its turret could traverse an arc of 360 degrees in contrast to the sponson-mounted gu on the General Grant with a traverse of about 30 degrees.

Kasserine Pass area. The enemy broke out of the pass on 20 February 1943. On the 21st he headed toward Tébessa and Thala. The attack on Tébessa was halted; the main attack toward Thala made some progress. A British armored force, with heavy losses in tanks and men, delayed the enemy until U.S. artillery got into position. On the 22nd the enemy pounded the defenses of Tébessa and Thala unsuccessfully. Allied planes attacked the enemy near Thala, and in the evening the Germans started to withdraw. The Kasserine push was the high point of enemy fortunes in Tunisia.

German armor. The Mark III medium tank, the standard German tank in Tunisia, had a high-velocity 50mm cannon which could penetrate the frontal armor of U.S. light tanks at 1,000 yards and the frontal and side armor of the General Grant at 500 and 1,000 yards respectively. The prototypes of both these vehicles existed in Germany in 1936 and were used until the end of the war.

Italian medium tanks left behind at Kasserine Pass. This model was the backbone of the Italian armor in Tunisia. By Allied standards it was inferior in practically every respect, but it was the best the Italians had.

The famous German Eighty-Eight. The original weapon, an Austrian 88mm cannon, was used in World War I. Restrictions imposed by the Allies after that war limited German experimentation on conventional offensive artillery but not on defensive artillery such as antiaircraft types (in photograph). With different sets of aiming fire instruments this antiaircraft gun could be used as an antitank gun or a conventional piece of artillery. It was tested as an antiaircraft gun under battle conditions during the Spanish Civil War in 1936. Encountered throughout the war in increasing numbers, it was probably the most effective all-around piece of artillery the Germans had.

U.S. tank destroyers. This tank destroyer was introduced in Tunisia after the Kasserine fight. The chassis was that of the General Sherman tank, the gun having a higher velocity than that of comparable Allied tank guns. The first time it saw action was in the vicinity of Maknassy during the middle of March 1943. The village of Maknassy was occupied by U.S. forces on 22 March 1943. (37mm gun motor carriage M6.)

U.S. half-track used as a mobile antiaircraft unit. AA units like this cut down the effectiveness of the German dive bombers. Half-tracks proved practical for many purposes not originally intended. First designed as a cavalry scout car, it became, with modifications, a gun carriage mounting anything from a 37mm cannon to a 105mm howitzer, a personnel carrier, an ambulance, or just a truck.

U.S. light tank, captured by the Germans. The main weapon of this tank was the 37mm gun. Its armor was light and riveted together as was the armor on the first models of the medium tanks. A glancing shell could rip off the outside heads of the rivets and send the rivets ricocheting through the interior of the tank with the velocity of bullets. Note German markings on this vehicle.

Sherman tank with "Scorpion" attachment, detonating mines during a test. The Scorpion was a revolving drum with chains attached; when in motion it acted as a flail, and could clear a path through a mine field for infantry and other tanks to follow. It was developed by the British and used extensively by them in desert warfare.

Jefna area, looking east to the plains of Mateur. The Jefna position, on the Sedjenane-Mateur road, was one of the strongest German defenses in northern Tunisia and included two heavily fortified hills commanding the road to Mateur: Djebel Azag (Green Hill) on the north and Djebel el Ajred (Bald Hill) on the south. On 13 April 1943, U.S. forces relieved the British and took positions on both sides of the road and the mountains along the valley. The fight for the two hills lasted until 3 May when the Jefna positions were outflanked by U.S. and French forces advancing toward Bizerte and the Mateur plain north of Jefna.

Infantry and armor advancing on Mateur. After the fall of Hill 609 the enemy pulled back leaving the road to Mateur open. This small village in the middle of a plain was the center of enemy road communications in the U.S. zone of attack. Its occupation on 3 May opened the way for the advance on Bizerte, the main objective of the U.S.-French drive.

Enemy prisoners near Mateur. Allied troops took 252,415 prisoners, together with large quantities of equipment and supplies, when the enemy surrendered in Tunisia on 13 May 1943. Because of Allied air and naval superiority the enemy was unable to evacuate his troops. Of those captured, the Germans were among the finest and best trained troops the enemy had and he could ill afford to lose them.

Military Aid to the French

French troops receiving instructions on U.S. equipment, in this case on the 105mm high-explosive shell. During the summer of 1943 shipments of arms and equipment for the French arrived in North African ports in increasing volume. Training was accelerated, and by the end of the year two fully equipped French divisions were fighting side by side with the Americans and British in Italy. As more equipment became available, additional French divisions were sent to the front.

Lend-lease equipment for the French Army. In January 1943, it was agreed that the United States would equip the French divisions formed from units then in North Africa, but comparatively little modern equipment became available for them in Tunisia until the summer of 1943. (P–38 Sherman tank M4.)

Quartermaster dump at Oran. Foodstuffs, stored in the open sometimes for months, suffered very little in spite of the hot African sun.

Bizerte, the main objective of the French and U.S. forces of II Corps, fell on 7 May. Bizerte's harbor and the important naval repair facilities at nearby Ferryville were to play important parts in future operations in the Mediterranean. The enemy had blocked the channel to the inner harbor by sinking ships at the entrance and had destroyed most of the port facilities not already wrecked by Allied bombings. The port, however, became operational a few days after capture; ships and supplies were assembled here for the invasion of Sicily.

Freighter burning in the harbor of Algiers. The cause of the fire was not determined. While air raids on Algiers caused little damage to shipping and military installations, serious accidents and fires, some of which aroused suspicion of sabotage, were not infrequent.

Army Forces in the Middle East and the establishment of a separate organization called the Persian Gulf Command.

Iran

The port of Khorramshahr, one of two Iranian ports operated by the United States, the other being Bandar Shahpur. These ports received lend-lease supplies en route to the USSR. By the fall of 1942, ports, highways, and railroads in Iran were sufficiently ready to handle increased traffic over the route through the Persian Gulf. The U.S. Army also operated the lighterage port of Cheybassi in Iraq.

The port of Bandar Shahpur on the Persian Gulf. The voyage from New York around South Africa to the Persian Gulf ports averaged 70 days. When the Mediterranean route became available in 1943, the time was shortened to 42 days. This port, built on swampy land where the river Jarrahi empties into the gulf, has a semitropical climate. Both here and at Khorramshahr much of the work was done at night, and even then the temperature was around 100 degrees Fahrenheit from March until October. The area is subject to torrential rains in winter. Docking space at both ports was often insufficient to accommodate all ships waiting to be unloaded, which necessitated the use of lighters.

Truck convoys with supplies for Russia. From the ports on the Persian Gulf, shipments went to Kazvin and Tehran by road and rail. From these points movements were regulated by the Russians. During the entire period of active operations, from August 1942 to May 1945, more than 5,000,000 long tons of lend-lease cargo were moved through the Persian Corridor to Russia. The greatest monthly movement of freight through the corridor took place in July 1944, when approximately 282,000 long tons were delivered. The bulk of this total was moved by rail, the rest by truck and air.

Freight train loaded with tanks bound for Tehran. U.S. troops from early 1943 operated the southern sector of the Iranian State Railway and the two Iranian ports. They constructed additional roads, docks, and other installations, and continued operation of aircraft and motor vehicle assembly plants. Diesel locomotives and rolling stock were brought in from the United States in large numbers. American responsibility for moving supplies to the USSR led to the separation of the Persian Gulf activities of the U.S.

The main railroad station at Tehran.

Qualeh Morgeh Airport at Tehran. This was jointly occupied by
U.S. and Russian air forces. Picture shows a Douglas C–47 transport and a B–24 bomber.

Russian pilots arriving at Abadan Airport,
Iran. This airport, on an island in the
Shatt al Arab near the head of the Per-
sian Gulf, was the main assembly field
for U.S. planes going to the Soviet
Union through the Persian Corridor.

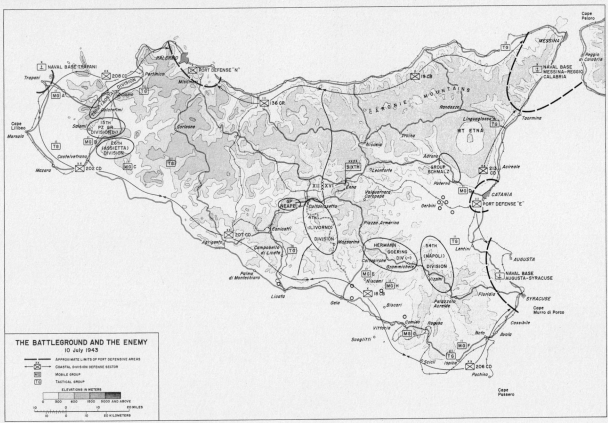

Map — Sicily

SICILY, CORSICA, AND SARDINIA

The decision to assault Sicily was made by the Chiefs of Staff at Casablanca in January 1943. After the conclusion of the Tunisia Campaign, plans were completed and preparations for the attack were accelerated (Operation HUSKY). The island of Pantelleria, located between North Africa and Sicily, occupied mainly by Italian troops, was bombarded by Air Forces and Navy units and fell on 11 June. Troops for the invasion were embarked from the United States, United Kingdom, Algeria, Tunisia, and the Middle East.

On the night before D-Day, a high wind of near gale proportions was encountered as the convoys approached their rendezvous. Shortly after H-Hour, 10 July, airborne landings, although scattered by the high wind, were to some extent successful in their effect on our beach assault. Three hours after the landing, beachheads were established from Licata to Scoglitti by th Americans and from Capo Passero to Syracuse by the British.

Despite the problem of supply during the first two days, by 12 July the Allied armies had seized the port of Syracuse and ten other Sicilian towns in addition to several airfields.

By the 23d, American tanks and infantry, driving across the western end of the island, took the key port of Palermo. The enemy, in the east, lodged in rugged mountain terrain, offered stiff resistance.

On 25 July King Victor Emmanuel III had announced the resignation of Premier Benito Mussolini and his cabinet, thereby exposing the weakness of fascist Italy. Italian resistance had crumbled, and in August the German army started to withdraw to the mainland across the Strait of Messina.

The British Eighth Army succeeded in taking Catania on the east coast early in August, and Messina was entered by both American and British units on the 16th. All organized resistance ceased on 17 August after 39 days of fighting.

Allief Force Headquarters' plan for the occupation of Corsica and Sardinia was confirmed at the Quebec conference held in August 1943. After the withdrawal of the German forces from Sardinia, the island fell into Allied hands without a struggle. The French army, given the mission of taking Corsica, met only slight resistance from the retreating German troops in October 1943.

Air bases established on both islands provided air coverage for future operations in northern Italy and southern France.

Sicily—Preinvasion Bombing

Flying Fortress bombing enemy installations in Sicily. For weeks prior to the invasion of the island, airfields, rail lines, and ports had been under aerial bombardment by Allied planes. Note black antiaircraft bursts.

Result of aerial bombardment on Napola railroad yard near Trapani, western Sicily. By the time of invasion the railroad net on the island was crippled and remained so throughout the campaign.

Men marching aboard landing craft in Bizerte Harbor. This port was one of the embarkation points for the invasion of Sicily, an island strategically important because its geographic location between Africa and Italy almost divides the Mediterranean Sea in two. In order to travel from one end of the Mediterranean to the other it was necessary to pass through the ninety-mile strait between Sicily and Tunisia. With Sicily in enemy hands, control of this strait was divided, and enemy aircraft and submarines interfered with Allied shipping to the Middle East. (Landing craft, infantry, large, LCI(L).)

Gela beach, Sicily. The invasion of the island took place on 10 July 1943. Gela was the center of the American invasion area which extended from Licata on the west to Scoglitti on the east. The British Army landed in the region between Capo Passero and Syracuse on the east coast of the island. Beach landings in both areas were preceded by airborne assaults. By sunrise, three hours after the first landing, the beaches were under control.

Licata beaches, looking westward along the coast. The highway in the foreground is the main coastal road. This was the western portion of the U.S. assault area, and Licata, located at the foot of the hill in the distance, was occupied by 1130 on D-Day.

An LST deck-loaded with men and equipment off Gela awaiting signal to approach the beach, while a U.S. cruiser fires on an enemy strongpoint.

Infantry landing on Gela Beach. Unloading equipment and supplies from LCVP's; in the background are two LST's. The sea ran so high during the morning of the landings that many craft were washed up on the beach and could not be refloated in time for turn-around to mother ships.

Half-track detouring through a side street. When the enemy retreated through the Sicilian villages he would often blow up buildings on both sides of the main street, thus blocking the passage for vehicles. If he had time he would also mine and booby-trap the road and ruins.

430

Troina. View from Troina toward the northwest showing Highway 120 winding over the hills to Cerami. Troina lies at the junction of Highway 120 and the road to Adrano and Paterno. The U.S. Seventh Army took Troina on 6 August after some of the fiercest fighting of the campaign.

The self-propelled gun of Italian manufacture is a 90mm cannon. It was used in North Africa as well as in Sicily.

Enemy artillery. The famous German 88mm gun. The pillbox in the background was sited to fire both toward the sea and along the road. The coast of the island was ringed with pillboxes, some of which had not been completed at the time of the invasion.

Self-propelled howitzer. This is the M7 howitzer motor carriage mounting a 105mm howitzer which was used for high-angle as well as direct fire. The .50-caliber machine gun is mounted in a raised pulpit-like structure which gave the vehicle the nickname Priest.

Sherman tanks entering Palermo on the day the city surrendered,
22 July 1943.

The city of Palermo. The port had been damaged by Allied bombing raids, and the Germans before withdrawing had demolished some of the installations. After the arrival of U.S. troops, the port was quickly made serviceable and was used as a supply base for troops advancing from here eastward along the coast toward Messina. It was later used as one of the embarkation ports for the invasion of Italy.

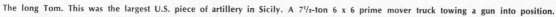

The long Tom. This was the largest U.S. piece of artillery in Sicily. A 7¹/₂-ton 6 x 6 prime mover truck towing a gun into position.

433

Digging a foxhole in an olive grove using a helmet as a shovel. These holes provided excellent protection against shell and bomb fragments. The steel helmet was used for a variety of purposes besides protecting the head. It made a fine wash basin, was used as a basket to carry post exchange items (paper bags were not available), and practically everyone used it as a seat while living in the field. In some cases it was used as a cooking utensil in violation of regulations, as excessive heat took the temper out of the steel, making it useless for the purpose for which it was originally intended. (The soldier in picture is wearing the fiber liner while he digs with the steel helmet, M1.)

Soldiers sterilizing mess kits after eating. When possible this was done before and after every meal. Such procedure was of the greatest importance in Sicily where sanitation as we know it was little practiced among the population as a whole. In spite of every precaution, dysentery of one kind or another was common among Allied forces.

Probing for mines at a bridge-crossing site. The mine detector reacts to metal; whether the metal was a mine or a shell fragment had to be determined by probing and digging, usually with a bayonet. (Mine detector SCR 625.)

San Fratello Ridge. Torrente Furiano in the foreground. San Fratello Ridge was taken on 8 August after bitter enemy resistance.

Scene from the northern coast of Sicily, looking toward the west. San Fratello Ridge and the village of Acquedolci. The fight for the San Fratello Ridge was unusually severe. Highway 113, the main axis of advance along the north coast from Palermo to Messina, follows the shore here. The enemy would blow the bridges, mine the approaches, and hold the top of each mountain ridge as long as possible, and then retreat behind the next ridge.

Coronia Valley, typical of the valleys separating the mountain ridges along the northern coast. The valleys provided little concealment from the enemy in position on top of the ridges. The bridge spans were usually long and easily demolished. Note that both highway and railroad bridges are blown in this picture.

435

Engineers repairing a break in Highway 113, on the north coast, caused by German demolition. The locality is Capo Calavà where the road practically overhangs the sea.

Brolo Beach on the north coast of Sicily. This is one of the several localities where U.S. forces made amphibious landings behind the enemy lines. Highway 113 runs along the hills, the railroad near the beach. The village of Brolo is at upper part of picture. The landing was supported by aircraft and naval gunfire.

A goumier of French Morocco. The goumiers, generally called "goums" by American soldiers, formed part of the French colonial troops. Serving with the Americans in Tunisia, Sicily, Italy, and southern France, they were greatly respected for their fighting ability. (The term "goum" literally means "company," and a goumier is a member of an infantry company. Not all native infantrymen, however, were known as goumiers, the term applying only to soldiers of certain Moroccan tribes.)

Pack mule. The interior and northern cost of Sicily were mountainous and had few roads fit for vehicles. Mules often had to be used to bring supplies to troops in forward areas.

LST's in Palermo Harbor. The very low altitude barrage balloons (above) protected the ships from dive-bombing attacks. They were flown at different altitudes from day to day.

Unloading equipment in Palermo. Even before the fighting in Sicily had ended, the buildup for the invasion of Italy started. The crane (left center) unloading pipe is a truck-mounted M2. Designed to handle 240mm howitzer materiel and 8-inch gun materiel in the field, it was a six-wheeled type with power supplied to all wheels and capable of accompanying convoy vehicles at a maximum speed of about 30 miles per hour. It was also used to facilitate unloading as above. The crew consisted of a chassis operator and a crane operator.

Smoke screen over Palermo Harbor area. The port, within easy reach of enemy bombers based in Italy, was subjected to air raids during the buildup period before the invasion of the mainland. The smoke screen obscured the port area and kept the bombardiers from aiming at any specific target.

Messina, with the Italian mainland across the strait. In the first two weeks of August the enemy started to withdraw to Italy across the narrow Strait of Messina under heavy bombing attacks. By concentrating antiaircraft guns in and around Messina as a means of combating these attacks, the Germans managed to ferry across thousands of their first-line armored and airborne troops, but much of their heavy equipment was left behind. U.S. patrols entered the city from the west on 16 August 1943 while British units entered from the south on the same day. The campaign had lasted 39 days. On 3 September 1943 British and Canadians of the British Eighth Army crossed this channel into Italy.

ITALIAN PENINSULA

Genoa
Bologna
Rimini
Leghorn
Florence
Elba
CORSICA
ROME
Anzio
Foggia
Bari
Naples
Taranto
SARDINIA
Salerno

SICILY

Gela
Pantelleria

ITALY: 9 SEPTEMBER 1943-5 JUNE 1944

The Allied victory in Sicily helped to bring about the surrender of Italy. The terms of the Italian surrender were signed on 3 September 1943 and announced on the night of the 8th. Allied troops received the news on shipboard while under way to invade Italy. Fighting did not cease with the surrender. Instead, the Germans took over the country with troops on the spot and sent reinforcements. The defeat of the Germans in Italy would strengthen Allied control over the Mediterranean shipping lanes and would provide air bases closer to targets in Germany and enemy-occupied territory. The Allied troops in Italy would also engage enemy troops which might otherwise have been employed against the Russians.

On 3 September, elements of the British Eighth Army crossed into Italy and advanced up the Italian toe in pursuit of the retreating Germans. On 9 September the main assault was launched when an Anglo-American force, part of the U.S. Fifth Army, landed on the beaches near Salerno, south of Naples. Since the enemy had expected landings in the vicinity of Naples and had disposed his forces accordingly, the Allies encountered prompt and sustained resistance. By 15 September, however, the Germans started to withdraw up the Italian Peninsula, pursued on the west by the Fifth Army and on the east by the Eighth Army. The port of Naples fell on 1 October and the Foggia airfields about the same time.

After crossing the Volturno River against stiff resistance, the Allies advanced to the Winter Line 75 miles south of Rome. In bitterly cold weather the troops slogged through mud and snow to breach the series of heavy defenses and advanced to the Gustav Line. In mid-January the main Fifth Army launched a new offensive across the Rapido and Garigliano rivers to pierce the Gustav Line and advance up the Liri Valley toward Rome. Bridgeheads were secured across the rivers, and footholds were obtained in Cassino and surrounding hills, but no breakthrough of the main German positions was effected. A few days after the initial attack against the Gustav Line, an Anglo-American amphibious force landed at Anzio and struck inland with the purpose of compelling the Germans on the southern front to withdraw. But the Allied beachhead force was contained by the enemy's unexpectedly rapid buildup, and was hard pressed to stave off several fierce German counterattacks.

After the Anzio front became stabilized and the effort to take Cassino was abandoned, the AAI (Allied Armies in Italy) regrouped and launched a new offensive on 11 May 1944. The Fifth Army, led by French troops and assisted by American troops, broke through the main German positions in the Arunci Mountains west of the Garigliano River while the Eighth Army advanced up the Liri Valley. A few days later the beachhead force effected a junction with the troops from the southern front, and advanced almost to Valmontone on Highway 6 before the axis of attack was shifted to the northwest. After several unsuccessful attacks toward Lanuvio and along the Albano road, the Fifth Army discovered an unguarded point near Velletri, enveloped the German positions based on the Alban Hills, and pushed on rapidly toward Rome, which fell on 4 June 1944 with the Germans in full retreat. Meanwhile preparations were being rushed for an invasion of southern France by Allied troops, most of them drawn from forces in Italy.

Golfo di Salerno. The plain of Salerno in Italy, ringed and dominated by mountains, provided observation posts and commanding positions for the enemy. Here, on 9 September 1943, landed elements of the U.S. Fifth Army, an Anglo-American force. The British 10 Corps of this army landed on the beaches shown in the center of the picture, the U.S. VI Corps on beaches at Paestum in distance. One division of the British Eighth Army landed at Taranto in the heel of Italy simultaneously with the main landings in the Golfo di Salerno. Just six days before these landings two divisions of the British Eighth Army had invaded Italy from Sicily. These two armies were to advance northward: the U.S. army along the west and the British army along the east side of the peninsula. Before the invasion of Italy the bombing of enemy rail communications leading into southern Italy had high priority. Naples and Foggia were the most important rail centers south of Rome, and both were heavily bombed prior to the landings.

The Salerno Invasion

DUKW's heading for Salerno beaches. The one the foreground is carrying gasoline in five-gallo cans. The maintenance of Allied forces for the fir few days depended largely on craft such as thes "ducks."

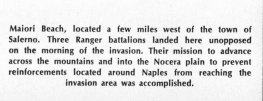

aestum Beach, on the Golfo di Salerno. At lower right is
aestum tower, the most prominent landmark on the beach.
his beach was the scene of the first invasion of U.S. troops
n the mainland of Europe. The landing took place before
aylight on 9 September, and the troops reached Monte
oprano before nightfall. The area did not contain many
xed defenses, but the enemy had a considerable number
of tanks and mobile guns.

Maiori Beach, located a few miles west of the town of
Salerno. Three Ranger battalions landed here unopposed
on the morning of the invasion. Their mission to advance
across the mountains and into the Nocera plain to prevent
reinforcements located around Naples from reaching the
invasion area was accomplished.

441

Invasion scenes at Paestum Beach. Infantry debarking from assault craft. The landing craft shown are all LCVP's.

D-Day. Five enemy air raids, each by a formation of eight fighter-bombers, were made against U.S. troops along the beach. Several smaller formations were sent against ships offshore. Casualties and damage caused were relatively slight on D-Day. Providing air cover from the Salerno area was a difficult problem because Allied fighters were based in Sicily. The longest-range fighter, the P–38, could stay over the beaches for only one hour, the A–36 (modified North American P–51 Mustang) 30 minutes.

Reinforcements coming ashore at Paestum Beach on D-Day. In background is a British-type tank landing ship (LST (1)). These were the first ships built specifically for tank landing purposes. They could land medium tanks over a low ramp carried within the ship and extended through low gates toward the beach. Load: thirteen 40-ton tanks or the equivalent. The tanks are the Sherman M4's.

Salerno, which fell to the British forces of the Fifth Army on D-Day. Until the port of Naples, which fell on 1 October, was cleared all reinforcements and supplies for the army came in over the beaches or through the port of Salerno. On 19 September the entire Salerno plain was securely in Allied hands. The German counterattacks which had started on 12 September had been checked by the 15th. On the 17th the Germans started to withdraw from the area.

Drive to Naples

Engineers repairing a bridge near Acerno. While part of the invading forces advanced westward toward Naples, part proceeded toward Benevento to the north. The enemy retreated slowly toward the river Volturno, the next natural line of defense, leaving rear guards to delay the advance, mine the roads, and blow the bridges.

Infantry advancing across bypass to bridge near Avellino on the way to the Volturno River. Blown bridges caused much delay; infantry, after crossing, generally ran into opposition that required the use of tanks, which had to wait until the engineers could rebuild the bridges.

U.S. troops in Naples. The city fell to the British 10 Corps, assisted by elements of some U.S. units, on 1 October 1943. When Naples fell, the Allies were in possession of three of Italy's best ports, Naples, Bari, and Taranto, as well as two of the most important airport centers, the Naples area on the west and the Foggia area on the east of the peninsula. The latter had fallen to the Eighth Army on 27 September, and soon became the base for the biggest concentration of Allied bombers in the entire Mediterranean theatre.

Caserta, near Naples. This area fell to the Fifth Army on 5 October 1943. The palace shown at end of tree-lined road became headquarters of the Fifth Army soon after the building was captured. Later it also became headquarters of the 15th Army Group (Fifth and Eighth Armies) and still later Allied Force Headquarters, the last named having control over the entire Mediterranean Theatre of Operations. The German surrender in Italy was signed in the palace.

The Garigliano River area on the Golfo di Gaeta. The area shown was the western anchor of the enemy Gustav Line as well as his Winter Line. By 15 November 1943 the Fifth Army was halted in front of the Winter Line, which consisted of well-prepared positions across the waist of Italy from the mouth of the Garigliano River on the west, through the mountains in the center, to the mouth of the Sangro on the east coast. The more formidable Gustav Line was located farther north except along the lower Garigliano where the two defense lines generally coincided. Little fighting took place in the area shown until the British 10 Corps crossed the river on 17 January 1944 to support the main Fifth Army effort to drive up the Liri Valley.

Volturno River above Capua. This was the first natural line of defense north of the Naples area. The Fifth Army had reached the southern bank of this river by 6 October. In the period between the landings on 9 September and the arrival at the Volturno, the Fifth Army had suffered 12,219 casualties of all kinds; 4,947 were U.S.; 7,272 were British. On 13 October the first successful crossing of this river took place above and below the hairpin loop. The river here is from 150 to 200 feet wide, its depth from 3 to 5 feet. U.S. troops crossed in assault boats or on rafts; some used life preservers, and some forded the icy stream with the use of guide ropes.

British soldiers searching a house in Colle, a village on Monte Camino. Soldier in foreground is covering his partner while the latter kicks open the door. The stone houses, typical of those in the mountain areas, with walls sometimes four feet thick, made fine strongpoints. They could be reduced by artillery, but in the Camino fighting, a joint British-American operation, there was no close-support artillery.

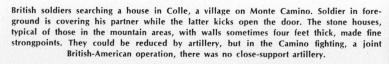

The Camino Hill mass. The hill mass with the Rapido River Valley in distance. The Winter Line continued along the south and east slopes of these mountains. The Camino Hill area fell to British and American troops on 9 December 1943, after several days of severe fighting.

Colli al Volturno. This typical Italian mountain village is located at the headwaters of the Volturno and was on the right flank of the U.S. Fifth Army. The mountains between this area and the left flank of the British Eighth Army fighting along the east coast of Italy were so rugged that no fighting took place there. Both Allied armies merely maintained small patrols to keep in contact. The lower road on the left runs through the mountains separating the Volturno and Rapido river valleys and leads to Atina north of Cassino.

Volturno River valley north of Venafro. River is in foreground. While German rear guards carried out delaying actions, the main enemy forces strengthened the Winter Line defenses in these mountains, which separate the Volturno River from the Rapido River. Hard fighting took place for control of the road leading from Pozzilli through the mountains to San Elia in the Rapido Valley. Initial attempts made by U.S. forces to cross the mountains failed because of the exhaustion of the troops, the difficulty of supply, the unfavorable weather, and the determined resistance of the enemy. The U.S. units were replaced by fresh French mountain troops, who in January 1944 fought their way across the mountains.

Flying Fortress returning from a mission. The moving of the heavy bombers from their bases in Africa to the Foggia area in Italy was a tremendous undertaking because of the equipment necessary to establish new runways, pumping plants, pipelines, repair shops, and warehouses. The move took place during the late fall and winter of 1943 and required about 300,000 tons of shipping. This was at a critical time of the ground fighting, and there was not enough shipping to take care of both the air and the ground fighters. So heavy were the shipping requirements that the buildup of Allied ground forces was considerably delayed.

Pack train in the mountains. These pack trains consisted mainly of mules, but horses and donkeys were also used. Without the use of pack trains the campaign would have been much more difficult. To supply the basic needs of an infantry regiment in the line 250 animals per day were required.

447

Hospital trains taking men wounded in the 1943–1944 winter campaign to base hospitals in the Naples area. Until the fighting had advanced beyond Rome, the main Allied hospital area in Italy was in and around Naples. The trains have German and Italian cars and U.S. locomotives.

Front-line soldiers being briefed on arrival in rest camp in Naples. Because of lack of food and housing in Italy it was found impossible to give a man a pass and let him seek his own recreation. Mlitary rest camps were set up in several localities, where the men could sleep late in clean beds, have good food, and some entertainment.

The Winter Line

Firing a mortar during a training problem near Venafro in the Volturno River valley. Mortars played an important part during the drive through the Winter Line mountains, and an intensive training schedule was maintained prior to and during the drive.

Christmas turkey on the hood of a jeep, Christmas 1943. Every effort was made to give the troops the traditional holiday dinners, complete with trimmings.

Camouflaged mobile antiaircraft unit near San Pietro Infine. Enemy air attacks were not very numerous during the Winter Line fight; the Germans had few aircraft to spare, and the weather tended to restrict the use of enemy as well as Allied aircraft.

Radar in operation near San Pietro Infine. The operating parts were mounted on a semitrailer towed by a tractor or truck. A van-body truck carried a complete stock of spare parts.

Howitzer in the Mignano area. This model was the largest U.S. artillery piece in Italy. It and the 8-inch howitzer were rushed from the States to help reduce the strong enemy fortifications of the Gustav Line; the most heavily fortified part of this line was in the Cassino area. (240mm howitzer.)

Infantry patrol entering Cervaro on 12 January 1944. A soldier carrying a tommy gun and covering the two men in front as they hunt for snipers. A few minutes after this picture was made, two men of this patrol were killed by Germans hidden in the ruins. Cervaro is on the western slopes of the Rapido Valley. By this time the Fifth Army had fought its way through the Winter Line mountains. Fighting in this area had lasted from 15 November 1943 to 15 January 1944.

Litter bearers take shelter along road near the Rapido River during the first crossing attempt. Casualties among medics were high during the Rapido River crossings. Visibility was generally poor because of mist or artificial smoke, and enemy automatic weapons had been zeroed in on likely crossing sites and the surrounding areas. The only means of protection for the litter bearers was the red cross markings on their helmets and sleeves, but at night and during periods of poor visibility in the daytime these identifications were not easily seen.

Changing tracks on a Sherman tank at Presenzano, a village located near Highway 6 a few miles behind the lines in Mignano Gap. Tanks had not played a big role during the Winter Line fight because of the mountainous terrain and the muddy lowlands. Tank units were kept ready for use once the infantry had cleared the way through Mignano Gap to Cassino and the entrance to the Liri Valley, the so-called Gateway to Rome.

Smoke pots used to screen infantry crossing the Rapido River near Cassino. The first attempt to cross was made south of Highway 6 by a U.S. division on 20 January 1944. It was a failure. Crossings attempted in the next two days by this division also failed. By afternoon of 22 January all assault boats had been destroyed, efforts to bridge the stream had been unsuccessful, the troops who had managed to cross were isolated, and supply or evacuation had become impossible. On 23 January the attack in the sector was ordered halted. Casualties were 1,681: 143 killed, 663 wounded, and 875 reported missing. On 24 January another U.S. division managed to cross the Rapido north of Highway 6.

Firing a mortar during the successful Rapido River crossing on 24 January. The attack was made north of Highway 6 and directed toward the mountains north of Cassino. The outskirts of the town were entered for the first time on the morning of 26 January. Tanks were not able to help during the first few days as the ground was too soggy and the engineers were unable to construct bridges. The entire area was under observation from Monte Cassino and the adjacent hills. Four tanks finally managed to cross during the morning of the 27th, but by noon they were all out of action. Two days later 30 tanks were across, the infantry had taken the village of Cairo high in the hills north of Cassino, and the Allies had made the first dent in the Gustav Line in the Cassino area.

The Anzio Beach area. The beach shown was the U.S. zone of the landing area. The British landing beach, about six miles northwest of Anzio, proved too shallow for unloading supplies. It was closed soon after the British forces had landed there, and supplies were handled mostly through the port of Anzio. The Anglo-American assault force consisted of almost 50,000 men and 5,200 vehicles.

While the Anzio landing was still in preparation, the Allied air forces had been bombing airfields and communication centers, and the army had started its drive (on 17 January 1944) to penetrate the Gustav Line. By the 22nd, the date of the Anzio invasion, the attempt to penetrate the Gustav Line had bogged down in front of the Cassino defenses.

Anzio D-Day

Morning of D-Day. Men coming ashore from LCI's. Enemy air raids started at 0850 and consisted of three separate attacks by an estimated 18–28 fighter-bombers. One LCI was hit and is shown burning.

The port of Anzio, which was taken intact with very little opposition on the morning of D-Day, 22 January 1944. The enemy had placed demolition charges to destroy the port and its facilities, but the assault was so sudden and unexpected that there was no opportunity to set off the charges. By early afternoon the port was ready to receive four LST's and three LCT's simultaneously. By midnight on D-Day, 36,034 men, 3,069 vehicles, and large quantities of supplies had been brought ashore, either through the port or over the beaches. The unloading area of the port was not suitable for Liberty ships or other freighters; these continued to be unloaded offshore, mostly by DUKW's. By May 1944, 1,051 pieces of antiaircraft artillery were on the beachhead, including 64 90mm guns.

The best-known of all the war correspondents in World War II was Ernie Pyle. Here he is talking to Captain Lonnie Thompson in the Anzio beachhead area, Italy, 18 March 1944. He was killed in combat with the 77th Division in the Pacific during the invasion of Ie Shima 18 April 1945.

Campoleone station near the Albano highway leading from Anzio to the Colli Laziali, the mountain mass overlooking the plains of the beachhead. By 31 January 1944 the Allies had advanced to Campoleone station, the front line being the railroad bed in foreground above, but the available forces could not hold the area. The enemy was bringing reserves toward the Gustav Line where the Allied drive had stalled. These enemy reserve troops were rerouted to contain the Anzio beachhead and, if possible, force the Allies back to the sea. The picture above, looking toward the sea, gives an idea of the flat, featureless terrain in the area. The group of buildings in the distance at right is the "Factory," scene of hard fighting.

Cisternia di Littoria. A thrust toward Cisterna di Littoria was made by the Allies on 25–27 January 1944, but was stopped about three miles southwest of the town. Another attempt made on 30 January–1 February met even less success. In the distance are the Colli Laziali overlooking the beachhead. Below the mountains is the town of Velletri. Highway 7 through Cisterna di Littoria leads past the mountains to Rome. Attempts to extend the beachhead failed: the first attempt along the Albano road was stopped at Campoleone; the second, the effort to cut Highway 7 at Cisterna di Littoria, was stopped within sight of the village. By this time the enemy outnumbered the Allies, and the latter consolidated their positions and waited for the counterattacks. On 2 February 1944, after the unsuccessful attempt to extend the beachhead, the Anzio force received orders to dig in and prepare for defense. By this date casualties totaled 6,487. Allied troops were on the defensive in Italy for the first time since the invasion at Salerno.

Radar set in operation. By 24 February 1944 the first sets of this type were in position on the Anzio beachhead. They were brought in to cope with enemy jamming techniques and "window" (small strips of metallic paper dropped from attacking planes) which had reduced the effectiveness of earlier types of radar. During the night of 24 February a flight of 12 bombers approached in close formation, using the "window" method of jamming. Forty-eight 90mm guns directed by radar of the improved type caught them at extreme range over enemy territory and brought down five with the first salvo. The remainder of the formation jettisoned their bombs and fled.

455

Laying an antitank mine. A soldier is arming a mine by pulling the safety fork. This type of mine contained 6 pounds of cast TNT and had a total weight of 10²/₃ pounds. The pressure of a man stepping on the mine would not detonate it, but any vehicle hitting it would set it off. Mines were generally laid at night or on foggy days behind a smoke screen. The task of laying minefields at night in the open, almost featureless terrain resulted at first in many improperly marked fields causing accidents. The practice was finally adopted of first marking a field, then recording it, and only then laying the mines.

On the night of 24 January 1944 a fully illuminated and marked British hospital ship was bombed and sunk while taking wounded on board. All evacuation from the beachhead was by sea. Air transportation could not be used, since the dust raised by planes landing or taking off brought on enemy shelling. Hospital ships were used whenever possible, but as these could not dock in the shallow port, LCT's were used to transfer patients from shore to ships. When storms and high seas interrupted this procedure, the wounded were loaded on board LST's at the Anzio docks for the 30-hour trip to Naples. For the period 22 January–22 May, 33,063 patients were evacuated by sea.

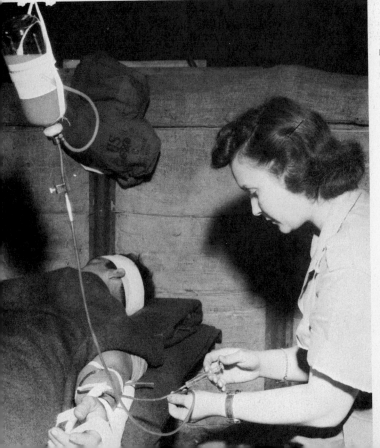

Nurse giving intravenous injection of plasma to a wounded soldier. In the period 22 January–22 May 1944, 18,074 American soldiers suffering from disease, 4,245 from injuries, and 10,809 battle casualties—33,128 in all—were given medical care and attention in evacuation hospitals at the beachhead. If recovery required 14 days or less, the casualty remained in the evacuation hospital; if the recovery period was estimated to take more than two weeks, the patient was evacuated to one of several base hospitals in the Naples area as soon as he was strong enough to be moved.

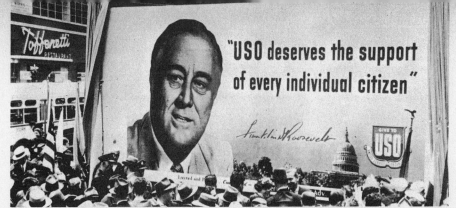

The USO's first national fund drive gets under way in New York's Times Square on 2 June 1941 with the unveiling of a billboard featuring President Franklin D. Roosevelt and the slogan that has been endorsed by every President since then: "USO deserves the support of every citizen."

THE USO

The USO has been serving the members of the Armed Forces since 1941 when camps were opening all over the United States to train the soldiers that would be needed if the country became involved in the war that had engulfed most of Europe. In an effort to make life a little more pleasant for those who were forced to leave their homes for an often bleak Army camp, six social and welfare organizations—the National Board of Young Men's Christian Associations, the National Catholic Community Service, the National Jewish Welfare Board, the National Board of the Young Woman's Christian Association, the Salvation Army and the National Travelers Aid Association—combined forces as the United Service Organizations, pledged to serve the military wherever and whenever needed. Some of the member organizations, notably the YMCA and the Salvation Army, had worked with the soldiers of previous wars. Using this experience and working with the Government, the USO planned and put into operation programs designed to serve the religious, spiritual, social, welfare and educational needs of the Armed Forces. USO clubs, camp shows, and other activities became a part of World War II service life from Alaska to the South Pacific, and the USO has gone wherever the soldier has gone ever since.

Supported by contributions from the people of the United States and responsible to the President and the Secretary of Defense, the USO primarily serves members of the Armed Forces and their dependents outside of military reservations when off duty or on leave. The USO sets up off-station clubs, community centers, and recreation and other facilities wherever there is a need for them that is not being met by the Department of Defense or some other Government agency. Currently the USO is active in cities near military bases in the United States, in Guam, Puerto Rico and the Canal Zone, and in overseas cities that are leave centers for United States troops.

The USO is the principal civilian agency for the procurement of live entertainment for performances at military installations in the United States and overseas, a service it has provided with notable success since World War II. Both professional and nonprofessional entertainers tour under USO auspices, as do popular sports figures.

With its camp shows and with its other activities the USO makes every effort to go wherever United States servicemen go—from the frozen north to the jungles of Vietnam—to provide a friendly greeting, entertainment, and a chance to relax in a homelike atmosphere for the young men and women far away from their own homes.

The USO troupes of World War II used many kinds of transportation to reach their audiences. Here, one member of a touring group travels by breeches buoy to a LST grounded off Leghorn, Italy, while the other members of the troupe wait their turn.

The beachhead faced a heavy concentration of German artillery, employed mostly in direct support of the infantry. Standard German divisional medium howitzer. The caliber was 150mm.

The German Panther tank. This heavy tank was probably the most successful armored vehicle the Germans developed, having relatively high speed and maneuverability, combined with heavy armor and a rapid-fire, high-velocity gun. It first appeared on the Russian front in the summer of 1943, and soon thereafter on the Italian front. No U.S. tank comparable to it appeared. The frontal armor could not be penetrated by Sherman tank guns at ordinary fighting range. In constructing this vehicle the Germans were influenced by the Russian tank, the T34. The corrugated surface is a plastic coating to prevent magnetic mines from sticking to the metal.

Used shell cases bound for the United States as scrap are loaded into a freighter from an LCT.

Beachhead ration dump. The failure of the main part of the army in the south to break through the Gustav Line and join the troops at Anzio necessitated maintaining the beachhead by sea for a longer period than planned. Shipping schedules were revised to take care of the gradually growing forces and to build up a reserve of food, fuel, ammunition, and other supplies. Food could be kept in a large dump, but fuel and ammunition presented problems. The beachhead area was so small that fuel and ammunition dumps, no matter where placed, were within enemy artillery range. These dumps were kept small and dispersed in order to keep losses to a minimum. Between 22 January and 10 March 1944 a little more than 1,000 tons of ammunition were destroyed, mostly by enemy bombing. Losses never became critical.

Malaria control. Soldier pouring Diesel oil in water-filled bomb crater to kill mosquito larvae. The Pontine Marshes near the beachhead had for centuries been notorious for the prevalence of malaria. In April 1944 large-scale draining projects were started, and patrols were sent out to dust or pour oil on canals, ditches, and pools. This activity was even carried right into no man's land at night. The program, combined with preventive measures taken by the individual soldier, such as the use of head nets, mosquito bars. insect repellents, and atabrine, kept malaria from becoming a medical problem. The division stationed in the worst area did not develop a single new case of the disease.

Inflating rubber dummy tank. Placing dummy tank in camouflaged position which had been vacated by a tank moving toward the front for the coming offensive. The dummy tank was designed by the British and manufactured in the United States.

Anzio Breakout

Watching the battle from observation point. The offensive from the beachhead started at 0545, 23 May 1944, when the artillery began firing. Allied medium and fighter bombers strafed and bombed enemy positions. At 0630 the infantry and tanks moved out. The artillery preparations, the most intensive thus far at the beachhead, had searched out command posts, assembly areas, and dumps, with the result that enemy communications and supply lines were severely damaged. The Germans recovered and put up a strong fight, but they could not make up for the initial disorganization.

Walking wounded on their way from the front to a hospital. Tags tell the nature of the wound and what has been done for it in the field or at the first-aid station. On the first day of the fight to break out of the beachhead, the Allies suffered the heaviest casualties of the Anzio Campaign. American combat casualties for the whole army on that day were 334 killed, 1,513 wounded, and 81 missing, a total of 1,928 and the high point in the entire Italian campaign. The U.S. and British combat casualties at the beachhead between 22 January and 22 May numbered about 30,000, including at least 4,400 killed and 18,000 wounded. The enemy captured about 6,800 prisoners. The noncombat casualties during this period amounted to about 37,000.

Infantry soldier in Cisterna di Littoria. This town on Highway 7 had been one of the German strongpoints facing the beachhead forces. It fell to tanks and infantry on 25 May. The main Allied drive had been launched in the direction of Cisterna di Littoria with the object of continuing straight north to capture Valmontone on Highway 6 and cut off the enemy forces retreating toward Rome from the shattered Gustav Line defenses.

The village of Campoleone with Campoleone station in upper left. The station area was reached on 31 January, when the first attempt to break out of the beachhead was made, but was soon lost to enemy counterattacks. It was not retaken by the Allies until 29 May 1944 during the drive on Rome. Starting on that day a tank-infantry attack fought a two-day action to penetrate the German defenses here, but without success. The area was heavily defended by infantry weapons supported by enemy tanks, self-propelled guns, artillery, and flak guns. On 31 May the U.S. armored division making the attack was withdrawn for maintenance purposes. Losses in both tanks and personnel had been severe. The breakthrough, when it came, was made across the eastern side of the Colli Laziali.

The Road to Rome

Howitzer. This piece fired its first mission in Italy in Mignano Gap, 30 January 1944. Howitzers were used with good effect during the Gustav Line fight in and around Cassino.

Monte Cassino Abbey. The Liri Valley, the so-called Gateway to Rome. On 15 February the abbey was bombed and shelled for the first time. Before that Allied soldiers had orders not to fire even a rifle shot at the structure. Enemy ammunition dumps were located close to the building, and gun emplacements in the vicinity were numerous. It had become a legitimate military objective. The bombing and shelling destroyed the abbey as a work of art, but its usefulness to the enemy was scarcely impaired. The rubble caused by the destruction of the upper parts of the building only served to strengthen the remaining lower parts.

The bombing of Cassino on 15 March. Although it had been repeatedly bombed before, the town was heavily bombed and shelled that day in preparation for the attack by the New Zealand Corps, at this time part of the Fifth Army. About 1,200 tons of bombs were dropped and 195,969 rounds were fired by artillery ranging in size from 3-inch guns to 240mm howitzers. The enemy's defenses were not destroyed. Protected by cellars, steel and concrete pillboxes, caves, and tunnels, the German troops suffered comparatively few casualties. The bombing and shelling neither overcame the enemy's resistance nor noticeably reduced his morale. When the infantry moved in for the attack they were met by heavy mortar fire; when the Allied tanks appeared they could not advance because of bomb craters and debris. The attack was repulsed.

German portable pillboxes. Some of these were found in the Gustav Line around Cassino, and others were later found in the Hitler Line in the Liri Valley. These steel pillboxes, camouflaged and usually connected by communication trenches to well-constructed bunkers, were impregnable to all but direct hits from artillery fire.

Goumier of the French forces leading a pack train into the Aurunci Mountains during the drive that started 11 May. Tank is U.S. M5 light tank manned by French crew, and armed with a 75mm howitzer.

Golfo di Gaeta. The high mountain at the right is Monte Petrella, which is 4,600 feet high; the one in the center is Monte Ruazzo, which is 4,000 feet high. The drive through the Gustav Line, started by the left flank of the Fifth Army, had reached Monte Petrella by 15 May and had advanced to the Itri Valley. U.S. forces in general advanced along the slopes facing the sea. The French mountain troops advanced across the mountains farther to the north, then turned right into the Liri Valley on the other side and threatened to cut off the German forces around Cassino and in the lower part of Liri Valley. This action by the French made the German position untenable, and the enemy started a general withdrawal from the Gustav Line.

Fifth Army entering Rome on 5 June only to continue through the city in pursuit of the enemy retreating along the roads north of Rome. During this retreat the Germans were under constant bombing and strafing attacks by Allied air forces. The roads of retreat were littered with vehicles of all kinds.

Valmontone on Highway 6, 25 miles southeast of Rome. This was the main escape route of the enemy forces trying to retreat toward Rome from the Cassino–Liri Valley area. The enemy kept the road open until 1 June. U.S. forces found the village unoccupied on the morning of 2 June when a battle patrol entered the town.

General Dwight D. Eisenhower, Supreme Commander of the Allied Armies, talks with U.S. Army paratroopers just before they board their planes. One British and two U.S. airborne divisions were dropped behind the Normandy beaches to secure routes of egress for the seaborne forces.

NORMANDY CAMPAIGN

On 6 June 1944 the Allied military forces invaded northern France. After long study of the German strength, including coastal defenses and the disposition of enemy troops, the Allied commanders selected the beaches along the Bay of the Seine for the assault landings. The two beaches to be used by the troops of the First U.S. Army were given the names of UTAH and OMAHA. Those on which the British and Canadians of the British Second Army were to land were named GOLD, SWORD, and JUNO. The assault began at 0200 on 6 June when airborne troops were dropped behind the beaches with the mission of securing exits from the beaches. Planes of the Allied air force bombed the coastal defenses, and shortly after sunrise the Navy began shelling the beach defenses. At 0630 the first troops landed on the beaches of Normandy. The sea was rough and the assault forces met varying degrees of enemy opposition, but the beachheads were secured and the assault and follow-up troops moved on to accomplish their missions. The U.S. forces landing on UTAH Beach moved northwest to clear the northern portion of the Cotentin Peninsula and capture the port of Cherbourg. Those landing on OMAHA Beach advanced southward toward Saint-Lô. The troops of the British Second Army were to advance in a southeast direction from Caen.

The enormous buildup of men and materiel began immediately after the assault. This operation was made most difficult because of the lack of port facilities, but before the invasion plans had been made for the construction of artificial harbors. The plans were quickly put into effect and the harbors were almost completed when a summer gale struck the Channel coast destroying most of the construction work. By using amphibian trucks and Rhino ferries, and by drying out LST's, the buildup over open beaches progressed much faster than was anticipated and men and supplies were poured into France in ever-increasing numbers.

While the beachheads were expanded and the buildup continued, the infantry and armored units fought their way through the hedgerow country toward their objectives. The fighting was slow and costly as enemy opposition stiffened in an unsuccessful attempt to prevent the Allied advance. With the capture of Cherbourg and Saint-Lô the initial missions of the U.S. forces were completed and the forces were then assembled in preparation for the drives south and west from the beachhead toward Avranches and the Brittany Peninsula. The British forces were to push southward from Caen exploiting in the direction of Paris and the Seine Basin. These attacks were scheduled to begin on 19 July 1944 but because of bad weather the supporting aerial assault was delayed and the breakout of Normandy did not get under way until 25 July.

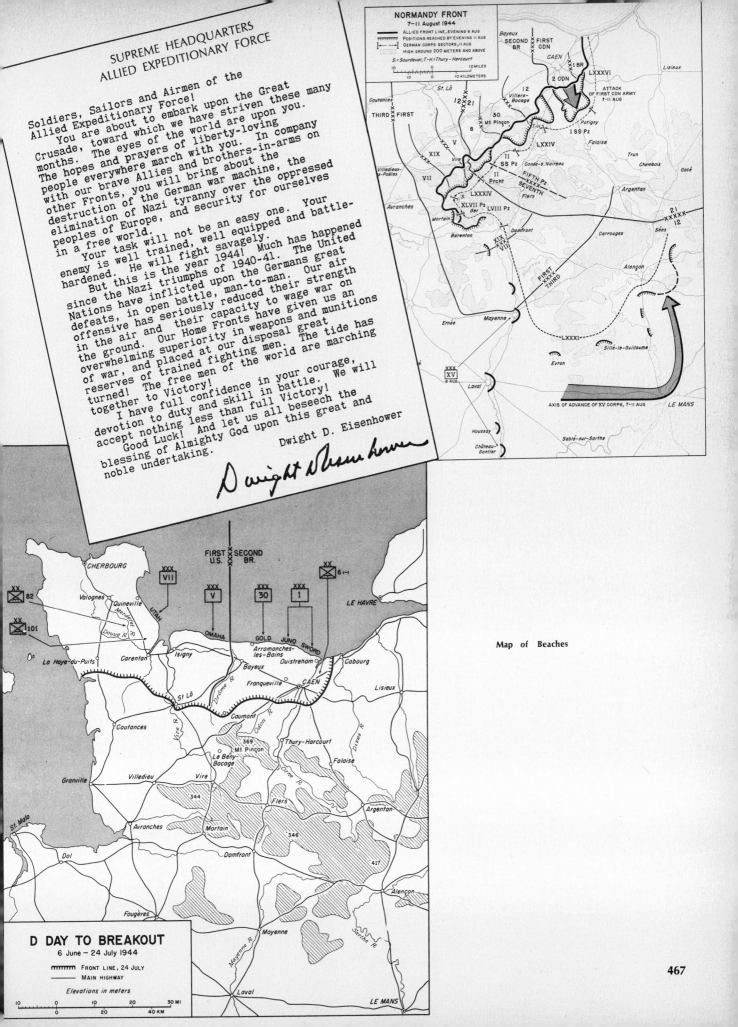

SUPREME HEADQUARTERS
ALLIED EXPEDITIONARY FORCE

Soldiers, Sailors and Airmen of the Allied Expeditionary Force!

You are about to embark upon the Great Crusade, toward which we have striven these many months. The eyes of the world are upon you. The hopes and prayers of liberty-loving people everywhere march with you. In company with our brave Allies and brothers-in-arms on other Fronts, you will bring about the destruction of the German war machine, the elimination of Nazi tyranny over the oppressed peoples of Europe, and security for ourselves in a free world.

Your task will not be an easy one. Your enemy is well trained, well equipped and battle-hardened. He will fight savagely.

But this is the year 1944! Much has happened since the Nazi triumphs of 1940-41. The United Nations have inflicted upon the Germans great defeats, in open battle, man-to-man. Our air offensive has seriously reduced their strength in the air and their capacity to wage war on the ground. Our Home Fronts have given us an overwhelming superiority in weapons and munitions of war, and placed at our disposal great reserves of trained fighting men. The tide has turned! The free men of the world are marching together to Victory!

I have full confidence in your courage, devotion to duty and skill in battle. We will accept nothing less than full Victory!

Good Luck! And let us all beseech the blessing of Almighty God upon this great and noble undertaking.

Dwight D. Eisenhower

Dwight Eisenhower

NORMANDY FRONT
7-11 August 1944

ALLIED FRONT LINE, EVENING 6 AUG
POSITIONS REACHED BY EVENING 11 AUG
GERMAN CORPS SECTORS, 11 AUG
HIGH GROUND 200 METERS AND ABOVE

S.= Sourdeval; T-H.=Thury-Harcourt

ATTACK OF FIRST CDN ARMY 7-11 AUG

AXIS OF ADVANCE OF XV CORPS, 7-11 AUG

Map of Beaches

D DAY TO BREAKOUT
6 June – 24 July 1944

FRONT LINE, 24 JULY
MAIN HIGHWAY

Elevations in meters

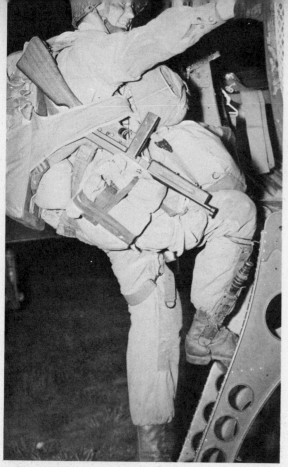

Fully equipped paratrooper, armed with a Thompson submachine gun, climbing into a transport plane to go to France as the invasion of Normandy gets under way. At aproximately 0200, 6 June 1944, men of two U.S. airborne divisions, as well as elements of a British airborne division, were dropped in vital areas to the rear of German coastal defenses guarding the Normandy beaches from Cherbourg to Caen. By dawn 1,136 heavy bombers of the RAF Bomber Command had dropped 5,853 tons of bombs on selected coastal batteries.

Gun crew alert aboard the cruiser USS "Augusta," as landing craft approach the coast of France during the invasion, 6 June 1944. The three landing craft nearest the "Augusta" are an LCT(6), an LBV, and an LBK. While the Allied air forces were bombing installations along the invasion beaches the Allied sea armada drew in toward the coast, preceded by its flotillas of minesweepers. Bad weather conditions and high seas had driven the enemy surface patrol craft into their harbors, and the 100-mile movement across the English Channel was unopposed. By 0300 the ships had anchored in the transport areas some miles off their assigned beaches, and the loading of troops into landing craft and the forming of the assault waves for the dash to the beaches began. At 0550 the heavy naval support squadrons began a 45-minute bombardment which quickly silenced the major coast-defense batteries.

D-DAY, OMAHA BEACH

An Army Air Forces B–26 medium bomber flying over one of the invasion beaches, early on D-Day morning. All planes which supported the invasion operations, with the exception of the four-motored bombers, were painted with three white and two black stripes for identification purposes. At dawn on D-Day the U.S. Air Forces took up the air attacks, and in the half hour before the touchdown of the assault forces (from 0600 to 0630) 1,365 heavy bombers dropped 2,746 tons of high explosives on the shore defenses. This was followed by attacks by medium bombers, light bombers, and fighter bombers. During the 24 hours of 6 June, Allied aircraft flew 13,000 sorties, and during the first 8 hours alone dropped 10,000 tons of bombs.

U.S. troops wading ashore from an LCVP at Omaha Beach during the assault. Elements of two U.S. infantry divisions, with engineer troops and tanks of an armored unit, made the first landings at 0630 6 June.

Infantrymen wading ashore from an LCT(6).

Troops leaving an LCVP to wade ashore. Half-tracks and 2½-ton amphibian trucks can be seen on the beach, and in the background men marching in columns start southward toward the bluffs. On the shelf the enemy strung barbed wire and planted mines. Lanes had to be cleared through these obstacles before the infantry could advance. Beyond this strip containing obstacles, the enemy laid out firing positions to cover the tidal flat and the beach with direct fire, both plunging and grazing, from all types of weapons. The men landing were fired upon from these positions, which for the most part had escaped destruction during the prelanding bombardment.

Army medics administering blood plasma to a survivor of a sunken landing craft on Omaha Beach. The highest proportionate losses were taken by units that landed in the first few hours, including engineers, tank troops, and artillerymen.

D-DAY, UTAH BEACH

Members of the follow-up division aboard an LCI(L) headed for Utah Beach on D-Day. Other LCI's in the background have barrage balloons flying overhead. These balloons were attached by cables to ships crossing the Channel to keep low-flying enemy strafing planes away from the craft.

Men and equipment along Utah Beach on D-Day.

Infantrymen resting along the sea wall and beginning to move inland, 6 June 1944. Fortunately, the first elements landed considerably south of the designated beaches in areas less thickly obstructed and where enemy shore defenses were less formidable than those opposite the intended landing beaches. While airborne troops seized the causeways through the inundated low ground to prevent enemy reinforcements from reaching the beach, the seaborne assault troops struck northwest toward Montebourg, on the road to Cherbourg.

An enemy shell hits the beach where U.S. troops are advancing.

German casemated fortification inland from the beach.

Obstacles on the landing beach. During 1943 the Germans had developed heavy frontal defenses at all the principal harbors from Den Helder to Brest. As the invasion threat grew, Cherbourg and Le Havre were further strengthened, while heavy guns were installed to block the entrance of the Bay of the Seine. Between the ports stretched a line of concrete defense positions and coastal and flak batteries. A program of casemating the coastal guns and strengthening the defense posts was still in progress on 6 June. The beaches were mined and obstacles were placed in the water offshore and on the beaches, but there was no secondary defense line behind the coastal defenses which the Germans thought would stop the invading troops.

A member of an engineer unit using a mine detector. The ground outlined with white tape had not been cleared of enemy mines, and enemy signs were used to mark the mined areas. Army and Navy demolition teams, following the assault infantry, found the beach less thickly obstructed than expected, and Utah Beach was cleared in an hour. Engineers prepared exits from the beach by clearing lanes through the mine fields.

An enlisted man looks up a number before placing a telephone call on a field telephone. The function of the Signal Corps was to furnish radio, wire, and messenger communications. Often Signal Corps personnel went inland, sometimes ahead of the infantry, to observe and correct the fire from the naval guns offshore.

Members of a shore fire control group operating Signal Corps radios. Man operating an SCR 284, while the second man operates the hand generator; a third man is using a hand-held radio set, "handie-talkie."

D-DAY PLUS

Gliders being towed by C–47 transports over the English Channel carrying reinforcements for the airborne divisions, 7 June.

A British Horsa glider wrecked while landing. Six thousand six hundred men of one of the two U.S. airborne divisions were scattered over an area 25 miles by 15 miles in extent, and 60 percent of their equipment was lost. In general, however, these men accomplished their mission successfully. Other gliders were flown in on 6 June but suffered considerable casualties.

Gliders and tow planes circling before the gliders are cut loose for a landing, 7 June. On the ground are gliders which landed the previous day, many of which were wrecked in landing.

An LCT(5) loaded with reinforcements moving toward the beach on 7 June. An LCT(R) and an LBV. In the background supply ships wait to discharge their cargoes.

Wrecked train. The trains were held up on this single track, in the vicinity of Chartres, when fighter bombers knocked cars off the track. With the track thus blocked, the movement of trains was stopped and much of the undamaged rolling stock later fell into Allied hands. Within an arc extending from the Pas-de-Calais through Paris to the Brittany Peninsula, 16,000 tons of bombs were dropped on coastal batteries, 4,000 tons on airfields, and 8,500 tons on railway targets between 6 and 11 June.

Utah Beach, 8 June. Men and supplies come ashore. Between 7 and 12 June the Allies concentrated their efforts on joining the beachheads into one uninterrupted lodgement area and on bringing in men and supplies.

A railroad bridge across the Seine destroyed by bombers of the Allied air force. Even though hampered by poor flying weather during the first week after D-Day, the Allied air force bombed bridges across the Seine and Loire rivers. This seriously hindered the movement of enemy troops and supplies, and trains had to be constantly rerouted in an attempt to reinforce the Germans trying to hold the assault forces in the area of the beachheads.

A 90mm gun of an antiaircraft battery firing near Vierville. Though enemy air attacks were not a serious threat to the Allies and very little opposition was encountered, antiaircraft batteries were always on the alert.

Multiple gun motor carriage with its four .50-caliber machine guns firing at the enemy in support of an infantry advance. This vehicle was a weapon of an antiaircraft artillery unit, but the lack of enemy air activity in Normandy made possible its use in other roles.

U.S. artillerymen emplacing a 155mm howitzer in a camouflaged position.

Formation of Douglas A–20's over France. The infantry and armored attacks were, when possible, preceded by concentrated air attacks. Employing carpet bombing methods, thousands of tons of bombs were dropped. Fragmentation bombs were used to break enemy resistance without causing extensive cratering which would hinder the advance of tanks. Although these attacks were temporary in effect, the results greatly aided the initial ground attack. Casualties to the enemy were few, but he was stunned by the weight of the bombing and considerable confusion ensued.

Engineers laying wire matting in the construction of a landing strip near Sainte-Mère-Eglise. An important factor in ensuring the success of the Allied close-support operations lay in the establishment of landing strips in Normandy, from which fighter planes could operate. Work began as soon as a footing was obtained on shore, and by 9 June planes were operating from these strips.

A quarry near Omaha Beach used by engineer units to supply rock and stone for the construction of roads. The tremendous amount of traffic on the roads in Normandy, as men and supplies were brought into France over the beaches, required the services of many engineer units to keep the roads in good repair. Most of the roads leading to the beaches were not hard surfaced but were constructed of rock and gravel.

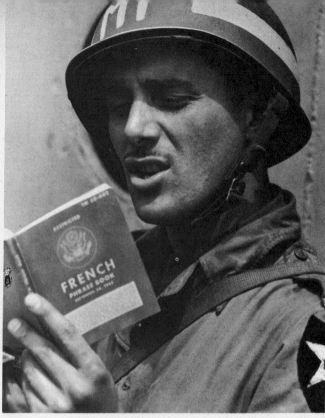

Enemy prisoners, taken during the first days of fighting, awaiting transportation to England. During the first week following the invasion landings the Germans lost some 10,000 men as prisoners. The enemy forces that manned the static beach defenses were largely Russians and other non-Germans, but were under German officers. Of the German troops, many companies were found to be composed of men either under twenty or over forty-five years of age. Many of these were of low medical categories, and their morale was not of the best.

A military policeman studying French.

THE MEDICS

Medical Corps men treating an enlisted man for a wrist wound. When casualties entered a battalion aid station within a few hundred yards of the front, they were immediately screened and sorted. Wounds were redressed. Those whose wounds permitted were evacuated to the rear, while those whose wounds did not permit further evacuation were held, treated, given plasma, and then moved farther back.

An evacuation hospital with a 750-bed capacity, Normandy, 24 July.

Army surgeons perform an operation out of doors. In World War II the number of deaths per hundred casualties was one-half of that during World War I. Responsible for this reduction was the surgical skill and painstaking care rendered by personnel of the Medical Corps aided by better surgery, the sulfa drugs, penicillin, plasma, and whole blood.

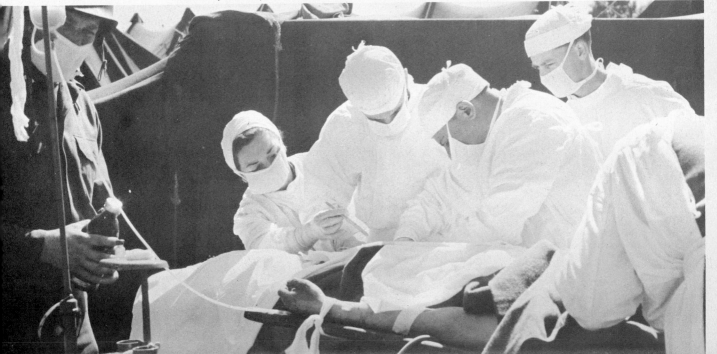

During the night of 11–12 June, Carentan was set ablaze by artillery and naval gunfire, and early on the morning of 12 June, U.S. troops entered the town. Its fall marked the effective junction of the two U.S. beachheads and the linking up of the two corps of the First U.S. Army.

CARENTAN

U.S. troops moving into Carentan, 12 June. A 105mm howitzer firing at enemy positions during the fighting at Carentan.

Douglas A–20's dropping bombs on a probable flying bomb launching site. The first flying bombs fell on England during the night of 12–13 June 1944, and the regular attacks began three days later. The smallness, the effective nature of camouflage, the comparative mobility, and the ease with which the V–1 launching sites could be repaired made effective bombing attacks on them difficult.

U.S. paratroopers patrolling the streets of Carentan in a captured German Volkswagen. The enemy counterattacks against the U.S. forces in Carentan were unsuccessful in their attempts to recapture the city, but were persistent enough to limit the U.S. advance to gains measured in hundreds of yards. However, on 17 June 1944 U.S. troops reached the west coast in the vicinity of Barneville, cutting the German forces into two groups, one south of the Carentan–Barneville line, the other in the Cherbourg area.

480

Part of a German rocket installation captured by U.S. troops. Many of these flying bomb sites were captured by the Allies as they advanced. Although the Air Force had destroyed some by bombing, most of the sites were taken by advancing troops and destroyed.

BRINGING IN MEN AND SUPPLIES

A portion of the artificial harbor at Omaha Beach. This harbor was in the Saint-Laurent-sur-Mer area of Omaha Beach and was known as "Mulberry A." Breakwaters were formed by sinking ships and concrete caissons, and steel bridging formed causeways to the beach. The harbor, construction on which began on 7 June 1944, was designed to provide moorings for seven Liberty ships and twelve coasters at one time. By 19 June it was 90 percent completed.

Vehicles moving from one of the piers over the causeway to the shore. These floating causeways to the beach rose and fell with the tide.

Engineers laying steel matting on Omaha Beach at the exits of the causeway which extend to the piers of the artificial harbor.

Damage to the artificial harbor and landing craft caused by the storm. The greatest detriment to the Allied buildup was not the enemy, but the weather. From 19–22 June 1944 one of the worst summer gales in Channel history hit the Bay of the Seine. Unloading operations were virtually stopped, the floating steel caissons broke free and sank, the concrete caissons moved or were broken up, and the beach was strewn with hundreds of stranded and damaged craft. The line of sunken ships remained fairly well intact, but as a whole the artificial harbor was destroyed and useless.

A truck on the beach (2¹/₂-ton) and one starting down the ramp of an LST (1¹/₂-ton). After the storm wrecked the artificial harbors, emergency measures, such as using 2¹/₂-ton amphibian trucks to bring men and supplies ashore and "drying out" landing ships and coasters, were employed. By "drying out" the vessels (as in picture) and unloading directly on the beaches, unloading operations were carried out.

482

Trucks fully loaded with men and supplies leaving a Rhino ferry
and being helped ashore by a bulldozer.

A ¾-ton weapons carrier rolling through the surf toward the beach
under its own power. All the vehicles which made these landings
through the surf had been waterproofed before leaving England.
Since they were able to travel only a short distance on land under
their own power when waterproofed, the waterproofing material
was removed soon after the vehicles landed.

Trucks and amphibian trucks (each is a 2½-ton
truck) on a beach in Normandy. In spite of the
damage caused by the storm, by 26 June Omaha
Beach was discharging 122 percent of its planned
cargo capacity. By this time 268,718 men, 40,191
vehicles, and 125,812 tons of cargo had been
discharged over Omaha Beach alone. By 1 July
the Allied commanders were not as much wor-
ried about a German counterattack that would
threaten the beachhead as about the possibility
that the enemy might bring in sufficient reserves
to create a stalemate in Normandy.

Unit advancing toward Cherbourg stops to inspect a German multipurpose gun. It was primarily an antiaircraft gun adaptable to antitank and general artillery use. In its role as an antitank gun it was fitted with a shield. In its mobile form it was towed on four wheels, usually with an 8-ton half-tracked tractor.

CHERBOURG

A 155mm howitzer firing on the defenses of the city of Cherbourg. An attack on Cherbourg was launched on the afternoon of 22 June, after an 80-minute air and artillery bombardment of the outer defenses.

Results of artillery fire and bombings in Montebourg.

Two U.S. infantrymen routing a sniper during street fighting in Cherbourg.

Fortifications around Cherbourg damaged by Allied shelling and bombardment. It was not until 24 June that the main defenses cracked, and the next day the three attacking infantry divisions, supported by heavy naval bombardment, reached the outskirts of the city.

German prisoners taken in Cherbourg. By 25 June U.S. forces were fighting in the streets of the city while the Germans demolished the port facilities. At 1500 on 26 June the German commanders surrendered. The Arsenal held out until the following morning, and fanatical groups had to be eliminated one by one. A certain number of the enemy still remained to be rounded up in the northwest corner of the Cotentin Peninsula, but on 1 July all resistance in the northern Cotentin came to an end.

A member of an Engineer unit, operating a bulldozer, clears a street in Cherbourg.

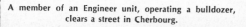

485

Members of an Engineer unit stationed in Cherbourg take time out to prepare a meal in the doorway of a house. C and K rations were generally issued to troops in combat. Where there was more time for the preparation of food, troops were given the "10 in 1" ration which contained more variety than the C and K rations. When units were more permanently settled, regular messes were set up, but during the early days on the Continent just after the invasion, and while the supply situation was still critical, troops resorted to eating rations that could be more easily transported and prepared.

An M5 light tank equipped with a hedgerow cutter. During the fighting in Normandy armored vehicles found the hedgerows a serious obstacle which they could neither cross over nor break through. An enlisted man of an Ordnance unit devised a method of attaching to the front of tanks rake-like cutters salvaged from underwater beach obstacles which the Germans had placed to wreck landing craft. During a period of 48 hours maintenance companies of the Ordnance Department turned out 300 of these cutters which enabled the tanks to open passageways through the hedgerows of Normandy.

The first ship-to-shore gasoline line, put in operation at Cherbourg. During the assault phase the Allied forces relied on canned gasoline, but by 3 July bulk supply was introduced by ship-to-shore pipeline.

Two German panthers, heavy tanks knocked out on a road near Le Désert. During the fighting in the Saint-Lô area the German forces included two corps with elements of no less than twelve divisions, including two armored divisions. The losses sustained by the enemy armored units removed the possibility of a further large-scale counterattack west of the Vire River.

JULY OFFENSIVE

An infantry patrol picking its way through the blasted ruins of Saint-Lô. Allied and German shelling and Allied aerial bombing reduced Saint-Lô to ruins. The original objectives of the July offensive were not attained except for the capture of Saint-Lô on 18 July 1944. However, the ground won was sufficient to give the troops more room and better jump-off positions which they needed to break out of Normandy.

Infantrymen firing from a hedgerow. Soldier is shown firing a fragmentation grenade using a U.S. rifle .30-caliber with a grenade launcher. The terrain through which the Allied troops fought was favorable to the defense. In the close bocage countryside, dotted with woods and orchards and with fields divided by tree-topped embankments where armor could not well be employed, the infantry had to wage a grim struggle from hedgerow to hedgerow and from bank to bank, harassed by snipers and machine gun posts. On 24 July the troops of the U.S. First Army were waiting for the weather to clear sufficiently for an air attack before they attempted to break out of Normandy in the area of the Périers–Lessay–Saint-Lô road.

Army medical aid men preparing to evacuate wounded. The U.S. losses during this campaign totaled nearly 11,000 killed, wounded, and missing. The Germans, as a result of the action, were prevented from regrouping and wore down their last immediate reserves for use against a breakthrough.

Infantrymen resting in their foxhole. Rain, which continued for six days, delayed the air bombardment and in turn the advance of the First Army which had scheduled an attack for 19 July 1944. During this period the men were compelled to huddle in their foxholes under the dripping hedgerows in conditions of extreme discomfort, while the enemy, also entrenched behind the natural defenses of the country, was alert to every movement. The low-lying country became a sea of mud, stopping further tank operations during this period.

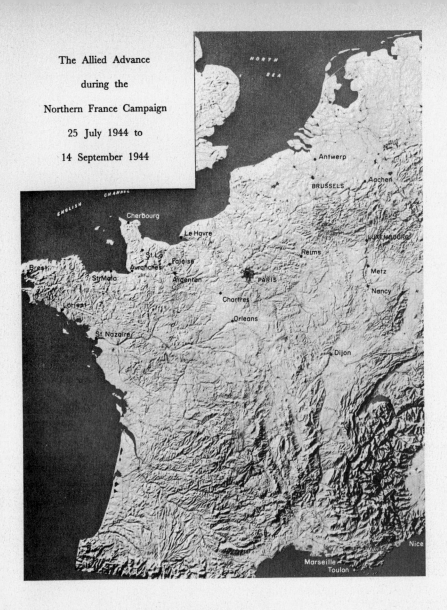

The Allied Advance

during the

Northern France Campaign

25 July 1944 to

14 September 1944

THE CAMPAIGN IN NORTHERN FRANCE

On 25 July 1944 the Allied forces fighting in Normandy were able to begin the offensive to break out of Normandy and carry to the German frontier. Preceding the ground attack, planes of the Allied air forces dropped more than 3,390 tons of bombs on enemy positions on a narrow front in the vicinity of Saint-Lô. The air attack's crushing power and its paralyzing effect on the German forces opened the way for a rapid and powerful drive by Allied armored and infantry units. Cities were captured in quick succession, and the enemy troops were forced to flee in a disorderly retreat.

The armored spearheads led the way out of the Brittany Peninsula which was quickly occupied with the exception of the fortresses of the port cities which were to continue to fight until after the German borders had been reached. While part of the U.S. forces were overrunning the Brittany Peninsula, the major portion turned toward the east in the direction of Paris, and British and Canadian troops moved southward from Caen along the road to Falaise. The battle of the Falaise-Argentan pocket was a disastrous defeat for the German forces who were trying to prevent the Allies from moving eastward. During the fighting in this area ele-

ments of two German armies were so disorganized and destroyed that their effectiveness was greatly impaired.

Paris surrendered on 25 August, and by the 27th all enemy resistance ceased there. The advance continued toward the eastern borders of France, where the Allies stopped their rapid drive, and though a few further advances were made, 14 September 1944 found them consolidating their positions along the Moselle River and northward in Belgium and Holland. The major port cities of Le Havre and Antwerp, which were badly needed by the Allies as ports of entry for men and materials, were captured.

During the Northern France Campaign the expanding Allied forces, reorganized. The Supreme Headquarters, Allied Expeditionary Force, moved to the Continent of Europe. The 21 Army Group was made up of the British Second and the Canadian First Armies. The 12th Army Group, composed of the First and Third U.S. Armies, became operational. In August 1944 Allied forces invaded southern France and moved northward to join those in northern France. This force, made up of the U.S. Seventh and French First Armies, made a junction with the northern group on 11 September. Also during this period the U.S. Ninth Army became operational and took over the reduction of the Brittany fortresses.

U.S. light tanks in Coutances, which fell to the Allies on 28 July after stubborn enemy resistance.

INTO NORTHERN FRANCE

Infantry troops set up a 57mm antitank gun. Advances south from Saint-Lô reached Tessy-sur-Vire on 28 July, while another attack farther east met wih severe resistance in the vicinity of Forêt de Cerisy. In the British-Canadian sector the advance had been halted by a strong enemy belt of antitank guns, dug-in tanks, and mortars.

Mail call at the front.

Frenchwoman, returning to her home after the German withdrawal, passes a knocked out German self-propelled antitank gun. Many of the civilians left their homes and towns during the fighting and returned afterwards, often to find that they had lost their homes during the artillery shelling and aerial bombing. However, in some cases the civilian population stayed in the towns during the fighting.

Motor column advancing along a road near Coutances. On 29 July U.S. armored divisions trapped an enemy column about seven miles southeast of Coutances. Fighter bombers came in and attacked the closely jammed columns of vehicles, destroying 137 tanks and over 500 other vehicles.

An armored column led by a light armored car stops for a few minutes during its advance to Avranches. On 30 July an armored division closely followed by an infantry division closed in on Granville. Another armored division entered Avranches and secured two bridges across the Sée River. The breakthrough was completed by 31 July, the area between Granville and Avranches was cleared of enemy pockets of resistence, and the U.S. forces struck southward in the direction of Villedieu.

Tankers of an armored unit reloading their .30-caliber ammunition belts during the drive southward.

Engineers using a truck-mounted revolving crane swing a section of a treadway bridge into place over the Vire River near Pontfarcy.

491

A medium tank rolls through a battered French village. After the rapid advances through the Brittany Peninsula, U.S. forces were left in front of the main port cities to contain the enemy. The Third U.S. Army turned eastward, driving with strong armored forces on the general axis of Laval–Le Mans–Chartres. On 4 August Mayenne was captured and contact with First U.S. Army units was established. During the next five days the drive to the east continued for a distance of 85 miles, and the cities of Angers and Le Mans were taken.

U.S. artillery observation post near Barenton, between Mortain and Domfront. After the failure of the German counterattack in the vicinity of Mortain, the only alternative for the enemy was to retreat, and a gradual withdrawal was made toward the Seine River. During this period two simultaneous battles were fought: one by First Army troops and those of 21 Army Group around the Falaise–Argentan pocket, the other by the Third Army which was driving hard to the Seine River.

TRANSPORTATION

Destroyed railroad equipment. So greatly had the French railroads suffered that over 900 locomotives and a third of the rolling stock used had to be supplied from Allied sources in England. In addition to replacing locomotives and cars, bridges had to be constructed, wrecked trains had to be cleared, and tracks had to be replaced. Damage by Allied bombings at every major junction and marshalling yard had to be repaired. These tasks fell to men of the Corps of Engineers and the Transportation Corps.

Railroad equipment being unloaded from a seatrain at Cherbourg. Motor convoys could not handle the vast quantities of supplies needed to maintain the Allied fighting forces, and it was necessary to supplement these convoys with rail transportation. The first scheduled run was made between Cherbourg and Carentan on 11 July 1944, using mostly salvaged French equipment. As soon as the Cherbourg port facilities were sufficiently restored, equipment was brought over from England and put into service.

THE FALAISE–ARGENTAN POCKET

Infantrymen picking their way through debris and rubble in Domfront in pursuit of the fleeing enemy. When the Falaise–Argentan pocket was closed, Allied divisions inside the pocket pressed in on the remnants of the German divisions. The enemy struggled to escape from the pocket through the gap between Falaise and Argentan and concentrated on removing his armored units, leaving the infantry to hold off the Allies. A considerable part of 8 armored divisions managed to escape from the closing Allied pincers but left behind a great proportion of their equipment. On 20 August the trap was closed on more than 7 infantry divisions and parts of 2 armored divisions. By 22 August the enemy in the pocket had been eliminated.

Infantrymen firing on
the enemy during the
house-to-house fighting.

Engineers of an armored division relax in a French town during
the advance of the U.S. troops. In the battle of the Falaise–Argentan
pocket the Allies did not accomplish the utter destruction of the
German forces in Normandy, but the enemy troops were broken as
an effective fighting force and the way across France was open.
During this period enemy losses included 70,000 killed and
captured.

Men and vehicles advancing toward Paris. Mopping-up the Falaise–Argentan pocket was assigned to troops of the 21 Army Group, while the First Army forces moved eastward. The Third Army was again moving eastward, and by the evening of 25 August the Allies held most of the Seine River west of Paris.

LIBERATION OF PARIS

The Allies had originally intended to bypass Paris so as to avoid its destruction in an assault. On 19 August 1944 fighting between the Germans and the French Forces of the Interior broke out in the city. The French were soon in need of relief, because of the shortage of ammunition, and Allied forces were shifted to take the city. Meeting with little resistance, a French armored division and a U.S. infantry division entered the city, and by noon on 25 August the German commander formally surrendered.

Parisians scatter as a German sniper fires at them during the celebration of the Allied entry into Paris.

U.S. troops march down the Champs Elysées during a victory parade in Paris. The last German resistance ceased in Paris on 27 August, and the next day the city was turned over to a French general who was to be the military governor.

An 8-inch gun M1 being towed into position by a high-speed 18-ton M4 tractor. The Canadian First Army cleaned up the enemy pockets west of the Seine by 31 August, and the U.S. forces regrouped to pursue the enemy east of the river and begin their drive toward Germany.

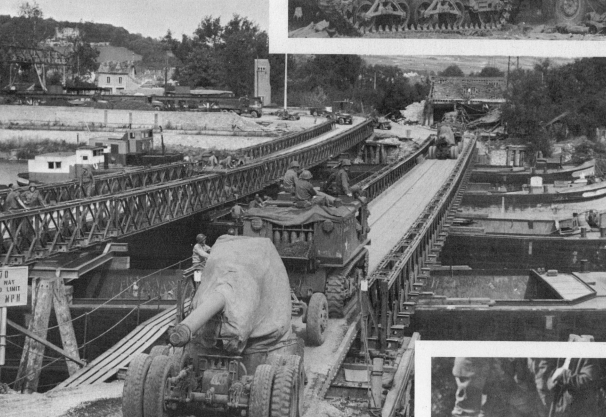

Towed 155mm guns cross a Bailey bridge over the Seine. U.S. troops advanced northeast from the Seine River bridgeheads to take Reims and Châlons-sur-Marne.

Engineers laying a gasoline pipeline in France. In an effort to transport fuel to the front-line units of the Allies, three fuel pipelines were laid across France. This also relieved the road traffic which became more and more congested as the number of Allied troops in France increased.

A wounded German is given medical aid by U.S. soldiers. By 3 September First Army troops had cleared most of the army's zone south of the Belgian border. On that day the remnants of 20 disorganized divisions were trapped before they could reach the Belgian border and 25,000 men were quickly liquidated. The British entered Brussels on 3 September and were also closing in on LeHavre, one of the major port cities on the coast.

A light armored car entering Belgium. On 1 September 1944, Supreme Headquarters, Allied Expeditionary Force (SHAEF), was established at Versailles and assumed the active direction of the 12th and 21st Army Groups. During this period the main problem was that of supplying the racing armored columns, since the only points of entry were the beaches and Cherbourg, a distance too far removed from the Allied forces advancing to the German frontier. By early September supply trucks were traveling 600 to 900 miles in round trips to carry fuel, ammunition, and rations to the combat units.

A 155mm gun motor carriage firing in Belgium. In spite of the shortage of supplies, the pursuit of the enemy continued between 4 and 14 September 1944, with the greatest Allied gains being made on the northern front. On 4 September the British forces captured the port city of Antwerp, one of the greatest prizes of the war. On 12 September the city of Le Havre surrendered. These two cities were of extreme importance because of their port facilities and their nearness to the battle-front. In both harbors the enemy had carried out measures to render the ports useless, but they were not too badly damaged to prevent repair. By 14 September 1944 the sustained drive of the First Army had stopped and the Germans were fighting on their own soil for the first time in many years.

Air Attacks Continue

Boeing B–17 flying through heavy flak over Germany en route to a target.

The Heinkel aircraft factory during an air attack.

499

Infantrymen cross the Moselle as a ¼-ton truck carries wounded men to the rear. On 10 September an attack was launched to secure bridgeheads over the Moselle below Epinal, which was reached on 14 September. The city of Nancy fell on 15 September.

Newly constructed treadway pontoon bridge over the Moselle River.

Infantrymen advancing in the outskirts of Brest. While the Third Army was battling a determined enemy on the Moselle, U.S. forces were still trying to reduce the fortress of Brest.

90mm gun motor carriage firing at an enemy pillbox in Brest. On 14 September the fortress of Brest was still for the most part in German hands, despite all efforts to reduce the strongly fortified positions.

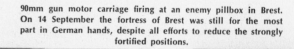

Smoke rising from waterfront installations as Liberators bomb Genoa, Italy, prior to the invasion of southern France. This was part of a plan to keep the enemy guessing as to where the assault would come. At the time of the Normandy landings most of the Allied troops intended for the simultaneous invasion of southern France were fighting in Italy.

SOUTHERN FRANCE

The offensive operation in southern France, originally scheduled to be executed simultaneously with the Normandy landings, was conceived with the aim of pushing northward from the southern coast, creating a diversion of enemy troops from the northern assault, and generally weakening the German Army in France. This operation was given the code name ANVIL.

A serious shortage of landing craft delayed the invasion until 15 August 1944. Meanwhile preparations for such a landing served as a threat and held a large number of German forces on the southern coast. Craft, used first for the Normandy landings, were then rushed to the Mediterranean for use in mounting ANVIL.

During June and July three divisions which formed the bulk of the U.S. VI Corps were withdrawn from the battle in Italy and sent to port areas for training and for participation in Operation ANVIL. At the same time all the French troops with U.S. Fifth Army were withdrawn to prepare for the invasion. The Allied strategic air forces began the process of neutralizing vital enemy communications and installations in southern France. As D-Day approached, a large naval force was amassed in the Mediterranean, and the ground forces, American and French troops, were embarked from Italy, North Africa, and Corsica.

An airborne task force of American and British units, with the mission of preventing the enemy from reinforcing the coastal defense, successfully jumped astride the Argens River behind the German lines before H-Hour. Landings took place on 15 August 1944 in the Cannes-Toulon sector against scattered and disorganized resistance from the enemy. The assault forces, assisted by members of the French Resistance forces, pressed their attack rapidly, defeated the enemy along the coastline, and pushed inland. The troops were met with enthusiasm by the French population.

Toulon and Marseille were captured by units of the French forces. By the end of August the combined American and French forces had broken German resistance in southern France, destroyed and put to flight the enemy, and advanced to Lyons. On 11 September 1944 they made junction with the Normandy forces west of Dijon, thereby sealing all of southwestern France.

Bombing of Rhône River bridges at Tarascon by Allied planes. Pre-D-Day bombardment wrecked all but one bridge across the Rhône, which helped to hamper large-scale movement of enemy troops. The Allied forces were to advance through the Rhône River valley which passes between two mountain masses, the Massif Central and the Alps, and forms a great natural corridor connecting the Mediterranean coast with the Paris basin.

B-24 over the Golfe de la Napoule. Smoke rising in distance, near village of Théoule-sur-Mer, is caused by bombing of railroad, highway, and bridges. At right is Cannes. The air offensive in support of the invasion actually began as early as 28 April 1944 when heavy bombers attacked Toulon. Between that time and August, the Mediterranean Allied air force dropped more than 12,500 tons of bombs on southern France. Beginning on 10 August the offensive was continued by attacking coastal batteries and radar stations, harassing coastal defense troops, and isolating the target area by destroying bridges across the Rhône.

Waterproofed Priest undergoing test in preparation for the invasion. The invasion training center at Salerno, Italy, established a school of one week's instruction in waterproofing vehicles for the coming assault. The 105mm howitzer motor carriage M7 was the principal artillery weapon of the U.S. armored division.

Vehicles assembled at the port of Naples for the invasion of southern France. The troop list of those landing during the first four days included over 155,000 personnel and 20,000 vehicles of all types, including personnel and cargo carriers as well as armored vehicles.

Loaded LST's in Naples Harbor in August 1944 before the invasion. By this time the Germans had been pushed north of Florence, their air force had been greatly reduced, and their airfields in the Po Valley were under constant air attacks by medium and heavy bombers.

Men on a beach near Naples waiting for water transportation to take them to nearby landing craft and transports in the Bay of Naples. This was the final loading before the invasion. Although the Germans were aware of the concentration of troops and shipping and knew that the invasion was in preparation, no enemy bombings interfered with the loading operations. The Allied air forces had rendered most of their airfields within range of Naples inoperative for all practical purposes.

Dropping supplies to paratroopers on D-Day, 15 August 1944. An Anglo-American airborne task force landed at various hours on D-Day beginning at 0430 near Le Muy and Le Luc to establish roadblocks, to prevent enemy movement toward the beaches, and to help reduce the defenses in the Frejus area. No air opposition was encountered and the paratroopers landed and came in contact with the enemy immediately, but resistance was light, primarily small arms fire. Preparations were made by the paratroopers for the landing of the glider-borne elements.

Infantrymen landing on beach from an LCI. In the center of the U.S. assault area troops landed under almost ideal amphibious conditions, four battalions abreast with little hindrance by mines and underwater obstacles and with light enemy resistance.

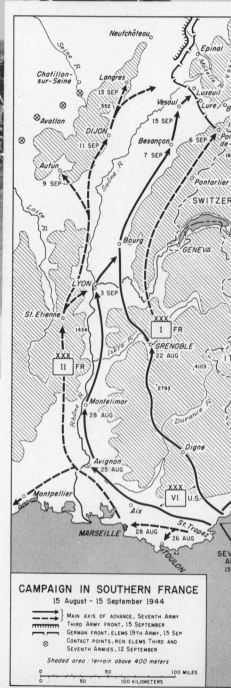

CAMPAIGN IN SOUTHERN FRANCE
15 August - 15 September 1944

- - → Main axis of advance, Seventh Army
  → Third Army Front, 15 September
⊤⊤⊤⊤ German Front, elems 19th Army, 15 Sep
⊗ Contact points, rcn elems Third and
   Seventh Armies, 12 September

Shaded area : terrain above 400 meters

0   50   100 MILES
0   50   100 KILOMETERS

Part of the beach on Baie de Cavalaire. On the left of the invasion coast in the U.S. sector, one division was to assault the beach area from Cap Cavlaire to the Cap de Saint-Tropez, including the town of Saint-Tropez. One battalion landing on the beach shown above advanced along the coastal road and cleared the town of Cavalaire-sur-Mer, and by 1330 on D-Day reached a roadblock, in the vicinity of Cap Nègre, held by the French.

The Cap Sardineau beaches. Another of the 3 assault divisions landed here in the center of the corps invasion area at H-Hour (0800) on D-Day. The three small beaches (shown left) lay along a curving bay between Cap Sardineau and Pointe de l'Arpillon. The divisional area extended inland 15 to 20 miles to Le Luc and Le Muy where the airborne troops had previously landed. After clearing the beaches, the division's mission was to contact the paratroopers to the north and the divisions on each flank.

Enemy pillbox. On the morning of 16 August 1944 troops moved through Saint-Raphaël clearing most of the resistance. There was considerable improvisation on the part of the enemy, such as the mounting of tank turrets on concrete to form pillboxes.

D-DAY PLUS

SOUTHERN FRANCE

The first French Partisans (French Forces of the Interior) to meet the invading U.S. troops at the beach in the Saint-Tropez area. The Partisans had been given a list of priority targets to be attacked on and after D-Day. They were to intensify their activities in the rear of the enemy forces, with special emphasis on the destruction of bridges, cutting and blocking highways and railroads, and seizing or controlling telephone and telegraph centers. At 2000 on D plus 1 a French army, consisting of 7 divisions, began landing on the beaches in the Saint-Tropez area, with the initial mission of capturing the port cities of Toulon and Marseille. The divisions assigned the taking of Toulon began the encirclement of the city on 20 August. Because of formidable enemy defenses, the combined efforts of the French army, the tactical air command, and the Allied naval task force were required before complete occupation of the city was accomplished. The German garrison surrendered to the French army on 28 August 1144.

Soldiers of the southern invading army meeting soldiers from the northern invading army. At 1500, 11 September, elements of a French armored division of the southern forces made junction with a French armored division near Sombernon, 150 miles southeast of Paris. The two invasion forces thus joined to form a continuous Allied front from the North Sea to the Mediterranean.

A little French girl giving a soldier a bottle of wine as a gesture of welcome as U.S. troops march through the streets of a liberated French town.

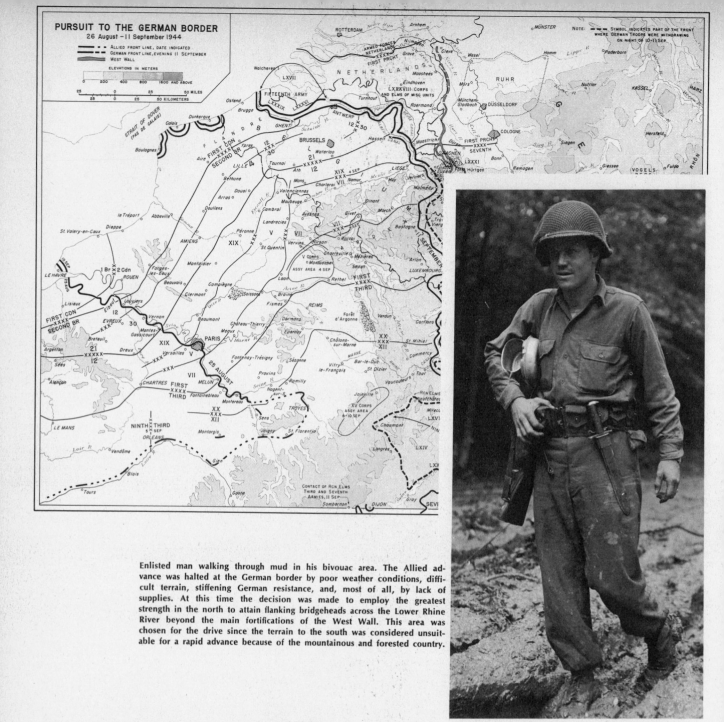

PURSUIT TO THE GERMAN BORDER
26 August – 11 September 1944

ALLIED FRONT LINE, DATE INDICATED
GERMAN FRONT LINE, EVENING 11 SEPTEMBER
WEST WALL

ELEVATIONS IN METERS
0   200   400   800   1600 AND ABOVE

25   0   25   50 MILES
25 0 25   50 KILOMETERS

NOTE: ⟶ SYMBOL INDICATES PART OF THE FRONT
WHERE GERMAN TROOPS WERE WITHDRAWING
ON NIGHT OF 10–11 SEP.

Enlisted man walking through mud in his bivouac area. The Allied advance was halted at the German border by poor weather conditions, difficult terrain, stiffening German resistance, and, most of all, by lack of supplies. At this time the decision was made to employ the greatest strength in the north to attain flanking bridgeheads across the Lower Rhine River beyond the main fortifications of the West Wall. This area was chosen for the drive since the terrain to the south was considered unsuitable for a rapid advance because of the mountainous and forested country.

THE RHINELAND CAMPAIGN: 15 SEPTEMBER 1944–15 DECEMBER 1944

On 15 September 1944 the Allied forces that had invaded southern France came under control of the Supreme Commander, Allied Expeditionary Force. This added the 6th Army Group to the forces opposing the enemy along the German frontier, making a total of 48 Allied divisions in the European Theatre of Operations. In a little over three months, 6 June–15 September 1944, the Western Allies had carried their offensives from the Normandy beaches to the western borders of Germany. During the next three months little, if any, progress was made. Several factors contributed to this general slowdown. As fall and winter approached, rain, mud, and snow greatly hindered operations and made living conditions extremely trying. The terrain became more difficult since many rivers and streams had to be crossed,

and rough, wooded, and hilly country was encountered. Enemy resistance stiffened as the Allies reached the German border. But more important than any other single factor was the problem of supplying the large forces which had advanced so rapidly that they had outrun their supplies.

During this period, as the Allies came to the West Wall and the Rhine, severe fighting took place all along the front. Some of the most difficult operations of the war in western Europe occurred during the Rhineland Campaign as battles were fought in the Arnhem area, the Schelde estuary, the Huertgen Forest, the Aachen sector, the Metz and Saar regions, and the Belfort and Saverne gaps. On 15 December the efforts of the Allies in the Rhineland were interrupted when the enemy broke through the lines in the Ardennes, causing a shift of troops to the Ardennes to reinforce the lines there.

Planes towing gliders take off for the invasion of the Netherlands, 17 September 1944. The First Allied Airborne Army launched its attack to secure a bridgehead across the Rhine in the Arnhem area. Complete surprise was achieved and the drops and glider landings were effective and in most cases were made in the prescribed areas. During the following ten days the fighting was severe with repeated German counterattacks. However, the railroad bridge across the Waal River in the Nijmegen area was captured on 20 September and remained in Allied hands. By the end of September the corridor was widened somewhat and the operation was considered a success even though the Allies were forced to evacuate most of the attacking troops after numerous casualties were suffered.

Paratroopers advancing under enemy fire in the Arnhem area. During the entire operation in the Netherlands which lasted for 30 days, from 17 September to 16 October 1944, over 5,500 planes and 2,500 gliders transported 34,000 men, and over 1,900 vehicles, 500 artillery pieces, and 5,000 tons of supplies. The airborne army suffered more than 13,000 casualties in killed, wounded, or missing.

Mine exploder attached to a medium tank. This model was an improvement over the earlier one because of its chain-driven exploder disks. On the first models the exploder disks rolled freely and were not power driven. The new model also had a higher degree of indestructibility and greater maneuverability and could be driven in mud 18 inches deep and across broken terrain.

Infantrymen of the Seventh Army advance through snow and sleet. The attack of 6th Army Group was to breach the Vosges Mountains whereupon the two armies would join in the Rhine plain to isolate the enemy's Vosges positions. Short of artillery ammunition, the troops slugged it out with the enemy over difficult terrain and in increasingly bad weather, with the infantry carrying most of the burden.

510

Infantrymen riding on an M4 medium tank-dozer through the West Wall, while others follow on foot. The last two weeks in September were spent by the First Army in probing the enemy's defenses along the frontier. On 2 October an attack was launched across the German border about 8 miles north of Aachen. Progress during the next two weeks was slow as troops fought their way through 6 miles of West Wall, or "Siegfried Line," fortifications. The German troops in Aachen refused a surrender ultimatum on 11 October 1944, and during the next three days the city was subjected to intense aerial bombardment and artillery fire. Infantrymen entered the city on 13 October and after fierce house-to-house fighting almost completely occupied Aachen by 20 October. The following day the garrison surrendered, making Aachen the first German city to fall to the Allies. The First U.S. Army then began preparations for a drive to the Rhine as soon as supplies and reinforcements should become available.

Thanksgiving dinner at the Front. During October and November 1944 the cold, rain, fog, and floods made living conditions of the front-line troops miserable. The battle against the weather was as difficult as that against the enemy.

Five-gallon water cans loaded in a quarter-ton trailer being filled at an Engineer water point. The Engineers were responsible for the purification of drinking water, and set up water points from which all units located in the area drew their daily supply.

Bridgehead across the Moselle south of Metz near Arnaville. While the U.S. First Army was driving toward the Rhine in the vicinity of Bonn and Cologne, the Third Army was holding its positions pending the improvement of the supply situation. The Ninth Army moved up from Brittany and took its position between the First and Third Armies in the Ardennes sector.

Infantry patrol entering Metz. For two months the U.S. Third Army was stalled in the vicinity of Metz, the fortress which would have to be captured before any substantial advance eastward could be made. Metz dominated three invasion routes into Germany from France: the valley of the Moselle through Trier and Coblenz; the Kaiserslautern Pass through Saarbruecken to Mainz and Worms; and the route through the Saverne Gap from Sarrebourg to Strasbourg and the Rhine. The capture of Metz was hindered by rain and floods which canceled the heavy air support and made the advance difficult for the ground forces. The attack started on 8 November with only artillery support and it was not until 22 November that the city was finally clear of all enemy pockets of resistance. The last of the forts which ringed the city was taken on 13 December. The Third Army was then confronted by one of the strongest sections of the West Wall, and since its reduction would require a vast amount of artillery support, the attacks were suspended until the necessary ammunition could be brought up.

512

Engineers hauling bridging equipment in flooded areas of the Moselle River. The flooded rivers and smaller streams made the task of bridging extremely difficult during this period of the fighting along the German frontier since, in addition to the wider than normal spans necessary to cross the rivers, the weather was cold and rainy, adding to the hardships of those employed in the task.

Medium tanks firing during the assault toward the Roer River. In spite of the elaborate preparations made for the attack and the great concentration of combat power, progress was extremely slow. Each of the towns was woven into a network in which each house had to be reduced, and each foot of the muddy ground was defended to the last by the enemy troops. The attack plowed on determinedly in the mud and cold, and on 3 December 1944 the Ninth Army came to the Roer. The First Army also attacked until the river was reached.

Infantrymen pushing through the Huertgen Forest near Vossenack, Germany. The Germans had strengthened this natural barrier by the clever use of wire, pillboxes, and mines, and U.S. infantrymen, restricted by the rough wooded terrain, were forced to fight for the most part without the aid of artillery or air support. Casualties to the two armies advancing in this area were high.

Firing rockets during the fighting in the Huertgen Forest area. In the picture 4.5-inch multiple rocket launchers are mounted on 2½-ton trucks, and consist of 8 tubes in a single bank. Two banks are mounted on each of the trucks with the rockets being fired at half-second intervals.

Tired, dirty, hungry infantrymen eat their first hot meal after fifteen days of siege of the town of Huertgen.

Battle-weary Germans who were among the last to surrender after the battle of the Huertgen Forest, which lasted for several weeks.

Infantrymen wait in a shallow zigzag trench before advancing. On 20 November Sarrebourg was captured and on 22 November Saverne fell. By 27 November Strasbourg and its ring of defending forts had been taken. After the collapse of the enemy positions in the Vosges, the Seventh Army attacked northward, and by the middle of December had crossed the German frontier on a 22-mile front and penetrated the West Wall defenses northeast of Wissembourg. In the meantime the German forces which had been driven from the Vosges maintained their bridgehead in the Colmar area, which became known as the Colmar pocket before it was finally liquidated. (right)

A 105mm howitzer motor carriage being fired on German positions in the Rhine Valley.

Five-gallon cans being filled with gasoline at a distribution point. On 15 December 1944 the armies had from a five- to nine-day supply of gasoline on hand.

Opening the valve on a gasoline pipeline. The critical fuel situation of September, which had stalled the armored divisions at the West Wall, was materially improved by late December. At that time three main pipelines were constructed or under construction: one for the northern armies, one for the central armies, and another for the southern armies.

Army supplies being unloaded at Antwerp. The greatest single factor in the improved supply situation was the port of Antwerp which became operational on 27 November. Despite heavy attacks from the German "V" weapons, the port discharged cargo which was badly needed by the forces fighting along the German frontier. Utah and Omaha Beaches ceased operations in November, and then only the larger port cities were used as supply ports of entry.

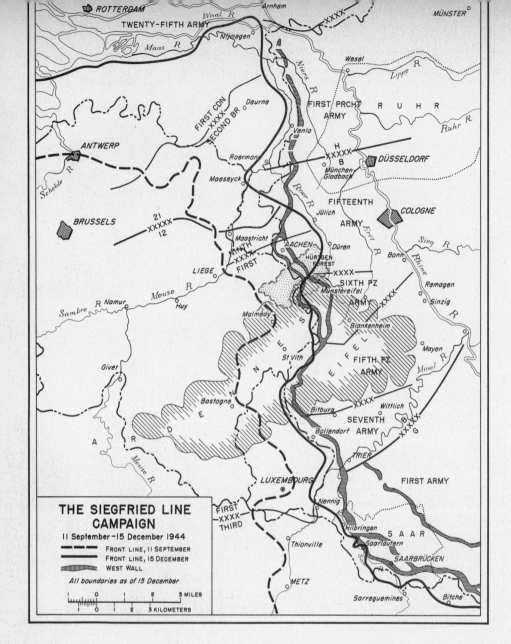

THE SIEGFRIED LINE
CAMPAIGN

11 September–15 December 1944

<pre>
━━━━━━ FRONT LINE, 11 SEPTEMBER
━━━━━━ FRONT LINE, 15 DECEMBER
▓▓▓▓▓▓ WEST WALL
</pre>

All boundaries as of 15 December

THE BATTLE OF THE BULGE

In mid-December 1944 the Allies stopped along the German border, but continued to attack in the Saar and Roer regions, while they concentrated the majority of their strength for an attack in the north. The Germans, taking advantage of their continuous front along the West Wall, planned a counterattack to strike the Allies in one of the weakest portions of the line—the Ardennes sector. The ultimate goals of this German operation were to capture the port city of Antwerp, sever the major Allied supply lines emanating from that port, and destroy the Allied forces north of the Antwerp—Brussels—Bastogne line.

Early on the morning of 16 December the German armies struck the Allied troops located in Belgium and Luxembourg. The Allies holding this portion of the line were too thinly dispersed to offer any great resistance against the powerful enemy attack and were forced to fall back. While the defenders fought the Germans, Allied armies shifted their drives, and troops were rushed to the Ardennes to reinforce the hard-hit units along the front from Monschau to Echternach. After severe fighting during late De-

cember 1944 and early January 1945 the Germans were defeated, and by 25 January the Allies were once more ready to move toward Germany through the West Wall defenses. During the Ardennes–Alsace campaign winter set in, and the cold weather and snow-covered terrain made operations and living conditions extremely difficult.

During this period the British forces in the north eliminated the Germans in the Roermond triangle and captured the enemy bridgehead west of the Roer River. The U.S. and French troops of the 6th Army Group fought a determined enemy in Lorraine and Alsace, and by 25 January had driven the attacking Germans back across the Moder River.

The Ardennes–Alsace campaign, which delayed the Rhineland campaign for six weeks, secured no major terrain objectives for either side. The Germans, who had employed some of their best remaining units, lost nearly 250,000 men, 600 tanks and assault guns, and about 1,600 airplanes. The Allies suffered 72,000 casualties.

On 6 January 1945 the Fifteenth U.S. Army became operational on the Continent and was assigned to the 12th Army Group, taking over many of that army group's responsibilities in the rear areas.

The rough, wooded tableland of the Ardennes in eastern Belgium and northern Luxembourg is broken by many small streams which become serious obstacles during periods of heavy rain or thaw. The Ardennes contained a fair primary but poor secondary road system. Because of the rough terrain the main centers of the road net assumed great importance during the Battle of the Bulge. Heavy snow made infantry maneuver difficult and seriously limited tank movement.

nemy troops pass burning U.S. equipment. The initial German attacks, following a heavy artillery prepa-
ation, were launched all along the front, roughly from Monschau to Echternach. The first objective was
 secure the high ground of the Hohe Venn, but the drive by the enemy met with stiff resistance and
 was forced to commit his armor before noon on 16 December. Further attacks in the northern sector
ere no more successful, and by night the Germans were still fighting at the approaches to the
Elsenborn Ridge.

A German soldier waving members of his unit forward. Spurred on by expressions of the German commanders such as "Forward to and over the Meuse" and "We gamble everything now—we cannot fail," enemy troops drove forward in a determined effort to defeat the Allies. South of the Elsenborn Ridge in the vicinity of the Losheim Gap U.S. troops were overwhelmed and forced to withdraw. By evening the enemy, though blocked in the north, had broken through the thinly held American line and drove toward Stavelot and Huy, the first objective on the Meuse River. Still farther to the south in the Echternach area, the U.S. forces stopped the enemy after he had made limited gains. The Allied situation along the front was extremely grave.

German soldier with ammunition belts moves forward during the enemy counterattack in the Ardennes. German morale was higher than at any time since the Allies had landed, partly because the individual soldier had been propagandized into believing that this was the opportunity to destroy the Allied troops in the west. At 0530 on 16 December 1944 three German armies attacked on a 50-mile front in eastern Belgium and northern Luxembourg. This battle was popularly known as the Battle of the Bulge.

Members of an airborne division moving up through the forest. On 18 December German patrols passed through a gap between Malmedy and Saint-Vith and continued as far west as Werbomont. Other enemy troops tried to push north through Stavelot but were stopped by a blown bridge over the Amblève River and by an improvised task force consisting of U.S. infantrymen, engineers, and tank detroyers. Engineer demolitions and effective use for the first time of the new proximity fuse by artillery strengthened the north shoulder of the growing salient. During the first week of the Battle of the Bulge most planes were grounded because of extremely poor flying weather.

German "King Tiger" or "Tiger Royal" heavy tank passing a line of captured U.S. soldiers being marched to the rear.

U.S. prisoners of the enemy taken during the early fighting in the Battle of the Bulge. Two U.S. regiments near Saint-Vith were surrounded and most of the men were taken prisoner before U.S. reinforcements could arrive on the scene. The enemy attacks on Elsenborn Ridge were stopped by these U.S. reinforcements on 17 December, but this help came too late to save from capture the men shown above and those of an artillery battery who were caught by an enemy armored column south of Malmédy.

Infantrymen batter down the door of a house where German snipers are holding out in the town of Stavelot. On 19 December the north and south flanks continued to hold, and road centers of Saint-Vith and Bastogne were still occupied by U.S. troops though almost surrounded by the enemy. The enemy captured Stoumont but the U.S. forces strengthened the line between Malmédy and Stavelot and with additional reinforcements began to attack the enemy east of Stoumont. To the south the enemy took up blocking positions south of the Sauer River with some troops as far west as the Arlon-Bastogne highway.

Crew of a multiple gun motor carriage M14 waiting to fire on an enemy plane as vapor trails fill the sky. On 20 December control of the First and Ninth U.S. Armies passed to the 21 Army Group, while the Third U.S. Army and a corps of the First Army remained under 12th Army Group control. On 23 December the weather cleared sufficiently for planes of the Eighth and Ninth U.S. Air Forces and the British Bomber Command to begin a large-scale aerial assault on German positions and installations. The German planes which were sent up in greater strength than at any other time since the invasion were no match for the Allies. On Christmas Day the First U.S. Army launched an attack and made contact with the British forces in the northern section of the front. For the first time since 16 December a continuous Allied front was established.

An infantryman pausing in his advance through the forest. During the first ten days of the battle, confusion reigned as hastily shifted troops arrived to reinforce the efforts of the isolated units attempting to halt the enemy attack.

Part of an armored division of the Third Army moving into the Ardennes. At the beginning of the Battle of the Bulge, Third Army was regrouping for an attack on the West Wall in the Saar area. On 18 December an armored division was turned north toward the Ardennes sector and was followed by an infantry division the next day. The 6th Army Group was turned north to take over the area held by the Third Army, which during a period of six days broke off its general attack in the Saar region, turned left, moved more than 100 miles over unknown winter roads, and mounted an attack with 6 divisions. While the Third Army was advancing to relieve the armored and airborne troops in Bastogne, the battle for the city was being waged. The enemy surrounding the city numbered 45,000, while within Bastogne there were about 18,000 U.S. troops. The commander of the troops in the city refused to surrender to the Germans and continued to hold out against all attacks. The defenders, cut off from their sources, were supplied by airdrops during this period. On 24 December over 100 tons of supplies were dropped.

Infantrymen fire at German troops in the advance to relieve the surrounded paratroopers in Bastogne. In Bastogne the defenders were badly in need of relief; they were attacked nightly by German aircraft; supplies were critically low in spite of the airdrops; and the wounded could not be given proper attention because of the shortage of medical supplies. After an advance which had been slow, U.S. relief troops entered Bastogne at 1645 on 26 December 1944.

Infantrymen advance on Bastogne.

Prisoners taken during the advance on Bastogne being evacuated. With the arrival of U.S. relief troops were 40 truckloads of supplies which were delivered during the night of 26 December. 652 wounded men were evacuated from the area, and the battle continued since the enemy had shifted a large portion of his attacking troops in this area. On the night of 26 December when the German advance was halted, the Third Army, consisting of 8 divisions and parts of 2 other battered divisions, faced elements of 11 German divisions between the Meuse and the Moselle.

Knocked-out U.S. medium tanks. During the last few days of December 1944 the main effort in the Third Army zone was concentrated in the vicinity of Bastogne, while the situation in the rest of the army area remained static. Armored and infantry attacks achieved small gains during which many German counterattacks were made. Echternach was reentered on 29 December, and all enemy forces south of the Sauer River were cleared. On 3 January 1945 the last German attack was made on Bastogne. It was unsuccessful.

Lieutenant General George S. Patton, Jr. (right) talks with Brigadier General Anthony C. McAuliffe and Lieutenant Colonel Steve Chapruis (center) after awarding them both the Distinguished Service Cross for their heroic defense of Bastogne. When the Germans demanded the surrender of Bastogne on December 22, General McAuliffe, commander of the besieged 101st Airborne Division, defiantly answered: "Nuts!"

Infantrymen bivouacking in the woods.

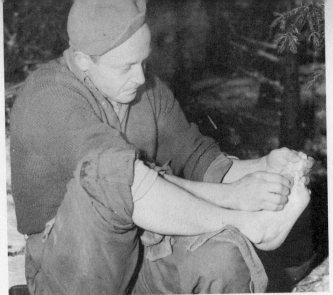

Soldier takes time out to wash his feet and put on dry socks. The cold weather combined with the snow and dampness caused many cases of trench foot during this period. It was difficult when wearing the regular leather shoes to keep one's feet dry and warm, but frequent washing and changing of socks helped.

Field mess. Living conditions during the best of times were not too pleasant for the combat soldier, but during the winter hardships were greatly increased.

Manhay, Belgium. On 3 January 1945 an attack was launched west of Manhay in the First Army zone. Visibility was reduced to 200 yards, and the temperature was near zero. The few roads were coated with ice, and the snow off the roads was waist deep, making it extremely difficult to maneuver. During the first day advances of almost 4,000 yards were made before a heavy snowfall halted the assault. On 5 January the attack was resumed and the La Roche–Vielsalm road was cut. La Roche was captured by the British on 10 January. The British troops were then withdrawn to regroup for the Rhineland Campaign. The Germans began to withdraw from the tip of the salient after becoming convinced that they had lost in their attempt to halt the Allies.

Airborne troops loading a shell into a 75mm pack howitzer. Between 16 and 27 December, First Army artillery units fired more ammunition than at any other time during the war except during the Normandy Campaign. An average of 800 weapons fired over 750,000 shells.

Two German prisoners being brought in.

An artillery plane with newly attached skis taking off.

523

Elements of the First and Third Armies made contact at Houffalize on 16 January. While the U.S. units were still under-strength, replacements to the theatre had increased. Despite heavy fighting and poor living conditions, morale was high. The junction of First and Third Armies at Houffalize marked the achievement of tactical victory in the Ardennes. On 17 January the First Army reverted to 12th Army Group, but the Ninth U.S. Army remained under 21 Army Group. With the enemy withdrawing from the Ardennes the Allies resumed their advance toward the Rhine.

A camouflaged 8-inch gun located in the southern portion of the Third Army zone. This gun was capable of firing a 240-pound projectile a distance of 20 miles. The troops left in this area were placed on the defensive during the fighting in the Ardennes sector. Heavy artillery in the area fired on enemy installations in the triangle of the Moselle and Saar rivers and West Wall fortifications.

Barbed wire being strung as a defensive measure in the event of another enemy counterattack. In mid-January the enemy was still able to maintain a cohesive line, but the critical situation on the Russian front made necessary the shifting of troops to the Eastern Front while withdrawing to the security of the West Wall all committed troops facing the western Allies.

First Army troops, wearing snow camouflage capes, advance. On 24 January the First and Third Armies' boundary was shifted north in the general line Saint-Vith–Losheim–Ahr River, and attacks were to be renewed on the Saint-Vith–Bon axis. The First Army was to breach the West Wall and secure the high ground in the vicinity of Blankenheim, while the Third Army was to attack with its left wing to cover the First Army.

Supplies moving through Bastogne, 22 January 1945, on their way to the front-line troops. By the first of the year materiel losses in the Battle of the Bulge had been replaced and the combat units were again prepared to move forward. From 17 to 24 January the Third Army continued to attack through Houffalize, and reached the northern tip of Luxembourg on 24 January. In an advance to the east bridgeheads north of Clervaux on the Clerf River were secured on 23 January. During this period most of the area between the Sauer and the Our rivers was cleared of enemy resistance. In a hurried effort to withdraw as many vehicles as possible the enemy lost over 1,700 vehicles to planes of the U.S. XIX Tactical Air Command.

A member of a glider regiment, armed with a rifle and a rocket launcher, returning from a three-hour tour of guard duty.

A tanker sews his clothing on an old sewing machine in front of his M4 medium tank.

THE ALLIES RESUME THE OFFENSIVE

Infantrymen advancing under enemy shellfire. On 15 January 1945, on the left of the First Army zone, an attack was begun from the Butgenbach–Malmédy positions. By 19 January the First Army had secured the defiles southwest of Butgenbach. The attack launched toward Saint-Vith continued to gain ground, and on 23 January Saint-Vith was recaptured.

An M5 light tank guarding a road in the U.S. Ninth Army area, 22 January. With the collapse of the German salient in the Ardennes, preparations were made for the offensive to the Rhine by 21 Army Group. The Germans held the triangle south of Roermond between the Meuse and Roer rivers. This was a serious threat to the left flank of the Ninth Army and had to be eliminated before the army could advance across the Roer to the Rhine plain. The task of eliminating this salient was assigned to the British Second Army, and by 26 January was completed.

Three-inch gun motor carriage firing on enemy positions at night. On 20 December 1944 the 6th Army Group abandoned its offensive and relieved the Third Army in the region westward to Saarlautern to defend against any enemy penetration in Alsace-Lorraine. The offensive was stopped even though many pillboxes in the West Wall had been taken, and during the last ten days of December the Seventh Army regrouped its forces and deployed its troops.

Seventh Army troops entering a fortress of the Maginot Line, near Bitche, France, which had been taken in the December fighting. Reduction of the strongly defended forts of the Maginot Line was halted when the Ardennes fighting began. The new Seventh Army front included the three following areas: the Saare Valley in Lorraine; the low Vosges Mountains; and the northern Alsace plain between the mountains and the Rhine.

The Seventh Army prepared an alternate main line of resistance along the old Maginot Line (Sarreguemines–Bitche–Lembach–Hatten–Sessenheim) and a final defensive position along the eastern slope of the Vosges. On 1 January 1945 the Germans attacked in the area between Sarre and Rohrbach and drove ten miles into the U.S. lines, where the appearance of powerful armored reserves of the U.S. forces and Allied counterattacks caused the enemy to curtail its operation. Another New Year's Day attack by the Germans in the Bitche area was a more serious threat. After stubborn fighting on the part of the Allied troops the attack spent itself on 7 January. In the Bitche salient the fighting continued until 20 January before becoming stabilized.

Tanks of an armored unit moving along a slippery road during a heavy snowstorm. In other 6th Army Group areas there was action along the front. As U.S. troops withdrew to the Maginot Line so that French troops could take over this portion of the front, the Germans followed closely. French troops in the Strasbourg area contained an enemy attack from the Colmar pocket. There was heavy activity in the U.S. zone near Hatten where the enemy, after suffering heavy losses, failed to break through the U.S. troops.

Camouflaged tanks and infantrymen, wearing snow camouflage capes, moving over a snow-covered field. Toward the end of January a heavy snowfall slowed operations, and on 25 January the enemy struck his final blow near Haguenau, France. On 26 January the Germans were driven back across the Moder River.

THE RHINELAND CAMPAIGN:
26 JANUARY–21 MARCH 1945

At the successful conclusion of the Ardennes–Alsace campaign the Allies again turned their attention to the Rhineland. Between 26 January and 21 March a major objective was achieved: the German troops which tried to halt the advance were cut off and destroyed, thus eliminating future enemy action west of the Rhine.

When the Rhineland campaign ended, the Allied Expeditionary Force numbered over 4,000,000 men organized into a well-balanced military machine, with combat elements ready to strike the final blow against the disintegrating enemy forces. On 21 March 1945 the First U.S. Army held a bridgehead across the Rhine about 20 miles wide and 8 miles deep and had 6 divisions on the eastern bank of the river, while the remaining Allied troops were prepared to cross in their respective zones.

Riflemen moving through snow-covered, wooded terrain. On 24 January the First U.S. Army was to begin an attack to breach the West Wall and secure the high ground in the vicinity of Blankenheim, while part of the Third Army was to attack with its left wing to cover the First Army. The rest of the Third Army front was to begin an aggressive defense.

Deep snow slowed military traffic. With the completion of the Ardennes-Alsace Campaign the Allies again began their advance to the Rhine after having been delayed for six weeks.

Advancing through the snow, men wearing camouflage suits blend in with the snow-covered ground, while those without white suits stand out plainly.

Infantrymen waiting in their snow-covered foxhole for an artillery barrage which will start an offensive.

Front of an M24 light tank showing its 75mm gun, newer type of track, and torsion bar suspension. When the offensive halted attention was given to attacking the Roer dams. The enemy took advantage of the wooded country, deep valleys, many streams, poor roads, and the fortifications of the West Wall in an effort to halt the advance. Bitter fighting developed but by 2 February the U.S. forces had reached a point within two miles of Schleiden. On 8 February the Canadian First Army struck the German forces west of the Rhine, the first of a series of attacks that were to destroy the enemy.

The town of Breisach, Germany, during a heavy artillery shelling. On 20 January 1945 U.S. and French troops of the 6th Army Group began an offensive converging in the direction of Breisach, Germany, on the eastern bank of the Rhine. This operation was aimed at the total reduction of the Colmar pocket west of the Rhine. On 1 February the U.S. forces had advanced to within three miles of Neuf Brisach while on the same day the French troops closed up to the Rhine. By 9 February the Colmar pocket had been eliminated.

Roer River treadway poonton bridge. Early on the morning of 23 February the Ninth Army jumped off after a heavy artillery preparation. Covering the right flank was a corps of the First Army. Because the enemy was surprised by this attack only moderate opposition was encountered, and by the end of the first day bridgeheads two to four miles deep were held, infantry troops were east of the Roer River, and seven bridges were being completed under a heavy screen of smoke.

530

Loading .50-caliber ammunition into the wing of a P-47 Thunderbolt fighter plane. On 22 February one of the greatest aerial operations of the war was carried out by nearly 9,000 aircraft taking off from bases in England, France, the Netherlands, Belgium, and Italy. The targets, the German transportation facilities, covered an area of over a quarter of a million square miles.

Destroyed rail yard at Rheine, Germany, on the main line leading from Berlin and Hannover into the Netherlands. One of the most important targets of this attack was the German railway system. The enemy's attempts at defense were completely ineffective as the bombs hit control points, railroad yards, roundhouses, and bridges. The attack so seriously crippled traffic that the railroad system did not recover during the war.

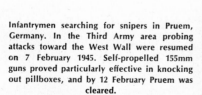

Infantrymen searching for snipers in Pruem, Germany. In the Third Army area probing attacks toward the West Wall were resumed on 7 February 1945. Self-propelled 155mm guns proved particularly effective in knocking out pillboxes, and by 12 February Pruem was cleared.

531

C-47's dropping supplies to infantry troops

2½-ton truck bogged down in the mud. Weather and terrain placed a heavy burden on engineer troops maintaining the roads. As the ground began to thaw, one of the main supply lines became impassable for a time. Over 190 planeloads of rations, gasoline, and ammunition were dropped to one division to maintain its attack.

Troops moving through dragon's teeth of the West Wall fortifications. By 23 February two corps of the Third Army had fought their way through the West Wall to the Pruem River.

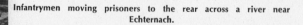

Infantrymen moving prisoners to the rear across a river near Echternach.

After crossing the Roer, the U.S. units advanced to within seven miles of the Rhine and closed in on München-Gladbach by 28 February. On 1 March one infantry regiment cleared the city which had a population of 170,000 and was the largest German city captured up to that time. Located 12 miles from the Rhine, it was one of the approaches to the Ruhr. On 3 March contact was made with the British, and by 5 March the U.S. Ninth Army had closed up along the Rhine on its entire front. By the end of February the Third Army was advancing toward Trier and Bitburg. By 5 March 1945 Trier was captured and preparations were being made for the final drive to the Rhine. During the first week of March the First Army advanced toward the Rhine with parts of its forces while others launched a strong attack from Euskirchen to converge on the Third Army area in the vicinity of Ahrweiler.

Tanks and infantry entering Andernach. The Rhine city of Andernach was captured on 9 March, and contact was made with U.S. First Army units the next day.

First Army men and equipment cross the Ludendorf railroad bridge which became known as the Remagen Bridge. This was the only bridge across the Rhine which was left intact. The attention of the First Army was focused at Remagen during the critical days of securing a bridgehead over the Rhine. The capture of this bridge was an unexpected windfall, because the retreating enemy troops had placed charges and were to blow the bridge at 1600 on 7 March. The first U.S. troops reached the bridge at 1550 and as the first charges began to explode army engineers cut the wires to the others. Thus the bridge, while damaged, was still intact and enabled the U.S. forces to cross the river.

The Ludendorf Bridge four hours
before it collapsed.

The bridge after it fell into the Rhine. After capturing the bridge troops were rushed across in pursuit of the retreating Germans while the engineers set to work to repair the damage. Enemy planes made repeated attacks on the bridge, and it was shelled by long-range artillery. At 1430 on 17 March the bridge buckled and fell into the river only a few hours before the repairs would have been completed.

Treadway bridge across the Rhine near Remagen. During the period 11–16 March the bridgehead was expanded north and south and all attacks gained ground despite the arrival of enemy reinforcements. Treadway and heavy pontoon bridges were built across the river. As the Rhineland Campaign came to an end, six divisions were east of the Rhine and six more were ready to cross in the First Army zone.

Pontoon boats and floats being
moved to the Rhine in
the Remagen area.

The city of Cologne on the banks of the Rhine. U.S. First Army forces took Cologne on 7 March. The enemy had withdrawn most of the veteran troops who had defended the city and left its Volkssturm troops to be battered by the advancing U.S. soldiers. By 9 March the First Army zone was cleared of enemy troops west of the Rhine.

Artillery shelling Bingen. From 11 to 13 March the Third Army cleaned out the Germans who remained north of the Moselle. The Third Army next regrouped its forces and started an attack toward Bingen and Bad Kreuznach to prevent the enemy from retreating across the Rhine. The attack was then to continue southeast to secure a crossing site somewhere between Mainz and Worms. At the same time a drive to Kaiserslautern was to begin and Coblenz was to be reduced.

535

Patton Dashes Across Rhine

Doughs Worm Out of a Nazi Where the Snakes Are

U.S. Army Signal Corp Photo

Taking nothing for granted, these 5th Division infantrymen accept with caution the directions of a German youth, who is pointing to snipers hiding in a building in Worms, Germany.

Nazis Say Russians Fight At Golzow, 30 Mi. from Berlin

Red Army troops smashed at both ends of the Eastern Front yesterday as German commentators reported new Soviet attacks along the central Oder River line due east of Berlin and indicated that a major offensive against the Nazi capital was imminent.

Berlin reports said Marshal Zhukov launched attacks in the Kustrin area, but claimed that the assaults broke down. Later, however, German Radio, quoting a front-line reporter, admitted that the Russians, attacking with infantry divisions and two tank columns, "managed to break through our front and spearheads reached Golzow." Golzow is about six miles due west of Kustrin and 30 miles east of Berlin.

Battered Troops Retreat

Farther south, battered German troops retreated toward the Sudeten foothills as Marshal Koniev's force accelerated its advance toward the great industrial center of Moravska Ostrava, focal point controlling German communications in Bohemia.

At least five German [...] barring the way t[...] the Moravi[...] by [...]

Ask That GIs Attend Frisco

WASHINGTON, Mar. 23 (ANS)—If Sen. Olin D. Johnston (D.-S.D.) and Rep. Henry M. Jackson (D.-Wash.) have their way, an American soldier would be included in the U.S. delegation to the world security conference in San Francisco next month.

They have introduced a resolution in the Senate and House respectively urging that a GI—with a rank no higher than a sergeant—be included in the American delegation [...]

[...] move followed a [...] a Detroit [...] [...]rish by [...]

Japs Admit Quitting Tokyo

Guam, Mar. 24 (Saturday) (AP).—American carrier planes destroyed or damaged 731 Japanese planes in raids on Southern Japan on Mar. 18 and 19, Adm. Chester W. Nimitz announced to-day. Previous Press reports said that 475 planes had been destroyed.

One-fifth of Tokyo's industry was crippled and an estimated 1,200,000 workers made homeless by the Superfort raid on Mar. 9, 20th Air Force HQ disclosed last night, while Tokyo Radio reported that nearly 3,000,000 persons have been removed from the Japanese capital in one of the greatest mass civilian evacuations of the war.

Brig. Gen. Lauris Norstad, 20th Air Force Chief of Staff, said it would be three months before 20 per cent of Tokyo's fire-blitzed industrial installations could be restored to operations. Between 200,000 and 250,000 homes and industrial buildings were destroyed.

Meanwhile, Home Minister Shigeo Odachi told the Jap Diet (Parliament), a Tokyo broadcast said, that the city now had fewer than 4,000,000 inhabitants and that more were scheduled to leave. The city's pre-war population was about 7,000,000 the world's third [...]

Site of Crossing Not Disclosed; Ruhr Ablaze from Raids

WITH U.S. 3rd ARMY, Mar. 23 (AP).—The 3rd Army crossed the Rhine without firing a shot during the night and today established a firm bridgehead on the east bank.

The first wave of doughboys paddled across the river at 10.25 PM, and ten minutes later sporadic shooting broke out as additional waves crossed the moonlit river.

(No indication was given where the crossing was made, but the Germans reported early yesterday that amphibious tanks had crossed at a point 12½ miles south of Mainz).

Caught completely by surprise, the Germans failed to fire a single round of artillery until two hours after the first doughboys were over the Rhine.

Germany's industrial Ruhr and the great plain leading to the north of the Reich was ablaze yesterday. Allied airmen, out for the third straight day of record operations to break the back of enemy forces in the path of Allied might massed on the Rhine, in the northern sector of the Western Front, struck again through towering clouds of smoke and dust at front-line targets, ammo dumps, oil supplies, troop concentrations, signal centers and suspected enemy HQ sites.

2,500 Heavies Hit Reich's Industries

The giant Allied air onslaught on the Ruhr roared into another day yesterday as an estimated 2,500 heavy bombers and fighters joined Continental-based tactical forces in blistering marshalling yards, railroad bridges and troop concentration centers in the Reich's smoldering industrial area.

The 8th Air Force led the attack with a salient of 1,250 heavies and 350 fighters which battled through intense flak to pound at ten marshalling yards and junctions in and around the Ruhr. Once again the bombers made their assaults through ideal weather, and airmen returned with precisely drawn accounts of bombs plummeting down directly on objectives.

The Fortresses and Liberators struck at yards in Osnabruck, Rheine, Munster and Coesfeld, on the northern fringe of the Ruhr; in Recklinghausen and Gladbeck, in the heart of the area; and in Hengstey, Unna-Dortmund, Holzwickede and Siegen, east and southeast of the R[...] [...] up in heavy bursts [...] [...]ts, was still [...] The [...] and [...]

'Can Cross Anytime, Anywhere'—Bradley

Operations on the northern stretches of the Western Front continued yesterday for the third day to combine great aerial strikes with the war of nerves. Allied airmen left wide areas east of the Rhine Elbow a seething mass of fire and smoke as they paralyzed German attempts to hurl in strength to meet the blow which enemy reports maintain will be launched across the river in the Wesel sector south of Arnhem.

From 21st Army Group HQ, which directs Allied operations on this sector, came only a report that "vigorous patrolling" was in progress on both sides. The Germans said that artificial fog continued to cloud the area and that British artillery had opened up on targets east of the Rhine.

Bradley Reviews Campaign

Lt. Gen. Omar N. Bradley, 12th Army Group commander, reviewing the campaign which carried out Gen. Eisenhower's dictum to destroy the Germans west of the Rhine, said yesterday: "The necessity of keeping the Remagen bridgehead small is now rem[...] [...]thing to

Stars and Stripes half page.

THE DRIVE INTO GERMANY

Soldiers watching vapor trails left by bombers on their way to bomb Germany.

Infantrymen using footbridges to cross a river while engineers complete a Bailey bridge. On 15 March three corps of the Seventh Army began attacks, one in the heart of the important Saar industrial area around Saarbrücken, the second driving toward Zweibrücken and Bitche, and the third from the Moder River.

Tube and recoil mechanism of an 8-inch gun M1 on the way to the front.

Infantrymen marching cross-country on their way to Germany.

Seventh Army troops entering Bitche.

537

Infantry platoon being briefed
before making an assault.

Soldiers taking a ten-minute break during
a march to the front lines.

Infantrymen climbing over obstacles as they advance through
the West Wall into Germany. The
advance of the Seventh Army
through the dense minefields and
fortification of the West Wall was
necessarily slow.

538

French commandos and Senegalese troops on an LCI in a Corsican harbor prior to the attack on the island of Elba. The troops were taken to Elba on 17 June 1944 in U.S. landing craft, and in two days the island had been secured.

Goumiers boarding an LST in Corsica for the attack on Elba. The attack, though not carried out by Fifth Army troops, was coordinated by Allied Force Headquarters with the advance on the Italian mainland, and was launched when the forces driving up the mainland were nearly opposite the island. The attacking force consisted of French, goumiers, and Senegalese.

ITALY: 5 JUNE 1944–2 MAY 1945

The Allies did not halt after taking Rome, but their northward progress was soon slowed by skillful delaying tactics of the retreating enemy and by the fact that all the French and some of the American divisions were being withdrawn from the U.S. Fifth Army for the operation in southern France. The Germans speeded construction of the Gothic Line in the north Apennines, and early in August 1944 the Allies paused for reorganization on a line running approximately from ten miles north of Ancona on the east through Pisa to the west coast. The Fifth Army held the territory south of the Arno River from the sea to a few miles east of Florence; the British Eighth Army was north of Ancona on the Adriatic.

During August, preparations were made by the Allied armies in northern Italy to penetrate the heavily fortified Gothic Line. This defensive system of the enemy extended in general from southeast of La Spezia through the mountains to Rimini. After regrouping and building up supplies, the Allied armies started their offensive on 26 August. They succeeded in breaching the Gothic Line in the center and along the coast, but fierce enemy resistance, bad weather, and a shortage of ammunition and replacements halted the offensive south of the Po River plain by the late fall of 1944. The winter of 1944–45 was spent in the mountains overlooking the Po Valley.

The spring drive by the Allied armies started on 9 April 1945. Bologna fell on 20 April, and armor and infantry overran the plain and divided the German forces. On 2 May 1945 the enemy in Italy surrendered unconditionally.

Engineers setting off enemy mines in a street in Leghorn on 19 July 1944, the day the city fell. The soldier at left is guarding engineers against snipers. The Germans had destroyed all the port facilities, mined the buildings in the harbor area, and made the latter unusuable by blocking the entrance with sunken ships. The drive from Rome to the Arno River was a pursuit action in which the Germans, by skillful delaying tactics, slowed the Allied advance so that completion of the Gothic Line defenses in the northern Apennines could be expedited. The mouth of the Arno River was reached by 23 July 1944.

THE ARNO RIVER AREA

Troops in Pisa. The southern outskirts of this town on the Arno River were entered on 23 July 1944. The enemy had destroyed all bridges across the river, and when the infantry entered the town they were met by heavy fire from across the river. The southern half of the city was found heavily mined and booby-trapped. During the approach to the Arno River, plans were being completed for introduction of antiaircraft units into the lines as infantry since enemy air activity had decreased to the extent that many AA units could be more profitably used as infantry.

Negro troops crossing the Arno near Pontedera on 1 September, during the drive toward the Gothic Line. The attack on this line was started by the Eighth Army along the east coast on the night of 25–26 August. On 1 September the line had been breached in that sector, but by the 6th the advance had been stopped a few miles below Rimini on the Adriatic coast. This advance by the British caused the German High Command to shift three divisions opposing the Americans to the British sector. The forces directly opposite the Arno drew back into the Gothic Line, a distance of about 20 miles.

Sherman tank fording the Arno in the Cascina area on 1 September. Little opposition was met until the Gothic Line was reached. The Germans had started to withdraw into this line during the last days of August. Before the withdrawal, it was estimated that the area between the Arno River and the Gothic Line contained about 350 enemy tanks, half of which were Panthers and Tigers.

Top of Il Giogo Pass in the Gothic Line, looking toward the north. The Fifth Army broke through this pass in the Gothic Line defenses outflanking the heavier prepared fortifications at Futa Pass on Highway 65. The scarcity of roads through the mountains made it possible for the Germans to concentrate their defensive works at a few key points such as the Futa and Il Giogo Passes.

Highway 65 at Futa Pass. This pass, at an altitude of 2,962 feet, is one of the lowest through the northern Apennines. Highway 65, the most direct route to Bologna and the Po Valley, became the main supply route and a principal axis of advance in the Fifth Army area, although the breach in the Gothic Line was not made here. Futa Pass fell on 22 September.

Infantry advancing over the hills in the area of Il Giogo Pass on 18 September, the day the pass was taken. The fight for the area started on the morning of 12 September. The mountains on each side of Il Giogo Pass are too steep to require antitank defenses other than roadblocks, but other defenses such as underground fortresses were numerous and well prepared. Barbed wire and antipersonnel minefields guarded approaches. Many of the hills were covered with pine woods, which made it difficult to locate enemy defenses by the use of aerial photographs. Some information was obtained from partisans who had worked on the Gothic Line.

542

German antitank ditch at Futa Pass. This ditch, about three miles long, crossed the road south of the pass. The ditch was covered with a network of infantry positions and bunkers for antitank guns. The area in front of the ditch was mined. Two of the bunkers in this area were topped by Panther tank turrets with long-barreled 75mm tank guns.

Bailey bridge in the Firenzuola area. The Bailey bridge was particularly suitable for operations in the mountains of Italy where sudden rains would swell the rivers and wash out pontoon bridges.

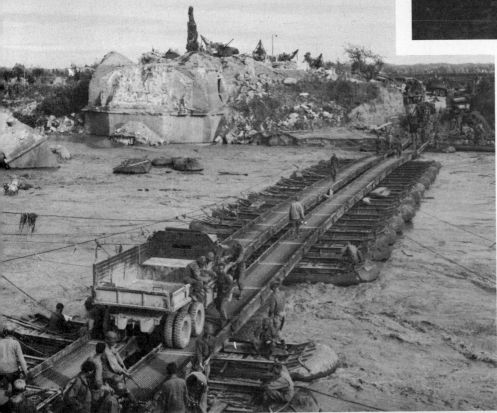

Repairing pontoon treadway bridge over the Arno at Pontedera. The supply situation of Fifth Army troops at the Gothic Line was made difficult by fall rains which raised the Arno River to flood level and washed out most of the bridges between Florence and Pontedera.

543

Loading mules with ammunition for 155mm howitzers in the Castel del Rio area on Highway 6524, between Firenzuola and the town of Imola in the Po Valley. After breaching the Gothic Line at Il Giogo Pass, an attempt to reach the Po Valley at Imola was made along the route above. Because of the exposed salient and stiff enemy resistance, the axis of attack was changed to Highway 65. On 1 October, the day the picture was made, bloody fighting for possession of the controlling height of Monte Battaglia, east of Castel del Rio, was in progress.

A tank battalion preparing to attack along Highway 65 toward the village of Monghidoro. The attack started on the morning of 1 October, and by evening of the 2nd the village was securely in Allied hands. The Sherman tanks pictured here are all armed with 76mm guns.

The jeep along the supply roads in the northern Apennines. This vehicle was capable of operating over unimproved roads and trails, and could be shifted into four-wheel drive for steep grades and muddy or sandy terrain. It could climb a 60 percent grade and attain a speed of 65 miles per hour over level highways. The jeep could also ford a stream 18 inches deep while fully loaded and a deeper stream when especially equipped with exhaust and air-intake extensions. The jeep, truck, and pack mule were always important in the advances made.

Terrain of the winter stalemate in the northern Apennines, looking toward the southeast. The high mountain peak in distance is Monte Vigese. This mountain was taken by the South Africans of the Fifth Army on 6 October 1944 after a three-day fight. The territory in the foreground was in enemy hands until the beginning of March 1945 when it was taken by American and Brazilian troops in a limited offensive to obtain better jumping-off places for the main attack toward the Po Valley.

Soldiers in the Apennines receiving an issue of woolen underwear, September 1944. Some of the peaks in the northern Apennines rise to well over 5,000 feet, and the weather is unpleasantly cold in winter. Fall rains, often turning to sleet, start in September, and the higher peaks are usually snow-covered by late October. Highway 65, the main axis of advance, runs mostly on top of the mountain ridges. Here the cold is particularly severe. There is nothing to break the winter winds, and part of the road is so high that it is often cloud-covered.

545

The ruins of Livergnano. The main highway through the village runs to Florence (upper right), and to Bologna (center left). Livergnano, taken in a five-day fight, became known as "Liver and Onions." During the final attack of this fall offensive toward Bologna, which started on 16 October and bogged down in mud toward the end of the month, the enemy concentrated his artillery fire on this village in an attempt to demolish the houses along the road and thus block the highway, the supply road for the area. The enemy managed to knock down some of the houses but did not succeed in stopping traffic. Bulldozers filled the craters in the road and pushed aside the rubble.

Patrol activity, December 1944. During the relatively quiet period of the first half of December, both sides sent patrols to probe the front lines and bring back prisoners. When the cold weather set in, winter clothing was issued, including the reversible, hooded coat known as the parka, shown below. One side was the conventional olive drab, the other side white for camouflage in snow. New-type shoepacs, combination wool sweaters and cotton field jackets, and sleeping bags left the troops better prepared for inclement weather than they had been during the previous winter, but there would be no possibility of keeping dry at the front during an attack when the rain lasted for days on end.

Pipeline pumping station at Leghorn. Construction of this line started soon after the capture of the port. By 23 November 1944 the pipeline had reached Highway 65 just a few miles behind the front, eliminating the trucking of gasoline over this already overcrowded road.

Members of a South African unit firing a Long Tom. This unit was stationed along Highway 64. During the winter of 1944-1945 the U.S. Fifth Army roster included Brazilians, South Africans, British, and Italians as well as U.S. troops, while the British Eighth Army along the east side of the peninsula contained New Zealanders, Canadians, Poles, Indians, Italians, and Jewish troops from Palestine in addition to United Kingdom units.

Ambulance evacuating wounded from the front lines near Highway 65, between Loiano and Livergnano. The flow of wounded from the battlefield was carefully controlled. Evacuation hospitals were kept as free of patients as possible, thereby affording immediate facilities for the most urgent cases. It was found desirable in daylight hours to direct the main stream of casualties to hospitals located farther in the rear, while during the night most of the patients were brought to the forward hospital units in order to reduce the delay caused by blackout ambulance driving over icy roads. ($^{3}/_{4}$ = ton 4 × 4 ambulance.)

547

Truck on Highway 65 near Loiano receives near miss, January 1945. This highway had been the main axis of advance during the October offensive in the U.S. sector and was the only good road in this area. During the winter stalemate and buildup for the spring offensive, a period of about five months, this road was under observed enemy artillery fire directed from Monte Adone, a commanding position between Highways 64 and 65.

Troops in a defense position near Highway 65. This area was thinly populated and houses were few and far between. Those still standing drew fire, and troops in support or reserve positions would dig in on the reverse slope of hills and make their foxholes as comfortable as possible. Roofs and walls were constructed from empty shell cases, food containers, and the like and reinforced with sand bags. Keeping warm was a problem: the area is almost bare of trees; most of the heating of the foxholes was done by gasoline stoves, sometimes issued, often improvised.

An infantry company moves into the line under a smoke screen to relieve another company. During the five-month static period starting at the beginning of November 1944, rotation of units for rest and recreation was a regular procedure.

Signal Corps linemen stringing communication wire in preparation for the coming spring offensive. During the winter stalemate many new lines were strung, and hookups were made to the Italian state underground cable system. Circuits linked all units of the Fifth Army, and an eight-mile line containing eight open-wire circuits was started in February 1945 from Filigare on Highway 65 near Monghidoro to the village of Lagaro on Highway 6620.

Reinforcements move up toward the fighting in the Monte Belvedere area. The men are equipped with M1 rifles and carbines, special shoes, and rucksack type pack.

THE SPRING OFFENSIVE

Members of an American engineer company working on a trail in the vicinity of Monte Grande. An Indian pack mule convoy is returning after taking supplies to the front line.

549

Monte della Spe area, looking toward the east. Highway 64 parallels the Reno River (in distance). The village of Vergato is shown on the west bank of the river. Monte della Spe is the rounded hill in foreground. It was taken on 5 March 1945 during an attack to secure a suitable jumping-off place for the spring offensive. Vergato, which was an enemy strongpoint, and most of the surrounding territory remained in enemy hands after the capture of Monte della Spe. The main offensive, the attack toward the Po Valley, started from here on 14 April 1945 and by the 20th Allied troops had broken into the valley.

Soldiers moving up into the line a few days before the start of the attack toward the Po Valley.

Easter service, 1 April 1945.

Self-propelled guns of a South African armored unit firing a mission a few days before the attack to break into the Po Valley. These vehicles are American Sherman tanks modified by the British as self-propelled guns. Prior to the jump-off, the units along the Fifth Army front had been engaged in a series of deceptive artillery fires.

Soldiers firing howitzers in support of the Nisei who were making an attack northward along the mountain ridges toward the towns of Massa and Carrara. The attack started on 5 April 1945. The Nisei were American soldiers of Japanese ancestry.

Bodies of American infantrymen killed during the opening of the spring offensive. Note stretcher bearer in background looking for casualties. The infantry was making an attack across the mountains toward Massa and Carrara on the west coast.

Pianoro on Highway 65, looking south toward the hills occupied by the Allies for almost six months. Pianoro, at lower left, was one of the keys of the German defense systems barring entrance to Bologna and the Po Valley. The fight for Pianoro started on 16 April. Entering what was left of the town on the evening of the 18th, the infantry found it booby-trapped.

Action during the Po River crossing at Ostiglia, 24 April. A 57mm antitank gun firing in support of an infantry assault across the railroad bridge to the north bank of the river. (The British 6-pounder was the forerunner of the 57mm gun. It was adapted for U.S. use and also manufactured for other United Nations under the lend-lease agreement as the 57mm antitank gun.)

Treadway bridge across the Po River at San Benedetto. Opened on the afternoon of 25 April, it was the first bridge across the river. The infantry had started to cross in this area on the morning of the 23rd in assault boats under heavy machine gun, mortar, and rifle fire as well as fire from enemy antiaircraft guns lowered to fire airbursts on a flat trajectory. Casualties were high, but by 1745 a bridgehead of 2,000 square yards had been established on the north bank of the Po. The bridge above is 915 feet long.

Weary U.S. troops in Bologna on the morning of 21 April. The city, entered from the south by U.S. forces and from the east by Poles of the Eighth Army, fell that day. Pressing forward, the troops pursued the fleeing Germans.

"Alligators" about to cross the Po River near Ostiglia. Developed by the U.S. Navy, the first shipment of these amphibian tracked vehicles arrived in December 1944 and training was begun. Great secrecy surrounded them and they were kept thoroughly camouflaged before the dash to the Po. They were armored and each had socket mounts at four locations for either .30- or .50-caliber machine guns. A stern ramp could be lowered to take on a vehicle. Maximum capacity was 8,000 pounds and a crew of three.

553

Infantry action at Vicenza, in the foothills of the Alps. The advance of the Allies across the plain was too fast to permit the Germans to halt, reorganize, and make a determined stand behind either the Po or the other rivers in the Po plain. Speedy thrusts by infantry-armor columns split the enemy forces and severed communications. After the crossing of the Po, the action on both sides developed into a race to the Alps, the enemy hoping to escape into Germany, the Allies determined to prevent them. Many isolated pockets of resistance developed behind the advancing columns, and special task forces were organized on 23 April to deal with them.

Prisoners were captured by the tens of thousands in the Po Valley and marched to the rear, often unguarded, or guarded by only one or two men. On 2 May 1945, the Germans signed the terms of the unconditional surrender of their forces in Italy. One week later the war in Europe was concluded with complete victory for the Allies. The Italian campaign had been a bitter one, lasting 607 days (3 September 1943 to 2 May 1945). Casualties of the Fifth Army, including all nationalities serving with that army, totaled 188,546. United States losses were 19,475 killed, 80,530 wounded, and 9,637 missing.

German prisoners and their equipment captured on the Po plain. For the first time in the Italian campaign, the enemy was retreating over terrain suitable for swift pursuit. Since the Germans lacked vehicles and gasoline, they had to rely to a great extent on horse-drawn transportation. They retreated across an open valley having a fine network of roads for mechanized forces, and were forced to cross wide rivers by ferries and pontoon bridges under constant attack by Allied air forces. The retreat became a rout.

THE CENTRAL EUROPE CAMPAIGN

The Central Europe campaign began on 22 March 1945 with units of the First U.S. Army across the Rhine in the Remagen area. On the night of 22–23 March elements of the Third U.S. Army crossed the river at Oppenheim. As the First and Third Armies crossed the Rhine the Fifteenth U.S. Army took over the area west of the river from Bonn to Neuss. On 26 March the Seventh U.S. Army crossed the Rhine north and south of Worms and, after meeting stiff resistance on the riverbank, broke through the enemy and quickly expanded the bridgehead. The Ninth U.S. Army crossed the river south of Wesel while the British Second Army crossed north of the city. Elements of the First Allied Airborne Army dropped east of the Rhine and linked up with the ground troops east of the river. In many respects this was the most successful airborne operation that had been carried out up to this time.

After the Allies were firmly established east of the Rhine, the great German industrial area of the Ruhr was encircled and the defending troops captured. The advance through Germany was rapid and met with little opposition except in scattered areas. The Russians drove into Germany from the east, and enemy troops in trying to escape capture by the Russians surrendered by the thousands to the western Allies. As the U.S., British, and Canadian troops in the north reached the line where it was expected they would meet the Russian forces, they halted. The Third and Seventh U.S. Armies continued their drives into Czechoslovakia and Austria where a junction was also made with the Russians.

On 2 May 1945 the German forces in Italy surrendered. Two days later elements of the Seventh U.S. Army met those of the Fifth U.S. Army, coming from Italy, at the Brenner Pass. On 9 May 1945 the surrender of all the German forces became effective, marking the end of the war in Europe.

Engineers constructing a pontoon treadway bridge over the Rhine. A steel treadway bridge was completed by 1800 on 23 March 1945, and the following day a heavy pontoon bridge was completed. By noon on 25 March a second treadway bridge was completed. The crossing of the Rhine in the Third Army area gained complete tactical surprise, and the enemy offered scattered resistance. By the evening of 24 March three divisions held a bridgehead ten miles wide and nine miles deep. These divisions were closely followed by two more, making a total of five on the east bank of the Rhine.

The Allied Advance

during the

Central Europe Campaign

22 March 1945

to 11 May 1945

An assault boat raft ferrying a 90mm gun motor carriage across the Rhine. Troops of the Third U.S. Army first crossed the Rhine at Oppenheim on the night of 22–23 March. Utilizing assault rafts and attacking without artillery or aerial preparation, six battalions were across the river before daybreak with a loss of only 28 men killed and wounded. Following the assault boats were landing craft and DUKW's. The LCVP's were manned by naval personnel who arrived at the river an hour after the assault began.

Jeeps and tanks crossing the Rhine at Boppard, Germany. On 24 March 1945 a crossing in the rugged Rhine gorge north of Boppard was made, and by 25 March a bridgehead eight miles wide and three miles deep was held. A treadway bridge was constructed at Boppard.

Crossing the Rhine near Worms, Germany. U.S. Seventh Army troops crossed the Rhine near Worms at 0230 on 26 March. These forces met small arms and scattered mortar fire while crossing and, after landing on the east bank of the river, met stiff enemy resistance north of Worms. South of Worms the troops reached the far shore with little opposition but as they moved eastward the resistance increased. Two panzer counterattacks were turned back during that morning. By evening of 26 March the bridgehead had been expanded to an area of 15 miles wide and 7 miles deep.

German prisoners being marched westward across the Rhine as troops of the Ninth Army move eastward into Germany.

556

An infantryman covers a German as he surrenders. In the First Army area an attack from the Remagen bridgehead was carried out, and preparations were made to advance to the Kassel area. On 28 March, First Army troops were closing up along the upper Lahn River. Infantry divisions quickly followed the armored spearheads to mop up enemy pockets of bypassed troops and to clear the areas which had been taken in the rapid advances. In six days the shallow Remagen foothold had been expanded to a lodgement area 65 miles deep.

Infantrymen entering Frankfurt. The bridgeheads along the Rhine were expanded and on 26 March Third Army troops entered Frankfurt. The advance moved northward toward Kassel. The Fifteenth Army was instructed to take over the west bank of the Rhine from Bonn to Neuss by 1 April, to assume command of the division which was guarding the Brittany ports, and to be prepared to occupy, organize, and govern the Rhine provinces as the 12th Army Group attacks progressed eastward.

Frankfurt on the Main River, showing the Frankfurt Cathedral. By 28 March Frankfurt had been half cleared of enemy troops and Hanau completely cleared. Part of a large enemy pocket west of Wiesbaden had been mopped up and contact was made between the First and Third U.S. Army troops.

Tow rope being attached to a glider as the First Allied Airborne Army prepares to take off for landings east of the Rhine in the 21 Army Group area. The mission of this army was to break up the enemy defenses north of Wesel and deepen the bridgehead to facilitate the linkup with the ground forces. The airborne troops took off from bases in England and France and converged near Brussels. The troops began landing on 24 March 1945 at 1000, and during the next three hours some 14,000 troops were transported to the battle area by over 1,700 aircraft and 1,300 gliders.

Members of first Allied airborne army after landing near Wesel. On the ground the airborne forces met with varying resistance. Bridges over the Issel were seized and 3,500 prisoners were taken. This airborne operation was the most successful carried out to this time. The attack had achieved surprise, and the airborne troops reorganized quickly after landing. Ninth Army troops held a bridgehead nine miles wide and three miles deep by the end of the day (24 March).

Signalmen roll a reel ashore on the east bank of the Rhine after laying a submarine cable on the bottom of the river from a DUKW.

EAST OF THE RHINE

Destroyed equipment left behind by the retreating enemy.

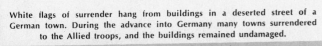

White flags of surrender hang from buildings in a deserted street of a German town. During the advance into Germany many towns surrendered to the Allied troops, and the buildings remained undamaged.

A transportation corps train moving over a bridge which was constructed across the Rhine at Wesel by the engineers. With all three Allied army groups established on the east bank of the Rhine, plans were made to encircle the Ruhr. By 1 April 1945 a trap was closed which formed a 4,000-mile-square pocket and included the Ruhr industrial area.

Seventh Army troops advancing after capturing the town of Mergentheim. On 28 March the Seventh Army launched its attack out of the Worms bridgehead. The assault was halted on 4 April when strong resistance was encountered at Heilbronn. On 31 March the French First Army crossed the Rhine at Speyer and Germersheim, and on 4 April captured Karlsruhe.

4.5-inch multiple rocket launcher mounted on a medium tank. The Germans stubbornly defended the industrial area of the Ruhr even though an army group was caught in the trap with little hope of escape. On the Allied flanks, advances were made as the enemy began to disintegrate.

Infantrymen and tankers take time out for a short rest during their rapid advance. On 4 April the Ninth Army was to start an attack southward, and the First U.S. Army was to drive to the north. While these two armies were eliminating the Ruhr pocket, the Fifteenth Army was to hold the line on the Rhine.

Machine gunners of a First Army division covering a road intersection. During the first fighting in the Ruhr the enemy showed spirit. On 4 April ten counterattacks were launched in an attempt to break out of the pocket. Heavy fighting continued in many towns with the civilians fighting alongside German soldiers. Dug-in self-propelled guns supported the German infantry. The line was drawn tighter by the Allies, and on 10 April Essen, home of the great Krupp armament works, was cleared by the U.S. assaulting troops.

Infantrymen pass a dead German as they cross a stream. On 10 April the Ninth, First, and Third Armies resumed the attack to the east with 22 divisions. Only in the Harz Mountains was any serious organized resistance encountered. The Germans had hurriedly assembled about 10,000 men to form an army which was initially to break through into the Ruhr pocket. When that failed it was to break through to the Thuringian pocket. This also failed, and the small army which represented the last of the German manpower was encircled by the U.S. forces.

Liberated slave laborers help themselves to food and supplies in a store in Hannover. With the liberation of the slave laborers who had worked in German factories, many problems arose, and Allied Military Government offices were established as quickly as possible to cope with them.

Prisoner-of-war enclosure. On 14 April the Ruhr pocket was split in two, and prisoners arrived in such large numbers that Allied facilities were taxed to the limit. On 16 April the eastern half of the pocket collapsed, and two days later the pocket ceased to exist. There were 325,000 prisoners, including 30 generals. This represented 21 divisions as well as many nondivisional units.

Vehicles of an armored division passing through a burning German town. On 18 April the three armies were along the Elbe River–Mulde River–Chemnitz–Plauen–Bayreuth line which was a restraining line established because of the probability of contact with the Russian troops advancing from the east. In the north the 21 Army Group was advancing on Bremen and the Elbe betwen Wittenberge and Hamburg.

Traffic moving across the Main River at Würzburg. On 5 April Würzburg was cleared after three days of heavy fighting.

Infantrymen moving down a street in Waldenburg during the Seventh Army advance. The French First Army cleared Baden-Baden and Pforzheim, and by 15 April Kehl was cleared.

Infantrymen climbing over rubble as they clear snipers out of Nürnberg. By 18 April part of the Seventh Army was in the battle for Nürnberg. Other troops of that army were halted for nine days around Heilbronn and along the Neckar and Jagst rivers.

Russian soldier grabs American soldier and hugs and kisses him gleefully when the two forces link up near Grabow, Germany.

U.S. officers and enlisted men meet Russian Troops in Germany. On 30 April a division of the Ninth U.S. Army made contact with the Russians at Apollensdorf. Troops of the First U.S. Army had met Russian troops earlier.

Soldiers crossing the Danube (Seventh Army). The two armies of the 6th Army Group lanuched a drive into southern Germany, the area where the remaining German forces supposedly were to make a determined stand.

564

German soldiers. The First and Ninth Armies, during the latter part of April and early May 1945, handled thousands of German soldiers and civilians who were trying to escape the advancing Russians by crossing the Elbe River into the American zone.

Capturing guards at Dachau, ten miles northwest of Munich. A few of the guards of the concentration camp remain standing with their arms raised while the majority lie on the ground, waiting to be taken prisoner.

An enlisted man gives his cigarettes to inmates at Dachau. On 29 April troops of the U.S. Seventh Army captured Dachau and released over 30,000 prisoners of many nationalities.

A German horse-drawn convoy moves along a winding mountain road in Austria to surrender. From 1 April 1945 until the end of the war the three armies of the U.S. 12th Army Group took over 1,800,000 prisoners.

Seventh and Fifth Army troops meet at Nauders, Austria. On 4 May, Seventh U.S. Army troops captured the town of Brenner in the Brenner Pass, and a few hours later contact was made with elements of the Fifth U.S. Army which had fought its way up the Italian Peninsula. On the same day Berchtesgaden was entered.

VICTORY

Members of "The Stars and Stripes" staff grab copies of the extra edition as they come off the press, proclaiming V-E Day.

A soldier being evacuated by plane from a German prison camp catches up on the news.

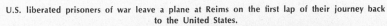

U.S. liberated prisoners of war leave a plane at Reims on the first lap of their journey back to the United States.

Men marching to the docks at Le Havre to board a ship that will take them home to be discharged under the new point system Men with the highest number of points were sent home first for discharge. These numbers were determined by the total number of months of service, total number of months overseas, number of awards and decorations, and the number of dependents.

Floodlights illuminate Big Ben on the Houses of Parliament as the lights go on again in London on V-E night after being blacked out during the war years.

BY THE PRESIDENT OF THE UNITED STATES OF AMERICA

A PROCLAMATION

The Allied armies, through sacrifice and devotion and with God's help, have wrung from Germany a final and unconditional surrender. The western world has been freed of the evil forces which for five years and longer have imprisoned the bodies and broken the lives of millions upon millions of free-born men. They have violated their churches, destroyed their homes, corrupted their children, and murdered their loved ones. Our Armies of Liberation have restored freedom to these suffering peoples, whose spirit and will the oppressors could never enslave.

Much remains to be done. The victory won in the West must now be won in the East. The whole world must be cleansed of the evil from which half the world has been freed. United, the peace-loving nations have demonstrated in the West that their arms are stronger by far than the might of dictators or the tyranny of military cliques that once called us soft and weak. The power of our peoples to defend themselves against all enemies will be proved in the Pacific war as it has been proved in Europe.

For the triumph of spirit and of arms which we have won, and for its promise to peoples everywhere who join us in the love of freedom, it is fitting that we, as a nation, give thanks to Almighty God, who has strengthened us and given us the victory.

NOW, THEREFORE, I, HARRY S. TRUMAN, President of the United States of America, do hereby appoint Sunday, May 13, 1945, to be a day of prayer.

I call upon the people of the United States, whatever their faith, to unite in offering joyful thanks to God for the victory we have won and to pray that He will support us to the end of our present struggle and guide us into the way of peace.

I also call upon my countrymen to dedicate this day of prayer to the memory of those who have given their lives to make possible our victory.

IN WITNESS WHEREOF, I have hereunto set my hand and caused the seal of the United States of America to be affixed.

Done at the City of Washington this eighth day of May in the year of our Lord nineteen hundred and forty-five and of the Independence of the United States of America the one hundred and sixty-ninth.

Harry Truman

By the President:

Joseph C. Grew

Acting Secretary of State.

Molly Pitcher at the Battle of Monmouth.

WOMEN IN THE ARMY

From the very beginning of our nation, women have shared the hardships and privations of pioneer life. The indomitable spirit of the American woman who defended her home and family has become legendary.

Tradition tells us that "Molly Pitcher" who gained her nickname by carrying water to the men on the Revolutionary battlefield at Monmouth, replaced her husband, Captain John Hays, when he collapsed at his cannon. One woman, Deborah Sampson Gannet, served in the Continental Army for three years under the name of Robert Shurtleff. She won a reputation for coolness and courage in action and was engaged in many daring exploits. During the Yorktown campaign she fell ill and her sex was discovered. She was discharged from the service and she received a letter of commendation from General Washington along with a bonus of money. In later years she was invited to the capital, where Congress voted her a pension and a grant of lands.

In later wars, women were frequently employed by the Army as laundresses, nurses, or clerks. But there was always one distinction. These women were civilian workers, not a corps of military women.

However, in due time the women won the legal right to serve their nation as career military personnel. Congress established the Army Nurse Corps in 1901 and the Women's Army Corps in 1942.

> Love and loyalty to one's country have never been the exclusive attributes of men. Women, too, throughout America's history, have given concrete evidence of their devotion. . . . American women have always taken their full share of responsibility. Today, as in the past, our women will meet the challenge.
>
> HELEN HAYES

Deborah Gannett, a woman, served in the armed forces of the United States during the Revolutionary War. She was enrolled as a private in the army under the name of Robert Shurtleff, was wounded in the battle of Tarrytown, witnessed the capture of Cornwallis, and was honorably discharged in November 1783. The document reproduced here is Deborah Gannett's deposition in her claim for pension. It is among the records of the Veterans Administration in the National Archives, Washington, D.C.

570

THE ARMY NURSE CORPS

It was as nurses that women were first accepted by the military, although full status as part of the military took nearly a century to achieve. The first war hospital was established in 1854 by Florence Nightingale, who organized a hospital unit of 38 women nurses for service with the British Army on the battlefields of the Crimean War. Ten years later, in the United States, Clara Barton went into the Union Army camps and hospitals of the Civil War to nurse the sick and wounded. After the war, she went abroad to work with the International Red Cross and gained experience with the German Red Cross during the Franco-Prussian War of 1870. Returning to the United States, she organized and became first president of the American Red Cross.

In the Spanish-American War of 1898, American civilian nurses served with the U.S. Army under contract. Even though they did not have the protection of military status, they served with the Army in Cuba, Puerto Rico, the Philippines, and on Army transports as well as in stateside camps.

In 1901, Congress recognized the wartime service of these nurses by establishing the Army Nurse Corps within the Medical Department of the Army. Army nurses, however, did not receive Army rank, officer status, equal pay, or benefits such as retirement and veterans' benefits. After World War I, members of the Army Nurse Corps were given relative rank and some retirement benefits, but full military rank and equal pay and benefits were not granted them until 1944, ninety years and several wars after the "Lady of the Lamp" established the first war hospital.

Third Division Hospital, Jacksonville, Florida.
Head of "Nurses Row." 7th Army Corps, 1898.

American Red Cross in France (Neuilly). Operation in American Military
Hospital #1, World War I.

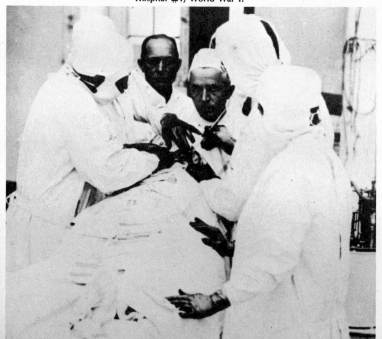

Army Nurse Corps nurse's aide dentist. World War I, France.

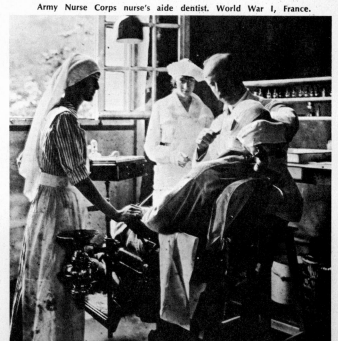

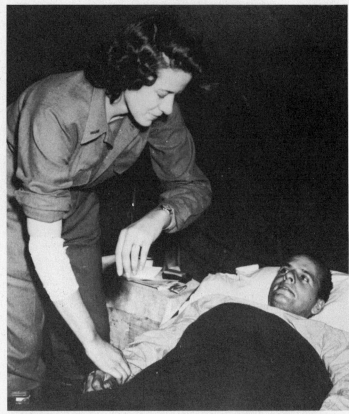

Lieutenant Cordelia Cooks, ANC, first U.S. Army nurse to be wounded in Italy. Presenzano Sector, 2 December 1943.

Nurses at the 5th General Hospital prepare plaster bandages. Carentan, France, 1944.

Nurse assists in operation on a soldier patient for the removal of shell fragments from the brain. 27th Evacuation Hospital, Xertigny, France, 1944.

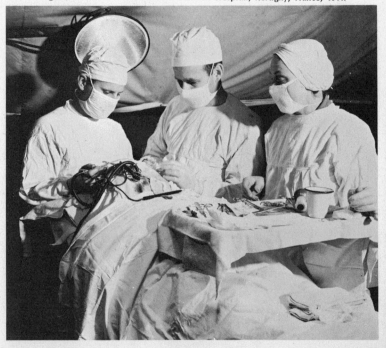

Army nurses taken prisoner by the Japanese at Bataan and Corregidor, freed from Santo Tomás University civilian concentration camp at Manila, are awarded Bronze Stars along with promotions before their departure for the United States. 20 February 1945.

Korea, 1951. An Army nurse off duty washes some clothes in the old combat standby, a steel helmet.

Army nurses in combat zone, Okinawa, wash out of steel helmets, 1945.

An Army nurse supervises an enlisted laboratory technician in making serology tests at the Tokyo Blood Bank. Occupation duty, Japan.

Wounded soldier shows picture of his children to flight nurse aboard an Army Air Forces Douglas C-54 air evacuation plane on the way back to the U.S. from the Pacific, August 1945.

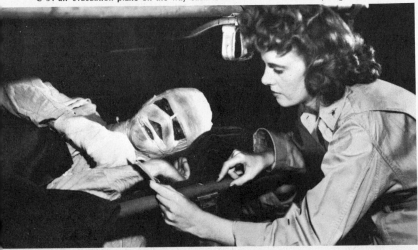

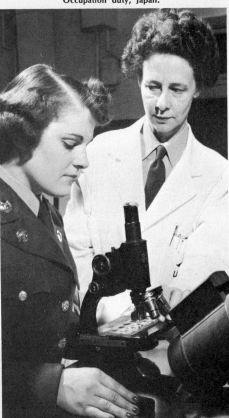

THE WOMEN'S ARMY CORPS

The desire of American women to be of service to their country found a ready champion in the Honorable Edith Nourse Rogers, Congresswoman from Massachusetts. For many years, Mrs. Rogers had been interested in the problems of women who had been employed by the Army during World War I, particularly those who had served with the American Expeditionary Force in France. From personal observation as a Red Cross worker in France during World War I, Mrs. Rogers knew the hardships they had undergone because they were not protected by Army status. They were not eligible for veterans' compensation, and in later years Mrs. Rogers saw many of them in sad circumstances because of this lack. She was determined that women would not undergo these difficulties in the event of another war. In the spring of 1941, therefore, Mrs. Rogers called upon General George C. Marshall, then the Army's Chief of Staff, to inform him that she intended to introduce a bill to establish a women's corps. During the month that followed, the War Department planned furiously for a bill that the Army could "safely sponsor."

Because the War Department was unwilling to incorporate women as part of the Army, Mrs. Rogers accepted auxiliary status for the proposed corps even though she felt strongly that its members should have the same rights of pension and disability allowance as male soldiers. The bill which she introduced into the House of Representatives on 28 May 1941 was entitled: "A Bill to Establish a Women's Army Auxiliary Corps for Service with the Army of the United States." The name Women's Army Auxiliary Corps was soon abbreviated to the familiar designation WAAC. The Women's Army Auxiliary Corps was to be a corps of 25,000 for noncombat service and, though not part of the Army, was to be the only women's organization authorized

to serve with the Army, exclusive of the Army Nurse Corps. In a decision which has been termed perhaps the most basic and vital in the Corps history, the mission of the WAAC, as defined by the Bill, was "to make available to the national defense the knowledge, skill, and special training of the women of the nation."

General Marshall and the Secretary of War threw their personal support behind the measure; but, because more urgent matters took precedence, passage of the WAAC Bill was delayed. At last, on 14 May 1942, the Bill was passed by the Senate, and, when signed the next day by President Franklin D. Roosevelt, became Public Law 554, 77th Congress, "An Act to establish a Women's Army Auxiliary Corps for service with the Army of the United States."

By a subsequent Act of Congress, the WAAC, on 1 September 1943, became the Women's Army Corps, a component of the Army of the United States. During World War II, more than 150,000 women served in the Women's Army Corps in the United States, Europe, Africa, the Southwest Pacific, China, India, Hawaii, the Philippines, and Alaska. On 12 June 1948, the President of the United States signed Public Law 625, Eightieth Congress, which made the Women's Army Corps an integral part of the regular and reserve elements of the United States Army.

Separate legislation at various times established five other components in the armed services, each composed completely or predominantly of women: the Army Nurse Corps, the Army Medical Specialist Corps, the Navy Nurse Corps, the Air Force Nurse Corps, and the Air Force Medical Specialist Corps. These components, with the Women's Army Corps, the Women in the Navy, the Women Marines, and the Women in the Air Force, are the nine women's components of the current U.S. military establishment.

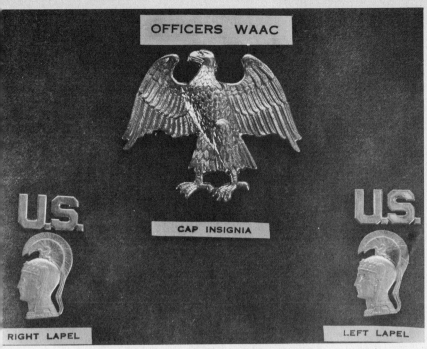

OFFICERS WAAC

CAP INSIGNIA

U.S.

RIGHT LAPEL

U.S.

LEFT LAPEL

Official insignia, Officers, Women's Auxiliary Army Corps.

"Mail Call" always caused the WAACs to fall out in a hurry for the precious letter from home or a boyfriend.

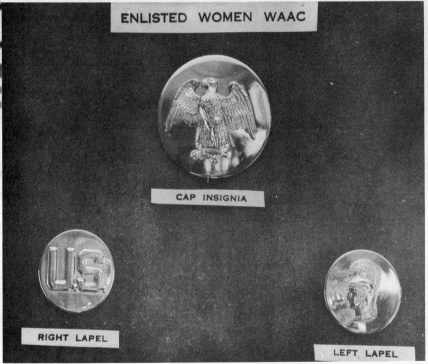

ENLISTED WOMEN WAAC

CAP INSIGNIA

US

RIGHT LAPEL

LEFT LAPEL

Official insignia, Enlisted Women, WAAC.

Daily calisthenics help keep the women physically fit and trim.

Representatives of the American Red Cross serving refreshments to WAACs who have just arrived in Scotland.

WAACs with full field equipment arriving at a North African port. Most Women's Army Corps duties in North Africa were of an administrative nature in offices of the various headquarters. Members of the Corps also worked in communications or other activities that could be handled as efficiently by women as by men.

Director Oveta Culp Hobby of the WAACs is shown taking the oath of office as a Colonel in the Army of the United States commanding the WAACs. Left to right are Brigadier General H. W. Lewis, acting Adjutant General of the Army; General George C. Marshall, Chief of Staff; Colonel Hobby and Lieutenant General Brehon B. Somervell, Commanding General of the Army Service Forces. 1943.

WAACs march in review at
Fort Des Moines, Iowa.

WAAC Corporal Geraldine Horne had one of the most
interesting jobs in World War II as the secretary to
Lieutenant General Mark W. Clark, Commanding
General, Fifth Army in Italy.

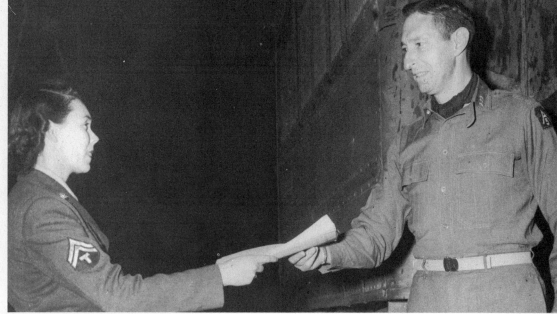

WAAC basic trainees at the WAAC Center at Fort Mc-
Clellan, Alabama, stand "at ease" while their sergeant speaks to them. Platoon sergeants work closely
with their trainees during the eight-week WAC basic
training course, guiding and helping them to adjust
to military life.

THE ARMY MEDICAL SPECIALIST CORPS

Dietitians, physical therapists, and occupational therapists have been employed by the Army since 1917. In recognition of their contribution as members of the professional medical team, they were given relative rank in 1943 and Army of the United States status followed in 1944.

The Women's Medical Specialist Corps was established by the 80th Congress, 16 April 1947, authorizing Regular Army commissions for these three groups of specialists. With authorization by Congress in 1955 for commissioning of men, as Reserves in the Corps, the name was changed to the Army Medical Specialist Corps.

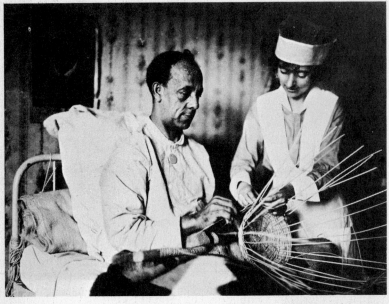

World War I—Army Medical Specialist Corps Occupational Therapist teaching a wounded soldier the art of basket-weaving.

World War I—AMSC Dietitian serving a specially prepared meal to a wounded soldier in a hospital in France.

AMSC Dietetic Intern checks up on patient at Brooke General Hospital in San Antonio, Texas, 1965.

WAACs working in the communications section of the operations room at an air force station. No opportunity was overlooked to replace men with personnel of the Women's Army Corps, both in the United States and overseas. WAACs were given many technical and specialized jobs to do, as well as administrative and office work. The Medical Corps employed the largest number of WAACs in technical jobs, but other technical services such as the Transportation Corps, Signal Corps, Ordnance Department, and Quartermaster Corps had many positions that could be performed by women as efficiently as by men.

The Soldier's Emblematic Link
with the Tradition of His Regiment —

DISTINCTIVE INSIGNIA

The Mark of a Distinguished Organization and Its Members

(The mottoes accompanying the insignia in this section are in conformance with the U.S. Institute of Heraldry. Where the motto is in English there is no foreign version; where it is in a foreign language, there is no English equivalent; where both are used, both constitute the official version.)

IN THE minds of many young soldiers, a distinctive insignia may be just another item of the required uniform—but to the old soldier, a distinctive insignia embodies a proud, personal sense of participation in the title of his organization, depicting the historic past to which he attaches great pride.

This soldierly feeling of identification with the accomplishments and traditions of the organization led to the use of heraldic coats of arms and distinctive insignia in the Army. Coats of arms, and the distinctive insignia derived therefrom, serve a twofold purpose—

▸ to depict the proud glory of the organization with the coat of arms emblazoned on regimental colors;
▸ to mark the soldier as a member of a proud and distinguished unit by the wearing of distinctive insignia on his uniform.

In 1957 the Combat Arms Regimental System (CARS) was established to permit continuity of the famous combat arms organizations carried on the rolls of the Army. Organizations selected for inclusion were designated parent regiments. These units, with their subordinate battle groups, now designated battalions, permitted the required flexibility in organizational structure for the modern Army without loss of historic achievements and tradition. The system also preserved for the soldier the privilege of membership in a distinguished unit.

The distinctive insignia worn by the soldier is not an item of issue from the supply stream. The Company Fund, administered by the fund custodian (Company Commander) and his enlisted fund council, is used to buy the distinctive insignia for each soldier of the unit. Only those assigned to the unit have the privilege of receiving it. Additional sets may be purchased by the individual at his Post Exchange or Post and Service School Bookstore.

To ensure that the distinctive insignia worn by Army personnel are manufactured authentically, a distinctive insignia painting and a manufacturing drawing are furnished the organization commander, on a loan basis, by The Institute of Heraldry, U.S. Army. These items are then made available to an insignia manufacturer. The resulting samples are examined by Quality Control Inspectors of the Institute, to ensure that they are correct in color, design, and detail, and are of high-quality material and workmanship. After the samples are approved, the organization commander notifies the manufacturer to complete the order. Subsequent orders may be placed with the approved manufacturer, but whenever another manufacturer is selected, the entire procedure must be repeated.

Those privileged to wear the distinctive insignia can truly feel that they are members of a distinguished Army outfit.

Following are the Distinctive Insignia of Armor, Cavalry, Armored Cavalry, Artillery, Infantry, and Airborne Infantry regiments of the active U.S. Army included in the Combat Arms Regimental System.

(Prepared by The Institute of Heraldry, U.S. Army.)

ARMOR

13th ARMOR
Organized 1 May 1901
It Shall Be Done

15th ARMOR
Organized 12 February 1901
Tous Pour Un, Un Pour Tous

16th ARMOR
Organized 1916
Strike Hard

32d ARMOR
Activated 15 April 1941
Victory or Death

33d ARMOR
Activated 15 April 1941
Men of War

34th ARMOR
Activated 1 October 1941
The Strong Arm for Victory

35th ARMOR
Activated 15 April 1941
Vincere Vel Mori

37th ARMOR
Activated 15 April 1941
Courage Conquers

40th ARMOR
Activated 15 April 1941

63d ARMOR
Organized 15 August 1942

64th ARMOR
Organized 1 June 1941

66th ARMOR
Organized August 1918

67th ARMOR
Organized 1 September 1929

68th ARMOR
Activated 1 January 1940

69th ARMOR
Activated 31 July 1940

70th ARMOR
Organized 15 July 1940

72d ARMOR
Organized 15 July 1943

73d ARMOR
Organized 1 June 1941

77th ARMOR
Organized 1 June 1941

81st ARMOR
Organized 1 October 1941

1st CAVALRY
Organized 4 March 1833
Animo et Fide

4th CAVALRY
Organized 26 March 1855
Paratus et Fidelis

5th CAVALRY
Organized 28 May 1855
Loyalty and Courage

7th CAVALRY
Organized 21 September 1866
The Seventh First

8th CAVALRY
Organized 21 September 1866
Honor and Courage

9th CAVALRY
Organized 21 September 1866
We Can, We Will

10th CAVALRY
Organized 21 September 1866
Ready and Forward

12th CAVALRY
Organized 8 February 1901
Semper Paratus

17th CAVALRY
Organized July 1916
Forward

2nd ARMORED CAVALRY
Organized 23 May 1836
Toujours Prêt

3d ARMORED CAVALRY
Organized 12 October 1846
"Brave rifles! Veterans! You
have been baptized in fire and
blood and come out steel."

6th ARMORED CAVALRY
Organized 18 June 1861
Ducit Amor Patriae

11th ARMORED CAVALRY
Organized 11 March 1901
Allons

14th ARMORED CAVALRY
Organized 19 February 1901
Suivez Moi

18th Armored
Cavalry

26th Cavalry

Headquarters and
Headquarters Company,
49th Armor Group

82d Cavalry

101st Cavalry

102d Armor

103d Armor

104th Armored Cavalry

105th Cavalry

106th Cavalry

107th Armored Cavalry

108th Armor

108th Armored Cavalry

109th Armor

110th Armor

Headquarters and
Headquarters Company,
111th Armor Group

112th Armor

116th Armored Cavalry

117th Cavalry

123d Armor

124th Cavalry

127th Armor

131st Armor

142d Armor

149th Armor

Headquarters and
Headquarters Company,
149th Armor Group

152d Armor

163d Armored Cavalry

172d Armor

185th Armor

Headquarters and
Headquarters Company,
185th Armor Group

194th Cavalry

195th Armor

196th Cavalry

198th Armor

210th Armor

223d Cavalry

230th Cavalry

238th Cavalry

246th Armor

252d Armor

263d Armor

Headquarters and
Headquarters Company,
264th Armor Group

303d Armor

632d Armor

DISTINCTIVE INSIGNIA OF
ACTIVE ARMY ARTILLERY REGIMENTS

1st ARTILLERY REGIMENT
Organized 1 June 1821
Primus Inter Pares
(First Among Equals)

2d ARTILLERY REGIMENT
Organized 1 June 1821
The Second First

3d ARTILLERY REGIMENT
Organized 1 June 1821
Celeritas et Accuratio
(Speed and Accuracy)

4th ARTILLERY REGIMENT
Organized 1 June 1821
Audacia
(By Daring Deeds)

5th ARTILLERY REGIMENT
Organized 18 June 1861
Faithful and True

6th ARTILLERY REGIMENT
Organized 23 March 1898
Celer et Audax

7th ARTILLERY REGIMENT
Organized 29 March 1898
Nunquam Aerumna
Nec Proelio Fractum
(Never Broken
by Hardship or Battle)

8th ARTILLERY REGIMENT
Organized 7 July 1916
Audacieux et Tenace
(Daring and Tenacious)

9th ARTILLERY REGIMENT
Organized 6 August 1916
Kulia-i-ka-nuu
(Hawaiian—Onward Still Higher,
Win the Day, Give the Victory)

10th ARTILLERY REGIMENT
Organized 1 June 1917
The Rock's Support

11th ARTILLERY REGIMENT
Organized 1 June 1917
On Time

12th ARTILLERY REGIMENT
Organized 1 June 1917
Nec Temere Nec Timide
(Neither Rashly nor Timidly)

13th ARTILLERY REGIMENT
Organized 1 June 1917
Without Fear, Favor,
or in the Hope of Reward

14th ARTILLERY REGIMENT
Organized 1 June 1917
Ex Hoc Signo Victoria

15th ARTILLERY REGIMENT
Organized 1 June 1917
Allons

16th ARTILLERY REGIMENT
Organized 21 May 1917
Macte Nova Virtute

17th ARTILLERY REGIMENT
Organized 6 June 1917
In Time of Peace
Prepare for War

18th ARTILLERY REGIMENT
Organized 1 June 1917
Per Aspera ad Astra
(Through Difficulties to the Stars)

19th ARTILLERY REGIMENT
Organized 1 June 1917
Per Scintillam Flamma
(Through the Spark, the Flame)

20th ARTILLERY REGIMENT
Organized 1 June 1917
Duty, Not Reward

21st ARTILLERY REGIMENT
Organized 1 June 1917
Progressi Sunt

22d ARTILLERY REGIMENT
Organized 10 July 1918
Labore et Honore
(With Industry and Honor)

25th ARTILLERY REGIMENT
Organized 2 August 1918
Tace et Face
(Be Silent and Act)

26th ARTILLERY REGIMENT
Organized 2 August 1918
Courage and Action

27th ARTILLERY REGIMENT
Organized 2 August 1918
Conjuncti Stamus
(United We Stand)

584

28th ARTILLERY REGIMENT
Organized 10 August 1918
We Support the Line

29th ARTILLERY REGIMENT
Organized 11 August 1918
Fidelis et Verus
(Faithful and True)

30th ARTILLERY REGIMENT
Organized 10 August 1918
Striving to the Highest

31st ARTILLERY REGIMENT
Organized 6 August 1918
In Periculo, Nos Jubete
(When in Danger, Command Us)

32d ARTILLERY REGIMENT
Organized 5 August 1918
Proud Americans

33d ARTILLERY REGIMENT
Organized 5 August 1918
Servabo Fidem
(I Will Keep Faith)

34th ARTILLERY REGIMENT
Organized 7 August 1918
We Support

35th ARTILLERY REGIMENT
Organized 9 August 1918
En Avant Toujours
(Forward Always)

36th ARTILLERY REGIMENT
Organized 7 August 1918
In Order

37th ARTILLERY REGIMENT
Organized 17 August 1918
On the Minute

38th ARTILLERY REGIMENT
Organized 17 August 1918
Steel Behind the Rock

39th ARTILLERY REGIMENT
Organized 9 August 1918
Celeritas in Conficiendo
(Speed in Action)

40th ARTILLERY REGIMENT
Organized 10 August 1918
All for One

41st ARTILLERY REGIMENT
Organized 10 August 1918
Mission Accomplished

42d ARTILLERY REGIMENT
Organized 10 August 1918
Festina Lente
(Make Haste Slowly)

43d ARTILLERY REGIMENT
Organized 7 August 1918
Sustinemus
(We Support)

44th ARTILLERY REGIMENT
Organized 6 March 1918
Per Ardua
(Through Difficulties)

51st ARTILLERY REGIMENT
Organized 21 July 1917
Fire for Effect

52d ARTILLERY REGIMENT
Organized 22 July 1917
Semper Paratus

55th ARTILLERY REGIMENT
Organized 1 December 1917
Vigilantia

56th ARTILLERY REGIMENT
Organized August 1922
Night Hides Not

57th ARTILLERY REGIMENT
Organized 11 January 1918
Veto
(I Forbid)

59th ARTILLERY REGIMENT
Organized 1 January 1918
Defendimus
(We Defend)

60th ARTILLERY REGIMENT
Organized 23 December 1917
Coelis Imperamus
(We Rule the Heavens)

61st ARTILLERY REGIMENT
Organized 9 March 1918
Non Est ad Astra Mollis e Terris Via
(The Way to the Stars Is Not Easy)

62d ARTILLERY REGIMENT
Organized 4 September 1921
Nitimir in Alta
(We Aim at High Things)

65th ARTILLERY REGIMENT
Organized 26 December 1917
Sursum
(Upwards)

67th ARTILLERY REGIMENT
Organized 21 May 1918
Memor et Fidelis
(Mindful and Faithful)

68th ARTILLERY REGIMENT
Organized 1 June 1918
Lolamy
(Can Do)

71st ARTILLERY REGIMENT
Organized 12 May 1918
Unique Venimus
(We Come from All Parts)

73d ARTILLERY REGIMENT
Organized 12 October 1918
No Motto

75th ARTILLERY REGIMENT
Organized 7 October 1918
Paratus Facere
(Prepared to Do)

76th ARTILLERY REGIMENT
Organized 13 June 1917
Duty, The Spirit of '76

77th ARTILLERY REGIMENT
Organized 23 May 1917
En Garde
(On Guard)

78th ARTILLERY REGIMENT
Organized 1 June 1917
Semel et Simul

79th ARTILLERY REGIMENT
Organized 1 June 1917
Our Country—Our Regiment

80th ARTILLERY REGIMENT
Organized 21 June 1917
Toujours l'Audace

81st ARTILLERY REGIMENT
Organized 21 June 1917
Libertas Justitia Humanitas

82d ARTILLERY REGIMENT
Organized 5 June 1917
Can and Will

83d ARTILLERY REGIMENT
Organized 5 June 1917
Flagrante Bello

84th ARTILLERY REGIMENT
Organized 3 October 1918
Performance Above All

92d ARTILLERY REGIMENT
Organized 8 January 1942
Brave Cannons

94th ARTILLERY REGIMENT
Organized 6 January 1942
Flexible

319th ARTILLERY REGIMENT
Organized 2 September 1917
Loyauté
(Loyalty)

320th ARTILLERY REGIMENT
Organized 29 August 1917
Volens et Potens
(Willing and Able)

321st ARTILLERY REGIMENT
Organized 2 September 1917
Noli Me Tangere
(Don't Tread on Me)

333rd ARTILLERY REGIMENT
Organized September 1917
Three Rounds

377th ARTILLERY REGIMENT
Organized November 1921
Firmiter et Fideliter
(Steadfastly and Faithfully)

517th ARTILLERY REGIMENT
Organized August 1925
We Sweep the Sky

562d ARTILLERY REGIMENT
Organized December 1929
Tuebor
(I Will Defend)

INFANTRY REGIMENTS OF THE
COMBAT ARMS REGIMENTAL SYSTEM

1st SPECIAL FORCE
Reconstituted 15 April 1960
De Oppresso Liber

1st INFANTRY
Organized 4 March 1791
Semper Primus
(Always First)

2d INFANTRY
Organized May–July 1808
Noli Me Tangere
(Do Not Touch Me)

3d INFANTRY
Organized Aug.–Sept. 1784
Noli Me Tangere
(Do Not Touch Me)

4th INFANTRY
Organized March 1812
Noli Me Tangere
(Do Not Touch Me)

5th INFANTRY
Organized May–June 1808
"I'll Try, Sir"

6th INFANTRY
Organized March–May 1812
Unity Is Strength

7th INFANTRY
Organized 1812
Volens et Potens
(Willing and Able)

8th INFANTRY
Organized 18 July 1838
Patriae Fidelitas
(Loyalty to Country)

9th INFANTRY
Organized 26 March 1855
Keep Up the Fire

10th INFANTRY
Organized March 1855
Courage and Fidelity

11th INFANTRY
Organized May 1862
Semper Fidelis
(Always Faithful)

12th INFANTRY
Organized 20 October 1861
Ducti Amore Patriae
(Having Been Led by Love
of Country)

13th INFANTRY
Organized 27 July–13 Nov. 1861
First at Vicksburg

14th INFANTRY
Organized 8 July 1861
The Right of the Line

15th INFANTRY
Organized Sept.–Oct. 1861
"Can Do"

16th INFANTRY
Organized August 1861
Semper Paratus
(Always Prepared)

17th INFANTRY
Organized 6 July 1861
Truth and Courage

18th INFANTRY
Organized Aug.–Nov. 1861
In Omnia Paratus
(In All Things Prepared)

19th INFANTRY
Organized 9 July 1861
The Rock of Chickamauga

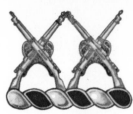

20th INFANTRY
Organized 6 June 1862
Tant que Je Puis
(To the Limit of Our Ability)

21st INFANTRY
Organized May 1862
Duty

22d INFANTRY
Organized 24 May–10 Dec. 1865
Deeds, Not Words

23rd INFANTRY
Organized July 1861
We Serve

26th INFANTRY
Organized 22 February 1901
Palmam Qui Meruit Ferat
(Let Him Bear the Palm Who
Has Won It)

27th INFANTRY
Organized 19 February 1901
Nec Aspera Terrent
(Frightened by No Difficulties)

28th INFANTRY
Organized March 1901
Vincit Amor Patriae
(Love of Country Conquers)

29th INFANTRY
Organized
5 March–3 June 1901
We Lead the Way

30th INFANTRY
Organized
12 Feb.–19 Aug. 1901
Our Country, Not Ourselves

31st INFANTRY
Organized 13 August 1916
Pro Patria
(For Country)

32d INFANTRY
Organized 7 August 1916
No Motto

34th INFANTRY
Organized 15 July 1916
Toujours en Avant
(Always Forward)

35th INFANTRY
Organized 8 July 1916
Take Arms

36th INFANTRY
Organized 27 July 1916
Deeds, Not Words

38th INFANTRY

Activated 1 June 1917

The Rock of the Marne

39th INFANTRY

Organized 1 June 1917

D'une Vaillance Admirable

(With a Military Courage
Worthy of Admiration)

41st INFANTRY

Constituted 5 July 1813

Straight and Stalwart

46th INFANTRY

Organized 4 June 1917

No Motto

47th INFANTRY

Organized 1 June 1917

Ex Virtute Honos

(Honor Comes from Virtue)

48th INFANTRY

Organized 1 June 1917

Dragoons

50th INFANTRY

Organized 1 June 1917

Play the Game

51st INFANTRY

Organized 22 May 1917

I Serve

52d INFANTRY

Organized 15 May 1917

Fortis et Certus

(Brave and True)

54th INFANTRY

Organized 16 June 1917

"I Will Cast My Shoe Over It"

58th INFANTRY

Organized 10 June 1917

60th INFANTRY

Organized 10 June 1917

To the Utmost Extent
of Our Power

61st INFANTRY

Organized June 1917

No Motto

75th Infantry

87th INFANTRY

Organized October 1918

Vires Montesque Vincimus

(We Conquer Mountains
and Men)

589

**187th AIRBORNE
INFANTRY**
Activated 25 February 1943
Ne Desit Virtus
(Let Valor Not Fail)

**188th AIRBORNE
INFANTRY**
Activated 25 February 1943
Winged Attack

**325th AIRBORNE
INFANTRY**
Organized 1 September 1917
Let's Go

327th INFANTRY
Organized 17 September 1917
Honor and Country

**501st AIRBORNE
INFANTRY**
Activated 15 November 1942
Geronimo

**502d AIRBORNE
INFANTRY**
Activated 2 March 1942
Strike!

**503d AIRBORNE
INFANTRY**
Activated 22 August 1941
The Rock

**504th AIRBORNE
INFANTRY**
Activated 1 May 1942
Strike—Hold

**505th AIRBORNE
INFANTRY**
Activated 6 July 1942
H-Minus

**506th AIRBORNE
INFANTRY**
Activated 20 July 1942
Currahee
(Stand Alone)

**508th AIRBORNE
INFANTRY**
Activated 20 October 1942
Fury from the Sky

509th INFANTRY
Activated 5 October 1941
All the Way

**511th AIRBORNE
INFANTRY**
Activated 5 January 1943
Strength from Above

DECORATIONS

**DISTINGUISHED
SERVICE CROSS**

MEDAL OF HONOR

For conspicuous gallantry and intrepidity at the risk of life, above and
beyond the call of duty, in action involving actual conflict with an enemy.

**DISTINGUISHED
SERVICE MEDAL**

PURPLE HEART

GOOD CONDUCT MEDAL

SILVER STAR MEDAL

LEGION OF MERIT

**DISTINGUISHED
FLYING CROSS**

SOLDIER'S MEDAL

BRONZE STAR MEDAL

AIR MEDAL

**COMMENDATION RIBBON
WITH METAL PENDANT**

591

CIVILIAN MEDALS

MEDAL FOR MERIT

MEDAL OF FREEDOM
Reestablished 22 Feb. 1963
with new design as
Presidential Medal of Freedom

**NATIONAL SECURITY
MEDAL**

**DISTINGUISHED CIVILIAN
SERVICE MEDAL**

**MERITORIOUS CIVILIAN
SERVICE AWARD**

**OUTSTANDING CIVILIAN
SERVICE MEDAL**

**EXCEPTIONAL CIVILIAN
SERVICE AWARD**

CAMPAIGN MEDALS

**CIVIL WAR
CAMPAIGN MEDAL**

**INDIAN
CAMPAIGN MEDAL**

**SPANISH
CAMPAIGN MEDAL**

**SPANISH WAR
SERVICE MEDAL**

**ARMY OF CUBAN
OCCUPATION MEDAL**

**ARMY OF PUERTO RICAN
OCCUPATION MEDAL**

**PHILIPPINE CAMPAIGN
MEDAL**

PHILIPPINE CONGRESSIONAL
MEDAL

CHINA CAMPAIGN
MEDAL

ARMY OF CUBAN
PACIFICATION MEDAL

MEXICAN SERVICE
MEDAL

MEXICAN BORDER
SERVICE MEDAL

WORLD WAR I
VICTORY MEDAL

ARMY OF OCCUPATION
OF GERMANY MEDAL

AMERICAN DEFENSE
SERVICE MEDAL

WOMEN'S ARMY CORPS
SERVICE MEDAL

AMERICAN CAMPAIGN
MEDAL

ASIATIC-PACIFIC
CAMPAIGN MEDAL

UROPEAN-AFRICAN MIDDLE
ASTERN CAMPAIGN MEDAL

WORLD WAR II
VICTORY MEDAL

ARMY OF OCCUPATION
MEDAL

MEDAL FOR
HUMANE ACTION

**NATIONAL DEFENSE
SERVICE MEDAL**

**KOREAN SERVICE
MEDAL**

**ARMED FORCES
EXPEDITIONARY MEDAL**

**ARMED FORCES
RESERVE MEDAL**

**UNITED NATIONS
SERVICE MEDAL**

**PHILIPPINE
DEFENSE RIBBON**

**PHILIPPINE
LIBERATION RIBBON**

**PHILIPPINE
INDEPENDENCE RIBBON**

**REPUBLIC OF VIETNAM
CAMPAIGN RIBBON**

SERVICE MEDALS FOR VIET NAM ACTION

**VIET NAM
SERVICE MEDAL**

**ARMED FORCES
EXPEDITIONARY MEDAL**

The Viet Nam Service Medal has been established by Presidential Executive Order 11231 to be awarded to members of the U.S. Armed Forces who serve in Viet Nam or contiguous waters or air space after 3 July 1965.

Armed Forces personnel who qualified for the Armed Forces Expeditionary Medal for service in Viet Nam between 1 July 1958 and 4 July 1965 shall remain qualified for that medal. They may choose which to apply for, but they may not be awarded both medals for service in Viet Nam.

NEW MEDALS SINCE 1967:

Vietnam Service Medal, Exec Order 8 July 1965
(for service in Vietnam after 3 July 65 to Mar 73)

Army Reserve Components Achievement Medal, GO 30,
29 June 1971

Meritorious Service Medal, Exec Order, 16 Jan 69,
(a non-combat award above the ARCOM and below LOM)

CHAPTER 15

WORLD WAR II-THE PACIFIC

Japan entered World War II with limited aims and with the intention of fighting a limited war. Its principal objectives were to secure the resources of Southeast Asia and much of China, and to establish a "Greater East Asia Co-Prosperity Sphere" under Japanese hegemony. In 1895 and 1905 Japan had gained important objectives without completely defeating either China or Russia; similarly in 1941 Japan did not seriously consider conducting an all-out war against the Allies.

JAPAN'S OBJECTIVES AND INITIAL GAINS

The operational strategy the Japanese adopted to start war in 1941 doomed their hopes to limit the conflict. Japan believed it necessary to destroy or neutralize American striking power in the Pacific—the U.S. Pacific Fleet at Pearl Harbor and the Far East Air Force in the Philippines—before moving southward and eastward to occupy Malaya, the Netherlands East Indies, the Philippines, Wake Island, Guam, the Gilbert Islands, Thailand, and Burma. Once in control of these areas, the Japanese intended to establish a defensive perimeter stretching from the Kurile Islands south through Wake, the Marianas, the Carolines, and the Marshalls and Gilberts to Rabaul on New Britain. From Rabaul the perimeter would extend westward to norwestern New Guinea and would encompass the Indies, Malaya, Thailand, and Burma. Japan thought that the Allies would wear themselves out in fruitless frontal assaults against the perimeter, and would ultimately settle for a negotiated peace that would leave Japan in possession of most of its conquests.

The Japanese were remarkably successful in the execution of their offensive plan, and by early 1942 had reached their intended perimeter. They had used relatively small forces and had dispersed them over a vast area. But the Japanese had miscalculated the effect of their surprise at-tacks at Pearl Harbor and in the Philippines, which brought into the war an aroused United States, and lost for Japan all chances of conducting the war on Japanese terms. Though defeated everywhere, the Allies did not seek a negotiated peace, but continued to resist and started striking back. In February and March 1942 small carrier task forces of the Pacific Fleet hit the Marshalls, Wake, and Marcus; bombers from Australia began to harass the Japanese base at Rabaul; Army bombers, flying off a Pacific Fleet carrier, delivered a hit-and-run raid against Tokyo during April. Meanwhile, the United States began to develop and fortify a line of communications across the southern Pacific to Australia, where the Allies began building bases from which to launch major counteroffensives. Buildup was also under way in Hawaii and Alaska. Once the Allies became strong enough to threaten the Japanese defensive perimeter from several directions, the Japanese would lose the advantage of interior lines, for Japan did not have and could not produce the means to defend and hold at all points.

Perceiving the danger, the Japanese decided to sever the Allied line of communications to Australia and simultaneously expand the existing perimeter. In the spring of 1942 they pushed southeast from Rabaul to Guadalcanal and seized Attu and Kiska in the Aleutians. Discarding as beyond their capabilities plans to invade Australia, the Japanese attempted to reach out in the center to Midway Island, northwest of Hawaii. Defeats the Japanese suffered during this second-phase expansion outweighed the strategic importance of their gains. In the naval battles of the Coral Sea in May and Midway in June, the Japanese lost the bulk of their best naval pilots and planes, as well as some carriers. These losses helped redress the naval balance of power in the Pacific and seriously curtailed the mobility of Japan's carrier striking forces.

LIST OF ABBREVIATIONS

BAR	Browning automatic rifle	LCVP	landing craft, vehicle and personnel
GHQ	general headquarters	LST	landing ship, tank
HB	heavy barrel	LVT	landing vehicle, tracked
LCI	landing craft, infantry	LVT (1)	landing vehicle, tracked, unarmored (Mark I) ("Alligator")
LCI (L)	landing craft, infantry (large)	LVT (4)	landing vehicle, tracked, unarmored (Mark IV
LCM	landing craft, mechanized	LVT (A) (1)	landing vehicle, tracked (armored) (Mark I)
LCM (3)	landing craft, mechanized (Mark III)		("Water Buffalo," turret type)
LCP (L)	landing craft, personnel (large)	LVT (A) (2)	landing vehicle, tracked (armored) (Mark II)
LCP (R)	landing craft, personnel (ramp)		("Water Buffalo," canopy type)
LCR	landing craft, rubber	LVT (A) (4)	landing vehicle, tracked (armored) (Mark IV)
LCT (6)	landing craft, tank (Mark VI)	PT	patrol vessel, motor torpedo boat
LCV	landing craft, vehicle	SCR	Signal Corps radio

Infantrymen during a field inspection in the Hawaiian Islands, January 1941. From 1935 on, the U.S. garrison in the Hawaiian Islands was larger than any other American overseas outpost. However, by 1940 there was a shortage of modern equipment and trained personnel, and not until February 1941 did troop reinforcements and up-to-date equipment begin to arrive in Hawaii.

Coast artillery battery training in Hawaii. Man at left is placing a round in the manual fuse setter of a 3-inch antiaircraft gun. A plan for the defense of the Hawaiian Islands had been set up and joint maneuvers (land, air, and naval forces) were held periodically to test the various security measures.

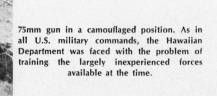

75mm gun in a camouflaged position. As in all U.S. military commands, the Hawaiian Department was faced with the problem of training the largely inexperienced forces available at the time.

596

Wreckage at the Naval Air Station at Pearl Harbor, after the enemy attack, 7 December. At 0730 on 7 December the first waves of Japanese aircraft struck the U.S. defenses. Although a few U.S. fighter planes managed to get into the air and destroyed some of the Japanese planes, the attack wrought severe damage. After neutralizing the airfields the Japanese struck at the U.S. Navy warships in the harbor.

The destroyer USS "Shaw" exploding during the attack on Pearl Harbor, 7 December. The first attack on the U.S. warships anchored in the harbor was delivered at 0758. By 0945 all the Japanese aircraft had left Oahu and returned to their carriers.

Wrecked planes at Wheeler Field after the 7 December attack. Of the Army's 123 first-line planes in Hawaii, 63 survived the attack; of the Navy's 148 serviceable combat aircraft, 36 remained. Only one small airfield on the north shore near Haleiwa was overlooked during the raid.

Destroyed hangar at Hickam Field, 7 December. During the attack the Army lost 226 killed and 396 wounded; the Navy, including the Marine Corps, lost 3,077 killed and 876 wounded. The Japanese attack was entirely successful in accomplishing its mission, and the U.S. forces were completely surprised both strategically and tactically.

Even more serious than the destruction of aircraft was the reduction of United States naval strength at Pearl Harbor. Three battleships were sunk; one capsized; one was badly damaged; and three others were damaged enough to require repairs. Three cruisers, three destroyers, and a seaplane tender also were hit. However, the Japanese victory was not total. Three U.S. aircraft carriers with their planes were safely at sea at the time of the attack.

A close-up of the battleships "West Virginia" and "Tennessee" side by side, burning and sinking.

Construction work at Wheeler Field, 11 December 1941. After the Japanese raid, many destroyed or damaged buildings were rebuilt.

Soldiers leaving pier to board trucks for Schofield Barracks, Honolulu. As a result of the disaster at Pearl Harbor, the Hawaiian command was reorganized. There was little enemy activity in the Central Pacific after the 7 December attack. The Japanese had seized Wake and Guam and were concentrating on their southern campaigns. As the buildup of men and equipment progressed, reinforcements began to pour into Hawaii for training and shipment to Pacific stations.

Deploying for advance inland after landing on the beach. During the war more than 250,000 men were given instruction in amphibious assault operations on Hawaiian beaches.

A battery of 105mm howitzers firing during maneuvers.

Cavite Navy Yard, Luzon, during a Japanese aerial attack. Early on the morning of 8 December 1941 the Japanese struck the Philippine Islands. By the end of the first day the U.S. Army Forces had lost half of its bombers and a third of its fighter planes based there. On 14 December the remaining 14 U.S. Army bombers were flown to Port Darwin, Australia, and the ships that were undamaged after the attack were moved south. After the destruction of the Navy yards at Cavite, the remaining 11 naval patrol bombers were flown to the Netherlands East Indies. The ground forces were left with little or no support.

Camouflaged 155mm gun parked on the Gerona–Tarlac road, December 1941. The Japanese forces moved down Luzon, forcing the defending U.S. troops to withdraw to the south. On 30 December a large-scale attack was launched and the U.S. troops were driven back 10 miles to Gapan. After another enemy attack they fell back 20 miles farther. A secondary enemy attack at Tarlac failed to achieve important gains. The northern U.S. force protected the withdrawal of the southern force by a delaying action. All troops were beginning to converge in the vicinity of Manila and the Bataan Peninsula.

Japanese prisoners, captured on Bataan, being led to headquarters for questioning. On 1 January 1942 the Japanese entered Manila, and the U.S. troops withdrew toward Bataan. Army supplies were either moved to Bataan and Corregidor or destroyed. The remaining forces on Bataan, including some 15,000 U.S. troops, totaled about 80,000 men. The food, housing, and sanitation problems were greatly increased by the presence of over 20,000 civilian refugees. All troops were placed on half-rations.

Japanese advancing during the drive on Manila. The medium tank is a Type 93 (1934), with a 57mm gun with a free traverse of 20 degrees right and left. It had a speed of 18 to 20 miles an hour, was manned by a crew of four, weighed 15 tons, and was powered by a Diesel engine.

Japanese soldiers firing a machine gun. This was the standard Japanese heavy machine gun.

Japanese firing a 75mm gun, normally found in an infantry regimental cannon company. Called a mountain (infantry) gun, it was replaced by a later model. Light and easily handled, it was very steady in action. When used as a regimental cannon company weapon it was issued on the basis of four per regiment.

Gun crew with a 3-inch antiaircraft gun. The U.S. troops moving southward down Bataan in front of the enemy forces continued their delaying action as long as possible. The Bataan Peninsula, 32 miles long and 20 miles across at the widest portion, is covered with dense woods and thick jungle growth. Through the center runs a range of mountains. The limited area and difficult terrain made the fighting more severe and added to the problems of the advancing Japanese. However, the situation became steadily worse for the defending troops, and on 9 April 1942 the forces were surrendered to the Japanese.

Japanese troops on Bataan during the spring of 1942. The Japanese commander insisted upon unconditional surrender of all the troops in the Philippines and was furious when he learned that only the U.S. forces on Bataan Peninsula had surrendered. The forces on Corregidor held their fire until the captured Bataan troops were removed from the area. (This picture was reproduced from an illustration which appeared in a captured Japanese publication.)

603

Aerial view of Corregidor Island off the tip of Bataan. On 25 December, Headquarters, United States Army Forces in the Far East, was established on Corregidor. Manila was declared an open city on the following day, and the remains of the naval base at Cavite were blown up to prevent its supplies from falling into enemy hands.

Twelve-inch-bore mortars located at Bay Battery on Corregidor Island. Corregidor's armament comprised eight 12-inch guns, twelve 12-inch mortars, two 10-inch guns, five 6-inch guns, twenty 155mm guns, and assorted guns of lesser caliber, including antiaircraft guns. The fixed gun emplacements were in open concrete pits and exposed to aerial attack and artillery shelling. The Japanese kept up strong concentrations of fire against the defenses on Corregidor until most of the defending guns were knocked out.

Coastal defense gun on Corregidor.

U.S. prisoners on Bataan sorting equipment while Japanese guards look on. Following this, the Americans and Filipinos started on the Death March to Camp O'Donnell in central Luzon. Over 50,000 prisoners were held at this camp. A few U.S. troops escaped capture and carried on as guerrillas.

Captured American and Filipino troops after the surrender on Corregidor. The 11,500 surviving troops on Corregidor became prisoners of war, and on 28 May 1942 were evacuated to a prison stockade in Manila. The fall of Corregidor on 6 May marked the end of the first phase of enemy operations. The Japanese had bases controlling routes to India, Australia, and many islands in the Central and South Pacific, and were preparing for their next assaults against the Allies. (This picture is reproduced from an illustration which appeared in a captured Japanese publication.)

Soldiers in Malinta tunnel on Corregidor, April 1942. With food, water, and supplies practically exhausted and no adequate facilities for caring for the wounded, and with Japanese forces landing on Corregidor, the situation for the U.S. troops was all but hopeless. The commander offered to surrender the island forts on Corregidor to the Japanese. When this was refused and with the remaining troops in danger of being wiped out, all the U.S. forces in the Philippines were surrendered to the enemy on 6 May 1942. Couriers were sent to the various island commanders, and by 17 May all organized resistance in the Philippines had ceased.

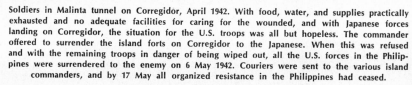

B-25's on the flight deck of the aircraft carrier USS "Hornet" before taking off to bomb Tokyo on 18 April 1942.

B-25 taking off from the flight deck of the "Hornet." In a small combined operation in the western Pacific by the U.S. Navy and the Army Air Forces, 16 planes, took off from the carrier "Hornet," 668 nautical miles from Tokyo, to bomb the city for the first time during the war. The Japanese were completely surprised because, even though they had received a radio warning, they were expecting Navy planes which would have to be launched from a carrier closer to Tokyo, and therefore would not reach the city on 18 April.

Lieutenant Colonel James Doolittle (fifth from left) poses with his crew after they bailed out in China returning from the Tokyo raid. Lieutenant Colonel Doolittle led the bombing raid on the Japanese capital. After dropping their bombs they flew on to China where they ran out of fuel before reaching their designated landing fields. The crews of only two of the planes fell into Japanese hands. The others lived in the Chinese mountains for about ten days after assembling, and were later returned to the United States. The news of the raid raised morale in the United States, and while the damage inflicted was not great, it proved to the Japanese that they needed additional bases to the east to protect the home islands of Japan.

U.S. troops arriving in Australia. In March the headquarters of the Allied forces in the Southwest Pacific was established at Melbourne. The Netherlands East Indies had fallen to the enemy, and it was necessary to build up a force in the Southwest Pacific area to combat the Japanese threat to Australia.

Coast artillery troops entraining at Melbourne, March 1942. The Japanese air attack on Darwin in February proved that the north coast of Australia was too open to attack by enemy planes, and thereafter the Allies concentrated their forces along the eastern coast from Melbourne to Townsville.

After firing, artillerymen open the breech of their 155mm howitzer.

Soldiers practice loading into small boats during training in Australia. Cargo nets on a transport could be used with a greater degree of efficiency than ladders as they could accommodate far more troops at one time.

An Australian sniper in a camouflaged position during training. Every effort was made to teach all troops all methods of jungle warfare so that they could better combat the enemy who was well trained in jungle fighting and living.

Completely equipped troops going up a gangplank at Melbourne on the way to their new station in the forward area. After receiving additional training in Australia, troops were sent out to carry the offensive to Japanese-held bases.

Troops en route to New Caledonia. Some troops arrived in New Caledonia directly from the United States while others went by way of Australia.

Army troops arriving at Nouméa, New Caledonia, in March 1942 aboard a transport.

Infantrymen and jeeps (¼-ton 4 X 4 truck) crossing a stream during training on New Caledonia, summer 1942.

Typical terrain of New Caledonia; the rugged terrain and dense woods and growth made maneuvering in the Pacific islands extremely difficult.

Interior of a native-type hunt occupied by U.S. troops stationed on New Caledonia. Huts of this type were used as troop quarters and as office buildings since the material for construction was easily accessible and the huts were also an effective camouflage measure against enemy aerial observation.

Amphibian truck, 2½-ton 6 X 6, nicknamed "the Duck," standardized in October 1942, proved to be an extremely valuable piece of equipment. It could operate on land or water, and was often used to bring supplies ashore where there were no ports or harbors available for larger craft. Supplies loaded from ships onto the Ducks could unload at the supply dumps, saving the extra handling involved when lighters or similar craft were used. This vehicle could carry approximately 25 men and their equipment or a 5,000-pound payload.

THE ALLIES START A COMEBACK

The Battle of Midway can be considered the turning point of the Pacific War. After that defeat the Japanese decided that they lacked the naval resources to push on and realized they were dangerously overextending themselves. They abandoned plans to cut the Allies' South Pacific line of communications and turned their energies to strengthening their perimeter. They had lost the strategic initiative, but they still intended to wage a protracted war of attrition in the hope of yet obtaining a negotiated peace.

Until mid-1942 the Allies were able to take only stop-gap measures to halt the Japanese, while the losses during the opening months of the war made it impossible for the United States to execute prewar plans for action in the Pacific. Moreover, the Allied decision to defeat Germany first prevented deployment of all available resources to the Pacific. The long lines of communication from the United States to Pacific bases, a general shortage of shipping, and the necessity for extensive base development throughout the Pacific further delayed offensive preparations. Nevertheless, by early summer of 1942, the Allies were able to launch a limited offensive. The U.S. Joint Chiefs-of-Staff, responsible for the direction of the war in the Pacific, decided that this offensive should be designed to protect the lines of communication to Australia, prevent the Japanese from consolidating their gains, and secure forward bases from which the Allies could mount future drives.

On 2 July, accordingly, the Joint Chiefs directed Allied forces in the South and Southwest Pacific Areas to begin a series of operations aimed at the ultimate recapture of Rabaul. Since the immediate seizure of Rabaul was beyond the capabilities of available forces, the Joint Chiefs decreed that the campaign would have three stages. First, forces of the South Pacific Area (under Vice Admiral Robert L. Ghormley until November 1942 and thereafter under Admiral William F. Halsey, Jr.) would seize base sites in the southern Solomons. Second, Allied forces of the South and Southwest Pacific Areas (the latter commanded by General Douglas MacArthur) would reoccupy the rest of the Solomons and move up the north coast of New Guinea as far as Lae and Salamaua. Third, the two theatres would cooperate to seize Rabaul and clear the rest of the Bismarck Archipelago. The first-stage offensives in the South Pacific were to be conducted under the general supervision of Admiral Chester W. Nimitz, whose vast Pacific Ocean Areas command included the North, Central, and South Pacific Areas as subtheatres. Second- and third-stage operations, including those in the South Pacific Area, would be executed under the strategic direction of General MacArthur. The Joint Chiefs-of-Staff, reserving to themselves final control of the assignment of tasks, allocation of resources, and timing of operations, would provide, in effect, unified command over Nimitz and MacArthur.

Guadalcanal: 17 August 1942

The offensive began on 7 August 1942 when a Marine division landed on Guadalcanal and nearby islands. The Japanese reacted vigorously, and six times from August to the end of November challenged American naval superiority in the South Pacific in a series of sharp surface engagements. Air battles were almost daily occurrences for a month or more after the landings, and the Japanese sent in strong ground reinforcements, gambling and ultimately losing substantial air and naval resources to hold Guadalcanal, for the Allies proved willing to sacrifice the planes, ships, and men necessary to assure the success of the amphibious assault. Ashore the issue was in doubt for months, and before the island was finally won the South Pacific Area had thrown in two Marine divisions, two Army divisions, and an Army regiment, to mention only the major ground combat elements. The last act came in February 1943, when an Army division moved into the Russell Islands, 35 miles northwest of Guadalcanal. In the Russells and on Guadalcanal, American forces constructed major air and logistical bases in preparation for subsequent advances.

MacArthur Papuan Campaign

Meanwhile, a Japanese overland drive toward Port Moresby in New Guinea had forced General MacArthur to begin an offensive of his own—the Papuan campaign. During the late summer the Japanese had pushed across the towering Owen Stanley Mountains toward Port Moresby from the Buna-Gona area on New Guinea's northeastern coast, and by mid-September were only 20 miles from their objective. Australian ground forces drove the Japanese back to the north coast, where the Japanese strongly entrenched themselves around Buna and Gona. It took two Australian divisions, one U.S. Army division, and another U.S. Army regiment almost four months of bitter fighting to dislodge the Japanese. Casualties were high, but as at Guadalcanal the Allied forces learned much about jungle fighting, the importance of airpower, and the need for thorough logistical preparation. They also learned that the Japanese soldier, though a skillful, stubborn, and fanatic foe, could be defeated. The myth of Japanese invincibility was forever laid to rest in the jungles of Guadalcanal and Papua.

After Papua and Guadalcanal the tempo of operations in the South and Southwest Pacific Areas slowed while General MacArthur and Admiral Halsey gathered resources and prepared bases for the next phase. The Japanese, in turn, undertook to reinforce their remaining bases in New Guinea and the Solomons. In March 1943 they attempted to send a large convoy to Lae in New Guinea, but in the Battle of the Bismarck Sea, lost some 3,500 troops and much valuable shipping, principally to Army land-based aircraft. During the following months Rabaul-based planes, reinforced by carrier planes flown in from the Carolines, sought unsuccessfully to knock out American air power in the Solomons.

ALLIED ADVANCE RESUMED JUNE 1943

The Allied advance resumed in late June when U.S. Army troops under MacArthur landed on Woodlark and Kiriwina Islands off eastern New Guinea and at Nassau Bay on the New Guinea coast northwest of Buna. About the same time U.S. Army units of the South Pacific Area went ashore on the New Georgia group in the central Solomons. Both sets of operations were designed to secure additional air bases. The Japanese did not leave the efforts unchallenged, and tried to reinforce New Georgia, losing combat ships they could not spare in an attempt to reduce American naval superiority in the Solomons. Army forces secured New Georgia and its Munda airfields by early August, but the campaign was not over until October, when United States and New Zealand Army troops had occupied Vella Lavella, between New Georgia and Bougainville.

At the end of October, New Zealanders and U.S. Marines landed on Treasury and Choiseul Islands to secure bases for a move to Bougainville. On 1 November Marines landed on Bougainville, a U.S. Army division soon following. Again the Japanese unsuccessfully challenged Allied air and naval powers in the Solomons, and launched strong ground counterattacks against the Bougainville beachhead. By late November 1943, the American beachhead was secure, and with the development of a major air base there, the South Pacific's share in second-phase advances toward Rabaul virtually ended. The advance had the support of land-based aircraft, and each forward move had been limited to the range of such planes. Japanese air and naval losses during the second phase crippled the Japanese fleet and immobilized it as a striking force for months to come.

Meanwhile, MacArthur's Southwest Pacific Area forces had continued their offensives, with Australian troops carrying most of the burden in New Guinea. In early September a U.S. Army parachute regiment, the first airborne operation of the Pacific War, seized an airfield at Nadzab, inland from Lae and Salamaua. Australian troops cleared Lae and Salamaua by mid-September and, flown into Nadzab, moved on to the Huon Peninsula. A U.S. Army division landed at the western end of the peninsula in January 1944 in an attempt to trap a large Japanese force, but by the time Australian and American units had sealed the western exits to the peninsula in February, most of the Japanese had escaped northwest to Hansa Bay and Wewak.

In the meantime, MacArthur and Halsey had assembled the forces to launch a final offensive toward Rabaul, but the Joint Chiefs had decided that the actual seizure of that objective would be too costly in terms of men, means, and time. They preferred to encircle Rabaul, neutralize it by air bombardment, and push on to seize an offensive base further west, in the Admiralty Islands. A new series of operations to these ends started on 15 December 1943 when U.S. Army units landed on the south coast of western New Britain, and on the 26th a Marine division under MacArthur's control landed on the north coast. In mid-February 1944 New Zealand troops of the South Pacific Area secured an air base site on Green Island, north of Rabaul, and on the last day of the month MacArthur began landing a U.S. Army division on the Admiralties, closing the western and northwestern approaches to Rabaul. Marines under Halsey seized a final air base site on Emirau, north of Rabaul, on 20 March, while Marine and Army units under MacArthur secured additional positions in western and central New Britain from March to May 1944. The major Japanese base at Rabaul, with its 100,000-man garrison, was as effectively out of the war as if destroyed. In the process of encircling Rabaul, the Allies had also left to wither on the vine another important Japanese base at Kavieng on New Ireland, north of Rabaul.

In the last phase of the campaign against Rabaul, a pattern developed that came to characterize much of the war in the Pacific. The Allies would mount no frontal attacks against strongly entrenched Japanese forces if they could avoid such action; they would not advance island-by-island across a vast ocean studded with myriad atolls and island groups. Rather, they would advance in great bounds, limited only by the range of land-based air cover or the availability of carrier-based air support. The Allies would deceive and surprise the Japanese; they would bypass major strongpoints and leave them reduced to strategic and tactical impotence.

While the Allied offensives against Rabaul were under way, the Allies had also pushed back the Japanese perimeter in the far reaches of the North Pacific. In May 1943 an Army division went ashore on Attu, and after three weeks of costly fighting through Arctic muck and over windswept ridges, in a cold, almost constant fog, destroyed the Japanese garrison. In August a combined United States-Canadian expedition landed on neighboring Kiska, only to find that the Japanese had evacuated three weeks earlier. With these advances the Japanese perimeter was back to the Kuriles, and the United States was ultimately able to effect a substantial reduction of its garrison in Alaska. The Allies had also opened another strategically important potential axis of advance toward Japan. However, commitments to other theatres, problems incident to operations in the northern regions, and a desire to avoid any chance of compromising Russia's existing neutrality vis-à-vis Japan, prevented exploitation of the approach. Further operations in the northern Pacific were limited to nuisance air raids against the Kuriles.

The campaigns against Rabaul and the Aleutians had been designed to halt the Japanese and secure bases from which to launch subsequent offensives. Allied strategy for these later offensives took into consideration the probability that an invasion of the Japanese home islands might prove necessary. To ensure the success of invasion, the Allies would first have to subject Japan to intensive aerial bombardment; sever Japan's line of communications to the Indies and Southeast Asia by air, surface, and submarine operations; and establish staging bases in the western Pacific to support the final assault. Planners decided that pre-invasion bombardment could best be undertaken from fields in eastern China. To develop air bases there, the Allies would have to secure a port on the south China coast, the overland routes from India being inadequate or too insecure for the purpose of moving men and materiel into China. To seize the needed port, and simultaneously cut Japan's lines of communication to the south, the Allies would have to gain control over the South China Sea. This in turn would require the establishment of major air, naval, and logistical bases in the strategic triangle formed by the south China coast, Formosa, and Luzon.

Strategic planners decided that the best way to reach the triangle would be across the Pacific rather than from the Aleutians, southeast Asia, or China. Long as they were, the lines of communication across the Pacific were shorter and safer than supply lines from starting points other than the west coast of the United States. Moreover, only in campaigns across the Pacific could the Allies employ to best advantage the growing strength of the U.S. Pacific Fleet.

Within this strategic framework, the intermediate objective in the western Pacific would be the central or southern Philippines. Here American forces would establish air bases from which to neutralize Japanese air power on Luzon before advancing into the strategic triangle. The Allies could follow two routes to the Philippines—one across the Central Pacific Area via the Gilberts, Marshalls, Marianas, Carolines, and Palaus; the other in the Southwest Pacific Area via the north coast of New Guinea and islands between northwestern New Guinea and Mindanao in the southern Philippines. The Central Pacific route promised to force a naval showdown with the Japanese and, once the Marianas were secured, to provide bases from which the Army Air Forces' new B-29 bomber could strike the Japanese home islands. The Southwest Pacific route was shorter, considering existing bases, and offered more opportunity to employ land-based air power to full advantage. Concurrent operations along both routes would serve to keep the Japanese off balance and offer the Allies many opportunities for surprise.

Here was the key to Pacific strategy after the campaign against Rabaul. The Allies would mount coordinated, mutually supporting drives toward the Philippines. Along both routes commanders would exploit every chance for surprise and acceleration, would bypass Japanese strongpoints whenever possible, and would concentrate air, naval, and ground strength at the decisive points and moments. American forces in the Pacific did not yet have the means to do everything at once, but with the nation's industry in full production the prospects for the successful execution of the strategy grew daily brighter.

THE CENTRAL PACIFIC OFFENSIVE BEGINS
NOVEMBER 1943

The Central Pacific offensive under the new plan started on 20 November 1943, when Admiral Nimitz sent Army and Marine divisions to the Gilbert Islands to seize airbases from which to support subsequent jumps into the Marshalls. Troops and supplies for the Gilberts loaded at Hawaii on newly developed assault shipping, and sailed over 2,000 miles to be set ashore by specially designed landing craft and amphibian vehicles. Makin, the Army objective, fell after four days of hard fighting. Tarawa, where the Marines went ashore, proved a bloody affair that provided a stiff test for American amphibious doctrine, techniques, and equipment. Naval gunfire vessels and carrier-based aircraft provided support during and after the assault.

The advance to the Gilberts disclosed that U.S. forces had not entirely mastered certain aspects of amphibious warfare, especially naval gunfire support, coordination of air support, and ship-to-shore communications. But valuable lessons were learned that, added to the earlier experiences of the South and Southwest Pacific Areas, established a pattern of island warfare which represented one of the major tactical developments of the war. First, air and naval forces isolated an objective and softened its defenses. Simultaneously, joint forces would attack or feint toward other islands to deceive the Japanese. The approach of convoys carrying the ground assault forces to the main objective signaled the opening of final, intensive air and naval bombardment of the landing beaches. Whenever practicable, small forces occupied neighboring islands as sites for the land-based artillery. Under cover of all these supporting fires, the landing forces moved from ship to shore in echelons, or waves, rocket-firing landing craft in the lead and amphibian tanks and tractors following to carry the assault troops directly onto the beaches and inland. Finally came landing craft with more infantry and with tanks, artillery, and supporting troops. Supplies followed rapidly as the assault forces secured and expanded the beachhead. Amphibious techniques were refined and modified to some extent after the Gilberts, but the lessons learned there made it unnecessary to effect any radical changes in amphibious doctrine throughout the rest of the war.

The Japanese did not react strongly to the loss of the Gilberts, and at the end of January Nimitz' Army and Marine forces moved into the eastern and central Marshalls to seize Majuro and Kwajalein. The strength employed in this operation proved so preponderant and Japanese defenses so weak that Nimitz was able to accelerate his next advance by two and a half months, and on 17 February 1944 landed Marine and Army units on Eniwetok Atoll in the western Marshalls. Concurrently, he conducted a long-awaited carrier strike against Truk in the central Carolines, considered Japan's key bastion in the Central Pacific. The raid revealed that the Japanese had virtually abandoned Truk as a naval base and the capture of the atoll, set for June, no longer appeared necessary. Nimitz now drew up plans to invade the Marianas in mid-June and move on to the western Carolines and Palaus in mid-September, again accelerating the pace of the advance.

Henderson Field, Guadalcanal, in the process of being built by the Japanese in the summer of 1942, was the immediate objective of the Marines who landed on the island on 7 August 1942. This broad, level, coastal plain on the north coast of Guadalcanal was the only territory in the southern Solomons offering terrain suitable for the construction of large airfields. The immediate objectives in the Guadalcanal Campaign were the Tulagi–Gavutu–Tanambogo area, the largest and best developed anchorage in the southern Solomons, and the nearly completed airfield on Guadalcanal. The Guadalcanal Campaign was the first amphibious offensive operation launched by the United States in World War II. On 7 August 1942, concurrent with landings on Guadalcanal, Marines landed on Tulagi, Gavutu, and Florida Islands.

Mortar crew in action on Guadalcanal. On the evening of 8 August, the airfield on Guadalcanal was in U.S. hands. During the following weeks, enemy attempts to retake the airfield were repulsed.

Near the front lines, December 1942. Natives of Guadalcanal, employed by the Army, carry supplies to the fighting lines.

Army troops landing on Guadalcanal to reinforce the Marines. Four 37mm antitank guns on the beach. On 13 October sorely needed reinforcements for the malaria-ridden Marines started to arrive, and by the end of the year U.S. forces were strong enough to begin the final offensive on the island.

Troops landing on Florida Island. Occupation of the island group, Tulagi and its satellites, was accomplished in three days. The enemy garrisons were wiped out except for about 70 survivors who made their way to Florida Island. Mopping-up operations on Florida continued for a few weeks.

37mm antitank gun in an emplacement guarding a bridge over the Matanikau River. The Japanese situation on the island had deteriorated rapidly by this time, partly because of the costly defeats suffered while attempting to bring in supplies and replacements.

Japanese transports afire off the coast of Guadalcanal, 15 November 1942. A group of 11 transports proceeding to Guadalcanal were intercepted by aircraft from Henderson Field. Seven ships were sunk or gutted by fire. Four were damaged and were later destroyed near Tassafaronga Point where they had been beached.

615

Muddy trail. Trails such as this made the use of chains on wheeled vehicles imperative.

Engineers, constructing a heavy-traffic bridge across the Matani-kau River, lay planking over framework of palm tree logs. Advance on Guadalcanal was difficult and slow. Troops cleared the areas from which the final drive was to begin, and pressure slowly increased against the enemy until the offensive was in full swing.

Evacuating casualties from the front lines. Casualties being unloaded near new bridge construction. The first part of their trip was in flat-bottom boats pulled through shallow rapids; the latter part was made in outboard motor boats. The procedure for moving supplies forward for the most part was reversed for the evacuation of the wounded.

Fire resulting from enemy bombs which fell into a bivouac area near a U.S. division headquarters on 22 January 1943. In mid-January ground force units attacked Mount Austen, the southern anchor of the enemy's position. While some Army units pushed through the jungle in an enveloping maneuver designed to cut off the enemy at Kokumbona, other Marine and Army units advanced along the coastal road.

Supply dump which was set up on Kokumbona beach after pushing the enemy back; note shell and bomb craters which were used as foxholes by the troops (bottom). The enveloping movement trapped several enemy units at Kokumbona which were then quickly destroyed. By the end of the month U.S. troops had reached the Bonegi River.

Japanese prisoners raising vegetables for their own table. The Guadalcanal Campaign drew to a close shortly after two U.S. forces converged on Cape Esperance where the Japanese were effecting their evacuation on 8 February 1943. The enemy had committed at least 36,700 men on Guadalcanal. Of these, some 14,800 were killed or drowned while attempting to land; 9,000 died of sickness, starvation, or wounds; 1,000 were captured; and about 13,000 were evacuated.

Convoy of ships moving toward Rendova Island from Koli Point, Guadalcanal, 29 June 1943. Only a few miles south of Munda Point in New Georgia, Rendova was first to be occupied in strength to provide positions for 155-mm. guns and a staging area from which the main thrust against Munda would be made. This operation was covered by fighter planes which shot down more than a hundred Japanese aircraft in a few days.

Munda Airfield on Munda Point, 8 September 1943. On 25 August, twenty days after the airfield was captured, all organized resistance on New Georgia ceased. During this operation Allied planes destroyed an estimated 350 enemy aircraft at a cost of 93 Allied planes.

Infantry reinforcements disembarking from LCI(L) on New Georgia, 22 July 1943. On 2 July 1943 troops had landed on New Georgia east of Munda Point. It was anticipated that these forces would be sufficient to seize the airfield and other objectives within thirty days, but because of the strong Japanese defenses encountered, reinforcements were ordered to New Georgia in mid-July to supplement the initial landing.

90-mm antiaircraft gun in action against enemy aircraft over Rendova. As soon as the Munda airfield and other strategically important points on New Georgia were taken, preparations were to be made for the capture of Kolombangara.

155mm howitzer in firing position on Arundel. Without success the Japanese continually attempted to reinforce their remaining garrisons in the New Georgia group of islands.

Men carrying mortar shells into the dense jungle while others rush back to the beach for another load. Arundel was one of the lesser islands in the New Georgia group, located between Rendova and Kolombangara.

B-25 medium bombers on raid over Bougainville. During the latter half of September 1943, before the New Georgia operation had ended, the Air Force turned its attention to the Bougainville area.

Marines in camouflage suits hit the narrow beach at Empress Augusta Bay, Bougainville, D-Day, 1 November 1943. Prior to the landing on Bougainville, the Treasury Islands were seized and developed as a staging area for landing craft, and diversionary landings were made on Choiseul in preparation for a surprise attack at Bougainville.

Coast Guardmen trying to free an LCVP after discharging its load of men and supplies during the initial attacks to secure a beachhead on Bougainville. Enemy action and heavy surf took their toll of many boats at the water edge. Enemy machine gun positions that caused some disorganization among landing boats were taken before the end of the day.

Infantrymen climbing down a cargo net of the transport "President Jackson," 5 November 1943, for the trip to Bougainville to reinforce the Marines. Note collapsible rubber raft (LCR) on side of transport. Before the assault on Bougainville, combat troops underwent rigorous training based upon lessons learned in the Guadalcanal Campaign.

C-47 dropping supplies and equipment on an uncompleted airstrip, 30 November 1943. By the end of the year three airfields had been put into operation. The mission of the forces on the island at this time was to maintain a defensive perimeter, approximately ten miles long and five miles deep, guarding installations in the Empress Augusta Bay area.

Infantrymen on guard near the Laruma River, 16 November, man a .30-caliber heavy-barrel automatic, recoil-operated, belt-fed, air-cooled machine gun.

Additional troops arriving on Bougainville, 25 December 1943. Trucks in foreground are 4-ton 6x6's. Troops continued to land at the base established on Cape Torokina for two months after the invasion.

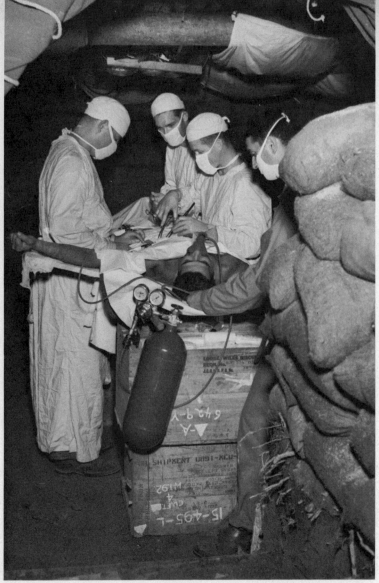

Emergency operation being performed in a dugout. This underground surgery room was dug about four feet below the surface, and the sides were built up with sand bags and roofed with heavy logs. The entire structure was covered with a pyramidal tent, shielding the occupants from the sun.

Infantrymen, walking through a lane between barbed wire, carry 60mm mortar shells to the front lines.

Infantrymen with bayonets fixed advance through jungle swamp, following an M4 medium tank, to rout out the enemy, 16 March. The conquest of the island necessitated much advance patrol work and many mopping-up operations deep in the tropical jungle. Casualties were heavier than in any operation since the Guadalcanal Campaign in the Solomon chain.

Infantrymen firing mortar, located on one side of bitterly contested hill, at Japanese positions on the other side of the hill, 8 March 1944. The Japanese forces had been ordered to drive the Allied forces from Bougainville because of the precarious situation at Rabaul. At the end of 1943, further offensive action on Bougainville had not been planned because of expected new strategic plans of operations against the enemy; however, renewed enemy activity evidenced in February 1944 necessitated further action.

The southeast slope of "Bloody Hill" after the last enemy had been routed. The enemy fought with his customary tenacity, and his resistance in defended positions won the grudging admiration of the U.S. troops. By 24 April 1944, ground forces had crushed the last important Japanese counteroffensive against the Bougainville perimeter.

Men wading across the Samboga, near Dobodura, New Guinea. The enemy fell back under the weight of the 28 September 1942 attack. Australians laboriously made their way over steep mountain trails of the Owen Stanley Range while most of the American troops, a total of about 4,900, were flown overland to Jaure in C-47's. This was the first large-scale airborne troop movement of the war.

Troops boarding a C-47 transport plane for New Guinea. During the last days of September 1942 the Allies launched a counterattack in Papua, New Guinea, thus starting the Papua Campaign. American troops for this action were sent to Port Moresby from Australia, partly by plane and partly by boat.

Aerial view of the terrain near Dobodura. The rugged terrain of Papua includes the high Owen Stanley Range, jungles, and impassable, malaria-infected swampy areas as well as coconut plantations and open fields of coarse, shoulder-high kunai grass encountered near Buna. Only one rough and steep trail existed over the range from the Port Moresby area to the front, taking from 18 to 28 days to traverse on foot; however, American troops and supplies flown over the range made the trip in about 45 minutes.

Constructing a corduroy road with the help of the natives in New Guinea. Constant work was maintained to make routes passable for jeeps. Construction of airstrips near Dobodura and Popondetta, under way by 18 November, was assigned the highest priority because of the lack of a harbor in the area. Some supplies were flown to the airstrips, and some arrived by sea through reef-studded coastal waters near Ora Bay. The last vital transport link was formed by a few jeeps and native carriers who delivered the supplies to dumps just beyond the range of enemy small-arms fire.

Airdrop at Nadzab at its height, with one battalion of parachute troops descending from C–47's (foreground), while another battalion descends against a smoke screen and lands beyond a hill (left background). White parachutes were used by the troops, colored ones for supplies and ammunition. The men were dropped to seize the airdrome at Nadzab, located some 20 miles northwest of Lae, on the morning of 5 September 1943.

General Douglas Mac-Arthur, in one of the waist-gun positions of a B-17, watches his paratroopers make the highly successful landing on Nadzab.

B-24 over Salamaua, on north coast of New Guinea, during an air raid, 13 August 1943. Smoke from bomb bursts can be seen on Salamaua. While the ground forces were battling with the enemy, aircraft were striking at his bases at Salamaua, Lae, Finschhafen, Madang, and Rabaul as well as at the barges and ships bringing supplies and reinforcements to the enemy in New Guinea.

Infantryman watching aircraft from his camouflaged foxhole. Five days after the landings the Americans had cleared the enemy from Arawe Peninsula.

American and Australian troops crossing a river near Salamaua. An advance on Salamaua was initiated by Australian troops with assistance from American units that had landed at Nassau Bay on 30 June. This drive was an attempt to divert enemy strength from Lae, the real objective of the Allies. As a result of this move, the Japanese did divert their reinforcements arriving at Lae to Salamaua to strengthen their defenses there as the Allies moved closer to the town. During the period from 30 June to 16 September, a total of about 10,000 Japanese had been overcome in the Lae–Salamaua area. About 4,100 and 2,200 were reported killed in the vicinity of Salamaua and Lae, respectively. The remainder made their way north as best they could.

U.S. Coast Guard gunners fighting against a determined Japanese aerial attack during the invasion at Cape Gloucester, New Britain. Bomb splashes can be seen in water, resulting from the enemy's attempt to hit the LST in foreground. This was the only effective resistance offered by the Japanese at Cape Gloucester. The invasion of New Britain was the climax of the drive up the Solomon–New Guinea ladder; at the eastern end of this island was Rabaul, chief enemy base in the Southwest Pacific.

Alligator, mounting a .50-caliber gun on the left and a .30-caliber water-cooled machine gun on the right, coming down a slope to a beach on Arawe for more supplies for the men on the front lines. Armored amphibian tractors proved to be valuable assault vehicles. They could be floated beyond the range of shore batteries, deployed in normal landing boat formations, and driven over the fringing reefs and up the beaches. One of the immediate missions of the forces landing on Arawe was to establish a PT boat base.

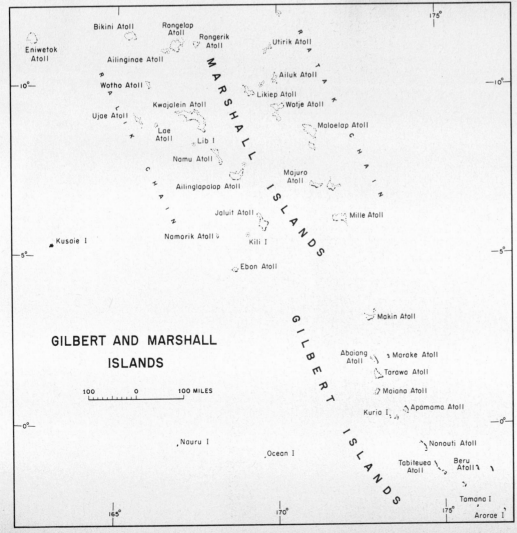

GILBERT AND MARSHALL
ISLANDS

100   0   100 MILES

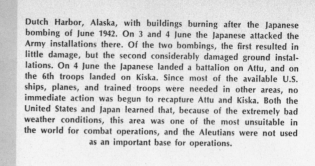

Dutch Harbor, Alaska, with buildings burning after the Japanese bombing of June 1942. On 3 and 4 June the Japanese attacked the Army installations there. Of the two bombings, the first resulted in little damage, but the second considerably damaged ground installations. On 4 June the Japanese landed a battalion on Attu, and on the 6th troops landed on Kiska. Since most of the available U.S. ships, planes, and trained troops were needed in other areas, no immediate action was begun to recapture Attu and Kiska. Both the United States and Japan learned that, because of the extremely bad weather conditions, this area was one of the most unsuitable in the world for combat operations, and the Aleutians were not used as an important base for operations.

Aleutian Islands

Landing beach in Holtz Bay area, Attu, as seen from atop the ridge separating Holtz Bay and Chichagof Bay. In the foreground can be seen a crashed Japanese Zero airplane. To the right, men and equipment are unloading from landing craft. It was soon found that the steep jagged crags, knifelike ridges, and boggy tundra greatly impeded the troops and made impracticable any extensive use of mechanized equipment.

Supplies being loaded into trailers to be taken to a supply dump back of the beach, 12 May or D-Day plus 1. The cloud of smoke in the background is from an enemy shell; the men in the area can be seen running to take cover.

American 105mm howitzer placed on wicker mats to help keep the gun from sinking into the tundra. Had the enemy used the guns which were found intact at the time of the invasion, the landing forces would have been greatly impeded.

Holding positions in the pass leading to Holtz Bay on 19 May; in right foreground is a strongpoint overlooking the area, in the background the enemy had gun positions above the fog line.

An oil and gas dump. The battle for Attu ended on 30 May but mopping-up operations continued for several days.

Troops aboard a transport headed for Butaritari Island in the Makin Atoll; landing craft which have been lowered into the water to take troops inland can be seen in the background. The Japanese, in September 1942, had occupied the Gilbert Islands. This group of islands included Makin Atoll and Tarawa Atoll. During the next year the enemy built garrisons on Butaritari Island and on Betio Island in the Tarawa Atoll. Only small enemy forces were placed on other islands in the Gilberts.

Men searching for snipers as they move inland from the beachhead on D-Day, 20 November.

Douglas Dauntless dive bomber (SBD) ready to drop its 1,000-pound bomb on Japanese-held island of Wake, 6 October 1943. During the planning for the seizure of the Gilberts, concurrent with action on Bougainville and in New Guinea, air attacks were made on Marcus and Wake, and the Tarawa Atoll, to soften Japanese installations and keep the enemy guessing as to where the next full-scale attack would be delivered.

The remains of a Japanese light tank which did not get into battle. During the morning of the first day American tanks could not make much headway against the combined obstacles of debris, shell holes, and marsh, but by afternoon they were able to render assistance to the infantry. The enemy had only two tanks on the island, but they were not used since when they were found wooden plugs were still in the barrels of their guns.

One of the antitank gun pits that ringed the outer defenses of one of the tank traps established by the enemy. Air observation prior to the operation had revealed most of defensive construction and led to correct inference of much that lay concealed, such as these antitank emplacements.

Marines leaving a log beach barricade, face fire-swept open ground on Betio Island in their advance toward the immediate objective, the Japanese airport. Landings were made under enemy fire on Betio Island in the Tarawa Atoll on 20 November, concurrent with the invasion of Butaritari Island, Makin Atoll. Tarawa, one of the coral atolls which comprise the Gilbert Islands, is roughly triangular in shape; about 18 miles long on east side, 12 miles long on south side, and 12½ miles long on northwest side. The Japanese had concentrated their strength on Betio Island.

War trophies consisting of chickens and ducks captured on the island, were cherished in anticipation of Thanksgiving Day when they could be used to supplement the K ration. On 22 November it was announced that organized resistance had ended, and on the next day forces on Makin were occupied with mopping-up activities.

631

Assaulting the top of a Japanese bombproof shelter. Once ashore, the marines were pinned down by withering enemy fire that came from carefully prepared emplacements in almost every direction of advance.

Captured Japanese command post with enemy tank in foreground. Shells and bombs had little effect on this reinforced concrete structure. Most of the command posts, ammunition dumps, and communications centers found here were made of reinforced concrete and were virtually bombproof. Powerful hand-to-hand infantry assault tactics were necessary to dislodge the enemy.

United States colors flying over Betio, 24 November 1943. The island was declared secure on 23 November; the remaining enemy forces were wiped out by the 28th. Betio, with the only air-field in Tarawa Atoll, together with captured Butaritari in Makin Atoll and other lesser islands, gave the Allies control of the entire Gilbert Islands archipelago. From these new bases an attack against the Marshall Islands was launched in 1944.

MacARTHUR'S SOUTHWEST PACIFIC TIMETABLE: APRIL 1944

Meanwhile, General MacArthur had also pushed forward the Southwest Pacific Area's timetable. Having landed in the Admiralties a month ahead of his original schedule, he decided to cancel operations against Hansa Bay and Wewak on the northeast coast of New Guinea in favor of a jump to Hollandia and Aitape, on the north-central coast, in April, two months earlier than previously planned. He would then continue northwestward along the coast in a campaign entailing the steady extension of land-based air cover by the seizure of successive air base sites.

On 22 April 1944 Army forces under MacArthur, supported by a Pacific Fleet carrier task force, landed at Hollandia and Aitape. At neither locale was the issue ever in doubt, although during July the Japanese bypassed at Wewak launched an abortive counterattack against Aitape. Protected by land-based aircraft from Hollandia, MacArthur's Army units next jumped 125 miles northwest on 17 May to seize another air base site at Wakde Island, landing first on the New Guinea mainland opposite the main objective. A ground campaign about a month and a half long ensued against a Japanese division on the mainland, but without waiting for the outcome of that fight other Army troops, on 27 May, carried the advance northwestward another 180 miles to Biak Island.

Now the wisdom of conducting twin drives toward the Philippines emerged. The Japanese Navy was preparing for a showdown battle in the Pacific, a battle it expected to fight off the Marianas in June. MacArthur's move to Biak put land-based planes in position to watch and harry the Japanese fleet, which was assembling in Philippines waters before moving into the Central Pacific. Because an American-controlled Biak would be an unacceptable thorn in their flank, the Japanese risked major elements of their fleet to send strong reinforcements in an attempt to drive MacArthur's forces off the island. They also deployed to bases within range of Biak about half their land-based air strength from the Marianas, Carolines, and Palaus—planes which their fleet would need for support during any battle off the Marianas.

Having undertaken two partially successful attempts to reinforce Biak, the Japanese assembled for a third try enough naval strength to overwhelm local American naval units, but just as the formidable force was moving toward Biak, the Japanese learned the U.S. Pacific Fleet was off the Marianas. The Japanese hastily assembled their naval forces and sailed northwestward for the engagement known as the Battle of the Philippine Sea. Having lost their chance to surprise the U.S. Navy, handicapped by belated deployment, and deprived of anticipated land-based air support, the Japanese suffered another shattering naval defeat.

Army and Marine divisions under Nimitz landed on Saipan in the Marianas on 15 June 1944 to begin a bloody three-week battle for control of the island. Next, on 21 July, Army and Marine units invaded Guam, 100 miles south of Saipan, and three days later Marines moved on to Tinian Island. An important turning point of the Pacific war, the American seizure of Marianas brought the Japanese home islands within reach of the Army Air Force B-29 bombers,

which in late November began to fly missions against Japan from Mariana fields.

At Biak Japanese resistance delayed capture of the best airfield sites until late June. On 2 July, MacArthur's Army forces moved on to Noemfoor Island, 90 miles to the west, in a combined parachute and amphibious operation designed to broaden the base of the Southwest Pacific's air deployment. On 30 July, an Army division continued on to the northwestern tip of New Guinea to secure another air base, and on 15 September MacArthur landed a reinforced Army division on Morotai Island, between New Guinea and Mindanao in the Philippines. On the same day Nimitz sent a Marine division ashore on Peleliu in the southern Palaus, and on the 17th an Army division from Nimitz' command landed on Angaur, just south of Peleliu. An Army regiment secured Ulithi Atoll, midway between Peleliu and the Marianas, on 23 September.

With these landings the approach to the Philippines was virtually completed. The occupation of Morotai proved easy and the island provided airfields for the support of advances into the Philippines and Indies. Hard fighting dragged on in the Palaus through November, but because of another acceleration in the pace of Pacific operations, these islands never played the role originally planned for them. The Allied forces of the Pacific had arrived in mid-September 1944 at the threshhold of their strategic objective, the Luzon-Formosa-China coast triangle. In seven months MacArthur's forces had moved forward nearly 1,500 miles from the Admiralties to Morotai; in ten months Nimitz' forces had advanced over 4,500 miles from Hawaii to the Palaus. The stage was now set for the reconquest for the Philippines.

THE LEYTE CAMPAIGN: OCTOBER 1944

The main assault at Leyte took place on 20 October 1944 with four Army divisions landing abreast in the largest amphibious operation yet conducted in the Pacific. Vice Admiral Thomas C. Kinkaid, MacArthur's naval commander, controlled the amphibious phases, including naval gunfire support and close air support by planes based on escort carriers. Ground forces were under Lieutenant General Walter Krueger, commanding the U.S. Sixth Army; land-based air forces of the Southwest Pacific Areas, in general support, were commanded by Lieutenant General George C. Kenney. MacArthur himself exercised unified command over the air, ground, and naval commanders.

The Japanese had originally planned to make their stand in the Philippines on Luzon, but the invasion of Leyte forced them to reconsider, and they decided that the entire Philippine Archipelago would be strategically lost if the U.S. Army secured a foothold in the central islands. Therefore, they started sending ground reinforcements to Leyte; they increased their land-based air strength in the Philippines in the hope of destroying Allied shipping in Leyte Gulf and maintaining local air superiority; and they dispatched their remaining naval strength to Leyte Gulf to destroy Kinkaid's invasion fleet and to block Allied access to the Philippines. The ensuing air-naval Battle of Leyte Gulf was the most critical moment of the campaign, and proved one of the most decisive actions of the Pacific war.

With the Leyte beaches secure, U.S. Army units proceeded with the destruction of the Japanese ground forces. Miserable weather bogged down the pace of operations, made supply difficult, delayed airfield construction, curtailed air support, and permitted the Japanese to continue to ship reinforcements to the islands. The reinforcement program came to a sudden halt early in December when an Army division executed an amphibious envelopment to Leyte's west coast, and by late December the Sixth Army had secured the most important sections of the islands, those required for air and logistical bases. Japanese troops in the mountains of northwestern Leyte continued organized resistance well into the spring of 1945, occupying the energies of large portions of Lieutenant General Robert L. Eichelberger's newly formed Eighth Army.

The choice of targets next after Leyte lay between Luzon and Formosa, and for months before the decision to go to Leyte the Joint Chiefs had debated the matter. Cogent arguments supported the seizure of either island, but military realities ultimately ruled in favor of Luzon. For one thing the Japanese, in the late summer and early fall of 1944, had overrun air base sites in eastern China from which the Allies had planned to bomb Japan prior to invasion. Since the Allies did not have the means to engage in extensive land campaigns in China to retake the airfields, the China coast had been eliminated from consideration as an objective, thereby reducing the importance of Formosa as a stepping-stone to China. Moreover, the Marianas already provided B-29 bases closer to Tokyo than Formosa. The Formosa

operation also promised to be logistically more inexpensive than Luzon, and, finally, MacArthur could move to Luzon three months earlier than Nimitz' forces could reach Formosa.

The Joint Chiefs decided that MacArthur would jump from Leyte to Luzon in December 1944. The forces that Nimitz was assembling for Formosa would be employed to seize Okinawa and other islands in the Ryukyus, 700 miles southwest of Japan, in March 1945. This operation would provide air bases close to Japan, and would give the Allies land areas on which they could develop major air and logistical bases for the support of the invasion of Japan. The Allies would also construct air and logistical bases on Luzon, while air and naval forces from Luzon, later aided by units from the Ryukyus, would sever the Japanese lines of communication to southeast Asia and the Indies.

The cancellation of Formosa and the scheduling of Okinawa for March left Nimitz' forces facing a lull in operations during the opening months of 1945, a lull inconsistent with the accepted principle of maintaining constant and unremitting pressure against the Japanese. The Joint Chiefs therefore directed Nimitz to secure Iwo Jima, 750 miles south of Tokyo, in January. The Army Air Forces were also vitally interested in Iwo, because the island could provide an emergency and staging base for B-29's making the long flight from the Marianas, as well as airfields from which fighter planes could escort the big bombers to and from Japan.

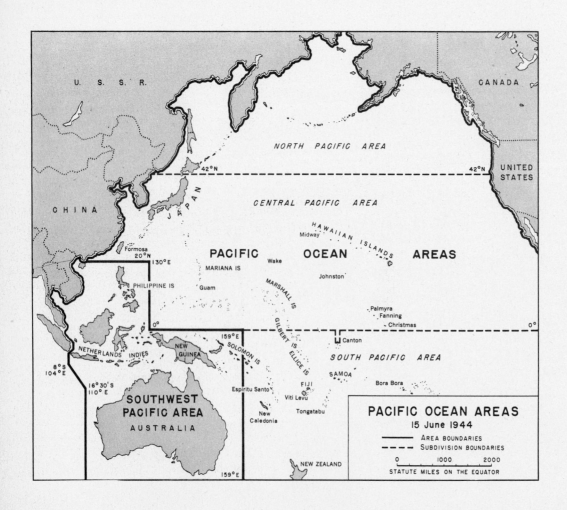

Training in the technique of uphill attack. In the early fighting against the Japanese, the tropical battlegrounds of the South and Southwest Pacific imposed severe difficulties on the U.S. forces. Operations were hampered by a jungle-wise enemy whose tactics and weapons were well adapted to the terrain. In October 1942 U.S. commanders were directed to begin a program of training which would include specialized training in close-in fighting, judo, firing from trees and other elevated positions, map reading, and use of the compass for movement through dense undergrowth.

Trainee jumping through burning oil. Emphasis was placed on specialized training in patrolling, ambushing, hip-shooting, stream-crossing expedients, and jungle living. Training was also given in the assault of fortified areas, hand-to-hand combat, and the use of demolitions. As the varied problems of assaulting the Pacific islands arose, the training was changed to suit the particular requirements.

Medical Corps men move a soldier off a field under machine gun fire during training at the Jungle Training Center. The course in first aid and sanitation emphasized those aspects of the subject which pertained to combat conditions in the Pacific. Training in jungle living covered all phases of survival in the jungle terrain, on the open seas, and on Pacific atolls.

Soldier wearing a camouflage suit fires a .45-caliber Thompson submachine gun during street-fighting course at the Jungle Training Center. The magnitude of the training given was vast. In the Hawaiian area alone, more than 250,000 men were trained for combat by these schools; additional men trained in the South Pacific and on Saipan brought the total to well over 300,000.

Medium tanks with 75mm guns going ashore on Kwajalein. The stacks at the rear of the tanks were used to extend the vented openings; unvented openings were sealed with tape and sealing compound to render the hulls watertight. Waterproofed vehicles could be operated satisfactorily in water deeper than otherwise possible, permitting them to wade in from landing craft halted at greater distances from shore.

Infantrymen, supported by a medium tank, move forward to wipe out the remaining enemy on the island. The fire raging in the background is the result of preinvasion bombing and shelling.

Routing the enemy from defensive positions, Kwajalein Atoll. Using a flamethrower to burn out the enemy from his positions; portion of rifle in right foreground is the .30-caliber M1 with fixed bayonet.

Gun motor carriage M10, used to blast pillboxes on Kwajalein. This weapon, called a tank destroyer, was mounted on the medium tank chassis and had a 3-inch gun in a semiopen turret, and a .50-caliber machine gun at the rear of the turret for protection against low-flying planes. Six days after the main landings had taken place, Kwajalein was in U.S. hands.

Consolidated Liberator heavy bombers, B-24's, raining 500-pound bombs on Truk in the Caroline Islands as part of a two-day strike executed to screen the assault on Eniwetok Atoll in the northwestern Marshalls. The strong enemy bases in the eastern Marshalls, bypassed when the western Marshalls were invaded, were continually harassed by air attack in 1944.

Enemy ship on fire, the result of direct hits during the 17–18 February air raid on Truk. During the two-day strike, 270 enemy aircraft and 32 of his ships were destroyed.

Invasion troops and supplies ready for the run in to Saipan, 15 June 1944. Craft in left foreground are LCVPs; an LCM(3) can be seen just behind them. The capture of the Marianas would sever the principal enemy north-south axis of sea communications through the Central Pacific, would become the initial step in the isolation and neutralization of the large enemy base at Truk, and would furnish staging areas and air bases for future offensives.

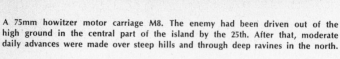

Infantrymen disperse for better protection as they approach the front lines. Prior to the invasion on 15 June, a two-day naval bombardment was directed at Saipan. During the first four days of the attack on the island, Japanese artillery and mortar fire exacted a heavy toll from the invaders.

A 75mm howitzer motor carriage M8. The enemy had been driven out of the high ground in the central part of the island by the 25th. After that, moderate daily advances were made over steep hills and through deep ravines in the north.

Street fighting in Garapan, Saipan. Enemy buildings and installations were set afiire by supporting artillery barrage before troops entered the town to engage the enemy. About 2,100 Japanese out of the original garrison of 29,000 on Saipan were taken prisoner. American casualties were approximately 3,100 killed, 300 missing, and 13,100 wounded.

Marine using a flamethrower to rout the enemy from a cave turns his face from the intense heat. The two men in the center fore-ground are watching to intercept any of the enemy who might try to escape. Note casualty on ground to the right of the two men. On 9 July organized resistance ceased, but thousands of the enemy remained scattered throughout the island in small groups.

638

Two burning medium tanks hit by enemy antitank guns near Yigo. As on Saipan, wiping out scattered enemy forces continued long after the main battle was over.

B-24's approaching for an attack on Yap Island, 20 August 1944. Aircraft operating from fields on Saipan had supported landings on Tinian and Guam and struck at enemy installations in the northern Marianas, and the Bonin, Volcano, Palau, Ulithi, Yap, and Ngulu islands. The next hop of the American ground forces was to the Palau Islands.

Marines pinned down by enemy fire on Peleliu Island in the Palaus. An American force from Guadalcanal assaulted Peleliu on 15 September and Anguar on 17 September, the two southernmost islands in the Palau group. Peleliu was the site of the major Japanese airfield in the group of islands, and Angaur was important as a suitable location for the construction of a large-size bomber base.

Men struggle up a steep slope on Peleliu. The assault of this island was met with considerable opposition. On D-Day the enemy, supported by tanks, launched a counter-attack against the landing forces. This attack was repulsed and the next day the airfield was captured.

The Vought Kingfisher two-seat observation seaplane OS2U–3 flies over firing ships and landing craft which carried invading forces to the shores of Angaur. The final loading of men used in the operations at Angaur and Peleliu was made in the Solomons. Compared with the battle on Peleliu, opposition was considered fairly light on Angaur. Angaur was declared secure on 20 September, though some fighting continued. In the Palau operation, U.S. casualties amounted to approximately 1,900 killed, over 8,000 wounded, and about 135 missing. Enemy casualties for this operation were about 13,600 killed and 400 captured.

Boeing B–29 Superfortress bombers leaving Saipan to bomb Tokyo. The B–29s made the first of a series of attacks on Tokyo on 24 November 1944.

640

Fires which resulted from the first raid on Tokyo.

LST's unloading troops directly on shore during the amphibious landing at Saidor on the north coast of New Guinea, 2 January 1944. This constituted the first advance of 1944 in the Southwest Pacific Area. Action in the Southwest and Central Areas was concurrent in 1944. In February reconnaissance planes reported that the Admiralty Islands were occupied by only a few small enemy units which were guarding the airfields there.

Aerial view of shore line near Saidor; ships along the coast are LST's. A regimental combat team landing here had the airstrip at Saidor in use on 7 January.

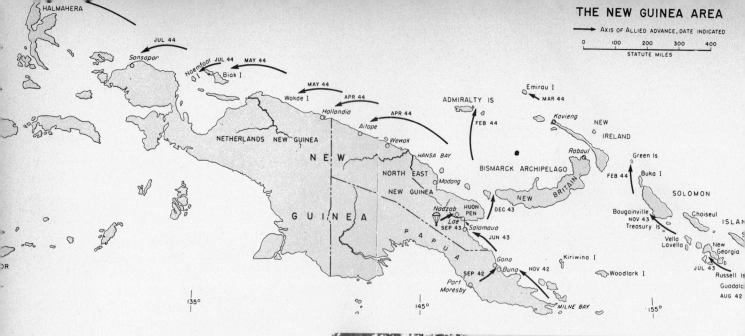

HALMAHERA

JUL 44

Sansapor

Noemfoor JUL 44 MAY 44

Biak I

MAY 44

Wakde I   APR 44

Hollandia   APR 44

Aitape

Wewak

NETHERLANDS NEW GUINEA

HANSA BAY

NORTH EAST

NEW GUINEA

Modang

NEW   GUINEA

PAPUA

Nadzab HUON
Lae   PEN
SEP 43   Salamaua DEC 43
JUN 43

Gona
Buna NOV 42
SEP 42

Port
Moresby

Kiriwina I

Woodlark I

MILNE BAY

135°   145°   155°

ADMIRALTY IS

FEB 44

Emirau I
MAR 44

Kavieng

NEW
IRELAND

Rabaul

BISMARCK ARCHIPELAGO

NEW   BRITAIN

Green Is

FEB 44   Buka I

SOLOMON

Bougainville   Choiseul
NOV 43
Treasury Is   ISLAN

Vella   New
Lavella   Georgia

JUL 43   Russell Is

Guadalc
AUG 42

Invading forces lounge on the deck of a ship taking them to Los Negros in the Admiralty Islands. These men landed on the east shore of the island near Momote Airfield on morning of 29 February 1944. Following an unopposed landing, the enemy guards at the airfield were overcome, leaving the field in U.S. hands. During the night of 29 February–1 March an enemy counterattack was repulsed.

155mm gun firing on Japanese positions on Manus Island from Los Negros, 23 March. Japanese reinforcements from Manus Island, separated from Los Negros by about 100 yards of water, were thrown into battle. By the 23d Los Negros, except for isolated enemy units, was captured and airfield was ready for operation.

Troops moving inland on 22 April found the way through the swampy areas near Hollandia difficult. The landings were virtually unopposed since the enemy had taken to the hills.

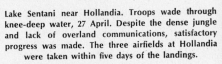

Lake Sentani near Hollandia. Troops wade through knee-deep water, 27 April. Despite the dense jungle and lack of overland communications, satisfactory progress was made. The three airfields at Hollandia were taken within five days of the landings.

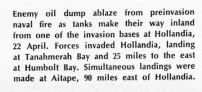

Enemy oil dump ablaze from preinvasion naval fire as tanks make their way inland from one of the invasion bases at Hollandia, 22 April. Forces invaded Hollandia, landing at Tanahmerah Bay and 25 miles to the east at Humbolt Bay. Simultaneous landings were made at Aitape, 90 miles east of Hollandia.

Main road at Arare being used to transport supplies, 24 May. On 18 May, with artillery support from the mainland, nearby Wakdé Island was assaulted. The next day the large airfield there was taken at a cost of about a hundred U.S. casualties.

Troops on Biak Island. While the positions on Wakdé and in the Arare area were being consolidated, other units assaulted Biak, about 200 miles to the west, on 27 May. Only slight opposition was met during the first day ashore; on the second day the advance inland was stopped by heavy enemy fire. On 29 May the enemy counterattacked and a bitter battle ensued.

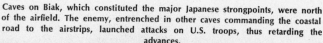

Caves on Biak, which constituted the major Japanese strongpoints, were north of the airfield. The enemy, entrenched in other caves commanding the coastal road to the airstrips, launched attacks on U.S. troops, thus retarding the advances.

Infantryman reading an issue of "Yank" magazine, just a few feet away from an enemy casualty. The Japanese attempt to reinforce his units on Biak was repulsed by U.S. air and naval forces, and by 20 June the ground forces had captured the three airfields on the island.

Command post set up on D-Day, 2 July, near Kamiri airstrip on Noemfoor Island. Note camouflaged walkie-talkie. The troops went ashore at points where reefs and other natural obstacles made the landings hazardous.

Airdrop at Kamiri Strip. The invasion forces on Noemfoor were reinforced by a parachute infantry regiment which dropped directly onto the airstrip. All three airfields here were captured by the night of 6 July.

LCI's unloading assault forces offshore at Morotai, northwest of Vogelkop Peninsula. The southern tip of Morotai Island was selected as the site for one of the last air bases needed before invading the Philippines. D-Day for this operation was 15 September, the same day that the invasion of Peleliu in the Palau group took place. On 30 September several airfields were made operational on the island.

Portion of a landing beach on Leyte where Philippine civilians left their hiding places to see the American forces. Fires smoldering in the background were caused by preinvasion aerial and naval bombardment. On one of the beaches heavy opposition was encountered. Enemy mortar and artillery fire sank several landing craft, and U.S. forces had to fight their way across the beach.

Unloading at a beach on Leyte, 21 October 1944. Beyond the two barges are several LCM(3)'s. An LVT(A) (2), the armored Buffalo, can be seen on the beach. On 20 October landings were made on three beaches: one in the Palo area; another between San José and Dulag; and the third about 55 miles to the south to control Panaon Strait between Leyte and the nearby island of Panaon.

646

Water supply point set up near a beach on Leyte, 21 October; note the collapsible water tank. By the end of the 21st, Tacloban, San José Dulag, and two airfields were captured. Heavy fighting continued at Palo. At the time of the invasion, the Japanese had only one division stationed on Leyte. Their vital supplies at Tacloban were lost to them on the 21st, and they appeared to have no organized plan of defense, offering resistance only at widely scattered points.

Direct hit on a Japanese warship by a B–25 in Ormoc Bay. Two transports and six escorting ships were sunk in the 2 November raid; however, by 3 November the Japanese had landed some 22,000 fresh troops at Ormoc Bay to reinforce the 16,000 original troops on Leyte.

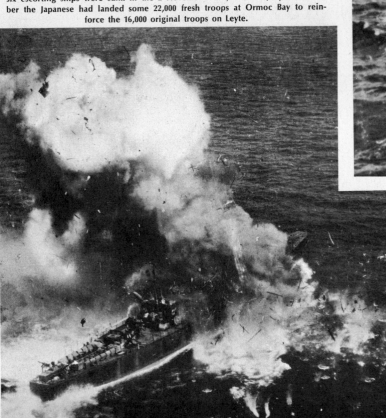

B–25 approaching a Japanese warship in Ormoc Bay. U.S. planes, operating from fields on Morotai, raided enemy ships in Ormoc Bay on 2 November in an atempt to keep the Japanese from landing reinforcements.

The Japanese, battling fiercely, delayed but could not stop the U.S. drive in the Ormoc Valley. By the end of November troops were closing in on Limon and were threatening Ormoc from the south. On 1 December 7 divisions were ashore and 5 airfields were in operation. On 7 December a division landed south of Ormoc, and by 10 December Ormoc was captured together with great quantities of enemy supplies and equipment. American motor convoy moving through the streets of a town on Leyte; vehicle in foreground is a cargo carrier. Valencia was taken on 18 December, Libungao on 20 December. After troops moved down from the mountains to take Cananga on 21 December, the enemy retreated westward. The Leyte Campaign was considered closed on 26 December but mopping-up activities continued for several months.

B–29's leaving their base on Guam for a strategic bombing mission on Japanese industry. As 1944 drew to a close, although the Allies had gained a foothold in the Philippines, the enemy continued to fight with the same fanatical zeal and tenacity of purpose as he did in the early days of the war. While his air, naval, and ground forces had been considerably reduced, he still had strong forces at his disposal for defense.

New York

London Edition

Paris

THE STARS AND STRIPES

Daily Newspaper of U.S. Armed Forces
in the European Theater of Operations
VOL. 5 No. 58—1d.

WEDNESDAY, Jan. 10, 1945

EXTRA   EXTRA

Yanks Land on Luzon

4 Lingayen Gulf Beaches Stormed, Held

Initial Losses Light; MacArthur Ashore

Front Lines Seesawing In Ardennes

With the front blanketed under winter's heaviest snowfall—drifts in the Ardennes were four feet deep— Allied troops continued yesterday to chip off chunks of the Germans' iced Belgian salient, compressing the northern flank of the bulge and battling to within three miles of the St. Vith-Houffalize road, the only main supply artery left to the enemy.

Indications of a Nazi withdrawal from the northern fringes toward the ridges protecting this highway were seen in reports that Allied forces were meeting "remarkably light artillery and mortar fire" as they advanced. Territory given up by the foe was sprinkled liberally with mines and booby-traps, a familiar German tactic when forced to retreat.

U.S. troops plodding southward west of the Ourthe River, which flows south-east to Houffalize, were about half a mile from the road junction of LaRoche, on the northeast, were about half a mile ther east, other doughboys were within ten miles of St. Vith, one of the enemy's main communications points in the salient.

While the Germans on the north flank fell back at some points for more than half a mile without fighting, the situation on the south flank was just the opposite. It was disclosed that 3rd Army troops at Bastogne had withdrawn Monday giving ground after a three-mile counter-attacks.

The Japs' New Order Changeth

The last amphibious step of Gen. Mac-Arthur's long road back to Bataan began yesterday when Sixth Army doughboys hit four beachheads in Lingayen Gulf, 110 miles from Manila and Corregidor. Map shows probable route of invasion convoys.

MacARTHUR'S HQ, Philippines, Jan. 9 (AP)— Gen. Douglas MacArthur today fulfilled his vow to return to Bataan when he and a great force of American doughboys landed on Luzon, major Philippine island, north of the Bataan Peninsula.

The Yanks poured ashore to secure a grip on four beaches in Lingayen Gulf about 110 miles northwest of the Philippine capital city, Manila, and the same distance north of Corregidor, from which starving and disease-ridden soldiers fought their heroic but losing defense in 1942.

Initial losses were described as light.

The landings were made by Sixth Army doughboys commanded by German-born Lt. Gen. Walter Krueger.

The landings for what MacArthur's communique called the "showdown" move in the Philippine campaign were made after U.S. surface vessels, carrier planes and land planes had subjected enemy defenses to almost continuous pounding for days. These softening-up blows hit the Japs everywhere from the Kurile Islands, north of the enemy's homeland, to the Philippines.

Though Japanese radio had been filled with invasion reports since Sunday, the actual landings were not made until 9.40 AM this morning. (The first flash in London came at 11.08 last night.)

The operation puts American soldiers in the Philippines within 525 miles of the China coast.

Though a blistering naval and air bombardment preceded the invasion, Japanese planes struck the landing forces repeatedly, inflicting some damage, MacArthur reported.

Final plans for the Luzon invasion were believed to have been mapped by MacArthur and Adm. Chester W. Nimitz, Pacific naval chief, when the two conferred in the Philippines late in December.

Meanwhile, other developments in the Pacific yesterday included raids by Superfortresses based both on Saipan, in the Marianas, and the China-based planes on the Asiatic mainland. The Saipan B29s struck Tokyo, while the China-based planes hit Formosa, enemy island stronghold 90 miles off the Asiatic mainland.

At Melbourne, it was announced that Australian and New Zealand soldiers had relieved sizable American ground forces in parts of New Guinea and New Britain and all of the Solomons.

Lingayen Gulf is one of the most important seaways on Luzon and was used by the Japanese for their invasion of the island in December, 1942. Practically the mile and its length about 35 miles. It is coral shelf, but this does not extend too amphibious army. These

FDR Submits Budget for 83 Billions

. . . message, President . . . . . year

Bill Mauldin in Stars and Stripes

"Maybe Joe needs a rest. He's talkin' in his sleep."

THE LUZON CAMPAIGN: JANUARY 1945

The first step of the Luzon Campaign was the seizure of an air base in southwestern Mindoro, 150 miles south of Manila on 15 December 1944, two Army regiments accomplishing the task with ease. The invasion of Luzon started on 9 January 1945, when four Army divisions landed along the shores of Lingayen Gulf. Within three days 5 Army divisions, a separate regimental combat team, 2 artillery groups, an armored group, and supporting service units were ashore and had begun a drive down the Central Plains of Luzon toward Manila. The Japanese were incapable of naval intervention at Lingayen Gulf, and their most significant reaction was to throw a number of kamikaze (suicide plane) attacks against Kinkaid's naval forces for four days.

General Tomoyuki Yamashita, commanding Japanese forces in the Philippines, did not intend to defend the Central Plains–Manila Bay region, the strategic prize of Luzon. Knowing he would receive no reinforcements and believing the issue in the Philippines had been decided at Leyte, he sought only to pin down major elements of MacArthur's forces in the hope of delaying Allied progress toward Japan. For this purpose he moved the bulk of his troops into mountain strongholds, where they could conduct a protracted, bloody, defensive campaign. But Japanese naval forces on Luzon, only nominally under Yamashita, decided to defend Manila and Manila Bay. Thus, when U.S. Army units reached Manila on 3 February, it took them a month of bitter building-to-building fighting to root out the Japanese. Meanwhile, operations to clear Manila Bay had begun with a minor amphibious landing at the southern tip of Bataan on 15 February. The next day a combined parachute-amphibious assault, involving two Army regiments, initiated a battle to clear Corregidor Island. Other forces cleared additional islands in Manila Bay and secured the south shore. By mid-March the Bay was open for Allied shipping, but an immense salvage and repair job was necessary before the Allies could fully exploit Manila's excellent port facilities.

In the meantime a reinforced Army division had landed near Subic Bay and had cut across the base of Bataan Peninsula to prevent the Japanese from holing up on Bataan as had MacArthur's forces three years earlier. An airborne division undertook both amphibious and parachute landings in southern Luzon to start clearing that region, and an Army regimental combat team made an amphibious assault in southeastern Luzon to secure the Bicol Peninsula. Turning against the Japanese mountain strongholds, MacArthur continued to pour reinforcements onto Luzon, and the land campaign there ultimately evolved into the largest of the Pacific war. MacArthur committed to Luzon 10 divisions, 2 regiments of another division, and 3 separate regimental combat teams, to mention only the major ground combat forces. Guerrillas also played a large role. One guerrilla unit came to substitute for a regularly constituted division and other guerrilla forces of battalion and regimental size supplemented the efforts of the Army units. Moreover, the loyal and willing Filipino population immeasurably eased the problem of supply, construction, and civil administration.

Except for a strong pocket in the mountains of north-central Luzon, organized Japanese resistance ended by late June 1945. The rugged terrain in the north, coupled with rainy weather, prevented Krueger's Sixth Army from applying its full strength to the reduction of this pocket. Eichelberger's Eighth Army took over responsibility for operations on Luzon at the end of June, and continued the pressure against Yamashita's last stand area, which held out until the end of the war.

ADVANCES IN SOUTHWEST PACIFIC CONTINUE: FEBRUARY 1945

While the Sixth Army was destroying Japanese forces on Luzon, the Eighth Army began its campaign by landing a regimental combat team on Palawan Island on 28 February 1945. Here engineers built an air base from which to help cut Japan's line of communications to the south and to support later advances in the southern Philippines and the Indies. On 10 March, a regimental combat team, later reinforced, landed near Zamboanga in southwestern Mindanao, and soon thereafter Army units began moving southwest toward Borneo along the Sulu Archipelago. In rapid succession the Eighth Army then landed on Panay, Cebu, northwestern Negros, Bohol, central Mindanao, southeastern Negros, northern Mindanao, and finally at Sarangani Bay in southern Mindanao, once intended as the first point of reentry into the Philippines. At some locales bitter fighting raged for a time, but the issue was never in doubt in the southern Philippines, and organized Japanese resistance there had largely collapsed by the end of May. Mopping up continued to the end of the war, with reorganized and reequipped guerrilla forces bearing much of the burden.

The last offensives in the Southwest Pacific Area started on 1 May when an Australian brigade went ashore on Tarakan Island, Borneo. Carried to the beaches by landing craft manned by U.S. Army engineers, the Australians had air support from fields on Morotai and in the southern Philippines. On 10 June an Australian division landed at Brunei Bay, Borneo, and another Australian division went ashore at Balikpapan on 1 July in what proved to be the final amphibious assault of the war.

Since slow base development at Leyte had forced MacArthur to delay the Luzon invasion from December to January, Nimitz in turn had to postpone his target dates for the Iwo Jima and Okinawa operations. The Iwo Jima assault finally took place on 19 February 1945, with two Marine divisions, supported by minor Army elements, making the landings. A third Marine division reinforced, while an Army regiment ultimately took over as island garrison. The Marines had to overrun fanatic resistance from firmly entrenched Japanese who held what was probably the strongest defensive system American forces encountered during the Pacific war, and it took a month of bloody fighting to secure the island. In early March a number of crippled B-29's made emergency landings on Iwo; by the end of the month an airfield was fully operational for fighter planes. Later, engineers constructed a heavy bomber field and another fighter base on the island.

The invasion of the Ryukyus began on 26 March when an Army division under Nimitz landed on the Kerama Islands, 15 miles west of Okinawa, to secure a forward naval base, a task traditionally assigned to Marines. On 1 April two Army and two Marine divisions executed the assault on the main objective, Okinawa. Two more Army divisions and a Marine infantry regiment later reinforced. Another amphibious assault took place on 16 April, when an Army division seized Ie Island, 4 miles west of Okinawa, and the final landing in the Ryukyus came on 26 June, when a small force of Marines went ashore on Kume Island, 50 miles west of Okinawa. Ground forces at Okinawa were under the U.S. Tenth Army, Lieutenant General Simon B. Buckner commanding, at first. When General Buckner was killed on 18 June, Marine Lieutenant General Roy S. Geiger took over until Lieutenant General Joseph W. Stilwell assumed command on the 23rd.

The Japanese made no attempt to defend the Okinawa beaches, but instead fell back to prepared cave and tunnel defenses on inland hills. Bitterly defending every inch of ground, the Japanese continued organized resistance until late June. Meanwhile, Japanese suicide planes had inflicted extensive damage on Nimitz' naval forces, sinking about 25 ships and damaging nearly 165 more in an unsuccessful attempt to drive Allied naval power from the western Pacific. Ashore on Okinawa, small unit tactics, combined with great concentrations of naval, air, and artillery bombardments, turned the tide of the ground battle. Especially noteworthy was the close air support provided the ground forces by the Army Air Forces and Navy and Marine aircraft.

The capture of Okinawa and other positions in the Ryukyus gave the Allies both air and naval bases within easy striking distance of Japan. By early May fighter planes from Okinawa had started flights over Japan, and as rapidly as fields became available bombers, including units from the Southwest Pacific Area, came forward to mount attacks in preparation for the invasion of the home islands. The forward anchorages in the Ryukyus permitted the Pacific Fleet to keep in almost continuous action against Japanese targets. The Ryukyus campaign had brought Allied forces in the Pacific to Japan's doorstep.

THE PHILIPPINE AREA

Men and supplies come ashore in the Lingayen Gulf–San Fabian area. After a heavy bombardment of the landing beaches, the first assault troops landed on Luzon, meeting little opposition. By nightfall the invading army had gained an initial lodgment, suffering but few casualties.

Filipinos working with U.S. engineer troops assembling steel matting on an airstrip at Lingayen, 14 January. On 17 January the Lingayen airstrip was completed, and the Far Eastern Air Forces assumed responsibility for the air support of ground operations. By this time the Japanese had stopped sending air reinforcement to the Philippines, and during the Luzon Campaign air superiority was held by U.S. forces.

U.S. casualty receiving plasma at the front lines near Damortis.

Japanese medium tank with 47mm antitank gun, knocked out near San Manuel. Forty-five enemy tanks were destroyed in the San Manuel fighting. Most of the enemy tanks encountered were dug in and used as pillboxes and were not used in actual armored maneuver.

105mm howitzers firing from the grounds of Santo Tomás University during the attack on Manila, 5 February. On the night of 31 January–1 February the attack on Manila began in full force.

Manila during an artillery attack. Rafts and amphibian tractors were used to ferry the attacking U.S. troops across the numerous streams because the enemy had destroyed all the bridges. When the enemy did not evacuate Manila, U.S. artillery was employed. It had previously been hoped that it would not be necessary to shell the city.

The Pasig River (foreground). The tall tower at right is part of the city hall, later occupied by GHQ.

Infantrymen on the alert in a street of Manila man their .30-caliber Browning machine gun. On 7 February 1945 the envelopment of Manila began, and by 11 February the Japanese within the city were completely surrounded. Cavite was seized on 13 February

240mm howitzer firing on Intramuros, where the walls were 16 feet high, 40 feet thick at the base, tapering to 20 feet at the top. During the night of 22–23 February all available artillery was moved into position, and at 0730 on 23 February the assault on Intramuros began. Once the walls were breached and the attacking troops had entered, savage fighting ensued. On 25 February the entire area of the walled city was in U.S. hands.

Infantrymen pick their way along a street of Intramuros as a bulldozer clears away the rubble. On 4 March 1945 the last building was cleared of the enemy and Manila was completely in U.S. hands. In background is the downtown business section of Manila, on the far side of the Pasig River.

653

Food and medical supplies being dropped to the Allied internees at Bilibid Prison Farm near Muntinglupa, Luzon, after they were rescued from the Japanese prison camp at Los Banos.

Bomb strike on a mountain west of Bamban. Progress was slow over the difficult terrain of the Zambales Mountains where the Japanese had constructed pillboxes and trenches and had fortified caves. The U.S. attack was made frontally, aided by daily air strikes, and the enemy strongpoints were eliminated one by one.

Crew of a 75mm pack howitzer being subjected to small-arms fire on Corregidor, 17 February. At first the enemy offered only spotty resistance but soon rallied and offered a stubborn defense.

U.S. paratroopers landing on Corregidor during the invasion of the island.

"Topside," Corregidor. On 16 February 1945 a battalion of a regimental combat team landed on the south shore of the island. A regimental combat team was flown north from Mindoro and landed two hours before the amphibious assault troops.

105mm howitzer motor carriage and infantrymen. By 15 March 1945 the enemy was being pushed back and the U.S. forces in northern Luzon were advancing columns up the roads to Bauang and Baguio.

View of the harbor at Manila showing the congested docking area and amount of shipping. Clearing Manila Harbor and restoring its dock facilities progressed rapidly and supply problems were soon helped by the full use of the excellent port, which was well located for supplying troops in the Philippines. By 15 March a total of 10,000 tons per day was passing through the port. By the middle of April almost 200 sunken ships had been raised from the bottom of the bay.

Mountainous terrain in northern Luzon. The Malaya River flows through the valley in the vicinity of Cervantes, Ilocos Sur Province.

Armor and infantry on a hillside overlooking Baguio; in the foreground is a 105mm howitzer motor carriage, while down the slope of the hill is a 76mm gun motor carriage. Vehicles, like the foot soldiers, found the going hard over the rough terrain.

Difficult terrain patrol moving through heavy undergrowth.

Vehicles fording a river in northern Luzon while engineer troops work on the road; in foreground is a 105mm howitzer motor carriage. Note destroyed enemy vehicles along road and in stream.

Medium tank M4A1 on a hill overlooking Baguio. Baguio was subjected to extensive bombardment by aircraft and heavy artillery, and the enemy's defenses around the former summer capital were reduced. Infantry troops led by tanks which had great difficulty maneuvering through the mountains entered Baguio on 27 April with practically no opposition.

155mm howitzer in Balete Pass shelling enemy artillery positions, 19 April. During March one division moved forward 10 miles after constructing more than 130 miles of roads and trails. The same problems of terrain were faced in this advance, and it was not until 13 May that the pass was seized.

Infantryman routing enemy soldiers hiding in a culvert near Aritao on the highway north of Balete Pass. U.S. forces broke through the Japanese defenses at Aritao and seized Bayombong to the north toward the Cagayan Valley on 7 June 1945. After this, the drive northward was rapid and met with little opposition.

Paratroopers landing near Aparri. The Northern Luzon Guerrilla Force had cleared the northwestern coast of Luzon, and by early June 1945 controlled practically all the territory north of Bontoc and west of the Cagayan Valley. On 21 June U.S. troops and guerrillas seized Aparri, and on 23 June a reinforced parachute battalion was dropped near the town. The paratroopers moved southward, meeting U.S. troops moving northward.

A phosphorus hand grenade exploding on an enemy position. The drive into the Cagayan Valley ended the last offensive on Luzon in June 1945. Enemy pockets of resistance were cleared out, and by 15 August, when hostilities officially ended, the U.S. forces had reported 40,565 casualties, including 7,933 killed. The Japanese lost over 192,000 killed and approximately 9,700 captured. While the fighting was still in progress on Luzon, other U.S. troops were engaged on other islands in the Philippine Archipelago. Mopping up was still in progress on Leyte and Samar; landings were made on Mindanao, Palawan, Marinduque, Panay, Cebu, Bohol, Negros, Masbate, Jolo, and Basilan; and other troops were being prepared for the invasion of Okinawa.

Troops wading ashore during the invasion of Cebu Island. During March landings were made on Panay, Cebu, and Negros.

Filipino residents of City of Cebu welcome infantry and armored troops.

Captured Japanese soldier being brought in on northern Cebu, May 1945.

Japanese prisoners at City of Cebu boarding a ship that will take them to a prisoner-of-war enclosure. Of the more than 350,000 enemy troops in the entire Philippine Archipelago only an estimated 50,000 were left when Japan capitulated. Of the original number relatively few were taken prisoner.

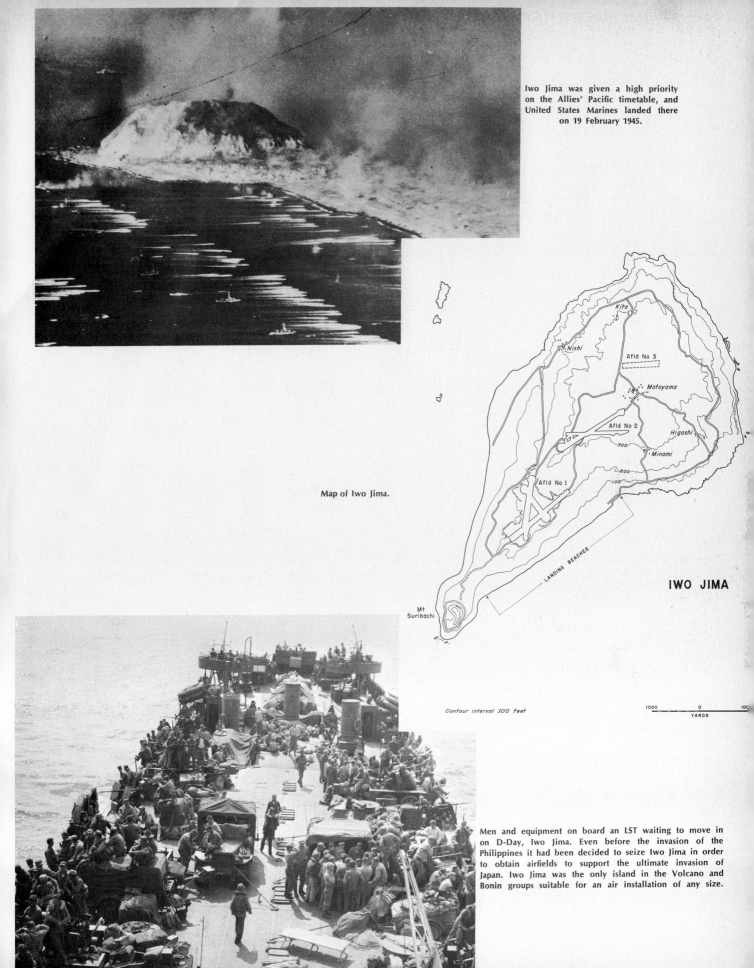

Iwo Jima was given a high priority on the Allies' Pacific timetable, and United States Marines landed there on 19 February 1945.

Map of Iwo Jima.

IWO JIMA

Contour interval 100 feet

1000   0   100
YARDS

Men and equipment on board an LST waiting to move in on D-Day, Iwo Jima. Even before the invasion of the Philippines it had been decided to seize Iwo Jima in order to obtain airfields to support the ultimate invasion of Japan. Iwo Jima was the only island in the Volcano and Bonin groups suitable for an air installation of any size.

661

Unloading on the beach on Iwo Jima. Initially during the landing on Iwo Jima all went according to plans. The water was calm, no underwater obstacles were found, and the heavy preinvasion shelling had destroyed some of the minefields. One hour after the first waves of Marines were ashore the enemy opened fire with automatic weapons, mortars, and artillery. Later in the day heavy seas hurled landing craft onto the beach, which added greatly to the difficulty of getting men and supplies ashore.

Steel matting being laid on the beach at Iwo Jima to facilitate the unloading of heavy equipment over the sand. Both on the beaches and inland the loose volcanic soil made the movement of vehicles extremely difficult. Trucks bogged down and supplies soon piled high on the beach.

4.5-inch automatic rocket launchers mounted on two ³/₄-ton trucks, firing on Iwo Jima.

Flamethrowers burning out enemy troops in a hidden cave while a rifleman waits behind the cover of a rock. One by one the Marines knocked out the enemy pillboxes and sealed the caves, gradually breaking down the defense system.

Marines firing on enemy soldiers hidden in a cave. Two Marines wait at the base of a rock while nearer the top one fires an automatic rifle and two others fire a rocket launcher and a .45-caliber submachine gun. The enemy had set up an elaborate system of defenses. The island was honeycombed with caves and connecting tunnels, camouflaged pillboxes and gun positions. Most of the caves had at least 35 feet of overhead cover and had not been damaged during the preinvasion bombing and shelling.

Men in surf enjoy their first bath since the invasion of the island began.

Admiral Chester M. Nimitz enjoys a glass of pineapple juice during an inspection tour of Iwo Jima.

1945 Easter services on Mount Suribachi for U.S. Army and Marine personnel.

Three Japanese coming out of their cave to surrender. On 16 March it was officially announced that all organized enemy resistance had come to an end, although mopping up continued for many days in the Kitano Point area. The exact number of casualties to the enemy is not known as many were lost in their caves and tunnels, but by 21 March over 21,000 dead had been counted, while only 212 prisoners were taken. Out of approximately 20,000 casualties the Marines lost over 4,000 killed, while Navy casualties amounted to over 1,000. Iwo Jima was probably the most strongly fortified island selected as an objective during the war.

OKINAWA ISLAND GROUP

10   0   10   20
MILES

Iheya I.

Yoron I.

Ie Shima

Aguni I.

Kume I.

OKINAWA I.

Keise Is.

NAHA

Kerama Is.

Aerial view of ships during the landings on Okinawa.

Flamethrowing medium tank firing at the entrance of a cave on southern Okinawa.

After a preliminary bombardment of the beaches, the heaviest to support a landing in the Pacific, the first assault troops landed on the Hagushi beaches against no opposition. Within the first hour over 16,000 men and some 250 amphibian tanks had landed. The airstrips at Yontanzam and Katena were seized against little resistance. As a result of the first day's operations a beachhead approximately 10 miles long and 3 miles deep was in U.S. hands. Both Army and Marine Corps troops made good progress during the next few days.

Japanese prisoner being searched at the entrance of a cave after he has surrendered.

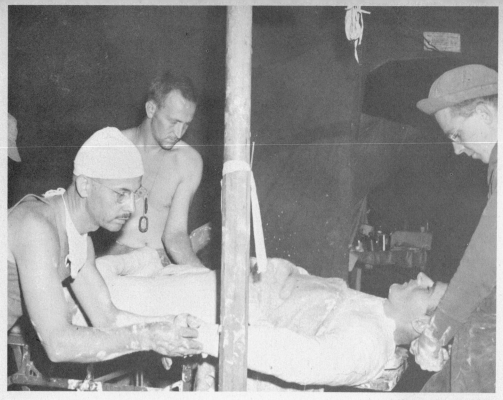

Medics at work in a hospital tent. During early April the U.S. troops were able to make only limited gains against a well-entrenched enemy. Heavy casualties were suffered.

An enlisted man washing in a water-filled foxhole following the heavy rains. The fighting continued on Okinawa until 21 June when the island was declared secure.

Prisoners waiting on a dock at Okinawa to be transported to Hawaii. In addition to the loss of a great base on the doorstep of Japan, the enemy lost 107,500 dead and 7,400 prisoners. U.S. Army casualties numbered 39,430, including 7,374 killed.

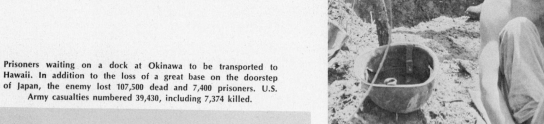

COMBAT ACTIVITY IN CHINA, BURMA AND INDIA

Except for some minor ground actions in Burma, U.S. Army combat activity in China, Burma, and India during World War II was largely limited to air operations against Japanese forces in China and Burma, and anti-shipping strikes over the South China Sea. But these combat operations amounted to only a small part of the U.S. Army's activities in these areas. The United States policy of keeping China in the war and increasing the potential of Generalissimo Chiang Kai-shek's ground forces required the Army to undertake a huge logistical effort in the CBI, an effort also aimed at supporting Army Air Forces operations in China.

Early in 1942 the Army sent Lieutenant General Joseph W. Stilwell to China with the missions of maintaining an overland supply line to China through Burma and coordinating American efforts to train, equip, and supply Chinese ground units. Stilwell also became Chiang's chief-of-staff in the latter's capacity as Allied commander of the China theatre, which nominally included not only China but also French Indo-China and Thailand. Burma, Malaya, the island of Sumatra in the Indies, Ceylon, and the waters of the Indian Ocean formed a separate Allied theatre, the Southeast Asia Command, established in August 1943 under Admiral Lord Louis Mountbatten. British Army forces in India remained under General Sir Claude J. E. Auchinleck. Stilwell, in addition to his other duties, commanded all U.S. Army forces in China, Burma, and India.

In May 1942 the Japanese drove British and Chinese forces (the latter operating under Stilwell) out of Burma and cut the overland route to China. For the next 18 months no significant ground activity occurred in the area, and American forces concentrated on the development of an aerial supply route to China and on training Chinese troops. From small beginnings the aerial supply operations grew until by the end of the war the Army Air Force was employing nearly 630 cargo planes to fly supplies into China over the dangerous "hump" in a continuous effort to support the Chinese Army and the Army Air Forces' own operations.

The aerial supply route could not support all needs—a land route was required to aid the Chinese, to build up means for planning campaigns against the Japanese, and to help develop the air bases in eastern China from which the United States intended to undertake bombardment of Japan in preparation for invasion of the home islands. Moreover, the air effort was expensive in transport aircraft, which, from the global point of view, were scarce. Work accordingly began in 1943 on the southwestern section of a new road (the Ledo Road) from India across northern Burma to China.

In October 1943 Chinese troops under Stilwell had started to clear northern Burma, and in the spring of 1944, a U.S. Army regiment, Merrill's Marauders, and parts of another Army regiment, spearheaded new offensives to secure the route for the overland road. Through most of 1944 operations in northern Burma were indecisive, although enough terrain was secured for engineers to push road construction and to start laying a pipeline 1,800 miles from India to China. Meanwhile, within China, U.S. Army Air Forces units under Major General Claire L. Chennault stepped up the pace of their operations, and B-29 bombers, based in India, began using a few fields in China to stage strikes against targets in Manchuria, Korea, and Japan.

The Japanese reacted strongly to the increased air effort, and beginning in April 1944 launched ground offensives that overran most of the existing fields and proposed air base sites in eastern China. By late summer the Japanese controlled most of the area from which bombers had been expected to fly against Japan. As already noted, this Japanese success had much to do with eliminating the China coast as a factor in the strategic plan for projecting Allied strength into the Luzon-Formosa-China coast triangle, and helped prompt the decision to move to Luzon rather than Formosa.

With the Chinese unable to halt the Japanese, the aim of Allied strategy in China became limited to keeping alive some semblance of Chinese resistance. Relations between Stilwell and Chiang became strained, and in October 1944 Major General Albert C. Wedemyer replaced Stilwell as Chiang's chief-of-staff and commander of U.S. Army forces

U.S. troops aboard a transport waiting to go ashore at a port in India. At the end of 1942 only about 17,000 American troops were in the China–Burma–India theatre, consisting almost entirely of Air Forces and Services of Supply personnel.

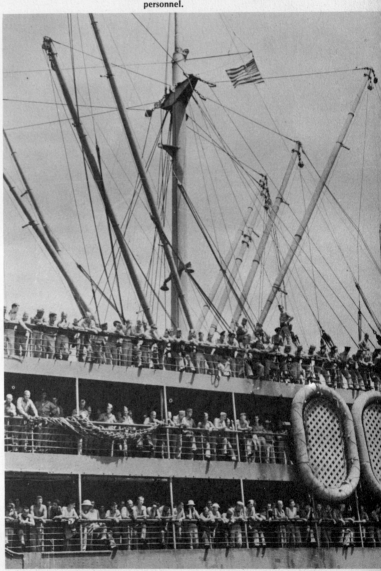

in China. Army units in Burma and India passed to the command of Major General Dan I. Sultan as Commanding General, India-Burma Theatre, an Army administrative and logistical organization. Sultan's missions were to push construction of the Ledo Road and the laying of the pipeline across northern Burma, to help the Army Air Forces step up the flow of supplies into China, and, in general, to support the China Theatre and Chennault's air operations.

U.S. Army ground combat operations in both China and Burma now ceased, and the Army turned its attention to training Chinese forces, providing advisors for Chinese divisions in the field, and planning a drive to the China coast that never transpired. The Chinese ultimately cleared part of northern Burma. British forces, whose offensive in central and southern Burma began to show results in late 1944, carried the rest of the combat load in Burma. By the end of the war Japanese resistance had collapsed in most of Burma, and the Japanese had begun withdrawing their forces from southern and eastern China to Manchuria and the homeland. From hopeful beginnings, the CBI had sunk to the status of a sideshow in Allied strategy for the defeat of Japan.

Chinese troops training at Ramgarh, India. Chinese troops learning to handle a .30-caliber Browning machine gun.

Transporting U.S. supplies in India, 1942. An American air force based in China was dependent upon the Hump air route, which was at the end of a 10,000-mile line of supply from the United States, for the much needed gasoline, bombs, and other munitions. In order for one American bomber in China to execute a mission against the enemy, a transport plane had to make an average of four separate flights over the Hump, the most hazardous mountain terrain in the world.

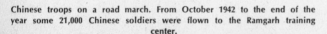

Chinese troops on a road march. From October 1942 to the end of the year some 21,000 Chinese soldiers were flown to the Ramgarh training center.

Snow-capped peaks of a spur of the Himalayas between the Salween and Mekong rivers. Some of these peaks are over 20,000 feet high. Cargo transported over the Hump increased from 10,000 tons a month during the summer of 1943 to approximately 46,000 tons a month by January 1945. The Curtiss C–46 Commando is pictured here.

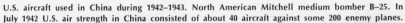

U.S. aircraft used in China during 1942–1943. North American Mitchell medium bomber B–25. In July 1942 U.S. air strength in China consisted of about 40 aircraft against some 200 enemy planes.

Pipelines showing the manifold valve installation on the pipeline near Myitkyina, Burma, September 1944. Engineers were to build two 4-inch pipelines for motor fuel and aviation gasoline starting in Assam, paralleling the Ledo Road, and extending through to Kunming, China. By October 1944 one of the lines reached Myitkyina, a distance of about 268 miles; 202 miles were completed on the other line by this date. Another 6-inch pipeline for gasoline was built in India from Calcutta to Assam.

Kowloon docks under air attack by U.S. planes, a portion of Hong Kong in foreground. A Japanese Zero can be seen just to the left of the smoke from a hit on the Kowloon docks and railroad yards. In Burma during 1942 most of the action following the Japanese conquest of the country consisted of limited air attacks and patrol clashes along the Burma–India border.

U.S. Services of Supply truck convoy starting across a temporary pontoon bridge just after its completion in 1944. Built across the treacherous Irrawaddy River, this bridge was approximately 1,200 feet long and served as a link in the Ledo Road for the combat troops and supply vehicles. When the torrential rains ceased a permanent structure was built to handle the tremendous loads of the convoys going to China.

Assembly of first convoy in Ledo, Assam, in January, 1945, to travel the Ledo–Burma Road, a route stretching over approximately 1,000 miles through Myitkyina, Burma, to Kunming, China.

The American Volunteer Group in China, the famous Flying Tigers, was organized by Claire Chennault, a retired United States Army Air Corps captain, to protect the Burma Road and provide the Chinese armies with air support. Chennault himself had gone to China in 1937 to build a Chinese air force that would help defend that country from Japanese aggression. As the Japanese army overran China, help came from America in 1941 in the form of a hundred Curtiss-Wright P–40B Tomahawks and volunteer pilots to fly them.

The American fliers were formed into three squadrons and trained so effectively by Chennault that the group produced no less than 30 aces during the short span of its history.

A row of shark's teeth was painted across the nose of each of the P–40's. Blood-red tongues and fierce eyes completed the picture of a tiger shark, and gave the members of the Volunteer Group their nickname, Flying Tigers.

The Flying Tigers flew against the Japanese in both Burma and China before they were inducted into the Army Air Forces in July, 1942. Chennault was recalled to active duty, promoted to the rank of brigadier general in the Army Air Forces, and early in 1943, given command of the Fourteenth Air Force, which had begun operations in China.

General Claire L. Chennault (far right) and members
of the 14th Air Force display the Flying Tiger emblem.

The most famous Flying Tiger was Colonel Robert L. Scott who wrote a best-selling book entitled "God Is My Co-Pilot." He is shown here in the cockpit of his P–40 shortly after shooting down a Japanese Zero.

The North American P–51 replaced the P–40 later in the war. Here is another well-known Flying Tiger pilot, Colonel David (Tex) Hill entering his P–51 for a combat mission.

Movie actress Ann Sheridan and her USO troupe entertain servicemen in northern Burma. During World War II the USO sponsored the overseas tours of over a thousand groups of entertainers.

Japanese warship under attack by an Army Air Forces B–25 near Amoy, China, 6 April 1945; some enemy survivors can be seen in the water as others cling to the side of the wreckage.

Allied military leaders confer on China–India–Burma strategy; (left to right), Brigadier General Claire L. Chennault, 14th Air Force Commander; Lieutenant General Joseph W. Stilwell, CBI Theatre Commanding General; and Sir John Dill, the British Commander.

The head of the Chinese government, Generalissimo Chiang Kai-shek and Madam Chiang Kai-shek discuss strategy with President Franklin Delano Roosevelt at the Cairo Conference (November 25, 1943).

ALLIES ATTACK JAPANESE HOME ISLANDS: SUMMER 1945

Since they could make no effort to restore the situation in China, Allied forces in the Pacific, during the summer of 1945, stepped up the pace of air and naval attacks against Japan. In June and July carrier-based planes of the U.S. Pacific Fleet and Army Air Forces planes from the Marianas, Iwo Jima, and Okinawa struck the Japanese home islands continuously. During July, Pacific Fleet surface units bombarded Japan's east coast, and in the same month a British carrier task force joined in attacking on Japan. Meanwhile, Army planes from the Philippines hit Japanese shipping in the South China Sea, and extended their strikes as far as Formosa and targets along the South China coast. At the same time American submarines redoubled their efforts to sweep Japanese shipping from the sea and sever the shipping lanes from Japan to the Indies and southeast Asia. Throughout the war submarines had preyed on Japanese merchant and combat vessels, playing a major role in isolating Japan from its conquests and thereby drastically reducing Japan's ability to wage war.

After Germany's surrender in May, the United States had embarked upon a huge logistical effort to redeploy more than a million troops from Europe, the United States, and other inactive theatres to the Pacific. The aim was to complete the redeployment in time to launch an invasion of Japan on 1 November. MacArthur and Nimitz had been sparing no efforts to expand ports and ready bases to receive the expected influx. They were also completing plans for the invasion of Japan, the Joint Chiefs-of-Staff having appointed MacArthur to the command of all U.S. Army forces

in the Pacific, simultaneously giving Nimitz control of all U.S. Navy elements.

By midsummer of 1945 most responsible leaders in Japan realized that the end was near. In June, those favoring peace began to come out in the open, and Japan sent out peace feelers through the Soviet Union, which they feared might also be about to enter the war. As early as the Yalta Conference of February 1945, Churchill, Roosevelt, and Stalin had discussed Russian participation in the war against Japan, and throughout 1945 American planners understood that Russia would come into the war three months after the defeat of Germany. At the Potsdam Conference in July 1945, Russia reaffirmed its decision to declare war on Japan. At this conference the United States and Britain, with China joining in, issued the famed Potsdam Declaration calling upon Japan to surrender promptly, and about the same time President Truman decided to employ the newly tested atomic bomb against Japan in the event of continued Japanese resistance.

Dropping the Atomic Bomb on Hiroshima: 6 August 1945

Despite the changing climate of opinion in Japan, the Japanese did not immediately accept the terms of the Potsdam Declaration. Accordingly, on 6 August a lone American B–29 from the Marianas dropped an atomic bomb on Hiroshima. On the 9th the Soviet Union came into the war and attacked Japanese forces in Manchuria; on the same day another B-29 dropped a second atomic bomb on Nagasaki. The next day Japan sued for peace, and with the signing of surrender terms aboard the U.S.S. **Missouri** in Tokyo Bay on 2 September the bitter global war had come to an end.

The U.S. Third Fleet off the coast of Japan. While the air strikes were going on, the surface warships were steaming up and down the east coast of Honshu shelling enemy installations. During these attacks by aircraft and surface vessels, steel-producing centers, transportation facilities, and military installations were struck; hundreds of enemy aircraft were destroyed or crippled; and most of the ships of the Japanese Imperial Fleet were either sunk or damaged.

Destruction of buildings by incendiary bombs in Osaka, Japan's second largest city. The bombing of Japan's key industrial cities was stepped up from less than 2,000 tons of bombs dropped during December 1944 to over 40,000 tons dropped in July 1945. More and more bombers were sent against Japan with less fighter opposition until, by the end of July, the targets were announced in advance of the raids. This did much to undermine the civilian morale, and the people began to realize that the end of the war was close at hand.

Enemy cruisers anchored in the Japanese naval base at Kure Harbor, Honshu, being bombed by U.S. naval carrier planes. On 10 July 1945 carrier-based planes struck the Tokyo area, concentrating on airfields. This was the first of a series of attacks by aircraft and surface warships of the U.S. and British fleets. In late July attacks were carried out against enemy warships anchored in the harbors of Honshu.

This is an atomic bomb of the "Little Boy," or uranium, type that was dropped on Hiroshima. It was 28 inches in diameter, 120 inches long and weighed 9,000 pounds. Its yield was equivalent to 20,000 tons of high explosive. Scientists were so sure that the "Little Boy" would work that it was not tested before it was used in combat.

The atom bomb was the result of long years of research into the nature of the atom and the energy that could be obtained by splitting it. By 1939 it appeared possible that an extremely powerful bomb could be created through the splitting of uranium or plutonium nuclei. The physicist Albert Einstein informed President Roosevelt of this, and urged that the United States develop such a bomb before the Axis powers did.

Research went forward in the United States, slowly at first, then more rapidly after the Japanese attack on Pearl Harbor. As the awesome nature of the atom bomb became more apparent, doubts were raised about using it as a weapon. Germany surrendered before the first bomb was ready, and it became a question of whether or not to use the bomb against the Japanese. The alternative was an invasion of Japan at the cost of millions of lives.

The decision was made to use the bomb as soon as it was ready, and in the B–29 the United States Army Air Forces had a plane capable of delivering such a bomb to the target.

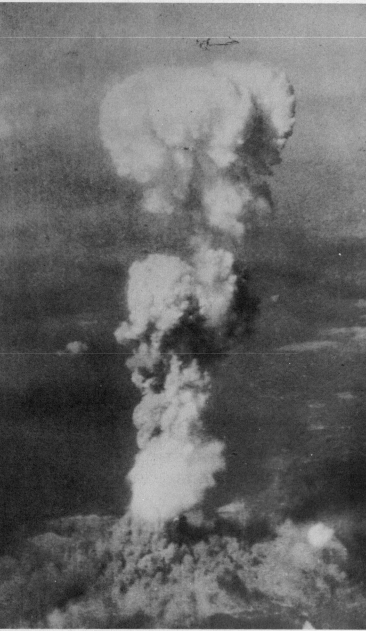

The bombing of Hiroshima with the first atomic bomb to be used against an enemy, 6 August 1945. With the refusal of the enemy to accept the unconditional surrender terms of the Potsdam Proclamation, it was decided to release a single atomic bomb from a Superfortress. The city chosen for the attack was Hiroshima, where important Japanese military installations were located.

676

Hiroshima was approximately 60 percent destroyed by the bomb. Ground zero (the point on the ground directly below the air burst of the bomb) was approximately in the center of the photograph. (The picture was taken a year after the atomic bomb was dropped.)

Atomic bombing of Nagasaki, 9 August 1945. This was the second atomic bomb to be dropped on a Japanese city.

An atomic bomb of the "Fat Man," or plutonium, type that was detonated over Nagasaki. It was 60 inches in diameter and 128 inches long. It weighed 10,000 pounds and its yield was 20,000 tons of high explosive. This bomb was tested by the Army at Alamogordo, New Mexico, on July 16, 1945. More advanced than the "Little Boy," its blast effect was greater.

A portion of Nagasaki after the atomic bomb was dropped. Nagasaki was a large industrial center and an important port on the west coast of Kyushu. About 45 percent of the city was destroyed by the bomb.

Damage at Nagasaki, showing large areas where most of the buildings were leveled. Buildings constructed of reinforced concrete suffered less than other types. The circular structure, at lower center, is the Ohashi Gas Works, approximately 3,200 feet north of ground zero.

General MacArthur signs the surrender documents.

Aboard the battleship USS "Missouri" just before the Japanese surrender ceremony, Tokyo Bay, 2 September 1945. This formally ended the three years and eight months of war in the Pacific and marked the defeat of the Axis Powers.

A Japanese watching U.S. troops landing on the beach at Waka-yama, Honshu.

With bowed heads, these Japanese prisoners of war at a POW camp on Guam listen to a radio broadcast made by Emperor Hirohito to announce the defeat and unconditional surrender of Japan.

U.S. B–29's flying over the USS "Missouri" during the surrender ceremony.

U.S. and Japanese photographers taking pictures of U.S. troops landing at Tateyama, Japan. Following the defeat of Japan, Allied troops landed on the Japanese islands to begin their occupational duties. The invasion of Japan had been planned, but the surrender of the enemy made assault landings unnecessary. However, many troops and much of the equipment landed over the beaches.

V-J Day Parade in Honolulu. The total of U.S. Army casualties in the global war was nearly 950,000, including almost 330,000 killed in battle. Of the total, the war against Japan accounted for approximately 175,000 casualties, including about 52,000 killed. In the South and Southwest Pacific Areas 72 combat landing operations were carried out in less than three years.

Waving the flags of the United States, Great Britain and Holland, Allied prisoners of war cheer wildly as units of the United States fleet aproach their camp in August, 1945.

General of the Army Douglas MacArthur greets Lt. Gen. Jonathan Wainwright (right), captured commander at Corregidor, and Lt. Gen. A. E. Percival (left), British commander at Singapore, after their release from a Japanese prisoner-of-war camp.

ARMY, CORPS, AND DIVISION INSIGNIA
(WORLD WAR II)

Army Ground Forces

Army Air Forces

Army Service Forces

First Army

Second Army

Third Army

Fourth Army

Fifth Army

Sixth Army

Seventh Army

Eighth Army

Fourteenth Army

I Corps

II Corps

III Corps

IV Corps

V Corps

VI Corps

VII Corps

VIII Corps

IX Corps

X Corps

XI Corps

XII Corps

XIII Corps

XIV Corps

XV Corps

XVI Corps   XVIII Corps   XIX Corps   XX Corps   XXI Corps

XXII Corps   XXIII Corps   XXXI Corps   XXXIII Corps

DIVISIONS

First Division   Second Division   Third Division

Fourth Division   Fifth Division   Sixth Division   Seventh Division   Eighth Division   Ninth Division   Tenth Light Division

Eleventh Division   Fourteenth Division   Seventeenth Division   Twenty-second Division   Twenty-fourth Division   Twenty-sixth Division

Twenty-eighth Division   Twenty-ninth Division   Thirtieth Division

Thirty-first
Division

Thirty-second
Division

Thirty-third
Division

Thirty-fourth
Division

Thirty-fifth
Division

Thirty-sixth
Division

Thirty-seventh
Division

Thirty-eighth
Division

Fortieth Division

Forty-first Division

Forty-second Division

Forty-third Division

Forty-fourth Division

Forty-fifth Division

Forty-sixth Division

Forty-eighth Division

Fiftieth Division

Fifty-fifth
Division

Fifty-ninth Division

Sixty-third Division

Sixty-fifth
Division

Sixty-sixth
Division

Sixty-ninth Division

Seventieth Division

Seventy-first
Division

Seventy-fifth
Division

Seventy-sixth
Division

Seventy-seventh
Division

Seventy-eighth Division

Seventy-ninth Division

Eightieth Division

Eighty-first Division

Eighty-third
Division

683

Eighty-fourth
Division

Eighty-fifth
Division

Eighty-sixth
Division

Eighty-seventh
Division

Eighty-eighth
Division

Eighty-ninth
Division

Ninetieth Division

Ninety-first
Division

Ninety-second
Division

Ninety-third Division

Ninety-fourth Division

Ninety-fifth Division

Ninety-sixth Division

Ninety-seventh
Division

Ninety-eighth
Division

Ninety-ninth
Division

One Hundredth
Division

One Hundred Second
Division

One Hundred Third
Division

One Hundred Fourth
Division

One Hundred Sixth
Division

One Hundred Eighth
Division

One Hundred Nineteenth
Division

One Hundred Thirtieth
Division

One Hundred Forty-first
Division

One Hundred Fifty-
seventh Division

Philippine Division

AIRBORNE DIVISIONS

Sixth Airborne
Division

Ninth Airborne
Division

Eleventh Airborne
Division

Thirteenth Airborne
Division

Seventeenth Airborne
Division

Eighteenth Airborne
Division

Twenty-first Airborne
Division

Eighty-second
Airborne Division

One Hundred First
Airborne Division

One Hundred Thirty-fifth
Airborne Division

CAVALRY DIVISIONS

First
Cavalry Division

Second
Cavalry Division

Third Cavalry
Division

Twenty-fourth
Cavalry Division

Sixty-first
Cavalry Division

Sixty-second
Cavalry Division

Sixty-third
Cavalry Division

Sixty-fourth
Cavalry Division

Sixty-fifth
Cavalry Division

Sixty-sixth
Cavalry Division

Armored Division

Americal Division

Checking medical records at a processing station at Le Havre, France. The "over forty-two" soldiers were being sent home for discharge in May, 1945.

CHAPTER 16

THE U.S. ARMY, 1945-1950

One of the chief reactions to the coming of peace in 1945 was the desire of Americans to return immediately to normal life. The meant converting industry from the production of armaments to civilian goods, drastically cutting armament expenditures, and sharply reducing military strength. Demobilization became the Army's most immediate and pressing problem.

DEMOBILIZATION PLANS

Planning for demobilization of the Army began in 1943, over two years before the end of the war. As a basis for planning, officials of the War Department assumed that (1) the United States would emerge as the world's foremost military power and would be prepared for action in many parts of the world; (2) the war in Europe would terminate before the Japanese surrender; (3) the United States would furnish an important share of large-scale occupation troops; and (4) public opinion would demand a rapid demobilization. The initial planning was based on the amount of shipping that would become available for transferring the troops, and the number of troops to be deployed to the Pacific to speed up the offensive against the Japanese. For planning purposes it was estimated that the war against Japan would last at least a year after the surrender of Germany. During this interim, the first demobilization period, the flaws that developed in the demobilization system could be eliminated and the system would undergo considerable revision before being used after final victory. The second period of demobilization would be that following the defeat of Japan but prior to the attainment of normal peacetime conditions; and the third period that in which the Army would be composed of permanent military personnel.

Although the unit system of demobilization had been the type most often used in the past by the United States Army and had many advantages, still the troops in World War II had been mobilized on an individual basis and, therefore, the proponents for the individual system argued, should be discharged individually. The natural outgrowth of this method was the Adjusted Service Rating or "point system." This method gave each individual a number of points for length of service, combat participation and awards, time spent overseas, and parenthood. By these impartial means those men who had been in the service the longest and participated in combat would be released from the service first.

The actual demobilization plan, including the basic policies and the execution, was set forth in draft form in August 1944 although the specific points were not finally decided on until 23 April 1945. Immediately on the surrender of Germany, 8 May, it was announced that redeployment would begin on 12 May. Planning was immediately started on the second period demobilization, based on the assumption that V-J Day would not take place for 18 months. But the surrender of Japan in August 1945 left the War Department with incomplete plans. Consequently the current plan was modified and emergency provisions quickly drawn up. At the end of fiscal year 1946 the Army's strength of 1,889,690 represented a decrease of 6,133,614 in the 9-month period that followed V-J Day. From then on the decline became more gradual. The reasons behind this rapid demobilization were varied. They included: public pressure on the Army to speed up the return of personnel to civil life; the lack of men under voluntary enlistment; a decreasing budget; the nonworkable selective service extension of 1946; and the terminal leave act of the same year.

The "General J. R. Brooke" arrives at Newport News, Virginia,
from Europe in July, 1945.

The War Department, meanwhile, had instituted an intensive recruiting campaign that brought in over one million volunteers by October 1946 and returned the Army to its authorized strength. Because of this the War Department decided not to induct any more men under the Selective Service Act, and the Act was allowed to expire. The Army then completed its demobilization program by 30 June 1947 when the last nonvolunteers were discharged.

THE NATIONAL SECURITY ACT OF 1947

Postwar changes in the Armed Forces were designed to attain effective military strength at a minimum cost to the economy and to provide the means of implementing national policy by coordinating military planning with that of other departments and agencies of the Government. Congress enacted the necessary legislation to effect these changes with the passage of the National Security Act in 1947. This legislation, as the act states, was intended "to provide for the establishment of integrated policies and procedures for the departments, agencies and functions of the Government relating to national security . . . to provide for the effective strategic direction of the armed forces and for their operation under unified control and for their integration into an efficient team of land, naval and air forces." The principal features of the act were creation of the National Security Council, organization of the National Military Establishment

headed by a Secretary of Defense, and establishment of the Air Force as a separate arm.

The National Security Council consisted of the President, the Secretaries of State and Defense, the Service Secretaries, and the Chairman of the National Security Resources Board. (This latter body also was authorized by the Act.) The National Security Council advised the President on matters of coordinating military, foreign, and domestic policies as they pertained to national defense. Specifically, the Council made recommendations to the President on national policies with relationship to the Nation's military strength. The Council also advised the Chief Executive on policies pertaining to national security as they affected the several departments of Government. Finally, the Council, as directed by the President, coordinated the policies of the several departments that related to national security.

Prior to World War II, proposals designed to bring the Armed Forces under unified command had few positive results. The World War II arrangements for joint strategic direction and for unity of command in the theatres were applied with outstanding success, but they did not carry with them any corresponding unity in the administrative establishments of the War and Navy Departments. And the wartime arrangements were temporary ones that gave way to separatist tendencies at war's end, particularly in the Pacific.

During the war a number of studies were made, and

plans drawn up by the War Department, the Joint Chiefs of Staff, and individual legislators, for uniting the Army and Navy under a single head. After the war the Army continued its efforts at unification but met strong opposition from the Navy. On the other hand, the Army Air Forces supported unification, with the additional objective of attaining status as a separate and equal service.

The unification provisions of the National Security Act were essentially a compromise between the Army's desire for strong centralized control vested in a single Secretary and the Navy's desire for separate and autonomous departments. The National Military Establishment, as provided by the Act, consisted of the Departments of the Army, Navy, and Air Force, and the Office of the Secretary of Defense. Included within the latter were the Joint Chiefs of Staff, the Munitions Board, and the Research and Development Board. The Secretary of Defense was made a member of the President's Cabinet and became responsible for formulating general policy in the Establishment, exercising general direction and control over the armed forces and supervision of the Department's budgets. He was also charged with coordinating the logistics systems of the various services to eliminate waste and duplication. In his efforts he was to have the assistance of the Munitions Board, charged with

planning for the military aspects of industrial mobilization and coordination of military production, procurement, and distribution plans, and of the Research and Development Board, charged with responsibility for formulation of the military research and development program. Each service retained most of its autonomy since all three were to be "separately administered" as executive departments under the Secretary of Defense, and each had direct access to the President and representation on the National Security Council through its civilian secretary. The act implicitly recognized the role claimed for air power by its proponents by making the Air Force a separate and independent service. Finally, the National Security Act made the Joint Chiefs of Staff a statutory body and charged them with the function of acting as "principal military advisers to the President, the National Security Council, and the Secretary of Defense." Under the direction and authority of the President and the Secretary of Defense, the Joint Chiefs were to be responsible for the formulation of strategic plans, joint logistic plans, joint training policies and policies for coordinating military education, for review of major materiel and personnel requirements of all armed services in the light of strategic plans, establishment of unified commands in strategic areas, and "strategic direction of the Military Forces."

Training recruits to fire the rifle grenade at Camp Crowder, Missouri, in 1946.

The Peacetime Army

Tank-infantry team instruction at Fort Benning, Georgia, in 1948.

688

Students at the Army's Mountain and Winter Warfare Training School, Camp Carson, Colorado, work out a field problem.

Root Hall at the Army War College, Carlisle Barracks, Pennsylvania. The War College, which reopened after World War II, prepares selected officers for high command and staff positions.

The National Security Act did not spell out the particular roles and missions of the three services or their relationship to the Joint Chiefs and the unified commands they were to establish. On these points broad interservice agreements were reached at Key West and Newport in 1948. By these agreements, the JCS were to have general direction of all combat operations but would not exercise this authority directly as a corporate body. Instead they would designate "one of their members as their executive agent" for each of the unified commands. In the division of service responsibilities, the Army was given the primary functions of organizing, equipping and training forces for operations on land, providing Army forces for air defense of the United States and occupation of territories abroad. The Navy and Air Forces were assigned similar functions of preparing forces for sea and land-based operations respectively. The Navy retained control of sea-based aviation and of the Marine Corps with the tactical aviation that supported it. Otherwise, Air Force jurisdiction over everything that flew was virtually complete, including strategic air warfare, air transport, and combat air support of the Army. No mention at all was made of the relatively new field of guided missiles.

689

CHANGES IN ORGANIZATION

Within the Army a number of changes took place in the tactical organization of field units as a result of both experience gained in World War II and the development of new weapons. Most of these changes reflected the great emphasis on firepower and mobility. For instance, the emergence of the tank-infantry-artillery team as a dominant factor in the tactical employment of ground troops led to the inclusion of a tank battalion in the organization of the infantry division and a tank company in the infantry regiment. At the same time the cannon and antitank companies were dropped from the regiment, but the loss of these weapons was made up by adding a 4.2" mortar company and recoilless rifles to the regiment. Division firepower was increased by adding an antiaircraft battalion and by upping the number of howitzers in each artillery battery from four to six. Research for better clothing, rations, engineer, transportation, signal, and other equipment resulted in vast improvement of these items. The success of airborne operations in the war and the necessity for rapid deployment of troops in combat led to further refinements in this form of troop employment. In the field of nuclear fission and jet and rocket propulsion the Ordnance Corps launched a long-range program to explore the use of these new forces. The Corps' research centered upon development of atomic artillery projectiles and guided ground-to-ground and ground-to-air missiles as a further addition to the firepower of field armies. At the same time the Ordnance Corps continued research to improve the standard weapons. One new type of weapon, the recoilless rifle, emerged from this research shortly after the end of the war. Light enough to be hand-carried, these rifles fired 57-m and 75-mm high explosive shells without any recoil, thereby greatly increasing the firepower of the infantry. During World War II the Navy and Air Force took over the mission of seacoast defense while the Coast Artillery Corps, which had been charged principally with harbor defense, devoted its efforts almost exclusively to antiaircraft artillery, which frequently performed a dual role by delivering fire on ground targets. Consequently, in the interest of flexibility and economy of force, the antiaircraft artillery was merged with the field artillery, and the Coast Artillery Corps was abolished. Similarly the mechanization of the Army made the horse cavalry obsolete. Before the end of World War II the horse cavalry had either been mechanized or fought as infantry. In the reorganization armor was made a continuation of the cavalry with all the traditions and honors of the earlier arm.

The Army's First Guided Missiles

A V–2 rocket, brought to the United States from Germany after World War II, is ready for testing at the Army's White Sands Proving Ground in New Mexico.

The WAC Corporal missile at the White Sands Proving Ground. The Corporal, a surface-to-surface missile, was developed to support ground operations.

The Army school system came in for its share of reorganization and refinement after World War II. The scope of instruction was broadened to keep abreast of the development of new weapons and new strategical and tactical concepts. The interdependence of foreign and military policies and the armed services, as illustrated in the war, placed greater emphasis on the joint aspects of all military operations while the technical advances made during and after the conflict called for highly specialized training of officers and enlisted men.

The requirements of a strong postwar force for national security called for changes in the status and organization of the country's Reserve components. As inheritors of the militia system that dated back to colonial times, the National Guard and the Organized Reserve Corps had played a major part in America's participation in both world wars. Now, the speed with which modern war can be initiated and the advances in the technology of warfare placed the emphasis on actual rather than potential strength. Because it was not economically feasible to maintain a large and permanent ground force, the Army, shortly after the end of the war, began reorganization of the Reserve components in order to make them an integral part of the Army of the United States and to bring them to a state of readiness for combat. The goal of this reorganization was a National Guard capable of immediate mobilization, with fully trained and equipped units ready to fight anywhere in the world in defense of the United States, and an Organized Reserve Corps trained and organized for rapid mobilization and expansion to supplement the Regular Army and National Guard. Both components began working toward accomplishment of their respective missions. With an authorized strength of 350,000 men (its actual strength was about 75,000 less) the National Guard organized infantry and armored divisions, regimental combat teams, artillery battalions, and supporting units. The Reserve Corps, with 750,000 men on its rolls, organized along similar lines. Both components established training programs under active Arm guidance. The enactment, in 1948, of Selective Service and legislation that authorized inactive duty training pay and retirement benefits added impetus to this program. As a result of these efforts the National Guard and Organized Reserve Corps contributed hundreds of thousands of trained men during the Korean conflict.

Since combat effectiveness is as dependent upon morale as it is upon training and weapons, the Army took steps to improve the welfare of its troops. In late 1945 the War Department appointed a board of officers, headed by Lieutenant General James Doolittle, to explore methods whereby the personal welfare of the individual soldier could be improved. The board put forward many recommendations that were adopted in one form or another. For instance, the board restated the well-known principle that **esprit de corps** depended on leadership, and that leadership could be improved by better selection of officers and noncommissioned officers. The board recommended that these leaders be given more effective training. The Department of Defense adopted the "Uniform Code of Military Justice" to apply to all the services. As another step, the troop information and education program, established during the war, became a permanent function of command. The chief objectives of this program were to impart to the individual soldier a cooperative spirit in accomplishing any mission, pride in his unit and himself, and appreciation of worldwide happenings in order that he might understand the necessity for his service. The program also continued the opportunity for the individual soldier to improve and increase his education so that he might better perform his current assignment and prepare himself for positions of increasing responsibility.

AMERICAN OVERSEAS FORCES

The U.S. Army overseas during this period was deployed over a large part of the world, carrying out a number of various missions. The larger part of this force was concentrated in Germany and Japan to carry out United States occupation policies.

American occupation policy in Europe stemmed from the agreements made by Prime Minister Churchill, President Roosevelt, and Premier Joseph Stalin at Yalta in February 1945 and elaborated upon at the Potsdam Conference in July 1945. In brief, these agreements called for the complete disarmament and demilitarization of Germany, elimination of all vestiges of the Nazi party, and reconstruction of political life on democratic principles. In the economic field Germany was forbidden to manufacture armaments, and the production of consumer goods and agricultural products was stressed. Also, Germany was divided into four zones of occupation—British, French, Soviet, and American—for purposes of administering the occupation, but economically it was to be treated as a single unit. The city of Berlin, deep within the Soviet Zone, was similarly divided, thus creating further fragmentation within a divided country and complicating the problems of occupation. Reparations were to be paid by the removal of stipulated industries and by the appropriation of external German assets. Each zone commander governed his own zone. Matters concerning Germany as a whole were dealt with by the Allied Control Council, which consisted of the four zone commanders.

The Army carried out its occupation responsibilities chiefly through the Office of Military Government for Germany. This office took measures to disband the German military forces in the American Zone. More than eight million German soldiers, sailors, and airmen were returned to civil life after careful screening. German military installations in the zone were disposed of or destroyed along with factories employed to manufacture arms. Military Government also prevented a resurgence of armament manufacture by keeping close surveillance of the remaining German industries and setting a level of production that restricted industries readily convertible to the making of arms.

Destruction of the Nazi party proceeded rapidly. Military and civilian personnel accused or suspected of war crimes and all members of the party who were more than nominal participants were apprehended. German courts of "denazification," closely supervised by Army personnel, tried over 800,000 German men and women on various charges. Meanwhile an international tribunal tried the major leaders of the Nazi party for crimes against humanity. Of these, 10 were eventually executed. Removal of Nazis from all public offices, from the courts, and from the police or-

The U.S. Army's 12th Armored Division passes in review in Schwäbisch, Germany, in the summer of 1945.

The Occupation Armies

An American infantryman on guard duty in Salzburg, Austria.

General of the Army Douglas MacArthur arrives at Atsugi Airport, Japan, to take over as Supreme Commander for the occupation of Japan.

General Lucius D. Clay, the American Military Governor of Germany.

ganization; abolition of party propaganda; and the institution of free elections completed the destruction of Hitler's organization. Meanwhile, in the absence of a German government, the Office of Military Government for Germany governed the zone. The edicts of Military Government for control of the population and for the general security of the United States Zone were enforced through the U.S. Constabulary. This special, highly mobile force operated throughout the whole zone as a police force to maintain order and discipline among the people and to detect and prevent uprising.

In contrast to the procedures adopted for the German occupation, the Big Three Powers did not lay down any general policy for governing Japan. Instead, the United States, acting for the United Nations, assumed exclusive control of the defeated nation and established the occupation policy to be followed. This policy, drawn up jointly by the War, Navy, and State Departments and approved by President Truman, stripped Japan of all her empire and limited her sovereignty to the Japanese home islands, disarmed and demilitarized the nation, encouraged the development of a democratic government, and permitted development of an economy to meet the peacetime require-

ments of the Japanese people. Finally, the policy called for military occupation under a Supreme Commander, Allied Powers, to enforce the surrender and control of Japan but charged the Supreme Commander to work through the Japanese Government, including the emperor, whenever possible.

General of the Army Douglas MacArthur became Supreme Commander for the occupation of Japan and immediately began implementing the program. In September 1945 General MacArthur directed the Japanese Government to demobilize and dissolve the country's armed forces. The Government accomplished the actual tasks without incident under the supervision of the occupation army. By December 1945 all elements of the military forces of Japan in the home islands were disbanded. At the same time high officials of the Army and Navy and of the Government were arrested and tried for war crimes. An international tribunal, similar to the one in Germany, sat in judgment on 25 of these officials Seven were given the death penalty and subsequently executed. Lesser officials were tried and sentenced by United States military commissions in Japan.

Removal of the militarists from power enabled the more democratic elements to transform the Japanese Gov-

On sentry duty in Tokyo.

Men of the First Cavalry Division raise the American flag over Tokyo in September 1945.

693

Two members of the U.S. occupation forces in Japan visit a Buddhist shrine.

The first Secretary of Defense, James V. Forrestal.

ernment into a constitutional democracy. Under supervision of the Supreme Commander, extensive political and governmental reorganization took place. By 1948 the legislation necessary to implement the new constitution, adopted the previous year, had been enacted and the Diet emerged as the representative body of the people.

Soviet counteraction to American efforts to rebuild the European economy came swiftly. Besides rejecting participation in the program, the Russians, in October 1947, announced the organization of a permanent committee for coordinating the activities of the Communist parties in Europe. Then, in 1948, Soviet military authorities in Berlin began cutting off the city from the rest of western Europe.

In Berlin each occupying power administered its own sector, and matters pertaining to the city as a whole were supposed to be settled in an Allied Control Council by unanimous agreement. But the discord that marked the deliberations of that body led to the division of the city into an East and West Berlin. In June 1948 the Russians cut off all land and water traffic between Western Germany and Berlin, and the only means of entry was by air. General Lucius D. Clay, the American Military Governor of Germany, then called on the Air Force to supply the city with food and other necessities by air. From June 1948 to May 1949 the Air Force and the Army, working together, kept the city supplied. Hundreds of American aircraft (there were also some British planes operating in this airlift) daily flew thou-

sands of tons of food, clothing, coal, and other vital goods into the western sectors of Berlin. By the spring of 1949 a daily average of 8,000 tons of supplies reached the capital by air.

In addition to calling for the airlift, General Clay immediately halted all shipments of goods from West Germany into the Soviet Zone of Germany. The British commander imposed a similar restriction, and by the spring of 1948 East Germany felt the shortage of industrial goods and materiel that she normally received from the West. The successful efforts of the Air Force and the Army to keep the city supplied and the Anglo-American counterblockade brought realization to the Communists that their efforts to drive the Western Powers out of Berlin had failed, and the blockade of the city was lifted 12 May 1949.

Although the failure of the Berlin blockade demonstrated American ability to counter Soviet moves, stronger measures were needed to block any further extension of Communist power. A beginning toward collective security in Europe was made in early 1948 when the Low Countries, England, and France signed a treaty of mutual economic and military assistance. This was followed by Senate authorization for the United States to enter into defensive alliances to preserve peace. This action cleared the way for the United States to join with Canada and the powers of Western Europe in the North Atlantic Treaty which provided for mutual assistance, including the use of armed force in the event of attack upon one or more of the signatory powers. To make the treaty an effective instrument rather than a paper agreement, the member nations established a supreme military headquarters in Europe under the command of General Eisenhower to organize and plan the defense of western Europe and its approaches. Each country earmarked forces to be placed under this command, which received the title of Supreme Headquarters, Allied Powers Europe.

While negotiations leading to the North Atlantic Treaty were under way in 1948, the National Security Council had been considering the matter of military aid to non-Communist nations. Under a number of different programs, some of them a continuation of World War II aid, the United States had made military equipment and training assistance available to Greece, Turkey, Iran, China, Korea, the Philippines, and the Latin American republics. The National Security Council now recommended that such aid be extended to the North Atlantic Treaty members and that all the separate aid programs be combined into one. Following President Truman's approval of the recommendation, legislation was drafted, and in October 1949 Congress passed the bill providing for a Mutual Defense Assistance Program. To implement the program the Department of the Army, as the executive agency, sent each recipient country a military assistance advisory group. Composed of Army, Navy, and Air Force sections, each group advised and assisted the government to which it was sent in determining the amount and type of aid needed. In addition, these advisory groups trained the armed forces of each country in the use and tactical employment of the materiel and equipment it received from the United States.

FURTHER DEFENSE REORGANIZATION

During this period the United Stated was looking to its own defense organization. The National Security Act of 1947 had brought the nation's armed forces under unified control.

But a major weakness was revealed when unified control began operating. As pointed out by Mr. Kenneth C. Royall, Army Secretary, this weakness lay in the fact that each Department still maintained its self-sufficiency within the framework of the National Military Establishment, and decisions thus had to be reached by mutual cooperation. He felt that military organizations could not operate on the voluntary cooperation theory, and that unification should be strengthened by giving the Secretary of Defense stronger control over the three Departments. The first Secretary of Defense, Mr. James V. Forrestal, brought the proposals of the Secretary of the Army to the attention of the President, who asked the Congress for legislation. In 1949 Congress changed the name of the National Military Establishment to the Department of Defense, enlarged the membership of the National Security Council to include the Vice President, increased the powers of the Secretary of Defense, and provided a Chairman of the Joint Chiefs of Staff. The Departments of the Army, Navy, and Air Force lost their status as executive departments and became separate military establishments under the control of the Department of Defense.

Following the unification of the armed forces the Congress passed the Army Reorganization Act in 1950. The chief objectives of this legislation, as stated by General J. Lawton Collins, then Army Chief of Staff, were to achieve simplicity and flexibility in the Army's statutory organization. The Act of 1950 eliminated or revised previous legislation pertaining to Army organization, some of which dated as far back as the War of 1812. It made the Secretary of the Army directly responsible for conducting all the affairs of the Army. At the same time it gave him the broad powers necessary to carry out this responsibility. It placed the Army staff under his direct control by permitting him the right to establish the duties and powers of the staff. In addition, the act permitted the Secretary of the Army to assign some of his duties to the Under Secretary and Assistant Secretary of

The U.S. 7th Division marches into Seoul in 1945 to occupy the city formally. The division was made up of veterans of the Okinawa Campaign.

the Army, although responsibility still rested with the Secretary of the Army. The Army Chief of Staff became responsible for carrying out the approved plans and policies of the Department of the Army. He had supervision of all personnel and units of the Army and was responsible to the Secretary of the Army for the Army's efficiency, combat readiness and plans for operational employment. Tactical organization of the Army was left to the Secretary of the Army, who could create such commands and forces as he deemed best. Field training came under the supervision of the chief of the Army Field Forces. His function was to supervise the Army's training, develop tactical doctrine, control the Army's school system, and keep the Chief of Staff informed on the status of the field units' combat readiness. The act also placed both the Transportation and Military Police Corps, organized on a temporary basis during the war, on a permanent footing within the structure of the Army. Finally, all the technical services, except the Medical Department, received the designation "Corps." The Medical Department became the Army Medical Service and embraced all phases of the Army's medical activities.

The home of the Department of Defense, the Pentagon, in Arlington, Virginia.

ARMY UNIFORMS OF THE TWENTIETH CENTURY

Representative of the reforms in dress since 1898 are these infantrymen in the Philippine Islands in 1903. Their uniform is the khaki tropical service dress with bronze buttons first adopted in 1898. Utility and suitability for field service were the keynote for this dress, simple in cut and with a minimum of ornamentation. The drab campaign hat, distinctively American, became the official head covering and was the most liked by the soldier.

In the left foreground is a first lieutenant with the gold hat cord and bronze coat of arms of the United States on his standing collar, both worn by all officers of the Army. On his coat he wears the silver shoulder bar of his rank, and on his collar bronze crossed rifles indicate his arm, the

infantry. The lieutenant's breeches are laced from the calf nearly to the knee and are close fitting to go under his russet leather leggings.

The sergeant in the right foreground is in the same uniform as the lieutenant. In place of the lieutenant's leather leggings he wears khaki canvas ones, and his belt is the blue-gray looped cartridge belt used with the .30-caliber Krag rifle.

The privates in the background are wearing the most frequently seen version of the khaki uniform without the coat—dark navy blue wool shirt, which was a holdover from pretropical service days.

The standard field uniform of both officers and enlisted men of the American Expeditionary Forces—the AEF—in France was the wool olive drab uniform introduced into the Army during the first decade of the 20th century. The vast amounts of this material required in World War I led to the color being anything between mustard green and brown. Another item of equipment widely used in the AEF was the British "basin"-pattern steel helmet painted a drab color.

In the front center is a lieutenant colonel of artillery with the silver leaf of his rank on his shoulder strap, and the bronzed crossed cannon of artillery and the block-style letters **U.S.** on the high standing collar. Two other distinctive features of his officer's rank are the brown braid on his sleeve and his brown leather Sam Browne belt, adopted by the officers of the AEF from the British and retained in the post-World War I Army. The colonel also wears the high, brown boots prescribed for officers, a pattern much favored by the mounted men of that period.

The machine gun company first sergeant in the left foreground wears an issue olive drab uniform with the wrap-around "puttees" adopted by the AEF during the war when production difficulties slowed procurement of the canvas leggings formerly worn. His grade is indicated by the three stripes and diamond on his sleeve, the chevrons now pointed toward his shoulder rather than toward his hand as in previous times.

Among the new types of troops added to the Army's order of battle as a result of World War II experience, none was to assume a more important role than the airborne soldier.

In the right and left foreground are a private first class and a first lieutenant, and in the left background is a first sergeant, all of the 82d Airborne Division in an airborne demonstration about 1963. They are dressed in the olive green field uniforms introduced during the 1950's and are carrying the M-14 rifle. Three features mark the men as airborne soldiers: the paratrooper's boots, the special chin-strap harness worn with the helmet, and the red, white, and blue AA" insignia—worn by the 82d Division in World War I—with the "airborne" tab, added during World War II.

In the right background is a Women's Army Corps (WAC) officer passing by in her Army blue dress uniform trimmed in gold. The green background on her shoulder straps and the green stripe on her sleeve indicate her branch.

This scene at a logistical base in Japan shows the kinds of uniforms worn there in 1951.

In the left foreground is a first lieutenant of artillery from the 25th Infantry Division. He is wearing the light tan tropical worsted summer service uniform. His cap has a russet leather visor and band, gilt buttons, and the gilt United States coat of arms first adopted around the turn of the century. His rank is indicated by the silver bars on the shoulder straps, and his branch of service by the crossed gilt cannons on the lapels. Light tan trousers and russet leather shoes complete his uniform.

In the right foreground is a Medical Service private. He is an aidman assigned to a nonmedical unit to give immediate medical assistance. He is in the fatigue or field uniform of the period, in which grayish green and a faded tan are the predominant colors. He wears a steel helmet, a loose, open collar, grayish-green cotton twill jacket with plain buttons, grayish-green twill trousers, and brown leather laced boots. He carries an individual medical packet and a medical supply haversack on his drab web cartridge belt. Around his right arm he has the Geneva Convention red cross armband.

Men of the 5th Infantry and 4th Armored Division, who fought as teammates in Lieutenant General George S. Patton, Jr.'s, Third Army, show the combat uniform worn in the European theatre in early 1945. The continued trend toward protective coloration and simplicity of style can be seen in these uniforms. All are olive green, varying only in the design of the individual pieces of apparel, which were adapted to the differing needs of the various branches of the service.

In the center foreground and right background are two infantrymen, a major and his radioman. They were wearing wool trousers, the latest style cotton cloth field jacket, wool scarves, and leather gloves, but they are still using the old natural leather field shoe with the buckle top added. The covers worn over their steel helmets show adaption for varying combat conditions—dark for field and forest activities and white for winter conditions.

In the left background is a Sherman medium tank with a 76-mm. gun and members of its crew. The tankers all wear the hard composition helmet prescribed for armored troops. The tank guard wears a field jacket of suiting lined with wool and with knitted cuffs, collar, and waistband over his tanker overalls and he also wears the new all-laced combat boot.

New dress uniforms, carrying on the Army's traditional blue, were adopted in the early 1950's and a new green service uniform came into use at the end of that decade. These two uniforms, the blue dress and the green service, are shown here.

In the left foreground is a master sergeant of the 1st Armored Division in the green service uniform. His single-breasted coat has a roll collar and gilt buttons. The sergeant's green service cap has a round gilt national coat of arms in the front and gilt buttons on the black leather strap. This color of leather—black—also seen in the cap visor and the sergeant's shoes, is a change from the russet leather worn in the Army from the Spanish-American War to this time.

In the right foreground stands a major of the Transportation Corps in the Army blue dress uniform. His dark blue, single-breasted coat has gilt buttons and the letters **U.S.** in gilt on the collar. His rank is shown by the gold oak leaves on his shoulder straps and the gold embroidery on the black visor of his dark blue cap. He wears the light blue trousers with the officers' gold lace stripe down the side.

In the center foreground of this scene at the U.S. Military Academy are shown a brigadier general, his aide, a captain of field artillery, and a bugler of the 10th Cavalry. The general and his aide are in the dark blue mess jacket authorized in 1938. The general has two stripes of gold lace down the seam of his dark blue trousers. His dress cap has gold oak leaves on the blue-black velvet band and on the visor. The aide's mess jacket and his cap band show the color of the artillery—scarlet. His cap has a plain black visor, and his trousers are light blue. The corporal bugler is a member of the squadron of the 10th Cavalry stationed at West Point. His uniform is the olive drab woolen service dress with the service cap of the same color. His grade is indicated by two olive drab chevrons outlined in black on his sleeves. He has on russet leather waist belt and buckle and laced boots of the same color.

In the right background are cadets of the Military Academy in their distinctive gray uniforms trimmed with black and yellow buttons, and gold lace insignia of cadet officers' rank.

CHAPTER 17

THE KOREAN WAR

In September 1945 the United States and the Soviet Union had arbitrarily selected the 38th parallel as a convenient boundary to accept the surrender of Japanese troops stationed in Korea. The Americans took the surrender below the parallel, the Soviets above it. By agreement, a joint commission from the two occupying powers was to develop a four-power trusteeship through which the United States, the Soviet Union, the United Kingdom, and China would guide a provisional Korean Government until the Koreans were able to govern themselves. But the commission made little progress toward formation of a trusteeship, principally because Soviet members obstructed settlement by deliberately presenting demands that were unacceptable to the Americans. Meanwhile, the Soviets sponsored and abetted a Communist regime in northern Korea.

In November 1947, the United States referred the problem of Korea to the United Nations. Two months later, in January 1948, a United Nations commissions entered Korea to supervise free elections throughout the peninsula. But Soviet authorities refused to let the Commission enter North Korea, and the North Korean people did not take part in the elections. The United Nations, therefore, sponsored an elected government that became the Republic of Korea in the southern half of the peninsula. After this action both the United States and the Soviet Union withdrew their forces from Korea, and the nation was left divided. From its inception as a republic, South Korea was a target of North Korean propaganda and terrorism. The North Koreans played on nationalism, always a strong feeling among the inherently proud Koreans, and began campaigning for new elections that would unify the divided country. But, quite clearly, the North Korean plan would have made Korea a communistic state, and South Korea rejected the proposal. North Korean authorities then decided on full-scale hostilities to bring South Korea into the Soviet sphere.

On 25 June 1050, a North Korean force equivalent to 10 divisions invaded South Korea. In its narrowest sense, the invasion marked the beginning of a civil war between peoples of a divided country. In a large sense, it represented an eruption of tensions between the two great power blocs that had emerged from World War II.

There is some evidence that the North Koreans were confident they could capture all of South Korea before any outside power could intervene effectively. Their confidence was based largely on the strength of the North Korean People's Army, formed around a hard core of veterans who had fought with Soviet and Chinese forces during World War II, and afterward, as a part of Chinese Communist armies, against Nationalist China. Equipped and carefully trained by the Soviet Union during and after the occupation of Korea, the North Korean Army was, except in air and naval support, an efficient fighting force; and the infantry and armored units that crossed the parallel in the initial attack constituted some of its best forces.

By contrast, the South Korean Army of 95,000 ill-equipped and poorly trained men was a highly ineffective force. Actually it was more of a constabulary than an army. During and after the American occupation of southern Korea, an American military staff assisted the South Koreans in organizing, equipping, and training a small army. But limited equipment, restricted command authority, and a policy that allowed the South Korean Military Establishment to become no more than an internal security force made it impossible for the Americans to create an army capable of meeting a well-armed and well-trained foe.

The very first engagement of the conflict, when the North Koreans crushed South Korean defenses at the 38th parallel, demonstrated the superiority of the North Korean Army. On 28 June, three days after the opening attack, a tank-infantry force leading the main North Korean thrust entered Seoul, the South Korean capital located near the west coast 35 miles below the parallel. Secondary North Korean spearheads in central and eastern Korea kept pace with the main drive. In the face of the onslaught, the South Korean Army retreated in disorder, leaving most of its equipment behind. Whatever effectiveness it may have possessed was already lost. The North Korean Army halted, and then only briefly, to regroup before crossing the Han River below Seoul.

Stunned by this planned Communist aggression, the free world turned to the United Nations. For the first time since its founding, this world body faced a full-scale war. The existence of the United Nations now depended on how well it met the challenge.

Evacuation of Americans from Korea. A litter patient being removed from a ship in Japan. Approximately 600 U.S. citizens were taken to Japan aboard the SS "Reinholt" of the Ivarian Line on 28 June. U.S. planes provided air cover for the journey, and the evacuation was carried out without incident.

Douglas C–54 military transport plane on fire after being strafed by North Korean fighter planes, 28 June. Seoul and Kimpo airfield reportedly fell to the North Koreans on the same day. U. S. planes went into action in support of the South Korean Government, which had moved to Taejon.

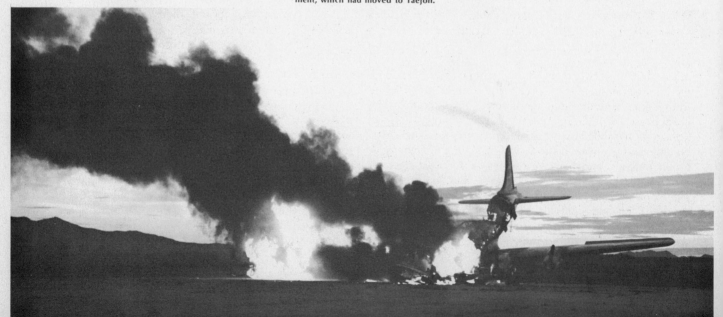

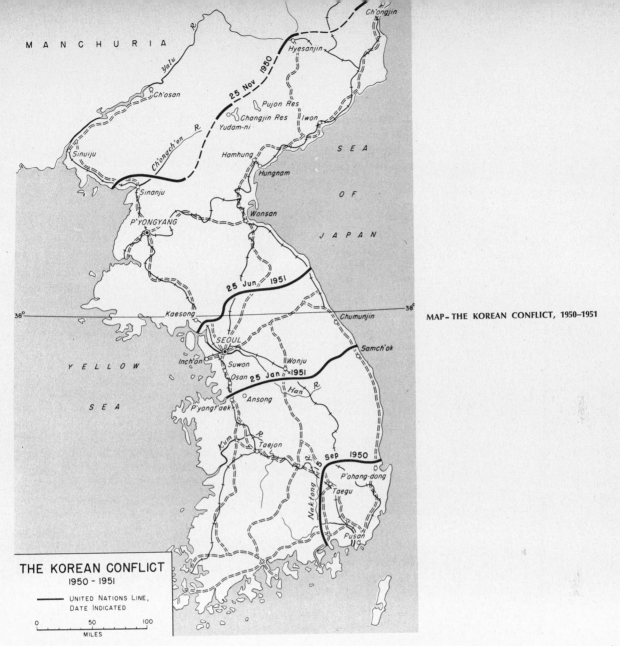

MAP – THE KOREAN CONFLICT, 1950–1951

THE KOREAN CONFLICT
1950 - 1951

—— UNITED NATIONS LINE,
DATE INDICATED

0   50   100
MILES

THE UNITED NATIONS CALLS FOR AID TO SOUTH KOREA: 27 JUNE 1950

The United Nations Organization swiftly denounced the North Korean armed aggression. On 25 June the U.N. Security Council demanded immediate cessation of hostilities and withdrawal of North Korean forces to the 38th parallel. When that failed, the Security Council, on 27 June, urged United Nations members to furnish military assistance to the South Korean republic.

Anticipating the Council's call, President Truman, on 26 June, authorized U.S. air and naval forces to attack North Korean troops and installations located in South Korea. Then on 29 June, he broadened the range of U.S. air and naval attack to targets in North Korea and authorized the use of U.S. Army troops to protect Pusan, Korea's major port at the southeastern tip of the peninsula. Meanwhile, General of the Army Douglas MacArthur, top military commander in the Far East, flew from his headquarters in Japan to Korea

to reconnoiter the battle scene. After watching South Korean troops fail in attempts to organize defenses south of the Han River, MacArthur recommended to Washington that a U.S. Army regiment be committed in the Seoul area at once and that this commitment be built up to two divisions. In response, Prsident Truman, on 30 June, authorized MacArthur to use all forces available to him.

MacArthur had at hand the 1st Cavalry, 7th, 24th, and 25th Infantry Divisions, all under the U.S. Eighth Army in Japan, and the 29th Regimental Combat Team on Okinawa. None of these was prepared for battle. Each division lacked a third of its organic infantry and artillery units and almost all of its armor, and its existing units were far understrength. The regiment on Okinawa was proportionately short. Weapons and equipment were warworn remnants of World War II. Some weapons, medium tanks in particular, could scarcely be found in the Far East, and ammunition reserves amounted to a 45-day supply. Since intensive combat training had been largely neglected for occupation duty, the undermanned Far East forces fell far below full combat efficiency.

703

American forces entered Korea piecemeal. On 2 July two rifle companies and a few supporting units of the 24th Division flew from Japan to Pusan and from there moved by train and truck to defensive positions near Osan, 30 miles below Seoul. The mission of this small group was to fight a delaying action to gain time for the movement of more troops from Japan. In the meantime, the North Koreans renewed their southward advance, and on 5 July a North Korean division supported by 30 tanks collided with a small American force. The Americans held their positions stubbornly for nearly five hours, then were outflanked and shoved back with heavy casualties and the loss of all equipment save small arms.

By that time the remainder of the 24th Division had reached Korea and had taken blocking positions along the Jum River north of Taejon (Taiden), 60 miles southeast of Osan. Strung out to the east, remnants of the South Korean Army held positions 50 miles above Taegu. The 25th Division landed in Korea on 14 July and occupied defenses east of the 24th; the 1st Cavalry Division arrived four days later.

Supplies and ammunition for the South Koreans being unloaded from a C–54 transport into a camouflaged truck at an airfield in South Korea, 28 June. Member states of the United Nations pledged their assistance to the Korean republic, offering ground troops, ammunition, supplies, air and naval support, and financial aid.

The 24th Division lost Taejon on 20 July, after North Korean forces established bridgeheads over the Jum River and encircled the town. Despite the arrival of the 29th Regimental Combat Team on 26 July, American and South Korean troops all along the line fell back steadily to the southeast under constant North Korean pressure; by early August the North Koreans had cornered them in a small portion of southeastern Korea.

Actual and probable commitment of military forces from the U.S. membership, meanwhile, posed a problem as new as the U.N. organization in one respect but as old as the unity of command principle in another. For greatest efficiency, the various national contingents entering the conflict had to be unified under a single command. By resolution on 7 July the U.N. Security Council asked the United States to form a unified command and to appoint a commander. The United States complied by establishing the United Nations Command, the first of its kind, in late July, and President Truman appointed General MacArthur to lead it. Thereafter, all military forces from contributing nations joined the U.N. Command as they reached the theatre of operations.

U.S. ASSIGNED COMMAND OF ALL U.N. AND SOUTH KOREAN FORCES

General MacArthur assigned command of ground troops in Korea to the U.S. Eighth Army under Lieutenant General Walton H. Walker. On 13 July General Walker established an advanced headquarters at Taegu, assuming command of all American ground troops on the peninsula and, at the request of South Korean President Syngman Rhee, of the South Korean Army. As ground forces from other U.N. member countries reached Korea, they, too, passed to Walker's command.

Alarmed by the rapid shrinkage of U.N.-held territory, General Walker early in August ordered a final stand along a 140-mile perimeter around Pusan. Although a long line and few troops left numerous and wide gaps in Walker's "Pusan Perimeter," he now held an important advantage over his adversary—shorter interior lines of communications. Pusan had become a well-stocked Eighth Army supply base, and was the hub of a fair rail line and road network leading to the battlefront. At the same time, the enemy's overland supply lines to North Korea had become longer, and less and less tenable under constant U.N. air attack. Moreover, British and American warships had wiped out North Korean naval opposition and had clamped a tight blockade on the Korean coast.

Thirteen North Korean infantry divisions and one armored division hammered at the Pusan Perimeter for a month and a half. Failing to recognize the value of concentrating forces for decisive penetration at one point, the North Koreans dissipated their strength in piecemeal attacks at various points along Eighth Army's line. Necessarily, Eighth

South Koreans move up to the front on flatcars. Note assorted dress of the soldiers; man in center foreground is armed with a .30-caliber carbine. Although the North Korean forces were still north of Suwon, U.S. field headquarters of approximately 290 men withdrew from Suwon on 1 July.

Army's defense hinged on a rapid shuttling of troops to block a gap or reinforce a position where the threat appeared greatest at a given moment. But by rushing his scant reserves from one critical area to another, General Walker launched short and quick counterattacks that inflicted heavy casualties on the North Koreans and prevented serious penetrations.

While the North Koreans lost heavily during repeated attempts to crack Eighth Army's defense, the Eighth Army's combat power grew. By mid-August the 2d Division (Army), the 1st Marine Brigade, and four battalions of medium tanks arrived from the United States, and the 5th Regimental Combat Team from Hawaii. Before the month was out Great Britain committed its 27th Brigade from Hong Kong, and American military advisers restored a semblance of order among five South Korean divisions. Thus, as the North Koreans lost irreplaceable men and equipment, U.N. forces acquired an offensive capability.

First U.S. troops to reach Korea. These men were flown to Pusan from Japan, then moved up to Taejon by train.

Airstrip at Taejon. Lockheed F–80 jet fighters being serviced for a takeoff to bomb enemy targets. As air attacks continued against North Korean targets, a small U.S. ground force made contact with the enemy on 5 July.

Panther jet fighter planes on the flight deck of a Navy carrier, lined up to take off on a mission against military targets in North Korea. On 3 July American and British planes started a two-day air attack in the P'yongyang–Sariwon–Ongjin area.

705

ROK forces, carrying 6.5mm Japanese rifles and wearing canvas-top shoes, move forward, 5 July. At this time the enemy was threatening P'yongt'aek on the west coast and was south of Suwon. On the east coast the enemy held Ulchin.

U.S. troops near Ch'onan, 7 July. Army .50-caliber Browning machine gun, camouflaged with rice straw. The enemy had taken P'yongt'aek by this date and held positions just north of Ch'onan across to Ch'ongju and through to the east coast.

Infantrymen mine a bridge in an attempt to retard the enemy forces which were bearing down in the direction of Taejon and Taegu, 9 July. At this time the South Koreans were engaging the enemy in the vicinity of Umsong, Ch'ungju, and Check'on.

Mortar emplacements. 4.2-inch chemical mortar M2 manned by a U.S. crew. On 10 July U.N. forces were fighting a defensive battle against overwhelming enemy forces and weapons. At the same time the North Koreans claimed the capture of Umsong from the South Koreans.

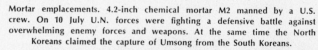

On 12–13 July U.N. forces made a planned withdrawal to the south bank of the Kum, leaving rearguard troops behind to delay the enemy's drive in the direction of Taejon and Taegu.

The General Chaffee light tank in action south of Ch'onan. Armament for tank included a 75mm gun, a 30-caliber machine gun, fixed, a 30-caliber machine gun, flexible, and a .50-caliber machine gun, flexible. On 11 July U.S. tanks saw action for the first time in the Korean conflict, engaging enemy tanks north of the Kum River, the last natural barrier north of Taejon.

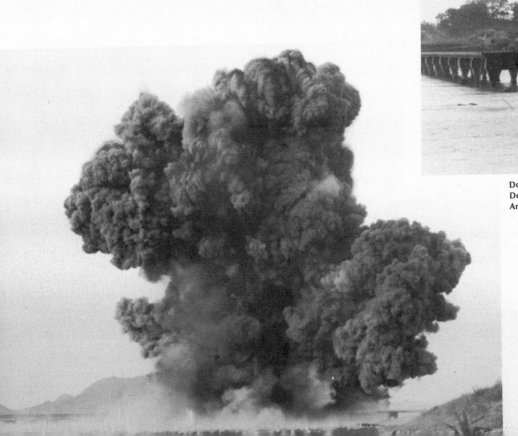

Destruction of a Kum River bridge. Demolitions set off on the bridge by Americans resulted in the wide gap.

American troops loading into landing craft from a ship off the east coast of Korea near P'ohang-dong, 18 July. These men were staged for this operation in ten days. U.S. carrier-based planes of the U.N. naval force provided air cover for the landing forces in addition to conducting a two-day air attack against enemy communications and supply lines in North Korea.

Landing craft shuttling from ship to shore with reinforcements and supplies. Note landing ship, tank (LST) at left.

Infantrymen wading ashore at P'ohang-dong, 18 July. This unopposed landing constituted the first amphibious operation of U.N. forces in Korea.

B–29 Superfortresses leave Japan for a raid on Korea. These giant bombers were active as early as 28 June in support of the ROK troops. On 13 July B–29's made the first large-scale strategic strike over Korea, dropping 450 tons of bombs on enemy installations.

Machine gun positions. .50-caliber Browning machine gun. As rearguard troops left Taejon on 20–21 July, defensive positions were set up southeast of Taejon. Units to the northeast continued to fight for Yech'on, and others recaptured Yongdok on the east coast.

American and ROK troops near Taejon. Scout Koreans were integrated with U.S. units and fought side by side with American soldiers.

709

Yongdong, southeast of Taejon. Units and equipment massed for action (foreground); note artillery bursts (center background). The numerically superior enemy, emplaced in the rugged hills around the town, forced the U.N. army to withdraw to Hwanggan on 26 July despite heavy artillery fire directed at enemy positions. Yongdong and other towns in this area, the scenes of heavy fighting, were wrecked.

Jeep brings ammunition to men who are trying to hold back the enemy with small arms fire.

ROK's proceed to new positions after a general reorganization of their forces. By 1 August Andong, Hamch'ang, and Sangju had been abandoned to the enemy; fighting in the Yongdok, Chirye, and Taegu areas continued.

U.S. troops preparing to move from a port area. Throughout August attempts were made to consolidate positions along the Naktong River line.

4.2-inch chemical mortar returning enemy fire on 6 August. Note shelters built by the troops with heavy logs, rice straw, and matting. The enemy, steadily building up strength for the attack on the Naktong River line, continued heavy pressure on ROK units south of Andong, established a small bridgehead about five miles southwest of Ch'angnyong, and in the southwest sector threatened U.N. positions near Chinju.

Pershing medium tanks made secure on flatcars. U.S. units abandoned Kumch'on as ROK forces, with supporting U.S. artillery and naval gunfire, recaptured Yongdok on 2 August.

An infantryman being comforted as a casualty tag is made out
for his buddy who was killed moments earlier.

Medical Aid men carrying a wounded soldier. Machine gun to right of men in foxhole is a .30-caliber
Browning, flexible. In the south, enemy units made
several sharp attacks on 29 August. West of Yongsan the North Koreans made three unsuccessful attempts to cross the river in small boats during the
night of 29–30 August, while on the east coast ROK
troops retook Kigye. North Koreans recaptured the
town again the next day.

Treadway bridge across the Naktong River constructed by U.S. engineers. Before the bridge was built, the only means of crossing the river was a small ferry operated by South Koreans.

Infantryman relaxes, reading the latest news while having lunch.

Field kitchen operating despite inclement weather. Whenever possible, combat troops received hot food, often prepared under great difficulties.

Men and equipment being unloaded on the beach during the invasion at Inch'on. The morning tide of 16 September gave U.N. forces their first opportunity to use the inner harbor at Inch'on for unloading heavy equipment and supplies. Meanwhile, the units holding beachheads at and near Inch'on met after making coordinated attacks, and then systematically began clearing the city of enemy forces.

MacArthur's Plan for the Inch'on Landing

Almost from the start of the conflict General MacArthur worked on plans for a decisive blow that would turn the tide of battle. His plan was based in large part on an evaluation of Korea's terrain. Korea is a peninsula of mountains. Main ranges run the length of the east coast, and spur ranges spread southwesterly across most of the peninsula. Myriad peaks and ridges forming these ranges, although not notably high, are unusually steep. Their number and precipitousness, as Walker's forces already had discovered, markedly curtailed the mobility of the highly motorized and mechanized U.S. forces. By and large motor movement was restricted to Korea's roads, which were few in number and indeed primitive. The main roads, and the rail lines, followed paths of least resistance through scant lowlands. Since the lowlands lay principally along the west coast, Korea's primary communications system was centered in the west. Most of the main roads and rail lines converged on Seoul from the south and southeast and wound through the western lowlands to the north.

Therefore, MacArthur planned an amphibious landing at Inch'on, a port on the Yellow Sea 25 miles west of Seoul, to be followed by an advance on the capital city to cut the main routes of communications over which most North Korean troops and supplies traveled south. In concert with this move, the Eighth Army was to make a general northward advance. Enemy troops who survived the Eighth Army's attack and withdrew over the main road net would walk into the guns of the amphibious force that had come in behind them. In the east, enemy forces could make only a slow and difficult escape through the precipitous, almost trackless mountains.

MacArthur's plan appeared dangerous to his superiors and to the Navy. Since MacArthur would be committing his last reserves to the landing, the U.S. Joint Chiefs-of-Staff anticipated serious consequences if Inch'on were strongly defended. Naval authorities considered the extreme Yellow Sea tides and narrow channel approaches to Inch'on as big risks to the shipping that would carry and support the am-

phibious force. MacArthur, nonetheless, held to his plan: he built up supplies and pieced together a landing force from the 7th Division, the greater part of the 1st Marine Division, which was sent from the United States, and the 1st Marine Brigade, which he pulled out of the line in Korea to fill out the Marine division. He assigned command of the landing to the newly activated U.S. X Corps, which would operate independently of the Eighth Army under the leadership of Major General Edward M. Almond.

General Almond's corps went into Inch'on on 15 September. Against light resistance, a Marine regiment covered by strong air strikes and naval gunfire quickly captured the port city proper, and, after the full division had landed, the Marines pressed toward Seoul. The 7th Division came ashore in the wake of the Marine advance. One regiment struck southeastward for Suwon, south of Seoul, while the remainder of the division joined the Marines in the fight for the capital city. On 29 September Almond's forces were in Seoul, and in a dramatic ceremony General MacArthur turned the city back to President Rhee.

General Walker launched the Eighth Army's offensive on 16 September, the day following the landing at Inch'on. His command, now consisting of the U.S. 1, ROK I, and ROK II Corps and within a week the U.S. IX Corps as well, made little progress at first. But when the portent of Almond's envelopment and Walker's frontal attack became clear to the North Koreans, they fled to the north and Eighth Army rolled forward and made contact with the U.S. X Corps on 26 September. Large numbers of enemy troops escaped to North Korea through the eastern mountains, but enemy casualties were high, and by 30 September the Eighth Army's prisoner-of-war cages held over 100,000 captives. Remnants of six North Korean divisions hid in the mountains of South Korea to fight as guerrillas, posing a large enough threat for Walker to commit his U.S. IX Corps against them. The North Korean Army, nevertheless, had ceased to exist as an organized force below the 38th parallel by the end of September.

Army units advancing through a Korean village six miles southeast of Inch'on, after landing over the beaches. By 20 September the U.N. forces were advancing against the enemy in all areas of South Korea.

North Korean prisoners, on their way to a PW camp, pass a knocked-out enemy T34 tank.

A convoy of U.S. and ROK Marines during an advance on Seoul. U.N. forces to the south recaptured P'ohang-dong on 20 September and advanced to the north. Light bombers and fighters continued close support of the ground forces all along the Pusan perimeter, while B–29's operating in small groups bombed targets in North Korea. Kimpo airfield, captured on 17 September, became operational.

M45 medium tank, with 105mm howitzer, crossing the Kumho River en route to the Naktong River. After breaking out of the Pusan beachhead, U.N. forces advanced to the Naktong River. On 18 September elements of the advancing forces crossed the Naktong, but the enemy still held the high ground five miles northwest of Yongsan.

Infantrymen overlooking enemy positions along the Naktong River during the drive toward Taejon. In one area units advanced 20 miles through Tabu-dong to the Naktong, two miles east of Sonsan. To the north U.N. forces were advancing into the outskirts of Seoul.

A soldier cooling his weary feet in a helmet filled with water.

THE STABILIZED FRONT
1952 - 1953

┬┬┬┬┬ UNITED NATIONS LINE
27 JUL 1953

0   10   20   30
MILES

U.S. troops advancing along the north side of the Han River on their way to Seoul. On 25 September Seoul was the scene of fierce battles, and the attacking forces broke through the defenses of the city. To the south Kumch'on was cleared, Andong was taken, and Army units entered Chinju.

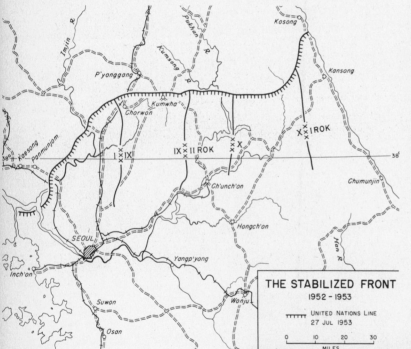

716

Men and tanks move through a street of Seoul during the battle for the city. On 26 and 27 September U.N. forces cleared the enemy pockets of resistance in Seoul. Shortly after 1100 on 26 September, units from the Inch'on beachhead and those from Pusan linked up, trapping the enemy remaining in southwest Korea. Osan, the first city lost by the U.S. forces to the North Koreans, was recaptured during the advance toward a linkup.

U.N. troops at the 38th parallel. The Commander in Chief, United Nations Command, restored Seoul to the President of the Republic of Korea on 29 September. While the west coast seaport of Kunsan was threatened, the advance in the north had almost reached the 38th parallel.

A destroyed bridge on the outskirts of Yongju in use after being repaired with sand bags.

717

THE U.N. FORCES INVADE NORTH KOREA

After driving the North Korean Army above the 38th parallel, U.N. forces awaited a decision whether to cross the parallel in pursuit. In making the decision American authorities, acting in behalf of participating U.N. nations, constantly kept in mind that crossing the parallel might, by sparking Chinese and Soviet entry into the conflict, bring on another world war. On the other hand, these authorities realized that failure to erase communism in Korea would leave the South Korean people in no better position than that of 24 June 1950. Choosing to risk Chinese and Soviet participation, President Truman on 27 September authorized U.N. forces to enter North Korea. On 3 October Communist China's Foreign Minister, Chou En-lai, warned that Chinese troops would enter the conflict if other than South Korean forces crossed the 38th parallel. This did not prevent the United Nations General Assembly from voting on 7 October for the restoration of peace and security throughout Korea, thereby giving tacit approval to entry into North Korea by U.N. military forces.

In the east, Walker's ROK I Corps crossed the 38th parallel on 1 October and advanced up the east coast to capture Wonsan, North Korea's major seaport, on 10 October. His ROK II Corps, meanwhile, crossed the parallel and advanced through central Korea. In the west, Walker's remaining forces relieved Almond's corps in the Seoul area, and on 9 October crossed the parallel to move on P'yongyang, the North Korean capital. Meeting but slight resistance, these forces covered the 90 miles to P'yongyang in 10 days. Three days later, Walker's troops were in Sinanju, 40 miles above P'yongyang. Within another week, Walker's westernmost division crossed the Ch'ongch'on River at Sinanju and reached a point only 18 air miles from the Manchurian border. Troops from a division farther to the east went even deeper: a South Korean regiment dashed northward and entered the town of Ch'osan on 26 October, to become the first contingent of U.N. troops to reach the Yalu River.

Some of the first Chinese communists captured by U.N. troops. The quilted cotton uniforms were typical of the winter uniforms worn by these troops. Some Chinese entered the conflict in North Korea against the U.N. army in October 1950. On 9 November it was estimated that 60,000 Chinese communists were in North Korea opposing the U.N. troops.

Sherman medium tank passing a disabled Russian-made T34 tank. While the majority of the U.N. units were preparing for action north of the 38th parallel, the first ROK units to cross into North Korea met rearguard enemy action while moving toward Wonsan.

Soldiers dispersed along a road take time out for a quick meal of C rations. On 9 October U.S. units crossed the 38th parallel north of Kaesong and met strong enemy resistance. Mopping up in South Korea continued with a total of more than 55,000 of the enemy captured by this time.

U.N. soldiers fighting in a railroad yard in P'yongyang. On 19 October U.N. forces entered P'yongyang, the capital of North Korea.

Landing craft heading for the beach during the landing at Wonsan. After waiting for six days for mine sweepers to clear the channel at Wonsan, units began unloading on the beach on 26 October.

Airdrop over the Sukch'on–Sunch'on area, 20 October. The drop was successfully executed and the paratroopers moved quickly to their assigned objectives. On the same day P'yongyang was captured and the mopping up of scattered enemy troops began.

719

LST's discharging cargo on the beach at Wonsan during the landing. After the U.N. forces landed, 26 October, they quickly deployed and began hunting out the enemy. ROK units were the first to reach the Yalu River and the Manchurian border.

Almond's U.S. X Corps, meanwhile, prepared a second amphibious landing, this time on the east coast of North Korea. After being delayed until mines could be cleared from Wonsan harbor, Almond's 1st Marine Division landed at Wonsan on 26 October; 3 days later, his 7th Division came ashore at Iwon, 80 miles farther to the north. Neither division met opposition since both landing areas already had fallen to the ROK I Corps.

Adding the ROK I Corps to his command upon landing, General Almond set out to capture the iron and steel mills, communications network, port installations, and power and irrigation plants of northeastern Korea. ROK I Corps followed the coastline toward the ironworks at Ch'ongjin, 120 miles above Iwon. The Marines moved 50 miles north of Wonsan to industrial Hamhung and its port, Hungnam, then struck inland for the Changjijn Reservoir, 45 miles to the northwest. From Iwon, the 7th Division attacked northwestward toward the Pujon Reservoir and the Yalu River.

Chinese Armies Turn Back U.N. Troops

The outlook for U.N. forces in the last week of October was distinctly optimistic. For all practical purposes the North Korean Army appeared to exist only as a "rabble at arms," and on 24 October MacArthur issued orders for attacks by U.S. Eighth Army and U.S. X Corps that he hoped would carry his forces to the Manchurian border and restore peace to Korea before the onset of winter. But brief clashes with Chinese troops between 25 and 28 October in both Walker's and Almond's sectors posed a new threat. Chinese prisoners taken during these engagements gave deceptive identities to their military organizations; hence, it was not clear whether a few makeshift units of Chinese volunteers had reinforced the North Koreans or whether the presence of Chinese troops represented full intervention by Communist China.

Battles with Chinese troops, costly to both sides, continued through the first week of November. In the face of the new opposition, Walker decided that he must advance on a broader front, and that he must build up his supplies before he could mount a large effort. He therefore withdrew his extended forces to the lower bank of the Ch'ongch'on River but kept a bridgehead over the Ch'ongch'on above Sinanju. Walker believed that 3 Chinese divisions, about 30,000 troops, opposed his army. Estimates placed 1, possibly 2, divisions ahead of Almond's forces in the east. Then, on 8 November the larger Chinese units abruptly broke contact with the U.N. forces and withdrew, obscuring their purpose and intentions in Korea.

The fact of Chinese participation in the conflict was a good reason for MacArthur to reconsider his plans for all-out attack to the Yalu River, but not reason enough to abandon them. He still planned to send Walker's forces northward through western and central Korea, starting on 24 November, while Almond's troops cut enemy supply lines in an enveloping movement to the northwest, beginning on 27 November. Between 8 and 23 November, Eighth Army and U.S. X Corps advanced cautiously against moderate resistance to gain favorable positions from which to launch their all-out offensive. Then on 24 November Walker attacked, with the Eighth Army and the ROK II Corps in line. His forces aimed for intermediate terrain objectives that would give him access to good routes for the final march to the border. His army was spread across as broad a front as its size would permit, not concentrated for a major advance along any single axis, thus not deployed in strict accordance with the principle of mass. For 24 hours the troops encountered only moderate resistance. But on 25 November Chinese forces stopped Walker's attack cold with a sudden and furious attack of their own which took the Eighth Army by complete surprise.

720

Psychological warfare leaflets being loaded into a bomb-type cluster adapter at an air base in Japan, 1 November. The adapter holds 22,500 five-inch by eight-inch leaflets. After crossing the 38th parallel, U.N. forces dropped leaflets and broadcast from aircraft in an effort to induce the North Koreans to surrender. Humane treatment was promised to those who did surrender.

Hyesanjin, near the Manchurian border, 21 November. Infantrymen advancing through its rubble-strewn streets. In a rapid advance north of Kapsan, U.S. units drove to the Manchurian border, reaching Hyesanjin against light enemy resistance on 21 November; ROK forces reached to within 15 miles of Ch'ongjin on the east coast.

The weight of the Chinese assault struck ROK II Corps on the Eighth Army's right flank, and the South Koreans fell away under the impact. Walker called out his reserves to restore the flank, but Chinese forces beat back the reserves and threatened to envelop the remainder of the Eighth Army after 4 more Chinese armies joined the attack on 27 November.

On the same day, 2 Chinese armies hit Almond's forces in the east, attacking along both sides of the Changjin Reservoir. After encircling 2 battalions of the 7th Division at Yudam-ni on the west, the Chinese cut the Americans' supply line and withdrawal route by blocking the road between the reservoir and Hamhung.

In the Eighth Army's sector, wave after wave of attacking Chinese struck the weakening U.N. line until defenders involuntarily fell back under the weight of the enemy's numbers. Walker countered by leaving one division to fight a delaying action while he pulled the bulk of his troops back to new defensive positions near P'yongyang. On 5 December, after Chinese forces again threatened his right flank, Walker withdrew his army from P'yongyang to positions along the Imjin River near the 38th parallel. During the withdrawal Walker evacuated his wounded and most of his supplies by water, rail, and air. Other supplies were burned. Thousands of fleeing Korean civilians clogged the Fifth Army's route of withdrawal, slowing trucks carrying U.N. troops to their new positions; but the Chinese had little motor transport to use in the pursuit, and the Eighth Army managed to break contact without serious interference.

Almond's forces also withdrew, retiring toward the east coast. His right flank units reached the coast with little difficulty, but the Marines and the 7th Division's two battalions encircled at the Changjin Reservoir had to fight their way out. Supplied by air drops, the Marine-Army force of about 14,000 men fought through successive Chinese roadblocks as it moved southeastward through steep, snow-covered mountains toward the port of Hungnam.

At the same time, the U.S. 3d Division, newly arrived from the United States, the ROK I Corps, and the rest of the 7th Division formed a perimeter around Hungnam. This consolidation was part of a plan by General MacArthur to evacuate the U.S. X Corps by water. Since he could perceive no tactical advantage in holding a beachhead on the eastern coast of North Korea, MacArthur had decided to move U.S. X Corps to South Korea to reinforce the Eighth Army.

North Korean prisoners of war, under guard on the beach at Wonsan, wait for shipment to Pusan. As of 3 November, the total number of enemy prisoners was reported as being 135,000.

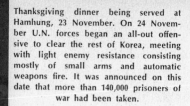

Thanksgiving dinner being served at Hamhung, 23 November. On 24 November U.N. forces began an all-out offensive to clear the rest of Korea, meeting with light enemy resistance consisting mostly of small arms and automatic weapons fire. It was announced on this date that more than 140,000 prisoners of war had been taken.

Combat engineers placing satchel charges on a railroad bridge near P'yongyang preparatory to destroying it to slow the communist advance. U.N. forces began evacuating their positions on the Manchurian border in late November.

U.S. Army units moving south from Sunch'on to P'yongyang as the U.N. forces were pulled back.

Men of an artillery battery preparing to put their 155mm howitzer motor carriages into action against the enemy north of Hamhung.

Barrels of aviation gasoline lined up on the beach at Hungnam. While the units defending the port area held off the communist forces, the evacuation of men and supplies continued.

Enlisted men using Korean A-frames carry mats, stovepipes, and other equipment during the withdrawal from the P'yongyang area to the 38th parallel. On 16 December Hamhung was abandoned and the bridges leading out of the city were destroyed. In northeast Korea the ROK I Corps was being withdrawn, and by mid-December this movement was completed.

Explosives being placed on a pier at Hungnam as the evacuation of the port nears completion. On Christmas Eve the last of the U.N. units were taken aboard ships at Hungnam. During this evacuation, over 105,000 soldiers and 98,000 civilians were removed from the area.

Actor Paul Douglas performs in a "tent theatre" in Korea in 1951.

A U.S. warship lying off the port of Hungnam as the docks are being destroyed. With the successful withdrawal of all the U.N. units in the area, all dock and other facilities were destroyed to deny their use to the communist forces. At the end of the year the U.N. forces had successfully completed their withdrawal from North Korea.

While U.N. ships gathered in the waters off Hungnam to take his forces out of North Korea, Almond sent a relief column inland to help hold the route of withdrawal for his men fighting their way to the coast. After the relief column met the retiring troops, the two groups made their way to the coast by 11 December. On the same day, Almond started his evacuation. While enemy troops continually attacked the Hungnam defenses, the perimeter gradually contracted and tightened about the port as Almond loaded his troops and supplies aboard ships in the harbor. On 24 December he pulled his rear guard off the Hungnam beaches, successfully completing the difficult operation of withdrawal from a hostile shore, and sailed for the Pusan area to join the Eighth Army.

U.N. FORCES ESTABLISH DEFENSE LINE AT 38th PARALLEL: DECEMBER 1950

In the west, the Eighth Army had fought no large-scale battle with the Chinese since the first week of December. After breaking contact with the Chinese, who were forced to wait at the 38th parallel for supplies and replacements, the Eighth Army organized a 140-mile, coast-to-coast defense line just below the parallel by the end of December. Along this line were 5 corps: the U.S. I and IX west and north of Seoul, the South Korean III, II,, and I to the east, in that order. The U.S. X Corps went into Army reserve.

As the Eighth Army developed its defenses, there was

an important change of command. On 23 December General Walker was killed in a motor vehicle accident and, at General MacArthur's request, Lieutenant General Matthew B. Ridgway was named Eighth Army commander. Ridgway's instructions from MacArthur were to defend his positions—if necessary, to fall back to successive positions to the south— but to keep his army intact at all costs.

On the other side of the 38th parallel, the enemy concentrated his ground strength above Seoul and pushed large quantities of supplies into his forward areas. Here was clear indication that he was about to resume the attack and that Seoul would be his next objective.

At daybreak on 1 January 1951 enemy troops attacked along Eighth Army's entire front. As expected, the major effort was directed against Seoul. Although the Eighth Army presented a stronger front than it had in November, the enemy offensive quickly gained momentum. Rather than risk destruction by defending in place, General Ridgway established a bridgehead around Seoul to delay the enemy and deny him the use of the Han River bridges, and pulled back the rest of his army to a line running along the south back of the Han below Seoul, then eastward to the coast through the villages of Yangp'yong, Hongch'on, and Chumunjin. By rolling with the punch, Ridgway believed he could conserve his strength until the enemy attack bogged down for lack of supplies and replacements, then could strike back.

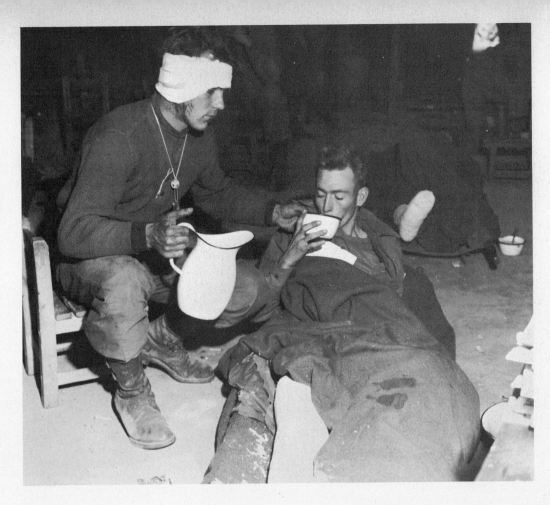

A Helping Hand

The Chinese Take Seoul

When enemy forces quickly followed up their initial success and crossed the frozen Han River to the east and west of Seoul, Ridgway ordered another withdrawal. Beginning on 3 January, he moved his forces to a line running from positions on the west coast 40 miles below Seoul eastward through the towns of P'yongt'aek, Ansong, Wonju, and Samch'ok. Enemy forces followed closely. In the west, the last of the Eighth Army pulled out of Seoul on 4 January, and engineers blew the remaining Han River bridges as enemy columns entered the city from the north.

Once Seoul fell, only light Chinese forces pushed south of the city, and enemy attacks in the west diminished. In central and eastern Korea, heavy fighting continued as U.N. troops in those regious withdrew to their new sectors, but by mid-January enemy pressure subsided along the entire front. Again, enemy ranks were depleted and supplies were low. As U.N. troops restored and developed positions along the P'yongt'aek-Samch'ok line, Ridgway's reconnaissance forces discovered that the enemy had set out light screening forces to maintain contact and had withdrawn the bulk of his troops to regroup and reequip.

General Ridgway gave his troops their objective for the next four months when he declared that he was no longer interested in land gains. "We are interested only in inflicting maximum casualties to the enemy with minimum casualties to ourselves. To do this we must wage a war of maneuver—slashing at the enemy when he withdraws and fighting delaying actions when he attacks."

Buildings burning in Seoul as South Korean government officials and U.N. troops leave the city for the second time, 3 January.

Troop-loaded tanks moving south after crossing the Han River.

Pontoon bridge spanning the icy Han is blown up after last of the U.N. forces evacuate Seoul, 4 January.

Hordes of refugees fleeing from Seoul clogging a dike across rice paddies, 5 January.

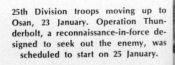

25th Division troops moving up to Osan, 23 January. Operation Thunderbolt, a reconnaissance-in-force designed to seek out the enemy, was scheduled to start on 25 January.

General J. Lawton Collins, Chief of Staff, U.S. Army, stopping for a conference in Japan before going to Korea, is greeted by General of the Army Douglas MacArthur.

General MacArthur visiting near the front lines north of Suwon, 28 January. He is accompanied by his military secretary, Major General Courtney Whitney (second from left), and Lieutenant General Matthew B. Ridgway, Commanding General, U.S. Eighth Army, wearing his characteristic grenade. Major General William B. Kean, Commanding General, 25th Division, is behind General MacArthur.

Ridgway's Probing Advances

To attain this objective, the Eighth Army began a cautious, probing advance on 25 January. Moving on a wide front through a succession of phase lines, Ridgway's troops attacked slowly and methodically, ridge by ridge, phase line by phase line, wiping out each pocket of resistance before making the next advance. Although enemy screening forces fought back vigorously and launched occasional counterattacks, the Eighth Army moved steadily and, by 1 March, regained the lower bank of the Han River.

By then the spring thaw had come to South Korea, swelling streams and turning the countryside into mud. Under those conditions the Eighth Army's advances were a test of endurance for both men and equipment. Ridgway's forces, nevertheless, succeeded in recapturing Seoul by mid-March, and by 19 March held a line that crossed Korea just below the 38th parallel.

Meanwhile, behind his screening positions a few miles above the 38th parallel, the enemy assembled troops and equipment for an offensive. Even though reentry into North Korea seemed a formidable undertaking in light of events of late 1950, Ridgway could not permit the enemy to prepare an attack unmolested. Therefore, on 5 April, he unleashed his troops in an attack toward an objective line designated Kansas, roughly 10 miles above the parallel whose capture would carry the Eighth Army through important enemy supply and troop concentration areas. On reaching this line at mid-April, Ridgway sent part of his force toward Line Wyoming, which looped above the western portion of Kansas through another important enemy supply area.

As Ridgway's forces advanced above Line Kansas, more evidence of the enemy's buildup appeared. As a precaution, Ridgway published on 12 April a plan for orderly delaying actions to be fought when and if the enemy attacked. This was one of his last acts as commander of Eighth Army. The day before, 11 April, President Truman had relieved General MacArthur of command in the Far East in one of the most controversial episodes of the conflict, and at the same time had named Ridgway as MacArthur's successor. On 14 April Ridgway turned over the Eighth Army to Lieutenant General James A. Van Fleet.

Lineman repairing telephone lines
between Tanyang and Chech'on.

C-119 Flying boxcar loaded with cargo flying over jagged mountains to a drop zone, January 1951.

Recovering an airdropped 55-gallon
drum of gasoline.

Back from captivity. Two American and four Australian soldiers in the 24th Division Medical Clearing Station after reaching U.S. lines.

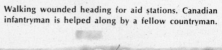

Walking wounded heading for aid stations. Canadian infantryman is helped along by a fellow countryman.

Bringing in enemy prisoners, 1st Cavalry Division area, 27 February. On 21 February Operation Killer was launched along 60 miles of the central Korean front to annihilate enemy forces and reestablish U.N. line east of Wonju.

Men of the 17th Infantry taking cover behind a stone wall, 20 February. On 18 February the 17th Regimental Combat Team, 7th Division, attacked northwest from Chech'on in the central sector.

At Chip'young-ni, 23 February. From left: General Ridgway; Major General Charles D. Palmer, Commanding General, 1st Cavalry Division; Colonel William A. Harris, Commanding Officer, 7th Cavalry Regiment; and Colonel John Daskalopoules, Commanding Officer of Greek Battalion attached to the 7th Cavalry Regiment.

Near P'yongch'ang, east-central sector.

7th Division troops moving north rest their weary feet during a break along the roadside.

On 11 April 1951, after a series of public utterances revealed sharp differences over national policy and military strategy, President Truman relieved General MacArthur of all his commands and replaced him with General Ridgway. Lieutenant General James A. Van Fleet was dispatched posthaste from Washington to take command of the Eighth Army and attached forces. He arrived and assumed command on 14 April.

General of the Army Douglas MacArthur addresses members of Congress in the Capitol. Behind General MacArthur are Vice President Alben Barkley (left) and Speaker of the House Sam Rayburn (right). General MacArthur arrived in Washington, D.C., on the morning of 19 April 1951 and spoke before Congress on that day. This was the first time the General had returned to the United States in 14 years.

THE ADDRESS TO CONGRESS

(in part)

By General Douglas MacArthur

Mr. President, Mr. Speaker, and distinguished Members of the Congress, I stand on this rostrum with a sense of deep humility and great pride; humility in the wake of those great American architects of our history who have stood here before me; pride in the reflection that this forum of legislative debate represents human liberty in the purest form yet devised. [*Applause.*]

Here are centered the hopes, and aspirations, and faith of the entire human race.

I do not stand here as advocate for any partisan cause, for the issues are fundamental and reach quite beyond the realm of partisan consideration. They must be resolved on the highest plane of national interest if our course is to prove sound and our future protected. I trust, therefore, that you will do me the justice of receiving that which I have to say as solely expressing the considered viewpoint of a fellow American. I address you with neither rancor nor bitterness in the fading twilight of life, with but one purpose in mind, to serve my country. [*Applause.*]

The Communist threat is a global one. Its successful advance in one sector threatens the destruction of every other sector. You cannot appease or otherwise surrender to Communism in Asia without simultaneously undermining our efforts to halt its advance in Europe.

With this brief insight into the surrounding areas I now turn to the Korean conflict. While I was not consulted prior to the President's decision to intervene in support of the Republic of Korea, that decision from a military standpoint proved a sound one. [*Applause.*] As I say, it proved a sound one as we hurled back the invaders and decimated his forces. Our victory was complete and our objectives within reach when Red China intervened with numerically superior ground forces. This created a new war and an entirely new situation, a situation not contemplated when our forces were committed against the North Korean invaders, a situation which called for new decisions in the diplomatic sphere to permit the realistic adjustment of military strategy. Such decisions have not been forthcoming. [*Applause.*]

While no man in his right mind would advocate sending our ground forces into continental China—and such was never given a thought—the new situation did urgently demand a drastic revision of strategic planning if our political aim was to defeat this new enemy as we had defeated the old. [*Applause.*]

Apart from the military need, as I saw it, to neutralize the sanctuary protection given to the enemy north of the Yalu, I felt that military necessity in the conduct of the war made necessary:

First, the intensification of our economic blockade against China.

Two, the imposition of a naval blackade against the China coast.

Three, removal of restrictions on air reconnaissance of China's coastal areas and of Manchuria. [*Applause.*]

Four, removal of restrictions on the forces of the Republic of China on Formosa with logistical support to contribute to their effective operation against the Chinese mainland. [*Applause.*]

For entertaining these views, all professionally designed to support our forces committed to Korea and bring hostilities to an end with the least possible delay and at a saving of countless American and Allied lives, I have been severely criticized in lay circles, principally abroad, despite my understanding that from a military standpoint the above views have been fully shared and passed by practically every military leader concerned with the Korean campaign, including our own Joint Chiefs of Staff. [*Applause, the Members rising.*]

I called for reinforcements, but was informed that reinforcements were not available. I made clear that if not permitted to destroy the enemy built-up bases north of the Yalu, to utilize the friendly Chinese force of some 600,000 men on Formosa; if not permitted to blockade the China coast to prevent the Chinese Reds from getting succor from without; and if there was to be no hope of major reinforcements, the position of the command from the military standpoint forbade victory. We could hold in Korea by constant maneuver and at an approximate area where our supply line advantages were in balance with the supply line disadvantages of the enemy, but we could hope at best for only an indecisive campaign, with its terrible and constant attrition upon our forces if the enemy utilized his full military potential. I have constantly called for the new political decisions essential to a solution. Efforts have been made to distort my position. It has been said in effect that I was a a warmonger. Nothing could be further from the truth. [*Applause.*] I know war as few other men now living know it, and nothing to me is more revolting. I have long advocated its complete abolition as its very destructiveness on both friend and foe has rendered it useless as a means of settling international disputes. Indeed, on the second day of September, 1945, just following the surrender of the Japanese nation on the battleship *Missouri,* I formally cautioned as follows:

"Men since the beginning of time have sought peace. Various methods through the ages have been attempted to devise an international process to prevent or settle disputes between nations. From the very start, workable methods were found insofar as individual citizens were concerned, but the mechanics of an instrumentality of larger international scope have never been successful. Military alliances, balances of power, leagues of nations, all in turn failed, leaving the only path to be by way of the crucible of war. The utter destructiveness of war now blots out this alternative. We have had our last chance. If we will not devise some greater and more equitable system, Armageddon will be at our door. The problem basically is theological and involves a spiritual recrudescence and improvement of human character that will synchronize with our almost matchless advances in science, art, literature, and all material and cultural developments of the past 2,000 years. It must be of the spirit if we are to save the flesh." [*Applause.*]

But once war is forced upon us, there is no other alternative than to apply every available means to bring it to a swift end. War's very object is victory—not prolonged indecision. [*Applause.*]

In war there is no substitute for victory.

There are some who for varying reasons would appease Red China. They are blind to history's clear lesson. For history teaches with unmistakable emphasis that appeasement but begets new and bloodier war. It points to no single instance where this end has justified that means— where appeasement has led to more than sham peace. Like blackmail, it lays the basis for new and successively greater demands, until, as in blackmail, violence becomes the only other alternative. Why, my soldiers asked of me, surrender military advantages to an enemy in the field? I could not answer. [*Applause.*] Some may say to avoid spread of the conflict into an all-out war with China; others, to avoid Soviet intervention. Neither explanation seems valid. For China is already engaging with the maximum power it can commit and the Soviet will not necessarily mesh its actions with our moves. Like a cobra, any new enemy will more likely strike whenever it feels that the relativity in military or other potential is in its favor on a worldwide basis.

The tragedy of Korea is further heightened by the fact that as military action is confined to its territorial limits, it condemns that nation, which it is our purpose to save, to suffer the devastating impact of full naval and air bombardment, while the enemy's sanctuaries are fully protected from such attack and devastation. Of the nations of the world, Korea alone, up to now, is the sole one which has risked its all against Communism. The magnificence of the courage and fortitude of the Korean people defies description. [*Applause.*] They have chosen to risk death rather than slavery. Their last words to me were "Don't scuttle the Pacific." [*Applause.*]

I have just left your fighting sons in Korea. They have met all tests there and I can report to you without reservation that they are splendid in every way. [*Applause.*] It was my constant effort to preserve them and end this savage conflict honorably and with the least loss of time and a minimum sacrifice of life. Its growing bloodshed has caused me the deepest anguish and anxiety. Those gallant men will remain often in my thoughts and in my prayers always. [*Applause.*]

I am closing my 52 years of military service. [*Applause.*] When I joined the Army even before the turn of the century, it was the fulfillment of all my boyish hopes and dreams. The world has turned over many times since I took the oath on the plain at West Point, and the hopes and dreams have long since vanished. But I still remember the refrain of one of the most popular barrack ballads of that day which proclaimed most proudly that—

"Old soldiers never die; they just fade away." And like the old soldier of that ballad, I now close my military career and just fade away—an old soldier who tried to do his duty as God gave him the light to see that duty.

Good-by.

Convoy Crossing the Soyang River. By 8 April the 7th Division put two battalions across the Soyang River, and by 19 April U.N. forces were in position along Line Utah.

Crossing the 38th parallel, 1 March 1951-21 April 1951

THE ENEMY'S OFFENSIVE: APRIL 1951

The threatened offensive came on the night of 22 April, when enemy forces launched strong attacks in Western Korea and lighter attacks in the east. After the enemy's attack in the west carried him below the 38th parallel, he concentrated his effort against Seoul. In the east, his attack also carried below the parallel but not in such depth as in the west.

According to previously laid plans, General Van Fleet withdrew through a series of delaying positions, finally establishing defenses along a line running northeastward across the peninsula from positions a few miles north of Seoul. Along this line the Eighth Army halted the enemy's attack by the end of April. When enemy forces withdrew to recoup their losses, Van Fleet used the lull in the battle to improve his defense line. Meanwhile, he planned an offensive designed to carry the Eighth Army back to Line Kansas, but signs of another enemy attack led him to postpone it.

Van Fleet had interpreted the signs correctly. After darkness on 15 May the enemy resumed his spring offensive. Expecting the next enemy assault against Seoul, Van Fleet had strengthened his defenses in the west, but this time the enemy drove a salient into the Eighth Army's east-central position. Adjusting forces to place more troops in the path of the enemy's attack and laying down tremendous amounts of artillery fire, Van Fleet exacted heavy enemy casualties and contained the enemy attack after it had penetrated 30 miles through Eighth Army lines. Determined to prevent the enemy from regathering strength for another attack, Van Fleet immediately ordered his forces forward in counterattack. Disorganized after their own attack, enemy forces resisted stubbornly only where their supply installations were threatened. Elsewhere, the Eighth Army advanced with almost surprising ease, and by 31 May was just short of Line Kansas. Van Fleet then prepared to advance part of his force back to Line Wyoming.

Marshaling yard on the main rail line leading south from Wonsan undergoing a fiery napalm bomb attack by B-26's of the 452d Light Bomb Wing, Fifth Air Force. Both Wonsan and Songjin were enemy communications centers for road and rail networks along the east coast of North Korea.

U.N. Forces withdrawing under the weight
of the enemy offensive.

M46 Patton tank towing a crippled mate through Uijongbu.

To this point, the conflict had been one of movement. Like a free-swinging pendulum, hinged above the center of Korea, it had changed direction several times, arcing first below and then above the 38th parallel. But each swing had been smaller as the pendulum lost momentum. For the Eighth Army, at least, there was little prospect of substantial reinforcement. As a result—in fact, as a gradual development since the time of Chinese intervention—U.N., and especially U.S., objectives in the conflict shifted from military victory to political settlement.

The United Nations' hope for a negotiated peace carried with it a restriction on military operations. After 1 June ground forces could not, without approval from Washington, make a general advance north of an east-west line generally along the 38th parallel. The only tactical operations permitted were those necessary to protect the Eighth Army, to maintain contact, and to harass the enemy. Here was the basic pattern of U.N. military operations through the rest of the conflict.

On 1 June, as part of his army advanced toward Line Wyoming and the remainder drove forward to consolidate on Line Kansas, Van Fleet ordered his troops to build a strong defense line once they gained their objectives. Van Fleet had no other choice since present objectives marked generally his limit of advance.

The Eighth Army reached Lines Kansas and Wyoming in mid-June. Recapture of these lines meant that all of South Korea except for a small area in the west was clear of enemy troops. To compensate for the enemy's hold south of the 38th parallel, Eighth Army held territory north of the line in central and eastern Korea. Upon halting, Van Fleet's forces began to fortify their positions and, aside from patrolling and clashing locally with enemy screening forces, spent the remainder of June developing their defenses. Enemy forces used the respite to reorganize after losing heavily. Indeed, as the first year of the conflict ended, the fighting took the appearance of a stalemate.

"Long Toms" of the 204th Field Artillery Battalion
firing north of Seoul.

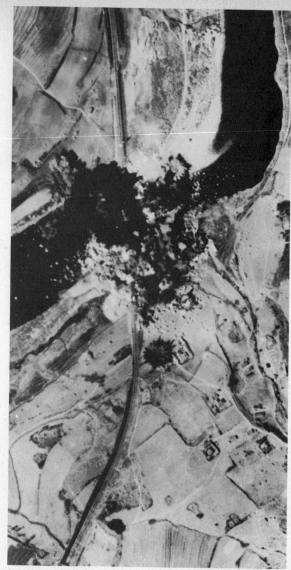

Railroad bridge across the Tae-
dong River, south of Tokch'on, is
blown up by Superforts of the
Far East Air Forces, May 1951.

Marshaling Yard Near Yangyang
on east coast undergoing a bombing attack by B–26 light bombers
of the Fifth Air Force.

The Hwach'on Dam Under Attack by Navy AD Skyraiders
using aerial torpedoes.

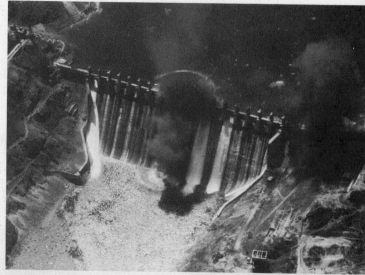

High-level conference. From left: Major General William M. Hoge, Commanding General, IX Corps; Major General Blackshear M. Bryan, Commanding General, 24th Division; Lieutenant General James A. Van Fleet, Commanding General, U.S. Eighth Army; and General Ridgway.

Marine patrol closing in on a Korean hut. Note feet of enemy casualty in the doorway. U.N. offensive, opened on 18 May, was slowed by heavy rains, mud, and stiff enemy resistance.

A casualty receives emergency first aid. On the 25th, elements of the 7th Division moved north of Ch'unch'on.

Elements of the 16th ROK Regiment move up to take over positions held by the 3rd U. S. Infantry Division.

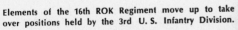

737

Evacuating 2d Division Casualties
across the Soyang River.

Supplies for the 187th Regimental Combat Team dropping near
Umyang-ni, south of Inje. On 27 May, the 187th drove into Inje.

Observation plane searching the rugged peaks for information on enemy positions
to relay to ground troops.

B-26 Invader over a target in North Korea

738

Medical corpsmen administer plasma.

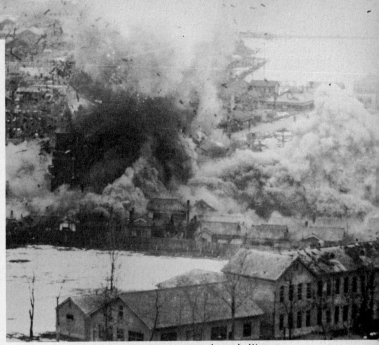
Direct hit on an enemy warehouse in Wonsan

F-86 Sabrejets ready to take off for "Mig Alley," an area in North Korea where Russian-built MIG–15 jets were frequently encountered.

A Sikorsky helicopter approaches a marker placed as a landing guide.

Marines hold down the helicopter after it lands on the windy slope.

United Nations Delegation at Kaesong. From left: Major General Laurence C. Craigie, USAF; Major General Paik Sun Yup, Commanding General, ROK I Corps; Vice Admiral C. Turner Joy, Far East Naval Commander (acting as chief delegate for the U.N.); Major General Henry I. Hodes, Deputy Chief of Staff, U.S. Eighth Army; and Rear Admiral Arleigh A. Burke, U.S.N.

TRUCE FEELERS: JUNE 1951

On 23 June 1951, Jacob Malik, the Soviet Union's delegate to the United Nations, made a public statement that implied Chinese and North Korean willingness to discuss terms of an armistice. Communist China's government followed Malik's lead with an announcement that indicated its own desire for a truce, and President Truman authorized General Ridgway to arrange an armistice conference with his enemy counterpart. Through an exchange of radio messages, both sides agreed to conduct negotiations beginning on 10 July at Kaesong, in what was then no man's land in the west but would become a neutral area.

At the first armistice conference the two delegations agreed that hostilities would continue until an armistice agreement was signed. Yet it seemed unlikely that either side would open any large-scale offensive as long as peace talks were in session, and action along the front, except for brief, violent episodes, never regained the momentum of the first year.

By 26 July the two armistice delegations had fixed the points to be settled in order to bring about an armistice. But immediately thereafter enemy delegates seemed more concerned with gaining concessions than compromising differences. To U.N. delegates it appeared that the enemy

Enemy delegation at conference site. From left: Major General Hsieh Fang and Lieutenant General Teng Hua, Chinese Army; Lieutenant General Nam Il, chief delegate for the Communists; Major General Lee Sang Cho and Major General Chang Pyong San, North Korean Army.

Conference site in Kaesong. Photograph was taken 10 July 1951, the day negotiations opened.

Orphaned Korean children received money, clothing, food and toys contributed by thousands of Americans.

sought to delay negotiations so as to gain time to strengthen his forces, and thus strengthen his position at the bargaining table and on the field of battle.

Van Fleet Improves U.N. Defensive Position

This last possibility did not escape General Van Fleet. While enemy delegates continued to delay and finally broke off

negotiations on 22 August, after charging that U.N. aircraft had attacked neutral Kaesong, Van Fleet launched a series of limited-objective attacks to improve the Eighth Army's defensive position. His U.S. X and ROK I Corps in east-central Korea fought for terrain objectives 5 to 7 miles above Line Kansas, among them Bloody and Heartbreak ridges, to drive enemy forces from positions that favored an attack

Hill 983, crest of Bloody Ridge.

Positions on the main line of resistance occupied by the Colombian Battalion, attached to the 24th Division, near Chup'a-ri overlooking the Kumsong Valley.

General of the Army Omar N. Bradley, Chairman of the Joint Chiefs of Staff, at 7th Division headquarters area. From the left: Lieutenant General William M. Hoge, Commanding General, IX Corps; General Bradley; Major General Ira P. Swift, Commanding General, 25th Infantry Division; Major General Frank F. Everest, Commanding General, 5th Air Force (shaking hands with General Bradley).

Wet and chilled, cavalrymen huddle around
a small can of burning gasoline.

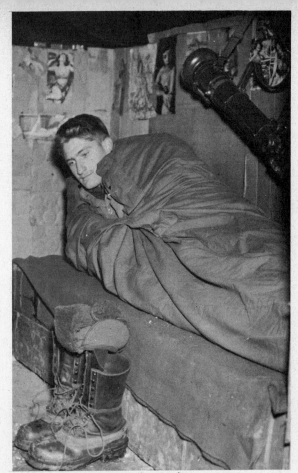

Now I lay me down to sleep. . . .

Wintry washday in
the 24th Division area,
24 November.

New Year's Day dinner
on its way up to Company L,
21st Infantry, near Kumsong.

743

on Line Kansas. These objectives were won by the last week of October. In the west, U.S. I Corps struck northeastward on a 40-mile front to secure a new line 3 to 4 miles beyond the Wyoming line in order to protect important supply routes that lay only a short distance behind the existing western front. U.S. I Corps met less resistance than its sister corps to the east, and captured the new positions by 12 October.

Successful advances in August, September, and October gave the Eighth Army possession of commanding ground along the entire front, and may have had an influence on the enemy, who now agreed to return to the armistice conference. Negotiations resumed on 25 October, this time at Panmunjom, a tiny settlement 7 miles southeast of Kaesong.

The Armistice Conference Resumes

Since the armistice conference was back in session, the possibility of peace loomed larger, and, since the Eighth Army now controlled excellent defensive positions, the cost of further assaults would be more than results could justify. For these reasons General Ridgway on 12 November ordered Van Fleet to defend his present front, limiting attacks to

those necessary to strengthen the main line of resistance and to establish an outpost line. Hope for an early armistice grew when, on 27 November, the two delegations agreed that a line of demarcation during an armistice would be the present line of contact, provided an armistice agreement was reached within 30 days. Thus while both sides awaited the outcome of negotiations, fighting tapered off to patrol clashes, raids, and small battles for possession of outposts in no man's land.

Discord over several issues, including the exchange of prisoners of war, prevented an armistice agreement in the 30 days between 27 November and 27 December. The prisoner-of-war quarrel heightened in January 1952 after U.N. delegates proposed to give captives a choice in repatriation proceedings. By the Geneva Conventions of 1949, which govern present-day warfare, prisoners are to be "set at liberty" at the end of a war. Accordingly, the United Nations maintained that those prisoners who did not wish to return to Communist control could be repatriated elsewhere. The enemy's representatives protested vigorously, insisting that all captives held by the Eighth Army be returned to their side. Thus, as 1952 opened, there appeared to be no easy path to an armistice.

Leaving warming tents to carry out a fire mission. The men are from Battery B, 37th Field Artillery Battalion.

January 1952. In this month the Eighth Army opened a sustained artillery-air campaign against enemy positions.

Medic treating injured 2d division infantryman, 14 February 1952, while a wounded ROK soldier is helped up the steep bank to await his turn.

Platoon leader briefing his men before leaving on a reconnaissance patrol, June 1952.

Searchlight, west of Ch'orwon. This searchlight, mounted on the bed of a converted 2½-ton truck, was used to illuminate communist position at night.

A Campaign Promise—Ike to Korea

President-elect Dwight D. Eisenhower in Korea, December 1952. The President-elect is with Major General James C. Fry, Commanding General, 2d Division.

He has dinner with 3d Division troops, south of Ch'orwon.

He leaves 3d Division area by jeep; in back seat are Lieutenant General Reuben E. Jenkins, Commanding General, IX Corps (left), and Major General George W. Smythe, Commanding General, 3d Division.

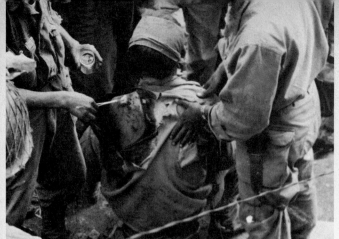

Treating a ROK soldier wounded on
Capital Hill, 8 September.

Battle-weary from fighting on Old Baldy.

T66 multiple rocket launchers in action, 40th Division sector, 26 November. Except for brief encounters with the enemy, most of the front remained relatively quiet during November and December.

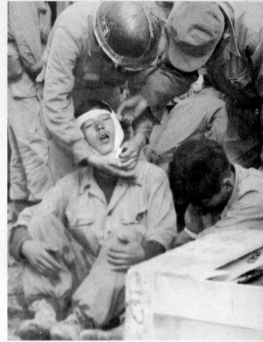

Medical Aid men dressing wounds at an aid station near base of White Horse.

White Horse (Hill 395), one of two key heights northwest of Ch'orwon attacked by enemy units in October. Vehicle is a 90mm gun motor carriage M36.

747

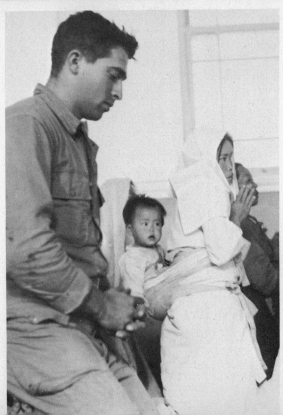

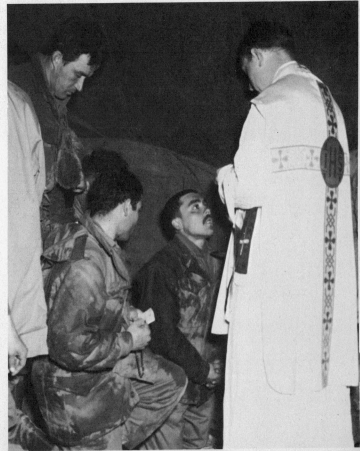

Negotiations Continue All Through 1952

While argument continued, both sides tacitly extended the 27 November provisions for a line of demarcation. This had the effect of holding battle action in 1952 to the pattern of the 30-day waiting period. Both sides fought artillery duels, dispatched patrols, set up ambushes, launched raids, and fought bitter contests for outpost positions. The tempo of battle followed the seasons, quickening during spring and summer, diminishing as winter approached. The men who fought small-scale but furious battles on oddly shaped land masses in no man's land such as Sniper Ridge, the Hook, the T-Bone, and Old Baldy, experienced all-out warfare, but the lines remained substantially unchanged as the year ended. In the meantime, the armistice conference recessed once again without coming to agreement. Indeed, peace prospects at the end of 1952 seemed as remote as at the year's beginning.

FIGHTING RESUMES IN 1953

Operations early in 1953 resembled those of the previous year. Through February, a month in which Lieutenant General Maxwell D. Taylor replaced General Van Fleet as Eighth Army Commander, and through March and April the front remained generally quiet. The pace of battle quickened in May when Chinese forces launched regimental-sized attacks against 5 outposts guarding approaches to the Eighth Army's western positions. A larger battle flared in central Korea on 10 June, when 3 Chinese divisions struck down both sides of the Pukhan River against the ROK II Corps's main defenses. Brushing aside South Korean counterattacks, the Chinese drove the right of the ROK II Corps two miles to the south before South Korean troops could contain the attack.

Armistice negotiations had resumed in April. The prisoner exchange problem finally was settled by providing each side an opportunity to persuade those captives refusing repatriation to their homeland to change their minds. With this obstacle removed, the delegates quickly negotiated remaining matters so that by 18 June terms of an armistice were all but complete. But on that date South Korean President Syngman Rhee, who from the beginning had objected to any armistice that left Korea divided, ordered the release of those North Korean prisoners who had refused repatriation. Within a few days most of the North Korean prisoners broke out of prison camp and disappeared among the cooperative South Korean people. Since these captives had been guarded by South Korean troops, United Nations Command officials disclaimed responsibility for the break, but the enemy's armistice delegates denounced the action as a serious breach of faith. It took more than a month to repair the damage done by President Rhee's order.

Enemy forces used this delay to wrest as much ground as possible from U.N. control. Again they attempted to penetrate the Eighth Army's line in central Korea. On the night of 13 July, 3 Chinese divisions opened the last battle with an attack down the U.S. IX Corps–ROK II Corps boundary, and in a short time the bulk of 5 Chinese armies reinforced the offensive. Under the heavy blow the ROK II Corps and the right flank division of the U.S. IX Corps fell back 8 miles to positions below the Kumsong River. To counter the enemy's offensive, General Taylor committed American divisions at the shoulders of the enemy penetration and sent the ROK II Corps in a counterattack toward the south bank of the Kumsong River. There, by Taylor's order, the South Koreans established a new main line of resistance on 20 July.

Troops boarding a helicopter to be airlifted up to the line.

Wounded 7th division infantry-man is rushed away from the fight on Pork Chop Hill.

General Mark W. Clark, Commander in Chief, U.N. Command (right), at the Greek Battalion headquarters. With him are (from left) Lieutenant General Reuben E. Jenkins, Commanding General, IX Corps; Lieutenant General Maxwell D. Taylor, Commanding General, Eighth Army; and Lieutenant Colonel George Koumanacos, Commanding Officer of the Greek Battalion.

THE PANMUNJOM ARMISTICE: 23 JULY 1953

Taylor made no move to restore the original ROK II Corps line, for by 20 July negotiators at Panmunjom had reached agreement on all armistice terms. At 1000, 27 July, the chief of each armistice delegation signed the agreement. A few hours later General Mark W. Clark, who had replaced General Ridgway as head of the United Nations Command, and the enemy commanders signed the papers. By prior agreement fighting was to stop 12 hours after the first signatures had been placed on the armistice documents. Thus, at 2200, 27 July 1953, hostilities ended.

By the terms of the armistice, the existing front line remained the boundary between North and South Korea. Troops on each side withdrew 2 kilometers, establishing a demilitarized boundary zone across which military trespassing was prohibited. The introduction of additional troops or of new weapons by either side was banned, though replacement in kind was permitted. Both a Military Armistice Commission, composed of U.N. and Communist officers, and a Neutral Nations Supervisory Commission with representatives from Sweden, Switzerland, Czechoslovakia, and Poland, were established to oversee the enforcement of these terms. Similarly, a Neutral Nations Repatriation Com-

mission, with India added as umpire and custodian of prisoners, was set up to handle the voluntary repatriation of prisoners. Finally, the armistice terms recommended the holding of a political conference for final settlement of the whole Korean question.

AIR SUPPORT

The circumstances under which the Communists fought the Korean war in the face of an accomplished United Nations air superiority allowed the United Nations air forces to operate at a greater rate than would otherwise have been possible. Of the three classical missions of tactical airpower —air superiority, interdiction, and close air support of friendly ground troops—the close support was the most complex, since it involved an intricate communications system between ground and air forces. Army commanders preferred to rely upon their own artillery for support within the first 1,000 yards of their fronts except in critical situation (32,482 such sorties); therefore air interdiction played a big role in Korea (192,581 such sorties). Interdiction is the employment of airpower to prevent, delay, or destroy enemy men, supplies, and equipment before they reach the battlefield.

Between 26 June 1950 and 27 July 1953, U.S. Air Force,

Marine, and friendly foreign aircrews claimed to have killed 184,808 enemy troops, hit 8,663 gun positions, 8,839 bunkers, 1,327 tanks, and 82,920 military vehicles. Extensive interrogation of North Korean prisoners of war revealed an estimate that interdiction and close air support destroyed 70 percent of their tanks, trucks, and artillery pieces and inflicted 47 percent of the casualties sustained by their troops.

In the Korean conflict, the United Nations Organization (Soviet bloc excepted) for the first time committed military forces to enforce its resolution against armed aggression. Under American leadership, the U.N. Command developed into an international group of ground, air, and naval forces representing the Republic of Korea, 20 U.N. member countries, and one other non-U.N. nation.

Of U.N. contributors, the United States, Great Britain, Australia, New Zealand, Canada, Turkey, Greece, France, Belgium, Luxembourg, the Netherlands, Thailand, the Philippines, Columbia, and Ethiopia furnished ground combat troops. India, Sweden, and Norway supplied ground medical facilities, and Denmark sent the hospital ship **Jutlandia.** Air forces came from the United States, Australia, Canada, and the Union of South Africa. Naval forces arrived from the United States, Great Britain, Australia, Canada, and New Zealand. Italy, a non-U.N. country, sent a hospital unit late in 1951.

The basic task of American leaders charged with creating an effective fighting force from the troops of a number of nations included in the Eighth Army was the development of standard organization and equipment. As a practical measure, since command and bulk of equipment were American, operations had to be conducted according to American methods. Although the problems were as diverse as the origins of the troops, a general cooperative attitude among the varied units allowed American leaders to build a cohesive war machine.

Among American units themselves, the biggest problems were those of insufficient numbers, inadequate training, and equipment shortages, but an expeditious flow of enlisted and officers replacements, accelerated training programs, and emergency equipment renovation and procurement procedures substantially reduced these handicaps.

In 37 months of fighting, U.N. forces lost almost 74,000 men killed and 250,000 wounded. Of those killed, 44,000 were South Koreans, 27,000 were Americans, and 3,000 were from other U.N. countries. The effect of U.N. firepower and the enemy's costly tactics is reflected in an estimate of 1,350,000 dead and wounded suffered by the Chinese and North Koreans. Thus the casualty ratio was 4 to 1 in favor of U.N. forces. In terms of territorial gain the enemy was the loser, winning 850 square miles of territory previously controlled by South Korea but giving up 2,350 square miles of North Korea.

Operation Little Switch, April 1953. On 11 April agreement was reached for the exchange of 605 U.N. prisoners for 6,030 enemy prisoners.

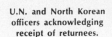

U.N. and North Korean officers acknowledging receipt of returnees.

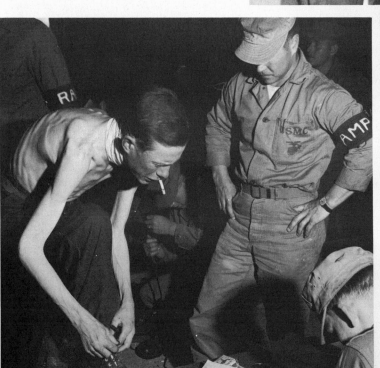

Emaciated and wounded American receiving new clothing at Freedom Village, Panmunjom.

Signing the Armistice agreement at 1000 hours, 27 July 1953, Panmunjom. Lieutenant General William K. Harrison, Jr., signs for the United Nations (left), and General Nam Il for the Communists (right).

Liberated Americans are escorted down the ramp of a C–124 upon arrival in Japan for medical treatment before continuing the trip back to the United States.

First shipment of repatriated men from Korea docking at San Francisco, 23 August.

DIVISIONS INSIGNIA (KOREAN WAR)

The shoulder patches of the major units of the United States ground forces who fought in Korea. The 11th Airborne Division patch is shown because men from that division made up the 187th Regimental Combat Team. The 1st Marine Division is no longer authorized a shoulder patch; the one shown was worn by members of the 1st Marine Division during World War II. Units of the 40th and 45th Infantry Divisions also participated in the Korean War.

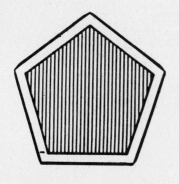

5th REGIMENTAL COMBAT TEAM

187th AIRBORNE REGIMENTAL
COMBAT TEAM

EIGHTH ARMY

I CORPS

IX CORPS

X CORPS

1st CAVALRY DIVISION

2d INFANTRY DIVISION

3d INFANTRY DIVISION

7th INFANTRY DIVISION

11th AIRBORNE DIVISION

24th INFANTRY DIVISION

25th INFANTRY DIVISION

1st MARINE DIVISION

General Dwight D. Eisenhower, Supreme Commander of NATO from 1951 February until 1952 April (left), in the field during a visit to the U.S. 12th Infantry Regiment in Germany.

CHAPTER 18

THE U.S. ARMY SINCE 1950

When the Korean War came to a close the United States was at the peak of a general rearmament effort to which the war had given the impetus. Military appropriations for fiscal years 1951–1953 totaled 155.6 billion dollars, almost five times what they had been during the previous three years. The Army's share came to slightly over one-third of this sum, approximately 54 billion. Rearmament involved a partial mobilization of both manpower and industry, and its aim was not simply to provide the sinews for the hot war in Korea, but to enable the United States to cope with the Communist threat on a worldwide basis. The goal was to provide a reasonable defensive strength in terms of balanced air, ground, and naval forces to serve as a deterrent to Communist aggression and to establish a mobilization base that could be rapidly expanded in case the deterrent failed.

The manpower goals of the rearmament program were generally reached by mid-1952. Total personnel in the Army, Navy, and Air Force increased from 1,460,000 to 3,636,000 in two years. The Army expanded from a skeleton force of less than 600,000 men to almost 1,600,000, enough to provide 20 divisions and supporting troops. This Army expansion took place in three stages. In the first, over 310,000 Reservists and National Guardsmen were called to active duty, both as individuals and in units, as trainers and for immediate defense missions. The next stage was the absorption of volunteers and selective service inductees, and the third the release of most of the reserves and their replacement by the men they had trained. Whereas 15 percent of Army strength in July 1951 was composed of National Guardsmen and Reservists, by July 1953 this proportion had fallen to 1.5 percent and the proportion of selectees had risen from 40 to 57.5 percent.

Progress in training the new units, and in equipping the expanded Army with modern military equipment, was necessarily slower than the recruiting of manpower. Training was vastly complicated by the tremendous turnover in personnel, almost 50 percent during the last year of the Korean War. Equipping of units was slowed by the long lead time involved in the production of major military items. Not until mid-1952 were the products of the partial mobilization begun in 1950 forthcoming in any significant volume.

American rearmament was closely tied in with the effort of the other nations joined with the United States in the North Atlantic Treaty Organization (NATO) to create a balanced force to protect the critical area in Western Europe. The initial American contribution to NATO consisted of 6 Army divisions and impressive air and naval forces. Moreover, American equipment furnished under the Mutual Defense Assistance Program (MDAP) and American economic assistance to NATO nations were both vital factors in enabling the alliance to maintain forces in the field.

ATOMIC WEAPONS

Though the major emphasis during the 1950–1953 period was toward making up previous deficiencies in conventional armament, the period also saw revolutionary developments in the field of atomic weapons. On 1 November 1952 the United States exploded its first fusion, or thermonuclear, device at its atomic testing grounds in the Pacific. The USSR was less than a year behind, setting off its own thermonuclear detonation in August 1953. The world soon learned that it would have to live with power great enough to destroy the largest cities at one blow.

Members of a Military Assistance Advisory Group liaison team explain the magneto timing of the 105mm howitzer to soldiers of the West German Army at Boostedt, Germany, in 1959.

During the 1950's the Army developed a mechanical ditch-digger to provide rapid protection for the troops. It could dig a trench 4 feet deep and 24 inches wide at the rate of 12 feet a minute.

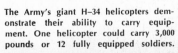

The Army's giant H–34 helicopters demonstrate their ability to carry equipment. One helicopter could carry 3,000 pounds or 12 fully equipped soldiers.

On 23 May 1953 the Army fired the world's first atomic artillery shell. The firing took place at Frenchman's Flat, Nevada.

The Army's experimental one-man helicopter during a test flight in 1957.

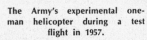

A logistical cargo carrier delivers supplies at Camp Century, Greenland.

The carbine in this picture is equipped with an infrared sight.

Miniature transmitting and receiving devices, developed during the 1950's, improved field communications.

Practicing with the new M14 rifle. The M14 was designed to replace the carbine, the .45-caliber submachine gun, and the Garand rifle.

Moving forward under fire at Camp Breckinridge, Kentucky.

757

A practice jump.

Counterinsurgents leave Ibu Dake, Okinawa, on a long-range patrol mission. The troops will receive some supplies by air, but they are also expected to live off the land.

A Nike Ajax site with 24 missiles in position. The picture was taken at Lorton, Virginia, in 1956.

The Nike Hercules
guided missile.

A Hawk missile crew
prepares for a launching.

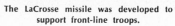

The LaCrosse missile was developed to
support front-line troops.

The Corporal, a surface-to-surface guided
missile on a transportation tractor at the
Army's Infantry Center, Fort Benning,
Georgia, in 1955.

Loading the Honest John, a free-flight
artillery rocket, onto a launching platform.

The H-bomb was the most fearsome product of an advancing atomic technology, but not the only one. The uses to which atomic energy could be put, both destructive and constructive, seemed limitless. The Navy developed an atomic-powered submarine that promised to revolutionize sea warfare in the future. More important for the Army, atomic science produce a wide variety of warheads of variant power ranging from a fraction of a kiloton to megaton-range weapons. At the atomic tests in the Pacific in 1955, a so-called "clean" bomb was exploded, one from which radioactive fallout was drastically reduced. These developments gave impetus to the search for practicable methods of using atomic explosives in ground warfare. By 1953 the Army had a 280mm cannon in operation capable of firing an atomic shell, but it was too immobile and unwieldy to be entirely satisfactory. Hopes for the future use of atomic warheads in land battle soon came to rest primarily on new developments in the field of ballistic missiles.

In truth, missile delivery systems promised to have almost as revolutionary an effect as atomic explosives themselves. In the United States, from 1945 until 1950, missile research went forward at a snail's pace; but by the end of the Korean War all three services were actively developing missiles, each seeking delivery systems best suited to its particular mission. In the USSR work on missile weapons apparently went forward full speed from 1945 onward. Both countries sought missiles within a wide field of ranges and purposes. At one end stood the Intercontinental Ballistic Missile (ICBM), which, combined with the H-bomb, many regarded as the ultimate weapon against which no defense was possible. At the other end were tactical missiles of short range primarily suited for land battle. In between lay a broad field of intermediate range (IRBM), ground-to-air, and air-to-ground missiles that could serve a multiplicity of military purposes.

Immediately on assuming office in 1953, the Eisenhower Administration began a review and reevaluation of the military posture of the United States in the light of both the worldwide nature of the Communist threat and the new weapons developments. The upshot of this reevaluation was a military program popularly identified as the New Look. The underlying philosophy of the New Look was that military preparations must not be geared to any one critical year but should be continued indefinitely into the future, and that these preparations must be carried out without placing an inordinate burden on the American economy. This new policy of long-range preparations at maximum economy clearly pointed to a greater emphasis on air-atomic power. As Secretary of State John Foster Dulles put it, the basic decision was to "rely primarily upon a great capacity to retaliate, instantly and at places of our own choosing." The doctrine of massive retaliation clearly meant that the United States would not in the future necessarily limit its effort to local defense as it had in Korea but would apply its air-atomic power to whatever degree and in whatever area it would be most advantageously employed. To achieve "more security at less cost," the stress would be on atomic weapons of all types as substitutes for conventional ones and the masses of manpower required to use them, and on concentrated mobile power rather than forces expensively dispersed around the world.

The New Look philosophy, taken in conjunction with the end of hostilities in Korea, produced a gradual reduction in Army strength in the years following. It is worth noting, however, that the Korean War was not followed by an immediate and drastic demobilization as all other American wars had been. The 1,534,000-man ground army in existence at the end of the Korean War was cut step by step to a level of around 900,000 men by June 1954. While an intensive effort was made to make as many cuts as possible in the service establishment, the number of active divisions also had to be reduced from 20 to 15, in large part by withdrawing divisions from the Far East. The 7 Army divisions in Korea at the time of the signing of the armistice was reduced to 2 in step with the training and equipping of Republic of Korea troops. The last Army division was withdrawn from Japan in 1957.

In view of the rapid strides the USSR was making in developing atomic bombs and building a strategic air force to deliver them, the United States had to look to the modernization of its air defenses. By 1957 a virtually complete radar warning net had been installed in cooperation with the Canadian Government. The distant early warning (DEW) line was constructed across Canada and Alaska, and was supplemented by other lines across middle and southern Canada, by extensions in the Aleutians chain, by radar towers offshore, and by naval picket ships and airborne early warning craft. Operational responsibility for air defense was entrusted to the Continental Air Defense Command (CONAD) for which the Air Force was executive agent, but all three services shared in the effort. The Army's main contribution lay in the field of ground antiaircraft defense. In this field the Army developed the first operational antiaircraft missile, the Nike Ajax, a weapon with far greater range, altitude, and accuracy than any existing antiaircraft gun. By mid-1956, Nike Ajax units were on site in 22 vital defense areas, and a new version had been developed, Nike Hercules, of even greater range and altitude. With an atomic warhead, a single Nike Hercules promised to make possible destruction of whole fleets of enemy bombers. By 1958 it was replacing the Ajax at selected sites. Meanwhile, work went forward on the Hawk, a missile designed to meet the threat of low-flying aircraft. While the ability to deliver a retaliatory blow remained the principal deterrent against atomic attack, improved air defenses heightened the value of the deterrent and promised to exact a high cost in any attack by manned enemy bombers.

THE ARMY'S RESERVE FORCES

It was becoming increasingly clear by 1953 that wars in the future would depend more on forces in being when the war started than on war potential, and that this country would never again have time to train its great reserves of manpower behind a shield provided by allies abroad. An essential feature of the New Look was therefore an effort to provide Reserve forces that could be mobilized rapidly to fulfill a wartime role without extensive additional training.

By legislation passed during the Korean War, Congress placed a theoretical "military obligation" on all physically and mentally qualified males between the ages of eighteen and one-half and twenty-six for a total of eight years of combined active and Reserve military duty. The Reserve was divided into two categories, the Ready Reserve, which could be ordered to duty on declaration of an emergency by the President, in numbers authorized by Congress, and the Standby Reserve, which could only be ordered to duty in war or emergency declared by Congress. To fulfill his military obligation, a young eligible male had several alternatives. By spending five years of his eight-year obligation on active duty or in a combination of active duty and membership in the Ready Reserve, he could transfer to the Standby Reserve for his last three years. Or he might join the National Guard at eighteen, and by rendering satisfactory service there for ten years avoid active duty unless his Guard unit were called into federal service. For college students there was also the alternative of enrolling in an ROTC course and, on its successful completion, spending two or three years on active duty and the remainder of the eight years as a Reserve officer.

This system had many weaknesses. There was really no compulsory military obligation beyond existing selective service arrangements, and draft quotas dwindled rapidly after the conclusion of the Korean War. The obligation to remain in the Reserve carried with it no compulsion either to enlist in a Reserve unit or to participate in continued training. Since enlistees in the National Guard required no prior training, Guard units had to spend most of their time drilling recruits. Thus the Reserve, while strong enough numerically, fulfilled none of the requisites for rapid mobilization in case of need, and there was no assurance that it would be kept up to strength by a steady input of young Reservists.

To remedy these weaknesses Congress, at the urging of the President, passed new Reserve legislation in 1955. While this act reduced the term of obligatory service from eight to six years, it imposed a requirement for active participation in Reserve training on those passing out of the armed services with an unexpired obligation. It also authorized voluntary enlistment of young men between the ages of seventeen and eighteen and one-half in the Reserve up to a total of 250,000 per year. These youths would receive six months of basic training after which they would pass into the Ready Reserve for seven and one-half years of additional service. As long as they participated satisfactorily they would be exempt from induction under selective service. All ROTC graduates were to receive Reserve commissions, but those in excess of current needs would serve six months on active duty followed by seven and one-half years in the Reserve instead of a two- or three-year tour within a six-year military obligation. The President was authorized, without further Congressional action, to call a million Ready Reservists to duty in an emergency proclaimed by him. He could also recall selected members of the Standby Reserve, and continuously screen the Ready Reserve to eliminate nonparticipants.

The Reserve Forces Act of 1955 was a major forward step toward the goal of organizing an effective Reserve that could be mobilized rapidly in war or emergency. A mobilization schedule was set up for the various units in both the Army National Guard and the Army Reserve. The tendency, as in the Active Army, was toward reducing overall numerical strength while concentrating on training those units that could be mobilized and deployed in the early stages of any conflict. While the irregularity of voluntary enlistments and restricted funds kept many of these units below their authorized strength, the efficiency of the Reserve forces as a whole rapidly improved from 1955 onward.

U.S. DEFENSIVE ALLIANCES

The worldwide nature of the Communist threat forced the United States to accept an ever-widening defense perimeter. By the end of the war in Korea, the United States had defensive alliances of varying nature with 14 NATO nations, 20 Latin American nations, Australia, New Zealand, and Japan. Recurrent crises in the years following produced new commitments.

The most difficult problem of all was in Southeast Asia. The end of the war in Korea enabled the Chinese Reds to step up their aid to the Communist rebels in Indo-China. Despite extensive American material aid, the French and loyal native forces in the area were unable to hold. Serious proposals of active intervention by American air and naval forces were made but finally rejected. In the end a settlement was reached in a conference at Geneva in 1954 providing for partition of Viet Nam much as Korea had been partitioned and for the withdrawal of the French from the area. The settlement left the whole of Southeast Asia dangerously exposed to further Chinese Communist aggression. To bolster defenses in the area, the United States extended military and economic aid to the remaining free Indo-Chinese states—South Viet Nam, Laos, and Cambodia—and entered into the Southeast Asia Collective Defense Treaty to provide the framework of an allied defense structure. This regional defense pact was signed on 8 September 1954 by the United States, France, Britain, New Zealand, the Philippine Republic, Thailand, and Pakistan. The contracting parties recognized that aggression in Southeast Asia should be regarded as a common danger, and that each party would act to meet it "in accordance with its constitutional processes."

In an effort to block the USSR in its attempts further to increase Soviet influence in the Middle East, the United States early in 1957 adopted the Eisenhower Doctrine. This doctrine pledged American military assistance to nations in the Middle East endangered by Communist aggression, and empowered the President to use the Armed Forces of the United States for this purpose. It was in consequence of this pledge that the United States sent military forces into Lebanon in the summer of 1958.

The far-flung commitments of the United States were not, except in the NATO area and Korea, supported by major overseas deployments of U.S. Army forces. The Army's role in supporting them lay rather in the maintenance of a mobile Reserve force and in its contributions to the equipping and training of foreign armies. By the end of 1956, the United States was furnishing military assistance to 38 different nations; the Army was represented in Military Assistance Advisory Groups (MAAG's) in 25 countries, and Army missions were performing MAAG functions in ten others. It was calculated that altogether the United States was assisting in training and equipping the equivalent of 200 ground divisions in other nations of the Free World.

THE CONCEPT OF LIMITED WARS

It was with the conviction that limited war was a likely contingency in the future and that even in a general atomic war, land action would be required before any victory could be decisive that the Army's leaders undertook the challenging task of revamping the Army's structure and doctrine to enable it to fulfill its mission in the atomic age. Within the limits of resources allotted to it, the Army in the years following Korea pushed ahead with the development of new concepts, new weapons, and new tactical formations. The basic premise behind these new concepts was that the Army must be versatile, maintaining a capability to fight with either atomic or conventional weapons. The emphasis was on mobility, both strategic and tactical, and on a high ratio of firepower to manpower with either type of weapon.

Improvements were registered in conventional weapons all along the line, and new short-range missiles were developed as the main reliance for an atomic capability. By 1958, the Corporal and Honest John, with ranges up to 75 miles, and the Redstone, with a range of 200 miles, were in operational units. New and lighter versions were under development. The Lacrosse, a shorter-range missile for close support of infantry, was emerging from the development stage. For battlefield mobility, the main reliance was on armored troop carriers that would not be roadbound, and helicopters and other short-range low-performance aircraft.

A new concept of tactical organization was introduced in 1956, centering upon the pentomic division and the missile commands. As opposed to the triangular infantry division of World War II with its three regimental combat teams, the pentomic infantry and airborne divisions were composed of five battle groups, each a self-contained force capable of independent operations. The armored division underwent less drastic change because it was already better adapted to the requisite pattern of mobility and dispersion. While the pentomic division had its own organic artillery and missiles with an atomic capability, the heavier and longer-range missiles were concentrated in supporting missile commands.

Reorganization of the Army for nuclear warfare called for a concurrent streamlining of the logistics system. In the atomic age, the Army could no longer count on supplying its troops on the lavish scale of World War II or Korea, or, at least in general war, on any sustained production of munitions once war began. Use of ports, large central depots, and rail lines might well be impossible. The new logistics system stressed reduction of requirements to absolute essentials, prestocking of depots in the United States and key overseas areas, lightning processing of requisitions by electronic machines, delivery of essential items by air transport or fast naval vessels, reliance on delivery over beaches by roll-on, roll-off vessels and aerial tramways rather than on fixed port installations, and use of supply carriers capable of cross-country movement. The working out of a new logistics system based on these principles was one of the most difficult of the many problems of preparing the Army to fight in the atomic age.

By the end of 1958 all of the 15 remaining Regular Army divisions had been reorganized along pentomic lines and deployed in keeping with the New Look concept of a highly mobile central reserve as a substitute for scattered ground garrisons. In Europe 5 divisions remained as part of the NATO forces, 2 were posted in Korea, and 1 in Hawaii. The other 7 were concentrated as a strategic reserve in the United States.

THE DEFENSE REORGANIZATION ACT: 6 AUGUST 1958

On 3 April 1958 President Eisenhower asked Congress for new legislation granting greater powers to the Secretary of Defense over the three services, strengthening the organization of the Joint Chiefs-of-Staff, and establishing a single chain of command running from the President through the Secretary of Defense to various operational commands. Though the President's plan encountered serious opposition in Congress and was considerably modified by Congressional action, its basic features remained intact in the Defense Reorganization Act of 6 August 1958. All military operations were placed under a unified command emanating from the President to the Secretary of Defense, with the JCS as principal planners and advisers in directing operations. The system of using service secretaries as executive agents was eliminated. The three service departments were to be "separately organized" but not "separately administered," and the Secretary of Defense was granted greater freedom in shifting functions among the services subject to the veto power of Congress in certain instances. A Director of Research and Development was appointed in the Department of Defense, replacing two of the assistant secretaries, to exercise supervision over the research and development programs of all services. The position of the Joint Chiefs as a corporate body was strengthened, and to free the individual Chiefs-of-Staff from routine duties and enable them to devote more time to JCS work, their Vice Chiefs were granted additional power to handle service matters. The Joint Staff serving the JCS was enlarged under the restrictions that it was not to "operate" or be organized as "an overall Armed Forces General Staff."

One by one, beginning with the U.S. Forces in Europe, various operational commands were removed from the executive agent system and placed under direct Department of Defense control. The service departments remained in control of raising, training, equipping, and organizing the forces to be furnished unified commands, and of developing the weapons and equipment they would use, operating under the general supervision of the Secretary of Defense. The service chiefs retained control of all those parts of their services not assigned to unified commands, and service components of those commands still received their support through channels of their own services.

FURTHER REORGANIZATION

In 1961 came ROAD (Reorganization Objective Army Division). In this reorganization, designed to provide forces tailored to specific missions, environments, terrain, and foe, the battle group structure of the pentomic division has been replaced by a battalion structure. Five types of divisions have been organized—airborne, airmobile, infantry, armored and mechanized—containing a semifixed base to which varying mixes of combat battalions are assigned, depending upon the location and mission of a division. ROAD was created to balance nuclear and conventional forces and to provide a flexible command and control structure, and an improved capability of operating with Allied forces.

ROAD divisions exemplify an increase in flexibility and combat effectiveness. Larger than the pentomic division by approximately 500 to 2,500 troops, ROAD is given more personnel carriers, light tanks, cargo trucks, and double the number of organic aircraft. Firepower is tremendously increased—artillery by a factor of 2, machine guns by 3, and recoilless rifles by 4. The ROAD organization, which began in early 1962 with two reactivated divisions, along with other changes, is blurring the hard-and-fast branch lines and developing combined arms officers.

The Army responded to Russia's launching of earth satellites in 1957 by speeding up its own astronautical developments. By June 1959 it had sponsored the launching of three earth-orbiting satellites, two lunar probes, and the Free World's first recovery of living creatures placed in space-flight trajectory. That autumn the Army's activities in this field were restricted to the development of tactical missiles.

The Strategic Army Corps (STRAC) was organized in 1957 to handle sudden great emergencies anywhere in the world. Composed of 4, and later 3, divisions, STRAC (renamed ARSTRIKE in 1961) is to a great extent self-contained and self-sufficient. ARSTRIKE is not a separate command, but one whose forces come from and remain a part of the Continental Army Command; these forces are designated the Strategic Army Forces (STRAF).

ARSTRIKE is the ground component of the U.S. Strike Command (STRICOM), whose air element is supplied by the Tactical Air Command. STRICOM, formed in 1961, was made a most effective force by combining the airpower and airlift capability of TAC with the land forces of ARSTRIKE.

In the Cuban crisis of 1962 STRAC demonstrated its importance when nearly 30,000 troops and over 100,000 tons of equipment assigned to the Strike Command were deployed as an augmentation to the operational command of the Commander-in-Chief, Atlantic. Army air defense battalions with their Hawk and Hercules missiles were deployed during the crisis; the Peninsula Base Command became established in Florida, and additional divisions were alerted.

In 1961 the United States began to place greater emphasis on limited war capabilities. When the country was brought into a semi-emergency by a new Berlin crisis, the Army saw its 870,000 authorized strength increased to 1,081,000, its active divisions made combat-ready, two additional divisions reactivated, tours of duty extended, Selective Service calls increased, and two National Guard divisions plus thousands of reservists called up.

With all its scientific achievements in the years after the Korean War, the Army did not forget its personnel—its most important ingredient. Conditions were improved and inducements were provided officers and enlisted men. The Army established new enlisted grades and a proficiency pay system, increased reenlistment bonuses, reinstated permanent promotions, and gave officers greater opportunities for promotion and provided them with more security while in service. A new emphasis was placed on training, and entrance and retention standards were raised. As a result of these and other improvements, the Army was able to meet the crisis in Viet Nam with a highly professional force.

Today, Army technology continues to provide benefits for our society. Many convenience foods found in supermarkets are an outgrowth of Army research in long-term storage, weight, and bulk. The list includes freeze-dried foods, canned bakery products, bakery mixes, and instant beverages —from fruit juices to dry milk.

Scientists and engineers at the Army Natick Laboratories have devised a system whereby the cellulose part of waste paper, cardboard, and plastic scraps, as well as other vegetable and industrial waste, may be converted into usable glucose.

American troops in Lebanon in July 1958, in response to a request from the Lebanese government for assistance in dealing with a threatened Communist takeover.

U.S. Army troops patrol the streets of Santa Domingo in May 1965. They were sent to the Dominican Republic when Communist-inspired violence and disorder threatened the safety of Americans and other foreign nationals.

THE GREEN BERETS

Special warfare is the term the U.S. Army applies to military and paramilitary actions related to unconventional warfare, counterinsurgency and psychological warfare. While all branches contribute to the Army's special warfare function, the Special Forces soldier concentrates all his activities in that area. He is the man that wears the green beret.

The mission of the Special Forces is to develop, organize, and equip guerrilla fighters in hot war situations and to teach underdeveloped countries to help themselves in combating insurgent forces and in initiating educational, medical, and economic programs. The men who carry out the Special Forces mission are volunteers for that duty. They undergo many weeks of intensive training in one of five specialties—demolitions, weapons, operations and intelligence, communications, and medical aid. When that is completed they receive cross-training in at least one other specialty; language training; and instruction in amphibious,

swamp, jungle, and arctic survival; jungle, mountain, and cold weather operations; underwater demolitions; and psychological warfare. Before his Special Forces Training begins the volunteer must have completed Airborne training.

The basic operating unit of the Special Forces is the 12-man A detachment—10 enlisted men led by 2 officers. A detachment always has two experts in each of the five Special Forces skills. At the invitation of the host country they train and advise indigenous military forces in maintaining and restoring internal security. The 12 men are capable of training as many as 1,500 guerrilla fighters. They also help build houses, schools, hospitals, and other facilities.

At times Special Forces men must work alone or with small groups under very dangerous conditions. Whether they operate as part of the standard A detachment or alone, the wearers of the green beret have one of the most demanding assignments in the modern Army.

A Special Forces demolitions expert uses demolitions in construction projects as well as in combat, and he can teach others what he knows about conventional and unconventional explosives.

All members of the Army's Special Forces are airborne-qualified. Here a group of trainees makes a jump.

Before he completes his training, the Special Forces soldier has acquired at least a working knowledge of the language of his host country.

Two Special Forces advisors at a ranger training center in Viet Nam (second and third from left) watch as a Vietnamese instructor explains combat tactics to his class.

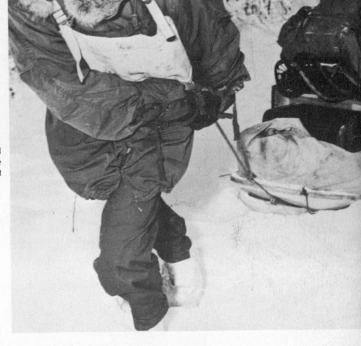

During arctic training Special Forces troopers learn to move themselves and their equipment through snow and ice.

Special Forces soldiers must be able to move quickly through all kinds of difficult terrain.

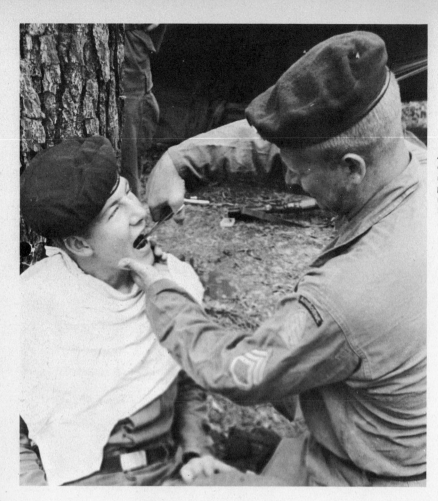

A medical specialist, who receives 37 weeks of intensive training, takes care of the other members of his detachment and the native people in his area when professional care is unavailable. He also teaches the native population the essentials of hygiene and disease prevention.

The primary job of the Special Forces soldier is to teach his skills to members of foreign military units.

Captain Roger Donlon of the Army's Special Forces, the first Medal of Honor winner since the Korean War. Captain Donlon, the commander of a Special Forces detachment in Viet Nam, won the nation's highest award for directing the successful defense of his camp against a heavy Viet Cong attack. Although he suffered four wounds during the five-hour battle, Captain Donlon moved from post to post within the besieged camp, helping his men move to new positions, caring for the wounded, retrieving abandoned weapons, and inspiring the defenders to renewed efforts. When the disorganized Viet Cong retreated into the jungle at dawn, they left 54 dead behind.

Since 25 November 1963, when a Special Forces sergeant placed his beret on the grave of President John F. Kennedy, there has been a green beret on the slain President's grave in Arlington National Cemetery. President Kennedy, who encouraged the development of the Special Forces, had called the green beret of the Special Forces soldier "the symbol of excellence, the badge of courage, the badge of distinction in the fight for freedom."

Map—Southeast Asia.

CHAPTER 19

THE ARMY IN VIETNAM

Although it is half a world removed from the continental United States, Vietnam has become a household word in America because of the massive effort being waged there to combat Communist insurgents who threaten the right of 16 million citizens of the young Asian republic to live in freedom and peace.

The Republic of Vietnam is about the size of the state of Georgia. It stretches in a 700- to 900-mile arc, for the most part 50 to 150 miles wide, lying next to Laos and Cambodia and bordering on the South China Sea. The country has a spine of dense jungle-covered mountains extending from north to south, almost reaching Saigon, its capital. South of the densely populated capital city area, the flat, fertile, canal-laced "Rice Bowl," or Mekong Delta, extends to the Gulf of Thailand.

Because of its strategic coastal location, Vietnam has for centuries been an important factor in southeast Asian affairs. Today its richness in natural resources, particularly food and rubber, makes South Vietnam a prize coveted by food-short North Vietnam and Communist China. Rice production in the rich Mekong Delta alone has the yet untapped potential of feeding the combined populations of South and North Vietnam with a surplus for export.

Although the Communist movement in South Vietnam goes back to the early 1930's, the present Viet Cong (Vietnamese Communist) structure dates from the signing of the Geneva Accords at the end of the Indochina War in 1954. Under the 1954 agreement Vietnam was divided at the 17th parallel by a temporary military demarcation line with the two areas to be administered by separate governments until the country could be reunited following elections planned for July, 1956.

Those elections have never taken place. With the passage of time, the two governments and the areas which they controlled became further divided in their international and economic affairs and in their forms of government. As a result, two Vietnams have been recognized—78 nations, including the United States, have recognized the Republic of Vietnam (South Vietnam) and 25 have recognized the Democratic Republic of Vietnam (North Vietnam). In other words, the United States and the other nations that maintain diplomatic relations with the Republic of Vietnam consider it to be an idependent national entity, exercising jurisdiction in the territory south of the 17th-parallel demarcation line.

American aid to South Vietnam began in 1950 when the Griffin Mission recommended help for the French in their war with Communist-led Viet Minh. Between 1950 and 1954 the United States contributed $4.2 billion to the French effort in Indochina. After January 1, 1955, the United States extended direct assistance to South Vietnam, both economic aid and aid in training the Vietnamese armed forces. The latter mission was handled by a U.S. Military Assistance Advisory Group (MAAG) of approximately 800 officers and men.

The program administered by MAAG allowed the United States to give important military assistance to South Vietnam without actively committing United States combat units. Under the program selected commissioned and noncommissioned officers were sent to Vietnam where they worked with infantry, artillery, armor, engineer, signal, aviation, medical, ordnance, quartermaster, military police, transportation and intelligence units of the Vietnamese armed forces. Many of the advisors were veterans of World

War II and Korea and others were highly qualified to assist with troop training, planning, and administration. An important part of their job was to persuade the Vietnamese to revise outmoded tactics and techniques.

Late in 1959 organized Communist activity increased sharply in South Vietnam. Directed by the government of North Vietnam, it took the form of guerrilla raids against army and security units, terrorism against local officials and civilians, and other subversive activities. The United States responded by increasing its economic and military aid to South Vietnam. In 1961 U.S. advisors, for the first time, were placed at the battalion level of Vietnamese military units and allowed to accompany the units on operations. This step greatly increased the advisors' usefulness because they could demonstrate techniques and observe and point out shortcomings at first hand. It also exposed the advisors to Viet Cong fire. When it became apparent that Viet Cong snipers were concentrating on the advisors, the advisors were authorized to fire back in self-defense.

An American advisor did not take command of a Vietnamese unit, but worked closely with a counterpart in the Vietnamese armed forces, giving advice and assistance of various kinds. As a member of the United States Armed Forces, an advisor received and carried out the orders of his superiors, and supervised subordinate advisors. He also observed and evaluated the performance of his counterpart and the Vietnamese unit to which he was attached. The advisor wore the shoulder insignia of the Vietnamese unit, lived as well as worked with it, and was actively concerned with its success in combat.

During combat the advisor was usually at his counterpart's side. If, however, the counterpart had to remain at a communications or command post, the advisor could visit subordinate units in the field, sometimes accompanied by his counterpart's staff officers. Advisors worked through interpreters, but most advisors learned to speak some Vietnamese. Important details were usually transmitted in writing to prevent mistakes. The successful advisor was the man who could get his counterpart to go along willingly with his recommendations, and he always made sure that the counterpart—and the unit—got the credit for a successful operation, not the advisor.

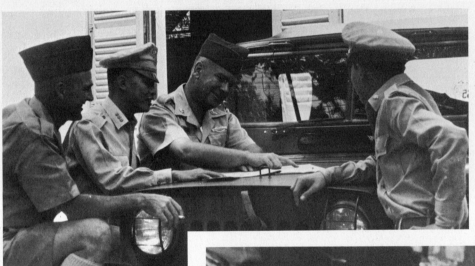

U.S. Army advisors (first and third from left) and Vietnamese officers at a military base in South Viet Nam.

A Vietnamese paratrooper and U.S. Army advisors confer on the dispatch of helicopters in support of Vietnamese army operations.

Lunch in the field. American advisors share a meal of rice, chicken, and fish with a Vietnamese battalion commander and his men.

With the help of an interpreter, an Army advisor explains the function of the military helicopter to Vietnamese infantrymen.

A U.S. Army captain checks rifles before Vietnamese infantrymen begin a training mission.

Because mobility is so important in fighting the elusive Viet Cong, Vietnamese soldiers receive extensive drill in helicopter-boarding techniques.

Disembarking from a helicopter
also requires training.

Their training completed, Vietnamese troops load up for a strike against
the Viet Cong.

Within a few seconds of landing, the
well-trained troops are out of the
helicopters and under way, rifles on
the ready.

Sweating out a mission. American
advisors wait at an airfield for helicopters to return a Vietnamese unit
from combat.

771

Because President John F. Kennedy was convinced that indirect Communist aggression involving the use of guerrillas would be the most likely form of warfare during the 1960's and because the fighting in Vietnam was definitely a counterinsurgency war, the U.S. Army moved to improve its counterinsurgency capabilities by establishing an Office of Special Warfare, inaugurating an accelerated program to train officers and men in guerrilla and counterinsurgency methods, and substantially increasing its Special Forces. Special Forces groups, trained in unconventional warfare, psychological operations, and counterinsurgency, had both a hot and a cold war mission. Their hot war mission was "to organize, supply, train and direct predominately indigenous forces in the conduct of guerrilla warfare in enemy-held or controlled territory to support the overall military effort." The cold war mission: "to train and assist indigenous leaders and forces in measures, tactics, and techniques required to prevent or eliminate hostile resistance and guerrilla groups" was their original mission in Vietnam.

Members of Special Forces teams, wearing the distinguishing green beret of their unit, gave the Vietnamese Special Forces the benefit of their own intensive training. The basic team had twelve members—two officers and ten men—each one an expert in demolition, communications, weapons, intelligence, operations, or medical aid, with cross-training in at least one other specialty. Because of the nature of their mission the teams operated in the remote, Viet Cong-dominated areas of South Vietnam.

In addition to acting as advisors to the Vietnamese military forces, Army personnel participated in the strategic hamlet program designed to consolidate the rural people of Vietnam into fortified villages under government control; to recruit, arm and train a local paramilitary force to defend the hamlets; and to win the support and confidence of the rural Vietnamese through economic and material assistance and sound advice.

In February, 1962, with the number of United States military personnel in Vietnam growing rapidly, the U.S. Military Assistance Command, Vietnam (USMACV), was established under four-star Army General Paul D. Harkins to provide centralized direction for the increased United States effort. The new command took immediate steps to improve the land, sea, and air mobility of Vietnamese forces, provide better communications and intelligence, and develop new counterinsurgency techniques and doctrine. In March, 1962, Army aviation in Vietnam and other supporting groups, mainly signal units, were organized into the U.S. Army Support Group, Vietnam. The Support Group is credited with developing many of the Army aviation tactics and techniques that have increased the mobility of the anti-Communist forces in Vietnam where the ability to move quickly is essential.

A Vietnamese soldier conducts a "house-to-house" search in the Mekong Delta area.

Bringing in prisoners after an encounter with the Viet Cong.

The two Army helicopter companies that arrived in December, 1961, were the first complete United States military units sent to Vietnam where, between July, 1962, and June, 1963, helicopters flew approximately 100,000 sorties and transported 275,000 troops and 9,000 tons of cargo. Since the Vietnamese Army had no organic aviation, U.S. helicopter units were assigned in direct support of Vietnam Army corps, but they remained under the operational control of the senior U.S. advisor to the corps who endeavored to provide a quick and adequate response to the needs of the Vietnamese commander. If necessary, helicopters transporting troops were escorted by armed helicopters or by Vietnamese-manned armed aircraft.

In addition to supplementing the troop-carrying capability of the United States Air Force in Vietnam, Army aviators have delivered supplies to outlying and isolated installations, and performed visual and instrument surveillance missions. The Army turned the intelligence derived from the surveillance missions over to the Vietnamese for use in planning ground and air operations and for target selection.

Late in 1963 the Communists stepped up their efforts in South Vietnam, and the situation there began to deteriorate. The Diem government, under increasing internal pressure, was overthrown in November, and during the ensuing political instability Communist terrorism and infiltration from the north continued. One indication of growing United States concern was the announcement on July 27, 1964, that several thousand additional advisors were being sent to Vietnam. The Pentagon had already moved to centralize and coordinate control of the United States military effort in Vietnam by deactivating MAAG, Vietnam, and placing all missions under the control of USMACV where General William C. Westmoreland had replaced General Harkins as commander on June 20, 1964.

On August 2, in the first of a series of incidents that eventually involved the United States in direct combat with the enemy, North Vietnamese torpedo boats fired on the destroyers U.S.S. **Maddox** and U.S.S. **Turner Joy** in the Gulf of Tonkin. The United States responded with bombing strikes against North Vietnam intended as a warning that the United States could not be frightened into stopping its aid to South Vietnam. When 100 Viet Cong guerrillas attacked the American compound at Pleiku on February 7, 1965, President Lyndon B. Johnson ordered "retaliatory" air strikes on North Vietnamese targets. The first United States ground combat unit, the Marine 1st Light Antiaircraft Missile Battalion (HAWK) arrived in Vietnam on February 9. It was followed by the 3d Battalion, 9th Marines and the Army's 173d Airborne Brigade (Separate). Other Army units deployed to Vietnam were the 716th Military Police Battalion and the 1st Logistical Command. On June 27 a 173d Airborne Brigade attack in War Zone D, north of Saigon, marked the first major U.S. combat offensive in Vietnam. Also in June, the B–52 heavy bombers of the United States Air Force began to attack Viet Cong installations in South Vietnam.

Under the watchful eyes of Vietnamese soldiers, captured Viet Cong suspects remove deadly "punji" stakes from a helicopter landing area.

U.S. troops, ready for combat, disembark from a CH–47A Chinook helicopter.

773

If necessary, helicopter crews can use their guns to clear an area before landing to discharge troops or cargo.

Helicopters deliver supplies as well as troops to the combat area.

Looking for the elusive Viet Cong.

A cautious group of U.S. infantrymen moves away from a landing area.

A UH-1B helicopter fires rockets
into the Vietnamese jungle.

Watching for the enemy
from a jungle foxhole.

Crossing a jungle river.

Good communications with other units
are essential in jungle fighting.

"Bastogne," a 175mm artillery
piece, fires at the enemy.

An Army corporal puts the fuse in a 105mm shell for the gun in the background.

A member of a 105mm gun crew makes elevation and windage adjustments prior to firing.

Another shell is on its way.

"Ready for fire."

776

The American combat troops found that in many ways fighting in Vietnam resembled the Indian wars of the nineteenth century. There was no front, no depth to the combat area, and operations were widely scattered and of a hit-and-run nature like the Indian raids on the frontier, but in Vietnam the enemy could usually be identified only after he committed an overt hostile act.

The enemy was a tough, fanatical fighter. He might be more afraid of his superiors than of his opponent, but under a good leader he fought well. He used a variety of weapons—American, French, Japanese, Chinese, and Russian. His heaviest were the 120mm and 81mm mortars and the 75mm recoiless rifles. He made effective use of the Soviet 12.7mm machine gun against helicopters and airplanes flying at altitudes up to 3,000 feet, and he had an antitank grenade launcher whose 40mm charge could pierce six inches of steel.

Booby traps and mines were a constant hazard, especially the deadly claymore mine—a pie plate weighing about 20 pounds and measuring 2 inches in thickness and up to 12 inches in diameter. The larger types contained 10 pounds of explosives and hundreds of steel pellets. Claymores on special mounts were used to attack headquarters buildings and barracks in Saigon and elsewhere. When United States convoys passed along the roads, buried, command-detonated claymores were exploded by operators hidden in the jungle. Sometimes two mines were buried close together. After the first had exploded and rescuers were at work, the second went off to increase the casualties.

Because the Viet Cong knew the country so well, they were hard to detect and pin down. This made it possible for them to attack United States bases, destroying aircraft and inflicting other damage before disappearing as silently as they had arrived. Dressed in the clothing worn by the Vietnamese peasants, a member of the Viet Cong could sit along a road near an American camp and count the number of soldiers leaving on a patrol, then take a shortcut through the jungle to help ambush the patrol, and return to the roadside to count the number of soldiers that returned from the patrol. The North Vietnamese soldier fighting in the south usually wore a nondescript gray uniform.

For military purposes, South Vietnam is divided into

Religious services for troops
recently relieved from the line.

Taking a bath.

An Army guard and his sentry dog on duty at an
American installation in Viet Nam.

four corps areas extending from the I Corps area in the north along the 17th parallel to the IV Corps area in the Mekong Delta south of Saigon. A Republic of Vietnam general officer commands each area. The United States Army has two field commands in Vietnam: I Field Force, Vietnam, in the central part where the commander is also senior United States advisor to the II Corps area, and II Field Force, Vietnam, in the III Corps area where the United States commander also serves as senior advisor. II Field Force has faced some especially difficult military problems because for years the III Corps area was a stronghold of the Viet Cong with few efforts made to dislodge them. Its Zone D, an area heavily tunneled and mined and full of booby traps, has been bombed by B–52's. On the ground the soldiers of the 173d Airborne Brigade and the 1st Infantry Division have conducted numerous search and destroy operations. In the II Corps area, I Field Force operates in the highland home of the Montagnards where, until recently, the only Americans were members of the Special Forces stationed at isolated camps and sector advisor teams.

Before 1965 the mission of the United States Army in Vietnam had been to advise Vietnamese forces and give them advice, support, and assistance in counterinsurgency operations, but the Army ended the year with its third major Vietnam mission well under way—active combat assistance, including offensive operations. The 173d Airborne Brigade was joined in Vietnam by the 1st Brigade, 101st Airborne Division, the 1st Cavalry Division (Airmobile), the 1st Infantry Division, the 25th Infantry Division, and the 4th Infantry Division. By June 30, 1966, the Army had 165,000 men in Vietnam.

The buildup of Army strength was accompanied by corresponding increases in artillery, aviation, and signal units and by the arrival of logistical support units of all kinds. In addition to handling its own supply system, the Army, operating through its 1st Logistical Command, provides common-user supply support for all Free World Forces fighting in Vietnam. The command operates hospitals, a replacement center, port facilities, field laundries, shower points, and other troop-support agencies.

In its active combat operations in Vietnam, the U.S. Army has concentrated on search and destroy missions designed to wipe out known or suspected Communist forces and their base areas. Although such missions are not intended to seize and hold territory permanently, they do disrupt the plans of the enemy and increase his casualties.

Secretary of Defense Robert S. McNamara (center) talks with General W. C. Westmoreland, Vietnamese Assistance Command commander, and Vietnamese General Tee during a visit to Vietnam in 1965.

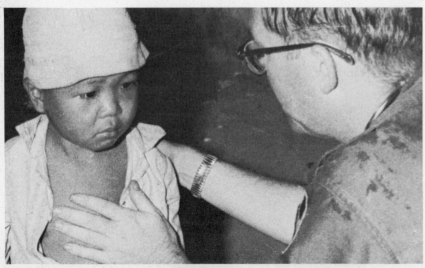

An Army doctor checks a child for possible respiratory illness, one of the many services rendered by the U.S. Army to the Vietnamese people.

Search and destroy missions in Vietnam have demonstrated the value of the Army's new airmobile 1st Cavalry Division. Designed, not to replace a standard infantry, armor, airborne, or mechanized division, but to carry out a special kind of mobile military operation, the 1st Cavalry Division is equipped with over 300 helicopters instead of the usual 1,500 wheeled and tracked vehicles. The helicopters allow the division to be both positioned and recovered vertically. Because combat elements can be moved quickly and directly over all kinds of terrain, commanders can maintain a rapid tempo of operations. In Vietnam the 1st Cavalry Division has been able to make a swift response to changing conditions, fight successive engagements at places a considerable distance apart, operate inside enemy-held territory, and provide a ready backup to offensives by other friendly forces.

The Army's standard infantry units in Vietnam have greatly increased their mobility by using helicopters. The infantryman often travels to battle in a helicopter, and helicopters deliver his supplies. The extensive use of helicopters has resulted in the development of lighter equipment for the soldier and the discarding of nonessential items that were once a part of his gear. "Shotgun riders," or helicopter door gunners, have been used with considerable success in Vietnam, and improved techniques have been worked out for clearing landing zones and for aerial evacuation.

At the beginning of 1965 the Army had four light helicopter companies and some small aviation detachments in Vietnam. A year and a half later, at the end of June, 1966, there were 64 company-sized U.S. Army aviation units there —45 helicopter units and 19 fixed-wing companies with 1,855 aircraft and 3,934 rated aviators.

After a series of encounters with the Viet Cong during the last months of 1965, United States forces (units of the III Marine Amphibious Force and the 1st Cavalry Division) and the Vietnamese Airborne Brigade launched Operation Masher/White Wing/Than Phong II on January 24, 1966. The operation was the largest attempted by Free World Forces up to that time, and cost the enemy 2,153 men.

After Masher/White Wing/Than Phong II, the Free World Forces continued to strike at long-held Viet Cong strongholds. With the help of aggressive air and artillery support, they inflicted heavy losses on the enemy. In one of the attacks in War Zone D, for example, the 1st Brigade, 1st U.S. Infantry Division and the Royal Australian Regiment overran and destroyed six enemy base camps and a hospital, and captured 388 tons of rice, 109 individual weapons, and 32 crew-served weapons. Enemy losses were 270 killed and one captured.

Members of the 1st Brigade, 101st Airborne Division, received a somewhat different assignment: protecting the farmers of Phu Yen province on the coast of central South Vietnam during the 1966 rice harvest. In the course of this duty the brigade and the Korean marines and South Vietnamese forces that worked with it met and routed a strong Viet Cong battalion, overran and destroyed a North Vietnam Army headquarters company, and met and defeated a regiment of North Vietnamese. As a result of the protection they received, the farmers of Phu Yen were able to harvest their rice and store it in government warehouses instead of losing it to the Viet Cong.

When this picture was taken, a Viet Cong plastic bomb had just exploded in a restaurant in Bac Lieu, southwest of Saigon.

The victims of the Viet Cong receive speedy medical attention.

Sniper fire from the woods
has pinned down these American soldiers.

In Vietnam, as in other wars, a clean
weapon is a soldier's best protection.

They continue to work with Vietnamese Special Forces who in turn recruit, train, and lead Civilian Irregular Defense Groups, a program developed to provide a defense force against Viet Cong or other Communist intrusion into South Vietnam. Special Forces units also assist district and province officials in the execution of civil and military duties until a secure community has been established.

The U.S. Army continues to assign advisors to Vietnamese commanders and staffs from corps down to battalions. Advisory detachments are also located in provinces and districts to advise units of the Vietnamese Regional Forces and Popular Forces. Members of the Army's 89th Military Police Brigade, who are responsible for most military police functions in the three southern Vietnamese Corps areas, advise the South Vietnamese Military Police on methods of criminal investigation, law and order, and the handling of prisoners of war.

Like the Army, the United States Air Force, Navy, and Marines now have both combat and advisory personnel in Vietnam. The Seventh Air Force is responsible for United States Air Force activities in Vietnam. It operates U.S. aircraft, advises the Vietnamese Air Force, and supervises overall air activity against the Viet Cong. U.S. Naval Forces, Vietnam, is responsible for the operation of most United States naval activities in Vietnam including harbor defense and mine countermeasures. Through its subordinate Naval Advisory Group, advisors are assigned to all echelons of the Vietnamese Navy. The III Marine Amphibious Force (III MAF) is responsible for operational control of U.S. Marine forces in the Vietnamese I Corps area, and the Commanding General, III MAF, is the senior advisor to the Vietnamese I Corps commander.

Free World Forces fighting in South Vietnam include units from the United States, Korea, Australia, and New Zealand as well as the South Vietnamese. Their overall objective is to make possible a stable and independent government free of Communist control. In pursuit of that objective they are conducting four major types of operations: search and destroy operations; clear and secure operations to eliminate permanently residual Communist forces from specified limited areas; reserve reaction operations designed to relieve provincial capitals and district towns under Communist attack and to reinforce friendly forces when needed; and operations in the defense of government centers. The strike elements of the United States and other Free World Forces are concentrating on the first type of operation and providing such help as might be needed by the South Vietnamese who have assumed primary responsibility for the others.

Although the various air units in Vietnam have contributed primary support through air strike, airlift, and reconnaissance missions, the nature of the conflict in South Vietnam has made it generally a ground war, and the role of the U.S. Army has been a major one. For the Army Vietnam has been a different and difficult kind of war, fought over unfamiliar terrain and under conditions that placed the heaviest demands on leaders and their men. In assisting the Republic of Vietnam in its fight against Communist terror and oppression, the U.S. Army met one of its greatest challenges. (Continuation of this history is in preparation.)

The first wave of Army of Vietnam paratroopers leaves the transports. The area into which they will drop has been worked over by the Vietnamese Air Force.

An Air Force CH–3C helicopter hovers over a 105mm howitzer as two U.S. Army men connect external carrying cables.

The most successful leader of the Republic of Viet Nam, Air Vice Marshal Nguyen Cao Ky, Prime Minister since June 1965, is shown here (left) in 1966 with General Hunter Harris, Pacific Air Forces commander.

Three members of U.S. Air Force Combat Control team watch as Vietnamese paratroopers drop into a Viet Cong infiltrated area. The combat control team jumped first to mark the drop zone for the paratroopers.

781

An Air Force forward air controller flies over the dense jungle in a light observation plane. Observation flights are made to locate guerrilla positions and to coordinate air and ground operations.

A B–52 unloads its 750-pound bombs onto Viet Cong positions along the coast of South Vietnam. The B–52 can carry 12 750-pound bombs under each wing and 27 bombs inside the aircraft. From 25 to 30 B–52's usually take part in each raid.

An F–5 of the U.S. Air Force 4503d Tactical Fighter Squadron Ekoshi Tigers drops three general-purpose bombs on Viet Cong positions in South Vietnam.

Craters in South Vietnam's Zone D after a B–52 attack. The B–52 has been especially useful in jungle areas where specific targets cannot be pinpointed for tactical bombing because of the heavy tree canopy.

782

A flight of four Thunderchiefs en route to a target in North Vietnam. Targets for the Thunderchiefs have included missile sites, bridges, railroads, highways, ammunition dumps, and radar sites.

Bombs away! Phantoms, which can carry a variety of ordnance, fly most U.S. Air Force night strikes over the Communist North.

One of the most popular of all USO entertainers, comedian Bob Hope, and the girls of his 1965 Christmas Show during a performance in Vietnam. Hope's annual Christmas tour is sponsored jointly by the Department of Defense and the USO.

Anita Bryant, touring the Far East with the 1965 Bob Hope Christmas show, sings to the troops at an air base in Vietnam.

783

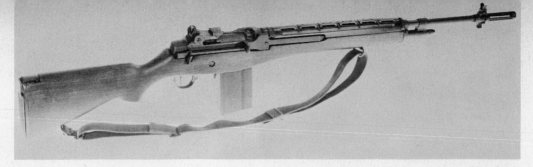

ARMY FIREPOWER AND MOBILITY

FIREPOWER

Combat effectiveness is a combination of firepower, mobility, and communications. These are three essentials necessary for winning any battle. They enable the soldier to move, shoot, and communicate.

The variety of new weapons available to the soldier today makes him a more versatile fighting man than ever before. He now has a rifle, the M14, which fires a 7.62mm cartridge common to the forces of NATO, and a smaller, lightweight weapon, the M16, which has been developed for use by specialized units such as airborne and Special Forces troops.

The SPIW, which stands for Special Individual Weapon, is a radically new development currently being evaluated. It is designed to incorporate the capabilities of both a rifle and a grenade launcher, thus making it a deadly double-purpose weapon. This weapon, complete with 100 rounds of point target and 3 rounds of area ammunition, weighs no more than an M14 rifle with 20 rounds.

The latest machine gun, the M-60 answers the need for a lighter, simpler weapon. It fires up to 600 rounds per minute and weighs about half as much as the older guns it replaces. It also uses the standard 7.62mm cartridge.

To provide the frontline soldier with firepower support, the Army has developed a new family of self-propelled artillery. These weapons will greatly improve the mobility, flexibility, and firepower especially of armored and mechanized divisions.

The 105mm self-propelled light howitzer and the 155mm self-propelled medium howitzer are Diesel-powered, full-tracked, amphibious vehicles which have a cruising range of about 250 miles. An atomic projectile has been developed to give the 155mm howitzer a nuclear capability.

The self-propelled 175mm and the 8-inch howitzer are in a class of heavier artillery; however, both are air transportable.

To provide the shock action of armor, the Army's main battle tank, the M60, combines improved firepower with greater mobility. It mounts a 105mm gun and has a cruising range of 250 miles, almost double that of older models.

The 105mm gun is being replaced on some of these tanks by the Shillelagh weapons system.

In Army tactical missiles, the first-generation Corporal has been replaced by the Sergeant, a missile with a range of 75 miles, as a corps support missile system. The Sergeant is more powerful and can be put into action with fewer crew members than the Corporal. Sergeant battalions are already on duty.

The Pershing missile system has replaced the Redstone as a field army support weapon. The Pershing has the advantages of lighter weight, solid fuel, and greater mobility. It has a self-propelled launcher which transports the missile to the firing site and acts as the launching pad. Its range is 400 miles.

The Lance, a missile system under development, is designed to replace the older Honest John and possibly the Little John in combat divisions. The Lance can be fired from its own tracked, air-transportable carrier at greater range than the Honest John.

Missile firepower has also been placed in the hands of frontline troops for antitank protection. One weapon is the ENTAC, a wire-guided antitank missile which is about a yard in length and weighs 27 pounds. It can knock out any tank in use today.

Another version of the wire-guided antitank missile is the SS11. It is used as an air-launched missile mounted on an Army helicopter. A newer missile scheduled to replace ENTAC, and possibly the SS11, is known as TOW which has greater range and accuracy. It, too, will destroy the heaviest known armor.

For the 1970's, the Army expects to have the General Sheridan, an airborne-assault armored reconnaissance vehicle mounting a 152mm gun/launcher. It can fire the Shillelagh, a direct fire, line-of-sight guided missile, as well as a high explosive round from the same 152mm gun launcher.

Ground-to-air missiles for air defense on the battlefield will include the Redeye in the future. This is a shoulder-fired weapon which one soldier can carry and use against low-flying aircraft. Redeye's infrared guidance system makes it extremely accurate.

SAM-D (Surface-to-Air Missile, Development) is a new air defense missile system under development by the U.S. Army with Navy participation for use on both land and sea. It is designed for battlefield and continental air defense roles in the 1970's, against low, medium, and high-flying jet aircraft and short-range missiles.

The M14 rifle and the weapons it replaced: (from front) the Browning automatic rifle; the M1 Garand rifle; the carbine; and the M3A1 submachine gun. The M14 is sometimes called the four-in-one weapon.

The new lightweight M16 rifle. First produced as the Colt AR15, the M16 will be used to equip specialized units such as airborne, air assault test units, and Special Forces.

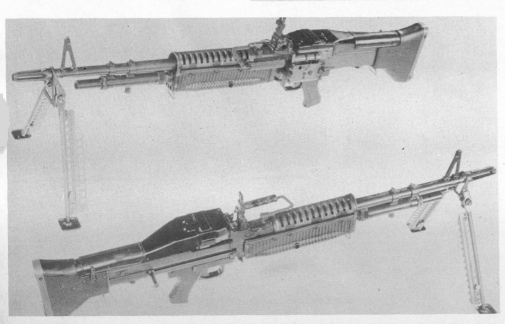

The M60 machine gun.

The versatile 23-pound M60 machine gun, shown here with the bipod in position, can be used for assault firing from either a prone or standing position.

The M60 machine gun can also be fired from a newly developed aluminum tripod.

The 105mm self-propelled light howitzer.
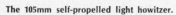

The 155mm self-propelled medium howitzer.

The modern Army's 175mm gun (the M107) performs on the firing range.

The M60 tank with the 105mm gun during a firing demonstration

The General Sheridan armored reconnaissance vehicle.

Test-firing the Shillelagh at the White Sands Missile Range.

The Sergeant, a surface-to-surface
ballistic guided missile.

The Pershing, a highly
mobile missile system.

The Lance ballistic missile in its
first firing test. The missile hit its
target.

The Hawk missile system was developed for
defense against low-flying enemy aircraft.

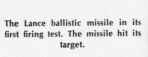

"Little John."

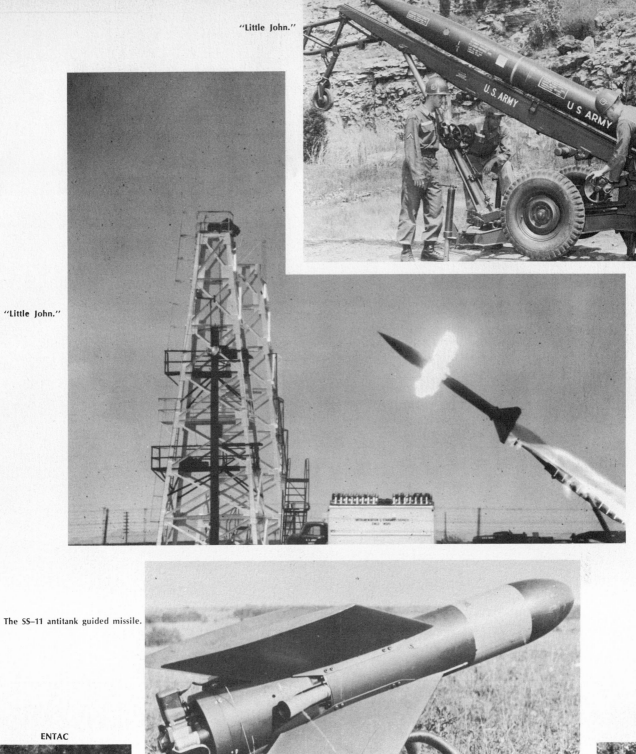

"Little John."

The SS–11 antitank guided missile.

ENTAC

The TOW missile launcher. The TOW is a tube-launched, optically tracked, wire-guided missile designed for use against tanks or field fortifications.

The Sprint, one of the Army's newest anti-missile missiles, shown here during a flight test, was developed as an interceptor missile for the Nike-X missile defense system.

The Redeye, the world's smallest guided missile, was developed to provide protection against low-flying enemy aircraft.

A soldier holding the Redeye guided missile in position.

The Davy Crockett, a hand or jeep portable weapons system, is capable of firing atomic or conventional warheads in support of the Army's front-line pentomic battle groups.

MOBILITY—GROUND

To the Army, mobility means more than being able to get from point A to point B. The Navy provides sealift and the Air Force airlift to move Army forces from one geographical area to another. That is strategic mobility. But the Army also needs mobility in the battle area. Tactical mobility must be combined with firepower and maneuver and support of combat units on the battlefield. Both ground and air vehicles are necessary to enable the Army to outmaneuver an enemy in modern warfare.

In addition to the new M60 tank and self-propelled artillery, the improved armored personnel carrier, the M113, has greatly increased the ground mobility of the Army. The carrier, transporting 13 combat soldiers, can reach a maximum speed of 40 miles per hour. It can also cross streams and rivers.

To keep up with tracked vehicles moving cross-country, the Army has developed the XM561, a 6-wheeled, 1¼-ton

truck. It is a two-part, jointed vehicle that looks like a jeep pulling a trailer; the rear element, however, is an integral part of the truck.

Some Army vehicles are used primarily for supply. One such vehicle is the Goer, which is similar in looks to commercial earth-moving equipment used on highway construction jobs. One model transports dry cargo such as ammunition, and another hauls liquid products such as gasoline. The LARC, a wheeled vehicle which operates both in water and on land, is also used for ship-to-shore hauling of cargo or personnel and is designed especially for amphibious operations.

The trend in cross-country vehicles is toward cargo trucks with an increased number of axles and individual wheel suspension. This design provides for maximum traction as each wheel comes in ground contact on the uneven terrain. Cargo trucks with 2½-ton and 5-ton capacities are being tested.

The M113 personnel carrier.

The Army's workhorse,
the 2½-ton truck.

The 5-ton truck.

LARC, an amphibious cargo carrier that
operates at 10 mph in water and 30 mph
on land.

The Army jeep.

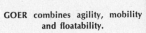
GOER combines agility, mobility and floatability.

The highly mobile XM561, a 1¼-ton, 6-wheeled cargo carrier, was especially developed for cross-country and off-road travel.

The Army's versatile ½-ton light weapons carrier has been called a "mechanical mule."

A four-wheel-drive moving platform that can take off in forward or reverse to carry supplies to front-line soldiers.

MOBILITY—AIR

Once looked upon as having a limited supporting role, Army aircraft are a common sight throughout the Army today. In 1950 there were about 700 aircraft in the ground forces; today there are over 6,000. An Army division now has some 100 aircraft, 97 of them helicopters.

Army aircraft live with the troops in the field. In today's modern warfare they are indispensable in transporting men and supplies within the battle zone.

With Army aircraft immediately available to the combat commander, reaction time on the battlefield can be reduced. Fast dispersal and rapid concentration for an attack are now possible as well as quick movement of reinforcements to forward areas.

Army aircraft are versatile. Three merit special mention—Iroquois, Chinook, and Mohawk.

The Iroquois is a utility and tactical transport helicopter designed for moving troops and supplies in the forward battle area. Also in the helicopter class is the Chinook, which can lift up to 6 tons of cargo, ramp loaded from the rear. It can also carry components of the Pershing missile.

The twin-engine Mohawk fulfills the Army's needs for short-range visual observation, day and night photography, and spotting of enemy targets. It is also equipped with side-looking radar.

The Army uses these and other aircraft to give the soldier the advantage of position in battle. There can be no substitute for the use of aircraft when required for troop maneuver and supply on the battlefield.

The UH–1 "Huey" Iroquois helicopter carries 11 passengers.

The CH–47 Chinook, developed as a cargo helicopter, can also carry 33 passengers.

The OV–1 Mohawk is used for battlefield reconnaissance.

The paratrooper of the future may wear flexwings which he can control to ensure landing in the right place.

The Army is studying Laser (for Light Amplification by Stimulated Emission of Radiation) for its communication applications.

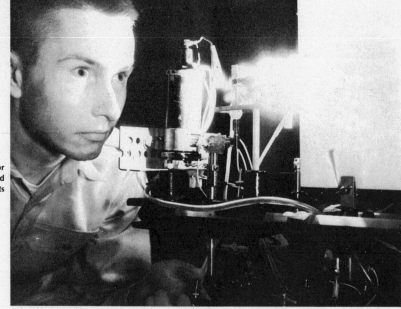

A LOOK TO THE U.S. ARMY'S FUTURE

Since its founding in 1775 the United States Army's mission has been to conduct prompt and sustained combat operations on land. While the Army's mission has remained unchanged over the years, the tools used to accomplish that mission have changed, and they will continue to change as the Army seeks to increase its effectiveness in placing the soldier at the right place at the right time with the right weapons and equipment to support national policy.

The Army constantly seeks to improve the efficiency of its organization and the professionalism of its personnel. This, plus the development of lighter, more effective conventional weapons, more accurate and reliable missiles, more mobile personnel and cargo carriers, new combat vehicles, and improved techniques for special and conventional warfare will enable the soldier of the future to defend the United States any time, in any place, in any kind of war.

The Army's experimental air car is designed to skim over land or water at speeds up to 50 mph. A recirculation system provides the supporting air cushion upon which the vehicle rides.

In areas where terrain, deep debris, or unfavorable flying conditions would make travel by other means impossible, the "Landwalker" will move Army personnel and cargo.

When nuclear power can be used to propel land vehicles, a train like this will carry Army supplies.

Automatic equipment such as (from left) the computer, the console that shows the status of all batteries, and the electric tactical map will improve the efficiency of the Army's artillery units.

Automatic alarm systems will warn the soldier when dangerous substances are present in the atmosphere. The device shown here detects nerve gas.

One-man flying belts will enable the soldier of the future to surmount formidable terrain barriers.

Using TV that intensifies starlight, moonlight, and skyglow, two Army officers watch a simulated night mission. The device may someday be used in combat.

APPENDIX

THE PRINCIPLES OF WAR OF THE UNITED STATES ARMY

Today, all great nations recognize certain principles of war and incorporate them in Army doctrine. The number of principles enumerated by the various powers varies, depending upon the interpretation. The United States Army recognizes nine. Their proper application, it holds, is essential to the exercise of effective command and to the successful conduct of military operations.

The principles of war are interrelated. They are not absolute and have been successfully violated at times, but only for very special reasons that had been carefully considered beforehand. The principles do not operate with equal force under all circumstances. They are applied in combination with specific situations. The combinations will vary according to the facts that influence operations, such as the nature of the terrain, day or night operations, the relative strength of the opposing forces—in terms not only of their numbers but also of their composition, their armament, their state of training, their morale, their supply—the effect of weather, and the mission of the command. The art of generalship is to be found in the application of the principles.

When determined for the conduct of a war or a lengthy campaign, the combination of principles selected is called strategy; when adopted for a single battle, the combination of principles is called tactics. There are further refinements. The broad policy decisions governing the overall conduct of war are known as grand strategy, the prerogative of the chief-of-state and his principal advisers. At the opposite end of the scale are minor tactics, the term used to describe the maneuvers of small units.

The nine principles governing the prosecution of war are concisely stated as objective, offensive, simplicity, unity of command, mass, economy of force, maneuver, surprise, and security.

Objective. Every military operation must be directed toward a decisive, obtainable objective. The destruction of the enemy's armed forces and his will to fight is the ultimate military objective of war. The objective of each operation must contribute to this ultimate objective. Each intermediate objective must be such that its attainment will most directly, quickly, and economically contribute to the purpose of the operation. It must permit the application of the maximum means available. Its selection must be based upon consideration of means available, the enemy, and the area of operations. Secondary objectives of any operation must contribute to the attainment of the principal objective.

Offensive. Only offensive action achieves decisive results. Offensive action permits the commander to exploit the initiative and impose his will on the enemy. The defensive may be forced on the commander, but he should adopt it deliberately only as a temporary expedient while awaiting an opportunity for offensive action or for the purpose of economizing forces on a front where a decision is not sought. Even on the defensive the commander seeks every opportunity to seize the initiative and achieve decisive results by offensive action.

Simplicity. Simplicity must be the keynote of military operations. Uncomplicated plans, clearly expressed in orders, promote common understanding and intelligent execution. Even the most simple plan is usually difficult to execute in combat. Simplicity must be applied to organization, methods, and means in order to produce orderliness on the battlefield.

Unity of command. The decisive application of full combat power requires unity of command. Unity of command obtains unity of effort by the coordinated action of all forces toward a common goal. Coordination may be achieved by direction or by cooperation. It is best achieved by vesting a single commander with requisite authority. Unity of effort is furthered by willing and intelligent cooperation among all elements of the forces involved.

Mass. Maximum available combat power must be applied at the point of decision. Mass is the concentration of means at the critical time and place to the maximum degree permitted by the situation. Proper application of the principle of mass, in conjunction with the other principles of war, may permit numerically inferior forces to achieve decisive combat superiority. Mass is essentially a combination of manpower and firepower and it not dependent upon numbers alone; the effectiveness of mass may be increased by superior weapons, tactics, and morale.

Economy of force. Minimum essential means must be employed at points other than that of decision. To devote means to unnecessary secondary efforts or to employ excessive means on required secondary efforts is to violate the principle of both mass and the objective. Limited attacks, the defensive, deception, or even retrograde action are used in noncritical areas to achieve mass in the critical area.

Maneuver. Maneuver must be used to alter the relative combat power of military forces. Maneuver is the positioning of forces to place the enemy at a relative disadvantage. Proper positioning of forces in relation to the enemy frequently can achieve results which otherwise could be achieved only at heavy cost in men and materiel. In many situations maneuver is made possible only by the effective employment of firepower.

Surprise. Surprise may decisively shift the balance of combat power in favor of the commander who achieves it. It consists of striking the enemy when, where, or in a manner for which he is unprepared. It is not essential that the enemy be taken unaware but only that he become aware too late to react effectively. Surprise can be achieved by speed, secrecy, and deception, by variation in means and methods, and by the use of seemingly impossible terrain. Mass is essential to the optimum exploitation of the principle of surprise.

Security. Security is essential to the application of the other principles of war. It consists of those measures necessary to prevent surprise, avoid annoyance, preserve freedom of action, and deny to the enemy information of our forces. Security denies to the enemy and retains for the commander the ability to employ his forces most effectively.

The mission of the United States Army has been stated in many ways:

To defend the security of the United States,

To fight and win wars,

To engage the enemy in sustained land combat,

To prevent a war, not to fight a war.

There is truth in all these statements. For, fundamentally, the Army supports our national objectives by being ready for any mission—in peace or in war. It has capabilities for deterring general war, preventing local aggression, and winning a war if we are forced to fight.

The Army does not and could not do all these things alone. It is part of a national defense team which also includes air and sea power. Each service, the Army, Navy, Marines, and Air Force, has distinctly different assigned responsibilities within the framework of the Department of Defense. However, each one complements the other. The total effort is what gives our nation its powerful military strength.

The mission of the Army has been tied to our nation's concern with its independence. We can go back to mid-April of 1775 when the embattled farmer-patriots of Massachusetts met the British regulars at Lexington Green. There the long struggle for our independence began with "the shot heard round the world."

On 14 June 1775, the Continental Congress, reflecting the mood of an aroused populace, determined to establish a regular Army that would later prove superior to the well-trained redcoats. It resolved:

"That six companies of expert riflemen be immediately raised in Pennsylvania, two in Maryland, and two in Virginia."

The Congress designated Colonel George Washington as commander-in-chief of the Regular Army and the volunteer Militia. So it was more than a year before the Declaration of Independence that the Army was established.

The Army has fought in a total of nine major wars in the interest of freedom. The price of national security is written in the history books under chapters entitled: Revolutionary War, War of 1812, Mexican War, Civil War, Spanish-American War, World War I, World War II, Korea, and Vietnam.

The Army is ready today to fight any war, anywhere, anytime, and in any manner to protect the nation and foster the cause of freedom.

The Army maintains its preparedness by accomplishing many varied tasks. These include the upkeep of forces deployed overseas, mobile strategic reserves, and responsive Army National Guard and Army Reserve units and individuals.

The Army is a major participant in providing the trained men and modern weapons employed in defending the United States against air attack.

The Army also has the primary responsibility for coordinating and controlling, through established service command channels, the military resources of all services for providing military support to Civil Defense authorities in an emergency.

The Army also assists our allies and other Free World forces by providing weapons and equipment, advice, and training assistance under the Military Assistance Program. In addition, assistance in economic and social betterment programs is provided by civic action teams.

These diverse and worldwide responsibilities can be carried out only by a modern and progressive Army such as our nation has today. It is dynamic, versatile, and responsive—as modern as tomorrow. Its progress is reflected n the well-trained soldiers and the modern arms and equipment organized into effective combat units to defend our national interest.

CREDO OF THE U.S. ARMY SOLDIER

I am the American soldier. For more than a century and a half I have been the guardian of our hallowed traditions of liberty and freedom—the American way of life. These ideals I dearly cherish and will defend with my life. I was with General George Washington at Valley Forge; I defended the principles of democracy at the Alamo and San Juan. I opened the door of the West for settlers in a budding continent dedicated to the principles of free men everywhere. I defended our heritage at Château-Thierry, Normandy, and Pork Chop Hill—symbols, all, of freedom from tyranny. I fought a "war to end all wars" and defended freedom's cause in conflicts whose reverberations still ring in the ears of Americans living today.

Today, as always, my fundamental mission is fixed, unchanged, determined, and inviolable—to defend the United States and its way of life. I fly the armed helicopters over the dense Vietnamese jungle. I walk the lonely outpost in Korea and patrol the Iron Curtain in Europe, the dividing lines between freedom and oppression. I man the missiles which stand ready to protect our country against the holocaust of total war. Whatever the need—for liberty, now and forever—I am an American soldier, the guardian of democracy—an essential force for freedom.

THE CAMPAIGN STREAMERS

The 145 streamers attached to the Army Flag staff denote the campaigns fought by the Army throughout our national history. Each streamer—2¾ inches wide and 4 feet long—is embroidered with the designation of the campaign and the year in which it occurred. The colors derive from the campaign ribbon authorized for service in that particular war.

The concept of campaign streamers came to prominence in the Civil War when Army organizations embroidered the names of battles on their organizational colors.

This was discontinued in 1890, when units were authorized to place silver bands, engraved with the names of battles, around their organizational color staffs. When AEF units in World War I were unable to obtain silver bands, General Pershing authorized the use of small ribbons bearing battle names. In 1921 all color-bearing Army organizations were authorized to use the large campaign streamers as now used with the Army Flag.

The 145 campaign streamers on the Army Flag represent participation in the following wars—

REVOLUTIONARY WAR

11 Streamers—Scarlet with a white stripe

TICONDEROGA ● BOSTON ● QUEBEC ● LONG ISLAND ● TRENTON ● PRINCETON ● SARATOGA ● BRANDYWINE ● GERMANTOWN ● MONMOUTH ● YORKTOWN

WAR OF 1812

6 Streamers—Scarlet with two white stripes

CANADA ● CHIPPEWA ● LUNDY'S LANE ● BLADENSBURG ● McHENRY ● NEW ORLEANS

MEXICAN WAR

10 Streamers—Green with one white stripe

PALO ALTO ● RESACA DE LA PALMA ● MONTERREY ● BUENA VISTA ● VERA CRUZ ● CERRO GORDO ● CONTRERAS ● CHURUBUSCO ● MOLINO DEL REY ● CHAPULTEPEC

CIVIL WAR

25 Streamers—Blue and gray, equally divided

SUMTER ● BULL RUN ● HENRY AND DONELSON ● MISSISSIPPI RIVER ● PENINSULA ● SHILOH ● VALLEY ● MANASSAS ● ANTIETAM ● FREDERICKSBURG ● MURFREESBOROUGH ● CHANCELLORSVILLE ● GETTYSBURG ● VICKSBURG ● CHICKAMAUGA ● CHATTANOOGA ● WILDERNESS ● ATLANTA ● SPOTSYLVANIA ● COLD HARBOR ● PETERSBURG ● SHENANDOAH ● FRANKLIN ● NASHVILLE ● APPOMATTOX

INDIAN WARS

14 Streamers—Scarlet with two black stripes

MIAMI ● TIPPECANOE ● CREEK ● SEMINOLE ● BLACK HAWK ● COMANCHE ● MODOC ● APACHE ● LITTLE BIG HORN ● NEZ PERCÉ ● BANNOCK ● CHEYENNE ● UTE ● PINE RIDGE

WAR WITH SPAIN

3 Streamers—Yellow with two blue stripes

SANTIAGO ● PUERTO RICO ● MANILA

CHINA RELIEF EXPEDITION

3 Streamers—Yellow with blue edges

TIENTSIN ● YANG-TSUN ● PEKING

PHILIPPINE INSURRECTION

11 Streamers—Blue with two red stripes

MANILA ● ILOILO ● MALOLOS ● LAGUNA DE BAY ● SAN ISIDRO ● ZAPOTE RIVER ● CAVITE ● TARLAC ● SAN FABIAN ● MINDANAO ● JOLO

MEXICAN EXPEDITION

1 Streamer—Yellow with one blue stripe and green borders

MEXICO 1916–1917

WORLD WAR I

13 Streamers—Double rainbow

CAMBRAI ● SOMME DEFENSIVE ● LYS ● AISNE ● MONTDIDIER-NOYON ● CHAMPAGNE-MARNE ● AISNE-MARNE ● SOMME OFFENSIVE ● OISE-AISNE ● YPRES-LYS ● ST. MIHIEL ● MEUSE-ARGONNE ● VITTORIO VENETO

WORLD WAR II

38 Streamers

ASIATIC-PACIFIC THEATRE

21 Streamers—Orange with two white, red, and white stripe groupings; with blue, white, red stripes in center.

PHILIPPINE ISLANDS ● BURMA, 1942 ● CENTRAL PACIFIC ● EAST INDIES ● INDIA-BURMA ● AIR OFFENSIVE, JAPAN ● ALEUTIAN ISLANDS ● CHINA DEFENSIVE ● PAPUA ● GUADALCANAL ● NEW GUINEA ● NORTHERN SOLOMONS ● EASTERN MANDATES ● BISMARCK ARCHIPELAGO ● WESTERN PACIFIC ● LEYTE ● LUZON ● CENTRAL BURMA ● SOUTHERN PHILIPPINES ● RYUKYUS ● CHINA OFFENSIVE

AMERICAN THEATRE

1 Streamer—Blue with two groupings of white, black, red, and white stripes; with blue, white, red in center.

ANTISUBMARINE 1941–1945

EUROPEAN-AFRICAN-MIDDLE EASTERN THEATRE

16 Streamers—Green and brown with two stripe groupings, one of green, white, red and the other of white, black, and white stripes; with blue, white, and red stripes in the center.

EGYPT-LIBYA ● AIR OFFENSIVE, EUROPE ● ALGERIA-FRENCH MOROCCO ● TUNISIA ● SICILY ● NAPLES-FOGGIA ● ANZIO ● ROME-ARNO ● NORMANDY ● NORTHERN FRANCE ● SOUTHERN FRANCE ● NORTH APENNINES ● RHINELAND ● ARDENNES-ALSACE ● CENTRAL EUROPE ● PO VALLEY

KOREAN WAR

10 Streamers—Light blue bordered on each side with white; white center stripe.

UN DEFENSIVE ● UN OFFENSIVE ● CC INTERVENTION ● FIRST UN COUNTER OFFENSIVE ● CC SPRING OFFENSIVE ● UN SUMMER-FALL OFFENSIVE ● SECOND KOREAN WINTER ● KOREA, SUMMER-FALL 1952 ● THIRD KOREAN WINTER ● KOREA, SUMMER 1953

Campaign Streamers Added to the Army Flag Since 1967*

Vietnam:
Advisory
Defense
Counteroffensive
Counteroffensive Phase II
Counteroffensive Phase III
Tet Counteroffensive
Counteroffensive Phase IV
Counteroffensive Phase V
Counteroffensive Phase VI

Tet 1969 Counteroffensive
Summer/Fall 1969
Winter/Spring 1970
Sanctuary Counteroffensive
Counteroffensive Phase VII
Consolidation Phase I
Consolidation Phase II
Ceasefire

American Revolution:
Lexington
Charleston
Savannah
Cowpens
Guilford Courthouse

*Note: Even though some of the Vietnam streamers pre-date 1967, they were not announced until December of 1968 and following. The total number of streamers is now 167.

TYPES OF ARMY DIVISIONS

The Army division is the cutting edge of our ground combat power. It is composed of combat arms, service and administrative troops as part of its organization.

There are 4 types of divisions in the Army—infantry, mechanized, armored, and airborne. (The "Airmobile Division"—such as the 1st Cavalry Division—will be developed as a new type of division.) All have a similar division base structure.

The base contains the division headquarters, service and administrative troops, and three tactical command headquarters called brigades. In addition, the base includes division artillery, a support command (provides supply, field maintenance, and medical service), an aviation battalion, engineer battalion, an armored cavalry squadron, and a military police company. To complete the division structure, combat battalions in various types and numbers are attached to the brigades.

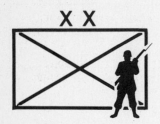

INFANTRY An infantry division has special capabilities for operating in difficult weather and terrain. The infantry meets the enemy, destroys him, and physically occupies the vital terrain. A "type" infantry division has about 15,500 men composed of 8 infantry battalions and 2 tank battalions. Active Army infantry divisions are the 1st, 2d, 4th, 7th, 9th and the 25th. The 1st Cavalry Division is also organized as infantry.

MECHANIZED A mechanized division also has about 15,900 troops when organized to include 8 mechanized infantry battalions and 2 tank battalions. A mechanized division is highly mobile, having special capabilities for fast pursuit and battlefield maneuver. The 4 mechanized divisions in the Army are the 3rd, 5th, 8th, and 24th divisions.

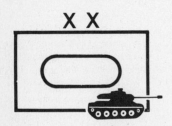

ARMORED Armored divisions are geared to mobile warfare, primarily offensive in nature. Their great firepower and mobility provide tremendous shock action on the battlefield. A "type" armored division has 15,900 men in 6 tank battalions and 5 mechanized infantry battalions. The 4 armored divisions in the active Army are the 1st, 2d, 3rd, and 4th.

AIRBORNE The successful use of airborne troops, both in World War II and in the Korean War, resulted in the retention of such forces in our peacetime Army. The special capabilities of airborne troops include rapid strategic movement by air and operations behind enemy lines. A typical airborne division of 14,000 strength may be composed of 9 airborne infantry battalions and 1 tank battalion. The 2 active Army airborne divisions are the 82d and the 101st.

Principal Wars in Which the United States Participated
U.S. Military Personnel Serving and Casualties [a]

Wars	Branch of Service	Number Serving	Casualties Battle Deaths	Casualties Other Deaths	Casualties Wounds Not Mortal [i]
Revolutionary War 1775–1783	Total	[j]	4,435	—	6,188
	Army	—	4,044	—	6,004
	Navy	—	342	—	114
	Marines	—	49	—	70
War of 1812 1812–1815	Total	286,730 [k]	2,260	—	4,505
	Army	—	1,950	—	4,000
	Navy	—	265	—	439
	Marines	—	45	—	66
Mexican War 1846–1848	Total	78,718 [k]	1,733	—	4,152
	Army	—	1,721	11,550	4,102
	Navy	—	1	—	3
	Marines	—	11	—	47
Civil War .... (Union Forces only) [b] 1861–1865	Total	2,213,363 [k]	140,414	224,097	281,881
	Army	2,128,948	138,154	221,374	280,040
	Navy	84,415	2,112	2,411	1,710
	Marines		148	312	131
Spanish-American War 1898	Total	306,760	385	2,061	1,662
	Army [e]	280,564	369	2,061	1,594
	Navy	22,875	10	0	47
	Marines	3,321	6	0	21
World War I .... (6 April 1917– 11 November 1918)	Total	4,734,991	53,402	63,114	204,002
	Army [f]	4,057,101	50,510	55,868	193,663
	Navy	599,051	431	6,856	819
	Marines	78,839	2,461	390	9,520
World War II .... (7 December 1941– 31 December 1946) [c]	Total	16,112,566	291,557	113,842	670,846
	Army [g]	11,260,000	234,874	83,400	565,861
	Navy [h]	4,183,466	36,950	25,604	37,778
	Marines	669,100	19,733	4,778	67,207
Korean War .... (25 June 1950– 27 July 1953) [d]	Total	5,720,000	33,629	20,617	103,284
	Army	2,834,000	27,704	9,429	77,596
	Navy	1,177,000	458	4,043	1,576
	Marines	424,000	4,267	1,261	23,744
	Air Force	1,285,000	1,200	5,884	368
Vietnam War .... (15 March 1962– 28 January 1973) [l]	Total	3,000,000			
	Army	1,600,000	30,716 [n]	7,193	96,811 [o]
	Navy	600,000 [m]	1,532	910	4,180
	Marines	400,000	13,020	1,684	51,399
	Air Force	400,000	1,334	603	939

a   Data prior to World War I are based upon incomplete records in many cases. Casualty data are confined to dead and wounded personnel and therefore exclude personnel captured or missing in action who were subsequently returned to military control. U.S. Coast Guard data are excluded.

b   Authoritative statistics for the Confederate Forces are not available. Estimates of the number who served range from 600,000 to 1,500,000. The Final Report of the Provost Marshal General, 1863–1866, indicated 133,821 Confederate deaths (74,524 battle and 59,297 other) based upon incomplete returns. In addition, an estimated 26,000–31,000 Confederate personnel died in Union prisons.

c   Data are for the period 1 December 1941 through 31 December 1946 when hostilities were officially terminated by Presidential Proclamation, but few battle deaths or wounds not mortal were incurred after the Japanese acceptance of Allied peace terms on 14 August 1945. Numbers serving from 1 December 1941–31 August 1945 were: Total —14,903,213; Army—10,420,000; Navy—3,883,520; and Marine Corps—599,693.

d   Tentative final data based upon information available as of 30 September 1954, at which time 24 persons were still carried as missing in action.

e   Number serving covers the period 21 April–13 August 1898, while dead and wounded data are for the period 1 May–31 August 1898. Active hostilities ceased on 13 August 1898, but ratifications of the treaty of peace were not exchanged between the United States and Spain until 11 April 1899.

f   Includes Air Service. Battle deaths and wounds not mortal include casualties suffered by American forces in Northern Russia to 25 August 1919 and in Siberia to 1 April 1920. Other deaths cover the period 1 April 1917–31 December 1918.

g   Includes Army Air Forces.

h   Battle deaths and wounds not mortal include casualties incurred in October 1941 due to hostile action.

i   Marine Corps data for World War II, the Spanish-American War and prior wars represent the number of individuals wounded, whereas all other data in this column represent the total number (incidence) of wounds.

j   Not known, but estimates range from 184,000 to 250,000.

k   As reported by the Commissioner of Pensions in his Annual Report for Fiscal Year 1903.

l   As set forth in AR 672-5-1, 3 July 1974.

m   Including offshore operations.

n   As of 30 June 1977—not including some missing in action.

o   Treated not hospitalized—104,725.

Dashes (—) indicate that information is not available.

THE JOINT CHIEFS-OF-STAFF
SINCE 17 SEPTEMBER 1947

CHAIRMAN*	From	To
General of the Army		
Omar N. Bradley, USA	16 August 1949	14 August 1953
Admiral Arthur W. Radford, USN...	15 August 1953	14 August 1957
General Nathan F. Twining, USAF...	15 August 1957	30 September 1960
General Lyman L. Lemnitzer, USA...	1 October 1960	30 September 1962
General Maxwell D. Taylor, USA....	1 October 1962	3 July 1964
General Earle G. Wheeler, USA....	3 July 1964	2 July 1970
General Thomas H. Moorer, USN..	3 July 1970	30 June 1974
General George S. Brown, USA....	1 July 1974	

*Position created by 1949 Amendment to the National Security Act of 1947.

COMMANDING GENERALS OF THE ARMY SINCE 1775

Name	From	To	Name	From	To
Gen. George Washington.......	17 June 1775	23 December 1783			
Maj. Gen. Henry Knox..........	23 December 1783	20 June 1784	Maj. Gen. Jacob Brown.........	15 June 1815	24 February 1828
Capt. John Doughty...........	20 June 1784	12 August 1784	Maj. Gen. Alexander Macomb...	29 May 1828	25 June 1841
Lt. Col. Josiah Harmar..........	12 August 1784	4 March 1791	Maj. Gen. Winfield Scott........	5 July 1841	1 November 1861
Maj. Gen. Arthur St. Clair.......	4 March 1791	5 March 1792	Maj. Gen. G. B. McClellan....	1 November 1861	11 March 1862
Maj. Gen. Anthony Wayne......	13 April 1792	15 December 1796	Maj. Gen. H. W. Halleck........	23 July 1862	9 March 1864
Brig. Gen. James Wilkinson.....	15 December 1796	13 July 1798	Gen. U. S. Grant..............	9 March 1864	4 March 1869
Lt. Gen. George Washington.....	13 July 1798	14 December 1799	Gen. W. T. Sherman...........	8 March 1869	1 November 1883
Maj. Gen. Alexander Hamilton..	14 December 1799	15 June 1800	Gen. P. H. Sheridan...........	1 November 1883	5 August 1888
Brig. Gen. Jasper Wilkinson.....	15 June 1800	27 January 1812	Lt. Gen. J. McA Schofield.......	14 August 1888	29 September 1895
Maj. Gen. Henry Dearborn......	27 January 1812	15 June 1815	Lt. Gen. N. A. Miles...........	5 October 1895	8 August 1903

CHIEFS OF STAFF SINCE 1903

Name	From	To	Name	From	To
Lt. Gen. Samuel B. M. Young....	15 August 1903	8 January 1904	General of the Army		
Lt. Gen. Adna R. Chaffee.......	9 January 1904	14 January 1906	Dwight D. Eisenhower........	19 November 1945	7 February 1948
Maj. Gen. John C. Bates........	15 January 1906	13 April 1906	General of the Army		
Maj. Gen. J. Franklin Bell.......	14 April 1906	21 April 1910	Omar N. Bradley.............	7 February 1948	16 August 1949
Maj. Gen. Leonard Wood......	22 April 1910	20 April 1914	Gen. J. Lawton Collins..........	16 August 1949	15 August 1953
Maj. Gen. Wm. W. Wotherspoon.	21 April 1914	15 November 1914	Gen. Matthew B. Ridgway.......	15 August 1953	30 June 1955
Maj. Gen. Hugh L. Scott.......	16 November 1914	21 September 1917	Gen. Maxwell D. Taylor........	30 June 1955	30 June 1959
Maj. Gen. Tasker H. Bliss.......	22 September 1917	18 May 1918	Gen. Lyman L. Lemnitzer.......	1 July 1959	30 September 1960
Gen. Peyton C. March..........	19 May 1918	30 June 1921	Gen. George H. Decker.......	1 October 1960	30 September 1962
Gen. John J. Pershing..........	1 July 1921	13 September 1924	Gen. Earle G. Wheeler..........	1 October 1962	2 July 1964
Gen. John L. Hines.............	14 September 1924	20 November 1926	Gen. Harold K. Johnson........	3 July 1964	2 July 1968
Gen. Charles P. Summerall......	21 November 1926	20 November 1930	Gen. William C. Westmoreland..	3 July 1968	30 June 1972
Gen. Douglas MacArthur........	21 November 1930	1 October 1935	Gen. Creighton W. Abrams.....	1 July 1972	4 September 1974
Gen. Malin Craig...............	2 October 1935	30 August 1939	Gen. Fred C. Weyand	7 October 1974	30 September 1976
General of the Army			Gen. Bernard W. Rogers.......	1 October 1976	
George C. Marshall..........	1 September 1939	18 November 1945			

SECRETARIES OF THE ARMY
SINCE 17 SEPTEMBER 1947

Kenneth C. Royall, 18 September 1947–27 April 1949
Gordon Gray, 20 June 1949–11 April 1950
Frank Pace, Jr., 12 April 1950–20 January 1953
Robert T. Stevens, 4 February 1953–20 July 1955
Wilbur M. Brucker, 21 July 1955–20 January 1961
Elvis J. Stahr, Jr., 24 January 1961–30 June 1962
Cyrus R. Vance, 5 July 1962–27 January 1964
Stephen Ailes, 28 January 1964–1 July 1965
Stanley R. Resor, 7 July 1965–30 June 1971
Robert F. Froehike, 1 July 1971–14 May 1973
Howard H. Callaway, 15 May 1973–2 July 1975
Martin R. Hoffmann, 5 August 1975–13 February 1977
Clifford L. Alexander, Jr., 14 February 1977–

NEW OFFICIAL ARMY SONG

BELOW are the words of the new official Army song, "The Army Goes Rolling Along," which was dedicated at Army installations throughout the world on Veterans Day, 11 November 1956.

Adoption of an official Army song climaxes eight years of search. After conducting a nationwide contest in 1948 and enlisting the aid of leading music composers, publishers, and recording studios in 1952, the Army finally found its song in words and music composed almost fifty years apart.

Basic melody of the new song is that of the rousing, familiar "Caisson Song" which was composed in 1908 by Lieutenant (later Brigadier General) E. L. Gruber, assisted by several of his fellow lieutenants of the 5th Field Artillery, then stationed in the Philippines.

Lyrics for "The Army Goes Rolling Along" were selected from some 140 contributions submitted by major Army commands. The new lyrics, based on the old "Caisson Song," were revised and adapted by Dr. Harold W. Arberg, Soldier Music Advisor, Special Services Division, the Adjutant General's Office.

The newly adopted song will be performed on all appropriate occasions throughout the Army Establishment.

"The Army Goes Rolling Along"

Verse:

March along, sing our song
 With the Army of the free.
Count the brave, count the true
 Who have fought to victory.
We're the Army and proud of our name!
We're the Army and proudly proclaim:

First Chorus:

First to fight for the right
 And to build the nation's might,
And THE ARMY GOES ROLLING ALONG.
Proud of all we have done,
 Fighting till the battle's won,
And THE ARMY GOES ROLLING ALONG.

Refrain:

Then it's hi! hi! hey!
 The Army's on its way.
Count off the cadence loud and strong:
For where'er we go, you will always know
 That THE ARMY GOES ROLLING ALONG.

Second Chorus:

Valley Forge, Custer's ranks,
 San Juan Hill and Patton's tanks,
And the Army went rolling along.
Minute men from the start,
 Always fighting from the heart,
And the Army keeps rolling along.

Refrain:

(Same as above.)

Third Chorus:

(slower, more freely)
Men in rags, men who froze,
 Still that Army met its foes,
And the Army went rolling along.
Faith in God, then we're right
 And we'll fight with all our might,
As the Army keeps rolling along.

Refrain:
(In tempo)

Then it's hi! hi! hey!
 The Army's on its way.
Count off the cadence loud and strong; (two! three!)
For where'er we go, you will always know
 That THE ARMY GOES ROLLING ALONG! (Keep it rolling!)
And THE ARMY GOES ROLLING ALONG!

INDEX